PLOWSHARES INTO SWORDS

Also By Arno J. Mayer

*The Furies: Violence and Terror in the French
and Russian Revolutions*

*Why Did the Heavens Not Darken?
The "Final Solution" in History*

The Persistence of the Old Regime: Europe to the Great War

Dynamics of Counterrevolution in Europe, 1870–1956

*Politics and Diplomacy of Peacemaking:
Containment and Counterrevolution at Versailles, 1918–1919*

Political Origins of the New Diplomacy, 1917–1918

PLOWSHARES INTO SWORDS

From Zionism to Israel

ARNO J. MAYER

VERSO
London • New York

This edition first published by Verso 2021
First published by Verso 2008
© Arno Mayer 2008, 2021

All rights reserved

The moral rights of the author have been asserted

1 3 5 7 9 10 8 6 4 2

Verso
UK: 6 Meard Street, London W1F 0EG
US: 20 Jay Street, Suite 1010, Brooklyn, NY 11201
versobooks.com

Verso is the imprint of New Left Books

ISBN-13: 978-1-78873-967-2
ISBN-13: 978-1-83976-168-3 (UK EBK)
ISBN-13: 978-1-83976-169-0 (US EBK)

British Library Cataloguing in Publication Data
A catalogue record for this book is available from the British Library

Library of Congress Cataloging-in-Publication Data
A catalog record for this book is available from the Library of Congress

Typeset in Sabon by Hewer Text UK Ltd, Edinburgh
Printed and bound by CPI group (UK) Ltd, Croydon CR0 4YY

CONTENTS

for Carl Schorske and Sheldon Wolin

PREFACE

This is a critical historical study of Zionism and Israel. I write as a non-Jewish Jew born into a Zionist family, my father, Franz Mayer, having embraced a left-humanist Zionism while studying political economy at the University of Heidelberg just after the First World War. In 1924 he and my mother Ida spent their honeymoon in Mandatory Palestine, and until the next war Franz, a wholesaler, presided over a Zionist reading society in our native Luxembourg. Following the Nazi assumption of power in Germany in 1933, he took the initiative in establishing a *hachshara*, or training farm, at Altwies on the Franco-Luxembourg border, where young Zionist refugees from Central and Eastern Europe could prepare for life on a kibbutz. My parents visited Palestine again in 1935. We were on the point of emigrating to the Holy Land when what I will deal with as the second Palestinian intifada erupted in 1936. Supported by both sets of grandparents, my mother demurred: she refused to endanger my sister, Ruth, and me.

The family fled Luxembourg on May 10, 1940, minutes ahead of the German Wehrmacht, which early that morning crashed into the Low Countries and France. During our flight we suffered the fears and agonies of a mass exodus on the roads of France: strafings, checkpoints, arrests, and shortages. Our uncertain and circuitous trek—Verdun, Chalons-sur-Marne, Troyes, Avallon, Lyon, Montpellier, Bagnères-de-Bigorre, Hendaye, Marseille, Oran, Oujda, Rabat, Casablanca, Tangiers, Lisbon—landed us in New York City in early 1941. There we became part of a vast and varied commonwealth of refugees, émigrés, and exiles from Central and Western Europe obsessed with the course of the war, trembling for the world that was ours, and desperate for news from the homeland. In February 1944 we learned, through the Red Cross, that my aged maternal grandparents, who had refused to flee with us, had been deported from Luxembourg to Theresienstadt (Terezin) in Czechoslovakia, where my grandfather Berthold died of malnutrition and medical neglect.

Without turning his back on our native land, my father, who now went by the name of Frank, continued in America to be an active Zionist. He raised money for the Keren Hayesod (the fundraising agency of the World Zionist Organization) and represented Luxembourg at meetings of the World Jewish Congress. Eventually, in 1959, my parents returned home. Frank was appointed Honorary Consul General of Israel to the Grand Duchy of Luxembourg.

All this time the family practiced a reflexive Judaism without faith. While I was circumcised and bar mitzvahed, and we observed the Passover Seder and Yom Kippur, we never lit a Shabbat candle, attended a Saturday morning service, or observed *kashruth*, the dietary laws. The Jewish Bible was literature: none of us believed that God had revealed the Ten Commandments to Moses on Mount Sinai or that we belonged to a chosen people. We were guided by a secular morality and ethics independent of the Torah and Talmud. Though Jews were confined to the margins of a society that was nearly 100 per cent Catholic, the idea of passing or converting was unthinkable. Because Luxembourg borders on Germany, France, and Belgium, our homes away from home, our marginality was anything but stifling. I recognize myself in Isaac Deutscher's profile of the "non-Jewish Jew," whom he places "on the borderlines of various civilizations, religions, and national cultures," whose "diverse cultural influences cross and fertilize each other."

It was with this background, in 1944, that I faced up to anti-Judaism during basic training in Company A of the Second Armored Replacement Battalion in Fort Knox, Kentucky. Early one evening after maneuvers, just after I had finished my assigned reading of the army's daily news bulletin to the men in my barracks, a fellow soldier rushed forward and handed me a poem to recite. Its closing strain ran, more or less: "Once we have defeated the Krauts and the Japs overseas we'll come home to kick the shit out of the Kikes and Niggers." When I brazenly proclaimed my Jewishness they jumped me, and in the melee that followed I lost two front teeth. A little later, as a 19-year-old corporal in U.S. Military Intelligence, I disobeyed orders to cosset the morale of rocket scientist Wernher von Braun, whom the U.S. had already hastened to enlist during the dawn of the Cold War: "Der kleine Judenbube"—the little Jew boy, as he called me behind my back—flew into a rage when he told me that Hitler's sole mistake had been his persecution of the Jews. Twenty years on, the dean of Princeton University called me to order for rescheduling, without his permission, a lecture that fell on Yom Kippur. For several years thereafter I changed any class coinciding with a Jewish holiday or festival, no matter how obscure, without warrant.

This was a time when most American academics of "Jewish faith" dissembled their identity to stay inconspicuous, and because they thought it incongruous with their by and large left-wing progressivism. Few at Princeton attended Yom Kippur services in the austere Corwin Hall, and practically none wore a *tallith*, or prayer shawl. Even Israel was not a particular concern. In time there were not only many more Jewish faculty and students, but nearly all of them came out of purdah, especially after the Six Day War of 1967. I was puzzled by this re-Judaization, measurable by the growing number and size of *tallithim* at Kol Nidre, now held in majestic Alexander Hall (Richardson Auditorium).

Having put away my shawl and prayer book along with my mechanical Hebrew the day after my bar mitzvah, I found this separatist Jewish subculture alienating. Jewish colleagues who rediscovered their ethnic identity revealed themselves to be ardent supporters of Israel. Not that they were about to make *aliyah*, turn Orthodox, or become card-carrying members of the insufferably pharisaic Anti-Defamation League. They favored Israel's Labor Party over Likud. But their level of tolerance for criticism of the pro-Israel lobby in the U.S., and of Israeli governments, was tightly calibrated.

In 1950, I made the first of several trips to Israel. I was drawn there by the village collectives and cooperatives, which embodied the ideal of the new Jewish man and woman "returning to the land" and valorizing manual labor. Only once I arrived did I learn that strategic considerations had dictated the location of so many *kibbutzim* and *moshavim*, and that the settlers were peasant-soldiers, with "one hand on the plough, the other on the sword." I spent the summer working in the orchards and fields of Ein Hashofet, 18 miles southeast of Haifa. A kibbutz named in honor of U.S. Supreme Court Justice Louis D. Brandeis, it was affiliated with the left-socialist utopian Hashomer Hatzair (Young Guard). The *chaverim* (comrades) who accompanied us on a trip to the Negev carried rifles, and the Arabs we met were Bedouin and Druze.

During several weekends in Jerusalem I stayed at the home of Ernst Simon, one of Martin Buber's faithful disciples and steadiest associates. My father and Ernst had become fast friends at Heidelberg, and our families had grown close. Having emigrated to Palestine in 1928, Ernst returned to Germany in 1934 for six months to assist Buber in a program of adult education to enhance Jewish self-awareness and solidarity—essential ingredients for spiritual resistance to Nazism. Ernst came to visit us in Luxembourg, and he again stayed with us, in New York, during his first trip to the U.S. soon after Israel's independence.

Before leaving for Israel, and while a graduate student in international relations at Yale University (on the GI Bill of Rights, which provided free education for veterans), I delved into the major publications and declarations of Brit Shalom (Covenant of Peace) and its successor, Ihud (Union). These were Zionism's premier associations of public intellectuals, dedicated to promoting Jewish–Arab understanding and a confederal state on the model of Switzerland, Belgium, or Canada. Among my readings one stood out: *Towards Union in Palestine: Essays on Zionism and Jewish–Arab Cooperation*, edited and with contributions by Buber, Judah Magnes, and Simon, published in early 1947. Ihud had submitted this volume articulating its position to the United Nations Special Commission on Palestine (UNSCOP) in support of the testimony of Magnes, its chief spokesman before that body in Jerusalem in mid-July the same year.

During the summer of 1950 Ernst spoke to me at length about the courageous political engagement of Magnes, the first chancellor, and then president, of Hebrew University, who had died in 1947. He also invited me to join him in two memorable visits with Buber. I continued my conversation with Ernst during four more trips to Israel—one to lecture in Jacob Talmon's course in European history at Hebrew University—and his two visits to Princeton. My last sojourn in Israel, in August 1988, sadly coincided with his death. When sitting *shiva* with his wife Toni and their children Uri and Hannah, I grieved for the passing not only of one of my mentors, but also of the noble vision of Ihud that Ernst had embodied. Yeshayahu Leibowitz, the last of the towering internal critics of the first hour, was among the mourners.

Since 1950 these dissidents have guided my thinking about the Yishuv—the pre-1948 Jewish community in Palestine—and about Israel. Their principles and guidelines inform my quest. Ahad Haam, the oracle of cultural and spiritual Zionism, and his heirs have above all convinced me of the centrality of the Arab Question in the establishment of a national homeland for Jews in Palestine. From the outset their cosmopolitan humanity moved them to warn, on both moral and pragmatic grounds, of the unwisdom of first disregarding and disdaining the Palestinian Arabs, and eventually condemning them as irreconcilable, benighted enemies. Their admonition about the danger of yesterday's victims becoming tomorrow's masters was rooted in a precocious awareness that the rise of Zionism coincided with not only the end of the Ottoman Empire but also the incipient decline of Europe's overseas empires, whose "civilizing mission" was being decried. They formulated a critique of orientalism long before Edward Said so powerfully conceptualized it in the 1970s.

Any book has its contingencies. In 1999, having finished a study on violence, terror, and vengeance in the French and Russian revolutions, I embarked on a memoir of remembrances, denials, and forgettings. Inevitably, as a refugee and exile from Nazi-occupied Europe, I found myself pondering the import of my Jewishness and early Zionist bearings at crucial junctures in my life. I was reading family papers and the émigré press when, on September 28, 2000, Ariel Sharon, then leader of the Likud opposition in Israel, visited the Temple Mount with an official bodyguard, and by leave of Prime Minister Ehud Barak's Labor-led government.

Outraged by this self-serving and provocative symbolic transgression, I resolved to devote some time to studying the Israeli–Palestinian conflict, which until then I had followed with no greater attention than other trouble spots around the world. After six months I wrote an opinion piece arguing that, if compromise and coexistence with the Palestinians were to have a chance, Israel would have to begin evacuating the occupied territories and repatriating its settlers from Gaza, the West Bank, and the Golan. I proposed a special *aliyah*, to be facilitated by tangible, government-supported inducements to colonists to return home with honor. Such a possibility, I argued, could only come to pass by balancing Theodor Herzl's canonical "dream and action are not so far apart as is often thought" against the late Faisal Husseini's cautionary reminder to both Palestinians and Israelis: "Dreams are not negotiable."

The difficulty of getting my screed published (*Le Monde* eventually ran it in June 2001), and the silent reproach among colleagues and friends for an unorthodox but hardly revolutionary proposal, prompted me to shelve my memoir, for which I had gradually lost my appetite. Although a relative outsider to the subject, I felt there might be room for an attempt to set the Zionist-Israeli quest in a broader historical context, much as I had done with the Judeocide and the revolutionary Furies. The urge to do so was all the greater since, with my background in international relations, I was especially sensitive to Zionism's primal resolve to implant a homeland for Jews in the Middle East—a geopolitical theater destined to become only more vital and volatile in world politics. Indeed, there may be no other region of the globe as susceptible to religious and ethnic discord, non-state intervention, asymmetrical warfare, and interstate conflict. Small states, in particular, are severely buffeted during such turbulence, and as a native of Luxembourg, arguably the world's smallest fully sovereign state, I am acutely perturbed by Israel's refusal to recognize that its future lies neither with its God nor its sword, but with the concert of world and regional powers. A sense of limits is the better part of valor.

I spent the next six years reading and writing with the skeptical eye of a left-dissident historian of modern and contemporary Europe, now reconfirmed in his sense of being a non-Jewish Jew, a non-Zionist Zionist, and an unreconstructed diasporist. Except in the Prolegomenon, I proceed chronologically. A number of themes emerge: the dire necessity of imperial protection; the persistent importance of the oil nexus; the congenital Zionist-Israeli disdain for Palestinians and Muslims; the unlooked-for Arab and Islamic awakening; the early hegemony of Jabotinsky's canon; the steadfastness of the Israeli consensus about the "Palestinian Question"; the Palestinian and Arab dissensus on how to contend with it; the enormous weight of American Jewry; the unqualified military, diplomatic, and economic supremacy of Israel; the humiliating powerlessness of the Palestinians; and the studied and perduring Zionist-Israeli prevarication on borders. Along the way I step aside from the narrative to reflect generally on founding violence, sovereignty, resistance, terror, and religious politics.

The polemical Prolegomenon lays out the ideological premises behind the rest of the book, and deals with those agents of the fiercely contested present who exploit the infinitely manipulable past in their struggle for the future. Its length and digressiveness are largely due to my propensity for thick contextualization. To reach for too much is to risk grasping nothing; but the failings of an holistic approach are inconsequential compared with those of a Judeocentric reductionism, whatever its variety, impetus, and intention.

Since, as Benedetto Croce suggests, all history is contemporary history, in the sense of being written from the vantage point of present-day concerns, concepts, and methods, any history of Zionism, Israel, the Palestinians, and the Israeli–Palestinian conflict is bound to be singularly problematic and tendentious. My transparently disenchanted viewpoint is informed, above all, by political Zionism's earliest internal critics: Ahad Haam, Martin Buber, and Judah Magnes, whose strictures deeply influenced Albert Einstein, Sigmund Freud, and Hannah Arendt. I am, of course, also indebted to Israel's left-"revisionist" historians, political scientists, and sociologists. I rely as well on a large corpus of secondary and memoir literature, though limited by my ignorance of Hebrew, Arabic, and Farsi. In an effort to partially mitigate this handicap, I became an assiduous reader, on the Internet, of *Haaretz, The Jerusalem Post*, and DEBKAfile.com, as well as of *The Daily Star* (Beirut), *Al-Ahram* (Egypt), and electronicInti-fada.net. This immersion in the discordant news and opinion of the region helped me penetrate the ideological environments, world-views, and linguistic codes that inform political discourse and dis-putation in the interpenetrating and conflicting territorial, as well as ideological, realms of the Middle East. But, of necessity, my study is not exhaustive and remains unfinished, like the situation it explores.

Like my *Persistence of the Old Regime* and *Why Did the Heavens Not Darken?*, this book is bereft of footnotes. As there, and as I said of the *Heavens* in the Afterword, it is a synthetic work based on the printed sources and secondary literature listed in the bibliography, which are well-known to the experts. For them, references would be superfluous; for general readers, overwhelming. *Plowshares into Swords*, like those two earlier works, chiefly raises "not factual but interpretive questions." To cite from my preface to the *Old Regime*, it is "in the nature of an argument [and] I make no pretense of presenting all sides of the question," so that once again I class myself as a "lumper" rather than as a "splitter."

Writing this book was more unsettling and solitary than I expected. Above all, I kept being brought up short by my prejudgments. The hypersensitivity of the subject made open conversations nearly im-possible. Jewish friends and colleagues, as well as family members, alternated between telling me what to write and urging me to give Israel the benefit of the doubt, so as not to incur the wrath of Jewish censors. Gentile friends and colleagues, fearful of giving offense, tended to keep their own counsel; several of them in America and Europe sheepishly confessed as much. Even so, I am indebted to two intellectual soulmates, the spirit of whose work and political inter-ventions has served to sustain me. As neither lived to read this manuscript, I will not invoke their names, lest I seem to suggest their sanctioning of arguments they did not vet and for which they bear no responsibility.

*   *   *

In all innocence Prudence Crowther agreed to help wrangle my prose, which, besides being written in what is not my first language, tends to circumlocute. Our exchanges have been wonderfully contentious and frankly a pleasure. In recompense I have bequeathed to her what of my army vocabulary she did not already command. Pamela Long once again typed and retyped successive drafts with her usual care and patience, often wondering if the endless revisions were indeed improvements; her skepticism was tonic. Charles Peyton was a gracious cryptographer and way more than a meticulous copy editor. Perry Anderson gave the book a berth at Verso as well as a wise and rigorous read; Tom Penn labored line for line with exemplary forbearance and saved me from frequent opacity—I must indemnify them both against my stubborn disinclinations.

Princeton—Chérence
December 2007

PROLEGOMENON

The Judeocide weighs heavily on how the history of Zionism, the Yishuv, and Israel is told. It is widely assumed and invoked to justify the Zionist project, as well as the establishment and development of the Jewish state. The teleological temptation is hard to resist: not a few historians and public intellectuals, with the privilege of hindsight, read first beginnings in terms of later outcomes. They consider the road to Auschwitz and Treblinka to have been linear, its victims and milestones ingrained in historical memory: the destruction of the First and Second Temples; torment during the First Crusade in the Rhineland and Jerusalem; expulsion from Inquisitorial Spain; pogroms in the Russian Pale of Settlement. In this construction, the Final Solution was the culmination of this exilic ordeal, redeemed finally by the establishment of a sovereign state in Palestine to protect the Jewish people, once and for all, against a uniformly hostile and relentlessly murderous gentile world.

This overdetermined, lachrymose narrative of the agony of exile and diaspora is woven into Israel's founding myth and self-understanding, which perpetuate a sense of victimhood and imminent aggression. Israel's Declaration of Independence of May 14, 1948 proclaims that "the catastrophe which recently befell the Jewish people" demonstrates "the urgency of . . . reestablishing . . . the Jewish state which would open the gates . . . wide to every Jew [as] survivors of the Nazi holocaust in Europe . . . continue to immigrate to the land of Israel, undaunted by difficulties, restrictions, and dangers." This was the first incantation of what gradually developed into the transnational religion or ideology of the Holocaust, with a capital H, whose high priests, rituals, and shrines make an idol of the state of Israel for its salvific mission.

Yet neither Theodor Herzl, Chaim Weizmann nor Arthur Balfour ever had the slightest foreboding of anything remotely like the Jewish catastrophe. Troubled by the ragged advance of emancipation across

Europe since 1789, Herzl imagined a homeland in Palestine as a refuge from traditional anti-Jewish discrimination and persecution. Should it take the form of a sovereign state, it would be modeled on France's Third Republic; this offspring of the Great Revolution remained Herzl's political model despite his having been profoundly disturbed by the infamous Dreyfus Affair.

A man of his own time, and like the leaders of France, Herzl took an imperialist view of non-Western cultures, although he probably embraced a progressive reading of Europe's *mission civilisatrice* overseas. He considered it altogether natural to establish a settler colony for European Jews in the Middle East under the military umbrella of one of the Great Powers. A link in Europe's "rampart against Asia," a Jewish commonwealth would serve as "an outpost of civilization against barbarism," in exchange for which "our existence . . . as a neutral state" would be guaranteed. Inspired by the ancient prophets, Herzl expected the Zionist homeland to become a "light unto the nations": a magnet for Jews from all over the Old Continent, and from Eastern Europe in particular. At the turn of the twentieth century, more than 60 per cent of Europe's Jews (over 5 million out of over 8 million worldwide) lived in the Russian empire, most in the Pale of Settlement. Herzl gave no thought to the diaspora Jews in North Africa and the Middle East—perhaps because for centuries they had seen nothing comparable to Christian anti-Judaism and anti-Semitism in the Islamic world.*

In the years leading up to the First World War nothing portended the cataclysmic turn that anti-Judaism and Judeophobia would take. And notwithstanding discrete eruptions of political and racial anti-Semitism, the unthinkable remained so past the middle of the Second World War, for Jews and gentiles alike. Between these dates, however, the leaders of political Zionism, who continued to gain on the advocates of cultural, spiritual, and religious Zionism, stepped up their drive for a sovereign state for the Jewish people in the Holy Land. Their success was destined to arouse the hostility and resistance of the indigenous Palestinian Arabs, who would experience Zionist immigration as an eleventh-hour European re-colonization. For most of the war the Zionist directorate invoked Nazi Germany's escalating war against the Jews to justify the whole of Zionist policy since 1917, and

---

* As in my book on the Final Solution, I distinguish between "Judeophobia"— prejudice on the part of individuals; "anti-Semitism"—the institutionalized forms taken by such prejudice (often but not always political) or their advocacy; and "anti-Judaism"—hostility directed against the Jewish religion or Jews as adherents of that religion (as opposed to "racial" prejudice).

to vindicate each and every one of emergent Israel's transgressions of the law. The Palestinians disputed this rationalization. Emboldened by their own national awakening and backed by the Arab and Muslim worlds, they refused to yield what they believed to be their land in expiation for Christian Europe's latest and most heinous torment of the Jews.

The Judeocide was less the culmination of age-old anti-Judaism and Judeophobia than it was the convergence, in Eastern Europe, of a uniquely ferocious total war with Nazi Germany's newly wrought racial anti-Semitism. The interpenetration of these two human enormities confirms that the history of Zionism and Israel provides a microcosm of the global history of its time; it cannot be explained in parochial, intramural terms. All major turning points in the life of the Yishuv, the Jewish settlement in Palestine pre-1948, and Israel, correlate with momentous world events: the First World War, the Russian Revolution, the fall of great European dynasties, the breakup of the Ottoman empire, the decline of Europe's overseas empires, the Fascist counterrevolution, the Second World War, the Cold War, the anti-imperialist nationalist revolt of the colonial and semi-colonial world, the ascendancy of the American empire, and the Islamic revival.

The tremors of this unprecedented, rolling earthquake shook the diaspora, the Yishuv, and Israel with special force. Zionism was nurtured and denatured by it. The British policy that made the Zionist project possible was itself bound up in the same rush of world events. The incongruous promises of an overextended empire—first to the Arabs in the McMahon–Hussein Correspondence of 1915–16, and then to the Jews in the 1917 Balfour Declaration—were forged in the crucible of the Great War of 1914–18.

The Zionist drive for a homeland for Jews and the Arab–Palestinian impulse for self-determination were therefore set to collide long before the Judeocide, the six Arab–Israeli wars, and all the Palestinian Arab intifadas from 1929 to 2000. The Jews brought with them the injuries of immemorial anti-Judaism; the Arabs bore the wounds of nearly two centuries of European colonial domination. If they were bound at first to battle each other, it was not the only prospect before them. Conciliation and coexistence would have been difficult, but not beyond the bounds of historical possibility.

The Zionist–Arab collision in Palestine occurred within a generally unsettled greater Middle East as the First World War reconfigured the spheres of influence, frontiers, and economic preserves of this exceptional crossroads of civilizations and religions. The McMahon–Hussein Correspondence, pledging Great Britain's support for an independent kingdom of most of the Arab lands of the Middle East, the secret British–French Sykes–Picot Treaty of 1916 dividing up so much of the region, and the Balfour Declaration—all three diplomatic instruments were premised on the demise of the Ottoman empire in the Middle East, and its replacement by Britain and, to a lesser extent, France. When the Second World War later diminished their dominance in the region, they in turn bowed to the U.S.

Between 1918 and 1922, following the First World War, London and Paris arbitrarily carved up Turkey-in-Asia into four newly imagined states with modern borders: Syria, Iraq, Transjordan, and Lebanon. In a typical example, the Foreign Office and Quai d'Orsay eventually agreed that the three Ottoman provinces (*vilayets*) of Mosul, Baghdad, and Basra should be joined to form a Sunni-dominated Iraq with a Hashemite sovereign, under British hegemony. With Sunnis accounting for roughly 22 per cent of the population, Shiites 55 per cent, and Kurds 14 per cent, London proposed to exploit deep-running ethnic, tribal, and sectarian divisions in order to sap the emergent Arab nationalism. More or less simultaneously, Great Britain tightened its hold on most of the Arabian peninsula (chiefly Saudi Arabia and Kuwait), Persia (Iran after 1935), and—to a lesser extent—Egypt. The boundaries of Palestine were broadly delineated and Zionism formally implanted during the last hurrah of European imperialism.

The statesmen of the Great Powers considered the Holy Land an inconsequential precinct in this final colonial partition—of not much account, that is, except for one piece of it: Palestine occupied a valuable location relative to a radically new and urgent factor in imperial power and politics: oil. By the end of the First World War, London, Paris, and Washington no longer doubted the economic and military importance of the region's petroleum deposits. Believed to be vast, the reserves of Mesopotamia, Arabia, and Persia intensely preoccupied the statesmen, generals, and oilmen who contrived the postwar borders, regimes, and energy concessions. Winston Churchill, then British colonial secretary and arguably the master architect of this new order, stands out for his foresight in anticipating the significance of black gold: in the early twenty-first century, the Persian Gulf countries, including Iran and Iraq, produce easily over 25 per cent of the world's oil, and hold over 55 per cent of its oil reserves. The same region commands 45 per cent of the world's natural gas reserves. London grasped the importance of controlling not only Middle Eastern oil but the Suez Canal and the Strait of Hormuz, vital arteries for shipments to Greater Britain and its allies, especially in wartime. It would take another Armageddon for the geostrategists of the West to appreciate these waterways as the world's most critical petroleum chokepoints. Oil transformed the geopolitical importance of the Middle East. The fate of Palestine and Zionism, inseparable from that of the Great Powers, was affected accordingly.

The U.S. emerged as a significant player in the geo-economics of oil in the Middle East before 1914, and between the wars developed into an even stronger one. In the second half of the 1930s the Arabian American Oil Company (Aramco) discovered and began to extract oil in Saudi Arabia; after 1944 the U.S. became the dominant petro-power. Oil was at the heart of President Franklin D. Roosevelt's astonishing meeting on February 14, 1945, on his return from Yalta, with King Ibn Saud aboard the cruiser U.S.S. *Quincy*, anchored in Great Bitter Lake in the Suez Canal. The potentate of Riyadh, self-styled protector of Sunni Muslims and fervent anti-Zionist, rebuffed the president's plea to support the opening up of Palestine to Jewish immigration, insisting that it was up to those who had oppressed and persecuted the European Jews to provide a haven, not the innocent Arabs. Apparently Roosevelt feared an Arab–Jewish collision in the region, and promised further consultation with Ibn Saud on the issue. But whatever their discord on Palestine, oil they could talk about. This meeting ushered in the era of relatively abundant, cheap, and stable supplies for the West, heavily dependent on the acquiescence of the Muslim Middle East. The Persian Gulf—until that time Britain's vital sea route to India and the Far East—became essential to the security of America's oil supply. Before long the U.S., by now the world's largest oil consumer, was importing over a quarter of its crude petroleum from the largest oil producer with the greatest reserves. In exchange for privileged access to these reserves, Washington guaranteed the integrity and independence of Saudi Arabia against domestic and foreign enemies. American air and naval bases in and near the King-dom became as conspicuous as Riyadh's and the United Arab Emi-rates' financial ties to the U.S. Treasury and Wall Street.

This relationship became the material and symbolic centerpiece of America's imperial engagement in the greater Middle East during the Cold War. In pursuit of its global interest, which included securing a regular supply of oil for Western Europe in the time of the crucial Marshall Plan, Washington made common cause with most of the Middle East's autocratic regimes. Oil was central to the CIA-engi-neered Anglo-American overthrow in 1953 of the government of the popularly elected and left-leaning Mohammad Mossadegh, prime minister of Iran. The chief motivations for this coup were geopolitical and geo-economic—notably the containment of Soviet Russia and the control of oil—rather than the democratization of the Middle East.

From Herzl onwards, the leaders of political Zionism acknowledged the necessity of support from one of the Great Powers to secure a state for Jews in Palestine. Prisoners of their own supremacist mindset, however, they were slow to realize that this backing became more problematic as anti-colonial nationalism swept through the Middle East, making it that much harder for the Yishuv, and then Israel, to establish a secure political, cultural and religious foothold in the region. The Zionists were also slow to grasp the waning of the European overseas empires, the burgeoning imperative of Middle Eastern oil, the ascendancy of Imperial America, and the fast-growing political weight of the transatlantic diaspora. Once they did, however, they put the American connection first.

During the 1950s, in furtherance of its own expansive national interest, Israel fell in ever more with U.S. policy. It gradually became a strategic outpost of the informal American empire in the Middle East, in exchange for much-needed military, diplomatic, and financial aid.

Before long, Washington alone had the leverage to empower, shield, or restrain Israel. By the grace of the U.S., Israel became a regional Goliath with an arsenal of ultra-modern weapons facing down a David: the would-be Palestinian nation.

Practically from the outset of modern Zionism, a galaxy of prophetic internal critics warned of the dangers of taking a narrow political road to Palestine. As they saw it, mainstream Zionism was proposing to establish a state for Jews in a land which was not theirs for the taking, and which was by no means without a people. To win through, besides needing imperial patronage, they would most likely have to fight an unconsenting local population. The internal critics of cultural and spiritual Zionism feared that a politics of violence and force would pervade the Zionist project, all the more so since statehood would have to be imposed on distrustful neighboring countries as well.

Starting with Ahad Haam in the 1890s, the internal critics discussed the "Arab Question," proposing ways to smooth the encounter between Jew and Palestinian. They stressed the cardinal importance of dialogue to the growth of mutual understanding and responsibility. Among their most prominent members, Martin Buber and Ernst Simon urged that the injunction to "love thy neighbor" cease being interpreted exclusively as applying to Jewish neighbors. They advocated revising the rabbinic tradition with regard to the non-Jewish

Other, opening it up to a "common humanity" embracing Jew and gentile equally. Theirs was a call for a universalist ethics and morality, without which there could be no positive encounter with the local and neighboring population.

Convinced that the attitude of the *olim* (immigrants) toward the Palestinian Arabs would be the touchstone of Zionism and true test of its intentions in the region, the internal critics were troubled from the beginning by the newcomers' behavior. Ahad Haam was the first of many critics to suggest that the persecuted past of the Jews, coupled with their Western supremacism, would predispose the settlers to act toward the subaltern natives like colonial masters. The only way to avoid such an outcome, the Zionist dissenters argued, was for the new arrivals to foster mutual understanding between the two communities by way of social, economic, and civic collaboration at the local and regional level—an essential first step toward a binational, single-state confederation providing equal powers and rights for Jews and Arabs, with guarantees against minority oppression.

Although retroactively marginalized as dreamers, Ahad Haam, Buber, and Judah Magnes were in fact no less sensible and pragmatic than Herzl and Chaim Weizmann, the prominent Zionist leader who would become Israel's first president. Until around 1946–8, their plan for a single binational state remained a feasible option, and only from a teleological perspective can a two-state solution be said to have been inevitable. Either outcome was contingent on the imperial interest and will of Washington, influenced by America's politically powerful Jewish community. And both solutions required the use of violence and force, with the U.S. playing a decisive if indirect role. In the short or long run the costs—human, political, social, economic, cultural— of establishing a binational state could not have been as forbidding as those, yet to be tallied, of dividing Palestine. Partition, the critics feared, would lead to endless cross-border and internal warfare fired by ultra-nationalism and xenophobia.

Zionism was born out of violence, not God or a golden vision: the physical and psychological violence of the pogroms in czarist Russia, and the rhetorical violence surrounding the Dreyfus Affair in Republican France and Karl Lueger's related municipal reign in Imperial Vienna; then the physical, psychological, and symbolic violence of the Zionist settlement in Arab–Muslim Palestine, a variant on the polymorphous violence of imperialist Europe's increasingly contested civilizing mission overseas.

Zionism's loyal opposition was not all-knowing. Most certainly it underestimated the violence inherent in establishing new states or new-model regimes even in relatively homogeneous cultural and religious settings. Hannah Arendt, echoing Machiavelli, stressed that, through the ages, there was no making a "beginning . . . without using violence, without violating." Each founding myth celebrates, romanticizes, and sanitizes the primal violence used in forging a new politico-legal order and fixing interstate boundaries, in the process transforming illegal violence into what comes to be accepted as legitimate force.

Struck by the "particularly close . . . relation between the state and violence" in Central and Eastern Europe during the era of the First World War, unsurpassed historical sociologist Max Weber formulated his incisive postulate: "The state is that human community which [successfully] claims or exercises the *monopoly of the legitimate use of physical force* within a given territory" (italics in original). Similarly, the eminent political theorist and proto-Nazi Carl Schmitt advanced an equally cogent axiom: "Sovereign is he who decides on the exception [state of emergency] in the face of grave political and social disorder."

Like most other nation-builders before them, between 1945 and 1949 the Zionists used both violence and force to establish the state of Israel. Warranted by the U.N. General Assembly, its governments claimed and exercised the monopoly of the legitimate use of physical force following the 1948 war. But Israel did not do so "within a given territory": to this day its borders—an essential criterion of the sovereign nation-state—are neither demarcated nor recognized internationally.

In its continued attempts to dictate a settlement and extend its sovereignty beyond the pre-1967 boundaries, Israel has invited a continuous confrontation. It presumes to decide when a state of exception exists in the occupied territories—and almost all Palestinian resistance has been deemed a "grave political and social disorder." But Israel's ensuing military response has never been recognized as legitimate by the people upon whom it has been visited, who continue to experience it as raw violence. Even after the establishment of the quasi-sovereign Palestinian National Authority in 1994 in part of the West Bank and Gaza, Israel continued to deny it the sovereign right to declare a state of emergency entailing resort to legitimate force.

In the mid-1920s, at the same time that the internal critics founded Brit Shalom in the hope of more effectively voicing their reservations about incremental political Zionism, Vladimir Jabotinsky came forward to demand that it be quickened and hardened. He and the emergent Revisionists (so-called because of their wish to revise the mandatory

borders) were polar opposites of the emergent Binationalists, led by
Magnes. However, Jabotinsky and Magnes did see eye to eye on one
pivotal point: both considered the Jewish–Arab encounter the crux of
the Question of Palestine. But whereas the spiritual heirs of Ahad
Haam wanted to mitigate the difficulty by reconciliation and compromise, Jabotinsky and his partisans proposed gaining the upper
hand by violence and force.

The prime mover of ultra-nationalist Zionism articulated in secu-
larized and traditional religious words and concepts, Jabotinsky called
for a unitary Jewish state from the Mediterranean Sea to beyond the
Jordan River, thus including all or part of the lands of the recently
fashioned Hashemite desert kingdom. In fact, he appreciated the
attachment of the Palestinian Arabs to their homeland and the
upswing of anti-colonial nationalism throughout the Arab–Muslim
world. Yet he held Islamic society and culture in contempt for what he
saw as its severe underdevelopment. Insofar as that meant military
ineffectiveness, however, he was all for it: he knew the Arabs would
never accede to the establishment of Eretz Israel Hashlema—the
Greater Land of Israel—without being compelled to do so by force
of arms.

Trusting in the sword and unilateral action, Jabotinsky called for an
"iron wall" of overwhelming military strength to break the Arabs.
With time, his *idée force* pervaded Israel's political and strategic elite
across the spectrum. David Ben-Gurion, Golda Meir, Yitzhak Rabin,
and Ehud Barak of Mapai—the dominant left party and precursor to
Labor—embraced it tacitly; Menachem Begin, Yitzhak Shamir, Be-
nyamin Netanyahu, Ariel Sharon, and Ehud Olmert of the right-wing
parties Herut, Likud, and Kadima did so unequivocally. Even the
religious ultra-nationalists, including the hardcore Orthodox, who
had once had faith-based scruples about statehood, came to believe in
the restoration of the Biblical borders of the kingdom of David and
Solomon by "blood and iron," as Bismarck had done for Germany and
Cavour for Italy. Because in their time the European state system had
been in near equilibrium, the Great Powers had forced a Machiavellian
sense of limits upon the Old Continent's two towering nineteenth-
century nation-builders and their immediate successors. In the Middle
East, no comparable constraint worked on Israel's military-political
caste, whose hubris matched the growth of a formidable and unrivaled
regional arsenal of the latest and most lethal weapons.

The Declaration of the Rights of Man and the Citizen of 1789
proclaims "resistance to oppression" among the natural and irrevoc-

able human rights. Every resistance to foreign occupation assumes the distinctive characteristics of its place and time. The stages are familiar: from spontaneous individual dissent and group remonstrance to increasingly willed, collective, and coordinated action. Following erratic Arab protests in the Holy Land during the early 1920s, there was a first intifada, or "shaking off," in 1929, and a second in 1936–9. Following the Second World War the Palestinian resistance and its external supporters found inspiration and validation in the anti-colonial nationalist rebellion that erupted throughout Asia and Africa. Demanding a place on the stage of world history, Nehru, Sukarno, Nasser, Chou En-lai, Ho Chi Minh, Nkrumah, and U Nu gathered in the Indonesian resort city of Bandung in April 1955 in a search of a nonaligned or third way between the Western and Soviet blocs in the Cold War. In the words of India's Nehru, "I propose to belong to neither bloc, whatever happens in the world"; and of Indonesia's Sukarno, "We the peoples of Asia and Africa, 1,400,000,000 strong, [represent] far more than half the world's population," who in Richard Wright's firsthand account (*The Color Curtain*, 1956) were "the despised, the insulted, the hurt, the dispossessed—in short, the underdogs of the human race." All the leaders in attendance at Bandung were confirmed secularists, whose piety was reserved for a nationalism informed by Socialist-Marxist aphorisms and Soviet-style economic development formulas. Yasser Arafat was the son of this pleiad from what soon became known as the Third World.

The Zionists, and subsequently the Israelis, were reluctant ever to concede the authenticity and legitimacy of the Palestinian cause—a negation anchored in their contempt for the Arab–Muslim world generally. It was but a short step from disparaging ordinary Palesti-nians to dehumanizing nonviolent protesters and militants, well before the advent of bomb-throwing terrorists and suicide bombers. By refusing all dialogue and indiscriminately vilifying the Palestinian resistance, the Israelis contributed to its radicalization. Extremists on both sides were both cause and effect of an ideological conflict over concrete, negotiable issues—borders, water resources, holy places, refugees, settlements—that became more and more religiously charged, hampering compromise. One side raised the specter of Arabs driving Israelis into the sea; the other, of Israelis driving Palestinians into the desert.

As resistance is a historical constant, so is terrorism. Its earliest source and sanction was revealed religion. Beginning with the French Revolution, however, it was more typically driven by ideologies, or civil religions, with political objectives: republicanism, nationalism,

Marxism, anti-imperialist nationalism. Only in the 1970s did religion again provide an impetus and rationale. Terrorism is contingent on a complex and unstable mixture of circumstance, belief, mind-set, and leadership. Few terrorists are simple desperadoes or fanatics. Poverty, anomie, rage, resentment, humiliation, frustration—all provide fertile ground for the recruitment of terrorists among Palestinians, especially among the children and grandchildren of the refugees of the wars of 1948 and 1967.

Community-based, decentralized and quick-footed terrorism is an expression of weakness, despair, and defiance. Given the imbalance of power between the Palestinian resistance and the Israeli army, in time the former ceased to field guerrilla forces that, to be effective, needed to secure physical control of a district or region, which was beyond its power. Instead the Palestinian terrorists used violence as an instrument of psychological warfare. With dramatic strikes on discrete targets and victims, they meant to provoke and unnerve the enemy, win recruits, rally sympathizers, and command the attention of world leaders and the media. In a classic division of political labor, individual terrorists now risk their lives, while their political leaders discordantly rationalize the violence: they condemn and justify it in public while supporting and seeking to restrain it behind the scenes. By and large terror is a means to an end, not an end in itself.

The Israelis consider and portray all armed Palestinian resistance—from stone-throwing to suicide bombing—as intrinsically fanatical, indiscriminate, and barbaric. By contrast, they characterize their own recourse to force and violence as defensive, necessary, and circumspect. In like manner Israel justifies its state terror—the collateral damage of its targeted assassinations, punitive raids, house demolitions, and mass arrests. But while modern arms are effective in deterring and fighting regular armies, and to a lesser extent disciplined guerrilla forces, they are ineffectual in battling an amorphous uprising composed of small groups of fighters operating without a central chain of command, and fitfully cooperating with rival rebel units. Adept at blending into supporting rural and urban surroundings, irregular forces easily replenish their ranks and renew their commanders. No matter how severe the losses, the insurgency reproduces itself at all levels; there is no vanquishing it by arms alone.

The role of religion in the escalation and persistence of the Arab–Israeli conflict is difficult to analyze, let alone understand. It was of little consequence until relatively late. The foremost figure of political Zionism, Theodor Herzl, was a child of Europe's nineteenth-century

Enlightenment, and thus of secularism. In his 1896 *Der Judenstaat* (*The Jewish State*, perhaps better rendered as *The State for Jews*), he presumed that Zionists would not allow the "theocratic impulses of clerics to get the upper hand," hoping they would be "kept in their synagogues" so as to make sure they would not "intervene in matters of state." Neither Herzl nor, as has been noted, Yasser Arafat later on, was religious, and both were loath to play the religious card. The issue here is not religion per se, however, but its gradual injection into politics: the use of religious beliefs and arguments in pursuit of profane objectives. In the process, politics invades religion as much as religion invades politics.

This interpenetration occurred as early as 1929, at the time of the first intifada, which was fuelled by the confrontation between Zionist and Palestinian zealots over control of the Temple Mount, or Haram al Sharif (the Noble Sanctuary). In both camps the militant vanguard comprised an unholy alliance of religious true believers and secular ultra-nationalists. The one side sought to liberate the Temple Mount, the site of the two hallowed Jewish temples thought to have been destroyed by the Babylonians and Romans in ancient times, with the idea of laying the cornerstone for a third; the other side rallied to protect the Al Aqsa Mosque and Dome of the Rock, standing on the hallowed ground from which the Prophet Muhammad was said to have ascended to heaven in the seventh century. Each party denied the other's claim to supremacy over Jerusalem and other holy places. Such were the beginnings of the instrumentalization of religion, which in years to come would take its toll both in blood and in growing distrust and tension between the two communities.

Brit Shalom instantly sounded an alarm: to mix politics and religion was to court disaster, particularly with rabbis and imams inciting and exalting the would-be soldiers of God. And sites holy to both religions have indeed ever since been among the most prone to violence: the Wailing Wall and Temple Mount in Jerusalem; the Cave of the Patriarchs in Hebron; Joseph's Tomb in Nablus; and Rachel's Tomb in Bethlehem. The religious investment of new states and regimes is no less dangerous. Machiavelli valued religion and the church for their critical role in the process of state-foundation—political leaders invoking the authority of teachings, myths, rituals, ceremonies, and chants to sacralize the embryonic state. But in so doing they risk freighting it with the intolerance, fanatical partisanship, and messianism that can accompany faith. Especially after the 1967 war, Jew and Arab have used and abused Biblical or Koranic commands for worldly ends. Finding humility, fear, and awe inconvenient, politically engaged laymen and clerics address God with pride and cunning, inviting Him to fortify their courage and witness their valor in the face of enemies to be defeated and slain.

A negative collective memory of Islam, Muslims, and Arabs is deeply embedded in the Christian West. Through the ages, until relatively recently, it was molded and perpetuated by medieval legends, chronicles, and poems that popularized antagonistic representations. Latin Christendom positively defined its own ethos in hostile interaction with the Muslim Other. The Crusades marked a low point in this clash of civilizations. With the rise of the West, the negative stereotype became largely dormant. In the meantime the West's revilement rankled among Muslims, whose sense of persecution was more keenly felt with the irruption of colonial imperialism. Presently the Jew became Christendom's indigenous negative Other, and the Christian world the home of the blood libel, Inquisition, and pogrom.

Today's renewed defamation of Islam stirs up this old resentment, in particular when the West—especially the U.S.—embeds it in fiery criticism of the region's lack of human rights, civil rights and liberties, gay and women's rights, electoral democracy, and free-market capitalism—self-serving ideological cover for latter-day economic, cultural, and political, not to say military, penetration. For Muslims, and not only the believers in political Islam, the invasion of Iraq, the treatment of prisoners in Abu Ghraib and Guantánamo Bay, the plight of Gaza and the West Bank, and the second disproportionate lashing of Lebanon breathe fresh life into latent memories.

The Arab national awakening is accompanied by an Islamic revival, which marks the great transformation of the Middle East and its place in the world since the First World War. The second-largest religion after Christianity, Islam is the fastest-growing. Its growth rate was 1.8 per cent for the twentieth century as a whole, and 2.6 per cent for the years 1970 to 2000. Moreover, in the last three decades the rate of conversion has risen considerably, to over 8 million annually. There were nearly 200 million Muslims in 1900, 380 million in 1950, 575 million in 1970, and 1.2 billion in 2000—and there will be an estimated 2 billion in 2025. In 1950 some 100,000 Muslims made the *hajj*, or pilgrimage to Mecca; in 2006, well over 2 million. Between 1970 and 2000, then, the number of Muslims doubled to make up one quarter of humanity. By the 1980s Islam was the dominant religion of the Third World. It is the majority faith in over forty countries, and Muslims make up a large minority in many others. Though Islam is Arab in origin, only one-fifth of the world's Muslims live in Arab countries.

Israel shares its problematic 1,000 km (621 mile) borders with four Muslim nations: Jordan's population is 95 per cent Muslim, Egypt's 91 per cent, Syria's 88 per cent, and Lebanon's 70 per cent. Regional neighbors Saudi Arabia, Iraq, and Iran are nearly 100 per cent Muslim. Islam divides chiefly into Sunnis (85 per cent) and Shiites (15 per cent), and the sectarian divide between them dates practically from the crisis of succession following the death of Muhammad, who according to Islam is God's last and final prophet, in 632. The Sunnis, who have dominated the history of Islam since its creation, have the ascendancy in eighteen out of twenty-one Arab countries. Non-Arab Iran, historically the defender of Shiism, is about 90 per cent Shiite. The proportion of Arab Shiites is 65 per cent in Bahrain, 25 per cent in Kuwait, and 20 per cent in Qatar. In Saudi Arabia Shiites are 10 per cent, concentrated in the oil-rich eastern province of al-Hasa. Some 70 per cent of the people living in the Persian Gulf region are Shiite. Iraq is between 55 per cent and 60 per cent Shiite.

To some degree Shiism may be said to resemble Catholicism in its emphasis on canonical infallibility, clerical hierarchy, and martyrdom. But like Catholics and Protestants, whatever their doctrinal and liturgical differences the Shiites and Sunnis share essentially the same profession of faith and observances: prayer, pilgrimage, fasting, and alms-giving. In the end the division between them is more profane than religious or theological. Except in Iran—and, more recently, in Iraq— the Shiites have been frozen out of political society. Since the sixteenth century they have been an intermittently persecuted—but permanently disadvantaged—social and economic minority. This subaltern condition renders them susceptible to the rhetoric of liberation, religious or secular, and to opposition or resistance to Sunnis, many of whose governors collaborate openly with the European and Atlantic West.

Judeo-Christianity and Islam may of course be practiced benevolently or inhumanely, and there is no significant difference in their attitudes toward violence. Both have had intensely violent and relatively temperate periods. Nothing is gained by attempting to weigh the Koran against the Bible to see which contains the greater number of overt or tacit warrants for armed conflict and violence—each has a superabundance. But in any straight contest between the history of Islam and the near Orient and that of Christianity and the West, the latter take the palm in man's inhumanity to man: the Crusades, the Inquisition, the Wars of Religion, the Napoleonic Wars, two World Wars, the Judeocide, Dresden, Hiroshima—the list goes on.

The doctrines of both Christianity and Islam lend themselves to political interpretation and perversion by clergy and laity alike. Yet the

West depicts Islam, broadly speaking, as a pagan and violent religion as well as a sectarian and benighted civilization. In 1835, in his classic "Minute on Indian Education," Thomas B. Macaulay professed that "I have never found one among . . . the Orientalists who could deny that a single shelf of a good European library was worth the whole native literature of India and Arabia." Islam was, however, a vital part of the non-European world that, in the words of Rabindranath Tagore, India's Nobel laureate in literature of 1913, "for centuries . . . held torches of civilization when the West slumbered in darkness" during its so-called Dark Ages. From the tenth to the fourteenth centuries, its Golden Age, the Islamic world soaked up the learning of the ancients, undertaking a vast translation program of Greek classics and making major strides in algebra, physics, astronomy, and medicine.

This age of intellectual enlightenment, when Jewish communities flourished in Islamic lands, came to a close with the completion of the Catholic reconquest of Spain in 1492. The Renaissance Popes doubtless nodded assent when Martin Luther maligned the Koran for its "errors" and for embracing "the insanity and wiles of the devil." Lately, moderate Muslims favoring a positive engagement with modernity, human rights, social reform, and the separation of state and mosque have been sailing against the wind. Because this progressive agenda was pressed on the Muslim world by Europe's colonial powers, from Napoleon's expedition to Egypt in 1798 until 1945, and thereafter by the American imperium, the headwinds are that much stronger. Even so, the greater Middle East, along with the rest of the Third World, continues to unbind Prometheus, no matter how Western he may be.

The latest spread of fundamentalism among Shiites and Sunnis is greatly conditioned by these same historical forces. The Iranian Revolution, which brought forth the Shiite Islamic Republic in Tehran in 1979, was an act of defiance against America and its European imperial inheritance. This ironic redemption of the overthrow of Mossadegh—anti-colonial nationalist, secularist, progressive, and modernizer—called forth a surge of pride among Shia and Sunni alike throughout much of the Muslim world, momentarily diminishing their sectarian discord.

The Taliban got started in overwhelmingly Sunni Afghanistan soon after the Iranian Revolution. A group of ultra-fundamentalists, they rose along with other rebels to fight the Soviet encroachment and occupation of 1979–89, and vowed to establish a theocracy to be governed by a strict interpretation of the *shariah*, the Islamic law. At first they were supported by Pakistan and Saudi Arabia. Both pulled back, however, once they realized that the Taliban considered the inbred, profligate, and American-supported regimes and elites of the Middle East as their paramount enemy. Obsessed with the containment of Soviet Russia, the U.S. briefly armed the *mujahedeen* (holy warriors), including the Taliban, among them Osama bin Laden. At the time Washington hailed them as freedom fighters.

Meanwhile, the popular fanaticism and violence that were perceived to have ensured the triumph of Shiite fundamentalism in Tehran informed the mutation of the Palestinian *fedayeen* (guerrilla fighters, drawn from Hamas, Islamic Jihad, and Hezbollah) into *mujahedeen*, at once homicidal and suicidal. Supported by Syria and Iran, these religiously fortified militant nationalists became increasingly important to the Palestinian resistance, which had previously been essentially secular and political.

This religious exaltation of mission occurred in Israel as well, especially in the wake of the Six Day War of 1967 and the Yom Kippur (Ramadan) War of 1973. The Torah-observant Jews rallied ever more around the embattled state, now on the final road to redemption following the conquest of Judea and Samaria (the West Bank). The ultra-Orthodox (*haredim*) and the religious Zionists came together: their *Weltanschauung* and way of life, as well as rigid religious practice, bear strong resemblances. But whereas the ultra-Orthodox scorn modern times and turn inward, most religious Zionists live and work in the real world.

The two main branches of religious Zionism transcend such differences as they have when it comes to encouraging and supporting the Judaization of civil and political society, and the settlement movement. During the 1970s they became the chief architects of Gush Emunim and the Yesha Council, important advocates of the settlers (although most did not share their fundamentalism). Following the right-wing Likud's momentous victory in the general elections of 1977, the two settler lobbies secured a pivotal place in the ascendant bloc of religious, conservative, and far-right political parties and factions. Eventually the rabbis of religious Zionism stepped forth as the most vocal and untouchable opponents of renouncing any of the settlements and outposts—the latest symbols of divine reclamation and deliverance. They also succeeded in securing public funding for the expansion of Israel's system of religious elementary schools (*heders*) and rabbinical seminaries (*yeshivas*).

At the start of the twenty-first century the religious fundamentalists stand at over 25 per cent of Israel's Jewish population of 5.4 million.

Their families have an average of 6.5 children—three times the national average for Jewish families as a whole. Between them the religious Zionists and ultra-Orthodox command between 20 and 25 per cent of the 120 seats in the Knesset. Where the original internal critics of political Zionism invoked the book of Isaiah—"Woe to those who go down to Egypt to seek help there, who build their hopes on cavalry, who rely on the number of chariots and on the strength of mounted men, but never look to the Holy One of Israel nor consult the Lord"—the Orthodox of later days heeded God's command to Joshua: rally the Israelites to conquer Canaan, "utterly destroy all that is in the city, both man and woman, young and old, and ox, and sheep and ass, with the edge of the sword . . . And they burnt the city with fire, and all that was therein, only the silver, and the gold, and vessels of brass and of iron, they put into the treasury of the house of the Lord."

The Koran offers a comparable range. It is mild and conciliatory: "God may plant affection between you and those whom you hold as enemies . . . God does not forbid you from showing kindness and dealing justly with those who never fought you over religion nor drove you out of your homes"; the faithful are enjoined to "fight in the way of God against those who fight against you, but do not begin hostilities, for God does not love aggression." And it is tough and fanatical: "Punishment for those who wage war against God and His messenger and strive for corruption in the land is to be killed or crucified or have their hands and legs cut off on alternate sides or expelled out of the land. This is their degradation in this world and they will have an awful punishment in the Hereafter." The current exhortation to fight the greater or major jihad, or struggle against the inner self and social iniquity both spiritually and physically, by tongue and sword, is drowned out by the summons and obligation to enlist in the lesser or minor jihad, or holy war, either defensive or offensive, to "slay enemies wherever you find them, and drive them out from whence they drove you out . . ."

Unlike the two other monotheistic religions of the Book, Judaism is not a religion of conversion. It means to preach by example and make a virtue of tribal separateness. Starting with Roman Emperor Constantine the Great, and well past the Crusades, Christianity prided itself on spreading the Word by the sword. Islam, like Christianity, is latently and intermittently crusading. There is today an offensive jihadist Islamism that knows neither territorial nor temporal borders. But this resurgent millenarianism that resorts to violence to spread the Koran is not the core of the Muslim revival, which is driven less by blind faith than by politics and culture. The objective is to block the West's—above all, America's—military, economic, and cultural penetration of the Muslim world, which it manages by its collaboration with the prodigal regimes of the Middle East and its one-sided backing of Israel.

This defensive Islamism is not of a piece; relatively few of its votaries are fundamentalists or terrorists. Would-be martyrs are in the mix along with adepts who mean to reconcile faith and modernity in both civil and political society. Islamism emerged to fill the vacuum left by the failure of secular forms of resistance: Third World nationalism, pan-Arabism, communism, socialism, and, more lately, American-style electoral free-market democracy. Its combination of the sacred and the profane mobilizes confederates aspiring to diverse outcomes.

To the extent that Islamism, in whatever guise, involves resistance, it is a product of pent-up anger and mortification. Such passions are more easily roused by language couched in religious and cultural idioms, and made more effective still for having been assailed by a West brandishing its ostensibly superior values. The attendant outbursts of nativism also attest to the syncretic nature of Islamism, which is *passéiste* and futuristic, reactionary and progressive. Ismail Haniyeh, the leader of Hamas ("Islamic Resistance Movement"), and Hassan Nasrallah, the leader of Hezbollah ("Party of God"), embody this "simultaneity of the unsimultaneous." So does President Mahmoud Ahmadinejad of Iran: not unlike President Gamal Abdel Nasser of Egypt, who, sworn to secular anti-Western nationalism, had reached for hydroelectric power and threatened to close the Suez Canal, Ahmadinejad, wrapped in the mantle of Islam, reaches for nuclear power and threatens to block the Strait of Hormuz.

Some forty years after the foundation of the state of Israel, several Israeli historians with access to previously unavailable documents began to bear out the Palestinians' contention that Israel must shoulder most of the responsibility for their mass exodus during and after the War of Independence. This revisionist reading has not, however, shaken a general conviction among Jews everywhere that, incited by their leaders, the Palestinians did not flee for their lives but left willfully in the hope of returning in the train of the Arab armies, which would win a lightning victory over the improvised armed forces of the fledgling state of Israel. When enacting the "Law of Return," allowing Jews the world over to emigrate to Eretz Israel, its new governors gave no thought to the Palestinians' own right to return.

According to Ilan Pappé, political scientist and then an historian at Haifa University, in 1948 between 700,000 and 800,000 Palestinians, or close to half the population, fled or were driven out of their homes and off their land. They left behind at least 500 devastated and depopulated villages, and abandoned ten urban neighborhoods. The state of Israel seized their property. During the third Arab–Israeli war of June 1967, about 400,000 Palestinians became refugees, not a few of them for the second time. By 2004 the number of refugees had passed the 7 million mark, owing to successive wars and natural growth. Over 3.5 million Palestinian Arabs are concentrated in the West Bank, the Gaza Strip, and East Jerusalem. Several additional millions live in the neighboring Arab states—the single largest community in Jordan, and the most straitened in Lebanon. Their main habitat is the refugee camp, of which there are fifty-nine. Taking account of the 1 million-plus Arab Palestinian citizens of Israel, the number of Palestinians is as big as the Jewish population of the Holy Land.

The ordeal of the Palestinian refugees became the original sin of Israel's foundation and the curse of Middle Eastern politics and diplomacy. By refusing to admit the problem, Israel contributes at least as much to the volatility of the region as the elites of the neighboring Arab regimes, who exploit the Palestinian cause to bolster their own anti-Western credentials. As a matter of course, the refugees have become the prime social carriers and moving spirits of the Palestinian resistance.

To nearly everyone's astonishment or exasperation, after nearly sixty years this resistance endures despite everything Israel has thrown at it: expulsion, expropriation, debasement, imprisonment, boycott, bombardment, assassination, immurement . . . At the start of the twenty-first century, even with steady and generous help from a broad donor community headed by the United Nations Relief and Works Agency (UNRWA), living conditions and standards in the occupied territories continue to decline. Hundreds of thousands of refugees are unemployed, and live below the international poverty line. Of the rapidly growing population, 40 per cent are under fifteen years of age, many suffering from malnutrition. This misery, multiplied by a general bitterness, guarantees recruiters a vast pool of potential militants, holy warriors, and activists. Literacy, often a contributor to militancy, stands at over 85 per cent in the West Bank and Gaza.

Regardless of political orientation, successive governments of Israel have disclaimed all responsibility for the Palestinian exodus and immiseration. This confident sense of inculpability is projected forward from the recent Judeocide, when the Jews of Europe had indeed been "blameless in life and pure of crime." But the statute of limitations on absolute innocence is expiring, and so is the Christian world's guilt for the Jewish catastrophe. Incongruously, many Israelis and Jews have all but forgotten the collective stain on the Germans and their legions of collaborators and collaborationists, but continue periodically to portray the militant Palestinian resistance and its supporters as Nazis redivivus. Israel's political class keeps alleging that, driven by unreconstructed anti-Semitism, the Palestinian demand for the right of return is its leadership's ploy to gut the Zionist-Israeli state by demographic, cultural, and political subversion. In many circles, fear of the Palestinian population time-bomb is as great as the fear of suicide bombers, medium-range artillery rockets, and long-range nuclear-tipped missiles.

Israel's leaders and citizens face two self-inflicted predicaments: Palestinian refugees and Israeli settlers. Both originate in a world-view and policy consensus that have congealed over the years, and have all the features of Revisionism.

While there is room for disagreement about the degree of Israel's responsibility for the Palestinian exodus, there can be none about its refusal to address the hard fate of the refugees. As for the incursion of the settlers into the Palestinian territories, Israel owns the problem wholly; there are no extenuating circumstances. Since 1967, all Israeli governments have promoted, financed, and protected the establishment and expansion of settlements in the occupied territories. The opening move of the new-model colonization drive was the Allon Plan, adopted immediately after the guns of the Six Day War fell silent. After the plan was conceived by Yigal Allon, prominent military commander and Labor minister, the Knesset voted its warrant and funding, backed by the quasi-official World Zionist Organization, the prime minister's office, and the security services. With time, the ministries of war, housing, construction, and justice were actively engaged, and their agents worked closely with the settlers. Civil society participated too: architects, urban planners, engineers, entrepreneurs, lawyers, physicians, teachers, rabbis. The U.S. provided essential financial support and fended off plaints about Israel's illegal settlement policy in the concert of powers and the Security Council. The American Jewish community became an unstinting backer and political mainstay, and its ultra-Orthodox precincts a wellspring of militant settlers.

Among the objectives of the Allon Plan, none were more important than military security—ensured by strategic depth—territorial expansion, and soft water sources. Like many of the kibbutzim in the past, the settlements became military strong-points, then way-stations from which to extend Israel's borders beyond the 1949 armistice lines. Another calculation was soon made: to locate not only the settlements but also the collateral roads and military bases in such a way as to preclude the formation of a viable, contiguous Palestinian state—the work of Yigal Allon, Moshe Dayan, and other senior officers. Compatible with the clamorous aspirations of secular and religious ultra-nationalists, this Greater Israel would comprise the entire area between the Jordan River and the Mediterranean Sea, with the Jordan Valley and Judean Desert perceived to be of vital military importance. Voicing a widespread assumption shortly before his assassination in November 1995, Premier Yitzhak Rabin stated that there would be "no return to the lines of June 4, 1967," and that Israel wanted the Palestinian territory "to be an entity less than a state."

The logic of this ambitious long-range plan dictated all that ensued: segregated roads, security zones, checkpoints, roadblocks, curfews, fences, walls, barriers, watchtowers, motion detectors, blockades. Even during successive so-called freezes of settlement activity, the colonizing and security drive continued, with Washington looking the other way. The exhortation to settlers in late 1998 by Ariel Sharon, then defense minister in a Likud administration, was typical: "Move, run, and grab as many hilltops as [you] can to enlarge the settlements, because everything we take now will remain ours." Yet the rate and scale of settlement activity was as great, if not actually greater, under Labor governments: Allon, Dayan, Rabin, Shimon Peres, and Barak were as sold on settlement expansion as Begin, Shamir, Netanyahu, Sharon, and Olmert.

By 2007 roughly 450,000 settlers, or close to 10 per cent of Israel's Jewish population, occupied over 140 settlements in East Jerusalem and the West Bank, linked to each other and to Israel by a network of roads. Some 210,000 of these settlers live in some fifty settlements west of the soon-to-be-completed separation/security wall. About 150,000 of the West Bank settlers now reside in eight major urban areas: Modlin Illit, Maale Adumin, Ariel, Givat Zeev, Pisgat Zeev, Alfei Menashe, Efrat, and Karnei Shomron. Close to 65,000 settlers live in seventy-five settlements east of the wall, and some 17,000 settlers are in thirty-three settlements on the Golan Heights. With a yearly growth rate of at least 5 per cent, half of which is among the ultra-Orthodox population, the settler population increases easily twice as fast as that of the nation as a whole. Some ultra-Orthodox settlements grow by 10 per cent each year.

Probably three-quarters of all the settlers went to the territories in search of subsidized, affordable housing, and otherwise to improve their standard of living and quality of life. Nearly 50,000 set forth for reasons of faith, of whom about half believed the land of Zion to be holier and more legitimate than the state of Israel. By predilection, these religious took root in a central part of Judea and Samaria (south and north of Jerusalem) dotted with sites recalling Biblical history, but also densely peopled by Arabs. The most fervent planted themselves in or near the biblically significant towns of Hebron and Nablus. The ultra-Orthodox, along with the religious nationalists, consider the Jews to have exclusive title to the as-yet-indeterminate land of Israel.

After 1967, beyond the provisional and controversial Green Line—the border established by the 1949 armistice agreements, before capture of the West Bank and Gaza in the Six Day War—Tel Aviv put in place a severe occupation regime. The settlers became the pretext for the carefully orchestrated takeover of the territories; the Palestinian refugees became the foot soldiers of the resistance that found expression in the third and fourth intifadas of 1987 and 2000.

Although the human cost of their encounter was high for both sides, it took a disproportionately heavy toll on the Palestinians. From the fourth intifada in 2000 to late 2007, the Israeli Information Center for Human Rights in the Territories (B'Tselem) counted over 4,000 Palestinian dead, of whom more than half were civilians, and over 850 of those minors. During this same period about 800 Israeli soldiers and over 700 civilians lost their lives, of whom close to 120 were minors. The ratio of Palestinians to Israelis killed was roughly three-to-one; for minors, at least four-to-one. The number of wounded (20,000 Palestinians) was similarly asymmetrical.

The Israeli armed forces outclassed the Palestinian resistance in every major respect: by far the mightiest military machine of the greater Middle East faced a virtually unarmed population. Yet the violence escalated, from militants hurling stones and Molotov cocktails at soldiers and tanks to *fedayeen* ambushing military convoys to *mujahedeen* murdering civilians in buses, markets, and entertainment centers inside Israel. Not surprisingly, the attacks on civilians swelled the ranks of Israel's intransigents and lent wings to the politics of fear.

Repression in the occupied territories grew uglier. Besides stepping up assaults by armored cars, tanks, helicopters, airplanes, drones, and remote-controlled missiles, Israeli forces made little effort to spare Palestinian bystanders. A policy of collective punishment and retribution meant the demolition of the homes and orchards of thousands of suspected militants and fellow-travelers, leaving scores without shelter or income. But imprisonment and administrative detention remained by far the most common punitive measures. During the two great intifadas tens of thousands of Palestinians spent extended terms in Israeli jails, where, in violation of Article 3 of the Geneva Conventions, and in the judgment of Israel's High Court of Justice, many were subjected to "cruel and inhuman and degrading treatment." The many killed and injured, and the many others imprisoned and made homeless, served to fuel Palestinian support for the active resistance. In 2007 there are some 10,000 Palestinians in Israeli jails. Many are sympathizers and activists; far fewer are terrorists. But all, more than likely, consider the scourge of occupation and disproportionate retaliation to justify even the most cold-hearted terrorist killings. Certainly they became the major radicalizers of both the Palestinian leadership and the rank-and-file.

The quest for a Greater Israel was latent and implicit in political Zionism, but did not become manifest and well defined until after the 1967 war. Not counting military expenditures, by 2004 the cost of the official settlement policy had exceeded $10 billion. Once the staggering military outlays are added, it becomes clear that successive Israeli governments, not the settlers, led the way.

The occupation ate away not only at the Palestinians, but also at the vitals of Israel's political and civil society. Inevitably, the enormous price of colonizing and policing the territories sapped the budgets for education, social welfare, and research unrelated to weaponry. The country witnessed a considerable rise in poverty, with nearly a million people living on or below the poverty line, including nearly 30 per cent of Israel's children. The creeping immiseration of the past thirty years has hit, in particular, the disfavored communities of the *Mizrahim* (Jews originally from the Near East and North Africa) and Arab Israelis. Among the nations of the First World, Israel has one of the greatest gaps between a small layer of super-wealthy and a large stratum of disadvantaged, along with an increasingly vulnerable and shrinking middle class.

At first the war against the Palestinian resistance was fought along traditional strategic lines, and with conventional forces. Before long, however, with the targets and foes becoming less distinct, the goal changed radically: to stamp out resistance fighters who melted into the countryside, refugee camps, and cities. Faced with an unconventional task, the so-called war on terror assumed a terrorist face of its own. Successive Israeli governments have sanctioned the use of state terror in the form of counter-insurgency operations that have again and again wrought more collateral than intended damage, human and material. The cross-border wars against Lebanon in 1982 and 2006, as well as the security drives in Gaza and the West Bank, intended to deracinate the partisans and infrastructures of the armed resistance, are cases in point. Israel has invariably represented such "surgical" operations—artillery rounds, air strikes, tank charges, home demolitions, dragnets, targeted assassinations—as acts of rightful retaliation or preventive self-defense. Since September 11, 2001, the Israeli leadership justifies its repression as part of the global war on terror, in which it claims to be the vanguard.

The self-glorified citizen army is debased by its serving as protector of the settlers and condoning of their despoliation of the land, vandalism, theft, dispossession, assault, and homicide. The suprema-cism behind such conduct leeches back into Israeli society. Both soldier and settler act with ever-greater impunity. With compulsory military service for men and women, and long-term reserve duty for men, hardly a family has not had a member or close friend helping to man roadblocks and border crossings, tear down houses, and carry out dragnets in the name of law and order, amid a population made ever more sullen, irate, and defiant.

The failure to build bridges between the Jewish and Arab populations, as urged by the internal critics, led ultimately to the construction of a formidable network of barbed-wire fences and concrete walls. Such immurements have historically been symbols of power, presumption, and intimidation, from Hadrian's Wall, to the Great Wall of China, to the Berlin Wall.

Compared with the great Roman and Chinese ramparts, the Berlin Wall was a runt, and was also short-lived, lasting only from 1961 to 1989. Its total length reached 155km, 106km of which consisted of concrete wall plates that were on average 3.6 meters high and 1.2 meters thick, topped by tubular cladding and reinforced by some 56km of mesh-wire fencing, some of it electrified. It also included over 300 watchtowers, and nearly sixty bunkers. It was patrolled by armed guards and police dogs, supplemented at night by searchlights.

Israel's rampart bears a familial resemblance. When completed, the eastern barrier fronting on the West Bank—its main section—will run between 650km and 670km (403 and 416 miles), or four times the length of the Berlin Wall. Most of it will consist of barbed- and razor-wire fencing 6 meters high; concrete slabs will make up the rest. Concentrated in and around certain cities, some of these walled segments measure up to 8 meters in height and 3 meters in width—as in and around Greater Jerusalem. Along its entire trajectory will run wide and deep trenches, roads for patrol cars, watchtowers, locked gates, and army posts, as well as motion sensors, video cameras, and aerial drones. By the end of 2005, at least one half of the network had either been built or was under construction, with the government hoping to finish it by 2008. The total cost is estimated at 10 billion new shekels, or about $2 billion.

At first sight, the wall's construction suggests that the country might be switching from an offensive to a defensive posture. After defeating the Arab states in 1948–9, Israel fought five more cross-border wars with countries that, in different degrees and ways, continued to support the Palestinians. Though it won these wars without difficulty, and despite its military predominance, the victories were pyrrhic. In due course Israel did secure a cold peace, as well as commerce with Egypt and Jordan, heavily subsidized by America. But it failed to impose its legitimacy in the greater Middle East and to break the Palestinian resistance, which only became more far-flung and virulent; its thick-growing web of autonomous and often rival groups, without much hierarchical structure, persevered despite heavy losses in its ranks and leadership.

The idea of the wall, like that of the settlements, originated with the Labor Party. Prime Minster Rabin was one of the first to broach it, following two bursts of violence in Jerusalem and Gaza in 1992 and 1994, before the rise of suicide terror. He ordered the construction of a fence to surround the Gaza Strip, hewing fairly closely to the 1949 Green Line. Rabin invoked the need for eventual clear borders that would mark the physical "separation between us and them," but went out of his way to add that Israel need not be bound by the line. Barak adopted the same position, through to Oslo; thereafter the idea took root on the composite Israeli right. In time nearly the entire political class embraced the security barrier, ostensibly to prevent suicide bombers from infiltrating into the country and settlements. Before long over 75 per cent of Israel's Jewish population approved of the Gaza and West Bank barriers, which drastically reduced the incidence of terrorist violence in the homeland. But this lull was bound to be no more than the calm before the storm.

Were it not for Israel's refusal to quit most settlements and enter upon sincere negotiations, there would be no need for "security" zones, fences, and walls. Such emplacements are anachronistic anyway, as the United Nations of Arms Makers, Merchants, and Traffickers rushes to furnish the necessary antidotes: rockets and missiles flying at higher altitudes, greater distances, and carrying heavier payloads. The ramparts also rouse militants to fresh ingenuity in tunneling their way under. Nevertheless, seizing on the idea of the "defensive" bulwark, Israel's generals and politicians both deceived the world and deluded themselves.

Initially they were discreet about the wall's invasive edge and purpose: it was meant to serve the occupation in the territories, with the eastern wall encroaching on the land of the Palestinians of the West Bank. Naturally there was no acknowledging that the contingent reason for it was to protect Israel from suicide bombings that its own policies had provoked in the first place. Instead, these abhorrent attacks were cited as further evidence of the innate savagery of the insurgents, and proof that the Palestinian leaders could not be trusted to negotiate in good faith and to crack down on their extremists. The armed resistance and terror, nearly all Israeli leaders maintained, sprang from Islamic fundamentalism and deep-rooted anti-Semitic anti-Zionism, independent of specific political circumstances. Embracing an ideological essentialism and determinism, these anti-temporal "intentionalists" beat out the minority of historicist "functionalists," who take account of not only the text but the context of the Palestinian fury.

Although the eastern separation barrier was aggressively promoted to foil suicide bombers, its advocates had several other largely unspoken objectives on the West Bank: to create Jewish territorial contiguity and Palestinian non-contiguity; to preserve military control; to push Palestinians out of certain regions; and selectively to expand Israeli territory beyond the Green Line.

This last objective entails routing the wall to include on the "Israel" side the three major settlement blocs or colonies: Maale Adumim, an eastward extension of Jerusalem with a population of over 30,000 in a municipal area the size of Tel Aviv; Gush Etzion, located between Bethlehem and Hebron, with a population of over 20,000; and Ariel, between Ramallah and Nablus, deep in the West Bank, with a population of about 20,000. East Jerusalem, with about 200,000 settlers, has long since been taken for granted as part of Israel, and is securely behind the wall.

The barrier is not intended to enclose the 6,200 Israeli settlers in the 35 settlements occupying nearly half of the fertile Jordan Valley atop the Eastern Water Basin, and with access to the water of the Jordan River. This strip of land in the far-eastern West Bank is intended to provide strategic depth, as well as a parapet to prevent the smuggling of arms and the infiltration of *fedayeen* from Jordan into the West

Bank. Although the political–military caste speak of it rarely, they are comforted that Ariel is an outpost halfway to Jordan's border. What matters is that any future border should preclude the formation of a geographically integrated, militarily credible, and economically sound Palestinian state with East Jerusalem as its capital.

Washington must have condoned this grand design. Although Israel's Supreme Court ruled on June 30, 2004 that a section of the barrier near Jerusalem violated the rights of the Palestinians, it judged the wall as an entity to be legal, upholding the government's argument that it was necessary for Israel's security. A week later the International Court of Justice issued a nonbinding advisory opinion: wherever the barrier crosses the 1967 boundary between Israel and the Palestinian territories, it violates international law. The two negative rulings prompted the Sharon government to make a correction: it reduced the challenged section by one half. But, mindful of demographics, it rerouted the wall in such a way as to simultaneously reduce from 100,000 to 10,000 the number of Palestinian Arabs who would find themselves on its "Israel" side. In a letter to Sharon of April 14, 2004, President Bush recognized that "in light of new realities on the ground"—a virtual paraphrase and blessing of Zionism's standard practice of creating "facts on the ground"—"including already existing major Israeli population centers," Israel could not be expected to consider a "full and complete return to the armistice lines of 1949." Both houses of Congress all but unanimously endorsed the letter, which Israel construes as a license to disregard injunctions to freeze the growth of settlements inside its anticipated territorial borders.

Indeed, before the unilateral and spurious pullout from Gaza in August–September 2005, Sharon declared that the Ariel bloc would be expanded and strengthened, and would "forever remain an inseparable part of Israel and . . . territorially connected with Israel, as will [the] other blocs." Shortly thereafter, with Vice-Premier Peres at his side, he told the Knesset that his government's development projects included "not only the Negev, the Galilee, and Greater Jerusalem," but also "the Jordan Valley, the settlement blocs, the security areas, and the Golan Heights." As for the "security fence . . . we will continue in full force to build [it], without any budgetary or political restrictions."

Ehud Olmert, Sharon's successor, also partnered by Peres (and Bush) assumes an identical posture: "The entire Ariel bloc is an integral [and] inseparable part of the state of Israel and will remain so forever"—along with the two other main settlement blocs, united

Jerusalem, and the Jordan Valley, "it being impossible to give up control over Israel's eastern border" along the Jordan River. Likewise the Golan, said to be of great strategic and aquiferous importance, "will remain in our hands forever." The fence-wall will be finished "as quickly as possible," in 2008, a widely popular position perfectly in keeping with Jabotinsky's rule: bring the Palestinian Arabs to heel, not to the table. Meanwhile outposts and settlements continue to be established on the far side of the Green Line, in the West Bank: in 2006 the settler population increased by 6 per cent, and in 2007 by 4.5 per cent.

Beyond its importance as a physical rampart and expansionist wedge, the wall is a state of mind—an act of cultural, emotional, and political separation. No doubt it will continue to keep down the number of suicide bombings inside the Green Line, which dropped from 50 in 2002, killing 210 Israelis, to 6 in 2005, killing 23. But this temporary tranquility entails a further seclusion. Having averted or thwarted bona fide negotiations, the leaders of Israel propose to find safety in a custom-built Western ghetto set in a vast Arab–Muslim neighborhood. As the separation barrier becomes coterminous with the state's coveted final borders, it stands starkly for the largely self-created impasse on the Palestinian Question.

Zionism's call to make *aliyah* was meant to inspire Jews to break loose from the ghetto. The "city on the hill" beaming "light unto the nations" was conceived as the antithesis of czarist Russia's Pale of Settlement, a magnet for people of the *galuth*, or the lands of exile. Except in times of dire threat, individuals and communities are moved to migrate by the push of despair and the pull of dreams. With the demise of the ghetto in the diaspora and its resurrection in Zion, the impetus for *aliyah* is at an all-time low, except among fundamentalist Jews who historically have flourished spiritually in the seclusion of the ghetto, whether forced or unforced. Conscription, overlordship, ethnic division, physical insecurity, and economic uncertainty overshadow the myth and romance of the kibbutz of yore. The kibbutzniks themselves, now less than 2 per cent of Israel's population, are an endangered species: only two members of the seventeenth Knesset live on a kibbutz, and one on a moshav (an agricultural cooperative).

There are today more Jews in the diaspora than in the Holy Land. In 2004, of the world's 13–14 million Jews, over 5.2 million were Israelis; about the same number were Americans. Between them, Israel and America are home to 80 per cent of the world's Jews. Most of the rest are divided between Europe, Latin America, and the

British Commonwealth. Jews who migrate now in search of a better life are more apt to move from one diaspora to another, with North America and Europe, including Germany and East-Central Europe, the preferred destinations. With slightly over 19,000 immigrants in 2006—down nearly 10 per cent from the previous year—immigration to Israel was then at its lowest point since 1988, the influx of immigrants from the former Soviet Union having largely come to a halt by 2002.

As Israelis come to realize the indispensability of America for the survival of their country, they are less disdainful of its diaspora Jews. Although, at between 5 and 6 million, Jews are about 2 per cent of the U.S. population, they exert a disproportionate influence in government, the foreign policy establishment, the academy, the learned and liberal professions, and the media, finance, and business sectors. American Jews enjoy unprecedented freedom, prosperity, status, and power. There are forty-three Jewish members of the 110th Congress (thirteen senators, thirty representatives), all but two of them Democrats. To date there is nearly unqualified bipartisan support for Israel, so that a change in the control of the House of Representatives and/or Senate is likely to make no effective difference. The American Israel Public Affairs Committee (AIPAC) is one of America's most powerful lobbies (alongside the American Association of Retired People, the National Rifle Association, the U.S. Chamber of Commerce, and the American Petroleum Institute). It has a multi-million-dollar yearly budget and a large staff. Although not registered as an agent of the Israeli government, AIPAC is in lockstep with it. Ever since its foundation in the 1950s, AIPAC has more or less uncritically backed all Israeli governments, but in recent years has tended to favor Likud, in keeping with its own increasingly conservative bent. It has not hesitated to join hands with predominantly white Christian Zionists or Evangelicals—an outreach publicly encouraged by Israel. In recognition of their support, in 1980 Prime Minister Menachem Begin awarded Moral Majority founder Jerry Falwell the Vladimir Zeev Jabotinsky Medal, while in 2004 Benny Elon, Israel's Minister of Tourism, presented televangelist Pat Robertson of the Christian Broadcasting Network with Israel's Ambassador Award. Two years later the televangelist Reverend John C. Hagee organized a lobby comparable to AIPAC—a "Christian" AIPAC—to make heard the voices of some 40 million conservative evangelicals in support of Israel. At its inaugural "Washington/Israel Summit" in the capital, in the summer of 2006, the roster of scheduled speakers included, besides the Israeli ambassador, several Republican senators, Reverend Jerry Falwell, and Gary Bauer, founder of the conservative political action committee, the Campaign for Working Families. Hagee characterized the Second Lebanese War as "a battle between good and evil" and support for Israel as "God's foreign policy."

Focusing on Congress, AIPAC initiates and helps pass pro-Israel legislation, including bills extending record grants and loans. Its effectiveness is neither hidden nor questioned: cumulatively Israel has received the largest amount of U.S. foreign aid of any country since 1948, running to some $100 billion. Since 1976 it has been the largest annual recipient of direct economic and military aid: in 2004 Washington extended $2.3 billion in military assistance and over $500 million in economic aid. Another $2 billion annually flows in from philanthropy and the proceeds of Israel Bonds. Domestically, AIPAC contributes indirectly to the coffers of critical congressional races, and helps mobilize the pro-Israel electorate in key states and cities with heavy concentrations of Jewish voters, who go to the polls in disproportionate numbers. From 1978 to 2000 it supported scores of candidates for the House and Senate, spending close to $34 million. It inveighs against its critics, and those of Israel, indiscriminately leveling the charge of anti-Semitism as a matter of course. AIPAC was most probably the inspiration for the foundation of the Middle East Forum, a right-wing research center that generally shares its positions. The Forum has an affinity with the website Campus Watch, launched in 2002 to "monitor Middle East Studies" at universities, which involves asking students to "send in names and information" about professors "suspected of anti-Israeli bias," and hence of anti-Semitism or Jewish "self-hatred." The kindred pro-Israel Committee for Accurate Middle East Reporting in America (CAMERA) keeps an eagle eye on the fourth estate.

To enlarge its reach, AIPAC collaborates closely with the American Israel Education Foundation (AIEF), which provides position papers to influential congressmen and opinion-makers. It has an interlocking directorate with the Conference of Presidents of Major American Jewish Organizations, representing over fifty Jewish organizations nationwide; CPMAJO formulates and articulates the ostensibly monolithic Jewish community's stance on the international politics bearing on the Arab–Israeli conflict, as broadly conceived. To bolster this effort, in 1985 AIPAC set up the Washington Institute for Near East Policy (WINEP), a think tank whose action intellectuals not only write position papers but occupy prominent posts in the mainstream media and councils of government.

It is a mark of AIPAC's exceptional, if questionable political status that, in May 2005, Secretary of State Condoleezza Rice addressed its national convention, and nearly half the members of the House and Senate attended the closing reception. In November of the same year, Kenneth Mehlman and Howard Dean—chairmen of the Republican and Democratic national committees, respectively—spoke at an AIPAC-sponsored "Salute to Congress." Both stressed that Israel had been a valuable pacesetter in the new global war on terror, although they differed on the wisdom of the war in Iraq. Just as Israel had had compelling reasons to make a preventive surgical raid against Iraq's nuclear reactor in Osirak in June 1981, Mehlman held, so the U.S. was right to attack Saddam Hussein in order to destroy his capacity to make weapons of mass destruction, and to prevent Iraq from becoming a base of operations for al-Qaeda. The logic of U.S.–Israeli collaboration was strengthened even though Israel was wary of the Bush administration's policy of promoting regime change by way of destabilization and managed elections, fearing an upsurge of the Islamists in the Arab street and at the polls. In August 2007, following the Second Lebanon War and Hamas' ascendancy in Gaza, AIPAC and the AIEF organized an all-expenses-paid trip to Israel for forty members of Congress from both parties, and their staff, in connection with the twinned initiatives of a Saudi Arabian arms deal and an Israeli military aid package. Responding to the threat from Iran, the U.S. extended to Israel an additional $30 billion, ten-year military aid package amounting to nearly $5,000 per Israeli citizen.

No doubt the leadership of the pro-Israel lobby as a whole is more hawkish and uncompromising than America's Jewish population in general. But since most Jewish US peaceniks are of the mainstream Peres–Barak persuasion, the largest and most powerful Jewish diaspora fundamentally mirrors the Israeli consensus. That consensus, after all, accords closely with the national and imperial interest of the U.S., which commands the first loyalty of American Jews—the great majority identifying themselves as Democrats.

Until recently, American Jews have in the main had an unskeptical emotional attachment to Israel—a badge of their Jewish identity in a time of declining religious observance, rising intermarriage (to over 50 per cent), and widespread acculturation. The greater number still venerate the state of Israel as their ancestors venerated God, with fundraising and lobbying serving as the rituals of a civil religion; and yet the fealty of young adults and the middle-aged has begun to weaken. The explosion of interfaith matrimony and the decline of religiosity coincide with the waning of American Jewry's cultural coherence. This dissociation, measured by a drop in annual giving and engagement in Jewish life beyond the synagogue, grows in response to the excesses of the occupation and the repression of the resistance. The Second Lebanon War of 2006 only sharpened a healthy skepticism about Israel's policy of unilateralism and militarism, unconditionally aided and abetted by the U.S. But in the spring of 2006, still confident in the sway of America's Jewish community, acting Prime Minister Olmert had good reason to aver, "Thank God we have AIPAC, the greatest supporter and friend we have in the whole world."

While immigration to Israel stalls, there is a *yerida*, or descent, into the *galuth*. This reverse *aliyah* is motivated by many of the same factors that deter potential immigrants: economic uncertainty, military service, and personal insecurity. On November 10, 2006, Israel's Deputy Defense Minister Ephraim Sneh chose to depict the future thus: Iran's acquisition of a nuclear bomb would prompt an exodus, since no one was keen on being "scorched," which would enable Ahmadinejad "to wipe out the Zionists without pushing a button." This fear-mongering recalls Yeshayahu Leibowitz's earlier wry observation that Jews "have never had it so good the world over" as they do today, "except in Israel, where they live in a state of permanent danger."

The protean world of Zion-Israel may be said to undergo what Weber, in another context, conceived as a "rationalization, intellectualization and, above all, 'disenchantment of the world.'" During any new state's transition from the poetry of foundation to the prose of consolidation and nation-building, "ultimate and more sublime values [retreat] from public life." As "the tension between religion and intellectual knowledge comes to the fore," one has to "choose between [the] religious dignity [of the] ethics . . . of the Sermon on the Mount and the dignity of manly conduct which preaches something quite different." In such moments "many old . . . and disenchanted gods ascend from their graves . . . and strive to gain power over our lives" as "they resume their eternal struggle with one another." The sacred and the profane, the moral and the political, the archaic and the modern—these currents, Weber argues, cross and combine with a particular power.

In the eyes of the Israelis themselves, as well as of the diasporists and the world at large, the nation's disenchantment is revealed in its loss of the aura of exceptionalism that has hitherto surrounded the innocence of its citizenry and the righteousness of its cause. One hundred years after the founding Zionist congress in Basel, and some sixty years after the Judeocide and independence, Israel is arguably a terror or rogue state—no longer a beacon unto the world.

This may well be the kind of disillusionment that inclines some of the new diasporists to embrace the dream of improving their and their children's life chances outside of Israel. In 2006 roughly 650,000 Israelis—12.5 per cent of the country's Jewish population—are estimated to be living abroad, 60 per cent of them in North America and 25 per cent in Europe. That same year 4,500 Israelis opted to become German citizens; numbering at least 100,000, Germany's Jewish population is Europe's third-largest. A brain drain has brought over 20 per cent of Israeli academics to the U.S., among them physicians, physicists, chemists, computer scientists, and economists. The transfiguration of Jerusalem, the deficit of democracy, and the narrowing of intellectual horizons are other factors in an unexpected *yerida* that, not unlike draft-dodging, seems to carry increasingly less of a stigma.

The Holy City demonstrates most radically Israel's religious and xenophobic turn. Political profiles of the presumed capital's three mayors tell the story: Theodor "Teddy" Kollek (1965–93), consummate Laborite who furthered Jewish dominance over the entire city and settlement beyond the Green Line, with calculated concern for everyday coexistence with the Palestinians; Ehud Olmert (1993–2003), zealous Likudist who defeated Kollek with a call for a unified Jerusalem and, supported by the religious, aggressively promoted Jewish settlement in the city's Arab neighborhoods; and Uri Lupolianski (2003–), Orthodox nationalist–Zionist rabbi who furthers the outright Judaization of the city. Sworn to making Jerusalem the capital of Israel, all three disregarded the fact that the city is Islam's third-holiest after Mecca and Medina, and sought to curtail the indigenous Palestinians' physical and political presence.

On June 7, 1967, the day the Israel Defense Forces (IDF) swept into East Jerusalem, Minister of Defense Moshe Dayan proclaimed, "we have united Jerusalem, the divided capital of Israel . . . We have returned to the most sacred of our Holy Places, never to part from it again." Gazing into the beyond, toward Biblical sites, he vowed: "We have returned to Shiloh and Anathot . . . forever." Later, Shlomo Goren, Chief Chaplain and Brigadier General of the armed forces, and future Ashkenazic Chief Rabbi of Israel, went to the Wailing Wall to pray for soldiers "who fell for their loyalty to God and the land of Israel, who fell for the liberation of the Temple Mount, the Western Wall, and Jerusalem, the city of the Lord." With the sound of gunfire in the background, he then blew the shofar—a ceremonial ram's horn—to herald the coming of the Messianic redemption. By the end of the month the Knesset voted to extend "the application of Israeli law, jurisdiction, and administration" to the eastern half of Jerusalem. In April 1968 Israeli authorities, including Kollek, approved the confiscation and leveling of the houses of two Palestinian neighborhoods to make way for an enlarged plaza in front of the Wailing Wall. On June 30, 1980, the city was formally annexed and declared the eternal and indivisible capital of Israel.

Jerusalem is Israel's first city, with over 10 per cent of the country's population. Extending over 50 square miles—or twice Tel Aviv and Haifa combined—its population has grown from some 84,000 in 1948 to nearly 700,000 in 2004, 470,000 of them Jews, 230,000 Arabs. East Jerusalem counts about 400,000 inhabitants, a good half of them Jews and their descendants who rushed to settle there after 1967; the other half are Palestinians. Some 32,000 Palestinians and 4,000 Jews live within the walls of the Old City.

The Jewish communities of Jerusalem are heavily religious, and have a much higher natural growth rate than the rest of the country—except for the Arab minority, which roughly matches it. Easily one of Israel's poorest cities, it has a disproportionately young population and a large number of seminarians, unemployed, and supporters of fundamentalist settlers. Lupolianski hails the latter for invigorating the new Jerusalem, their prized public stage. Over one-third of the city's Jewish population are *haredim* and religious Zionists. Another third claim to be secular, compared with some 75 per cent in Tel Aviv and Haifa. About 45 per cent of the more than 200,000 pupils in Jerusalem attend ultra-Orthodox elementary schools, most of them publicly funded; and well over half of its *haredi* men are lifelong *yeshiva* students who forbear gainful employment and are exempt from military service. The political nerve center of Israel's Orthodox, Jerusalem posted an 18.5 per cent vote for Shas—the party representing primarily Sephardic ultra-Orthodox Jews—and 12.5 per cent for the National Union–Religious Party alliance—a coalition representing far right and religiously anchored constituencies, with a heavy settler component. By comparison, only 12 per cent of voters in Tel Aviv supported those two formations combined.

Both the national government and municipal administration intend to cement Israel's full sovereignty over Greater Jerusalem, with the establishment of a clear Jewish majority in annexed East Jerusalem at the top of the agenda. By early 2006 the projected separation wall was designed to enclose all of the city, including the main settlement blocs to the far side of what has already been annexed. Rather than expand its perimeter to the limit, the political architects of the wall will so draw its line as to expel by dejurisdiction a minimum of 55,000 of the 200,000 Palestinians, leaving about a quarter of the city's Arab population cut off from essential social and municipal services. The unspoken objective is to solidify mastery over the undivided capital by increasing its number of Jews, reducing its number of Palestinian Israelis, and forcibly expanding Jewish Jerusalem deep into the West Bank. Once the idea of the separation barrier reached its season, this Greater Jerusalem, defined to include two of the three major settlement blocs, was bound to be enclosed by a rampart. In mid-June 2006, Olmert characteristically declared that

> I, as prime minister of Israel, will never, ever, ever agree to a compromise on the complete control over the Temple Mount. And not only the Temple Mount, but also the Old City, the Mount of Olives, and every place that is an inseparable part of Jewish history.

A year later, to mark the fortieth anniversary of Israel's capture of East Jerusalem, the U.S. House of Representatives, by a near-unanimous voice vote, adopted a nonbinding resolution congratulating Israel for its "reunification" of the Holy City, and urging that America officially recognize it as "the undivided capital of Israel."

There is no ignoring the breathless rise of Israel's warfare state, with its military/high-tech complex and advanced weaponry, lately buttressed by a redoubtable barrier-wall. This anatomy of power bears out Martin Buber's worst fears. In the midst of the nation's difficult birth he had held that, without a radical reorientation toward the Palestinian Arabs and the neighboring states, any armistice would be tenuous; the new state would "be compelled to maintain a permanent posture of vigilance." Yet even he could never have imagined that Israel would develop one of the world's strongest armed forces, a nuclear capability, and one of the world's major armaments industries, which exports two-thirds of its output.

The armed forces (it is as specious to speak of Israeli "Defense" Forces as it is of the American "Defense" Department) have become a pivotal institution of Israeli civil and political society. On reaching 18 years of age, men are called to arms for three years, women for two. Until middle age, men report, service gun in hand, for active reserve duty for one month every year—a practice that prompted a senior officer to extol the national reserve as "soldiers on eleven months'

vacation." The army inculcates such values as unquestioning patriotism and obedience, and teaches a military code that extenuates
"excessive excess" in battle and in "security" operations in the
occupied territories. This pedagogy becomes part of the integration
of new immigrants to Israel. The military establishment has also
become closely intertwined with the universities, especially the facul-
ties of physical, natural, and computer sciences. The weapons industry
in particular is a large sector in the national economy, given its
phenomenal budget; and the armed services, including the intelligence
services Mossad and Shin Bet, are regular customers of nearly all other
major sectors. Unsurprisingly, two-thirds of the aid the military
receives from the U.S. must be spent on made-in-America ordnance.
Naturally this proviso invites steady collaboration between Israeli and
American arms firms, with active and retired senior officers on both
sides trading on their access to the military and political corridors of
power.

Apart from its sheer power and ubiquity, the Israeli military
establishment is barely subject to civilian control. Although the
Knesset approves the defense budget after it has been vetted by the
free-market economists of the Finance Ministry, it tends to use the
rubber stamp. High-ranking officers hold key political positions, from
prime minister to the ministries of war, intelligence, and foreign
affairs. They also become expert advisors, political operatives, and
pundits. Active, retired, and reserve officers form a cohesive and
immensely influential corps with a shared temper and way of thinking.
The military's influence is all the greater because of the fundamental
consensus of the political parties on major diplomatic and military
issues.

A permanent state of alert, recurrent resort to arms, and long-term
emergency rule in the occupied territories degrade a democratic civil
and political society. To be sure, Israel has free presidential and
parliamentary elections. But with the occupation and colonization of
the territories operating as a pervasive concern, elections are more
often than not in the nature of referenda. The electorate is asked to
choose between two alternatives that differ in rhetoric only: the major
parties swear by the quest for absolute security, the pursuit of "facts
on the ground," and the imposition of a dictated final settlement. As
merchants of fear, they drastically narrow the marketplace of ideas
about foreign and domestic policy. There is barely a whisper about a
broad range of fundamental issues. Living way beyond its means, the
country is hooked on its limitless American credit card, which under-
writes the oversized military budget. (Aptly, this account is currently

managed by Stanley Fischer, an American executive once high up in
the World Bank, International Monetary Fund, and Citigroup—until
2005, when he became governor of the Bank of Israel.) Also scanted in
electoral debates are the absolute priority of guns over butter, the
neglect of the *Mizrahim*, and the unchanging discrimination against
the Arab-Palestinian minority. Passed over in silence is Israel's political dependence on the U.S.: at crucial moments Washington exercises
its veto on behalf of Tel Aviv in the U.N. Security Council, as it did
most recently during the Lebanese War of 2006. Nor is there much
discussion of repeated violations of U.N. Security Council Resolutions
242 and 338, international law, and the Geneva Conventions. As for
Israel's wager on weapons of mass destruction, it is beyond the bounds
of electoral debate.

In terms of per capita military spending, Israel ranks first in the
world—even ahead of the U.S., which ranks third. Although largely
paid for by the U.S. and the diaspora Jews, the outsized military
outlays—10 per cent of GNP—squeeze social spending at a time of
heightened strains and stresses in Israeli society, intensified by the side-
effects of laissez-faire capitalism and globalization. In 2005 roughly 34
per cent of Israelis, including Palestinian Israelis, earned the minimum
wage or less; some 50 per cent of high school students failed to
graduate. Politicians channel social discontents into the perennial
"existential struggle" with the Palestinians, as many Israelis heed
the piercing ultra-nationalist, religious, anti-Arab, and Islamophobic
sirens.

The legal system, too, is formally democratic but also gravely
compromised by the security imperative, the state of emergency in
the occupied territories, and the abuse of eminent domain. For the
most part higher courts validate legal legerdemain in cases pertaining
to the expropriation of the property of Palestinians. Judges and
members of the Knesset's Committee on Constitution, Law, and
Justice invoke security and sectarian considerations when denying
and restricting the civil and human rights of Arab Israelis and
Palestinians in the territories. In like manner, they shrug off targeted
killings and the collateral injuries to innocent bystanders. As for the
broad privileges and immunities of the religious estate, they are
guaranteed by a state that defines itself as at once democratic and
sectarian. On the whole, the separation of state and religion is treated
more as a vexed and embarrassing question than as a vital and pressing
constitutional and political issue. There is only a politically worn-
down, though intellectually vigorous challenge to the broadly defined
Orthodox rabbinate's virtually divine prerogative as regards rites of

passage, citizenship, and conversion, as well as state-funded religious schools, the law of return, blue laws, parochial schools, and special status for seminarians.

A democratic system corroded by fear and devitalized by a national consensus on the Palestinian Question further narrows debate of serious alternatives. With the major parties representing a heavy majority all but agreed on Israel's policy toward the Palestinians at home and abroad, and with the minor parties being supplicants of power, there is no steady, loyal opposition of significance on the core issues of borders, settlements, refugees, security, and Jerusalem.

Following Brit Shalom and Ihud, Israel's peace camp tried to fill this void. While the leaders and activists of the Peace Now and Gush Shalom extra-parliamentary movements have been largely associated with the left—mainly Labor—they have also drawn from the center-left. Peace Now for a time drew support from Meretz (a left-wing secular and social reformist party) and Shinui (anti-clerical and free-market); all three parties were intermittently critical of Gush Shalom for allegedly pandering to the Palestinians by not insisting on an unconditional end to all violence and terror as a sine qua non for cooperation between peace advocates on both sides. In the 2006 elections, Meretz won five seats in the Knesset, down one from the preceding legislature, while Shinui, by then hawkish, lost all its fifteen seats through factional infighting.

Against enormous odds, Peace Now and Gush Shalom, headed by Yariv Oppenheimer and Uri Avnery respectively, resolutely hold to their informed opposition, and occasionally rally massive popular support around their banners, as they did after the 1982 massacres in the Palestinian camps of Sabra and Shatila in Lebanon. Both groups benefit from the remarkable investigative work of B'Tselem, the Israeli Committee Against House Demolitions (ICAHD), and the Center for the Defense of the Individual (HaMoked). Yet they lack public intellectuals of the stature of the first internal critics, and despite a broader popular base than Brit Shalom and Ihud, remain at the margins. The Sisyphean nature of their task combines with the fear of random terrorist and rocket attacks to discourage left-radical activist dissent.

The 2006 Lebanon War confirmed the discomfiture of this stunted, but steadfast and tenacious opposition, which rallied around the Olmert–Peretz government, agreeing that Israel had "the legitimate right to defend itself," and stood "with the mainstream of Israelis." A week into the war, on July 20, 2006, when Israel's disproportionate reaction was plain to see, the noted novelist and pro-Labor peace activist Amos Oz claimed that Israel was "not invading Lebanon," but was "defending itself from a daily harassment and bombardment of our towns and villages by attempting to smash Hezbollah where it lurks." Rejecting any "moral equation between Hezbollah and Israel," he insisted that, whereas the former was "targeting Israeli civilians wherever they are," the latter was "targeting mostly Hezbollah." Oz summoned the "Israeli peace movement . . . to support Israel's attempt at self-defense, pure and simple, as long as this operation . . . spares, as much as possible, the lives of Lebanese civilians"—admittedly difficult, because "Hezbollah missile-launchers often use Lebanese civilians as sandbags." His literary peer and advocate of Arab–Israeli conciliation David Grossman held that "no country in the world could remain silent and abandon its citizens when its neighbor strikes without any provocation." Both passed over their government's part in the escalation of an ordinary border incident into a deadly conflict.

It was not until practically a month after the start of the thirty-four-day war that Peace Now and Meretz called for what turned out to be a small demonstration to protest not the war as such, but simply and solely its flawed conduct. Billed nevertheless as an anti-war protest, the rally was all but overshadowed by a swelling right-wing campaign damning the government, intelligence services, and high command for their misjudgments, missteps, and failures of nerve, and calling for a better-executed war next time. The pounding of Lebanon, especially Beirut, went unaddressed, while the concurrent punishment of Gaza was entirely out of mind.

Peace Now and Gush Shalom, compared with Brit Shalom and Ihud in their day, have less resonance in the diaspora. Their counterparts and sympathizers in the U.S.—Americans for Peace Now, Jewish Alliance for Justice and Peace (Brit Tsedek v'Shalom), Jewish Voice for Peace, Meretz USA—have so far had little influence and no power. AIPAC and its confederates all but ignore them.

Although Yeshayahu Leibowitz had the learning, wisdom, and civic courage of his contemporaries, Magnes and Buber, he had none of their international recognition, and remained a relative loner. A professor of chemistry who had studied philosophy at Heidelberg, Leibowitz was both Orthodox and a man of the European Enlightenment. Between 1967 and 1994, the year of his death, Leibowitz articulated the principles of critical Zionism. As a political fundamentalist, he stressed the separation of synagogue and state: political

Zionism and nationalism were carriers of secular, not religious, values. To place God "in the service of politics" was to tempt idolatry.

Victory in the Six Day War moved Leibowitz to caution against becoming "intoxicated by national pride, military arrogance, and fantasies of Messianic deliverance." To occupy Arab territories, let alone conquer them, would be to destroy Israel "morally," transforming its state into an instrument of "domination and repression." Indiscriminate reprisals were not simply immoral, but counterproductive. *Fedayeen* stabbing Israeli civilians in the streets of Tel Aviv, or Israeli soldiers firing on Palestinian teenagers with live bullets in the streets of Ramallah—how were these not equivalent? The founder of Gush Shalom, Uri Avnery, saw a similar moral equivalence between the murder by hit squad of Rehavam Zeevi, Sharon's Tourism Minister, in October 2001 in Jerusalem, and the assassination by missile of Sheikh Ahmed Yassin, co-founder and spiritual guide of the Islamist Hamas, in March 2004 in Gaza. An ultra-nationalist, Zeevi had advocated the negotiated "transfer" of Palestinian Israelis to Arab countries as a "cure" for the country's "demographic ailment," insisting that transfer, a euphemism for expulsion, was preferable to killing. In the same period, Leibowitz had continued to encourage and support soldiers who, for reasons of conscience, refused to serve in the occupied territories, and pilots who objected to flying punitive missions that put civilians at risk.

Leibowitz had in fact been the inspiration for the foundation of Yesh Gvul ("There is a Limit") in 1982, in reaction to the First Lebanon War. A small organization of limited means, it continues to provide moral, financial, and legal support to conscientious objectors. Those rallying to its banner declare that, as

> candidates for service and soldiers in the IDF, men and women, [and] as responsible citizens . . . we will take no part in the continued repression of the Palestinian people in the occupied territories and we will not participate in policing actions or in guarding the settlements.

Nearly 200 refuseniks served prison terms during the third intifada, and at least again as many during the fourth. By the end of 2005, over 1,000 had taken a stand. Few stepped forward during the Second Lebanon War. But under the banner of "Breaking the Silence," soldiers and reservists, jolted by their own transgressions, are stepping forth to relate what they "saw and did during their tour of duty" on the West Bank and in Gaza.

Israel's hegemonic institutions, including the universities, have long since made their peace with the warfare state, their neglect of the refugees, the occupation, the settlements, the expropriations, and the annexation of East Jerusalem. Politically engaged academics, writers, and artists were largely pro-Labor and favored Oslo, or the exchange of land for peace. Sorely disappointed by Oslo's failure, which most blamed on Arafat, they turned inward, and away from the peace camp. Relatively few academics and literati signed petitions, let alone took to the streets to decry the excesses of the occupation and warfare state. Typically of its species, the greater part of the intelligentsia disengaged politically to get on with its professional life.

By their silence, university faculty and students acquiesce in Israel's many questionable policies. With such policies being implemented practically next door to their homes, offices, and classrooms, they are deprived of the proverbial excuse that they "did not know" anything about them. In 1982 Bar-Ilan University, near Tel Aviv, even set up an annex near Nablus called the College of Judea and Samaria; in 1991, this was relocated to Ariel, the second-largest settlement on the West Bank. Except for the ultra-religious, Israeli faculty and students perform their military service, some no doubt in the occupied territories. Professors of several disciplines are advisers to the government and intelligence agencies, with not a few of the natural scientists closely tied to the R&D establishment of the armed forces and weapons industry.

The universities have seen little organized political dissent. Students and faculty are more likely to raise their voices to further their corporatist interests than to protect the few students and teachers of Arab origin in higher education, let alone highlight the plight of the Palestinians generally. The academy remains virtually unschooled in the life, language, culture, and history of the Palestinians and the neighboring Arab and Muslim world. "Arab Studies" have little foothold in secondary and higher education, and American English, not Arabic, is Israel's second language. The little there is of Arabic-language instruction in secondary schools is being cut back.

For the Jews, Zionism and Israel hold out not only the promise of great benefits, but also the prospect of considerable costs. As early as 1918, Thorsten Veblen, America's premier sociologist and author of the classic *The Theory of the Leisure Class*, had speculated about a likely mutation in the Jewish intelligentsia in the event of the onward march of Zionism. During the Wilsonian moment in the era of the First World War, he saw Zionism, almost universally considered *sui generis,* as one of "many claims to self-determination." From its creation, the movement presupposed a thick "demarcation between Jew and gentile" that entailed "isolation and inbreeding." It was too bad that the bid for Jewish nationhood, like other such efforts, could not have been made earlier, before modernity made "national isolation impracticable." Zionism also came too late for an uncontested neo-colonial implant in the non-European world, he might have added.

But Veblen's main misgiving was that, by founding their own state and "turning in upon themselves," the Jews would cease to contribute "more than an even share to the intellectual life of modern Europe." He considered the Jews to have been, through the ages, "the pioneers, the uneasy guild of pathfinders and iconoclasts in science, scholarship, and institutional change and growth." By breaking out of the tradition-bound shtetl and ghetto, gifted Jews engaged in intellectual "cross-breeding," becoming a "nation of hybrids" and "disturbers of the intellectual peace." Their "intellectual preeminence" came out of an immersion in gentile culture in which they remained "skeptics"; in part because of the "animus with which the community of safe and sane gentiles" met them, the Jews played "their part of guidance and incitement" and wound up "in the vanguard of modern inquiry."

Like the Jewish-American philosopher Morris Cohen twenty years later, Veblen feared that Zionism would impoverish what had been the singularly Jewish addition to the life of the mind. If its founding fathers' project came to pass, Zionism might well "be crowned with a large national complacency and, possibly, a profound and self-suffi-cient content on the part of the Chosen People domiciled once more in the Chosen Land." In the event that

> the Jewish people in this way turn inward on themselves, their prospective contribution to the world's intellectual output should, in the light of historical evidence, fairly be expected to take on the complexion of Talmudic lore, rather than that character of free-swung skeptical initiative which their renegades have habitually infused into the pursuit of the modern sciences abroad, among the nations.

In Philip Roth's 1993 novel *Operation Shylock*, the character imper-sonating "Roth" shares many of the concerns of Buber and Veblen. He is perturbed by the ethical and spiritual price of the state's over-reliance on military metaphysics. Should the Israelis resort "not merely to breaking the hands" of stone-throwing protesters but to deploying "nuclear weapons to save themselves from their enemies," they might "save their state," but at the cost of "destroying their people." Even now, "they barely have the wherewithal to survive morally . . . in this tiny place, surrounded on all sides by tremendous hostility . . . Better to be marginal neurotics, anxious assimilationists, and everything else that the Zionists despise, better to *lose* the state than to lose your moral being by unleashing a nuclear war."

Since Zionism has "outlived its historic function . . . the time has come to renew in the European Diaspora our preeminent spiritual and cultural role"—that diaspora remaining "to this day, the most authentic Jewish homeland there has ever been . . . the birthplace of rabbinic Judaism, Hasidic Judaism, Jewish secularism, socialism [and], of course, of Zionism, too." Jews were part of "the civilization that gave to mankind Sholem Aleichem, Heinrich Heine, and Albert Einstein." Writing halfway between Veblen and Roth, the critical Marxist Isaac Deutscher added Spinoza, Marx, Rosa Luxemburg, Trotsky, and Freud to the honor roll of hybrids who "found Jewry too narrow, too archaic, and too constricting"—as did Proust and Kafka.

Shylock uses the recent evolution of the Holy City to examine Zionism-cum-Israel's failed and dangerous success. The *faux* "Roth" wonders what "owning *Jerusalem*, of all places, has to do with being Jews in 1988," and whether that is not perhaps "the *worst* thing that could possibly have happened to us." He doubts the wisdom of the solemn invocation "Next year in Jerusalem!" during the Passover reading of the Hagadah, celebrating the Exodus from Egypt, and imagines future seders where the cry will be "*Last* year in Jerusalem! Next year in Warsaw!" To complete "a historical as well as spiritual victory over Hitler and Auschwitz" Jews should "return to where we belong and to where we have every historical right to resume the great Jewish European destiny." No reason to "be driven for all time from the continent that nourished the flourishing Jewish worlds of Warsaw, of Vilna, of Riga, of Prague, of Berlin, of Lvov, of Budapest, of Bucharest, of Salonica, and of Rome." Edward Said (who said Roth should get the Nobel Prize for literature) might well have criticized the Occidentalism of the character, who should perhaps also have called for a return to Alexandria, Algiers, Baghdad, Cairo, Casablanca, Damascus, Fez, Tehran, and Tunis.

As already noted, in 2003 over 55 per cent of the world's oil reserves and 45 per cent of its natural gas were centered in the Persian Gulf. Saudi Arabia was the greatest regional exporter, followed by the United Arab Emirates and Iran, for a total of close to 65 per cent of oil and gas combined. Nearly 90 per cent of local oil exports transited by tanker through the Strait of Hormuz, linking the Persian Gulf with the Gulf of Oman and the Arabian Sea and fronting on southern Iran. This 34-mile narrows has a one-mile-wide channel for inbound and another for outbound tankers; that year the oil passing through amounted to about 40 per cent of oil traded worldwide. The Gulf supplies the U.S. and Western Europe with over a quarter of their oil imports, and Japan with nearly two-thirds. Of this Gulf oil, most of it crude, the U.S. and Europe brought in about 70 per cent and 50 per cent, respectively, from Saudi Arabia; Europe and Japan, over 30 per cent and 17 per cent from Iran.

The geo-economic importance of Middle East oil and natural gas is even more pronounced than these figures suggest, since global oil production is rapidly peaking in the face of an infinite increase in demand for energy worldwide, with the result that consumption of a finite resource is driving up production costs and market prices. The severity of this crunch can only be somewhat softened, primarily by oil and natural gas supplies from Russia, which has the greatest proven and estimated energy reserves outside the OPEC nations, and the sixth-largest worldwide, making it the largest oil exporter after Saudi Arabia. Broken as a military superpower, Russia is returning to the international stage as an energy-exporting heavyweight, though its own rising energy consumption will foreshorten its advantage. Overall, for the foreseeable future, much hinges on the as yet halting development of alternate energy sources, some of them renewable and clean (coal, hydrogen fuel cells, biofuels, wind, solar, nuclear), which remain uncertain and problematic.

Although the American-dominated energy and infrastructure multinationals favor control of the Middle East in pursuit of market share and profit, Washington's first objective is to shore up its political leverage with the region's oligarchic energy-producing regimes. Besides looking after its own fuel supply, the U.S. means to continue carrying disproportionate weight in the global marketing of energy in order to be able to reward or punish allies, enemies, and fast-growing, energy-hungry competitors like China and India, each with a billion-plus population and fast-growing economy. By 2000 China was beginning to overtake Japan as the world's second-largest consumer of oil, and by 2015 it will probably import 65 per cent of its crude oil from the Middle East. Beijing is investing huge sums in the development of Iranian oilfields and pipelines running to the Caspian Sea.

America's grand scheme in the Middle East, then, began to take shape well before the surge of political Islam or the attack of September 11, 2001. Israel favors the enterprise, naturally, and so do Egypt, Jordan, Saudi Arabia, and the Emirates. All are prepared, with their usual caution, to aid and abet the reining in of Iraq, Syria, and Iran. Israel in particular urges the containment of these three states that, besides challenging its regional military supremacy, will probably continue to support the militants of the Palestinian resistance. It is also emphatic about the need for the West to get a firm hold on Lebanon.

Washington's removal of Saddam Hussein was intended as a prologue to the recasting of the region's political and civil societies in the West's image. Next it would coach the pro-American regimes to embark on gradual democratization, social reform, and ethnic conciliation; Iraq, Syria, and Iran would be shoved in the same direction. But Washington must be careful not to exert too much pressure for domestic reform on the autocratic regimes that sit on vast energy reserves, trade their oil and gas for dollars, host vital strategic bases, and invest billions in the U.S. economy. Their special relationship with America is at least as important as Israel's, and Tel Aviv is panicked that the Arab world might eventually come to matter more to the West. Will Washington one day force Israel to meet the Palestinians halfway?

Following the occupation of Iraq, control over its oil—estimated to constitute the third-largest reserves in the world—is expected to reduce American dependence on Saudi Arabia and make a breach in OPEC, which pumps about 40 per cent of the world's crude. More leverage is timely, since several OPEC members question the economic and political rationale for maintaining the U.S. currency as the coin of the world's energy realm. Concerned about the risk of a weakening dollar as America's budgetary and trade deficits reach record levels, and the costs of the Iraq war climb, these members are prompted to invest more of their oil revenues in the East and the European Union, as well as in their own economies. Because of its interdependence with the U.S. economy and bond market—it owns some $300 billion, or about 8 per cent, of the U.S. government's publicly held debt—China shares these misgivings. In addition, Iran and Venezuela have political reasons for diversifying out of dollars. Washington seeks to contain this centrifugal disorder in petro-politics and petro-finance, which risks unsettling the U.S. economy and weakening America's position in the Middle East, thus endangering Israel.

Contrary to initial U.S. expectations, Iraq may turn into a loose and precarious Shiite-dominated confederation of three semi-autonomous regions, with a weak central government allocating oil revenues, managing a common currency, controlling the armed forces, and handling foreign affairs. Alternatively, consumed by religious, sectarian, and ethnic conflicts, as well as untoward foreign interventions, it may fracture, Yugoslavia-style, into three separate states, with the Kurds in the north and Shiites in the south splitting the greater part of Iraq's oil wealth, around Kirkuk and Basra respectively, at the expense of the minority Sunnis, confined to the landlocked and uncertainly endowed western and central provinces. Either way, Iran, OPEC's second-largest exporter, and possessing the world's second- or third-largest oil and natural gas reserves, stands a good chance of emerging as the main beneficiary of the political emancipation of the long-oppressed Shiites next door. Both the U.S. and Israel sound the alarm, claiming that Iraq's Shiites will support Tehran's drive to become a major power in the Middle East by developing the ultimate weapon and by backing Islamic terrorism. Seizing on the incendiary rhetoric of President Ahmadinejad, Shiite fundamentalist zealot and fierce critic of Israel, Washington now portrays Iran as its "biggest single strategic challenge," allegedly bent on forcing its hegemony on the entire region.

Since before the end of the Second World War, America has considered the Persian Gulf central to its national interest, and control over it an absolute prerogative. From Roosevelt and Truman onward, all presidents and their foreign policy advisers have been transparent on the subject. Jimmy Carter was the most concise:

> Let our position be absolutely clear: an attempt by any outside force to gain control of the Persian Gulf region will be regarded as an assault on the vital interests of the United States of America, and such an assault will be repelled by any means necessary, including military force.

This pronouncement was at the core of his Farewell Address of January 1980, more than a year after Camp David I, and just weeks after the start of the hostage standoff in Tehran and the Soviet invasion of Afghanistan. He spoke with greater candor than his predecessors or successors, stressing that the Soviet troops in Afghanistan not only "threaten" a region that "contains more than two-thirds of the world's exportable oil," but also stand at the ready "within 300 miles of the Indian Ocean and close to the Strait of Hormuz, a waterway through which most of the world's oil must flow."

Following the Soviet Union's implosion, Iran became America's new spectral enemy. U.S. support for Saddam Hussein's secular Sunni republic in its eight-year war with Ayatollah Khomeini's theocratic

Islamic Republic was a prologue to the direct confrontations with Iran and Iraq—both medium-sized powers fronting on the Persian Gulf, both overflowing with oil, and both contesting the American–Israeli regional hegemony. During the Cold War the U.S. routinely berated the Soviet empire as an evil "outside force" with nefarious designs on the Gulf. After 1989 the rhetoric had to change: too obviously the pot would be calling the kettle black.

Washington advanced a rash of reasons for the invasion of Iraq: to remove a world-class tyrant, to deactivate weapons of mass destruction, to foreclose an al-Qaeda base. Not a word was said about Iraq's importance for the West. It remained unspoken until the drive to establish a Western-friendly and secular regime began to falter and degenerate into a protean civil war. With Saddam Hussein toppled in Baghdad, the August 2005 election of Ahmadinejad as president in Tehran proved helpful. His inflammatory anti-Israeli and anti-American broadsides made it easy to charge Iran with inspiring, financing, and arming the terrorist insurgencies in Iraq, Lebanon, and Palestine as part of a concerted campaign to dominate the Gulf and the Middle East, in the process expanding the reach of Shiite Islam.

In a July 2006 opinion piece, former Secretary of State Henry Kissinger updated the Carter Doctrine, which had become a relic of the Cold War. If Iran "insists on combining the Persian imperial tradition with contemporary Islamic fervor," he pontificated, "it simply cannot be permitted to fulfill a dream of imperial rule in a region of such importance to the rest of the world." Defense Secretary Robert M. Gates, speaking in Kabul in mid-January 2007, served notice that the U.S. would continue to have "a strong presence in the Gulf for a long time into the future," a resolve that America was reaffirming "with the current naval and military buildup through the region." A week later, speaking in Dubai, Undersecretary of State for Political Affairs R. Nicholas Burns declared that "the Middle East isn't a region to be dominated by Iran"; nor was "the Gulf . . . a body of water to be controlled" by it. The U.S. was stationing two carrier battle groups there so Iran would "understand that the U.S. will protect its interests if Iran seeks to confront us." In May 2007, speaking to 3,500 service members on the flight deck of the U.S.S. *John C. Stennis*, positioned in the Persian Gulf some 150 miles off Iran's coast, Vice-President Dick Cheney said again: "We'll keep the sea lanes open [for oil] . . . we'll stand with our friends in opposing extremism and strategic threats . . . we'll stand with others to prevent Iran from gaining nuclear weapons and dominating this region."

The Iraq Study Group's report of December 6, 2006 left no doubt that it was not so much concerned with the turmoil on the Tigris per se as it was with its impact on the greater Middle East and America's overall imperial position and momentum: "Iraq is vital to regional and even global stability, and is critical to U.S. interests." Besides running "along the sectarian fault lines of Shiite and Sunni Islam, and of Kurdish and Arab populations . . . [i]t has the world's second-largest known oil reserves." It has also become "a base of operations for international terrorism, including al-Qaeda." In sum, "Iraq is a centerpiece of American foreign policy, influencing how the United States is viewed in the region and around the world." Although concerned about a blow to its "global standing" if America were to leave, the report affirmed that

> even after the United States has moved all combat brigades out of Iraq, we would maintain a considerable military presence in the region, with our still significant force in Iraq and with our powerful air, ground, and naval deployments in Kuwait, Bahrain, and Qatar, as well as an increased presence in Afghanistan.

Marx and Engels wrote *The Communist Manifesto* mere weeks before the social–political uprisings that shook Europe in 1848 were easily quashed. Its opening paragraph was both prescient and timeless: "A specter is haunting Europe—the specter of communism. All the powers of old Europe have entered into a holy alliance to exorcise this specter: Pope and Tsar, Metternich and Guizot, French Radicals and German police-spies." Those powers denounced communism, then embryonic at best, as a ubiquitous mortal threat lurking behind every popular protest. It was to "meet this nursery tale" that the two penned "a manifesto of the party itself," to set communists apart from left reformists, utopian socialists, and anarchists.

Today a specter is haunting the West, and the powers that be have entered into a holy alliance to exorcise it. By portraying and battling ideological Islam as another monolith, they render it larger than life. But Islamism is not a uniform calling. Social, political, and nationalist forces, whether Sunni or Shiite, are censed with religion, not subsumed by it. Movements and programs are composite. The Arab Shiites have through the ages rebelled against the ruling Sunni minority, under which they were often socially scorned, economically outclassed, and politically disenfranchised—not to mention seen as religious apostates. This divide is centered in the Persian Gulf. The surrounding area is home to three-quarters of the world's Shiites; the oil-rich eastern provinces of Saudi Arabia and southern provinces of Iraq are heavily Shiite.

The threat of the Shiite rebellion and the urgent need for oil underpin the West's denunciation of Islamism. Potentially a vast fifth column, the minority Shiites are said to be poised to lock arms to form a crescent of terror, putting at risk not only the Gulf states but Egypt, Jordan, Lebanon, and Israel—as well as the oil and natural gas supplies fueling the world economy. The situation is complicated by emergent non-state actors that invite foreign intervention and challenge the traditional Arab regimes whose autocratic authority, backed up by their ties to America, is increasingly called into question by the Arab street. Uncomfortable with the liberal-democratic cate-chism, whose allure is in any case limited to sectors of the new middle classes of the cities, the leaders of the conservative Sunni polities and societies use religious tropes in an effort to preempt the attraction of the Islamists. Rushing to fill an ideological vacuum left by the failure of postcolonial secular social nationalism and pan-Arabism, Islamism offers up a syncretic credo. Social, political, and cultural appeals playing on latent anti-American, anti-Western, and anti-Zionist re-sentments are expressed in religious rhetoric.

In Palestine, as in Beirut and Baghdad, sectarian animosity is profane rather than religious. In Gaza and Ramallah, sectarian strife—between Sunnis and Shiites—is driven by conflicts over con-crete issues: foreign occupation or intervention, power-sharing, modes of resistance, economic equity, and social welfare. But religious motives are latent, and political leaders rouse the rank-and-file—not just the extreme faithful—by expressing temporal anxieties in ancestral religious idioms.

The leaders of both the inchoate "axis of evil" and the incipient "axis of virtue" have two closely entwined concerns: the regional balancing of military power and security, and the vicissitudes of internal, if not civil war in Palestine, Lebanon, and Iraq—as well as Pakistan and Afghanistan. Besides intervening directly in support of local proxies, the U.S. maneuvers indirectly to destabilize the Iranian and Syrian governments. Typically, in September 2006 Congress passed the Iran Freedom Support Act, allocating $85 million for a campaign of psychological warfare to "sharpen the contradictions between the Iranian people and a regime that does not respect them." It funds exile organizations; pro-democracy radio and television stations broadcasting into Iran to incite disaffected notables, intellec-tuals, and professionals; and civil society forces disposed to promote political and human rights along with market capitalism. Optimally,

Washington looks to trigger a "velvet," "color," "flower," "cedar," or "pinstripe" revolution to overthrow the government and bring about regime and societal change in Tehran. Covert and overt intervention goes hand in hand with diplomatic, economic, and military pressure, accompanied by rolling rhetorical thunder.

Tel Aviv and Washington denounce Tehran as the epicenter of demonic Islamism, and Ahmadinejad as its evil genius. Yet radical Islamism has two major strains: Shiite extremism that is heavily dependent on the Iranian Islamic Republic, and Sunni extremism that is embodied in the Taliban and al-Qaeda. Israel and America conflate the worst aspects of both in order to magnify the Islamist phenomenon, with willful disregard for its temporal complexities. At the same time, they foster sectarian strife between Fatah and Hamas in Palestine; between the Fouad Siniora government and Hezbollah in Lebanon; between Shiites and Sunnis in Iraq; between Shiite Iran and the Sunni Arab states. They back whichever side or combination of forces best serves their interests. This manipulation of deep-seated religious and ethnic hostilities for profane ends not only stirs enmity between Shiite and Sunni state and non-state actors, but also risks ensuring that the Western jihadists' prophecy of a "clash of civilizations" will be self-fulfilling.

The stratagem is not new. Soon after the Second World War, the Western powers and Israel proceeded to support Islamic groups with the idea of impeding the growth of nonreligious nationalist parties and left-leaning popular movements. The British began by helping Egypt's Muslim Brotherhood, the progenitor of Hamas. The Americans followed suit after Nasser's rise to power in 1954. Starting in the 1970s, Israel backed Hamas in an effort to weaken support for the secular Palestinian resistance and block the consolidation of the PLO. In each case unintended consequences trumped the game plan, as they will continue to do. The outsiders attempt to set against each other parties that share core elements of faith, culture, and history. Moreover, Hamas and Fatah, Siniora and Hassan Nasrallah, Iran and Saudi Arabia, and Syria and Lebanon have in common a perception of the intervening Judeo-Christian powers as the absolute and imperious Other.

America's crusade to turn the greater Middle East into a haven for secular democracy, human rights, and gender equality also did not go as intended. Iraq was to be the first stop. A surgical operation of overwhelming force was expected to break open political and civil society for the scripted change; scared neighboring regimes would fall into line. And Israel, though skeptical of democratization and fearful that the Arab street would gain power through free elections, as Hamas did in Palestine, enthusiastically supported the war.

But any kind of victory for Washington in Baghdad would redound to Tel Aviv's advantage. Israel was first to favor the breakup of Iraq—especially the secession of the Kurds, which, in addition to reducing Iraq's strategic regional weight, would improve chances for an airbase closer to Iran, beholden as the Kurds are to the U.S. Chastened by the misadventure in Mesopotamia but determined to continue its imperial mission by forcing a showdown with Iran, the U.S. now shies away from pressing for open-ended reforms in the moderate Arab states, and resumes its tried and tested collaboration—ongoing since 1945—with their ingrown, self-perpetuating elites. While Israel discreetly welcomes the end of the crusade to make the Middle East safe for democracy, it publicly embraces the latest attempt to keep it safe for the American empire. With Washington intent upon linking the impasse in Baghdad and the defiance in Tehran, Israel fully approves the new course of rallying the now so-called moderate Sunni Arab states to help isolate and contain Shiite Persia. By inflaming and exploiting sectarian and ethnic animosities to this end, Washington and Tel Aviv help convert temporal conflicts of power and interest into religious wars akin to those of early modern Europe. Comparison of that epic to the present situation in the Middle East suggests how devastating these machinations could yet prove to be.

There are, of course, vast historical and institutional differences between the reform of Christianity and that of Islam. Islam has no papal authority to justify and defend, to denounce and attack. Even so, the two reformations-cum-counter-reformations, as immature as Islam's is, are homologous in purpose, exhortation, and incitement, as well as in the twining of the sacred and the profane. Doctrine and faith are invoked and contorted to legitimize and promote conflicting political, social, economic, and cultural orientations. Like such Christian reformers as John Calvin, today's Islamic reformers mean to reclaim the purity of the faith and restore a strict moral code. Analogous to Calvin's reign in Geneva, the *shariah* that is to implement this renewal has both a regressive and a progressive side. But what is singular about the Islamic Reformation is its effort to adapt to a modernity widely viewed as a foreign import—an instrument of the Western intruder. Even in Europe, free of the wounds of colonial–imperial subjection, the confrontation between the Reformation and the Counter-Reformation was marked by massive fanaticism, violence, and cruelty spread over more than a century. How much more terrible might a Middle Eastern religious conflict be if the variables include that external humiliation?

The 1948 partition of Palestine was the first major blow to the subaltern state system established in the Middle East by the Western powers after the First World War. America's invasion and unintended dislocation of Iraq was the second. The aftershocks of both earthquakes continue to be felt throughout the region. The Gulf Arab states, unlike East and Southeast Asia and Africa, never experienced the romance and blood sacrifice of anti-colonial nationalist uprisings for independence. All along, the region's phenomenal oil reserves and strategic chokepoints were a blessing and a curse: they were the material base for the close alliance between Western governments, big energy conglomerates, and the local ruling elites. Yet with those elites diverted by collaboration, secular and reformist Arab and Persian nationalism was deprived of experienced leaders and the mass base it might have rallied. When Mossadegh and Nasser did seize the day, their respective overthrow and defeat signaled the West's limited tolerance for secular-cum-radical decolonization. Without leverage of their own, Lebanon and Jordan marked time and, like Israel, had compelling reasons for continuing to rely, anxiously, on the protection and backing of the West. Governed by a Shiite minority, Sunni Syria was the exception. Even today, it tenaciously adheres to a secular nationalist course.

The Arab ruling and governing classes and the Western powers are paying for having locked the Middle East's civil and political societies into a generalized stasis. Islamism is one of the costs, its adherents multiplied by the demographic explosion and the spillover of refugees from Palestine and Iraq. Indeed, by May 2007, America's deeply flawed invasion and regime change in Iraq had created the largest population displacement in the region since 1948: some 2 million refugees, most of them Sunnis, scattered primarily throughout Syria and Jordan, with about the same number uprooted inside Iraq. These 4 million, and the more than 50 per cent of Iraqis who were unemployed, enlarged the potential for discord.

The pressures within the fragile state system coincide with an incipient general crisis in Middle Eastern polity, society, and culture that does not respect national borders. This crisis is more the cause than the effect of the Islamic revival. In the Israeli–Palestinian conflict, without the abominable conditions in the occupied territories and the refugee camps in neighboring countries, Hamas and Hezbollah would not have a mass following. Similarly, the civil war in Iraq is as much political, social, and economic as it is sectarian and ethnic. Of course, as always in times of transnational general crisis, politics and ideology are tightly entwined, and it is difficult to accurately gauge their respective weight in crucial moments.

The greater Middle East has rarely been as volatile and unpredictable as it is now. Destabilized by bloody internal wars in Iraq, Lebanon, Palestine, Afghanistan and Pakistan, as well as by the related rise of radical Islam far and near, it will be difficult to brake the rising danger of a region-wide nuclear arms race, with the attendant risk of a nuclear mishap in one of the world's most treacherous precincts. Israel is the premier nuclear power of the Middle East, and Iran is presumed to be bent on adding nuclear warheads to its panoply of weapons of mass destruction—a program aggravating the danger of regional nuclear proliferation. Under Riyadh's leadership, the Gulf Cooperation Council of six Sunni Arab states (Bahrain, Kuwait, Oman, Qatar, Saudi Arabia, and the United Arab Emirates) is about to launch a nuclear research and development program for peaceful purposes; Turkey and Syria are likely to follow. Egypt is about to resume its civilian nuclear program, suspended since 1986.

In recent times Israel has taken to denouncing Iran as a life-and-death threat not only to itself but to the West as a whole. With or without a nuclear bomb, Iran is almost certain to change the balance of forces significantly in southwest Asia. For Israel, this change has less to do with the shadow of imminent destruction than with a challenge to its half-century of regional military and diplomatic primacy. Its super-hawks even go so far as to assert that, in extremis, Israel must be prepared to act on its own, if necessary resorting to atomic warheads for a first-strike raid on Iran's nuclear facilities. But Iran's armed forces are not about to match Israel's, which, with scores of nuclear warheads and missiles, are the second- or third-mightiest in the world. Israel and the U.S. know full well that Iran presents no imminent threat to either of them, and that their animus and bellicosity predates the election of President Ahmadinejad and Tehran's nuclear ambitions. Even so, separately and jointly they sound the alarm and whip up fear.

In October 2005 Israel's foreign minister, Silvan Shalom, stressed the "urgency" of dealing with Iran's "threat" lest it be too late—but not by way of negotiation, which would be tantamount to "appeasement," which had led to the Second World War and "the attempted genocide of the Jewish people in Europe just sixty years ago." In January 2006 Robert Joseph, hard-line assistant US secretary of state for arms control, told an AIPAC committee that America "cannot accept a nuclear-armed Iran" because doing so "could embolden [its] leadership . . . to advance its aggressive ambitions in and outside the region, both directly and through the terrorists it supports." Tehran would be a "direct threat to U.S. forces and allies in the region" and "an existential threat to the state of Israel." Later that month Dan Gillerman, Israel's U.N. ambassador, forewarned the General Assembly that by calling for Israel to be "wiped off the map" and putting in doubt the Holocaust, President Ahmadinejad was "preparing the next one."

By February 1, 2006, when asked whether the U.S. would "rise to Israel's defense," President Bush replied, "You bet." Three weeks later he made it clear again "that we will use military might to protect our ally Israel." AIPAC's annual policy conference, held in Washington on March 7, with Vice-President Cheney and UN Ambassador John R. Bolton among the star speakers, focused on mobilizing America's "pro-Israel community . . . to demand that Iran be referred immediately" to the Security Council "in order to keep the world's leading state sponsor of terror from acquiring the world's deadliest weapons." Before 4,500 delegates, Cheney declared that the U.S., with other nations, would "not allow Iran to have nuclear weapons" and would support the removal of its "fanatical regime." America's commitment to Israel's security was "solid, enduring, and unshakable," he vowed. Howard Kohr, AIPAC's executive director, invoked the Holocaust analogy with a video suggesting that Iran's Islamic Republic and Germany's National Socialist regime—Ahmadinejad and Hitler— were cast in the same mold.

Back in Israel, Olmert decried the Iranian president as a "psychopath of the worst kind [who] like Hitler speaks . . . of the extermination of the entire Jewish nation," as had Hitler before the Nazi assumption of power in January 1933. On Yom Hashoah (Holocaust Memorial Day), April 25, 2006, the prime minister warned that "concessions and weakness amount to a recipe for holocaust." At Yad Vashem, the Holocaust Memorial in Jerusalem, President Moshe Katsav exhorted the West "not to stand silently in the face of nations trying to acquire nuclear weapons and preaching the destruction of the state of Israel." Defense Minister Shaul Mofaz warned against being "indifferent to the declarations of one of the most radical leaders in the world since Hitler," adding that "more can be done from outside Iran to raise the Iranian people's awareness that the current regime will bring destruction upon them."

Israel seized on the Second Lebanon War of July–August 2006 to bolster its contention about the gravity of the Iranian threat. The war, triggered by two unexceptional border incidents that spiraled out of control, was fanned by miscalculations all around. Apparently Hamas, Hezbollah, and their foreign patrons underestimated Israel's readiness to strike back forcefully. Rather than dampen the fire, the U.S. and Israel most probably stoked it, accusing Iran and Syria of having started it in the first place. The moment was deemed auspicious to crush Hezbollah, which Jerusalem and Washington presented as containing the shock troops of Iran's drive to impose itself as the new regional heavyweight.

In October 2005, after years of fulminations against the Iranian Islamic Republic by the U.S. and Israel, President Ahmadinejad revived the Muslim world's primal anti-Zionist scream. He invoked his mentor Imam Khomeini's charge that "This regime occupying Jerusalem must vanish from the page of time," one he deemed "very wise." He went on to predict that "[just] as the Soviet Union disappeared, the Zionist regime will also vanish and humanity will be liberated." Granting their ambiguity, these phrases still do not call for the destruction of Israel or the Jewish people. Yet the Israeli and Western media routinely accuse Ahmadinejad of calling for "Israel to be wiped off the map," just as in the 1950s and 1960s, during the high tide of secular anti-Western nationalism and pan-Arabism, Nasser was denounced for intending to drive the Israelis into the Mediterranean.

Ahmadinejad's declarations about Israel and the Holocaust, no matter how fiercely tendentious, have a logic that is widely subscribed to by the Muslim world: if the Holocaust was the primary reason for the establishment of a Zionist state, it was up to the Europeans, the perpetrators of this unpardonable scourge, rather than the Palestinians, in his words, to "pay the price" of ceding some of their own land to the Jews who had "suffered at [their] hands." Ahmadinejad considers Zionism to be "a Western ideology and a colonial idea," and Israel "a European appendix with a Zionist and anti-Islamic nature in the heart of the Islamic world." By implementing their project "in the name of the Holocaust," the Zionists "have created a myth which they regard to be worthier than God, religion, and the prophets," and which is used to justify the full sweep of Israeli policy.

As for the designation of new Hitlers, that reflex also goes back to Nasser, the reborn "Hitler on the Nile." He was the first Middle Eastern leader to be so defamed, not only by Israel's political class but also by Britain's Prime Minister Anthony Eden and Hugh Gaitskell, leader of the Opposition, at the time of the Suez crisis. Eventually Arafat was reviled for allegedly taking the "Hitler-loving [Grand]

Mufti [of Jerusalem]" as his model, and making the Führer his "ideological and anti-Semitic idol." From the run-up to the American invasion of Iraq until his overthrow and execution, Saddam Hussein was likewise vilified as a modern-day Hitler by a spokesman for George W. Bush.

Ahmadinejad is the latest candidate. Like Prime Minister Olmert, Benjamin Netanyahu, leader of Likud and of the Opposition, reached eagerly for the Hitler analogy: "The time is 1938 and Iran is Germany . . . No one cared then and no one seems to care now"—and this despite Iran's military buildup "in the service of a mad ideology" that not only seeks "the destruction of Israel" but has a "world-wide range." "To prevent genocide" the West should choke the Iranian economy so as to undermine the regime and encourage a domestic opposition that is presumably ready and eager to rise up.

Renouncing some of his original theses, Benny Morris, one of Israel's left-critical "new historians," accepts this line of argument, insisting that the nation's latest peril calls for a radical course. With the country vulnerable to total destruction by only "four or five [remote-controlled] hits," when all else fails there can be no hesitation about a preemptive attack on Iran's nuclear installations, missiles, and launching platforms. In February of 2007, the *Jerusalem Post* Likudist columnist Michael Freund warned that "less than 1,000 miles east of Tel Aviv . . . the would-be Hitler of Persia" was preparing "a new Auschwitz" where "in place of Zyklon-B gas, the agent of choice is now uranium." With diplomacy at a dead end, the time has come, "before it is too late . . . for Israel or the U.S. to bomb Iran."

There is something hysterical about this diabolization of Ahmadinejad—whose power is limited, and who may be removed overnight without slowing or halting Iran's quest for regional and nuclear power—and the drumbeat for war. Both responses are disproportionate to the present danger, and overrate Israel's autonomy. For protection against ever more high-powered Palestinian rockets and Iranian missiles, Israel ultimately depends almost entirely on the U.S.

There should be a moratorium, too, on branding autocrats, despots, or nationalist leaders as would-be Hitlers. By abusing historical analogy to vilify the Iranian president, Israel distorts and trivializes the contingent uniqueness of Hitler, the Nazi regime, and the Judeocide, and falsifies the present. Nearly all analogists—politicians, journalists, academics—are intentionalists who attach absolute primacy to ideology, discourse, and rhetoric, disconnected from their relevant historical, political, diplomatic, and military contexts—local, regional, and global.

Israel presents Iran as the latest evidence of its perennial mortal endangerment, and as a clarion call to the Jewish diaspora. But Iran serves as a useful bogeyman in other ways, notably in Bush's declaration of war on global terror and radical Islam. According to Raanan Gissin, a former senior advisor to Ariel Sharon, Israel is "on the front line of Iran's war against the West," and to fight Hamas and Hezbollah is to be the vanguard in the battle against the "axis of evil."

The Palestine problem, it is now increasingly acknowledged in the Israeli press, was never merely the Palestinians, whom Israel could easily have mastered, but the Arab–Muslim world, which by supporting them against Israel has been fighting the West as a whole. Israel's self-serving version of the present historical juncture presents the Israeli–Palestinian troubles as merely part of the larger Arab–Israeli deadlock, which is being redefined by the transformation of the Middle Eastern balance of power and state system.

A potentially nuclear-armed arch-enemy suits Israel's military, which like America's is geared for operations of "shock and awe" rather than "search and destroy." Israel's Second Lebanon War and America's Second Iraq War testify to the inconvenient nimbleness of non-state actors whose old–new organization and technology enable them to challenge ultra-modern state actors whose armies have feet of clay. Understandably, the Israeli General Staff prefers to engage Iran and Syria electronically rather than to fight their proxies on ill-defined and rapidly shifting battlefields. In March 2006, Moshe Ya'alon, Israel's former chief of staff, stated that, though Iran's eight to ten major nuclear facilities were widely dispersed and well hidden, Israel had the capability to destroy them "in several ways and not only by air." The likely targets would be the underground uranium enrichment complex at Natanz, as well as the above-ground heavy-water reactor at Arak and the uranium conversion plant near Isfahan. Any such attack presupposes that Israel's anti-missile defense system could intercept Iran's improved Shahab-3 long-range surface-to-surface ballistic missiles, which might be carrying nuclear, chemical, or biological payloads. Should it take this wager on Mutually Assured Destruction, Israel would do so with additional insurance: a second-strike capability in the form of several German-made missile-launching submarines roaming freely in the Persian Gulf and Mediterranean Sea.

In early November 2006 President Bush and Secretary of State Rice raised the possibility of Israel striking Iran's nuclear installations. The following December, Olmert vowed that with Iran threatening to "wipe Israel off the map," there was no tolerating its aspiration "to have a nuclear weapon like the U.S., France, Israel, and Russia." Tehran could not be trusted to master even the basics of enriching uranium for nuclear energy, the first step toward developing atomic weapons—a process that Israel claims will take months rather than years. Meanwhile Iran, like Israel, is perfecting its long-range delivery systems and mobile missile launchers. In July 2006 Howard Friedman, president of AIPAC, told its members that Israel was "fighting a pivotal war for its life" in Lebanon; because of American Jewry, the U.S. was the "only nation in the world" to have a "clear and unambiguous view of the situation," and so would allow Israel to "finish the job" there. Hezbollah "must be defeated," but much more was at stake, since its offensive was intended to "divert attention away from Iran's nuclear weapons program." AIPAC's work, then, was only just beginning. American Jews should "stand up and tell our elected officials that they must demand that Iran halt its pursuit of atomic arms." On July 18 and July 20, the Senate and House passed nonbinding bipartisan resolutions expressing unqualified support for Israel's military action in Gaza and Lebanon, and calling on Bush to impose sanctions on Iran and Syria. The Senate vote was unanimous; the House was in favor by 410 votes to 8.

Israeli officials and Jewish leaders used AIPAC's annual conference of March 12–13, 2007 to publicize their case against Iran, relying again on Vice President Cheney to set the tone. Presenting the latest rationale for persevering in Iraq, he stressed that a "precipitous American withdrawal . . . would be a disaster for the United States and the entire Middle East." Should the "allies" of the Tehran regime prevail, its "designs . . . would be advanced," magnifying "the threat to our friends in the region." It was

> simply not consistent for anyone to demand aggressive action against the menace posed by the Iranian regime while at the same time acquiescing in a retreat from Iraq that would leave our worst enemies dramatically emboldened and Israel's best friend, the United States, dangerously weakened.

Although no less aware than the Vice President that the majority of American Jews, along with Americans generally, were critical of the Bush administration's resolve to stay the course in Iraq, Olmert and Foreign Minister Livni did not hesitate to express their full support. Speaking by video-link, Israel's prime minister stated that "Those who are concerned for Israel's security, for the security of the Gulf states, and for the stability of the entire Middle East should recognize the need for American success in Iraq." A "premature" exit could have disastrous consequences, especially as regards "those threats emerging from Iran." In short, "when America succeeds in Iraq, Israel is safer." Moreover, added Livni, at the conference in person: "If we appease the extremists—if they feel that we are backing down—they will sense victory and become more dangerous not only to the region, but the world"; to "address extremism" in Iraq is "to address Iran [which] is a regime that denies the Holocaust while threatening the world with a new one." Both backed Netanyahu's call for economic, financial, and psychological warfare to force the Islamic regime to the wall and spur disaffection among the youthful and swelling middle class in the cities, and separatism among the non-Persian ethnic minorities of the border provinces—Kurds, Azeris, Baluchis, and Ahwazi Arabs (nearly 50 per cent of Iran's population of 70 million are non-Persian). Both Washington and Tel Aviv covertly foment this nascent unrest in the Islamic Republic's outlying areas. An imposing array of representatives, senators, members of the Executive, and presidential candidates mingled with several thousand aficionados at the customary gala dinner. The next morning, AIPAC's operatives and foot-soldiers went to Capitol Hill to lobby for an inflexible course toward Tehran and every kind of support for Israel.

But neither Jerusalem nor Washington neglected the international arena. Ahmadinejad's intemperate anti-Zionist screeds and specious Holocaust conference gave them enough ammunition to mount a campaign in the U.N. General Assembly to isolate the Islamic Republic and restore Israel's fading image of an innocent and endangered nation in the court of world opinion. In January 2007, U.S. Ambassador Alejandro Wolff introduced a nonbinding resolution that "condemns without any reservations any denial of the Holocaust" and calls on member-states "unreservedly to reject any denial of the Holocaust as a historical event, either in full or in part, or any activities to that end." Co-sponsored by 104 nations, the resolution was approved by consensus, without a vote. Predictably, the Iranian mission to the U.N. denounced America and Israel for manipulating the Jewish catastrophe "for political purposes."

In April 1956, a half-year before the Suez War—and midway between the War of Independence and the Six Day War—Roi Rutenberg, a young Israeli, was killed in an attack on Nahal Oz, a three-year-old kibbutz strategically located at the northern tip of the Negev, just across the eastern border of the Egyptian-controlled Gaza Strip. Presumably the *fedayeen* who had carried out the raid were residents of the nearby Jabalya refugee camp.

In an astonishing eulogy, Moshe Dayan, then chief of staff, reflected upon the deadly struggle between Israelis and Palestinians. Rather than simply "cast the blame on the murderers," he traced the Palestinians' "burning hatred for us" to their "sitting for eight years in . . . the refugee camps in Gaza" watching Israelis transform "the lands and villages, where they and their fathers dwelt, into our estate." The causes for the loss of "Roi's blood" were to be found "not among the Arabs in Gaza, but in our own midst." There was no "shutting our eyes . . . to our fate," nor to the vision, "in all its brutality, [of] the destiny of our generation," embodied in "the young people dwelling at Nahal Oz bearing the heavy gates of Gaza on their shoulders." Beyond the borders Dayan saw "a swelling . . . sea of hatred and desire for revenge" waiting for the day when, "serenity having dulled our path . . . we will heed the call of ambassadors of malevolent hypocrisy . . . to lay down our arms." It was this generation's "fate . . . and choice to be prepared and armed, strong and determined, lest the sword be stricken from our fist, and our lives cut down." That meant never losing sight of "the loathing that inflames and fills the lives of the hundreds of thousands of Arabs who live around us." When Roi left Tel Aviv "to build his home at the gates of Gaza" that became "a [protective] wall for us, [he] was blinded by the light of his heart and did not see the flash of the sword."

Extraordinarily, Dayan had brought himself to see the Palestinian Other. Yet over half a century later the causes and dynamics of the cycle of violence are essentially unchanged: the two sides remain trapped in a war of words waged by zealots both religious and profane. In the standoff, the Israelis keep the upper hand in every respect but one. The Palestinians and their Middle Eastern sympathizers have regained the moral advantage: they and they alone can confer legitimacy on the state of Israel by granting it absolution for its original sin—a process that is reciprocal, not one-way. Although Arafat knew that the pen—in tracing his signature—was his ultimate weapon, during the Oslo moment he all but squandered it by extending recognition without securing what he and his associates deemed to be fair and adequate consideration.

But no matter how intense the mutual distrust, fear, and hostility, Jewish Israelis are destined to live together with Palestinians in Israel and Palestine, as well as with the Muslims of the greater Middle East. To be sure, given the intensity of reciprocal suspicion, the likelihood of good-faith and consequential negotiations anytime soon—on borders, security, settlements, refugees, water resources, Jerusalem—are slim. Perhaps after all these years it goes beyond reason to expect, in the disingenuous words of Bush, "the establishment of a Palestinian state that is viable, contiguous, sovereign, and independent." Meanwhile, even at this late hour, no harm can come from taking significant confidence-building steps toward an eventual and inevitable dialogue, détente, and reconciliation. As the early internal critics kept insisting, it was up to the Yishuvniks first, and then the Israelis, to take the initiative: after all, it was they who had settled in a land that was emphatically not "a land without a people for a people without a land," and to this day most Palestinians perceive them as invasive and predatory colonists. Besides, given its superior strength, Israel can afford to make overtures to the Palestinians—at home and abroad—without in the least endangering its security. For the Palestinians, such steps would be like going to Canossa.

Although Israel does not really want a final status peace except on its own extravagant terms, it cannot say so publicly. Instead, it keeps setting impossible preconditions, making nonnegotiable demands, and lamenting the absence of a "partner for peace" among the Palestinians. This unilateralist diplomacy calls for military preparedness for the next military confrontation which, given the chaos in the Middle East, risks escalating out of control. Resolving or de-escalating the Israeli–Palestinian conflict can remove one of the major catalysts for the region's gathering general crisis.

Pointing to the critical situation in Iraq, Afghanistan, Pakistan, and the Gulf, and conscious of Iran's great-power aspirations, in September 2004 President General Pervez Musharraf of Pakistan, at the time highly valued by both Washington and Tel Aviv, reminded the U.N. General Assembly that "the tragedy of Palestine is an open wound inflicted on the psyche of every Muslim." Wherever the U.S. and its allies intervene in southwest Asia, they heighten Arab–Muslim self-awareness, along with a sense of injured dignity in their societies and corridors of power. Israel is widely viewed as being involved in this latter-day Western incursion, and as a symbol of it; by cold-shouldering the Arab League's peace initiatives in 2002 and 2007, it has remained a convenient lightning rod for the Middle Eastern street, drawing anger away from their own ruling classes, who have their own grounds for favoring Western intervention.

For the moment there is neither incentive nor pressure for Israel's leaders to come forward with a reasoned and reasonable peace initiative: at home the conciliatory left—or what remains of it—is in disarray, and the hardliners carry the day; in Washington, the bipartisan pro-Israel consensus remains nearly intact. Although it has yielded substantial returns, unilateralism has not secured the promised land. Bona fide steps to freeze the expansion of settlements, the construction of the separation barrier, and the arrogation of East Jerusalem while significantly releasing prisoners and relaxing the occupation regime—all these would help break out of straits that are internal and external, political and diplomatic. The irenic force of such actions would be magnified by their being made part of an effort to broach the refugee problem candidly and flexibly, rather than dismiss it summarily. In March 2007, Ehud Olmert restated the dictum that recognizing a "right of return" or allowing even a single refugee to come home was "out of the question." Since the plight of the Palestinians stemmed from the Arab states' attack on Israel in 1948, he did not think Israel "should accept any kind of responsibility for the creation of this problem."

This was a full five years after Arafat had declared that "we understand Israel's demographic concerns and understand that the right of return of Palestinian refugees, a right guaranteed under international law and United Nations Resolution 194, must be implemented in a way that takes into account such concerns." However, "just as we Palestinians must be realistic with respect to Israel's demographic desires, Israelis too must be realistic in understanding there can be no solution to the Israeli–Palestinian conflict if the legitimate rights of these innocent civilians continue to be ignored." If "left unresolved, the refugee issue has the potential to undermine any permanent agreement between Palestinians and Israelis."

Pace Olmert, Israel must answer for most of the problem, though there is widespread agreement that the return of a significant number of Palestinian refugees to Israel, whatever its final frontiers, is unthinkable. A comprehensive reparations settlement is not. This would involve acknowledging partial responsibility for the Nakba and paying partial compensation for physical harm and material loss. Adopted in 1948 and invoked by Arafat, UN Resolution 194 prescribes that "the refugees wishing to return to their homes and live in peace with their neighbors should be permitted to do so at the earliest practical date, and that compensation should be paid for the property of those choosing not to return."

The postwar compensation agreement between West Germany and Israel might provide some guidelines. Signed in Luxembourg in September 1952, it paid reparations to victims and survivors of the Judeocide and to the infant state. A year before, Chancellor Konrad

Adenauer had solemnly declared in the Bundestag that the "unspeak-
able crimes [that] have been committed in the name of the German
people . . . against the Jews of Germany and the occupied
countries . . . demand restitution, both moral and material," which
he hoped would "ease the way to the spiritual settlement of infinite
suffering." Perhaps Adenauer's Catholic roots moved him to seek
absolution and do penance for West Germany, though he most
certainly also had compelling political and economic reasons for
paying the indemnity: the Federal Republic was in urgent need of
international recognition and foreign loans.

The claimants' motives and aims for seeking payment were also
complex. Ben-Gurion and Moshe Sharett for Israel and Nahum
Goldmann for the World Jewish Congress sought not only compensation for victims and survivors, but also financial and economic aid for
forced-draft nation-building. Over the next fourteen years, Germany
transferred more than $3 billion in cash and capital goods to develop
the railways, port installations, power plants, pipelines, and irrigation
systems that underlay Israel's phenomenal economic growth. But there
was also opposition. Herut, the embryo of Likud, led a vehement
campaign to refuse what Menachem Begin disdained as "blood
money": to accept German marks was to pardon Nazi Germany's
crimes—though recognition of sin, remorse, empathy, and restitution
are not exactly beyond the spirit or practice of rabbinic Judaism.

Funding a program of Palestinian compensation would not be easy,
financially or politically. Israel's exchequer is strained by inordinate
military expenditures, and short of credit for essential social programs
for the disadvantaged, including the Arab minority. But it should be
possible to supplement state monies with foreign loans and credits,
both public and private. Besides, an overture along these lines would
probably resonate with Saudi Arabia and the other Arab oil states and
emirates, which seem disposed to provide compensation to refugees
looking to settle in the new state of Palestine and to finance the
improvement of living conditions in the refugee camps of the economically hard-pressed neighboring Arab countries. The U.S. could hardly
avoid contributing its share; nor could the European Union.

Israel remains adamant that recognition of it by the Palestinian
authorities is a precondition for negotiation. But recognition is a
reciprocal matter. Neither Israel nor would-be Palestine has internationally recognized territorial boundaries—a defining attribute of
statehood and sovereignty. Inevitably, questions arise. Were the
Palestinians to unilaterally recognize Israel, which borders would

they be recognizing? And would recognition not imply acquiescence to an ethno-religious Jewish state consigning 20 per cent of its population—the Arab minority—to second-class citizenship, especially given Tel Aviv's latest and additional sine qua non that the Palestinians recognize Israel "as a Jewish state"?

And what of Jerusalem? Following the dramatic conquest of the eastern part of the city during the Six Day War, Israel proclaimed reunified Jerusalem its eternal and indivisible capital. In 1967 the Holy City was 74 per cent Jewish, 26 per cent Arab. Within 40 years the population has risen from 266,300 to 732,000, of whom 66 per cent (480,000) are Jewish, and 34 per cent (250,000) Arab. It is estimated that within twenty-five years the population of Jerusalem will reach virtual parity between Jews and Arabs. Among Jewish Israelis there is a gnawing worry about the city's shrinking Jewish majority. On the eve of the fortieth anniversary celebrations marking the city's reunification, its *haredi* mayor, Uri Lupolianski, declared that to avoid "losing the city to Hamas," Israel needed urgently to adopt "a long-term strategic plan" to assure its Jewish future. For good measure, he added that "anyone who does not recognize [unified] Jerusalem as the capital of the state of Israel does not recognize the state of Israel."

The ultra-Orthodox not only make up about 30 per cent of the Jewish population and 20 per cent of the total population of Jerusalem, but also exert disproportionate political and cultural power in the city. Their heavy hand, along with poor economic prospects, discourages secular Jews from either moving or staying there.

During the anniversary year of 2007, without regard for Arab and Muslim sensibilities, the municipality of Jerusalem gave the green light to the renovation of the Mughrabi Gate in the Old City, near the Western Wall of the Temple Mount; for the construction, on behalf of the American-based Simon Wiesenthal Center, of a Museum of Tolerance on the asphalt-covered site of one of Jerusalem's oldest Muslim cemeteries, dating from the Middle Ages; for the ascent of the Temple Mount by a score of religious Zionist rabbis. During this same season the national government allocated over $1.5 billion for the development of some 20,000 new housing units for over 85,000 settlers on the outskirts of the eastern part of the city, which now has a Jewish population of over 200,000. Meanwhile, the wall crisscrossing the Arab neighborhoods of East Jerusalem, and all but separating them from the West Bank, is being rushed to completion. Behind this wall, especially in East Jerusalem, the Arab Israeli population suffers severe social, economic, and political discrimination.

Just as Israel cannot command recognition of its statehood, and of its borders, by force, so it cannot legitimize its sovereignty over Great Jerusalem *manu militari*. In mid-2007, not a single U.N. member-state recognizes the annexation of East Jerusalem and the reunified Holy City as the "eternal" capital of Israel: the U.N.'s 194 members persist in their refusal to move their embassies from Tel Aviv to Jerusalem, and even the ambassadors from the U.S. and the European Union begged off the official celebration of the jubilee. Nettled by this boycott, Foreign Minister Tzipi Livni insisted that "even if the world has not yet recognized a united Jerusalem," its connection with Israel was "inseparable." Besides, "it is not dependent on the position of non-Jewish nations." Easily half of the Knesset members press for an undivided Jerusalem, with Netanyahu warning that to leave any part of the Holy City will be to allow "militant Islam to walk in."

Of course, the Palestinians are no less fixed on East Jerusalem as their future capital—an aim, not to say yearning, shared by the Sunni and Shiite Muslim states as well. Master of the situation in Jerusalem but in want of legitimacy, it behooves Israel to propose parameters for a viable compromise along the lines of either a conjoint or re-divided municipal sovereignty.

Israel continues to tighten its stranglehold on the West Bank and Gaza. Military, police, administrative, and economic controls splinter the territories into small, discontinuous enclaves, while the occupation forces fortify the settlements. In the Jordan Valley, which makes up about 30 per cent of the West Bank, they preside over the expansion of settlements that are intended to define Israel's "eastern border." For the occupied Palestinians, meanwhile, economic and social conditions go from bad to worse, with destitution gaining on poverty. Daily harassment at over 100 checkpoints, more than 400 road blocks, and all border crossings wounds pride and feeds despair. So do travel restrictions, curfews, segregated roads, and targeted killings. The Palestinians must be made to feel in all ways strangers in a strange land, and depart.

Despite Israel's unilateral but contingent evacuation of Gaza, conditions there are even more draconian and explosive: completely besieged and quarantined, the strip is crowded, poverty-stricken, and isolated. Consisting of about 140 square miles, Gaza has close to 1.5 million inhabitants, making it one of the world's most densely populated territories; the annual demographic growth rate is close to 4 per cent. Nearly 50 per cent of its people are under 14 years of age, and

65 per cent under 20; nearly 70 per cent are refugees. Except for its Mediterranean coastline, with an apparently promising offshore natural gas reserve, Gaza is poorly endowed economically, and financially asphyxiated by Israel, the U.S., and the European Union. Well over half the labor force is unemployed, and almost two-thirds of the population live near or below the poverty level—many in squalid, overcrowded refugee camps.

Under such circumstances, today's young adults are likely to be even more disposed to radical politics than their parents and grandparents. It is hardly surprising that from Gaza, which is a hotbed of temporal and religious extremism and terror, Hamas challenges the Palestinian Authority, the PLO, and Fatah. Nearly half the younger generation despairs of peace in their lifetime. It is not within the power of the forces loyal to Palestinian Prime Minister and Fatah leader Mahmoud Abbas to prevail over the political Islamists without the financial and military support of the Quartet (the U.S., the E.U., Russia, and the U.N.) and the moderate Arab countries. Israel is providing them with instructors, arms, and ammunition. It also continues to seal off lines of communication between Gaza and the West Bank—a distance of about 40 miles. This separation is in keeping with the policy of forestalling the creation of a fully viable and sovereign Palestinian state.

In their struggle for self-determination the Palestinians have engaged in a horrific level of fratricide, an effect of postponed statehood and a ruptured society, and a guarantor of both. But Israel bears a heavy responsibility for this infighting. With time, this prophylactic strategy has given rise to an ever fiercer rivalry between secular and Islamist factions and militias, and has helped to raise what Israel now considers a Frankenstein: Hamas.

With a decisive military victory out of reach, in May 2007 Israeli officials served notice that it considered the entire Hamas leadership, including Prime Minister Ismail Haniyeh, appropriate targets for assassination. Ephraim Sneh, Labor deputy minister of defense, warned that "no one in the circle of commanders and leaders in Hamas is immune from a strike"; Ze'ev Boim, Kadima minister of immigrant absorption, said "we must strike their leaders . . . from the first to the very last . . . with all our might." On May 23, Israeli soldiers and security agents arrested thirty-three prominent Palestinians in the West Bank—the bulk of them affiliated with Hamas, and among them the minister of education, three members of the Palestinian legislature, and seven mayors and councilmen. In jail they joined the other forty-one Hamas members of the 132-seat Palestinian

Parliament arrested in the summer of 2006. Hamas' takeover of Gaza is the most dramatic expression so far of Israel's policy of divide and rule. The campaign to weaken Arafat and the PLO by playing on internecine conflicts eventually escalated into a near civil war, with a separation between Gaza and the West Bank. In both halves of their fractured land Fatah and Hamas visit atrocities on each other.

The political Islamists won the upper hand in Gaza first at the polling stations in January 2006, and then in the streets in June 2007. They did so less because their supporters and sympathizers clamored for an Islamic theocracy and the *shariah* than because they approved of Hamas' social and charitable work, its political program, and its resistance to occupation. Israel, the U.S., and the E.U. ascribe Hamas' success to its religious fanaticism, terror, and Iranian–Syrian support, in order to discredit it (along with Hezbollah) as a model in the eyes of Islamists throughout the region. Fearful of contagion, the Middle Eastern regimes are also worried that Gaza will turn into a beachhead for Iran and Syria—particularly with the perennial political instability in Lebanon. Certainly Washington, spurred on by Tel Aviv, endorses this reading, which accords with the creed of the war on terror.

But how to break Hamas' hold on Gaza? One way is to tighten the quarantine, backed by overwhelming military force; the other is to encourage Hamas to meet Fatah halfway in the interest of achieving full Palestinian statehood. The U.S., Israel, and Europe favor the first course. Conjuring the specter of fast-spreading Islamism and resurrecting old talk of dominoes, they redouble their support for Abbas and Fatah—previously disprized for weakness, incompetence, and corruption—with dollars, weapons, and advisers. The idea is to strengthen Abbas' emergency government in "West" Palestine, and to raise its prestige over against Hamas' breakaway rule in the "East."

On June 14, 2007 Abbas, in a move backed by the Quartet, dismissed Prime Minister Haniya and severed all relations with Hamas, denouncing its leaders and rank-and-file as "murderous terrorists" and "revolutionists" whose lies "even the devil cannot match." In a show of solidarity with Fatah, President Hosni Mubarak of Egypt and King Abdullah II of Jordan hastily convened a four-way summit with Abbas and Olmert at the Red Sea resort of Sharm El-Sheikh. Cairo and Amman are beholden to Washington, but each has its own good reason for bolstering Abbas: to head off a radical regime next door that would incite Egypt's Muslim Brotherhood and Jordan's Islamic Faction Front. Abdullah II naturally is forever concerned about the Palestinian refugees who account for over half of his Hashemite Kingdom's population of 5.6 million.

Though equally anxious about the growing threat to the status quo, Saudi Arabia advocates a less confrontational course of action. Rather than push Hamas to the wall, Riyadh proposes to mediate a dialogue and reconciliation between the two principal Palestinian factions. Oil leverage and proximity to the Strait of Hormuz give the Saudi kingdom greater room to maneuver, vis-à-vis the U.S., than Egypt or Jordan enjoy. By the same token, it has a global rather than local perspective on the greater Middle East and the emergence of Iran as a major regional power. Abdullah of Saudi Arabia means to keep alive the Arab Peace Initiative that, as crown prince, he floated unsuccessfully in March 2002 and then revived as king in 2005–06, to become the basis of the Mecca Agreement of February 2007. Riyadh's proposal, backed by the twenty-two governments of the League of Arab States, calls for Israel to withdraw to its 1967 borders, recognize a sovereign Palestinian state in the West Bank and Gaza with East Jerusalem as capital, and agree to a "just solution" for the refugees. In return, the Arab states promise to recognize Israel and establish full diplomatic relations.

The House of Saud's disarmingly simple and sober starting point was rejected out of hand by Israel, and consequently failed to reduce the gap between Fatah and Hamas over whether, or on what terms, to engage diplomatically with Israel. Following Hamas' victory in the parliamentary elections of January 2006, the rift between Gaza and the West Bank turned fratricidal. To curb the violence and break Israel's economic quarantine, the Saudi monarch organized the summit in Mecca. Momentarily overcoming its own inconsistency, the Arab League prevailed on Fatah and Hamas to form a national-unity government expected to set in motion the peace initiative of 2002. Israel and the Quartet restated their preconditions for negotiating: the Palestinian side must abjure violence, recognize Israel, and accept all previous agreements and obligations of the Oslo accords—which to date Israel has honored only in the breach. Determined to stamp out Hamas, Tel Aviv, backed by Washington, spurns any agreement reconciling the two factions. The prospect of a renewed push for negotiations premised on the Arab Peace Initiative is abhorrent to Israel.

In the meantime, Israel and the West intensify their support for Abbas, his quasi-legal emergency government, and Fatah, confident that, rattled by Hamas' takeover in Gaza, they will strike a bargain inordinately favorable to Israel—whose top priority will be to make the West Bank safe for nationalist forces that are moderate, secular, and tractable. The scale of that challenge can be measured by the outcome of the 2005 elections, in which Hamas won seventy-four of 132 parliamentary seats, scoring heavily in both Gaza and the West Bank, and confirming its considerable sway in Ramallah, Bethlehem, Nablus, and Kalkilya.

Backed by the West, Abbas and Prime Minister Fayyad seem prepared to fight Hamas to unconditional surrender, even at the risk of separating the West Bank (population, 2.5 million) from Gaza (1.5 million). But should Abbas and Fayyad or their successors ever seriously consider a rapprochement with Hamas, Israel is likely to bear down on them as it did repeatedly on Arafat. In any case, Israel will persevere in what Moshe Dayan in 1977 called "living without a solution," which allows for continuing consolidation and distension of facts-on-the-ground.

In the wake of the Second Lebanon War, Washington, in accord with Tel Aviv, expressed its wholehearted support for President Abbas and Fatah in the showdown with Hamas. Congress hastened to allocate $59 million and the White House $18 million to train, arm, and expand the Palestinian Authority's security forces under the direction of Lieutenant General Keith Dayton, the U.S. security coordinator in the Palestinian territories. In October 2007 Washington allocated an additional $400 million, and upon meeting the Palestinian Authority's security officials in Nablus, Dayton assured them that by "succeeding in Nablus, you will send a message to the entire West Bank and our neighbors that you are serious about law and order and that you can do the job." Within weeks, the U.S. was funding the training and equipping of Abbas's security forces, and Israel authorized the delivery of twenty-five armored personnel carriers to them. Dayton harmonized the growing American intervention with the more modest interventions by Egypt and Jordan, which are increasingly nervous about the spread of Islamic movements next door—in Palestine, Lebanon, and Iraq, backed by Iran and Syria. Apparently the chief operatives of all three countries worked closely with Muhammad Dahlan, Abbas' national security advisor and strongman whose Fatah militia in Gaza was preparing to overpower Hamas.

Judging by the tenor of the Knesset's postmortem on the Second Lebanon War and the reaction of the Israeli street, no substantive rethinking is in the wind. The parliamentary inquest focused almost exclusively on the "severe failures . . . of judgment, responsibility, and prudence" of the generals and the dysfunction of civil–military relations. Its goal was to apportion blame for the conduct of a war that had come to an impotent conclusion, not to question the fundamental logic behind going to war in the first place. Public criticism of the war was conducted along similarly one-dimensional lines.

All this time, Hamas and Islamic Jihad have continued to fire outdated Qassam rockets and Katyusha missiles into the western Negev from the Gaza Strip, striking in particular Sderot and Ashkelon. Since the start of the fourth intifada, thirteen Israelis have been killed by shrapnel, and some 300 wounded. Many more suffer from shock and post-traumatic stress disorder. In 2006 and 2007 a total of about 1,400 projectiles killed two Israeli civilians and wounded 122. On top of the setback in Lebanon, this rocket-firing, though taking a relatively minor toll, is politically and psychologically unnerving. Generals and politicians seize on it to justify continuing in the old ways. Except for several NGOs, Israel's "left" opposition and peace camp are politically extinct. Labor partners Kadima with an eye trained only on the next general elections. Having lost its identity and ideological bearings, it is not about to reconsider the main thrust of Israeli policy. Between them the center-right Kadima and center-left Labor claim fifty-three of the Knesset's 120 seats. Most of the remaining sixty-seven seats are divided among a half-dozen secular and religious parties whose stand on essential issues of foreign and domestic policy is to the right of the governing coalition. In mid-2007 it appeared that, in the event of early elections, Likud, led by Netanyahu—who favors expanding settlements, denying the Palestinians sovereignty, forcing regime change in Iran, and spurring free-market capitalism—has every chance of increasing its parliamentary seats from twelve to between thirty and thirty-five. Similarly, the far-right Yisrael Beiteinu (Israel Our Home) party, led by Avigdor Lieberman, will probably double its representation to twenty seats. The blowback from the Second Lebanon War and the so-called Gaza pullout has unquestionably pushed the center of political gravity further rightward. Whereas the "left of the left" has all but evaporated, the "right of the right" is at its apogee: confident of the support of the political reserve army of the religious Zionists and ultra-Orthodox, it can make or break governments.

To shore up his coalition, in October 2006 Prime Minister Olmert invited Lieberman to join his cabinet. One of Israel's most vituperative ultra-nationalist politicians, Lieberman lives in Nokdim, a settlement deep in the West Bank. Sworn to create a virtually "homogeneous Jewish and Zionist state," he advocates expelling or transferring large numbers of Israeli Arabs across Israel's expansive post-1967 borders, and confirming the second-class citizenship of those who remain. Previously he has called for the infrastructures of the PLO and the terrorists to be deracinated, for Egypt's Aswan Dam to be bombed in retaliation for Cairo's support of Arafat, and for Palestinian prisoners held in the occupied territories to be drowned in the Dead Sea.

Without significant protests at home or in the West, Olmert appointed Lieberman as one of his deputy prime ministers and a as member of his inner cabinet. He also made him the first ever "minister of strategic threats," charged with developing the government's overall policy in the showdown with Iran, which Lieberman considers "the biggest threat to the Jewish people since the Second World War." The significance of Lieberman's political ascent is succinctly summed up by Ilan Pappé:

> The problem with Avigdor Lieberman is not his own views but the fact that he reflects what most Israelis think, and definitely what most of his colleagues in the Olmert government think but do not dare to say, or do not think is desirable to say for tactical reasons.

But, sooner or later, most Israelis—whether generals, politicians, public intellectuals, or citizens—will have to face the increasingly unstable world system—including its non-state actors—in which their small, self-estranged country will have to secure its regional recognition and position.

For now Israel's leaders proceed on the assumption that the U.S.-led war on terror will advance their goals, in uneasy coalition with the Western powers and the axis of so-called moderate Arab kings, presidents, and princes. All see and present themselves as fighting an essentially abstract, occult, and de-territorialized enemy sworn to a dark, messianic, and universalizing creed. Yet, as usual, not only the leaders and activists but the rank-and-file of al-Qaeda and the Mahdi Army, of Hamas and Hezbollah, are flesh and blood, battling as much for profane objectives as for religious–ideological articles of faith. While the political and religious leaders are from the middle classes, the militants, followers, and sympathizers originate in the poor and powerless sectors of society.

A belated embodiment of the postcolonial anti-Western revolt of the wretched of the earth, the Palestinian cause remains hugely exemplary for Muslims everywhere. Barring mass starvation or collective suicide in the open-air prison that is Gaza, the Palestinian question and resistance will not vanish; nor can they be stamped out, except at the risk of a regional calamity. The refugees defy Ben-Gurion's prediction that "the old will die and the young will forget." But having done virtually nothing to assuage their plight since 1949, the

Israeli leadership is not likely to change course now, short of strong and sustained American pressure.

To focus on recognition and borders is to look through the wrong end of the telescope. The problems of the Palestinian refugees and the Jewish settlers are far weightier. So are those of the rights of the Arab minority in Israel, the relations of state and synagogue, and the ties between Israel and the diaspora. Whatever its borders and place in the regional state system, Israel will have to reckon with this second cluster of essentially intramural problems.

History suggests that it may be even more difficult to forge the political and civil society of a new state than it is to negotiate its international frontiers. The primacy of international over domestic politics would seem to be incontrovertible: "national security" trumps all other arguments in the official formulary of reasons for Israel's refugee and settler policies. Yet the origins of these policies are ideological, and their motive forces eminently political. From the Zionist and Israeli perspective, whatever the causes of their exodus, the Palestinian refugees and their descendants are self-deluded: they persist in feeling, conceiving, representing, and affirming themselves as Palestinians. This obstinacy runs counter to the Israeli belief that the Palestinians are simply indigenous Arabs belonging only to a vast and motley pan-Arabic world without national borders. They therefore lack any authentic tie to the Holy Land, and are not entitled to imagine, much less claim, a nation-state of their own. When members of the Palestinian elite began to formulate nationalist yearnings and precepts, they were impugned for fabricating a national identity and catechism out of whole cloth—as if the Israelis had engaged in no imagining of their own. Soon Jabotinsky's assurance that Jewish militias would know how to deal with them reinforced the political Zionists' confidence that the aborigines would eventually yield to superior force or decamp to nearby Arab lands.

The uprisings of 1929 and 1936–8—in effect the first and second intifadas—were an expression of the growing self-awareness and self-assertion of the Palestinians, and saw the start of their demonization as anti-Semites, terrorists, and murderers. By their failure to recognize the reality and legitimacy of a Palestinian resistance, the Yishuv and the nascent Jewish state unwittingly aided its radicalization and religionization, driven by a purblindness rooted in the orientalism of the Zionists' apprehension and experience of the Middle East. From 1947 to 1949, some 750,000 of Mandatory Palestine's nearly 1.5 million Arabs fled or were expelled to become refugees dispersed unevenly in the neighboring Arab countries. These settlements were facilitated by strong religious, cultural, and political affinities between the refugees and their host countries. Bound by shared suffering and nostalgia, this universe of diasporas became the forcing bed of the Palestinian resistance.

The "Arab-Palestinian question" does not exist apart from the Zionist-Israeli question. From the first, the ideological representation of the Arabs and everyday relations with them were a measure of the unfolding policies of the Zionist movement, and of its balance of forces. During the Yishuv, Brit Shalom and the far left alone warned against holding the Arabs in contempt, insisting that such conduct would not only be incendiary but corrosive of the Jewish ethic and of Zionist lifeblood. No matter what its borders, if informed by this conceit the future homeland for Jews would be fundamentally warped by the subjection and segregation of the Palestinian Arabs.

Israel emerged as a democracy for Jews, not for the Palestinian Israelis, though they benefited from the right to vote and to field political parties. In Mandatory Palestine, Israel, and the diaspora, only Brit Shalom, Ihud, and the far left insistently called for equal civil and political rights. With the headlong advance of the nascent country's manifest destiny, the voices of internal critics became voices in the wilderness.

Through the years, the Arabs voted for Mapai, and its political heir, Labor, as the lesser evil. But as Labor increasingly took them for granted, they became more irate about their social condition, the torment of their kinfolk in the territories and camps, and the elusiveness of peace. The political forces pressing for equality and equal opportunity under the law for *all* citizens are now worn to a shadow. Most of Labor keeps tergiversating, at a time when one half of all Israelis living at or below the poverty line are Palestinian Israelis. Meretz remains, but has a mere handful of deputies in the Knesset, and its extended political family commands at best 5 per cent of the popular vote.

Some 500,000 registered Arab voters are free to cast their ballots for either Jewish-Israeli or Palestinian-Israeli parties. As Labor's traditional Jewish electorate has migrated to right-wing parties—its Knesset seats have declined from forty-four in 1992 to nineteen since 2003—the party has sought to stem the defection of the Arabs. In the general election of 2006 it ran three Arab candidates on its list for the Knesset—two successfully. Despite the injuries of discrimination, many Palestinian Israelis realize that they are better off than most other Palestinians under Israel's heel or in neighboring countries. But with their own condition worsening, Palestinian Israelis become increasingly susceptible to the lure of Palestinian nationalism and political Islam.

In the elections of March 2006, their radicalized leaders managed to further reduce the Arab vote for Labor while increasing the vote for the three ethnic parties: United Arab List, led by Sheikh Ibrahim Tzartzoour; Democratic Front for Peace and Equality (Hadash), led by Mohammad Barakeh; and National Democratic Assembly (Balad), led by Azmi Bishara. With roughly 253,000 votes and 8 per cent of the national vote, they elected ten representatives—two more than in 2003. But they are completely marginalized in a parliamentary system that would be closed to them even were it not dominated by hard-liners.

In the wake of the Second Lebanon War, Labor decisively elected Ehud Barak as party chairman, clearing the way for him to succeed Amir Peretz as Olmert's defense minister and to become Labor's standard-bearer in the next election, most likely against Netanyahu. To make his political comeback, Barak defeated two formidable rivals who, like him, had notable careers in the defense and security establishment: Amir Ayalon, former commander-in-chief of the Navy and director of Shin Bet, who by mid-September 2007 had joined the government's security cabinet as minister without portfolio; and Dani Yatom, former head of the Mossad. Ophir Pinez-Paz, Olmert's minister of science, culture, and sports, also entered the lists. But having resigned his post to protest Olmert's appointment of Avigdor Lieberman to the cabinet, he finished last, with less than 8 per cent of the vote.

In his victory speech Barak promised to invest "all our knowledge in strengthening the defense establishment and the IDF and restoring Israel's power of deterrence." At Defense he has set about making contingency plans for lightning preemptive ground and air incursions into Gaza, Lebanon, the West Bank, and Syria. Apparently he has since had second thoughts about the wisdom of the Oslo peace process, and opposes any major territorial withdrawal for three to five years—the time needed to perfect and deploy a new rocket defense system to intercept short- and medium-range Palestinian missiles fired from Gaza and southern Lebanon. He has solicited help from the Pentagon to develop mid-range and long-range defensive missile systems to intercept ballistic missiles from Iran and Syria. Together with Ephraim Sneh, he means to rush the deployment of a missile defense system to cover all of Israel in anticipation of a showdown with Iran. Save for the cautious support of Meretz and several associations of civil society, the three Palestinian Israeli parties are entirely on their own, something that prompts the Palestinian leaders within Israel to intensify their call for the transformation of the state for Jews into a state of and for all its citizens, with equal political and legal rights as well as separate but equal cultural and religious spheres.

With the start of the fourth intifada in late 2000, the Arab minority in Israel came increasingly to be viewed as a fifth column, and its Knesset members as arch-traitors. The security services took to keeping a watch on them, beginning with Bishara, their most prominent and forceful tribune. The Palestinian Israeli leaders never hid their sympathy for the Palestinian resistance, including Hamas and Hezbollah. During the Second Lebanon War some were in contact with like-minded politicians in the occupied territories; Bishara was arraigned for collaborating with the enemy and for money-laundering while traveling abroad. With his parliamentary immunity lifted and a fair trial highly improbable, Bishara resigned from the Knesset (denying all charges) and continued to plead the Palestinian cause from neighboring countries. Right-wing members of the Knesset hastened to denounce him as a traitor and a criminal. In the words of Zevulum Orlev, chairman of the National Religious Party, "The suspicions against Bishara prove that Trojan horses . . . have infiltrated the Knesset" and that he "must be captured wherever he hides, and brought to justice in Israel."

Zionism saw it as a given that the state for Jews would be built by and for the "chosen people"—a notion in accord with the Western supremacism it also took for granted. These two kindred conceits inform Zionism's construction of the Palestinian Other.

The chosenness of the Jews is central to Judaism. Anchored in the covenant said to have been revealed by Moses at Mount Sinai, it has pride of place in the Hebrew Bible and the most solemn prayers. The Friday evening *kiddush*, blessing wine and bread, thanks God for having "chosen us and hallowed us above all nations." The daily prayer *Aleinu* exalts God for not having made the Jews "like the nations of other lands [nor] the same as other families of the Earth"; for not having placed them "in the same situations as others," and for not having made their "destiny the same as anyone else's." It is not uncommon for the Orthodox to conclude this prayer with language that had been widely forgotten since the Middle Ages, especially by the Ashkenazi: "Others bow to vanity and emptiness and pray to a god who cannot save." Lately this sentence has been restored to the service and prayer books of many Orthodox.

While the tenet of divine election does not imply racial superiority, it does display a profound ethnocentrism. Jews generally, and Israeli Jews in particular, are imbued with a notion of uniqueness that is historical and circumstantial, with emphasis on the unremitting torment of discrimination and persecution at the hands of the Christian worlds, culminating in the Judeocide. Israel conjures this teleological narrative to sacralize its *raison d'être*. Through the ages, Europe's Jews were segregated in ghettoes that became ever more conscious and affirming of their singularity. Today, by opposing the ethnocentric state, the Muslim world unintentionally furthers Israel's gradual and partly self-imposed transformation into a ghetto with a siege mentality rooted in a chronic sense of victimhood and immanent peril. In the past, the Jewish people survived without a state, though at an ever steeper cost to themselves. Hereafter their future is said to depend on a Jewish state able to fight fire with fire, trusting in weapons of mass destruction as its *ultima ratio*. That Israel could serve as a home and guarantor of last resort for the Jews of the diaspora is transparently a myth.

The doctrine of chosenness can of course be read antithetically: God entrusted the Jews with the Torah, intended for all humanity, thereby laying a unique burden upon them. This universalist interpretation started with the enlightenments and emancipations in the epoch of the French Revolution, and eventually became a source for reform Judaism, secular Jewish reformism, and left Zionism. The revisionists of the canon give particular weight to the Mosaic code of ethical and moral precepts in the Ten Commandments, shared by Judaism, Christianity, and Islam. Israel is an expression of these two takes on godly election. The Book of Joshua—the Biblical story of Moses' successor, the zealous warrior who set out to conquer Canaan at God's direction and for the "chosen people"—is said to prefigure the new state's destined course, and is used to legitimize it. Immediately to the west of the Jordan River and north of the Dead Sea, Jericho was the first city to be charged and captured by the trumpet-sounding Israelites: "They devoted the city to the Lord and destroyed with the sword every living thing in it—men and women, young and old, cattle, sheep and donkeys." The zeal of Joshua, which Judah Magnes explicitly abjured, is the spirit of Israeli policy in Lebanon and the occupied territories—and toward much of the Muslim world.

The prophet Isaiah articulated another concept of chosenness: the Lord "called you in righteousness" and took "hold of your hand" to "keep you safe" and "give you a covenant for the people, and a light for the nations . . . so that you may be my salvation to the end of the earth." This exceptional civil and political society, unlike any other, was Herzl's dream. His state, imagined in his novel *Old New Land*, would diffuse the light of a modernizing social and cooperative utopia that would reclaim the desert, be a haven for *aliyah*, and an example to the Arabs. As what light there was grew murkier, the Israeli leadership shifted to vaunting the country as an exemplary democracy, unique to the region, despite convincing evidence to the contrary.

Isaiah intuited that it was difficult, if not impossible, to balance a Joshuan mailed fist abroad and an open society at home. In weighing the issue, rather than consult the Hebrew prophets, David Ben-Gurion eventually turned to the ancient Greeks, Thucydides and Plato especially. There was no guaranteeing the survival of a Jewish Athens in the Middle East, he believed, without alloying it indeterminately with Spartan elements: oligarchic rule, military education, garrison state, and social castes.

Perhaps Ben-Gurion, master realist, fought shy of Isaiah for the latter's having glimpsed the punishing tensions between a cosmopolitan polity and a warfare state way back in biblical times. As a critic of power, the prophet saw that to keep faith with the covenant the people would have to "beat their swords into ploughshares, and their spears into pruning hooks." Only by turning from Joshua's path would "[nation] not lift up sword against nation"; neither should they "train for war anymore."

How much more difficult to forge a post-conquest policy in a corner of the earth that is so much more hostile and turbulent now than it was in Biblical times. Afflicted by the memory of the Judeocide, and anxious for the embattled state of the Jews, the leaders of Israel and the Jewish diaspora are not disposed to temper Sparta with Athens, Joshua with Isaiah. Nor is there a popular groundswell to do so. Yad Vashem and the Wailing Wall, the binding memorials of Israel's civil religion, are instrumentalized to exalt a memory that neither forgets nor forgives, thereby tightening the grip of the dead hand of the past.

Yad Vashem, Israel's official memorial to the "Martyrs and Heroes of the Holocaust," takes its name from Isaiah: "To them will I give in my house and within my walls *a memorial and a name* [*yad vashem*] better than that of sons and daughters: I will give them an everlasting name which will not be cut off." The mission of the Remembrance Authority is confined to commemorating the 6 million Jewish victims of an unprecedented global war that consumed over 55 million lives, the majority of them civilians. The only non-Jews to be honored are those who, at their own peril, actively assisted endangered Jews.

Truer to Isaiah would have been a more inclusive credo, even if in the spirit of a chosen people's universal calling: "Let not the foreigner say 'The Lord will surely separate me from his people': Let not the eunuch say 'I am just a dry tree.' . . . The time has come to gather all the nations and tongues." By celebrating a narrow ethno-religious memory, Israel becomes more dry tree than beacon. Since 1959 this solipsism has been hallowed on Yom Hashoah, or Holocaust Martyrs' and Heroes' Day, and increasingly this holy day is observed in the diaspora as well.

The Wailing Wall drew devout Jews from early modern times; by the early twentieth century, secular and Orthodox Zionists revered it as well. Following victory in the 1967 war, the Wall and its plaza became the state's supreme open-air shrine. But before long the religious Zionists and ultra-Orthodox—their social and political influence on the rise—began to reclaim the Wailing Wall for their theologically informed reading of the mission of the state.

Peres and Olmert are sworn secular political Zionists in the spirit of Joshua, not Isaiah, looking to Sparta, not Athens. Neither has ever hesitated to use religion as a justification for and energizer of public policies and military campaigns. By so doing, they encourage the religious Zionists and ultra-Orthodox to flex their cultural and political muscles. As early as 1929, the year of the first Zionist–Palestinian collisions over holy places in Mandatory Palestine, Gershom Scholem, then a member of Brit Shalom, took exception to a would-be Messianic Zionist movement "using a religious terminology for political purposes" and calling for "religious redemption" in some remote future. He balked at "pursuing 'political' exigencies and nostalgias of a distinctly nonpolitical and religious nature." The further interpenetration of the profane and the sacred made it increasingly difficult, in the words of Matthew, to "render unto Caesar the things which are Caesar's, and unto God the things which are God's."

Today the ultra-Orthodox community makes up some 800,000 of a Jewish population of 5.4 million: with an average of close to seven children per family, their offspring make up some 23 per cent of Israel's first-grade pupils, all of them in parochial schools. Judaism is the state religion, and the Orthodox are its guardians. Their chief rabbis arrogate to themselves functions that recall those of the Roman Curia's Congregation for the Doctrine of the Faith. The true believers are like a state within a state. Combining their aura of sanctity with political influence, they exert considerable power over society, culture, and polity. Besides lording it over the principal civic registers, rites of passage, and the rules of conversion, the Orthodox have secured a state-funded but completely autonomous system of primary and secondary education. The public exchequer substantially subsidizes the 60 per cent of ultra-Orthodox men who do not work in order to devote themselves to full-time Torah study. As a consequence, over 50 per cent live below the poverty line, yet they receive disproportionate welfare subsidies as well as grants from the *yeshivas*. Perhaps most revealing of the privileges extended to the Orthodox community are the laws exempting them from universal military service. Between 1975 and 2007 the deferments of draft-age men for reasons of religious faith rose from about 2.5 per cent to about 11 per cent, or 50,000, the equivalent of some four divisions—a striking increase given the hardline settlement and occupation policy championed during these same years by most ultra-Orthodox and religious Zionists.

The religionization of politics and the politicization of religion foster growing social dissension and political inconsistency in Israel. They also complicate relations with the diaspora, where the officially countenanced rise and encroachment of ultra-Orthodoxism disconcert the younger generations in particular, at a time when they are in doubt about both their Jewish identity and their bond to Israel. After 1967, Israel inspired a renewal of Jewish self-awareness and self-assurance in the diaspora, along with a prodigious increase in financial support. For close to forty years Israel could do no wrong. Jews abroad all but blindly endorsed Israel's self-representation as the harmless and beleaguered nation forced to keep fighting for its survival against deadly enemies—the latest being Iranian nuclear warheads and Palestinian fertility.

Israel's destiny is only partially in its own hands. The country is as much at the mercy of world politics in 2007 as it was at its creation in 1947–9, and as were Zionism and the Yishuv during the preceding half century. Should Israel ever deign to define its borders, it can never dictate them, no matter how mighty its armed forces, barbed its fences, high its walls, deep its trenches, wide its buffer zones, or effective its anti-missile missiles. After sixty years the Palestinian resistance is unlikely to fade away, especially given the growing restlessness of the Arab street and the surge of radical Islam throughout the Middle East.

Israel's political class is largely responsible for its estrangement from the Middle Eastern state system and cultural environment, perpetuating an inordinate dependence on imperial patronage. In 1898 Herzl had commended a Jewish homeland in Palestine to imperial Germany as a "link in Europe's rampart against Asia," and after the Balfour Declaration, Weizmann had reassured imperial Britain that such a settlement would be "a safeguard [to England] in particular in respect to the Suez Canal," its gateway to India. Following the Suez War of 1956, which spelled the end of the British and French colonial presence, Israel relied more heavily on the U.S., becoming a combination client state, proxy, and proving ground of the American empire. The U.S. became Israel's armory and paymaster, military and diplomatic shield, economic and cultural model.

After the implosion of the Soviet Union, the U.S. stepped up its drive for global hegemony, taking advantage of the temporary absence of a countervailing coalition of powers. Unlike past empires, the U.S. is a nonterritorial imperium without borders, dominating indirectly. Its military became the strongest the world has ever known. Preponderant on sea, in the air, and in space, it has an awesome capacity to project its power over enormous distances with uncommon speed. America spends at least 25 per cent of its annual budget on defense, almost as much as the rest of the world combined. In addition to at least sixteen secret intelligence agencies, it commands a giant-size navy and air force. Rather than establish colonies and dependencies to be ruled by proconsuls or governor-generals, it rings the globe with over 700 military, naval, air, and intelligence bases, in over 100 countries.

At present the U.S. has twelve aircraft carriers. All but three are nuclear-powered, designed to carry over eighty war planes and helicopters, as well as sizable contingents of marines, sailors, and pilots for rapid deployment of military power to the four corners of the earth. Prepositioned in forward bases and constantly patrolling strategic sea lanes, the U.S. Navy provides the new-model empire's spinal cord and arteries.

The American military presence in the Persian Gulf, Indian Ocean, and surrounding waters is emblematic of its powerful reach. The greatest concentration of overseas military outposts is in the Middle East, as measured by the web of U.S. army, navy, air, and intelligence facilities in Egypt, Jordan, Saudi Arabia, Bahrain, Kuwait, Oman, and Qatar. Not counting Iraq, the U.S. has 40,000 troops, mostly Marines, on land bases and staging grounds in the Gulf, some of them close to the Iraq–Iran border. The headquarters of the U.S. Army Central Command are in Qatar, those of the Fifth Fleet in Bahrain. Numerous U.S. warships, including at least two world-class aircraft carriers, are crisscrossing the Persian Gulf, Arabian Sea, and Indian Ocean, with some of the accompanying seaborne fortresses carrying landing crafts, tanks, jump-jets, and cruise missiles. The chief intent of this display is to maintain a firm grip on one of the world's most critical geopolitical and geo-economic regions, with its phenomenal energy reserves.

The American empire has reached its peak, or an incipient stage of its decline. Yet its military might remains unequaled, as does its political, cultural, and economic energy and radius. Admittedly its ground forces are stretched thin, but new-model mercenaries are being recruited to remedy this shortfall: in 2007 in Iraq they contribute more boots and contractors on the ground—many of them on the cheap from Third World countries—than America's military. The dollar may no longer be the pivot and sole reserve currency of the international monetary system, but it is not broken. Middle Eastern and Asian magnates and sovereign wealth funds continue to invest heavily in the U.S. economy, including its major financial firms. America is still the epicenter of the global capitalist economy, despite the embattled dollar and shrinking manufacturing base, and its wild financial and economic quakes create seismic shocks far and wide.

The U.S. is a status quo empire; it defends rather than expands its overextended realm. As yet it has the military and economic muscle to keep other powers from defying or threatening its positions. Likewise, although increasingly contested, its belief system and soft power remain relatively resilient. But stymied by the asymmetries of postmodern irregular warfare, the U.S. is bound to become embroiled in new difficulties, as in Iraq, Palestine, Lebanon, Pakistan, and Afghanistan. These costly involvements accentuate political conflicts among Washington's power elite in the face of rising class divisions, fiscal constraints, and monetary upheavals. Their infighting, however, is never about questioning the logic or rightness of empire, but only about securing it more effectively. Mounting trouble along the periphery and dissension at the center lead to a loss of influence and prestige on the world stage. In reaction, the wounded empire's Caesars, senators, and proconsuls trumpet their universal virtue more loudly, while becoming more prone to rattle the saber and favor preventive war.

American neoconservative pundits like Martin Kramer celebrate the present "geopolitical situation" as uniquely favorable and enviable in the history of the Jews: they have "one foot planted in a Jewish sovereign state and the other in the world's most open and powerful society," in addition to having "a strategic alliance with the greatest power on earth." Whereas in the past Jews "were revolutionaries," nowadays they are "a status quo people" and do not "need the world

to change," even in the Middle East. Along with Israel they are
"generally confident or complacent enough to prefer the status quo
to the risks of [change]."

Israel's negotiations with the Palestinians and the Arab countries
reflect this attitude. Its leaders persist in the objective of forcing the
former to settle for a fragmented and demilitarized state with all the
trappings, but none of the substance, of independence and sovereignty.
Israel probably means to reserve the right to control the skies,
electronic airspace, border crossings, and territorial waters of a virtual
Palestine. Convinced that Israel is still at the zenith of its power, few in
the Establishment dare admit, at least publicly, that this potency will
perdure only as long as the country has the unswerving support and
protection of the U.S.

For the foreseeable future, Israel will continue to benefit from
Washington's having turned the greater Middle East, now including
Pakistan and Afghanistan, into the main theater of military deployment and political engagement in its open-ended war on terror. This is
the third phase of the American war to make the world safe for
democracy—a crusade started during the First World War and
resumed during the Second World War in the form of the Cold
War, until 1988–90. Because of its uneasy conscience and latent
penitence for the Judeocide, which is likely to fade, the West, led
by the U.S., has unequivocally backed Israel in its conflict with the
Palestinians and with its neighboring Arab states.

But hereafter in the American-orchestrated global war on terror
Israel will count less as an exceptional state than as a troublesome
if highly proficient client state in the volatile Islamic world. Its
formidable military machine and giant armaments industry can
compensate neither for its small population in the midst of a vast,
inhospitable regional environment nor for its economic and military
reliance on the U.S. government and diaspora. Tel Aviv's decision-
makers become irate whenever Washington shows signs of deviat-
ing from the straight and narrow pro-Israel path. Even so, they
continue to bet only on America, as if determined to go for broke.
Out of a long habit of largely self-willed diplomatic isolation, they
now have difficulties imagining and seeking openings to other
major powers.

Whereas the U.S. represents Iran's pursuit of its own security and
regional interests as a challenge to American imperial prerogatives,
Israel represents the Islamic Republic as an existential threat. In fact,
for both Washington and Tel Aviv, balance of power and regime
change are at issue, not Iran's nuclear menace. They know well that

Tehran has neither the capability nor the proclivity to attack them, not least because of America's and Israel's daunting retaliatory power.

Iran's military posture and capacity are essentially defensive, and for obvious reasons. The country is three times the size of metropolitan France, with a population of close to 70 million animated by a deep sense of its historical past and national identity. It borders on Afghanistan in the east, Iraq in the west, and—since the collapse of the Soviet Union—five new countries in the north. The neighborhood is not exactly demilitarized. Neighboring Russia and Pakistan are nuclear-armed states. More to the point, the U.S. has an array of strategic air and naval bases, as well as aircraft carriers in the Persian Gulf, along with air bases in Iraq, Pakistan, Afghanistan, Kyrgyzstan, Tajikistan, and Turkmenistan. And Israel has several hundred atomic warheads, as well as a credible missile defense system and second-strike capability.

In the event of an attack, Iran is ready to retaliate with medium- and long-range missiles charged with deadly warheads aimed not only at Israeli cities, but also at U.S. warships and at energy installations in the Gulf. To assert, however, that Iran is the urgent danger for Israel, the Middle East, and the world is to turn reality upside down. The country's preparedness is a response to longstanding and rising external threats. As time passes the Israeli–Palestinian conflict, the quagmire in Iraq, the unsteadiness of Lebanon, or the insurgencies in Afghanistan and Pakistan matter less in themselves than in their effects on the confrontation with Iran—now allegedly the nerve center of the axis of evil and Mecca for jihadists. What the Soviet Union and Communism were to the Cold War, Iran and Islamism—"Islamo-fascism"—are to the War on Terror. Only yesterday Moscow was denounced for controlling every Communist party down to the last cell; today Tehran stands accused of funding and masterminding each and every terrorist movement and militia down to the last suicide bomber.

In times of general transnational crisis it is difficult to determine the respective importance of the geopolitical and ideological factors— even more so when the geography is the Middle East, and oil is a major constant. Afghanistan and Pakistan may not have any, but both countries border on oil-rich Iran, and Pakistan borders on the Gulf of Oman, southeast of the oil-strategic Strait of Hormuz. Although the Taliban and al-Qaeda are predominantly radical Sunni organizations, they matter less for their impact on the borderless Sunni–Shiite religious and ethnic strife than for their effects on the political conflicts in host countries, where the outcome will further unsettle the balance of power, in which Iran is certain to be an increasingly weighty player. The leaders of the U.S. and Israel, like Iran's, are over-ideologizing what is a normal change in a regional balance of power that, like any, is impermanent. Invariably, status quo powers strain to slow down or obstruct what they perceive to be re-equilibrations unfavorable to them. As Iran asserts itself, with increasing support from a resurgent Russia and a fast-rising China, the U.S. looks to reaffirm its predominance by keeping things as they are. Tel Aviv is reduced to following in Washington's train, though it has the capacity and conceit to complicate the politics and diplomacy of its indispensable protector.

Confronted with ever stronger and more complex countervailing forces, the U.S. and Israel steel themselves for the painful task of scaling back their overreach: Washington to manage its imperial retrenchment, Tel Aviv its territorial contraction. Domestic politics decides on whether the stance is to be minimal flexibility or outright intractability. At the moment there is less of a contest in Israel, where the secular diehards still trust the leverage of their transatlantic acolytes. But as Washington wavers in its support, the political pendulum in Tel Aviv is likely to swing further to the religious right, whose position is, in effect, *après nous le déluge.*

American and Israeli hardliners readily entertain the idea of preventive war to hedge against the ostensible growth in the enemy's strategic advantage, or to forestall a future attack. This kind of wager has notable precedents in recent history: the Central Powers' rush to war in 1914; Nazi Germany's invasion of Soviet Russia in June 1941; Japan's attack on Pearl Harbor in December 1941; Britain and France's move on the Suez Canal in 1956; America's invasion of Iraq in 2003; Israel's thrust into Lebanon in 2006. In each instance the imminence and scale of the enemy's threat is exaggerated, and adverse unintended consequences take over.

In 2003 the U.S. and its willing coalition partners launched a preventive war against Iraq to overthrow Saddam Hussein, whose alleged weapons of mass destruction and links to al-Qaeda were said to threaten the national security of America and its allies. In 2006 and 2007, the super-hawks in Washington and Tel Aviv call for preventive and admonitory strikes on Iran's nuclear installations, to destabilize the Iranian regime and set back its putative resolve to join the nuclear club. Bogged down in the region, the U.S. considers seizing on Iran's nuclear ambitions as a pretext to redeem itself through a fresh show of force. Not to act, it is feared by many Beltway insiders, would be taken as a sign of general weakness and failure of nerve. As Geoffrey

Morrell, Pentagon press secretary, put it in November 2007: "At a time that we have our hands full in Iraq and Afghanistan" the U.S. needs to "remind the rest of the world . . . that we are still very much engaged globally."

A nuclear power by the grace of the West, Israel exceeds the U.S. in its resolve to prevent Iran from acquiring not so much the ultimate weapon itself as the diplomatic status and leverage it presumably confers. Nearly the entire political and military class is determined to escalate diplomatic and economic coercion to force Iran to swear off military nuclearization and yield to regime change. Should this non-violent stratagem of diplomatic and economic coercion fail to do the trick, Tel Aviv will spare no effort to bring Tehran to heel, if need be by unilateral military force.

Israel is readying itself for a showdown. In the words of former Assistant Defense Minister Ephraim Sneh in October 2007: "In the event no one stops Iran on its way to the bomb, a military option for Israel must still be kept on the table . . . only a nuclear Iran is worse [than] the final option." In November, Defense Minister Ehud Barak added that, in the standoff with Iran, "we cannot take any option off the table and we need to study operational aspects." And in December, General Gabi Ashkenazi, Chief of Staff, commented, "In the coming years . . . the capability to act both defensively and offensively against various threats [and targets] will be upgraded greatly with a strong emphasis on long-range capability." The military, assured of the requisite funds, largely provided by the U.S., will re-equip Israel with state-of-the-art offensive and defensive weapons and weapons systems, as well as ammunition. Meanwhile the Israeli Air Force carries out training flights of long-range attack planes (F-15s and F-16s), covered by fighter jets and accompanied by refueling aircraft.

Israel's geostrategists and politicians call into question American estimates that, should Iran stay on the nuclear path, it will not have enough enriched uranium for a bomb until some time between 2009 and 2015. In tune with most of the Israeli intelligence community, Efraim Halevy, former director of the Mossad, insists that Israel has to operate "on the basis of the worst-case scenario": Iran is moving ahead not only with uranium enrichment to military grade, but also with the "development of long-range ballistic missiles." He expects 2009, when Tehran is likely to cross "the weapons threshold," to be the "year of decision."

Senior political and military figures, though agreeing with Halevy that "the future of the region cannot be determined with Israel outside the door," and that the "option of last resort" cannot be precluded, differ among themselves on whether or not to go it alone. Giving voice to a broad national consensus, Netanhayu, leader of the opposition, holds that "we always prefer international action, led by the United States, but we have to ensure that we can protect our country with all means." Even if Israel were to attack unilaterally, would or could it do so without giving advance notice to Washington? Were wisdom to prevail, Israel would not ignore the U.S., which would have to assume overall responsibility for the potentially far-reaching unintended military, diplomatic, and political consequences, especially given Tehran's fast-improving defensive and retaliatory capabilities. Tel Aviv cannot lightly risk provoking Iran into striking nearby U.S. land and naval forces, and partly paralyzing the world's premier energy complex.

Will Israel continue to contribute to widening the general crisis and escalating political violence in the greater Middle East, in which Islamic revival and ethno-religious discord play an inevitable role? So far, Israeli governments have done little, if anything, to pour oil on the waters. To the contrary, they have troubled them further, helping to turn Israel into a convenient scapegoat for Arab–Muslim societies and polities. Practically every other sensible soul is urging Israel's governors—out loud or on the quiet—finally to make a virtue of necessity, and give peace a chance. Yet they do so fully aware of the difficulty of loosening the political and ideological grip of the secular and religious hawks and their opposite numbers in the U.S., where the more flexible of those favoring the imperial status quo intermittently check their power.

Israel contravenes America's effort, in its own imperial interest, to forge a coalition of "moderate" Arab states to help contain the Shiite Islamic Republic and stabilize the Middle East. Washington's promise to pay them off by prevailing on Israel to enter good-faith and equitable negotiations with the Palestinians particularly galls Tel Aviv. Israel's hardliners are convinced, however, that the leaders of the Sunni Arab oligarchies, including Egypt and Jordan, are so frightened of Tehran's military ascendancy and religious clarion call that they will sign on to America's terms unconditionally.

Instead, America's refusal to check Israel bolsters the resolve of the Gulf Arab states to seek a middle way between Washington and Tehran. To be sure, they are disquieted by Iran's warnings that any U.S. or Israeli attack will touch off retaliatory strikes certain to further unsettle a region where popular restlessness is being fed by the grossly unjust distribution of oil and natural gas wealth. But Tehran also speaks in another voice: senior envoys visit the six members of the Gulf Cooperation Council (Saudi Arabia, the United Arab Emirates, Kuwait, Qatar, Bahrain, Oman)—most of them host to American bases—to reassure them that Iran's nuclear program is for peaceful purposes. In October 2007 King Abdullah of Saudi Arabia conferred with President Ahmadinejad in Riyadh. A week after the Annapolis Conference of November 27, the latter attended the annual meeting of the GCC in Doha, Qatar. After reiterating that Iran's nuclear program was nonmilitary, Ahmadinejad stressed the "need to achieve peace and security in the region without foreign intervention" at a time when "the security of all countries in the region is interconnected, and any security disturbance would affect all its countries." The Saudi sovereign, breaking with precedent, even invited Ahmadinejad to be his special guest for the yearly *hajj* to Mecca in mid-December, where he joined over 2 million pilgrims from scores of Muslim countries.

In a special address to the pilgrims, Ayatollah Ali Khamenei, Supreme Leader of the Islamic Republic, declared that "Islamic unity and solidarity are definite religious duties." He challenged "the organizers of the hegemonic centers and expansionist and aggressive powers which consider the Islamic awakening a great threat to their illegitimate interests and their oppressive domination over the Muslim world." Terrified, these powers exploit the "disunity and conflicts among the parts of the Muslim Ummah." Sowing the "seeds of discord among our brothers . . . proved to be effective in Palestine, Lebanon, Iraq, Pakistan, and Afghanistan, and some people in these Islamic countries were instigated to oppose some of their own countrymen and to spill their blood." As Islam tries to overcome "the humiliating backwardness . . . imposed on it in recent centuries," it comes up against enemy "media and propaganda which . . . try to attribute any freedom- and justice-seeking movements in any part of the world to Iran or Shiism." Khamenei concluded:

> The astonishing patience and perseverance of the legal government of Palestine and its self-sacrificing people and many other signs of the revival of Islam in Muslim countries are all accused of being linked to Iranism or Shiism in order to impede the unanimous support of the Muslim world.

Leaders of the Gulf countries, emboldened by Moscow and Beijing, are susceptible to this reasoning, however nervous they may be about Iran's ascendance. In December, when their security officials met with Defense Secretary Gates in Manama, Bahrain, they not only contested

America's unchanging position on Israel, including its nuclear arsenal, but also questioned Washington's unwillingness to negotiate directly with Tehran. After underscoring the seriousness of Iran's nuclear and political thrust, Gates offered the Gulf countries an anti-missile shield, an upgrade of strategic weapons, and support for their incipient collaborative program for nonmilitary nuclear energy. While the GCC countries half-cynically placed their orders for advanced weapons, which they can afford but scarcely need, Israeli officials and AIPAC hastened to lobby against this sale in Washington, to no effect.

Israel may be reaching a point of no return. But rather than take stock, its leaders, in denial and as ever blinded by hubris and self-righteousness, go to any lengths to preserve a state and society that, though walled in, remains vulnerable. Israel can, of course, develop and acquire more lethal and sophisticated weapons, delivery systems, anti-missile shields, and second-strike capabilities, just as it can build longer and higher sensorized walls and safer nuclear shelters.

Though there is no such thing as absolute security, Israel's leaders, with broad popular support, continue to pursue this holy grail. Contemptuous of diplomacy, they keep trusting in the sword. But with the rest of the world, including the West, increasingly disabused, they do so at enormous risk—perhaps because they are prepared to have recourse to the Samson Option as a last resort.

"Will suspicions cease? Will there be an end to vengeance?" Martin Buber posed these pained questions immediately following the first Arab–Israeli War of 1948–49. "Won't we be compelled, and I mean really compelled, to maintain a position of vigilance forever, without being able to breathe?" He brooded on Nehemiah: "Everyone with one of his hands wrought in the work, and with the other held a weapon"; and lamented that while so employed, "you can build a wall, but not an attractive house, let alone a temple."

Buber had foreseen that life in the garrison state would not be the sanctuary Herzl had envisaged in the *Old New Land*.

1

THE IMPERIAL CONTEXT:
1890 TO THE FIRST WORLD WAR

Like any civil and military struggle that entails a fight to the death over a Holy of Holies, the Arab–Israeli conflict resists sober analysis. In much of the First and Second Worlds, political opinion and public sentiment tend to be distinctly more favorable to the Israelis than to the Palestinian Arabs. Among the many reasons for this partiality, three stand out.

First: a lingering, Western-supremacist contempt for and suspicion of "natives"—non-Christian and formerly colonized peoples. Having emerged during the high noon of Western colonial imperialism, the Zionist project matured during its sunset and became its last avatar. While the Zionists did not assume the White Man's burden in their drive to establish a Jewish commonwealth in Arab Palestine, they went in with his attitude; the state of Israel was consolidated in a region seething with anti-imperialist nationalism.

Second: displacement of a deep-seated guilt for age-old anti-Judaism, seared by the Judeocide of 1941–5. In god's good time, in an access of New Testament charity and Old Testament reversion, the Christian nations of Europe and the Americas embraced Zionism and Israel in atonement for their persecution of Jews through the ages, of which the Final Solution was the nadir. It was for the Europeans—not the Arabs—to atone, make reparation, and provide a haven for the refugees and displaced persons of the Jewish catastrophe.

Third: a Manichaean view of the Arab–Israeli conflict. In the reigning perspective, innocent, imperiled, and peace-seeking Israelis are set against treacherous, swarming, and aggressive Arabs. Law-abiding citizens, reputable politicians, and noble citizen-soldiers confront a "beast with many heads"—devious timeservers, and barbarian terrorists. Fear of being driven into the sea eclipses any Israeli disquiet that the Palestinian Arabs might be driven into the desert. Where one right of return is consecrated, another is execrated.

The Palestinian Arabs perceived the Jewish immigrants of successive *aliyah*s as foreigners bent on imposing a colonial regime. In fact,
by the 1920s they considered the Zionist settlers a greater peril than the
British and French satraps in the Middle East: the latter understood
that they were strangers in the land, certain to return to the metro-
polis; the former deemed Palestine their home and, until recently,
neither would nor could imagine returning to the commonwealth of
the diaspora.

The Zionists and the Palestinian Arabs invented their nations
almost simultaneously, and ever more interactively. The Zionists
adopted the liberal nationalism of nineteenth-century Europe. Forcibly
exiled by the Romans in AD 70, and having wandered for nearly two
millennia, they recast the mythologized and ritualized Jewish memory
of the Holy Land as a presumptive right to a sovereign territorial
nation-state with legendary boundaries. The Palestinian Arabs embraced the anti-imperialist nationalism of the twentieth-century Third
World: the land their people had been living on continuously since the
seventh century (apart from a hiatus during the Crusades) belonged to
them. Each plaintiff claimed the high ground, the Zionists essentially
from the common-law position "first-in-time is first-in-right"; the
Palestinians, "last-in-time is first-in-right."

Would-be nation-states, artificially contrived, are equidistant from
god and the devil. Defined by contested boundaries with neighboring
nations, sovereign states are finally made up by, or in accord with, the
shifting will of the great powers of the day. As a ward of successive
empires, Palestine lacked not only clear borders but also a vested
authority to draw them. At the outset, and for years on end, the
Zionists assumed that the concert of great powers would decide the
fate of Palestine as it had started to decide the fate of Asiatic Turkey
and of Africa at the Congress of Berlin, in 1878 and 1885 respectively:
at both summits Europe's statesmen had peremptorily delineated
frontiers and bartered sovereignties. The early Zionists had good
reason to assume that, should the indigenous Arabs oppose a Jewish
homeland in Palestine, in due time the great European chancelleries
could be prevailed upon to have that population moved across
mysterious desert boundaries into Mesopotamia or Arabia.

Historically the Jews may be said to have mistimed their claim to a
territorial nation in Palestine. Had they advanced it a century earlier,
they could have borne down on the Palestinian Arabs as freely as the
Spanish conquistadores had on the Mayans and the North American
colonists on the native Indians. (Had the Zionist movement emerged a
third of a century later, after Lenin and Wilson had universalized the

gospel of self-determination, it would have been stillborn.) But Palestine was not "a land without a people," and expulsion or extermination of people in peacetime was going out of favor, at least for the time being.

As might be expected, the Zionists' legal, historical, and religious reasons for settlement were challenged by the Palestinian Arabs. By repudiating the latter-day return, they constituted their own legitimacy. In what became an all-out struggle between two increasingly irreconcilable claims that turned adversaries into enemies, one side's lawless aggression and terrorism became the other's self-defense and justified revenge.

There is no understanding the Israeli–Palestinian imbroglio without exploring the dialectics of the vexed "Arab Question" in the unfolding of the Zionist project. For Martin Buber, a towering internal critic of Zionism, this question concerned "the relationship between Jewish settlement and Arab life, or, as it may be termed, the intra-national [intraterritorial] basis of Jewish settlement." From the outset, starting with Ahad Haam in the 1890s, eminent lone Zionist voices in both the diaspora and the Yishuv upbraided the principal founders and leaders of modern Zionism for their ingenuous but stubborn neglect of this crucial problem. Eventually Judah Magnes sadly concluded that the failure to make Arab–Jewish understanding and cooperation a major policy objective was Zionism's "great sin of omission." Instead of taking the true measure of the majority Arab-Palestinian population, most early Zionists ignored, minimized, or distorted its nature and reality. Even over time they either remained blind to the potential for an Arab awakening or dismissed Arab nationalism as an inconsequential European import.

Buber spoke for the critics who had all along insisted on the urgency of the Arab Question, and on the importance of addressing the fears of Palestinian Arabs, as well as respecting their political aspirations. He became convinced that the issue would be the "touchstone" of Zionism and its intentions. He deplored the early settlers' "basic error": they neglected to "gain the confidence of the Arabs in political and economic matters" and by so doing caused the Jews "to be regarded as aliens, as outsiders" uninterested in "seeking mutual trust."

Buber took to task Zionism's "political leadership" for "paying tribute to traditional colonial policy," and for being "guided by international considerations" to the exclusion of attention to "intra-national" affairs. On the whole, Zionist policy not only neglected

Arab–Jewish relations inside Eretz Israel, but also failed to "relate the aims of the Jewish people to the geographic reality in which these aims would have to be realized." As a consequence, the nascent Jewish commonwealth was "isolated from the organic context of the Middle East, into whose awakening it [needed to] be integrated, in accordance with a broader spiritual and social perspective." As early as February 1918, Buber demurred when ultra-Zionists advocated "creating a majority [of Jews] in [Palestine] by all means and as quickly as possible." Fearing that "most leading Zionists (and probably also most of those who are led) are thoroughly unrestrained nationalists," he predicted that unless "we succeed in establishing an authoritative [Zionist] opposition, the soul of the movement will be corrupted, maybe forever."

This reaction was the germ of the idea that informed the foundation of Brit Shalom (Alliance for Peace) in 1925, and was carried on by Ihud (Union) in 1942. The members and fellow-travelers of these two societies of dissidents formed an influential but powerless opposition on the Arab Question, and emerged as the racked conscience first of Zionism and then of Israel. By virtue of being severely marginalized, these faithful internal critics were unable to inspire and encourage their Palestinian and Arab counterparts, who were as weak and beleaguered as they themselves.

In 1947–8, following the proclamation of the problematic and contested Jewish state, Buber reflected on the creed and role of those public intellectuals who, "equally free from the megalomania of the leaders and the giddiness of the masses, discerned the approaching catastrophe." He claimed that, as the embodiment of Cassandra in their time, this "spiritual elite . . . not merely uttered warnings but tried to point to a path to be followed, if catastrophe was to be averted." In "speeches which were so many deeds" these critics, among whom Buber was one of the most forceful, conceived of another road "to a Jewish revival in Palestine" and to the "rescue of the Jewish people." Envisioning an alternative to the "Jewish state" promoted by Theodor Herzl and his political heirs, they put forth a farsighted program for a "binational state" aimed "at a social structure based on the reality of two peoples living together." They cautioned that "any [Jewish] national state in vast and hostile [Middle Eastern] surroundings would be the equivalent of suicide," largely because "an unstable international basis could never make up for the missing intra-national one." Only an "agreement between the two nations could lead to Jewish–Arab cooperation in the revival of the Middle East, with the Jewish partner concentrated in a strong settlement in Palestine." Buber expected the logic of multi-ethnicity to favor the reemergence of "national universalism," the Jewish people's "unique truth," to inform the "struggle against the obstacles chauvinism places in our way."

In October 1948, in the midst of the first Arab–Israeli war, Buber questioned the credo that, since the Jewish state had been attacked, it was "engaged in a war of defense." "Who attacked us?" asked Buber, ever attentive to the Other. The aggressors were "those who felt that they had been attacked by us, namely by our peaceful conquest" under an imperial umbrella, and who "accuse us of being robbers." Israelis and Zionists countered with the claim, as Buber put it, that "this was our country two thousand years ago and it was there that we created great things." Though a sworn Zionist, he found their logic incredible: "Do we genuinely expect this reason to be accepted [by the Arabs] without argument, and would we accept it were we in their place?"

As Buber recalled, in their own time these loyal critics struggled to preserve their ideal against its replacement "by the Asmodeus [evil spirit] of a political chimera." Contemptuously referred to as "certain intellectuals," "quislings," and "defeatists," they overcame "despair" by keeping the faith and by invoking "the helpful power of reason."

Two radically different, even incompatible, societies were destined to coexist in Palestine—the one dynamic, the other relatively changeless. Though coming out of the traditional shtetl life of Eastern Europe, most settlers of the first *aliyah*s had the advantage of formal education, openness to technology, access to capital, and ideological commitment. By comparison, the host Palestinian society was static, ritualized, and hierarchic. But whatever the hard facts of the great divide between Jewish and Arab Palestinians, they were magnified by mutual misperception and stereotyping, fed by ignorance of each other's history, culture, and language. In this uneven encounter, Zionism was the invasive and ascendant party. The Jewish immigrants, even if only half-consciously, carried Western civilization into an Oriental world that they disdained and saw through a glass darkly; and they did so under the aegis of imperial powers. A heavily urban and manufacturing society, the Yishuv became a fast-growing center of dynamic modernity in a torpid rural society.

By 1940 one-third of the Jewish population of about 500,000 lived in greater Tel Aviv. The per capita income in the Yishuv vastly exceeded that of nearly 2 million Palestinian Arabs who still owned and worked 90 per cent of the land. Zionists scanted this reality by characterizing their mission as the redemption of the land, the revaluation of manual labor, and the recovery of an unaffected communal life. The Arcadian kibbutz, not fast-growing cosmopolitan Tel Aviv, heralded the New Jerusalem. Although many of the Arabs benefited from the modern and modernizing enterprise of the Yishuv, the greater number viewed it with a mixture of ambivalence, wariness, and *ressentiment*. Tensions between the Zionist and Palestinian spheres were analogous to the perennial urban–rural friction everywhere. Locally, however, they were compounded by the volcanic animus peculiar to the contemporary confrontation of imperial master and colonial subject.

Both intra-nationally and internationally, to use Buber's terms, the conflict over Palestine was profoundly conditioned by the twilight of European imperialism and the dawn of the colonial rebellion. Both coincided, at the end of the nineteenth century, with the birth of Zionism. Just as the Balfour Declaration, the Mandate, and the Partition of 1947–8 were late expressions of imperial legerdemain, so the Palestinian resistance and clamor for a nation-state were part of the far-flung struggle of colonial peoples for self-determination and independence.

The Zionist bid for a homeland in Palestine and, later, the establishment of the state of Israel were impossible without the backing of an imperial power. Like most national liberation movements, Zionism was both liberating and repressive. The emancipation of Jews having stalled in Europe, the Zionists proposed to consummate it in the Holy Land. But to achieve their goal, they cast their lot from the start with Europe, and came to adopt elements of its colonial mindset and operating code.

The members of the first *aliyah* (1883–1903) settled in Palestine at a time when the Great European Powers had begun to carve up the Arab lands of the failing Ottoman empire. The founding Zionist Congress met in Basel in 1897. The following year, Theodor Herzl met the Emperor of Germany, first in Constantinople and then in the Holy Land, to urge him, unsuccessfully, to press the Sultan of Turkey to grant the Jews a charter for an autonomous precinct in Palestine. That was the year the United States took possession of the Philippine Islands, Guam, Puerto Rico, and Hawaii. Where Mark Twain took umbrage and became a founding member of the Anti-Imperialist League, Rudyard Kipling celebrated America's joining in the parade with his rousing poem, "The White Man's Burden," calling on the citizens of the civilized nations to uplift "Your new-caught, sullen peoples, Half devil and half child." He wrote this ode to empire in 1899, the year Britain secured a protectorate over an as yet oil-less Kuwait and an Anglo-Egyptian condominium over the Sudan.

In 1902 Joseph Chamberlain, colonial secretary in the cabinets of Lords Salisbury and Balfour, grudgingly offered Herzl an autonomous region for Jewish settlement in Uganda, in Great Britain's East African protectorate. In 1905, the year following Herzl's death, and just before the large pogroms of that and the following year in czarist Russia, the Seventh World Zionist Congress, again meeting in Basel, spurned this option as forswearing the dream of Palestine. Finally the bitter fortunes of the First World War presented the Zionists with an unhoped-for opening: trapped in a severe military and diplomatic crisis, and desperate for every scrap of support, in November 1917 Lord Arthur James Balfour, His Majesty's foreign secretary, promised that England would "facilitate the establishment in Palestine of a national home for the Jewish people." With the future of Turkey's wards in Mesopotamia and Arabia undecided and contested, London did not yet wield the scepter over Palestine, putting in question its legal right to map the Holy Land's destiny.

Britain's policy in Palestine was an integral part of its designs on the greater Middle East. These reached their zenith between the mid 1870s and the early 1880s, when England gained control of the Suez Canal and established a protectorate over Egypt, with a view to securing a quick sea route to India. Flaunting its ambition, Britain titled Queen Victoria Empress of India in 1876. For the time being the declining Turkish empire kept a tenuous hold on Greater Syria, including Palestine, Mesopotamia, and most of the Arabian peninsula. Well before that empire collapsed, having joined the losing coalition during the First World War, England and France in particular were waiting impatiently to carve up its Asiatic provinces.

By then the geostrategic importance of the Middle East had been magnified beyond measure by the new factor of "black gold." In the last quarter of the nineteenth century, governments and entrepreneurs began to realize the vital importance of oilfields worldwide. Although the oil rush started in America and Mexico, it had spread to the Middle East before 1914. With the growing economic and strategic importance of fuel, the Great European Powers, with no petroleum deposits of their own, woke up to a future vulnerability that would be exacerbated in times of war. They would have to secure not only their own production of oil overseas, but also the ocean lanes for its transport home. In July 1913, First Lord of the Admiralty Winston Churchill, eyeing Persia—where oil had begun flowing in 1908—and the Middle East, insisted that Britain "must become the owners, or at any rate the controllers, at the source, of at least a portion of the supply of natural oil which we require." In 1874 Prime Minister Disraeli had bought for Britain 44 per cent of the shares of the Suez Canal Company; in 1914 Churchill purchased half the shares of the Anglo-Persian Oil Company (later British Petroleum, or BP—rival of Exxon and Shell).

The First World War confirmed the indispensability of oil for the Great Powers: French Prime Minister Georges Clemenceau declared it to be "as necessary as blood"; Marshal Ferdinand Foch insisted that "we must have oil . . . or we shall lose the war"; Lord Curzon, British foreign secretary and former viceroy of India, said simply that "the Allies floated to victory on a wave of oil." Looking ahead, oil was certain to be critical to diplomacy and war, and to industry and transport.

With Russia and Germany *hors de combat*, it was left to England and France to wrangle over the succession of Asiatic Turkey, two regions of which, in Mesopotamia, were thought to have large oil deposits. The ground for this division of spoils was prepared during the 1914–18 war. Steeling the Entente for an unexpectedly difficult and protracted conflict, in March–April 1915 France and Britain underwrote Russia's annexation of Constantinople (Istanbul) and control of the Bosphorus, the strait joining the Black Sea to the Mediterranean. And with the Sykes–Picot agreement of May 1916, the British and French delimited their respective spheres of influence in Asia Minor, arbitrarily allotting eastern Syria and the Mosul province of Mesopotamia to France, and southern Mesopotamia, with Baghdad and Amman, as well as the ports of Haifa and Acre, to Great Britain. In late 1918, Paris ceded oil-rich Mosul—in what is now northern Iraq—to London in exchange for a quarter share in the region's oil deposits, to be exploited by France's state-controlled Compagnie Française des Pétroles. The bargain of Syria for France and Iraq for England was all but consummated.

These grand imperialist transactions were typically negotiated and signed in utmost secrecy, and typified the old diplomacy about to be exposed following the Russian Revolution and America's entry into the Great War. On November 22, 1917, the new Soviet government, having unlocked the czarist archives, published the secret wartime agreements in *Izvestia* as part of its call for an early negotiated end to the war. The Allied governments in vain asked their newspapers to exercise discretion. In December Lord Balfour indignantly declared in the House of Commons that "the documents in question ought not to have been published, and I do not propose to republish them." But on January 8, 1918, Woodrow Wilson all but endorsed the insolent

démarche of Lenin and Trotsky in the first of his Fourteen Points
laying out the basic premises for a just and lasting peace: following the
imminent peace, "there shall be no private international understand-
ings of any kind but diplomacy shall proceed always frankly and in
public view."

While excoriating the double-dealing of both enemy camps, the
Bolsheviks universalized the right of national self-determination. On
December 3, 1917, the newly constituted Soviet Union renounced
Imperial Russia's claim to Constantinople and withdrew from Persia,
exhorting the "Moslems of the East! Persians, Turks, Arabs and
Hindus" to throw off their colonial shackles. This was in keeping
with Lenin's insistence, as early as 1915, that self-determination "was
a thing of the present and future . . . in the Orient, Asia, Africa, the
colonies . . . which have a combined population amounting to a
billion."

Wilson's pronouncements on the subject were in large part a
response to Lenin's. The fourth of his Fourteen Points called for
the "adjustment of colonial claims with concern for the wishes and
interests of the inhabitants as well as for the titles of rival claimants."
Although the president, who was loath to renounce America's own
overseas possessions, did not sanction the Soviets' outright condemnation of colonial imperialism, he did stress, on February 11, that
"people are not to be handed about from one sovereignty to another
by an international conference or an understanding between rivals and
antagonists." After insisting that "national aspirations . . . be respected" and that people be "dominated and governed only by their
own consent," he declared that " 'self-determination' [would] not [be]
a mere phrase [but] an imperative principle of action which statesmen
will henceforth ignore at their peril." No wonder Wilson, like Lenin,
touched a sympathetic chord with emerging nationalists throughout
the non-European worlds, including semi-colonial China.

Not that the British were deaf to the rising nationalism in the greater
Middle East and in South Asia, notably India. But their response was
to channel it toward their own ends. During the Great War, London
enlisted the politically traditional but restless Arab elites to launch
military attacks against the Turks and help form a British-controlled
confederation of nebulous Arab states to replace the Ottoman imperium. Stealth diplomacy was again to be its mode of operation. His
Majesty's Government decided to make overtures to the Supreme and
Sanctified protector of Arabic-speaking Asia: a member of a family
with a common ancestry with the Prophet Muhammad, Sherif Hus-

sein, oversaw the holy places in Mecca and Medina, in the region known as the Hejaz. A lordly and respected nationalist, he proposed the reestablishment of a grand Arab sultanate, with himself as supreme king of the Hejaz. His elder son, Feisal, was to be suzerain of Syria and Iraq, and Abdullah, the younger, suzerain of Palestine.

Sir Henry McMahon, the British high commissioner for Egypt, was charged with the negotiations. After exchanging numerous letters with Hussein between mid 1915 and early 1916, he pledged Great Britain to support and recognize "the independence of the Arabs" in a territory bounded, in broad terms, in the north by the 37th parallel; in the south, by the future states of the Arab Gulf; in the east, by the future Iranian border running down to the Persian Gulf; in the west, by the Red Sea and the Mediterranean coast, exclusive of a zone "lying to the west of the districts of Damascus, Homs, Hama, and Aleppo." The correspondence did not mention Palestine by name, nor Lebanon or parts of the future Syria, reserved for possible inclusion in a French sphere of influence. Keeping his side of the bargain, in early June 1916 Hussein announced the start of a necessarily limited Arab revolt against the Turks. London charged Colonel T.E. Lawrence with helping him and Feisal to organize and direct this uprising in Mesopotamia and Palestine, and among the Bedouins. Until the end of the war and the fall of the Ottoman empire, the British continued to pay court to the Arabs, who then expected to gain a free hand.

Disclosure of the secret Sykes–Picot agreement in late 1917 complicated matters—and not just for Lawrence, who had been kept in the dark. The disparity between the McMahon–Hussein letters and the Anglo-French accord could not have been more flagrant. That the former predated the latter by six months made the perfidy all the greater in the eyes of Hussein and the disquieted Arab elites; the Balfour Declaration of November 2 compounded the breach of faith still further. In an effort to lay the dust, on January 4, 1918, the British government assured the king of a would-be Arab commonwealth of nations that the return of Jews to Palestine would go only "so far as is compatible with the freedom of the existing situation." Following this confidential and perfectly ambiguous message, in June London issued a public declaration to the Arab world that "future government . . . should be based upon the principle of consent of the governed"— unambiguous, given the then clear majority of the Arabs. And on November 7, Great Britain and France jointly reassured the Arabs of their continuing commitment to "the complete and definite emancipation of the peoples so long oppressed by the Turks and the establishment of national governments and administrations deriving their authority from the initiative and free choice of the indigenous population."

True to Sykes–Picot, and scorning Wilson, let alone Lenin, the conservative governments of France and Britain continued to wrangle over the fabulously rich but divisive legacy of Asiatic Turkey. Not until 1921 did they reach a definitive settlement. After having driven King Feisal out of Damascus, the French convinced the British to recognize their supremacy in Syria, in violation of London's promise to Hussein. In turn, Great Britain placed Feisal, who had taken refuge in Palestine, on the throne of a brand-new Iraqi state, and overnight created the Hashemite emirate of Transjordan, with Abdullah on another custom-made throne in Amman. Syria, Iraq, Transjordan, and Palestine became Class A Mandates under the League of Nations, to be administered by the "advanced" member countries for "people not yet able to stand by themselves." Determined by imperialist logrolling and mired in unchanged colonial conditions, their future was, to borrow a phrase from a contemporary play, "only the past again entered through another gate."

This is the geohistorical context in which Zionism burst upon the world stage. All three diplomatic interventions—Sykes–Picot, McMahon–Hussein, and the Balfour Declaration—were made possible by the impending collapse and reorganization of Turkey-in-Asia. France and England were its chief architects, with London primarily disturbed by France's rival ambition. Next in importance were the Arabs, and then the Jews.

The year 1917 was a fateful hinge for the Allies. Their troops were mired in the killing fields of the Western front, and the French armies were riven by mutinies. Meanwhile, its forces spent, Russia was turned upside down by revolution, and the fragile Provisional Government was under intense pressure to quit the war, leaving Britain and France to face the Central Powers alone. It was this dangerous conjuncture that precipitated the unique understanding between the Zionist leadership and the British government. The two parties were agreed that Russian Zionists might strengthen the hand of the non-Bolshevik left, in the Provisional Government and the country at large, that opposed a separate peace with Germany and favored continuing the war on the side of the Allied and Associated Powers.

Not that the outlook was uniformly bleak for the Western Allies. America entered the war, and so became an unanticipated source of hope and financial support. Overwhelmingly anti-isolationist, American Jews could be counted on to enthusiastically back "the war to end all wars," especially now that their country was leagued with a democratic rather than an autocratic-pogromist Russia. By this time both key British officials and Zionist leaders expected that American Zionists would carry increasing weight in U.S. politics and in the Zionist movement more generally. Though Britain's leaders curried favor with the Jewish diaspora in Russia and America partly for the sake of the war, they did so also with a view to reinforcing His Majesty's interests in the Greater Middle East. They considered Palestine a vital land bridge between Africa and Asia, and an essential outpost near the Suez Canal and Baghdad, between Egypt and India.

Lord Balfour's Declaration favoring the establishment of a Jewish homeland in Palestine took the form of a letter addressed to Lord Lionel Walter Rothschild, one of the most eminent and influential members of Britain's Jewish community. The text was problematic from the outset. As its wording was being discussed by British officials, Chaim Weizmann—an eminent Zionist leader known to Balfour, and from 1920 president of the World Zionist Organization—and his associates submitted a draft that called for "the re-establishment of Palestine as *the* Jewish National Home" (italics added). Following deliberations spread over a period of three months, the operative clause was revised to read "the establishment in Palestine of *a* national home for the Jewish people"—a formulation considerably short of what the Zionist leaders had wanted.

Ahad Haam, who was well-informed, noted that the British government, not wanting "to promise anything which might injure the present inhabitants of Palestine [refused] to make the Jewish people the absolute ruler in the country." Balfour himself wanted it "clearly understood that nothing shall be done which may prejudice the civil and religious rights of the existing non-Jewish communities in Palestine." Although the Zionist leaders publicly construed the text of the Balfour Declaration as corresponding to the intent of their draft proposals, they realized its failings: the worm was in the bud. Weizmann was "angry" with Ahad Haam for stating that in the Balfour Declaration the Zionists were "promised a National Home in Palestine, and not Palestine as a Jewish National Home." As for the proviso that the Jewish project not be furthered at the expense of the indigenous population, Weizmann took offense at Balfour's seeming to "imput[e] possible oppressive intentions to the Jews"; he complained that it could also be "interpreted to mean such limitations on our work as completely to cripple it."

In 1917 the Jews in Palestine were a minority of between 50,000 and 60,000—a population whose size was roughly 10 per cent of an Arab population of between 600,000 and 700,000 that was subsumed in the Balfour Declaration under "non-Jewish communities." The failure to mention the preponderant native Other by name most likely sprang from the sense of Western superiority shared by Britons and Zionists. In 1919 Balfour confided that "in Palestine we do not propose even to go through the form of consulting the wishes of the present inhabitants of the country," as some Americans were suggesting. In his view, what mattered was that

> the four great powers are committed to Zionism and Zionism, be it right or wrong, good or bad, is rooted in age-long tradition, in present needs, in future hopes, of far profounder import than the desires and prejudices of the 700,000 Arabs who now inhabit that ancient land.

The Zionist project troubled Wilson, however. Officially, he expressed support for the Balfour Declaration: "I am persuaded that the Allied nations, with the full concurrence of our Government and our people, are agreed that in Palestine shall be laid the foundations of a Jewish Commonwealth." But, seconded by the King–Crane Report of August 28, 1919, an American study on the feasibility of the Balfour letter, he knew that in Palestine neither the British nor the Zionists were about to foster representative institutions capable of putting Arabs in charge. In 1922 the League of Nations made Great Britain the guardian of Palestine, and the Holy Land became a Class A Mandate. The document entrusting Britain with this charge cited the Balfour text, perpetuating the ambiguities of the earlier pledge and holding out no prospect of a self-determined sovereign polity for the Palestinians.

Although the Jews of Eastern Europe—the reserve army of Zionism—had been shaken up by the First World War and the Russian Revolution, the outlook of the Zionist leaders remained parochially Central and Western European, as well as Judeo-centric. They failed to appreciate the world-shaking events that had converged in 1917 to redefine the terms of the Jewish–Arab confrontation in Palestine.

The loyal opposition, personified by Ahad Haam and Buber, stood out for their effort to understand the new epoch breaking in upon European Jews and Zionism. They reflected on how (not whether) Zionism's future would be contingent on a sympathetic understanding of the Arab resurgence and a reasoned effort to mediate between the West and the Orient. Even before Wilson was disavowed by the Congress in Washington and the Allies at Versailles, and before the Mandate system was chartered, Buber worried about the Jews returning to Palestine as "servants of a mighty but doomed Europe," and in partnership with a perduring "colonialism and imperialism." By the spring of 1919 he stressed the importance of Zionism's distancing itself from the values of the League of Nations by "making it clear that we have nothing to do . . . with imperialism masquerading as humanitarianism."

In the early 1880s, Theodor Herzl, then living in Vienna, had been tormented by the fury of the pogroms in Russia and, while in Paris during the 1890s, by the violent mutation of traditional anti-Judaism into ideological anti-Semitism during the Dreyfus Affair in France. He proposed to secure, in Palestine and away from Christian Europe, the elusive emancipation of its Jews. In this quest he was impelled by the ideas of the Enlightenment, Western liberalism, and progressive nationalism, all infused by him with Romanticism. For Herzl the "Jewish Question" was national and political, not cultural or religious, to be resolved by the establishment of a sovereign nation-state, which he prized as the highest good of historical development and human achievement. He was ignorant about Judaism per se, and alienated from it.

The founding father of political Zionism was a cosmopolitan Jew who knew neither Hebrew nor Yiddish. His faith in individual emancipation paired with assimilation, as promised by the French Revolution, had been shattered. But he remained faithful to the republican project of 1789, which made the pluralistic nation-state the principal agent of progress, as measured by the advance of reason over religion and church. After his visit to the Wailing Wall in 1898, Herzl said it stood for "superstition and fanaticism on every side"; he had nothing "in common with these degenerate exploiters of our national mourning." Jerusalem proper was, like Lourdes and Mecca, freighted with ages of "inhumanity, intolerance, and uncleanness." With republican France as a prototype, the future Jewish state would be national and secular. Its civil society would reshuffle the Jewish occupational pyramid: where commerce, trade, and skilled crafts constituted the broad base in the diaspora, that stratum would henceforth belong to manual labor, both on the land and in the factory workshop.

There was something Arcadian as well as archaic about this celebration of farming and manufacturing as levers of social regeneration. A man of the upper classes, Herzl, along with the Jewish notables he associated with, distrusted the *Ostjuden*: besides breeding a surfeit of revolutionaries, as immigrants in Central and Western

Europe they encouraged anti-Jewish prejudice by dint of their exoticism, thereby slowing the march of assimilation. These were good reasons to exhort militant Jewish intellectuals and unreconstructed ghetto Jews to make the *aliyah* to Palestine to build their own "city upon a hill." And like the capitalism of the Third French Republic, that of the Jewish Republic would strive to assume a human face, in allegiance to the ideals of *liberté, égalité, fraternité.* In short, Zionism was to secure for the Jews a democratic state and open society whose chief influences and languages would be English, French, and German. Besides becoming a "light unto the nations," this non-Jewish Jewish civil and political society would grow into a peerless partner in Europe's mission overseas. The *Judenstaat*, as Herzl conceived it, would "form part of a defensive wall for Europe in Asia, an outpost of civilization against barbarism."

In Herzl's messianic secular vision there was little, if any, place for the Arabs of Palestine. Nahum Goldmann, urbane Zionist statesman during the three decades following the foundation of Israel, was to note that they do not figure in Herzl's two seminal books, *The Jewish State* (1896) and *Old New Land* (1902). Nor do they figure in his public pronouncements. Herzl's blind spot was altogether unexceptional for a thoroughly assimilated, acculturated Jew of Central and Western Europe's educated bourgeoisie. In his diary there is a hint of his position on the Arab Question: on June 12, 1905, without mentioning Palestine's Arabs by name, Herzl noted that, as the Zionists pursued the occupation and acquisition of land, they would have to "try to spirit the penniless population across the border by procuring employment for it in the transit countries, while denying it employment in our own country." Though confident that the local landowners would cooperate, he nevertheless reasoned that "both the process of expropriation and the removal of the poor [would have to] be carried out discreetly and circumspectly."

For Herzl, the Jewish resettlement on "a piece of Asia Minor" was frankly "something colonial," as he wrote to Cecil Rhodes, the ultimate imperialist of his time. In this Herzl followed the German Jewish socialist Moses Hess, who, in his *Rome and Jerusalem* (1862), had imagined the Jews becoming "the bearers of civilization to the primitive people of Asia . . . under the protection of the European powers," preferably France. From the outset, Herzl realized that Zionism could not hope to secure a place for itself without the umbrella of at least one of the Great Powers, inevitably motivated by its own national interest. And because diplomacy came naturally to him, he invested most of his energy in that rather than in the intraterritorial aspects of settlement in Palestine. With the advice and intercession of establishment Jews, he waited on crown and chancellery in search of land for the Jews. Kaiser Wilhelm II of Germany, King Victor Emmanuel III of Italy, Pope Pius X, Sultan Abdul Hamid of the Ottoman empire, key ministers of Czar Nicholas II of Russia, the colonial secretary of the British empire (Chamberlain): these were Herzl's courts of appeal.

In its uphill rivalry with London, Berlin itself was courting the Turkish empire, of which Palestine was a province. In August 1898, Wilhelm stopped off in Constantinople on his way to the Holy Land. There, in a secret audience, Herzl urged him to press the Sultan to grant a charter for the establishment of a Jewish homeland in the region, hinting that such a colony might become a useful bridgehead for Germany in the Middle East. In Jerusalem three months later, when Herzl again met the Kaiser and his foreign minister, Prince Bernhard von Bülow, he learned that the Sublime Porte had declined his proposal.

Now Herzl turned to Britain. In a speech in London in 1899, while still pursuing other avenues, he noted that since England had been the "first to recognize the necessity of colonial expansion in the modern world," and since "the Zionist idea [was] a colonial idea," he expected Great Britain to understand it "easily and quickly." The following year, at the Fourth Zionist Congress, meeting for the first time in London, he extended the thought: given its global outlook and interests, "mighty . . . and free England [should] understand . . . our aspirations . . . and [make] the Zionist idea soar further and higher than ever before."

Herzl's fall trip to Palestine in 1898 had been timed only to abet his supplication of Wilhelm II, not to dally with the Yishuv and the local population. He disembarked in Jaffa, Palestine's main seaport, which at the time counted fewer than 3,000 Jews in a population of 32,000. In the country as a whole, at just over half a million, Arabs outnumbered Jews nearly ten-to-one. And yet, as Herzl traveled through the towns and villages of Eretz Israel, he looked at the Arabs without really seeing them, except as a "mixed multitude of beggars, women, and children."

As a Westerner, Herzl could conceive of the indigenous people neither as political citizens of the secular and democratic republic he espoused nor as potential bearers of a national destiny of their own. This myopia predisposed him to focus on the European powers while consigning the reigning potentates of the Middle East to his peripheral vision. Herzl's legacy, then, was twofold: an inspiring and closely reasoned idea, and a narrow and time-bound political praxis.

2

PREFIGURATION: THE 1920S

Even before Herzl journeyed to "old new land," skeptics within Zionism had begun to voice the danger of not giving serious thought to the Arab Question. In 1897, at the founding Zionist Congress in Basel, A. S. Yahuda, born in Jerusalem and a promising Orientalist, unsuccessfully tried to direct the attention of Herzl and his associates to the importance of seeking mutual understanding with all classes of Arabs in the Middle East. The following year Leo Motzkin, born near Kiev and both witness and student of the latest pogroms in Russia, spoke to the winds when he told the same assemblage that more than 500,000 Arabs occupied "the most fertile parts of our land" and that by now there were "innumerable clashes" between Jews and Arabs in a country that was a "colorful mixture of wilderness, tourism, and pilgrims."

But in the 1890s it was Asher Zvi Ginsberg (known by his pen-name Ahad Haam—"One of the People") who emerged as the wisest and most prestigious challenger of Herzl's political Zionism. Born in Ukraine to a well-off Chasidic family, Ahad Haam was an accomplished Talmudist before traveling widely in Central Europe, in the wake of ferocious pogroms in czarist Russia, to read philosophy and social theory, from 1882 to 1884. On his return to Odessa, where he made his home in 1887, Ahad Haam became a guiding spirit among the Lovers of Zion, who promoted migration to Palestine and the purchase of land for the establishment of Jewish agricultural colonies. Like Simon Dubnow, renowned historian of Chasidism and of Eastern European Jews, Ahad Haam looked for a rebirth of the Jewish nation by way of cultural autonomy rather than by statehood. Uniquely among Zionists, he visited the Holy Land frequently, staying for several months in 1891, 1893, and 1900. The pogroms attending the Russian Revolution of 1905 were especially murderous in Odessa, and foreshadowed a new-model political reaction by the czar's ministers, which prompted Ahad Haam to move to London in 1908. Finally, perplexed by the unsteady light of heaven following the Russian upheaval of 1917, he settled in Palestine in 1922.

In his public interventions Ahad Haam was moved by a complex mixture of theoretical positivism and empirical practical idealism. He advanced two reasons for what he diagnosed as a weakening of the theological and cultural foundations of Judaism: first, the dead hand of the past, which throttled any dreaming about the future; second, young Jews imitating the dominant gentile culture, which accelerated the rush to assimilation and entailed the "loss of Judaism's best minds" to the non-Jewish world. Ahad Haam sought to enlist the rationalist but not the teleologically charged reason of the Haskalah—the Jewish offspring of the Enlightenment—to loosen the hold of the past without transvaluing time-honored values, a move he deemed risky and futile. Secular knowledge, education, and civil rights were to advance, concurrent with a revival of Hebrew culture. What concerned Ahad Haam most, however, was the atrophying of Judaism, and the cruel plight of the Jews, most acute between the Dniester and the Vistula rivers, in large precincts of the diaspora.

Even before the First Zionist Congress, which he attended as a skeptical observer, Ahad Haam criticized Herzl's Zionism for being narrowly political, with little if any attention to the spiritual–cultural element. He faulted Herzl himself for his neglect of Jewish religion, history, and culture, as well as of the mental world and agony of the Jews of Eastern Europe. The insensitivity toward them was especially deplorable, since they were not only the principal carriers of cultural Judaism, but also the foot soldiers of Zionism. In a radical departure from the tenets of the Zionist movement, Ahad Haam posited a minimalist expression of it: the establishment in Palestine of an exemplary spiritual–cultural center, rather than Herzl's prosaic sovereign state. Such a place would spark a renaissance of Judaism that would spread throughout the diaspora, which he was convinced would remain the home of most Jews.

To Ahad Haam's mind, the essence of Judaism was not a set of religious practices and ceremonies but a decalogue of tested moral and ethical precepts that had guided the conduct of the Hebrew people in exile. He argued, extravagantly, that by virtue of their stateless condition and history, the Israelites had lived a continuous protest against force and violence. He prized this alleged refusal, which made him question the bid for a home that would grow into a sovereign nation-state like any other. A state would necessarily have to wield the sword not only against hostile neighboring countries but also domestically, to keep down the resentful, subaltern Arab population.

In his essay "Truth From Eretz Israel," written and published immediately after his first visit to Zion in 1891, Ahad Haam insisted that Palestine was no empty, virgin space, but was inhabited by a vast Arab population that owned and worked nearly all the land. He cautioned against the prejudice, common among Zionists, that these Arabs "are wild desert savages who, like donkeys, neither see nor understand what is happening around them." "Like all Semites," he said, reaching unwittingly for a stereotype of his own, "they have a sharp and cunning mind." The urban elites in particular "see and understand our actions and aspirations" in their land for what they are. It may well be that, for reasons of momentary self-interest and weakness, they "keep silent and pretend not to notice what goes on around them." But all the while, "in their heart of hearts they mock us . . . and harbor rancor and vengeance." Ahad Haam warned that, once Jewish settlers started to "drive out" the natives "on a small or large scale," the Arabs would no longer "easily step aside."

Ahad Haam was revolted to see Jews treating Arabs "with hostility and cruelty, unjustly trespassing on their land and shamefully beating them for no good reason, and even boasting about it." Having witnessed the subjugation of his own people in the Pale of Settlement, he was appalled that Jews who only yesterday had been "slaves in their lands of Exile" should act despotically upon tasting freedom. Such abuse ensues whenever "a slave becomes a king," but "past and present history" should have taught Zionists "to treat these people with love and respect as well as . . . with justice and good judgment." By 1910, although he had long been troubled by the latent but simmering hostility between Palestinian Arabs and Jews, Ahad Haam voiced surprise at its rising to the surface at a time "when our power in this land is as yet limited and unobtrusive." Three years later, when the settlers boycotted indigenous labor in favor of Jewish farmhands, he deplored the fact that the Zionists should be "morally capable of so mistreating another people." Should such behavior prefigure Zionism's practice after "we become masters of Eretz Israel," let the Messiah appear, "but may I not live to see him."

Max Nordau, one of Herzl's most trusted deputies and a fiery political Zionist, lost no time taking issue with Ahad Haam. Like Herzl he was born in Budapest, was attuned to the intellectual currents in Paris, where he lived, and was virtually de-Judaized. A physician by profession, he became a prolific and widely translated social critic, novelist, and playwright. Nordau was best known and is best remembered for *Degeneration* (1893), a polemical diagnosis of Europe's pre-1914 "world of yesterday." In addition to charging Ahad Haam with being a fainthearted Zionist, Nordau dismissed him as a philistine ghetto Jew who could hardly be expected to understand that Zionism was one of the finest flowers of Europe's culture of Enlightenment, and that the Jewish pioneers would bring tolerance and civilization to the land of their ancestors. Apolitical and impractical, Ahad Haam's ideas were also dated and defeatist; the man was blind, Nordau claimed outrageously, to the forlorn condition of the Eastern European Jews, the flame-keepers of Judaism, for whom Palestine would be "a refuge for the oppressed, a refuge in time of trouble." Relatively dead to the Arab Question, he chose not to raise it in his impeachment of Ahad Haam.

The matter of the Arabs soon became central and irrepressible. In 1907, with the encouragement of Chaim Nachman Bialik, poet laureate of modern Hebrew, Yitzhak Epstein had published "A Hidden Question." Originally a lecture delivered in the shadow of the Zionist Congress of 1905, it was one of the most forceful and widely debated essays on an issue that haunted more than a few thoughtful Zionists. Born in Belorussia in 1862 but settled in Palestine since 1886, Epstein became a Hebrew scholar and teacher before studying at the University of Lausanne from 1902 to 1908. His geographic remove sharpened his critical perspective and yielded this blunt assessment: "Among the complex questions raised by the grand design for the rebirth of our people in its own land one question outweighs all others: the question of our relations with the Arabs." "Fundamental" as it was, Zionists had all but "ignore[d]" the issue and "scarcely addressed it honestly in their literature," thereby exposing a certain "superficiality that racks our movement."

Epstein, inspired by Ahad Haam, argued that while Zionists "feel the love of homeland . . . for the land of our fathers," they tend to "forget that the people living there . . . are also strongly attached to [their] homeland." The Arabs of Palestine "form only a small part of a great nation—composed of Syria, Mesopotamia, Arabia, and Egypt—that surrounds" the Holy Land. It was all-important not to "ignore [their] rights" and not to take advantage of their still living in virtually pre-modern, pre-Enlightenment conditions. This retardation, which Epstein called on Zionists to help overcome, should not detract attention from the "smoldering embers" of Arab self-assurance and pride, which the tempest of foreign oppression might stir into a "wildfire." Already "mighty and numerous," the Arab people needed "no rebirth because it never died and ceased existing." He warned that the Arabs saw the Jews as "sworn enemies" and were "harboring revenge." Zionists should take care not to "provoke the sleeping lion."

In Palestine there was an entire people strongly attached to "our beloved land" by "moral [bonds to] the graves of [their] ancestors." There were "no empty fields": 80 per cent of the "more than half a million Arabs . . . live off the land." In an agrarian society stuck in the sixteenth century, land purchases by Zionists generated resentment, particularly among the *fellahin*, the peasants who tilled the soil. To accord the Arabs "human and political sensitivity" and to respect their "individual and national rights" would call for Jewish settlers to become "properly acquainted with . . . their attributes, inclinations, aspirations, language, and literature," and to acquire a "deep understanding of their life, customs, suffering, and torments." Epstein considered it a "disgrace" that by and large Zionist actions failed to take account of the "spiritual condition" of the local population, largely because no one was studying "the psyche of our neighbors." To this task, "so far not even one Jew has devoted himself," he charged. As a consequence, "we are *complete illiterates in anything concerning the Arabs*, and all of our knowledge about them is folk wisdom" (italics in original).

Israel Zangwill is perhaps best remembered for characterizing Palestine as "a land without a people for a people without a land." Since 1897, when he coined it, the slogan had become Zionism's legitimating myth and rallying cry. A novelist and playwright, Zangwill was a prominent English Zionist, with a fine feel for London's Jewish East End, as evident in his novel of 1892, *Children of the Ghetto*, whose inhabitants he both deprecated and celebrated. In no time he gainsaid his own dictum. By 1905 he conceded that the Jews "accounted for only 12 per cent of [Palestine's] population and owned only 2 per cent of the land." Rather than risk a grand Arab refusal, Zangwill first fixed upon the British offer of Uganda as, in the words of Sigmund Freud a quarter-century later, "a less historically burdened land." But once the territorialists dropped that prospect, he believed the Zionists were in a predicament: "[We] must be prepared either to drive out the [Arab] tribes in possession as our forefathers did or to grapple with the problem of a large alien population, mostly Mohammedan and accustomed for centuries to despise us." By 1920, Zangwill advocated pressuring the Palestinian Arabs, perhaps in the form of compensation, to resettle in neighboring lands. The Arabs, who were culturally and economically "backward," could not be allowed to block the Zionists' "valuable reconstruction." Mostly "semi-nomad" and contributing nothing to the Holy Land, they were "not entitled to the rules of democracy." They should " 'fold their tents and silently steal away,' " as was "their proverbial habit." They needed to be "persuaded to 'trek'" and leave behind "these few kilometers," given "they have all Arabia with its million square miles" to go to. Despite his misgivings, then, Zangwill became one of the first to argue—anticipating Jabotinsky and Ben-Gurion—that the Palestinian Arabs should cede their land to the non-tent-dwellers, since the Jews had no refuge of their own.

The First World War changed the diplomatic, political, and ideological climate for realizing the still indeterminate Zionist project. The fall of the Romanov and Habsburg empires led to the creation of successor states, most of whose large Jewish populations were at risk of becoming more imperiled because of a heavy anti-Jewish past. By contrast, the collapse of the Hohenzollern empire augured well not only for the Jews of Germany but for the Zionist cause. Under the Weimar Republic, the Jews reached a pinnacle of emancipation, assimilation, and acculturation, and became a model for others seeking to unbind themselves from the world of their fathers and mothers. Just as momentous, the demise of the Second German empire spelled the end of the Ottoman empire. With Berlin knocked out of the colonial scramble, Britain and France were free to apportion the Porte's possessions in the greater Middle East in line with their wartime promises and treaties, however inconsonant those last might be. The McMahon–Hussein correspondence, Sykes–Picot, the Balfour Declaration, the artifice of the Mandate System—all served to magnify rather than mask the contradictions in the overlap of the decline of European colonial hegemony and the rise of anti-colonial nationalism.

Once Lenin and Wilson, grand ecumenical adversaries, had universalized the Western concept of territorially bounded national self-determination, there was no keeping it out of the greater Middle East. The internal Zionist critics probably agreed with Lawrence, who concluded from his engagement with the Arab anti-Ottoman rebels that though "the East remained Muslim," its public life was increasingly driven by a "craving for national independence and self-government." As the future Lawrence of Arabia saw it, "this new condition of a conscious and logical political nationalism in Western Asia was . . . too widespread to be temporary." Sworn to saving the life of the overstretched British empire, Lawrence urged engaging with the new Arab states. In order to prevent the Arabs from becoming Great Britain's "last brown colony," Lawrence proposed to give them dominion status, the alternative being "to hold on to them with ever-lessening force, till the anarchy is too expensive and we [will have to] let go." Provided London met the Arab world halfway,

Lawrence expected it to become "as loyal" as the other dominions, and that it "would not cost England a cent."

As for the Jews, Lawrence approved of Europe's "least European people" returning to "the Orient," since they brought with them "samples of all the knowledge and technique of Europe." He expected the Zionists to make Palestine "as highly organized as a European state," raising the Arab population "to their own material level." His only concern was that they might some day devise a "new confederation" of the Arab world liable to become "a formidable element of world power" potentially threatening to British interests. Such an undertaking would "to a very large extent stand or fall" with the Zionists—whose success, he may have thought, would depend on their not dismissing the new nationalist consciousness outside Europe.

This, then, was the context for the Arab Question during the 1920s. Ahad Haam's advocacy of an extraterritorial spiritual–cultural center versus a martial sovereign state struck the ear of the next generation of passionate but critical and nonsectarian Zionists: they sought a political formula for Jewish–Arab collaboration premised on a shared humanity. Many of these *engagé* intellectuals came from assimilated Western and Central European families. They were university graduates; many were academics, including Hugo Bergmann, Buber, Epstein, Hans Kohn, Arthur Ruppin, Gershom Scholem, Ernst Simon, and Robert Weltsch. Judah Magnes, who had studied in Berlin and Heidelberg, stood out as the only American and the only (Reform) rabbi among them. Chaim Kalvarisky, Shlomo Kaplansky, and Moshe Smilansky, who had been born in the Pale of Settlement and gone earlier to Palestine, became brothers-in-arms. All were profoundly shaken by the rabid military and patriotic vehemence of the First World War. Their experience, as soldiers or civilians, goes a long way toward explaining their visceral but reasoned skepticism of the quest for a sovereign Jewish state with an army of its own. They were sympathetic to the Russian Revolution but uncertain about its outcome. They were wary too of the new order in East Central Europe and the great mutation in the imperialist galaxy. Unreconstructed votaries of the Enlightenment and the Haskalah, they nevertheless showed a renewed and respectful interest in the waning but tenacious world of their people.

Their studied empathy for the ways of traditional Judaism predisposed these fraternal critics of mainline Zionism to fully "encounter," in Buber's sense, the Arabs of Palestine and the greater Middle East. The viability of Zionism would depend, they were convinced, on cooperating with the leaders and native people of the Holy Land and

the surrounding Arab–Muslim world. Arthur Ruppin—an early sociologist of Judaism and a founder of the kibbutz movement, and,
beginning in 1908, head of the World Zionist Organization in the
Yishuv—was another who worried about the growing estrangement
between Jews and Arabs. Just as before the Great War Smilansky had
lamented that it was not the Arabs who had "remained alien to us but
we to them," immediately after it Ruppin voiced the conviction that
"the Arab hatred towards us is to a great extent our own fault."
"Zionism will end in catastrophe," he warned, "if we do not succeed
in finding a common platform" and "unless we gain friends and
understanding to our interests in the wider Arab world . . . in
Baghdad, Cairo, and Damascus," where he expected "Arab policy"
to be made. Ruppin had reason to regret that "only a few of us" were
sufficiently "familiar with the whole complex of the Arab problem" to
be able to "foresee the awakening of the Arab world."

Buber agreed. A utopian and communitarian socialist, he had studied
in Berlin with Georg Simmel, the left-leaning pioneer of formal sociol-
ogy. Buber's Zionism was strongly marked by Ahad Haam, but also
bore the marks of eighteenth-century mystical Judaism. He shared the
humanist and anarchist socialism of Gustav Landauer, his political
mentor and soul mate. Starting in 1915, this courageous critic of German
Social Democracy's unconditional wartime super-patriotism began
advocating a compromise peace without victory on the grounds of
moral necessity. Deeply disturbed by Landauer's brutal murder by the
White Guards during the repression of the Munich Commune in the
spring of 1919, Buber soon had his misgivings about Wilsonian idealism,
suspecting it of concealing the devilry of power politics in general, and of
political Zionism in particular.

His reproof to Herzl's realpolitik centered on the Arab Question,
which demanded the integration of ethical concerns into Zionist
politics and diplomacy. Buber was critical, above all, of "hypertropic"
nationalism, whose champions exalted the longed-for and emergent
Jewish homeland as an absolute principle and truth. He warned
against the Jews' returning to Palestine under the protection mandated
by the League of Nations, fearful that it stood for "imperialism
decorated with the flags of [Wilsonian] humanism." Such auspices
were unsuited to the urgent task of "instituting a permanent and
friendly accord with the Arabs in all spheres of life . . . in our common
land." Its outcome would hang on "whether we face the awakening
East as hated agents and spies or as beloved teachers and creators."
Following the first anti-Zionist riots in Palestine in 1920–1, Buber
presented a resolution to the Twelfth Zionist Congress in Carlsbad

calling for "redoubled efforts to secure an honorable entente with the Arab people" and urging the delegates to "emphatically declare that the work of Jewish settlement shall not infringe on the rights and needs of the working Arab nation." This text was diluted nearly to the point of travesty for reasons captured in the address of Berl Katznelson, militant labor organizer in the Yishuv, future editor of the Labor–Zionist paper *Davar*, and advocate of the "absolute justice" of the Zionist cause: "[E]xposed to danger . . . we must secure our life and property before negotiating with the Arabs [and we must do so] by strengthening our self-defense and consolidating our position in Palestine."

The conspicuous rise of Jewish immigration after 1918 and the prospect of unrestricted immigration in the future, heralded in Zionist rhetoric, stirred a growing disposition to resistance among Palestinian Arabs. In early April 1920, the celebration of a Muslim holiday (Nabi Musa) became the occasion for the first violent anti-Zionist remonstrance in the Holy Land, not accidentally in Jerusalem. A random harassment of Zionists escalated into several clashes in the Jewish Quarter of the Old City. The nine dead included five Jews; they made up most of the more than 200 wounded as well. Within a year there would be another uprising, this one more far-flung and deadly.

The implementation of the three major wartime agreements bearing on the Middle East was contingent on the final collapse of the Ottoman empire, which made the Sick Man of Europe's Arab-speaking lands available for division, as they had been in 1648 and 1814–15, providing opportunities to earlier victors. The Allies and Associated Powers redrew the borders of existing states and fashioned frontiers for previously "stateless" spaces. They invented *ex nihilo* the territorial frontiers of Iraq, Syria, Lebanon, Transjordan, and Palestine. Britain also compelled Ibn Saud, founder and first king of Saudi Arabia, to accept a map fixing formerly nonexistent borders between Saudi Arabia, Kuwait, and Iraq.

Prime Minister Lloyd George's coalition cabinet and His Majesty's proconsuls acted with imagination, boldness, and recklessness—all the more so since they were acutely aware, following the exertions of war, that the empire was militarily overextended and financially wasted. Amorphous Mesopotamia became Iraq, composed of the three Ottoman provinces of Mosul in the north, Baghdad in the center, and Basra in the south. Feisal, of the Hashemite dynasty, who had never set foot in Iraq, was fancifully placed on its new-wrought throne. To make his accession appear popularly determined, the British saw to his confirmation by a specious plebiscite. Like Yugoslavia, its contemporary, Iraq turned out to be a multi-ethnic construction: the population of three million was 50 per cent Shiite, 25 per cent Sunni, and over 20 per cent Kurd. Not so incidentally, when Churchill—as colonial secretary one of the chief inventors of Iraq—wavered, the prime minister reminded him, though he hardly needed reminding, that should England depart from Mesopotamia within "a year or two," it might discover that it had "handed over to the French and Americans some of the richest oilfields in the world." At this same moment, Lawrence also noted that "nature may have bestowed . . . an abundance of cheap oil on Mesopotamia." If that were so, the region would "inevitably take the headship of the Arab world in the future." With "five times the population of Syria, and many times its wealth," Baghdad, not Damascus, would be "the master of the Middle East, and the power controlling [Mesopotamia's] destinies will dominate all its neighbors."

The creation of Transjordan was an equally imperious maneuver. Interpreting loosely the calculated ambiguities of McMahon–Hussein and Balfour, London decided to divide Palestine along the Jordan River. To the east, the British established an all-Arab Emirate. Abdullah, Feisal's younger brother, would reign there. To the west, the Jews would be able to build their homeland as set out in the controversial Declaration.

In so constituting these borders and regimes, Britain felt no need to seek the consent of the native people; nor did France in shaping Syria and Lebanon. Between themselves, and within their respective spheres of influence, the British and French proceeded as if neither Wilson nor Lenin had made a dent in the ethos of that imperial–colonial era. True, England granted Iraq, as it had Egypt, a semblance of autonomy. But this bow to the zeitgeist was still compatible with the exercise of complete military, economic, and diplomatic control. The same control would obtain in Palestine and Transjordan, notwithstanding their separate-but-equal status under the Mandate system, which was widely expected in times of trouble to replace the velvet glove with the mailed fist.

In April–May 1920 at San Remo, on the Italian Riviera, the victor powers formalized the broad outlines of the redrawn Middle East. Throughout the Arab world the anti-colonial nationalists, elitist and popular, protested against what was perceived as a massive betrayal of wartime promises and the vaunted creed of self-determination. Thousands of Arabs were moved to rise up in protest, even in arms, in Iraq, Palestine, Transjordan, and Syria. Iraq witnessed the largest and most deadly uprising against British troops rushed in from India: between July and October 1920, the insurgency claimed the lives of over 3,000 Arabs and 400 Britons, with the number of wounded running to nearly three times as many. Presently Churchill found it "extraordinary" that the British civil administration "should have succeeded in such a short time in alienating the whole country to such an extent that the Arabs have laid aside the blood feuds they have nursed for centuries and that the Sunni and Shia tribes are working together."

Churchill called a conference in Cairo for March 12–22, 1921, to make last-minute but minor revisions to the projected new territorial and political order. The roughly forty participants were the cream of Britain's leading officials in and experts on the Middle East, most prominent among them Sir Edmund Allenby, high commissioner for Egypt; Sir Herbert Samuel, high commissioner for Palestine; and Lawrence. The colonial secretary had three preoccupations: to reassure France that Syria and Lebanon were not subject to Britain's hegemony in the region, to cut the costs of maintaining His Majesty's presence there, and to contain Arab nationalism. It was in Cairo that Churchill, disregarding such dissent as there was, made final the partition of historic Palestine. In keeping with recent colonial transactions, he confirmed the arbitrary conjuring of the Hashemite Kingdom of Transjordan, wedged between a reduced Palestine and Iraq. Palestine was pared down to one-fifth of its size and a large fraction of its population. As a quid pro quo for his perch in Amman, King Abdullah, backed by British bayonets, was expected to be a loyal satrap. Churchill sealed Britain's compact with Abdullah personally in Jerusalem on March 24. Though Churchill distrusted the left Zionists, his reasons for severing Palestine were neither anti-Zionist nor anti-Jewish, but simply pro-imperial.

While in the Holy City, Churchill met with local Arab and Zionist leaders. The newly formed Palestine Arab Congress was less accommodating than the brother-kings in Baghdad and Amman. In addition to reiterating their unqualified opposition to a Jewish national home in Palestine and to unrestricted immigration, the delegates demanded the right to self-determination and to create ties with sister Arab states. Churchill then met with representatives of the Yishuv. In his response to their high-flown homage to Great Britain, he urged them to bear in mind the "great alarm" felt by the Arabs, before reminding them that, were it not for the Zionist movement, "there would be no need for Britain to keep up such a large garrison at so great an expense in this country."

New disorders broke out a month after Churchill's visit. On May 1, 1921—May Day for communist Zionists, Easter for Orthodox Chris-

tian Arabs—in defiance of an official ban, some fifty Jewish Bolsheviks took to the streets of Jaffa, brandishing red flags and carrying
posters that called, in Yiddish, for a Soviet Palestine. Soon they clashed
with a considerably larger, authorized demonstration of Jewish socialists. In this melee opposing the adepts of Lenin and Karl Kautsky,
the police weighed in and helped put the communists to flight. Local
Arabs watched from the sidelines before themselves assaulting the
Jews and pillaging shops in Jaffa's Jewish quarters. By the end of the
day, 27 Palestinian Jews lay dead, with 104 wounded; there were 5
dead and 34 wounded among the Palestinian Arabs. With Jews arming
and retaliating during May 2–6, there were also deadly scuffles to the
north in Tel Aviv, Petah Tikva, and Tul Karm; to the south in
Rehovot; and to the southeast in Ramla. By May 7, when the unrest
subsided, a total of some 50 Jews and 50 Arabs had been killed, and
140 Jews and 70 Arabs wounded.

Sir Herbert Samuel, the first high commissioner for Palestine, was
also the first Jewish member of a British cabinet. Pro-Zionist but
initially lukewarm about the Balfour Declaration, he was jolted by the
scope and intensity of the animus between Arabs and Jews. Having
underestimated the "great alarm" among the Arabs, Samuel hastened
to assure them that England "would never impose upon them a policy
which [they] had reason to think was contrary to their religious, their
political, and their economic interest." In a gesture to the moderates
among them, on May 8 he cleared the way for Haj Amin al-Husseini to
succeed his deceased brother as Grand Mufti, probably in part to
recognize his contribution to dampening the embers of revolt in
Jerusalem. Shortly thereafter al-Husseini also assumed the presidency
of the Supreme Muslim Council. Sir Herbert was not nearly so
conciliatory with the Jewish notables, speaking the same day to the
leaders of the Yishuv in the language of Zionism's internal critics.
There was "only one way" to move forward, and that was by means
of "an agreement" with the Palestinian Arabs. To date, Zionism "had
not . . . done a thing to obtain [their] consent." Without it, "immigration will not be possible." The Zionists were offended to be told,
and by a *Landsman* no less, that they were "inviting a massacre which
will come as long as you disregard the Arabs."

As part of his effort to reduce tensions, Samuel appointed a
commission headed by Sir Thomas Haycraft, chief justice of Palestine,
to inquire into the recent uprising. Published in October 1921, its
report found the Arabs responsible for starting "the racial strife [that]
rapidly developed into a conflict of great violence between Arabs and
Jews, in which the Arab majority, who were generally the aggressors,

inflicted most of the casualties." But the causes of the Jaffa riots, both precipitant and underlying, were also discussed. The "immediate cause" was the "unauthorized demonstration of Bolshevik Jews" and their ensuing "clash with an authorized demonstration by the Jewish Labour Party." As for the "fundamental cause," it sprang from "a feeling among Arabs of discontent with, and hostility to, the Jews, due to political and economic causes, and connected with Jewish immigration, and with their conception of Zionist policy as derived from Jewish exponents."

Churchill conferred with Samuel before issuing his White Paper of June 1922, which was intended to make clear that the Balfour Declaration of 1917 did not "contain or imply anything which need cause either alarm to the Arab population of Palestine or disappointment to the Jews." Attentive to "unauthorized [Zionist] statements," the Arabs took this Declaration's hidden agenda to be "a wholly Jewish Palestine," complete with the "disappearance or subordination of the Arab population, language, and culture" there. His Majesty's Government did not "contemplate that Palestine as a whole should be converted into a Jewish National Home." Having addressed, if not appeased, the worst apprehensions of the Arabs, Churchill contested their presumed construction of McMahon's wartime assurances. McMahon had not promised "that an independent national government should be at once established in Palestine." Although London intended to "foster" such a government, because of "the special circumstances of that country, this should be accomplished by gradual stages and not suddenly." In countering the Arabs' interpretation of the confines of the projected Arab kingdom, Churchill affirmed that "the whole of Palestine west of the Jordan was . . . excluded from Sir Henry McMahon's pledge."

The White Paper also spoke to Zionist anxieties, brought on by what Churchill may have considered Samuel's overly stern predication to the Yishuv. The Jews in Palestine were fearful that the British Government might "depart from the policy embodied in the Declaration of 1917. It is necessary [therefore] once more to affirm that these fears are unfounded, and that that Declaration . . . is not susceptible of change." It was no less "essential" to reassure them that they were "in Palestine as of right and not on sufferance," and that this right was "internationally guaranteed, and . . . formally recognized to rest upon ancient historic connection." To pursue its project, the Jewish community in Palestine "should be able to increase its numbers by immigration." It would have to be understood, however, that "this immigration cannot be so great in volume as to exceed whatever may be the economic capacity of the country at the time to absorb new arrivals." Nor should the immigrants become "a burden upon the people of Palestine as a whole . . . and deprive any section of the present population of their employment."

Where the White Paper was a cruel defeat for the Palestinian Arabs, it was an almost total triumph for the Zionists. It sanctioned their right to a national home in Palestine, which the Arabs continued to contest on principle, and unequivocally.

Both sides joined battle over immigration, an issue the Hashemite Kingdom had made incendiary: with the east bank of the Jordan River closed to Jewish colonization, Palestine risked becoming over-populated. Convinced demographics were their only major political asset, the Arabs clamored for a complete stay of Jewish immigration. The Zionists, conscious that only superior numbers would in the long run give them an advantage at the ballot box, were equally resolute in their drive for higher quotas, if not for a completely open door.

The Arabs were ill-fitted for the struggle with the Zionists, who were backed by the strong arm of Britain and the moral authority of the League of Nations. Their own national movement in Palestine was as yet rudimentary and the local political elite sorely divided, largely by clan-like rivalries. Although anti-colonialist nationalism had made greater strides in some of the neighboring Arab countries, these were disunited by competing dynastic, diplomatic, and economic interests, and all were wards of the British empire (or in Syria's case, the French). In terms of access to the world's centers of political, economic, and cultural power, the Arabs were no match for the Zionists. With fast-expanding im-migration as their imperative, the Yishuv proceeded to build a virtual state, develop a vibrant political economy, and fashion a distinctive cultural identity with modern Hebrew as its catalyst and vital center. And Jews throughout the diaspora, Zionist and non-Zionist alike, lent their indispensable political and financial support.

In Palestine, meanwhile, Britain continued to divide and rule. Certainly there was nothing to suggest that London would bestir itself to encourage Arab–Jewish understanding. Equally clearly, neither the Palestinian Arabs nor the Zionists were about to advocate mutual empathy and cooperation at any level of society.

To this standoff, the internal critics of Zionism responded that it was up to the Jews, returning to their ancestral land after hundreds of years, to meet the indigenous Arabs at least halfway, and to go the distance first.

Between 1922 and 1925 Ahad Haam's heirs agreed on the postulate, eventually formulated by Magnes, that "Arab–Jewish cooperation is not only necessary . . . but possible." It pained them to expose what they considered Zionism's grave failing: the Jewish Agency, like the mandatory power, failed to make cooperation with the Arabs a "major policy objective." They agreed, in Magnes' words, that the establishment of a Jewish state "against the will of the Arab people—inside and outside Palestine—could not be achieved except through armed conflict, and that to maintain a state thus engendered would require endless violence and warfare." To prevail, the Jews would have to "prostrate themselves before the idols of economic imperialism and militarism."

In 1925, in Jerusalem, at the initiative of Arthur Ruppin and Martin Buber, the phalanx of "conscientious objectors" to statehood founded Brit Shalom (Alliance, or Covenant, for Peace) along with the journal *Sheifotenu* (Our Aspirations). Their aim was to advance a respectful reciprocity between the Yishuv and Palestinian Arabs. By this time Palestine was home to 750,000 Arabs and 75,000 Jews. Taking note of this inescapable fact, Ruppin told the delegates to the Fourteenth Zionist Congress in Vienna the same year that, like it or not, Palestine would be "a state of two nations." Simultaneously Robert Weltsch, one of Buber's close associates, wrote in the *Jüdische Rundschau*, the leading Zionist weekly in Germany, if not in Europe, that Palestine would "always be inhabited by two peoples" in need of "mutual trust." There was no realizing the Zionist project without "integrating it into the ever stronger nationalist awakening of the neighboring Asian peoples." With world opinion aware of "a large native population in Palestine" and showing "growing sympathy" for the revolt of colonial peoples, Zionism risked becoming "unpopular in many quarters, not out of anti-Jewish feelings but out of consideration for the natural rights of Arabs."

As an alternative to Herzl's *Judenstaat*, the guiding spirits of Brit Shalom projected a binational country of Jews and Palestinian Arabs based on the principle of parity. They imagined a society where the members of both ethno-religious communities would have equal rights (including suffrage) and equal representation, regardless of the numerical balance between them. To further the Israelites' reabsorption into an alien Middle East, the Judeo-Arab entity would eventually join its fortunes with a regional Arab confederation.

According to the skeptics, Zionism's drive for massive immigration in a quest for local ascendancy was as reckless as its reliance on the Great Powers to establish a Jewish island in the middle of an Arab sea.

Both policies courted violence and portended a garrison state: one called for outsized police forces to keep watch over a sullen and unconsenting Palestinian Arab population, the other for outsized military forces to guard the hostile borders. Brit Shalom envisaged another possibility. With equal rights for both people and diplomatic relations with neighboring countries, binationalism would reconcile Jew and Arab in an open political and civil society with minimal burdens of sovereign statehood and imperial dependency.

Brit Shalom was the first and only Zionist association ever to force an open discussion of the Arab Question and present an alternative to the official blueprint. Though indeterminate, it plainly implied two main axioms: first, Jews and Arabs had an equally valid claim to the Holy Land; second, it was incumbent on the leaders of the Yishuv and the World Zionist Organization to defuse the righteous and rising hostility of Palestinian Arabs by exploring true compromise. Brit Shalom was chartered in November 1925, during the most benign days of the halcyon break in the thirty years of crisis and war of the twentieth century. Jews benefited from these good times throughout Europe, in the Soviet Union, and in the United States. In Palestine, between 1920 and 1923 the Jewish population rose from about 56,000 to over 90,000, and between 1924 and 1929 by another 82,000, most of the migrants of the third and fourth *aliyah*s coming from Poland and settling in the major cities. Demographic growth was matched by considerable economic and cultural development, as well as by an increase in the number of kibbutzim and moshavim. This general boom was striking, yet its pace and scale were moderate, there being no headlong rush of European Jews to Palestine. Besides, largely because of a sluggish local economy, an estimated 23,000 of the latest immigrants actually returned to the diaspora. By 1930–1, Mandatory Palestine counted about 175,000 Jews and 840,000 Arabs.

While the Palestinian Arabs continued to oppose the encroachment on their land and daily life, the inconstancy of the Zionist incursion seemed to ease their fears. Several political groups, animated by the longstanding Nashashibi clan, turned toward greater collaboration with both the British and the Zionists. In contacts with Mandate officials, these moderates pressed their demands for a legislative council and self-government. Although in public they execrated Zionism, covertly they entertained relations with its officials. The two major Arab newspapers of this less hidebound orientation understandably took an interest in Brit Shalom. One editorial asked, in late 1929, whether "the Jewish question will be settled by sober and more reasonable leaders such as Dr. Magnes and Dr. Bergmann, or whether the advocates of peaceful and constructive policies will be removed from the political arena."

Nineteen twenty-five also saw the inauguration of the Hebrew University in Jerusalem. Twelve symbolic foundation stones had been laid on Mount Scopus in July 1918, bringing to term an idea conceived at the first World Zionist Congress in 1897. Ahad Haam and Buber, as well as Albert Einstein and Sigmund Freud, joined the embryonic advisory council. At the opening of the School of Natural Sciences in 1922, the first faculty of the university, Einstein lectured on his relativity theory. Two years later, Magnes, the first chancellor, and under the sway of Ahad Haam, established the Institute of Jewish Studies. The School of Oriental Studies opened in 1926. In shaping the latter, Magnes was counseled by Josef Horowitz, later a faculty member and leading Western Orientalist—Magnes had met him at the University of Berlin. They were agreed on the desperate importance of learning about and engaging the culture of the ambient Arab world, starting with the study of Arabic itself, to be followed by Arabic literature and Islamic art and philosophy. Construing the scholarly and intellectual mission of Hebrew University as cosmopolitan from the outset, Magnes insisted that Mount Scopus remain autonomous, and not be turned into a Zionist Olympus.

But the chief statesman of the project was Chaim Weizmann, president of the World Zionist Organization. With Zionism in danger of losing its charge, he decided that "what was needed was some strong stimulus to galvanize the whole thing," with special stress on mobilizing "friends, Jewish and non-Jewish, in the diaspora." Conceding that there existed only "the germ of a university," Weizmann nevertheless thought a ceremonial opening was warranted, and this was set for April 1, 1925. Although the tally of guests fell short of the 12,000–14,000 he anticipated, the attendance was large and distinguished. For a start, there was the triumvirate of Balfour, Allenby, and Samuel; next, a veritable pantheon of local and world Zionists, among them Ahad Haam, Norman Bentwich, Bialik, Buber, Meir Dizengoff, Ruppin, Nahum Sokolov, and Menachem Ussishkin. Also present were Professor William E. Rappard, until recently secretary of the Mandate Commission, who represented the University of Geneva, and emissaries from several other Western universities and learned societies. Ahmed Lufti El-Sayyid, rector of the Egyptian National University, was the sole representative from an Arab institution.

As Weizmann had intended, Balfour was the honored guest and lodestar of the occasion. His sojourn had the character of an apotheosis. At the ceremony, and wherever he traveled and visited during his two-week stay in Palestine, he was welcomed and cheered by adulatory crowds. Though retired from politics and 77 years old, he had the aura of an historical personage transcending his long and distinguished career as His Majesty's prime minister, first lord of the Admiralty, and foreign secretary. Landing in Alexandria on March 23, Balfour traveled to Cairo, where he was the guest of Lord Allenby. Two days later he and his party continued by train to Suez, on their way to Palestine. Before and after the pomp of April 1, Balfour made a triumphal tour of the British Mandate. Tel Aviv, Richon Le'Tsion, Petah Tikva, Haifa, Nazareth . . . their roads and streets were thickly lined with impassioned well-wishers waving British and Zionist flags.

On Mount Scopus, when Balfour walked onto the platform for honored officials and guests, the audience broke into sustained applause and jubilant cheers. He stood tall and erect in his academic robe with the colors of Cambridge and Edinburgh, as the Chief Ashkenazi Rabbi Avraham Yitzhak Kook, speaking in Hebrew, invoked the blessing of the Almighty for King George, Balfour, and the High Commissioner for Palestine, followed by a prayer for the success of the university, and an expression of disquiet about the pursuit of free inquiry. After a stirring introduction by Weizmann, Balfour praised the founders for embracing the principle of disinterested research, saying that "we are now engaged in adapting Western methods and a Western form of university to an Asiatic site and to an education which is to be carried on in an Eastern language." According to Rappard, the British empire's chief rabbi, J.H. Hertz, asked for a divine blessing for this "venture of brotherhood and understanding that the Jews of Palestine sought to undertake in collaboration with the Arabs, whose semitic background and land they shared." He was interrupted by boisterous clapping, which he cut short with an emphatic gesture.

Balfour hoped to visit Damascus and Beirut before returning to Alexandria to embark for his voyage home. It was during this leg of his trip that he ran into outright anti-Zionist and anti-British demonstrations. Not that his time in Palestine had passed without protests—though Weizmann downplayed them, saying there had been only "fairly peaceable demonstrations in the form of a strike, and the closing of a few Arab shops in Jerusalem, Haifa, and Jaffa." The Arab Palestinian resistance was at best in gestation, and the mandatory authorities had mounted exceptionally tight security measures. Still, in Damascus and Beirut, crowds in support of an Arab Palestine were sufficiently threatening that Balfour never ventured into either city.

Since the dramaturgy of Balfour's visit to the Holy Land was exclusively focused on the Yishuv, it was certain to incense not just the Arab Palestinians but the entire Arab–Muslim world, especially with the father of the eponymous Declaration playing his role so willingly. And, like Herzl, Balfour was largely oblivious to the local Arabs. Chronicling his travels in Palestine with Balfour, Weizmann refers to them only twice: first, during their "short tour of the Judean colonies," when Balfour "met some of the Arab sheiks who came in from near-by villages"; second, in an encounter with three Arab youths outside Nazareth who told them that "a very great Jew"— Balfour—had "come to 'hand over' Palestine to the Jews." Although Weizmann records that "it was all said quite without bitterness, indeed lightly, and half-banteringly," he took it as evidence "that Arab propaganda had already made considerable progress."

As chancellor of the university, Magnes was centrally involved in the planning and production of the convocation. From the first, however, he was deeply troubled by its blatant political instrumentalization. He had grave reservations about making Lord Balfour, the patron saint of the Jewish National Home, the *spiritus rector* of what he considered and hoped would be essentially an academic affair. Just to secure Balfour's safety, the authorities had to deploy 100 extra constables on the university campus, giving it the appearance of a British imperial bastion. But Magnes worried about needlessly pouring oil on the simmering fire of Arab resentment and wounded pride— in Palestine and beyond. In a morose letter to Ahad Haam, he wondered whether Hebrew University "could not have been inaugurated without stirring up the Moslem world against us?"

In his autobiography, recalling that Magnes tended to "deprecate the ceremony as too much of a political act," Weizmann asked himself if, even assuming it were one, the occasion "should lose any value thereby." He took the position that "the creation of any great institution in Palestine—or anywhere else, for that matter—[was] always a political act." Professor Rappard was not the only guest from afar to conclude that the inauguration "was the supreme consecration of the Jewish National Homeland in Palestine."

Coincident with the founding of Brit Shalom and the Hebrew University was the formation, in Paris, of the Zionist Revisionist movement, a far-right faction within the World Zionist Organization. Vladimir "Ze'ev" Jabotinsky was the force behind this suddenly powerful crosscurrent. Born in Odessa, he had studied in Bern and Rome between 1898 and 1901, returning to Russia only to have the Kishinev pogrom of April 1903

radicalize his Zionist persuasion. During the First World War he raised a
legion of Jewish volunteers to fight alongside the British Army in the
Middle East, and by 1920 had begun to organize Jewish self-defense
units. These became the embryo of the Hagana (Defense), the military
force under the Yishuv, and its offshoot, the underground paramilitary
group Irgun Zvai Leumi ("national military organization," now known
by its Hebrew acronym, Etzel). From the start he had no doubt that
military force and violence would decide the struggle for the Jewish
Homeland in Palestine.

While Herzl's Zionism was indebted to the liberal nationalism of
the long nineteenth century that began in 1789 and ended in 1914,
Jabotinsky's came out of the messianic nationalism rampant during
the First World War and its aftermath. Although he celebrated the
hardy frontier spirit of the kibbutzniks, he rejected their socialist
assumptions and their romance with class conflict. A champion of free
enterprise, Jabotinsky sought to rally the middle classes—mainly the
lower-middle classes—of the towns and cities in Palestine and the
diaspora of Eastern Europe. A cross between Gabriele D'Annunzio
and Benito Mussolini, he gave priority to the political and military
struggle for a sovereign state, postponing discussion of its cultural,
social, and economic contours until doomsday.

Jabotinsky, like Herzl, was a Western supremacist, but he fixated
more on just whom Westerners were superior to. He considered "the
Orient . . . an inferior and wanton civilization," closed to reason and
progress. This cultural zone harbored archaic societies whose "har-
ems, veils, and patriarchal sheiks" had outlived their time. While Islam
was an "intelligent and noble religion," it was problematic in so far as
its emirs were forever tempted to "implant it in all spheres of civic
life." Though the Jews may have originated in the Middle East, they
"have nothing in common with what is called the 'Orient,' thank
God." Jews were going to Palestine primarily for their "national
convenience [but also] to thoroughly sweep out of Eretz Israel all
traces of the Oriental . . . and Islamic soul," the Muslims being a
"yelling rabble dressed up in gaudy savage rags."

Notwithstanding his blanket indictment of the whole Arab–Muslim
world, Jabotinsky made a relatively equitable assessment of the
Palestinian Arabs before 1925, particularly of their senses of place
and self. As Palestine was their "birthplace," it was "the center and
basis of their own national existence." The land was "full of Arab
memories," and they "[love] it as much as we do." Although he
claimed that, of the "two truths" that were on a collision course in
Palestine, the Jewish truth "is greater," Jabotinsky recognized that,

despite their "cultural backwardness . . . the instinctive patriotism of the Arabs is just as pure and noble as our own." Since their rising national movement refused to be bought off with "words, gifts, and bribery," it could only be "curbed" by superior force.

Perhaps even more clearly than the seers of Brit Shalom, Jabotinsky understood that, for the Zionist project to have a future, the ancient and swelling Jewish–Arab discord must be overcome. But the two camps meant to take divergent paths: Brit Shalom looked to mutual tolerance and reconciliation, Jabotinsky to the sword. Convinced that, demographically, time was against the settlers, he called for rapid immigration from Eastern Europe, along with a double-quick military buildup. As "a colonizing venture . . . in a land in which the people already living there" were certain to resist, Zionism was destined to "stand or fall on the question of armed forces" fitted for both defensive and offensive warfare.

Precisely because he discerned the new nationalisms sweeping the world, Jabotinsky understood that the friction between Jews and Arabs was not simply a "misunderstanding but a natural conflict" between two equally authentic nationalist movements. Bound to defend their ancestral land, the Palestinian Arabs would "not accept Zionism [until] confronted with an 'iron wall' [of] Jewish bayonets." After his previous execration, Jabotinsky now admitted frankly that, because the Palestinian Arabs were "not a rabble but a living people . . . as long as they had a glimmer of hope . . . of getting rid of us nothing in the world" would make them get out of the way. It would take superior power and resolve to force the "extremist Palestinians" who were sworn to "the slogan No" to yield to "more moderate groups" that would be willing to "compromise . . . and bargain with us on practical matters, such as guarantees against pushing them out and equality of civil and national rights." An equally vital accord with the "Arabs of Baghdad, Mecca, and Damascus" would also depend on the Yishuv's military forces, which, given their outright technological edge, would have no difficulty joining battle with the outdated Arab–Muslim armies.

This confidence in defying the neighboring countries moved Jabotinsky to challenge the chief Zionist policymakers. At the founding congress of his party-movement in 1925 he called for a revision of the geographic terms of the Mandate: the nullification of Britain's severance of the eastern bank of the Jordan from historic Palestine and its closure to Zionist colonization. Zionism could settle for nothing less than a Jewish state and majority on *both* sides of the river, primarily as a refuge for the Jews of Eastern Europe.

Revisionism gained a greater hold upon the Zionist movement and decision-making elite than Brit Shalom, its antithesis. Jabotinsky's precepts began to persuade Zionists across a spectrum of belief, not least because he proposed to solve the largely unvoiced but always pendent Arab Question by making it disappear altogether. The champions of binationalism were apprehensive: they were afraid the Revisionist idea would come to tempt the Yishuv, and incite the Arab world.

By the mid 1920s, the Zionist stance vis-à-vis the Arabs became a public political issue. In the fall of 1925, David Ben-Gurion, speaking for the fast-growing labor movement, declared that, whereas Zionists had "completely ignored" the Arab community and proceeded "as if Palestine were completely uninhabited . . . the time for such naïveté had long since passed, never to return." After recognizing that the Arab community was an "organic and inseparable part of Palestine and that its members were rooted and working in it and here to stay," he maintained that Zionism had not come "to inherit this community's place or rise on its ruins." Certainly, some Zionists were pointing to the forcible "dispossession [in 1923] of hundreds of thousands of Greeks from Turkey and hundreds of thousands of Turks from Greece" to justify a forced transfer of Palestinian Arabs to nearby lands. But "only a madman or a scoundrel could impute some such design to the Jewish people in Palestine." At exactly the same moment, Weizmann, head of the Zionist Executive and doyen of the centrist General Zionists, told the delegates to the Fourteenth Congress in Vienna that "Palestine must be built without violating by even one iota the legitimate rights of the Arabs." Rather than invoke "Platonic formulas," Zionists should realize that Palestine "was not Rhodesia" and that "according to the world community's sense of justice" the Arabs living in the Holy Land had "exactly the same rights as we have to a National Home."

But this incipient quasi-official acknowledgment of the Other alternated sporadically with a quite different position, endorsed by Weizmann, that shortly became an article of faith: Ben-Gurion asserted that Zionism would realize "the immigration of masses of Jews" to establish a "new economy . . . designed to absorb a large Jewish majority that will live in Palestine together with the Arab people settled in it." In 1927 he served notice that, just as the Jews had no intention of depriving a single Arab of his rights, "the Arabs should not deprive us of ours." Where Jabotinsky proposed to rely on the force of arms to secure Jewish dominance, Ben-Gurion trusted in the force of economics: with vast stretches of Palestine, including the

Negev, underpopulated and undeveloped, the Jews had a moral and natural right to develop "all those unsettled and unformed areas." Since the Arabs were economically unfit, they "must not be allowed to interfere with us." They had a "right only to that which they have created and to their homes."

This sense of moral entitlement derived from the European assumption of cultural superiority. And, starting with the second *aliyah*, the Zionists also believed that by furthering the uplift of the Palestinian people they would reconcile the Arabs to the irruption of strangers into their land. But in the words of T. E. Lawrence, which could have been those of the internal critics, "we have increased [their] prosperity—but who cares for that when [loss of] liberty is in the other scale." This same skepticism was articulated by Chaim Arlosoroff, a young Berlin-educated socialist labor leader and theorist influenced by Ahad Haam and Buber, who warned against thinking of the Arab Question as a socioeconomic one. Disabused about the alleged benefits of Europe's civilizing mission, he argued that the political issue was foremost, as defined by "an Arab national movement."

Yet even during the glorious 1920s, when nothing was yet foreclosed, there were no Zionist voices raised in advocacy of concrete measures for making a virtue of the necessity of living together apart from the critical public intellectuals of the elitist Brit Shalom, centered in Jerusalem, and the popular tribunes of the newly fledged Hashomer Hatzair (Young Guard) of the kibbutz movement.

The great crash of the American stock market in the fall of 1929 shattered the relative serenity in Europe. In the Holy Land that same autumn, and not unrelated to world events, the latent hostilities between Jews and Arabs broke out in the form of the first generalized revolt, or intifada, of Palestinian Arabs. Opposition to the relentless Zionist drive, local and international, for a Jewish national home in their country combined with bitterness over the continuing influx of colonists, some of them settling on hallowed ancestral lands. Distrust made for a spontaneous and explosive fusion of religious and national sentiment.

Jerusalem, with its contiguous Jewish and Muslim religious sites, was a mecca for zealots. The Western Wailing Wall (Kotel Ma'areve) and Haram ash-Sharif (site of the Omar and al-Aqsa Mosques) provided an ideal focal point for a confrontation between the worshippers of mutual non-recognition. The Wailing Wall is the sole shrine of Judaism—a religion all but indifferent to holy places, its Biblical temples having long since become imaginary monuments kept alive by the study of the Torah. Even so, the Wall was easy to politicize and exalt by reason of its location on the southwestern hill of the City of David, which symbolizes Jerusalem, the Promised Land, and the Messianic hope conjured by the term Zionism. Built on top of the surviving Western Wall of the Second Temple, destroyed by Titus in AD 70, the Haram ash-Sharif of AD 687, known to Muslims as the Noble Sanctuary, is Islam's third-holiest site, after Mecca and Medina.

Under late Ottoman rule there was a certain constriction of the rules governing Jewish worship at the Wailing Wall. But that by itself did not intensify the minor running altercations there between the Jewish and Muslim faithful—a mark of their relatively peaceful, if cold, coexistence. Rising political extremism, not religious fanaticism, scorched this sacred ground. Starting in 1928, ultra-nationalist Zionists, cheered on by Jewish fundamentalists generally, challenged the status quo at the Western Wall. For Yom Kippur they set up a *meritsa* (the screen separating men and women), stools, and ceremonial lamps for prayer in the venerable plaza. A Pro-Wailing-Wall Committee, presided over by Professor Joseph Klausner (tied to the Revisionists and author of *Jesus of Nazareth*, portraying Jesus as "the most Jewish of Jews"), and the Va'ed Leumi, the National Council of the Jews of Palestine, called for the Wall to be placed under exclusively Jewish jurisdiction.

The Arab–Muslim counterparts of these secular and religious Jewish extremists understood their moves as harbingers of a cultural offensive to inspirit the Zionist drive for demographic, economic, and political primacy. They rightly suspected that the steady push for higher immigration quotas and more land purchases was meant to prepare the way for complete ascendancy in Palestine. Control of the Wailing Wall and its plaza was likewise intended to secure a stepping stone to the 35-acre Temple Mount, where Muslims feared Jews aimed to raze their al-Aqsa Mosque and build the Third Temple. The Central Islamic Council denounced this presumed stratagem, and a Society for the Defense of al-Aqsa, animated by fundamentalists, organized a minimal protest on the esplanade of the Haram. A denial by the Zionist Executive of any such design counted for naught.

On August 14, 1929, some 6,000 militant Zionists marched and rallied in Tel Aviv, harkening to the slogan "The Wall is Ours." In the evening, half as many gathered for a would-be prayer meeting near the Wall in Jerusalem. The next day, a crowd of religious Jews came to pray in observance of Tishah b'Ab (destruction of the First and Second Temples). Determined to appropriate a religious rite for their cause, some 300 exercised Revisionists from Tel Aviv joined them, which alarmed both non-Zionist religious Jews and internal critics near and far. The Jewish flag was unfurled, speeches were made, the Zionist anthem (*Hatikvah*, or "hope") sung. Then they dispersed to proclaim their word in other parts of the Holy City.

After morning prayers the next day, Friday—the Prophet's anniversary—there was a mass counter-demonstration on the Haram, organized by the Islamic Council. The meeting swung out of control, and the Arab–Muslim protesters spilled down the steps toward the Wailing Wall. After rallying there, they burned objects left behind for a service the following day, as well as Jewish prayer books, and even notes to God in the Wall's crevices. Lay and religious leaders tried to calm the atmosphere, but in vain. On Saturday, there were several scuffles in the heart of Jerusalem that took one Jewish life and claimed a small number of wounded on both sides. Zionist militants exploited the funeral of the Jewish victim for their own ends. Jews feared a pogrom, Muslims an assault on the Noble Sanctuary.

Tensions remained high in Jerusalem and spread to other cities of mixed population, as well as to the countryside. The virus of rebellion fed upon a host body of Arab frustration and anger. Here and there, rumors that Jews had seized the Holy of Holies on the Haram incited a number of *fellahin*, perhaps goaded by mullahs, to reach for cudgels and knives, and march in small bands to nearby towns. There they joined urban militants in anti-Zionist and anti-Jewish demonstrations that escalated into riots leading to plunder and murder. During the week of August 23–30, about 130 Jews and 115 Arabs were killed in Jerusalem, Hebron, Nablus, Jaffa, Haifa, Safad, and Tel Aviv. In Jerusalem, after the unrest of August 15–18, the two communities remained on edge and susceptible to incitement by religious and political ultras. The Jews feared another confrontation, which came on August 23, when Arab militants, advancing from the Haram, broke into the Jewish quarters of the city. That same day, in the ultra-Orthodox district of Mea She'arim, two Arabs were killed by Jewish extremists.

The week's bloodiest incidents, which claimed the bulk of Jewish victims, took place in Hebron and Nablus. Hebron had a population of over 15,000 Arabs, many of them devout Muslims, and about 700 Jews—largely long-established Sephardim and non-Zionists. When reports of the mayhem in nearby Jerusalem reached the city, a muster of primitively armed Arab townsmen hastened to the capital, 22 miles off. Meanwhile, peasants from neighboring villages rushed to take their place in Hebron, home to the Tomb of the Patriarchs, where the Biblical Abraham, Isaac, and Jacob are believed to be buried. Here they joined hands with local militants, who on August 24 ran riot in the Jewish quarter, killing between sixty-five and seventy Jews, fifteen of them women and children. Many, apparently, were relative new-comers to Hebron from Eastern Europe. These the Arabs saw as Zionists, seeking to disinherit them of their land—not desecrate their religion and culture. Many of the Sephardic Jews found safety in the homes of their Arab neighbors, with whom they shared a language and various customs. But, taking the turbulence all in all, it is impossible to weigh the anti-Zionist against the anti-Jewish motives.

The risings in all the cities shared similar sources: fear, cynicism, and religiously or temporally prompted wrath. The mechanisms too were alike: a blend of educated urban youth and illiterate peasants, and inadequate forces of law and order. In every instance, except in Jerusalem and Tel Aviv, the Arabs were the assailants, even if most assaults gave rise to cycles of revenge.

Whereas the targets and objectives of Arab and Jewish extremists may have had a certain logic, their victims were guiltless. Yet opposing sides in civil conflict will always and naturally dramatize each other's brutality and cruelty. Following this first intifada, the Yishuv and the Zionist Executive gave these predictable accusations an Orientalist coloring: they portrayed Arab rage, with its attendant savageries, as non-Western and typical of barbarians in what would soon be called the Third World. Eastern European Jews in Palestine and the diaspora even compared Bloody Week to earlier pogroms in the late czarist empire's Pale of Settlement. Ben-Gurion, for instance, likened the rising in Hebron to the 1903 slaughter in Kishinev. Such comparisons stressed only similarities, not differences: unlike the Russian autho-rities, British officials neither organized nor condoned the Palestinian destruction of Jewish life but were caught off-guard, largely for lack of security forces. Christian and Russian anti-Semitism, moreover, bore little resemblance to Arab anti-Zionism. To the extent that Zionists acknowledged Arab–Muslim nationalism and resistance, they con-sidered it a transgression of the law manipulated by al-Husseini, the Mufti of Jerusalem who, in both his religious and political capacity, kept calling for an end to Jewish immigration. In fact, he and his adjutants had tried, albeit unsuccessfully, to rein in the runaway Palestinian radicals.

London chartered the Shaw Commission to inquire into the first intifada of 1928–9, and the subsequent report became an important source for a White Paper of 1929, authored by Lord Passfield (the renowned Fabian socialist Sidney Webb). Discussing the underlying causes of the uprising, both the report and White Paper, like the earlier

British investigation of 1920–1, placed more of the blame on the Zionists than on the Arab Palestinians, in arguments analogous to those used by the internal critics. The Shaw report, published on March 30, 1930, described an undercurrent of resentment among Palestinian Arabs, fueled by the lack of self-government and of access to His Majesty's Government. And it forcefully pointed up

> the fundamental cause[s] without which . . . the disturbances either would not have occurred or would have been little more than a local riot: the Arab feeling of animosity and hostility toward the Jews consequent upon the disappointment of their political and national aspirations [and the] twofold fear of the Arabs that by Jewish immigration and land purchases they may be deprived of their livelihood and in time pass under the political domination of the Jews.

After adducing "the long series of incidents" brought about by Jews and Muslims around the Wailing Wall, the report held that the incident that "most contributed to the outbreak was the Jewish demonstration at the Wailing Wall on August 15, 1929." Yet it deemed the role of the Society for the Protection of the Muslim Holy Places more provocative than that of the Pro-Wailing-Wall Committee. There were also the inflammatory articles in the Arab and Jewish press, as well as "the propaganda among the less educated Arab people of a character calculated to incite them." Last, the official report mentioned the "inadequacy" of the British military and police.

The Shaw Commission recommended that, "with the least possible delay," His Majesty's Government define "in clear and positive terms the meaning" they attached to "the passages in the Mandate providing for the safeguarding of the rights of the non-Jewish communities," particularly with regard to such "vital issues as land and immigration." Above all, there was need for "a clear and definite declaration of the policy . . . regarding the regulation and control of future Jewish immigration." To help the local administration, London should consider giving the Palestinian Arabs some measure of self-government and should appoint "an ad hoc commission to determine the rights and claims in connection with the Wailing Wall."

The "tragic events" of August having "further poisoned" the atmosphere of "racial antagonism and mutual suspicion," there was little prospect of a détente between Jews and Arabs "unless cooperation between the two races, the composure of their differences, and the removal of causes of suspicion are by some means brought about." Shaw and his colleagues looked to the Jewish leaders "not to allow their most natural feelings to deter them from exploring to the full the possibility of . . . cultivating a better understanding between the two races." They added dryly, "it would seem that, so far, little effort has been expended in this direction"—a reflection reminiscent of Sir Herbert Samuel's assertion, in 1921, that Zionism "had not done a thing to obtain the consent" of the Palestinian Arabs and that "without that consent immigration will not be possible."

In May 1930, as a follow-up to the Shaw report, London sent Sir John Hope-Simpson to Palestine to review Britain's immigration and land policy. Pending his assessment the Labour government, sensitive to the economic plight of the underclass of Palestinian Arabs during the Depression, restricted land sales and virtually suspended immigration.

In the Yishuv and the diaspora the Shaw report was excoriated as evidence of what it was felt would become England's anti-Semitically driven betrayal of the Balfour Declaration in favor of the Arabs. A general strike in the cities and towns of Palestine was followed by anti-British demonstrations in Europe's major capitals, with the single greatest mobilization in the streets of Warsaw on June 11, 1930. American Jews also protested in several cities.

Along with the Hope-Simpson report, the Passfield White Paper was published on October 21, 1930. The Zionists took it to confirm their worst fears. Besides recommending the establishment of a joint Legislative Council in Palestine, it proposed a further restriction of immigration and land sales, on account of the level of Arab unemployment and the country's "economic capacity." The campaign of Jewish protest resumed. Finally, under mounting political pressure, on February 13, 1931 Labour Prime Minister Ramsay MacDonald, in a letter to Chaim Weizmann, all but abrogated the contested provisions of the White Paper. Here was another example of the Zionists having greater access to British officialdom—this time in London—than the Palestinian Arabs. Immigration, which for Zionists was the crux, thereupon rose to unprecedented levels, reaching about 40,000 in 1934 and 60,000 in 1935.

How did relatively moderate Zionists see this critical moment, with the first intifada as its pivot? Weizmann may be taken as speaking for the vital center. For him, the "Palestine pogroms of 1929" were an indication that the Arabs realized the scale and speed of Zionism's progress. To thwart any further advance, they precipitated "the riots, appealed to religious fanaticism, whipped up blind mob passions, and deliberately misrepresented Zionist aims." So far, "the riots were the strongest effort . . . to frighten us, by mob action, from continuing our work in Palestine." Of course, "they came too late [and] they failed." Even so, as Weizmann wrote to Buber, the Arabs remained "confident of victory," a disposition "encouraged by Britons, Anti-Semites, Catholics, and perhaps also Moscow." Rather than put part of the blame on the Jews, as the White Paper did, His Majesty's Government should realize that "there is only one quarter from which disaffections, disorder, violence, and massacre originated." As if to corroborate Ahad Haam's plaint about official Zionism's purblindness, Weizmann added, "we do not massacre; we were the victims of a murderous onslaught."

Weizmann considered Lord Passfield, secretary of state for the colonies, to have "little sympathy"—perhaps even "hostility"—for Zionism. His White Paper was intended "to render our work in Palestine impossible" and was London's "most concerted effort . . . to retract the promise made to the Jewish people in the Balfour Declaration." That pledge was not to "one hundred and seventy thousand people as against seven hundred thousand people, a small minority juxtaposed to a great majority." Rather, the Mandatory Power was under obligation to "the Jewish people, of whom one hundred and seventy thousand are merely the vanguard." By the same token, Weizmann "energetically"—to use his own word—took issue with London's presumed "obligation toward both sections of the Palestine population."

Weizmann was hardly a meek advocate of the Zionist cause or a cautious critic of the Shaw Commission, the Hope-Simpson report, and the White Papers. Even so, the Revisionists, backed by the Orthodox Mizrachi, corralled sufficient hard-line votes to force him to resign the presidency of the Zionist Organization at the World Zionist Congress in Basel in June 1931. Tellingly, even many centrist General Zionists deserted him.

The internal critics had a more nuanced view of the heightened estrangement from the Palestinian Arabs and descent into violence. Buber traced the cause to the sad reality that "we have not lived nor do we now live 'together with' the Arabs, but merely live 'alongside' them." In the matter of the Wailing Wall, the "immediate occasion" for the riots, this "'alongside' turned into an 'against,' and we ourselves are not blameless for this 'against' having found expression in the form of religious fanaticism." Buber made a special point of stressing how much the Wailing Wall meant to Judaism and to him personally. But he lamented that of late it had been desecrated "not only by an Arab mob but also by a misguided part of our youth who

made it an object of nationalist propaganda and demonstrations."
Buber even dared to say that, whereas on the Arab side the militants
appeared to have been "genuine believers," on the Jewish side they
seemed to have been "both believers and nonbelievers." He embraced
the heretical view that by allowing themselves to "be exploited by the
misuse of a holy shrine . . . the Jews fell into a trap . . . and got
themselves into a quagmire."

Buber made two proposals to begin restoring a modicum of serenity
and trust to intercommunal relations. He suggested that "the question
of the Wailing Wall . . . become the subject of negotiations" between
Jewish and Muslim leaders, and urged Zionists and non-Zionists alike
to "intervene [and] demonstrate" for the commutation of the death
sentences of Arabs convicted of murder during the disorders. When
Weizmann proved indifferent, Buber advanced the gesture as moral
and political: it would "help decontaminate the atmosphere and
hearten wavering sympathizers." Against the argument that the Arabs
would interpret such a protest as a "sign of weakness," Buber said, on
the contrary, it would be a sign of "strength and consciousness of
strength to save my enemy's life."

Since 1925 Magnes had had close ties with the members of Brit
Shalom, though he stopped short of joining for fear of compromising
his stewardship of the university. The intifada of August 1929 changed
his mind. He chose his address opening the new academic year "to
express before you [faculty and students] my position with regard to
the basic problem of the shared lives in the land which is holy to two
nations, Arabs and Jews, and to three religions, Judaism, Christianity,
and Islam." Of necessity "ways must be found—and I think that none
of us has been sufficiently diligent in this respect—to share life and
work in the cultural, economic, social, political, and all other senses."
But any such efforts would be "in vain" should the Jewish National
Home have no other backing than the "bayonets of some Empire."

In a letter to Weizmann on September 7, 1929, Magnes implied that
official Zionism was increasingly open to the political logic of
Jabotinsky, as opposed to that of the internal critics. This "imperialist, military, and political policy is based upon mass immigration . . .
and the creation (forcibly if necessary) of a Jewish majority, no matter
how much this oppresses the Arabs . . . or deprives them of their
rights." In following such a course, he insisted, "the end always
justifies the means." A Jewish Home "built upon bayonets and
oppression is not worth having, even if it succeeds, whereas the very
attempt to build it up peacefully, cooperatively, with understanding,
education, and good will is worth a great deal, even though the

attempt should fail." The question was, "do we want to conquer Palestine now as Joshua did in his day—with fire and sword?" The alternative was to take "cognizance of Jewish religious development since Joshua—our Prophets, Psalmists, and Rabbis, and repeat the words: 'Not by might, and not by violence, but by my spirit, saith the Lord.'" A week later, Magnes wrote to the prominent non-Zionist American banker, Felix Warburg, that "unless the whole aim of Zionism is changed . . . there will never be peace" in the Holy Land. Since Palestine "does not belong to the Arabs, nor to Judaism or Christianity or Islam . . . nothing there is possible unless Jews and Arabs work together."

Magnes continued to profess his belief that the "eternal and far flung" Jewish people could survive without a state in Palestine, convinced as he was of the necessity and vitality of the diaspora. The last thing the Israelites needed, he insisted, was a "normal nation like any other" in Palestine—Herzl's notion—one that could not be born or survive except by the use of force, at inordinate human cost, for want of an agreement with the Arab peoples beyond its borders. That fall, Magnes set about developing the idea of binationalism for a pluralistic civil and political society. What Brit Shalom had only adumbrated, Magnes began to fill in: parity between the two na- tions—Jewish and Arab—would be embodied in a bicameral system with a lower house elected by popular vote and an upper house divided, equally, by nationality. Although the idea was instantly attacked for being naive and impractical, it has persevered against wind and tide.

The first intifada had jolted Ruppin, too, but he responded by veering away from the internal critics. Pessimistic about prospects for Arab–Jewish understanding, he moved closer to the General Zionists, who were more than ever convinced that, demographically, time was against the Yishuv. But his seasoned sense of the centrality and urgency of the Arab Question was un-dulled. He stuck to his operating premise: the objective of Zionism—"to bring the Jews as a second nation into a country which is already settled by a nation—and achieve this by peaceful means"—was without precedent in history. No nation had ever before "freely agree[d]" to another nation's barging in to demand "full equality of rights and national autonomy at its side." Having "initially overlooked the existence of the Arabs," Zionism had gone on to minimize the "immense difficulties" of reconciling conflicts over land acquisitions, immigration quotas, and wage inequalities. Since "all the Palestinian Arabs are opposed to Zionism," it would be difficult to "convince them with logical arguments that our interests correspond with theirs." Ruppin even expressed the fear that, with "most of the Arabs being illiterate, the masses will follow a few leaders . . . who will exploit their religious and national fanaticism against the Zionists."

It was too late now to "find a formula" likely to meet the vital interests of both Jews and Arabs. With the "political position of the Arabs very much strengthened," they were "much less inclined to make concessions today than 10 years ago." At best, Ruppin concluded dispassionately, the Arabs were willing to give the Jews "minority rights . . . in an Arab state, following the pattern of minority rights in Eastern Europe," as yet untested. In any case, to make the "fate of the Jewish minority in Palestine . . . dependent on the good will of the Arab majority holding the reins of government . . . would certainly not satisfy the Jews of Eastern Europe, who are the majority of the Zionists."

Whereas Ruppin, like Buber and Magnes, remained a tried and true Zionist, Hans Kohn, a founding member of Brit Shalom and one of Buber's disciples, returned to the diaspora and renounced the faith. For him, the disturbances of August were "eye-opening," calling for a reappraisal of "the moral and spiritual foundations of Zionism" and a search for a "new solution" to the Arab Question. As an early student of comparative nationalism, Kohn scorned the official Zionist policy of "portraying the Arab national movement . . . as the wanton agitation of a few big landowners." Of late, all too often "the most reactionary imperialist press in England and France [has] portrayed the national movements in India, Egypt, and Iraq in a similar fashion—in short, wherever the national movements of oppressed peoples threaten the interests of the colonial power." There was no denying that "the Arabs attacked us," but their "barbaric acts" were, without doubt, "characteristic of a colonial revolt."

Rather than feign victimhood, Zionists and Jews should delve down into the "deeper causes." During the twelve years since the Balfour Declaration, Zionists had not "made a single serious attempt to secure the consent of the indigenous people by way of negotiation" or concrete "constitutional proposals." Instead, they had "relied exclusively on Great Britain's military power." With the Arab national movement growing stronger by the day, it would become harder "to reach an agreement." In Kohn's judgment, even "tens of thousands" of additional immigrants could not prevail. A growing Yishuv could naturally "hold Palestine . . . for a long time." But to do so, it would have to "rely first on British aid," and then ever more on "our own bayonets."

*   *   *

The reactions of Freud and Einstein to the events of 1929 typified the discomfort of pro-Zionist, non-Jewish Jews in the diaspora with the rise of ultra-nationalism and religious fundamentalism in the Yishuv. Following the disorders, the Keren Hayesod (the overseas fundraising arm of the World Zionist Organization) called on eminent Jews to write letters in support of the Jewish claim to unfettered control over the Wailing Wall. Freud begged off. On February 26, 1930, he wrote to the Fund's Viennese representative: "Even under the critical circumstances of the moment," and given his "sober judgment of Zionism," he could not issue a statement that "to influence the multitude . . . would have to be resounding and enthusiastic." He "sympathized" with Zionism's "aspirations" and was also "proud of our university in Jerusalem" and of the "success of our settlements." But he did "not think that Palestine could ever become a Jewish state," in part because "the Christian and Islamic worlds" would never accept to "have their holy places under Jewish control." It "would have been more reasonable to establish a Jewish fatherland in a historically less encumbered land," though he realized that "such a rational viewpoint would never have fired either the enthusiasm of the masses or the support of the wealthy." He "concede[d], with sorrow, that the unrealistic fanaticism of our 'national comrades' [was] partly responsible for the awakening of Arab distrust." He "[could] not muster any sympathy whatever for a misguided piety that turns a piece of Herod's Wall into a national relic, thereby hurting the feelings of the natives."

The same day, Freud repeated his train of thought in a letter to Einstein. Answering the request in similar terms, Einstein conceived "the essential nature of Judaism [to be] at odds with the idea of a Jewish state with borders, an army, and a measure of temporal power no matter how sparse." Concurrently, he wrote to Weizmann that, should Zionism "be unable to find a way to honest cooperation and honest pacts with Arabs, we shall have learned nothing from our 2,000 years of suffering and will deserve our fate." A straight line runs from this to his affirmation, in 1938, that he would "much rather see reasonable agreement with the Arabs on the basis of living together in peace than the creation of a Jewish state." He feared the "inner damage to Judaism . . . especially from the development of a narrow nationalism in our ranks."

Both Freud and Einstein were troubled by the prospect that Zionism would entail the Jews', in the words of Veblen, "withdrawing . . . within the insulating frontiers of the Holy Land," thereby losing the advantages of "hybridization." While both retained a strong Jewish identification, intellectually they had "escaped from their cultural

environment" to become men of "divided allegiance," released "from
the dead hand of conventional finality." Writing his essay in 1918, for
all one knows Veblen had Freud and Einstein in mind:

> When and in so far as the Jewish people . . . *turn inward on
> themselves*, their prospective contribution to the world's intellec-
> tual output should, in the light of the historical evidence, fairly be
> expected to take on the complexion of Talmudic lore, rather than
> that character of free-swung skeptical initiative which their rene-
> gades habitually infused into the pursuit of the modern sciences
> abroad.

Freud and Einstein were of the party of Ahad Haam, Buber, and
Magnes in their advocacy of an open cultural–spiritual home in
Palestine. They apprehended lucidly all the perils—as brought into
the open by the first intifada of 1929—of the quest for a territorial–
political state, contested by the Arab world, and in a land possessed by
indigenous Arabs.

3

GATHERING STORMS

The first intifada served to actualize the Arab Question: thereafter there was no ignoring, hiding, obfuscating, or evading it. The seismic eruption of mutual distrust and fear ended in a great divide. The Yishuv and its supporters faced the coming struggle with a triumphalist fervor and sovereign self-confidence; Palestinian Arabs and the Arab–Muslim world seethed with frustration and tasted gall.

The rebellion served to make more dauntless the resolve of Zionists everywhere, and validated, in particular, Jabotinsky's core precepts. The dissipation of what little there had been of a moral concern for the Arab Other was reflected in a broad-scale attack on Brit Shalom. Its associates were pilloried for pinning much of the blame for the recent violence on the Jews, for their naïve political grasp of the Arab world, and for an unconscionable disregard for the plight of eastern European Jews. Implied in this censure was the ultimate condemnation: in criticizing Jews more than Arabs, Brit Shalom was a de facto traitor, aiding and abetting the enemy by the impious questioning of Zionism's official ideology and course of action.

The free-spoken dissidents were also upbraided for their failure to bring forward credible interlocutors on the other side. Although there were few conciliators among the Palestinian Arabs, it is doubtful they were any less numerous and influential than their Zionist counterparts. Stentorian hardliners in both camps claimed that all efforts to reach out to open-minded and moderate respondents were sabotaged by the other side, thereby confirming the self-fulfilling prophecy of bad faith and enmity. The Jewish Agency was not inclined to meet the native elite any part of the way, as the internal critics kept urging. Haim Kalvarisky—an agronomist, head of the Arab Department of the Zionist Executive in Jerusalem, and close to Brit Shalom—judged that on those rare occasions when Zionist officials "stretched out the hand [they] withdrew it as soon as the other party expressed a willingness to act," confounding the Arab doves. The impasse was "not the fault of the other party only . . . 'if any one tell thee, I have striven and have not found, then believe him not.' " In this same key, Arlosoroff, mysteriously assassinated in 1933, maintained that with "no [Arab] policy" to speak of, official Zionism remained guided mostly by "vague . . . and abstract generalities" at a time when Arab public opinion was starting to coalesce.

In this tense atmosphere, the spokesmen for Brit Shalom felt it necessary to reaffirm, in the words of Buber, that "we are all good Zionists" before laying out their new program, which consisted mainly of these two tenets: Jewish immigrants should not exceed half of the Arab population, and land purchases should be kept within reason. In exchange for such a self-limitation, the appeasers asked the Arabs to agree to a shared sovereignty. Brit Shalom envisaged a solid bargain, not a sellout. It also urged reducing the dependence of tomorrow's binational Palestine, along with its immediate neighbors, on any imperial power.

In the early 1930s, and following several prominent defections, Brit Shalom began to dissolve. The severest blow was Ruppin's renunciation of binationalism to devote himself to helping to settle the more than 200,000 immigrants of the fifth *aliyah* (1933–9), overwhelmingly from Poland and Germany. He did so with open eyes. On April 25, 1936, just weeks before the second intifada, he acknowledged that, like it or not, "we shall live in a state of perpetual war with the Arabs, and there will be no avoiding casualties."

Brit Shalom never had more than 200 members, nor did *Sheifotenu* ever reach many more readers. Even so, by default and unwittingly, this sect of binationalists, both in the Yishuv and the diaspora, became the conscience of Zionism. Its irreproachable voices continued to call attention to the antinomies of Zionist nationalism and the moral values of Judaism and the Enlightenment as they bore on the matter of violence and the Other.

Although these conscientious objectors were on the whole of liberal-democratic persuasion, after the first intifada and with the premature dissolution of Brit Shalom and *Sheifotenu*, they developed an elective affinity for the Social Democratic and Marxist left, notably for the center-left labor party, Mapai, and the class-driven Hashomer Hatzair, including their respective kibbutzim. And to a large extent the composite left endorsed the internal critics' critique of the Zionist right. The pull of Mapai, representing most wage-earning workers, became particularly strong once it became the dominant political force in the Yishuv, during the 1930s, politically outpacing Hashomer Hatzair and the Communist Party, whose ideological aura gave them considerable influence but little power.

After 1929 the fervently colonizing Hashomer Hatzair, marrying Jewish nationalism to utopian Marxism, became the most emphatic champion of binationalism. But it broke new ground by seeking social and political parity between Jews and Arabs. Under the motto "a socialist binational society," Hashomer Hatzair advocated proceeding simultaneously on both fronts in both communities, including the Arab–Muslim world beyond Palestine. This would mean promoting the cooperation, even solidarity, between "the working Jewish people and the working Arab people," perhaps firstly by organizing a binational Histadrut, or trade union. Hashomer Hatzair stressed the need to constrain the small, reactionary "exploiting class" of an essentially feudal society that "runs . . . the Arab national movement" in its own "interests."

Committed to providing a refuge for the mass of Eastern European Jews, the heart of its movement, Hashomer Hatzair rejected the elitist notion of a spiritual–cultural center in Palestine. Rather than a limited Zionism, it favored a large-scale Jewish immigration into a socialist society with "complete equality" between the two peoples. While the respective blueprints of Brit Shalom and Hashomer Hatzair remained general, they both stood out for reflecting in broad daylight upon the magnitude and gravity of the Arab Question.

The degradation of Arab–Zionist relations in 1929 served to shock both sides into an attempt at conciliation and cooperation. Whatever their differences, they had vulnerability in common, and a shared suspicion of the Mandatory power's scepter. In October the Mufti, though skeptical of how much political leverage the binationalists actually had, told a British intermediary that he was inclined to accept a Jewish National Home of the sort previously envisaged by Magnes, which would respect the integrity of Arab Palestine. Magnes himself proposed that Arabs and Jews each have such a home in the Holy Land. Neither community would lord it over the other, while both jointly prepared the ground for a confederation on the Swiss or Canadian model that would eventually forge a common national identity.

This was the moment when Ben-Gurion gave up on the idea of improving the economic and social condition of the Palestinian Arabs with the intention of making them forget about their "political rights" and agree to become "strangers in their own land." The conflict would be political, not socio-economic. He embraced the idea of two autonomous cantons, but without giving thought to the development of common institutions. For the time being, Britain would keep control of the army, police, and external relations. His political star rising, Ben-Gurion also proposed to step up immigration, the elixir of Zionism, with the final goal a clear Jewish majority. He refused to think in terms of equality or parity, and told Magnes he was not prepared "to sacrifice immigration for peace." Palestine had an altogether "different meaning" for the Jews, who had no other refuge, than for the Arab people, which "possesses many countries whose area in Asia alone is one third that of Europe," with a mere fraction of Europe's population. For that reason, "the existence of a Jewish nation with a population of several million in Palestine would not endanger the culture, independence, or existence of the Arab nation." But the Arabs of Palestine? Ben-Gurion's position spoke of Revisionism, with the eventual transfer or expulsion of the Palestinian Arab majority the unspoken subtext.

For the time being, however, Ben-Gurion rallied to the formula that Weizmann and the Jewish Agency kept putting forth, starting in December 1929: although the Jews neither "contemplated" nor "desired" political domination in Palestine, they were resolved not to be dominated by the Arabs. In 1934, a year before becoming head of the Jewish Agency and the Zionist Executive in Palestine, he declared that "not tactics" but "political reality" warranted the principle of mutual "nondomination."

Privately, Ben-Gurion held fast to his conviction: with the irrepressible growth of the Yishuv, the formula would have to be reconsidered. The "whole question of an agreement" might founder less because of intensifying "bitterness and hatred . . . than because of the basic political contradictions between ourselves and the Arabs, primarily on the question of immigration." Peace was "vital," of course, and it was "not possible to build up a country in a situation of permanent war." But the end was the "complete and absolute fulfillment of Zionism," with peace only a means to it. Two types of agreement could be contemplated: "an all-inclusive agreement on the final aim; and a temporary agreement." In mid 1936, at the onset of the second intifada, Ben-Gurion insisted that, whereas it was not "absolutely impossible to reach a temporary agreement. . . a comprehensive agreement was out of the question." The Arabs would not "accept a Jewish Palestine" until overcome by "despair" born of their failing resistance and appreciation of "our growth in the country." There is no missing the similarity of his reasoning to Jabotinsky's "iron wall" argument. And the Revisionists, having overtaken the centrist General Zionists, had become, after Mapai, the second-strongest political force in the Yishuv.

*   *   *

From the early 1930s onwards, world history once again broke in violently upon the question of Palestine. With the growing insecurity and endangerment of the Jews in Central and East-Central Europe the Zionists ratcheted up pressure on the British to open wide the gates of immigration to the Holy Land: the Zionist executive wanted a figure of 60,000 a year, Weizmann 40,000, and Magnes 30,000. Even this last seemed out of all bounds to the Arabs in Palestine and the greater Middle East. They were incensed to be asked—that is, forced—to pay for Christian Europe's latest eruption of Judeophobia and anti-Judaism in the form of political and racial anti-Semitism, especially with so many countries closing their doors to refugees. In reaction, the leaders of the Palestinian Arabs called more forcefully for a complete halt to immigration and land sales. London was caught in the middle with scant room to maneuver, particularly given its growing military and diplomatic predicament under Europe's darkening skies.

For Zionists and Palestinian Arabs, immigration became more than ever the gravamen. During the first decade of the Mandate (1922–32), 125,000 Jews settled in Palestine; during the second decade, 250,000 more. On the eve of the Second World War, Jews in the Holy Land approached half a million. The fifth *aliyah*, from 1929 to 1939, was the largest since the birth of modern Zionism. In both 1935 and 1936 the number of immigrants exceeded 60,000 per year, breaking all records. A Jewish majority, or at least parity, in Palestine seemed possible within ten years. Between the wars the Arab population increased from about 700,000 to 1,100,000.

The newcomers raised the urban profile of the Yishuv and deepened the estrangement between the dynamic cities and the static countryside. During the 1930s the population of Tel Aviv more than tripled, from 45,000 to 165,000. Under the transfer agreement with the Nazi regime, between 1933 and 1939 some 50,000 German Jews, allowed to leave with only limited monies, arrived in Palestine. Unlike so many Eastern European Jews, they took residence in the three major cities. The decade also saw the establishment of some 130 rural settlements, including fifty kibbutzim, outposts of modern farming in a land of ancestral agriculture.

While the imminent Judeocide was still inconceivable, leading Zionists actually considered the rise of National Socialism in Germany and of fascism in East-Central Europe potentially helpful to their cause. Although Ben-Gurion hoped for the quick defeat of Hitler, he did not hesitate to exploit the Nazi menace "for the good of Palestine." Until after the fall of France in June 1940, he put the continuing growth of the Yishuv ahead of the rescue of Europe's endangered

Jews: their latest plight should be used as "a political force and lever to speed up" the establishment of the "Hebrew nation in its land." He and his associates worried that Jews would be perceived as refugees deserving asylum the world over, thus easing pressure on the Mandatory Power, which was already resolved to virtually close the Holy Land to immigration. Even after Kristallnacht, on November 9, 1938, when Neville Chamberlain offered a refuge for Jewish children in England, Ben-Gurion confided that, given the choice between saving "all the Jewish children of Germany [and Austria] by sending them to England" and saving "only half of them by taking them to Palestine," he would opt for the latter. Settlement of the refugees elsewhere would harm the Yishuv, costing it the financial support of Jewish organizations that was Zionism's mainstay.

Until the outbreak of war, the flux of immigrants continued largely unabated, although the second intifada of 1936–9 gave some second thoughts. According to Lloyd George's memoirs, cited by Weizmann, when the Imperial War Cabinet acceded to the Balfour Declaration, it did not preclude the prospect that, should the Jews "become a definite majority of the inhabitants, then Palestine would thus become a Jewish Commonwealth." The "notion that Jewish immigration would have to be artificially restricted in order that the Jews should be a permanent minority never entered the head of anyone engaged in framing the policy." In 1929, when objecting to the suggested restrictions in the Shaw and Passfield reports, Weizmann had asserted, as we have seen, that it should be clear to anyone that "the one hundred and seventy thousand [Jews now in Palestine] are merely the vanguard." In 1935, by which time the "annual immigration figure [had] passed the sixty thousand mark," he and his associates "thought that if this would only continue another few years we would be past the difficulties which have given us most trouble." As we will see, this surge was interrupted in 1938–9. But already the intention was clear, and it coincided with the rising fears of the Palestinian Arabs.

They and the Arab world at large could hardly have been expected to look the other way, or to have resigned themselves to being disregarded or cowed. Like the Zionists, their instinct was to exploit international rivalries to advance their cause and interest. They would go to all lengths to hold back the flood of Jewish immigrants. And for the most part, this resolve was driven by anti-Zionism rather than anti-Judaism or anti-Semitism.

The first intifada of 1928–9 and the second of 1936–9 were similar in dynamics and purpose, though different in scale and intensity. During the years separating the two, the rise in immigrants stimulated Palestinian Arab resistance. By the mid 1930s the Yishuv was a community of 400,000, resting on solid institutional foundations. On Britain's sufferance, over 120,000 Jewish newcomers disembarked in the Holy Land in 1935–6, a time of growing economic malaise and anti-colonial nationalism throughout most of the non-Western world. When Palestinian Arab notables raised their voices against this swelling tide, they were ignored.

On April 15, 1936, a band of Arabs attacked a bus on the road between Jaffa and Tel Aviv, killing several Jews and robbing several passengers, most of them non-Jewish. This incident touched off a cycle of violence in these twin coastal cities, leaving about twenty dead, sixteen of them Jewish, and a total of some 150 wounded in both camps. The frenzy spread, escalating into the largest colonial uprising in the British empire between the two world wars. General Sir Arthur Wauchope, the High Commissioner, declared a state of emergency and requested urgent military reinforcements.

By April 25 the Palestinian governing class had set up an Arab Higher Committee, presided over by Haj Amin al-Husseini, the Grand Mufti. Its membership was formed mainly by the heads of the six major political parties that had begun to supersede the clan-like factions. This Committee, which meant to control and direct the formless Arab rebellion, called for the end of immigration, the prohibition of land sales, and the right of self-government for Arab Palestine. To advance these aims, it proclaimed countrywide strikes and boycotts, and looked to street demonstrations and tax protests to incite further participation in civil disobedience and political resistance.

The effort lasted six months, and was marked by acts of violence. Nearly eighty Jews were killed, mostly in cities but also on open roads; there were several attacks on agricultural settlements as well. These armed raids were better planned and executed than those of 1929, but the Yishuv was also better prepared. The irregulars of the Hagana, a conglomerate of clandestine paramilitary militias, were well-trained and disciplined, and intermittently collaborated with the British security forces. Strategically located kibbutzim were turned into military outposts primed for self-defense.

In the mid 1930s Palestine was still a largely feudal society, with an agrarian economy dominated by a handful of big landowners in uneasy symbiosis with a small peasantry, the Mandate's main social formation. Among the former, many of them eager to sell land to the Zionists, the Husseini and the Nashashibi families continued to loom large, and to feud with one another. The political base of the Husseini clan was rural and clerical; the Nashashibi reached out to the urban, upper-middle class of the Mediterranean littoral, with whom it shared misgivings about contemporary nationalism's religious propensity, as practiced in the holy cities. The intifada of 1936–9, then, unlike the first, was at once a nationalist rebellion and a war between brothers.

The newly formed Arab Higher Committee—the permanent executive organization representing the major Palestinian groups—was split between radicals, led by the Mufti, Amin al-Husseini, and moderates opposed to violence. This division informed the internecine clashes between and within partisan bands that eventually accounted for more than half of all Arab casualties. Overall, however, most of the insurgents were, once again, "primitive rebels" bound together more by ancient dreams and grievances than by contemporary calls for anti-Zionist national liberation and religious reawakening. Compared with 1929, the uprising—though still part-jacquerie—was more sophisticated, with the involvement of an enlarged stratum of educated city dwellers. This emergent middle class was the probable source of the agents who, hearkening to the Committee, politicized the rebellion. Apprehensive about the groundswell, in October 1936 the sovereigns of Iraq, Transjordan, and Saudi Arabia—who, like the Nashashibi, were troubled by the Mufti— prevailed on the Committee to suspend the second intifada and trusted "our good friend Great Britain" to intercede.

As early as mid May 1936, London had intimated that, once order was restored, Stanley Baldwin's National Government would appoint a royal commission to investigate "the causes of unrest and alleged grievances of Arabs or of Jews." This commission, chaired by Lord Robert Peel, was formed in August, and repaired to Palestine between mid November 1936 and mid January 1937 to hold hearings and collect written evidence. Its findings and recommendations, published that July, challenged the assumption that "some measure of compromise or reconciliation between the races can [still] be expected, and that on vital issues some Arabs [can] be found to vote with Jews and some Jews to vote with Arabs." The Mandate was past use, "the aspirations of the Jews and Arabs [having become] mutually contradictory," making their coexistence problematic, if not impossible. Not that the Mandate had failed in all respects: "Broadly speaking the Arabs had benefited by way of example from the development of the country owing to Jewish immigration." Whatever these benefits, however, rather than their having had a "conciliatory effect," they had contributed to the "deterioration of the political situation." The Peel Report was plainspoken: "In short, the problem is a political one."

Under the circumstances, His Majesty's commissioners urged abandoning the search for parity, cantonization, and other variants of binationalism in a unitary Palestine, in favor of its partition into two separate, if uneven states. The Arabs would get the center of the country as far as the Jordan River (today's West Bank), the southern confines to the strip along the Mediterranean coast, and the Negev, or a total of close to 80 per cent of the land (20,000 square kilometers, or 7,722 square miles). The Jewish realm would consist of the rest—the coastal plain from south of Rehovot to Acre, the valley of Jezreel, and eastern Galilee (5,000 square kilometers, or 1,930 square miles). For the time being, Great Britain would retain control over Jerusalem and its environs, including Bethlehem, Ramla, and Lod, and a narrow corridor running to the coast at Jaffa. To make the two projected states more homogeneous ethnically, the report suggested an exchange of populations: the transfer of some 1,250 Jews out of the Arab state and of some 225,000 Arabs out of the Jewish state, especially out of Galilee. Until this ground plan could be considered, Britain would limit Jewish immigration to a "political high" of 15,000 annually.

The Peel Report, especially its rationale and proposal for partition, struck Zionists of all persuasions like a bolt from the blue. Because of its enormous implications for the future, it sparked a heated and wide-ranging debate, shaped by two concerns: the gathering storm in Europe, with its devastating consequences for the Jews, and the Palestinian Arab resistance, whose import for the Yishuv could no longer be dismissed. Religious Zionists bound to the Torah and Talmud, notably Mizrachim, inveighed against partition as flouting God's prophetic promise of the Jewish people's return to the Kingdom of Solomon or the Land of Jacob and Abraham—which, though it was geographically ill-defined, they proclaimed one and indivisible. This fundamentalist refusal carried little weight compared with the Revisionist excoriation of the proposal for leaving the lion's share of Palestine to the indigenous Arabs. Jabotinsky was particularly galled, since he considered the Peel Report a reiteration of the first partition in 1922, when Churchill had severed 90,000 square kilometers, or 34,750 square miles, east of the Jordan River from the Mandate to re-found the Hashemite Kingdom. He stuck to his position that "the River Jordan does not delineate the frontier of Palestine but flows through its center." With the rising friend–enemy dissociation between Jews and Arabs, he more than ever trusted in the sword, not god, to secure Eretz Israel. Presently the Revisionists turned to subversion and to running immigrants into Palestine—especially from Eastern Europe. But Jabotinsky exercised caution, mindful that in the short term there was no alternative to making the best of the exigent relationship with perfidious Albion.

Although deeply influenced by Revisionist precepts, the official leadership, supported by General Zionists and Mapai, reacted prudently but with firmness to the Report. When Weizmann had testified before the Peel Commission in Jerusalem in November 1936, he had begun by calling attention to the "deterioration of Jewish life in Central and Eastern Europe," and to the division of the world between "places where [Jews] cannot live and places where they may not enter." To counter any notion that the Balfour Declaration was "vague" and merely a "wartime expediency," he cited Lord Robert Cecil's one-time formula to capture its presumed intent: "Arabia for the Arabs, Judea for the Jews, Armenia for the Armenians." But Weizmann went on to say, wryly, that although he knew "that God [had] promised Palestine to the children of Israel, [he did] not know what boundaries He [had] set." Even so, Zionism's elder statesman reckoned the borderlines "were wider than the ones now proposed, and may have included Trans-Jordan": having "forgone the eastern part," the Jewish people were now being "asked to forgo some of the western parts" as well.

Following the publication of the Peel Report, when Weizmann addressed the future Jewish National Home's Mandate and its attendant intraterritorial conflict, whatever its frontiers, he was brazen. In a letter to a high British official, before the resumption of the second intifada, he vilified the Arab leaders for running a "terrorist campaign . . . from their hiding places . . . for the liquidation of the Mandate and for Jewish acceptance of a minority status." The Jews were "not going to Palestine to become, in their ancient home, 'Arabs of the Mosaic Faith' or to exchange their German or Polish ghetto for an Arab one." Zionists were not making the "supreme effort" in Palestine "for the purpose of subjecting the Jewish people, which still stands in the front rank of civilization, to the rule of a set of unscrupulous Levantine politicians."

As for Ben-Gurion, whose voice carried at least as far as Weizmann's, he celebrated the partition as an astonishing advance for a movement that had started from nothing forty years before: it would mean the instant foundation and recognition of a sovereign Jewish state invested with the power to regulate immigration without British or Arab interference. Brought face-to-face with another uprising, Ben-Gurion conceded that the Palestinian Arabs were not fearful of "losing land, but of losing [their] homeland"; that "no government in the world can prevent individual terror . . . when a people is fighting for its land"; that it was not "easy to suppress a popular movement strictly by the use of force"; and that, were he "an Arab with a nationalist political consciousness [he] would rise up against an immigration likely . . . to hand the country and its Arab inhabitants over to Jewish rule." But he would not allow empathy to cloud his discernment of Peel's proposal. Like so many others across the political spectrum, he worried about the military and economic viability of the proffered mini-state, set in a hostile geopolitical environment. Still, Ben-Gurion was confident its borders, like all borders, could be changed, and that future generations could be trusted to extend them.

So, at the urging of Weizmann and Ben-Gurion, the Jewish Agency and the Zionist Congress of August 1937, by a vote of 299 to 160, accepted Peel's blueprint. In the course of it, Ben-Gurion extrapolated from the idea of population transfer: Arabs in strategic areas within the National Home could be removed in large numbers to neighboring and nearby countries, notably Transjordan and Iraq. Within less than a year, and following Herzl and Jabotinsky, he repeated his support for "compulsory transfers," which he eventually insisted had "nothing immoral about them."

With the idea of partition twice approved, the Jewish Agency set up several committees to plan its implementation. Ben-Gurion, Ruppin, Moshe Sharett (head of the Jewish Agency's Political Department), and Ussishkin participated, as well as leading economists and land experts, among them Alfred Bonné, Abraham Granovsky, Dov Joseph, and Joseph Weitz. All served on the pivotal "Committee for the Transfer of Population," working behind closed doors from mid November through mid December 1937. Its charge was to gather data about the Palestinian Arabs within the state for Jews delineated by the Peel Report, with an eye to their voluntary or compulsory "resettlement." To be considered, too, were their economic prospects—especially in Transjordan, but also in Syria—and a reasonable timeframe (and with what combination of carrot and stick) for carrying out the transfer to neighboring countries. Ultimately they concluded that the diminutive *Judenstaat* would not be viable with a large Arab population, which would be a security risk and occupy land needed to settle and feed untold thousands of future immigrants. More than 225,000 Arabs, as specified by the Peel Report, would have to be removed somehow. The Transfer Committee agreed that, since the Palestinian Arabs were not about to leave voluntarily and the Arab states were unlikely to take them in, diplomatic pressure and military force would be required. Only Britain, perhaps with international support, could accomplish such a feat, but this was altogether improbable. Weitz, Ruppin's successor as head of settlement at the Jewish Agency, later concluded that there was "no room for both peoples together in this country." There was no solution other than "a Palestine, at least Western Palestine (west of the Jordan river), without Arabs." Nor was there another way "than to transfer the Arabs from here to the neighboring countries, to transfer all of them."

Whereas, broadly speaking, the Zionists responded to Peel with deliberation and made a virtue of necessity, the Arabs were enraged. They rejected outright the very idea of what they considered a severe amputation of their homeland, whose population was overwhelmingly Arab–Muslim. Colonial–imperialist legerdemain once again benefited the Zionists. What is more, since the Palestinian Arab political class closely monitored the running debates, it had good reason to suppose that the Zionist leaders would consider their misbegotten state a staging area for the investment of the whole of Palestine.

The second intifada resumed in the fall of 1937 and continued through mid 1939, with the peak of violence during the second half of 1938. Aimed against both the Mandatory power and the Yishuv, this second phase of the second Arab eruption, unlike its first, was broad-based and widespread. The British broke up the Arab Higher Committee and arrested certain of its nationalist leaders. The Grand Mufti hastened to Syria. Although lacking central direction and inner cohesion, the rebellion persisted, and took a far heavier toll than the 1936 overture: 400 Jews lost their lives, out of a total of approximately 500 for the entire second intifada. Most Arab losses, totaling between 4,000 and 6,000, were likewise in this second phase. Many were killed by Britain's reinforced military and police forces, though fratricide too did its fell work. Some 5,500 Arabs were arrested. Both Jews and Arabs suffered considerable material damage, beyond the 2,000 houses the British leveled in Arab towns, villages, and neighborhoods for their allegedly serving as rebel strongholds or hideouts. Some 120 English soldiers and policemen also lost their lives.

Some of the hit-and-run attacks on Jews were not just deadly but savage, feeding the underlying prejudgment that Arab culture and the Muslim religion were intrinsically violent and barbarian. As Weizmann expressed it: "on the one side the development of the forces of destruction and of the desert; on the other the resolute forces of civilization and development." In this timeless struggle, "we shall not give ground." And, loyal to his Western Manichean outlook, he affirmed the complete innocence of the Yishuv. He rejected out of

hand British intimations that the Jews shared responsibility for the
insurrection. He was all too familiar with the "procedure of
blaming . . . the victims . . . after pogroms in czarist Russia [but]
never expected to see it adopted by a British Administration." Besides,
in defending themselves "in the face of the utmost provocation," the
Jews "resolutely followed the policy of *Havlagah*, or self-restraint." In
so doing, Weizmann wrote in a letter to the high commissioner, they
had performed "one of the great moral political acts of modern
times."

There were bursts of savagery on both sides; civil war was ever thus.
This was the moment when the Irgun, the Revisionists' paramilitary
arm, mounted its first terrorist attacks: in July 1938 its partisans set off
a bomb killing twenty Arabs in an open-air market in Haifa. Another
explosion soon followed, making a total of some forty victims.

It is worth recalling that the second intifada coincided with the
coming of the Second World War, the purges in Soviet Russia, the
Civil Disobedience Movement in India, and the growth of militarism
in Nazi Germany and Imperial Japan. Seen in a "larger setting," the
situation in Palestine was also, according to Weizmann, "the mirror of
[the Civil War] in Spain, at the other end of the Mediterranean, where
England and France 'persisted in maintaining that there was no
connection' between the rebels and the Axis powers." Enlisting such
questionable analogies to serve his cause, he told William Ormsby-
Gore, Britain's colonial secretary, that the fundamentally "crude"
Arab national movement, which was "trying to work up hatred of the
British and the Jews . . . looked to Mussolini and Hitler as its heroes,
and was supported by Italian money."

During discussions of the Peel Report it became apparent that these
universal troubles affected the actions and reactions of the three major
actors in the Holy Land. The British government embraced partition
as the surest way out of the Palestine quagmire. In January 1938 it
appointed a commission, chaired by Sir John Woodhead, to fix precise
borders for two independent states and devise a means for their
separation. As the taskforce worked, the second intifada reached
its peak, the Third Reich annexed Austria, and the fate of Czechoslovakia was sealed at Munich. The Woodhead Commission published its report on November 9, hours before Kristallnacht. The
historical season was not propitious for mutual understanding and
compromise.

The Woodhead Commission reported back that there was no
breaching the gap between the two camps, making partition impracticable. In response, Malcolm MacDonald, Ormsby-Gore's successor

at the Colonial Office, summoned Zionist and Arab representatives to a roundtable conference in London, slated for February 1939. The aim was to lower tensions and break the impasse by updating the Mandate delineated in Churchill's White Paper of 1922. The initiative was stillborn: the Arabs would not sit at the same table with the Zionists; the Zionists would not deal with the representatives of the five neighboring Arab countries who were part of the Arab delegation. The Zionists demanded all but unrestricted immigration and land purchases; the Arabs would have none of it.

In 1915–17 Britain had made inconsistent commitments to Arabs and Jews in the midst of a war that became increasingly taxing, and erosive of the Europe-centered imperialist order. By 1938–9, with Germany invading Czechoslovakia and Poland, His Majesty's Government prepared to engage in another round of hedging, in anticipation of a second war that would probably strain its forces even more. Once again, and notwithstanding their greater gravity, Jewish interests and aspirations were secondary; nor did Jew or gentile as yet feel necessity's sharp pinch. Besides, no matter how intense the plight of the Jews in Palestine—and the diaspora—they had no choice but to cast their lot with London.

The Arab–Muslim world did have a choice. Middle Eastern oil was the lifeblood of Britain's economic power, and the Suez Canal was its lifeline to India, which encompassed a large Muslim community. The political elites of this critical region were of course animated by anti-imperialist nationalism. And after the duplicity of the McMahon–Hussein correspondence, Sykes–Picot, and the Balfour Declaration, they were cynical about British promises. The Arabs assumed that the threat of their defection to the Axis, eventually carried out by the Grand Mufti of Jerusalem and by India's left-nationalist Subhas Chandra Bose, would count even more than the Ottoman empire's support of the Central Powers during the Great War.

The Zionists denounced any Arab approach to the Axis and any British conciliation of the Arabs as anti-Semitic. In the Zionist logic, although London stopped appeasing Nazi Germany after the fall of Czechoslovakia and the guarantee to Poland, it continued to placate the Arabs at the expense of the Yishuv. Predictably, with its security forces strained in the colonial realm and its armed forces deficient for war on the continent, Great Britain, in pursuit of national and imperial interests, decided to continue the Mandate rather than take on the forbidding task of implementing and enforcing a two-state solution in Palestine.

Britain's third and final White Paper on Palestine was issued on May 17, 1939, and remained in force until the end of the Mandate nine years later. Its purpose was to chart a new course following the rejection of partition by the Woodhead Commission and the failure of the London roundtable. After twenty-two years, London acknowledged "the ambiguity of certain expressions in the Mandate, such as the expression 'a national home for the Jewish people.'" Since "the resulting uncertainty as to the objectives of policy [was] a fundamental cause of unrest and hostility between Arabs and Jews," there was an urgent need for "a clear definition of policy and objectives." Although the Balfour Declaration, as "embodied" in the Mandate, did not "preclude . . . an ultimate Jewish State," it did not intend "Palestine to be converted into a Jewish State against the will of the Arab population of the country." Britain at no time "contemplated . . . the disappearance or the subordination of the Arabic population, language or culture in Palestine." The Declaration had never stipulated "that Palestine as a whole should be converted into a Jewish National Home, but that such a Home should be founded *in* Palestine." To remove all doubt, His Majesty's Government now declared "unequivocally, that it was not part of their policy that Palestine should become a Jewish State," and "would indeed regard it as contrary to their obligations to the Arabs under the Mandate, as well as to the assurances which have been given to the Arab people in the past."

Yet London reiterated that the Jewish people were in Palestine "as of right and not on sufferance." As evidence that Britain stood by them, the White Paper noted that since 1922 "more than 300,000 Jews [had] immigrated to Palestine, [raising] the population of the National Home to some 450,000, or approaching a third of the entire population of the country." This growth was accompanied by "achievements in many fields," testimony "to a remarkable constructive effort which must command the admiration of the world and must be, in particular, a source of pride to the Jewish people."

How to make a Solomonic choice without aggravating Britain's predicament? The Arabs took their stand upon Palestine having been "included within the area" in which Britain, in 1915–16, had undertaken "to recognize and support Arab independence." And where Zionists invoked Balfour to support their claim to a homeland, the Palestinian Arabs invoked McMahon–Hussein to claim that "Palestine should be converted into an Arab State." The British, however, stuck with the view that "the whole of Palestine west of the Jordan was excluded from Sir Henry McMahon's pledge."

In short, Jews and Arabs would have to continue cohabiting in an undivided cis-Jordanian Palestine, with neither side imposing its nationality and control on the other. But it would be "contrary to the whole spirit of the Mandate system that this population should remain forever under Mandatory tutelage." The White Paper looked to the establishment, within ten years, of a self-ruling, independent state in which "the two peoples in Palestine, Arabs and Jews, [would] share . . . a government in such a way as to ensure that the essential interests of each community [would be] safeguarded." During "a transitional period," the British government would "promote good relations between the Arabs and the Jews." They would "be given an increasing part in the government of their country," and their representatives would be invited "to serve as heads of Departments approximately in proportion to their respective populations," if need be "with the assistance of British advisors."

After specifying transitional steps to a binational solution, the White Paper broached the fraught issues of immigration and land purchases. By the terms of the Mandate, Great Britain was required to "facilitate Jewish immigration under suitable conditions," but with care not to prejudice "the rights and positions of the [local] population." While to date "the sole criterion" limiting immigration had been "the economic absorptive capacity of the country," it need not remain so "for all time and in all circumstances."

Just as the cultural repercussions of "advanced" economic development called for attention, "damaging" political effects too "should not be ignored." The Arabs were aghast at the prospect of an "indefinite Jewish immigration" whose ultimate objective they presumed to be domination of the country. If continued, it might well perpetuate "a fatal enmity between the two peoples" and turn "the situation in Palestine [into] a permanent source of friction amongst all peoples in the Near and Middle East." Since unlimited growth of the Jewish National Home through immigration was likely to require "rule by force," the British proposed to make "further expansion" contingent on Arab consent. Not that London was about to heed the call for an instant closing of the borders, being "conscious of the present unhappy plight of large numbers of [European] Jews seeking refuge" and believing that "Palestine can and should make a further contribution to the solution of this pressing world problem." Accordingly, during the next five years (1939–44), 10,000 immigrants would be admitted annually. In addition, 25,000 Jewish refugees would be taken in, "special consideration being given to refugee children and dependents . . . bringing the Jewish population up to approximately one-third of the total population." At that point, however, "no further immigration will be permitted unless the Arabs of Palestine are prepared to acquiesce in it."

The practice of transferring land from Arabs to Jews, like recent immigration, had not prejudiced "the rights and positions of other sections of the population," and had been unrestricted. But, "owing to the natural growth of the Arab population," this situation was changing. In some areas there simply was no further Arab land to be transferred, "whilst in some other areas such transfers . . . must be restricted if Arab cultivators are to maintain their existing standard of life and if a considerable landless Arab population is not soon to be created." From here on, then, the high commissioner would assume the power "to prohibit and regulate transfer of land." The White Paper concluded that, in view of the complexity and contentiousness of key issues, London could not "hope to satisfy the partisans of one party or the other." Even so, its "purpose [was] to be just as between the two peoples in Palestine whose destinies . . . have been affected by the great events of recent years, and who, since they live side by side, must learn to practice mutual tolerance, goodwill, and cooperation."

Nevertheless, on the vital day-to-day issues of immigration quotas and land sales, the British leaned toward the Arabs. By all but stopping immigration after five years, and limiting the Yishuv to one-third of Palestine's total population, Chamberlain's National Government marked a shift of partiality from Jews to Arabs, who now bid fair to be ascendant in tomorrow's independent Palestinian state. Helped by the threat of the Arab world's defection to the Axis, almost despite themselves (the second intifada having been put down) the Palestinian Arabs recovered much of the diplomatic ground they had just lost.

The leaders of the Yishuv and of Zionism worldwide denounced the White Paper of 1939 for so flagrantly violating the spirit and letter of the Balfour Declaration and the Mandate. For Weizmann, while the Peel and Woodhead reports had begun to undermine Balfour, the White Paper accomplished "its actual nullification." Ben-Gurion decried "the greatest treason perpetrated in this day and age by the government of a civilized people . . . formulated and expressed by men expert in the art of feigning high-mindedness." In a statement issued on May 18, 1939, the morrow of the White Paper, the Jewish Agency charged the Mandatory power with denying the Jewish people "the right to reconstitute their national home in their ancestral country" and with restricting them, instead, to "a territorial ghetto" there. The new policy for Palestine was "devoid of any moral basis and contrary to international law," and the Jewish people "[would] not accept it." Great Britain's "breach of faith [was] a surrender to Arab terrorism." Although the Jews had not "retaliated" against Arab terror, they would not "submit to it," not even after the Mandatory government had "reward[ed] the terrorists by surrendering the National Home to them." The Yishuv had benefited all the inhabitants of Palestine and had not exerted "an adverse effect upon the life and progress of the Arab countries." While insisting that the Jewish people had "no quarrel with the Arab peoples," the Jewish Agency protested, once again, that "the Arabs [were] not a landless or a homeless race like the Jews, nor [did] they need a place of refuge."

Through Zionist eyes, in the late 1930s, after trying to prevent war by appeasing Nazi Germany at the expense of the Czechs, Britain turned to preparing for war by appeasing the Arabs at the expense of the Jews. It did so confident of having redeemed its pledge: to help bring about the implantation of a broadly based and solidly institutionalized Jewish National Home, not a Jewish state, in Palestine. But what the British took to be the beginning of the end of their Mandatory support, the Zionists considered merely the start of their need for continuing international patronage, if not protectorship, by Great Britain—or some comparable imperial power. Fate itself could occasionally assist the Zionist cause. Even during the second intifada, driven by surging anti-Semitism on the continent, nearly 100,000 immigrants arrived in Eretz Israel, and some fifty new kibbutzim were founded. By the outbreak of the Second World War the Yishuv was 450,000-strong, and in the diaspora support for Zionism was at an all-time high. Although during the war years only some 50,000 immigrants made it to the Holy Land, the Yishuv's proto-state continued its quick development, abetted by the British, of modern industry and infrastructure, and of police and military forces.

The uprising of 1936–9, for which Zionist leaders denied all responsibility, strengthened the hand of the Revisionists and their sympathizers, including Ben-Gurion. The White Paper, the hardliners argued, proved that violence had lent wings to the Arab cause. Readiness to resort to force and violence assumed a central place in Zionism's political and diplomatic formula, and in its ethos. An enlarged auxiliary Jewish police force collaborated ever more closely with the British constabulary, while the Yishuv's military and paramilitary forces—Hagana, Palmach, Irgun, Lehi—grew apace. Many of the collective and cooperative settlements also began to acquire a certain military mien, though the Zionists claimed their sword, unlike the Arabs', had only a defensive edge. Wielding it was wholly in keeping with Zionism's ultimate aim. In so far as the core objective was a large and predominantly Jewish state, force would be necessary to establish and consolidate expansive borders and to further ethnocultural homogeneity, if need be by coercive relocation of Palestinian Arabs to Arab countries.

The idea of resettlement or deportation, as Herzl had sketched it out, gradually took hold in many sectors of Zionism's political elite, before surfacing as an enduring idea in the Yishuv's civil and political society. Jabotinsky was its first prominent public precentor; despite his secularism, many religious voices joined in chorus. But as the most unrighteous "solution" to the Arab Question, transfer was initially not clearly enunciated. During the 1930s, however, Weizmann, Ben-Gurion, and Sharett themselves began to entertain transfer as a vector of Zionist policy. By recommending the exchange of a large number of Arabs with a small number of Jews, to ease the acceptance of a proposed partition, the Peel Commission had broken the taboo. Where once the injunction had been to "think of transfer, always, but speak of it, never" (to adapt Léon Gambetta's phrase about France's loss of Alsace-Lorraine in 1871), hereafter the consensus was to wait for an opportune moment to go public—or to prevail on others, preferably the British, to propose it.

Looking further ahead, the extreme recourse of forced expulsion seemed politically less out of bounds and risky given the continuing incoherence, through lack of unity, of the Palestinian Arabs and their supporters throughout the greater Middle East. Within Palestine there was the persistent division between the irreconcilables, led by Grand Mufti al-Husseini, and the moderates, led by Raghid al-Nashashibi, the ex-mayor of Jerusalem. Rivalries between and within urban elites, rural clans, and armed gangs exacerbated the in-cohesion. Beyond Palestine, the Arab countries were too deeply divided to act in unison, Transjordan being the weakest link in the chain of neighboring states. As yet the Arab streets and villages were quiescent, even if the mullahs were beginning to play on the resentments of the underclass and the failings of the incumbent elites.

This etiology of relative powerlessness would be incomplete without taking account of three additional deficits: the absence of an Arab Palestinian proto-state comparable to the Jewish Agency; the non-existence of their own equivalent of a Zionist movement; and a dearth of influential Arabs with access to the political society of the Great Powers. As war approached, Arab leverage consisted almost entirely of the Middle East's oilfields and vital geostrategic arteries, supplemented by the specter of unrest throughout the Arab–Muslim world, with the risk of a spillover into Southeast Asia. Those conditions would enable the Arabs to best the Zionists only momentarily in the international system.

Zionist leaders exploited the generalized Arab disarray without considering the psychic or political consequences of their own hubris. Reassure the Palestinian Arabs that their intentions were peaceful, equitable, and empathetic, to be consummated by mutual cooperation and compromise—this they could not do, because they could not imagine any of it.

The internal critics were alarmed by the Peel Commission's major proposals—especially by the renunciation of the principle of binationalism. They warned of the danger of abandoning the quest for Jewish–Arab understanding. Convinced that the very future of Zionism was at stake, Magnes for the first time went before the Council of the Jewish Agency, probably with a view to appealing to its non-Zionist members. He pleaded for a continuation of the search for a peaceful way to an undivided Palestine that "would be neither a Jewish nor an Arab state, but a Jewish–Arab state under the protection of. . . Great Britain." The Arabs would not leave a Jewish state "voluntarily," and "the irredenta which would be created in [it] would become an insoluble problem" and "bring war with the Arabs." His entreaty was both severely criticized and shrugged off. Norman Bentwich, professor of politics at Hebrew University and former (and first) attorney general in British Palestine, later said that, while "many Jews and non-Jews" shared Magnes' view that "the surgical separation of Palestine . . . should be averted," and "the possibility of an understanding" had not been "sufficiently explored," the proposal for a "regional autonomy of Jews and Arabs with a central government for common concerns" had been "somewhat brusquely dismissed."

Between 1936 and 1939 Magnes gave all his energies to unofficial Arab–Jewish encounters, serving as facilitator, intermediary, and interlocutor in informal conversations with prominent and responsible Palestinian nationalists in Palestine and abroad: George Antonius (author in 1938 of *The Arab Awakening* , in which the text of the McMahon–Hussein correspondence of 1915–16 had first been published), Jamal Husseini (active in the second intifada, but looking for a nonviolent way forward), Musa al-Alami, and Rashid Haj Ibrahim. He was also centrally involved in the talks between the British scholar Albert Hyamson and Colonel Stewart Newcombe, which fashioned the most compelling, if finally futile, framework for mutual accommodation during the prewar years. Both the Jewish Agency and the Arab Higher Committee made a point of treating those engaged in these explorations as mere meddlers—to be used when convenient, but in general to be disavowed.

The issue of immigration remained paramount: Ben-Gurion refused any negotiation that might entail a "limitation of Jewish growth in Palestine"; the Mufti was implacable on its cessation. Against all odds, Magnes and his associates sought to break what they considered a disastrous deadlock. They held fast to the premise, shared by their Arab counterparts, that since the Zionists were perceived as latter-day colonial intruders, they should make the first gestures of reconciliation. Magnes kept insisting the Zionist leadership reformulate concrete terms on immigration, land sales, and borders that could serve as a basis for genuine discussion.

Here too he and his brethren were roundly, and incoherently, disparaged: they were called both credulous and perfidious, and said to have no plausible Arab partners. The internal critics in turn charged the official Zionists with jejune intransigence, most perfectly expressed in their refusal to settle for anything short of an outright majority in a Jewish-dominated state. In mid 1938 the American Consul General in Jerusalem appeared to refer to this bad faith when he said that "a number of conversations with colleagues and British officials" close to the Hyamson–Newcombe discussions confirmed his impression that "any Zionist talk of having vainly extended or of readiness to extend the hand of friendship to the Arabs is pure and simple eyewash."

Doubtless the political Zionists were ill-suited for the craft of negotiation. According to Robert Weltsch—a Prague-born Zionist writer and editor close to Buber—their focus was excessively "inward" on intramural politics, with the result that they represented "all attempts at partnership with the Arabs" as so many magnanimous "concessions" and "spoke of [mutual] understanding . . . in terms certain to frighten them." Rather than discuss the "objective factors" underlying the "Jewish–Arab hatred [these Zionists] attributed it exclusively to the wickedness and moral inferiority of the Arabs." In 1939 Weltsch ruefully noted that there was no way of reaching an "agreement with the Arabs by demanding 100 per cent fulfillment of Jewish demands and meeting zero per cent of Arab demands." Kalvarisky, who by now had given up the directorship of the Jewish Agency's Department of Arab Affairs, similarly considered it "fatal" that most Zionists and their leaders persisted in thinking "that the Palestine problem, though the main factor, could be solved without the Arab neighbor and against his will."

Ernst Simon was another forceful early champion of Jewish–Arab reciprocity. A religious humanist profoundly influenced by the German–Jewish existentialist and religious philosopher Franz Rosenzweig, he later explored, in Palestine, the pedagogic theory of Johann Heinrich Pestalozzi, the Swiss educational reformer. Simon contributed to the public discourse in the Yishuv and in Israel with essays probing the complex links between faith, reason, and politics, exemplified in his classic article, "Are We Israelis Still Jews?" written in 1952, after Independence. In it, he was among the first to call for a "Protestant" or open Judaism, as against a "Catholic" or closed, holistic Judaism that negates all values and obligations not grounded in the Torah. Simon stressed that the Jews, individually, could open themselves to the wider world and other value systems without being any less steadfast in their faith than Orthodox true believers and religious Zionists sworn to a Torah state.

Philosophically, politically, and personally close to Buber, Simon stressed the importance of acknowledging that Arab apprehension was "sincere" and that "the Palestinian Arab National movement had become an adversary to be taken seriously," just as Arab nationalism throughout the Middle East was authentic and not to be denied. Instead of continuing to practice evasion, the official Zionists ought to "work to gain Arab sympathy for the creation of a Jewish National Home in Palestine." They needed to wear away the "Arab fear" of the Jewish presence in order to secure "agreement to a binational state" that eventually, under British protection, would join "a larger Arab federation." Although sympathetic, like Buber, to far-left Zionism, Simon considered Arab–Jewish tensions to be grounded in "national–political" conflict, to be dealt with on "the national not . . . the economic . . . and class plane." In 1939 he related the second intifada to his anguish over the soaring distress of European Jews: recognizing that the Arab rebellion "was partly the fault of the Zionists," he deemed it all but impossible to "give shelter to masses of Jewish refugees" without greater Arab–Jewish mutual recognition,

Humbled but not broken by the lame and impotent conclusion of the Jewish–Arab negotiations after the second intifada, and alarmed by events on the continent, the internal critics persevered in their search for a minimal accord. Soon they abandoned politics and diplomacy for confidence-building efforts of a social, economic, and cultural nature. The League for Arab–Jewish Rapprochement and Cooperation was founded in April 1939 at the initiative of Buber and Kalvarisky. The organizing committee included, besides Simon and other stalwarts of Brit Shalom, the American-born Henrietta Szold, founder of Hadassah, and S. Y. Agnon, Hebrew novelist and future Nobel laureate. The League proposed to rally, on both sides of the Great Divide, "each and every one who recognizes the need for

Jewish–Arab rapprochement . . . and considers it necessary that the question of Palestine be solved on the basis of economic advancement and freedom of national, cultural and social development of both nations—Arab and Jewish—together." It launched a monthly, *Be'ayot Ha-Yom* (Problems of the Day), to provide a platform for the discussion of its ideas.

Before long, Hashomer Hatzair, Poalei Zion (Workers of Zion), and the Socialist League all fell in with the new League. This composite left, tracing its origins to czarist Russia, provided a welcome social and political base for an essentially elite-driven voluntary association. In early October 1939, following the invasion of Poland, a League-sponsored conference called for Jewish–Arab cooperation during and after the war—a war certain to complicate the inherently difficult task of developing a network of Arab contacts in Palestine and the neighboring countries. Soon thereafter a delegation of the League, led by Buber, called on Ben-Gurion to press for its plan for a binational state and to urge that Jewish immigration be limited to 45 per cent of Palestine's population. Ben-Gurion was said to have asked, as he had Magnes years earlier, whether Buber had "come to Palestine with the consent of the Arabs or against their wishes"— clearly, he had come only "against their wishes, and with the force of British bayonets." Ben-Gurion knew of "no example in history of a nation opening [its] gates [simply] because the nation wanting to enter explained its desire to do so." He assured Buber that he was confident "an agreement will be reached [with the Arabs] because [they believe] in our power, in our power which will grow."

4

REALIGNMENTS

By the outbreak of the Second World War the search for a Jewish–
Arab accommodation had come to practically nothing: few members
of the Arab Palestinian establishment were willing to accept a Jewish
homeland or state in any part of Palestine; few members of Zionism's
political class conceded the stubborn fact, let alone legitimacy, of the
Palestinian Arabs' nationalist aspirations. Bitter foes saw each other
more and more as irreconcilable enemies. The anti-Semitic furies in
Europe were bound to intensify the Zionist sense of mission and
urgency, especially with regard to speedier and unrestricted immigration. This fixity of purpose further eroded any tentative disposition to
meet the Arabs partway. Among the Allies, the renewed torment of the
Jews raised sympathy and support for the Zionist cause. At the same
time Zionist hardliners were emboldened by the momentary demor-
alization of the Palestinian Arabs following the quelling of the second
intifada.

The World Zionist Congress, having convened in Geneva in August
1939, disbanded for the duration of the war. Delegates set up an
Emergency Council to be headquartered in the U.S.—not only for
reasons of security but also to turn to good account the burgeoning
primacy of American power and American Zionism. It had taken some
time for U.S. Jews to acquire influence in the World Zionist Movement. At the time of the founding congress in 1897, they were 1 million
strong, but barely a handful were Zionists. Not surprisingly, only one
delegate went to Basel that year. Following the abortive Russian
Revolution of 1905, 2 million Jews left Eastern Europe, most for
America. By 1914 its Jewish population had swelled to 3 million, of
whom 150,000 considered themselves Zionists, although by 1917, the
year of the Balfour Declaration, America's amorphous Zionist Federation had a scant 10,000–20,000 members, fewer than 1,000 in New
York, with a vest-pocket budget. By championing a Jewish Homeland
in Palestine as an Allied war aim, U.S. Supreme Court Justice Louis

Brandeis and President Wilson, each in his own way, gave a boost to American Zionism, making it concordant with patriotism. Within two years the number of declared Zionists—affiliated with several organizations about to be leagued in the nascent Zionist Organization of America—rose to more than 175,000.

In America, as in Europe, the Eastern European Jews became the main carriers of Zionism. They clung to a pre-emancipated, self-isolating Judaism and *Yiddishkeit* that separated them from the established Reform Jews who assimilated and took up the local culture. Notables like Brandeis, Justice Felix Frankfurter, and Rabbi Stephen Wise, who had roots in Central Europe, also embraced the Zionist cause, but in the spirit of the less conservative internal critics, not the official leadership. Palestine for them was a land of refuge for the endangered Jews of the Old Continent, not a home for the "chosen" and sheltered Jews of the New World.

As the members and offspring of the Eastern European *aliyah*s to the US began to constitute more of American Jewry, they provided susceptible recruits for a Zionism that in turn reinforced conservative Judaism. Zionism thereby fortified what from early on Solomon Schechter—theorist of conservative Judaism and chancellor of New York's Jewish Theological Seminary—foresaw would be a potentially "great bulwark against assimilation." Unlike socialism, which was inherently universalizing and secularizing, Zionism was compatible with the synagogue and the Torah, and with the continuing observance of immemorial traditions and rituals.

The wildfire of fascism and Nazism, which intensified anti-Semitism and ignited the conflagration of the Second World War, inevitably had a profound impact on America's Jewish communities in general, and on its Zionist movement in particular. During the 1930s the Jewish refugees from Germany and Austria, including the charmed circle of intellectual exiles among them, were welcomed in many quarters, both Jewish and gentile. They were, however, too few, too emancipated, and too moderate to overshadow America's increasingly militant Eastern European Jews. These found their spokesman in Rabbi Abba Hillel Silver of Cleveland, whose call for "the constitution of Palestine in its historic boundaries as a Jewish commonwealth" was adopted by the annual conference of the Zionist Organization of America in the fall of 1941. The intransigents even began to win over the membership of Hadassah, the flagship in America of humanistic and non-confrontational Zionism.

Ben-Gurion had concluded, meanwhile, that American power and American Jewry would soon hold the key to Palestine. Unlike Weiz-

mann, who continued to look to Britain and, like Herzl, to trust the
ways of the old diplomacy, Ben-Gurion proposed to mobilize popular
support for his forward policy in the political corridors of Washington
and the local precincts of American Zionism. Ben-Gurion came to
America for a one-year stay in November 1941. With the capital his
base of operation, he collaborated with Silver, a master of public
relations and pressure politics. Their attempt to organize a de facto
Jewish lobby coincided with a major drive not so much for Weizmann
and the General Zionists, who backed the call for an unalloyed Jewish
state, as against Wise and Magnes, who fought a rearguard action
against the hawks.

Once America was at war, the Zionist Executive of the World
Zionist Organization and the American Emergency Council representing the U.S. Zionist leadership prepared to press the Allies to proclaim
that one of their cardinal war aims was to end, once and for all, the
wretched homelessness of the Jewish people. Unrestricted entry to
Palestine was placed at the top of the agenda: the issue promised to
rally broad-based support for the defiance of Britain's White Paper of
1939, which was "cruel and indefensible in its denial of sanctuary to
Jews fleeing from Nazi persecution." In effect marking the shift of
Zionism's diplomatic center of gravity from the U.K. to the U.S., a
lopsided World Zionist Congress met at the Biltmore Hotel in New
York City on May 9–11, 1942—a time of already lethal Jewish
persecution in Europe, but before any awareness of the Final Solution,
formalized at Wannsee in January of that year. The Zionist Organization of America convoked the gathering, together with Hadassah,
Mizrahi, and Poale Zion. Although there were representatives from
seventeen countries, most of the 600 delegates were American. Goldmann and Weizmann were much in evidence, but they were overshadowed by Silver and Ben-Gurion, who demanded "a clear and
unequivocal reaffirmation of the original intention of the Balfour
Declaration and the Mandate to reestablish Palestine as a Jewish
Commonwealth."

The delegates would hear no objections. Overwhelmingly they
adopted eight resolutions, soon known as the Biltmore Program.
At its heart was the call "that the gates of Palestine be opened; that
the Jewish Agency be vested with control of immigration . . . and
with . . . authority for upbuilding the country, including the development of its unoccupied and uncultivated lands; and that [the whole
of] Palestine be established as a Jewish Commonwealth integrated into
the structure of the new democratic world." The hardliners had
prevailed without affronting the moderates. Emanuel Neumann, an

advocate of the massive transfer of Arabs and Silver's closest associate, boldly averred that if "we can effectively mobilize our forces and talents throughout [this] country, if we go in now for an all-out effort for winning the battle of America, there is a good prospect that we will win the battle of Palestine." Before the end of the year, with worsening news from Europe, and in observance of the twenty-fifth anniversary of the Balfour Declaration, 68 senators and 194 congressmen, along with scores of other public figures, signed a manifesto advocating the establishment of a Jewish National Home in Palestine.

By formally laying claim to the full expanse of the Mandatory territory for tomorrow's *Judenstaat*, the Zionist leaders had taken a momentous turn. The Arab Question was effectively expelled from discourse. Virtually the entire world Zionist movement and the Yishuv, including their governing bodies, aligned with the new orientation. Once again Ben-Gurion and Weizmann stood shoulder to shoulder, backed by Labor, the General Zionists, and Mizrahi. This broad coalition still comprised elements that continued to trust in diplomacy, suspect populist rhetoric, and forswear violence. But these latter-day centrists were more than counterbalanced by the Revisionists and their sympathizers, who criticized the Biltmore Program for not laying claim to the borders of the historic Palestine of 1917, before the British had truncated them to establish Transjordan. Especially in the Yishuv, but with increasing encouragement from overseas, this faction also advocated the use of naked force.

Yet Biltmore itself had delivered another severe blow to those in favor of binationalism and Jewish–Arab understanding, who were horrified by the program's presumptuous unilateralism. Magnes noted in his diary that the "slogan 'Jewish State' (or Commonwealth) is equivalent, in effect, to a declaration of war by the Jews on the Arabs." It was intended to "mobilize the Jews for a diplomatic onslaught upon the Arabs," to be followed by "agitation" for a Jewish army, possibly including "storm troops," which at a "proper time" could be used "as a conquering force in the tradition of Joshua."

As despairing as anyone over the Jewish ordeal in Europe, Magnes still approvingly quoted George Antonius: no moral case "can justify the persecution of our people in an attempt to relieve the persecution of another." Specifically, "Jewish distress" ought not to be alleviated "at the cost of inflicting a corresponding distress" upon the Palestinian Arabs. Although Magnes "understood the mood and reasoning" behind the Biltmore position, he allowed himself to think that "if there is no other way, then the whole thing is not worthwhile." His foreboding was shared by the members and friends of the defunct Brit

Shalom, the League for Jewish–Arab Rapprochement and Cooperation, Hashomer Hatzair, and Poale Zion. All remained loyal to
binationalism (although Hashomer Hatzair was reluctant to cap
immigration), and all opposed the maximalists on both sides of the
Great Arab–Jewish divide. The Biltmore Program, they felt, had
served only to reconfirm the Palestinian Arabs' deep suspicion, despite
sporadic disclaimers, that the official Zionists were intent on taking
possession of the whole of Palestine.

Magnes resolved to rally the secular dissidents for an open challenge
to Biltmore. With Buber, Kalvarisky, Simon, Smilansky, and Szold he
organized Ihud (Union) to keep the urgent issue alive. In what turned
out to be her last public pronouncement, Henrietta Szold declared that
"if we do not give [everyone] the opportunity to consider the Arab–
Jewish Question, we will be committing . . . an unpardonable sin."
More than ever "convinced that politically as well as morally" it was
"the decisive question," Szold beseeched the Zionists to "find a way in
common with the Arabs living in this country." She was "almost
certain" that it would be "easier" during than after the war to bring to
bear "our influence on those who determine the course of affairs."

Ihud held its first public meeting in Jerusalem on August 11, 1942. In
his opening remarks Magnes spoke against drawing borders by fiat. A
state and civil society with self-proclaimed frontiers would tempt fate:
it would run the risk of a deadly war with the Arabs and of a fatal
imprisonment in a hostile regional environment. Besides breeding
lasting resentment and hatred, this forced implantation would probably end in a "pagan" rather than a Jewish state of any kind.

Magnes also drafted Ihud's platform, published in September. Jews
and Arabs were to have equal rights in a binational Palestine affiliated
with an Arab confederation, itself to be associated with the Western
powers. Britain should appoint Jews and Arabs, in equal numbers, to
responsible positions in the Mandatory administration and should
create autonomous, communally based cantons or districts with joint
organs of government intended to further "cooperation between the
Jewish world and the Arab world in all branches of life—social,
economic, cultural, political." In other words, Ihud renewed the
internal critics' support of a Jewish National Home in Palestine. It
also pressed again their demand for the resumption of immigration
during the remaining life of the Mandate at a rate that would avoid
fulminating Arab fears of Jewish domination and the Arab ultra-
nationalism those fears would feed.

The Zionists realized at once that Ihud presented the clearest and
potentially gravest challenge to their working plan, not least because

of the intellectual and moral standing of its master spirits. The relatively moderate, well-grounded, and accommodating program might well appeal to wavering and confounded Zionists the world over, but especially in America, and—perhaps most dangerously—to official circles in Washington and London. Ben-Gurion set the tone for the denunciation of Ihud. He vilified its leading lights as "national apostates" whose visions of binationalism and autonomous districts were the "sick phantasmagoria of Jewish boys . . . with muddled brains" who lacked the courage to admit that "the Arabs were unwilling to allow Jewish immigration." Supporters of Ihud were seeking to "destroy organized Zionism." Sharett reviled them as "a pack of anti-Zionists," and Yitzhak Ben-Tzvi, prominent Mapai leader and president of the Yishuv's would-be National Assembly, considered them an "anti-Zionist constellation." Labor's associates on the right and left were equally virulent, accusing Ihud of knifing the Yishuv, betraying Zionism, and inviting "the suicide of the Jewish people."

In the Yishuv Ben-Gurion was most concerned with the looming defection of Hashomer Hatzair, a polestar of the kibbutz culture and a pioneer in the development of its military disposition. Since this utopian-socialist group commanded some 20 per cent of the vote in the Histadrut, it could not be ignored at a time when the leaders of Mapai were making every effort to transmute Zionism's inspiring social poetry into a practical-minded political prose. In the U.S., Zionist leaders were more fearful of Ihud's impact on sectors of the Jewish and gentile elites than on rank-and-file Zionists. Silver worried especially about the non- and anti-Zionist pillars of Jewish society, among whom Magnes was highly respected. The editorial page of the *New York Times* was open to him through his privileged relationship with Arthur Hays Sulzberger. In New York Magnes also had access to the *Nation* and *Foreign Affairs*, and in London to the *Economist* and the *Times*.

Ihud's pull in the Yishuv, however, was less political than moral, and the official Zionist leadership engaged it accordingly. In 1940 the Executive of the Jewish Agency had established an advisory committee on the Arab Question, and Kalvarisky, Kaplansky, and Magnes, among others, had agreed to serve on it. Shortly following the organization of Ihud, the Agency invited Buber, Kalvarisky, Magnes, Smilansky, and Szold to meet. Ben-Gurion and Sharett took turns saying they disapproved of Ihud's continuing encounters with Arab politicians and intellectuals. Exasperated, Magnes defended his "perfect right" to explore ideas of cooperation and joint governance, in his home or theirs, without being charged with punic faith for allegedly carrying on "negotiations" that he quite agreed were the province of the "recognized institutions." Smilansky seconded the importance of informal contacts in the search for common ground, and argued there "could be no agreement . . . as long as the idea of a [Biltmore-like] state was on the agenda."

Sharett's rejoinder revealed the Executive's basic stance. Although he considered the Ihud program an "anti-Zionist document," he did not mean to "suggest that the personalities [subscribing to it] were anti-Zionist." Even so, it was "shameful [that] a group of notables," including Szold, who was a member of the Zionist Executive, should call for "far-going concessions, above all in the matter of immigration." The Zionists would give the impression of being divided among themselves. Ben-Gurion sounded a more peremptory note. Though he claimed to value "the process of conversation" with Arabs "so as to explain a number of things to them," he reminded his audience of the official "premise that Jews who have a political position different from the Jewish Agency may not have discussions with Arabs."

The unfolding of the Zionist project was conditioned more than anything by the wrathful thirty years that shook the world in the twentieth century. In 1917 Weizmann had successfully exploited the military predicament of the Allies. But that had also been the year of the Russian Revolution and the American intervention in the Great War. Events of the following two years were no less momentous and determining: the collapse of the Ottoman and Austro-Hungarian empires; the defeat of Germany and its halting regime change; the eruption of the idea of national self-determination around the globe; and the growth of anti-Semitically-minded right-wing parties throughout most of postwar Central and East-Central Europe. These rolling paroxysms reverberated in Zionist politics and diplomacy.

The internal critics were unusually clear-eyed about the tempest of their time. Cosmopolitan Zionists, they decried sectarian nationalism without exception and in all quarters, and never allowed themselves to be penned within Euro-, Judeo-, or Ziono-centrism. Their disciplined ecumenism naturally extended to the perplexing question of Palestine.

The Second World War only confirmed the cogency of their wide-angled view of the issues facing Zionism. To be sure, the Judeocide was still unthinkable, and even in 1942–3, like all the world, they were slow to realize that the European Jews were caught in a trap of unprecedented mass slaughter. As Jacob Talmon, author of *The Origins of Totalitarian Democracy*, noted later: "The theory of catastrophic Zionism . . . soon was confirmed in a way which even the gloomiest prophets could never have imagined." But rigor required the dissidents to reject all such teleological and theological interpretations. In their disconsolate reading, the Judeocide was an historical and profane event that, for all its monstrousness, demanded a reasoned and principled Zionist response. The furies of the Second World War had not forever changed the contours and dynamics of the conflict over the Jewish Homeland—they were merely rigidified: immigration, land, Arab resistance, imperial dependency, and violence.

These remained the prevailing exigencies between the end of the war and the foundation of the state of Israel in 1947–8. Thirty years after the Balfour Declaration the insolvent British empire turned over its League of Nations Mandate to the United Nations for Trusteeship, simultaneously pleading with Washington to take over its watch in the eastern Mediterranean, Arabian Sea, and Persian Gulf. India, led by Mahatma Gandhi and Jawaharlal Nehru, took care of itself, wresting away its independence, albeit at the price of ferocious Hindu–Muslim intercommunal violence and geographic partition. The future of a sovereign National Home for Jews in Palestine was inevitably wrenched by the demise of British hegemony, as it was by the death throes of the European empires, the rise of American imperial power, the beginning of the second Cold War (the first having involved the containment of Bolshevism after 1918), the further spread of other national liberation movements throughout the Third World, and the trauma of the Judeocide.

Backed by Ihud and the League for Arab–Jewish Rapprochement and Cooperation, Magnes kept urging the Zionist leadership, given the need for large-scale immigration, to spare no efforts to reach a compromise with the Arabs. The exhortation was out of season: Field Marshal Erwin Rommel captured the Libyan port city of Tobruk and advanced toward Alexandria in mid 1942, and the Grand Mufti called on Mussolini and Hitler; in Berlin he declared that "the Arabs were the natural friends of Germany because they had the same enemies: the British, the Jews, and the Communists." But within a few months, once Field Marshal Bernard Montgomery had routed the German panzers in Egypt at Alamein and the Red Army had crippled the Wehrmacht in Russia, the political atmosphere appeared to take a turn for the better. By early 1943 the US envoy in Cairo reported to Washington that, fortunately, there were "certain individuals and groups . . . on the Jewish side in Palestine that increasingly realize the necessity of working out a peaceful solution with the Arabs," among them Szold, Magnes, and Mordakhai Bentov, leader of Hashomer Hatzair. He urged that these "moderates" be asked to visit America to press for "additional homes for the Jews in Palestine," as well as to bolster those Zionists who opposed the "extreme position of the Jewish Agency."

Weizmann journeyed to Palestine in February 1945. Accompanied by Sharett and Elias Sasson, head of the Arab Section of the Jewish Agency, he met with Buber, Kalvarisky, and Magnes, all three of whom voiced their concern about the local leadership, who would not admit any open discussion of the Biltmore Program. Though the Jewish Agency alone was authorized to come to "an agreement with the Arabs," Magnes again insisted that dissidents had the right, even the obligation, to use their "contacts" to "prepare the ground" for a rapprochement. The Agency should not only allow such contacts, chimed in a colleague, but should stop "libeling" whoever sought ways of "reaching a solution" through dialogue.

On the ground, the balance of power kept shifting in favor of the Yishuv—demographically, economically, and militarily. It was further strengthened in the international community, with Britain increasingly less anxious about the loyalty of the Arab world and the U.S. ever more supportive of the Zionist project. Admittedly, an Arab League was called into life in March 1945, but its backing of the Arab Palestinians, who were no match for the Jewish Palestinians, was woefully weak. Although the Soviet Union secured its place in the court of the Great Powers by dint of the Red Army's unexpected military feats and blood sacrifice, the U.S. and Great Britain were about to lay down the law in the Middle East. By late May 1945, prominent Zionists the world over summoned Britain to abrogate the White Paper of 1939 and open up Palestine to immigration, overseen by the Jewish Agency. After the Judeocide, insisted Ben-Gurion, the creation of a Jewish state had become only more urgent and more just.

Financially drained and militarily spread too thin, Britain was in no position to restore control over its vast imperial periphery. In Palestine it faced rising Jewish violence, including terrorist acts, against British military and civilian officials; this defiance coincided with escalating Hindu–Muslim tensions in India. Clement Attlee and Labour replaced Churchill and the Conservatives in July 1945, three months after the death of Roosevelt had raised Harry Truman to the American presidency. Attlee was as eager to enlist the U.S. to help in Palestine as Truman was disposed to entertain his request. Just as he began to heed the increasingly vocal Jewish lobby, he realized that Britain's colonial exhaustion in the Middle East might redound to America's advantage.

By virtue of its Mandate, Britain found it more difficult than the U.S. to disregard the hostility seething among the Palestinian Arabs and in the wider Arab world as it faced the pressing Zionist demand for open immigration and for a Jewish state. The Labour Party having supported their cause all along, the Zionists now charged the new Labour prime minister, Clement Attlee, and Ernest Bevin, his foreign secretary, with playing them false by not disavowing the White Paper outright. Bevin particularly was suspected of anti-Zionism, if not anti-Semitism, for taking account of London's Mandatory obligations, as well as its global and economic interests, in his uphill search for a solution acceptable to both Jews and Arabs. But the imperial sunset in Southeast Asia and the greater Middle East correlated with Britain's even more vital diplomatic–economic relations with the U.S., to which both Bevin and Attlee assigned absolute priority. Without continuing American aid, they could neither slow the headlong decline of Britain's standing in the international system nor afford to relieve its financially fatigued civil society and underwrite the seminal Beveridge plan for the expansion of the welfare state. Eventually this transatlantic dependency worked to the advantage of hardline Zionism.

In mid 1945—both out of genuine empathy and pressed by the Jewish lobby—Truman asked Attlee immediately to admit 100,000 Jewish Displaced Persons (DPs) to Palestine. But Attlee and Bevin, bound by the White Paper of 1939, were reluctant to do more than raise the annual immigration quota from 15,000 to 18,000, though they were willing to do that much without Arab approval. The DPs soon became a matter of contention between Washington and London. On the European continent the war had left a heinous legacy of millions of refugees: between 1945 to 1955 some 20 million either fled their homes or were forcibly expelled, transferred, or exchanged, entailing untold physical and mental suffering. The displaced Jews were only a small fraction of this human flotsam, but, unlike the gentiles, most were either unable or unwilling to return to their countries of origin, fearful of aftershocks of anti-Semitism and anti-Judaism.

Only some 50,000 Jews had survived in Germany and Austria by hiding, or by using false identities. Of the 750,000 Jews remaining in the Russian-controlled Eastern European countries, some 250,000 fled or moved westward, primarily from Poland. Within one year from the end of the war, these 300,000 or so Jews were languishing in rudimentary camps, desperately waiting for papers to a safe haven. Although there were rising, if random, cries for visas, the governments of the free world, rather than open wide their own doors, merely kept them ajar, as they had since 1933. Despite this continuing ostracism in a time of extreme adversity, at least 50 per cent of the Jewish DPs expressed a preference for resettlement in Western countries, especially the U.S., rather than Palestine. In 1945 America's annual immigration quota for Germany was 26,000; for all the Eastern European nations combined, 13,000. Men and women of good will, Jews and gentiles, called for a revision to meet the emergency. But both the Congress and public opinion demurred strongly. Even though America had been spared the disasters and miseries of war on its own soil, the opposition successfully invoked the expected postwar economic hardships and the danger of communist infiltration to keep out the homeless and stateless. Anti-Judaism and Judeophobia probably played a role as well.

The leaders of American Zionism were not among those supporting the call to ease immigration to the U.S. In this they were at one with the Jewish Agency, which opposed settling refugees anywhere except in Palestine: more American visas would only reduce the pressure for 100,000 certificates for Eretz Israel. Instead of working on the admission policies of their own countries, Jewish leaders of the First World generally abetted the Zionist stratagem of using the cause of the DPs to legitimize and energize the campaign to open up Palestine and nullify the White Paper of 1939. Bevin did not assent to this one-refuge solution. Surely, he felt, a substantial number of Jews could find a haven in Europe or the U.S., or elsewhere overseas. Here he followed Churchill, who in August 1945 doubted that "a vast dumping of the Jews of Europe into Palestine" would solve the Jewish problem, and advised against being "in too great a hurry to give up the idea that European Jews may live in the countries where they belong." But few governments, if any, ever seriously explored the option of opening countries other than Palestine for the DPs.

Of course, both statesmen knew that to settle the DPs in Palestine under Zionist and American pressure would only serve to further inflame Arab nationalism and resistance—which would then have to be contained by British soldiers. On June 12, 1945, speaking at the Labour Party Conference in Bournemouth, Bevin alleged, without offering refugees a haven in Great Britain, that though driven by the "purest of motives," the Americans wanted to put 100,000 Jews into Palestine because "they did not want too many of them in New York." Unconcerned with geopolitics, Rabbi Silver spoke not just for himself in accusing His Majesty's foreign secretary of "a coarse bit of anti-Semitic vulgarity reminiscent of the Nazis at their worst." The two Democratic Senators from New York, Robert Wagner and James Mead, said the same: Bevin's remarks were an "echo from Nazi dogma." In July, fervid American Zionists expressed their support for their counterparts in the Yishuv with a mass rally at New York's Madison Square Garden, a march on Washington by several thousand Jewish war veterans, a rash of picket lines in front of the British Embassy and consulates, and a spate of telegrams and letters to the White House and Capitol.

In the fall of 1945, Bevin looked for a way to defuse rising tensions with the U.S. over Truman's push to settle displaced Jews in the Holy Land. He was less concerned with Palestine as such than with London's privileged relationship with Washington. At stake was Britain's economic recovery and standing as a major, if weakened, Great Power in the concert of nations generally, and in the Middle East in particular. After 1918, in the words of T. E. Lawrence, England had "control[ed] nine parts out of ten of the Arab world, and inevitably call[ed] the tune to which the French [had to] dance." A quarter-century and a world war later, America had become the dancing master.

In November, Washington agreed to the establishment of an Anglo-American Commission of Inquiry to study the dilemma of Palestine, with special attention to the Jewish refugees. Among its twelve members, the most prominent were Frank Aydelotte, director of the Institute for Advanced Study in Princeton and former president of Swarthmore College; James G. McDonald, former League of Nations high commissioner for refugees and a member of the editorial board of the *New York Times*; and Richard H. S. Crossman and Lord Robert Morrison, both Labour members of parliament. The Commission's charge was "to examine political, economic, and social conditions in Palestine as they bear upon the problem of Jewish immigration and settlement . . . and the well-being of the people now living there." After taking testimony from "competent witnesses and . . . consulting representative Arabs and Jews," the Commission would make recommendations "for an ad interim handling of these problems as well as for their permanent solution." In March 1946 it held plenary hearings in Cairo and Jerusalem. The Commissioners also broke up into subcommittees: some went to investigate conditions in camps for Jewish DPs in five European countries (Germany, Czechoslovakia, Austria, Poland, Italy); others traveled to five Arab capitals (Damascus, Beirut, Baghdad, Riyadh, Amman) to "hear the views" of their governments and of other "representative bodies."

Although the Peel Report of 1937 had remained a dead letter, the Commission made the earlier diagnosis of the situation in Palestine its own. Since the conflict was "primarily political . . . it was as much about the future as about the present," leaving the big question: "Who, in the end, will govern Palestine?" The Commission found that, since 1937, "the gulf between the Arabs of Palestine and the Arab world on the one side, and the Jews of Palestine and elsewhere on the other has widened still further," with neither side inclined to "reconcile either their superficial or their fundamental differences." While the Arabs viewed the Mandatory government with "misgivings and anger," it was "attacked with bombs and firearms by organized bands of Jewish terrorists." In an effort to "keep the situation under control," and with the jails bulging with political prisoners, the local administration was obliged to resort to "the display and use of very large forces." Spending close to four times more on "law and order" than on health and education, "Palestine has developed into a semi-military or police state." The Commission reported the "fear of experienced [British] officials that tomorrow may produce circumstances in which military operations will be necessary."

From the outset the Zionists distrusted the Anglo-American Commission. Having "had [his] fill of inquiries and investigations," Weizmann was angered that "instead of generously recognizing the original purposes of the Balfour Declaration," British Labour went with "the old, shifty double emphasis on the obligation toward the Arabs of Palestine as having equal weight with the promise of the Homeland to the Jews." The Arabs already had several countries of their own; the Jews had none. Although there might be "some slight injustice politically if Palestine were made a Jewish state . . . the line of least injustice demand[ed] that the Jews be given their chance." He knew it was a "radical solution of the Jewish problem" but recommended "the evacuation of the remnant of European Jewry to Palestine." Both in written statements and public hearings in Washington, London, and Jerusalem, the Zionists, with few exceptions, advocated the Biltmore Program, coupled with a call for the instant admission of 100,000 immigrants. They asked the Mandatory power to meet three cardinal demands: cede control of immigration to the Jewish Agency; abolish restrictions on the sale of land; and "proclaim as its ultimate aim the establishment of a Jewish state as soon as a Jewish majority has been achieved." Ben-Gurion stressed that since the Jews lacked "security . . . even in countries where they seem secure," they had come to Palestine to ensure it for themselves.

The Anglo-American Commission recognized the Biltmore Program had "the support of the overwhelming majority of Zionists," even if "many Jews" questioned the "wisdom of formulating these ultimate demands." It noted that Mapai, by far the biggest party, "largely determined the official line." The Jews in Palestine were becoming more obdurate. They were convinced that the "terrorism" of 1936–9 had paid off for the Arabs, whose revolt had precipitated "Jewish terrorism . . . and a general militarization of Jewish life." In turn, though it amounted to only "some 1 per cent of the Jewish community," the Revisionist party "openly support[ed] the present terrorist campaign." Many of its members were "boys and girls under twenty, of good education, filled with a political fanaticism as self-sacrificing as it is pernicious."

The objectives of the Arabs, according to the Commission, were the reverse of the Zionists': "the immediate stoppage of Jewish immigration; the immediate prohibition of the sale of land to Jews; and the concession of independence to a state in which the Arab majority would be dominant." Standing on their more thatn 1,000 years in Palestine, the Palestinian Arabs contested the "Jewish historical claims" to their land and the right of the British "to give away something that did not belong to [them]." The Mandate, along with Jewish immigration forced upon the Arabs, violated their right of self-determination. They insisted they were "as fitted for self-government" as the adjacent Arab states that had been granted their own. This account was replete with references to the "promises and assurances" given to Arab leaders by the British during the First World War, beginning in 1915, and by the Americans during the Second World War, starting in 1942.

The Commission found that, since the adoption of the Biltmore Program, indigenous Arab opposition to a Jewish national home had become "more intense and bitter" and was being whetted by "the suggestion that self-government should be withheld . . . until the Jews have acquired a majority." As matters stood, "the absolute, unqualified refusal of the Arabs to acquiesce in the admission of a single [additional] Jew to Palestine is the outstanding feature of Arab policy." Yet Arab spokesmen, the Commission reported, denied they were anti-Semitic, and "professed the greatest sympathy for the persecuted Jews of Europe." But since the Palestinian Arabs were not "responsible" for this persecution, it was "not just that they should be compelled to atone for the sins of Western peoples by accepting into their country hundreds of thousands of victims of European anti-Semitism." "Some Arabs even declared that they might be willing to do their share in providing for refugees on a quota basis if the United States, the British Commonwealth, and other Western countries would do the same."

Although the fast takeoff of nationalism in the Middle East, including the Holy Land, had invigorated the Palestinian Arabs, the influx of Western capital and equipment "represented by the Jewish population" had "overwhelmed" them. Their "sense of inferiority" became more acute once they realized they were at a great disadvantage when it came to "stating their side of the controversy to the Western World": the Arabs had fewer prolocutors in the great capitals, and they were "less familiar with modern methods of propaganda."

Albert Hourani—English-born, Christian Lebanese by descent, and subsequently Britain's leading historian of the Arab world at Oxford—drafted and presented the brief of the Arab League. In his reading, the Zionists were using immigration as a "weapon" to gain control of Palestine. Should they fail to equal or overtake the rapidly growing Arab population, they would "consider evacuating at least part of the Palestinian population to other countries." The Zionists meant to impose their ascendancy upon the Arabs, who were offering them "communal autonomy" and political participation in proportion to their share of the total population. In any case, there could be no agreement "as long as the Zionists refuse to understand that they cannot get in London and Washington what is refused to them in Jerusalem." Having outlined the Arab League's general position, which defied official Zionism, Hourani addressed Ihud's project. He told the Commission that in the absence of "a certain spirit of cooperation . . . and trust," without which there were no "neutralizing communal differences," a binational state, as proposed by Magnes, could only "lead to one of two things: either a complete deadlock involving perhaps the intervention of foreign powers; or the domination of the whole life of the state by communal considerations." In that event, it was probable that "the majority of Zionists would use what Dr. Magnes had obtained for them in order to press their next demands," which might make him "the first victim of political Zionism."

The Palestinian Arabs were very much daunted by the Jewish Agency, noted the Commissioners, who for their part considered it "one of the most successful colonizing instruments in history" as well as "the most important nongovernmental authority in Palestine and, indeed, in the Middle East." Even the Peel Commission had spoken of the Zionist Executive as "a Government existing side by side with the Mandatory Government," and the former was "generally believed to have an unofficial, but nonetheless powerful, influence over the Hagana, the so-called Jewish Army whose strength is estimated over 60,000." Now that the Jewish Agency was obstructing the implementation of the White Paper of 1939, it was actively "undermining the authority of the [British] Administration," which regarded the Agency "as a distinctly dangerous influence." Unless the relations between these two authorities were "corrected" in the interest of promoting "the general welfare and the cause of peace . . . Palestine might well be plunged into a civil war, involving the whole Middle East."

Ihud was perhaps the most influential and respected Zionist group critical of the Biltmore Program to give evidence before the Anglo-American Commission of Inquiry. In fact, according to Magnes, the central Jewish institutions had "decided to prohibit the appearance before the Committee of any public bodies or personalities who would voice opinions which could not be fitted into the official Zionist scheme." Ihud appeared anyway convinced that "minorities like ourselves have a right to . . . voice the opinion of the Zionist opposition about the political course of the Jewish people." It submitted a position paper and delegated Magnes and Buber, accompanied by Smilansky, to present it. On March 15, 1946, before beginning their testimony, Magnes told the panel that he and Buber would speak

"not in the name of Hebrew University . . . but as residents of the country and as Jews who feel it their duty to give voice to a view that, though differing from the official Zionist program, is nevertheless shared . . . by large numbers of the population."

After assigning responsibility to all three parties—Arabs, Jews, and Britons—for failing to further Jewish–Arab cooperation, Ihud's statement argued that the confrontation of the two nationalisms turned on "three main elements: immigration, land, and self-government." In this dire hour the group fully supported the prompt admission of 100,000 displaced persons to Palestine. Thereafter the rate and level of immigration must be calibrated to take account of the local economy's "absorptive capacity (bearing in mind Arab unemployment)," but not to exceed numerical parity between Jews and Arabs. Ihud envisaged a time when, with a binational Palestine tied to a confederation of Middle Eastern states, the continuing arrival of Jews would cease to alarm the Arab peoples. To prepare for that state's self-government, Ihud called, once again, for the appointment of Jews and Arabs to administrative positions in the Mandatory bureaucracy. It also advocated establishing a temporary U.N. Trusteeship composed of representatives of the British High Commission, the Jewish Agency, and the Arab League, who would share executive, legislative, and administrative power. Concrete actions, not futile words, would make for everyday Jewish–Arab cooperation and understanding.

Buber opened for the three-man Ihud delegation with a discourse on the meanings of Zionism. Initially his own espousal of the Zionist cause was "prompted and intensified, but not caused, by modern anti-Semitism," and he could never have conceived a destination other than Palestine for a people who had "survived for nearly two millennia by their trust in their return, in the fulfillment of the promise, in the realization of the idea." Modern Zionism was making three "irreducible demands": the acquisition of sufficient soil "to bring about a renewed connection with the primal form of production . . . without which no original spiritual and social productivity can arise"; a large-scale "influx of settlers" to keep advancing "the work of reconstruction" and to protect it from the elements of "degeneration" that even Buber thought threatened "colonization in the Levant"; and "self-determination" for the Jewish community's "way of life and . . . institutions," including "an assurance for its unimpeded development as a community."

In returning to Palestine "in the age of national movements, Judaism was not simply creating another national movement of the European type, but a unique one, a 'Zionism,' the modern expression of the tendency towards 'Zion.'" This Zionism's three demands, embodied "in the concept of a 'National Home' . . . must be carried out without encroaching upon the vital rights of any other community"; "one's own independence must not be gained at the expense of another's"; the Jews must neither "oust" Arab peasants nor "cause the political status of the present inhabitants to deteriorate." Both the Jewish "tradition of justice" and "historical circumstances" commanded the "regenerated Jewish people in Palestine" to live peacefully and cooperate fully with the Arabs, without violating their "fundamental rights." The political form of this National Home, even given "the demand for autonomy," and contrary to what "the greater part of the Jewish people thinks today," need not entail a Jewish state and majority. What was required was "an internationally guaranteed agreement between the two communities . . . that defines the spheres of interest and activity common to the partners and those not common to them," with a warranty of "mutual noninterference" in the respective self-governing spheres.

It was left to Magnes to develop further the idea of binationally grounded parity. And why, he was asked, did he oppose partition? His foreboding was frank: the creation of two separate states would make for chronic hostility between the two states, as well as between the majority and minority within each state. He saw a

> day when, in a few years' time, after this partition, you will get a
> group of young Jews, and a group of young Arabs, on both sides of
> this irredentist border, going after one another in just the same way
> the militarists today want to have the field for a trial of arms.

Insisting that, with wise mediation, the two peoples could "find a way . . . to work together," Magnes adjured the Committee: "You don't have to do this partition." The members of the Commission listened carefully to "Dr. Magnes and his small Ihud group," whose importance they suspected was "far greater than its numbers."

Although Hashomer Hatzair did not appear, they published a pamphlet in support of binationalism while the Inquiry was in progress. The far-left Zionists also blamed Britons, Jews, and Arabs for not having promoted Arab–Jewish understanding. It was "natural" for the Arabs to want to remain "masters and keep the majority . . . in the country they live in" as well as to "gain their independence." And with the prospect of immigration continuing "at the rate of 100,000 yearly for some twenty years," as was advocated even by Hashomer Hatzair, there was no denying the "fact of Arab fear of Jewish domination." From its world socialist perspective, Hashomer Hatzair traced the inefficacy of the Arab national movement to a fatal contradiction between "political slogans which serve to disguise the ambitions of reactionary leaders" and "economic and social interests" that seek "a national emancipation of a progressive character." A binationalism rooted in political and economic equality for both peoples could alone resolve the conflict inherent in each side's contention that "its ends can be achieved solely by converting Palestine, respectively, into either an Arab or a Jewish national state."

The Anglo-American Commission of Inquiry published its report on May 1, 1946. It agreed with the Peel Commission's conclusion: the burning problem could not be solved "by giving either the Arabs or the Jews all they want. The answer to the question 'which of them in the end will govern Palestine?' must surely be 'Neither.'" But where Peel had recommended partition, only to see it "f[a]ll to the ground," the Inquiry could not: "no partition would have any chance unless it was basically acceptable to Jews and Arabs, and there is no sign of that today." Embracing the "principle that . . . Palestine shall be neither an Arab nor a Jewish state," the Commission advised a "period of tutelage" for the two communities to develop the "will to work together" to set up self-governing institutions, in the process overcoming their mutual "fear of dominance" by the other.

The report reaffirmed the "reality" of the Jewish National Home, "established under international guarantee." Fortified by its "historic connection," this National Home had struck "deep roots" in the soil of Palestine, giving it "a right to continued existence, protection, and development." Even so, "Palestine is not, and never can be, a purely

Jewish land," situated as it is "at the crossroads of the Arab world." The local Arab population, "descended from long-time inhabitants of the area, rightly look upon Palestine as their homeland." Since it would be "neither just nor practicable" to have Palestine ruled by either majority, it "must be established as a country in which the legitimate national aspirations of both Jews and Arabs can be reconciled, without either side fearing the ascendancy of the other." Until this shared animosity "disappears," the Holy Land "must remain under some form of Mandate or Trusteeship."

Sensitive to the grievous plight of the DPs, the Commission recommended that 100,000 Jewish "victims of Nazi and Fascist persecution" be admitted to Palestine "as far as possible in 1946." But Palestine alone "could not meet the emigration needs" of all the Jewish victims, for which the "whole world" shared "responsibility." Inasmuch as the Jewish National Home could not be "argued out of existence," the Inquiry "rejected the view that there shall be no further Jewish immigration without Arab acquiescence, which would result in the Arab dominating the Jew." Restrictions on Jewish land purchases should likewise be eased. Yet, with equal certainty, it repudiated "the insistent Jewish demand that forced immigration must proceed apace in order to produce as quickly as possible a Jewish majority." In short, the "well-being" of the one community ought not to be "subordinated" to that of the other.

To insure against just such an outcome, "the mandatory or trustee" in this tutelary period should proclaim "the principle that Arab economic, educational, and political advancement in Palestine was of equal importance with that of the Jews." Preparing the ground for conciliation and joint governance would require a "deliberate and carefully planned policy" to reduce the "great disparity" between the Arab and Jewish standard of living that "makes it easier for Arab political leaders to keep alive anti-Jewish feelings in the minds of the masses." Education would be essential, and it was past time for "the Arab community to assume the same responsibility" in the matter as the Zionists. The Commission suggested the "introduction of compulsory public education within a reasonable time." There was, however, a caveat: the Jewish schools, "financed by the community . . . having become most effective agencies for inculcating a spirit of aggressive Hebrew nationalism," the Commission "urged most strongly" that the interim authorities exercise "adequate control . . . over the education of both Jews and Arabs."

A section on "Jewish Relations with Arabs" was at the heart of the Inquiry's concluding chapter, and circled back to an earlier concern.

Reduction of the widening socioeconomic gulf between Jews and Arabs "might be quite as important for the growth and security of the National Home as the drainage of swamp lands or the creation of Jewish industry." The prospects seemed none too promising: there were, "unfortunately . . . signs of a hardening of the Jewish attitudes towards the Arabs." Jews "find it almost impossible to look at [such] issues from the Arab point of view and to realize the depth of the feeling aroused by their 'invasion' of Palestine."

A last, devastating judgment remained, offered almost apologetically: the Inquiry considered it "not unfair to say that the Jewish community in Palestine *has never, as a community, faced the problem of cooperation with the Arabs.*" Surely it was "significant that in the Jewish Agency's proposal for a Jewish State, *the problem of handling a million and a quarter Arabs is dealt with in the vaguest of generalities*" (italics added). The Commissioners, "with pleasure," mentioned a few "rare" instances of Arab–Jewish collaboration, singling out "the proposals for cooperation with the Arabs made by Hashomer Hatzair and by the Ihud group."

The publishing of the Anglo-American Commission's report was the internal critics' finest hour. Magnes rightly claimed that the Inquiry "adopted a great deal of what we said, sometimes in the very words of our statements." The essential points were these: Palestine should be neither a Jewish nor an Arab state; the Jewish National Home should not be founded at the expense of the Palestinian Arabs; immigration should not be unlimited; confidence-building in both civil and political society should be given high priority; there was need for an interim trusteeship; and an overture to the neighboring Arab states was imperative.

The Inquiry's report was a stinging setback for Ben-Gurion and Silver, among the main movers of the Biltmore Program of 1942. Despite the murder of millions of Jews since then, the Commissioners, attentive to their governments' leanings, resisted the demand for open immigration and for a Jewish state to extend over the whole of Palestine. Ben-Gurion's worry about Magnes and his associates proved to have been warranted: they had put forth a plan that engaged significant elements of the British and American political class as much by their own moral authority as by its prudent workability. But, whereas the advocacy of official Zionism's peremptory program stumbled in the international forum, among the Yishuv and the Jewish community in America it continued to make strides.

There was one glaring lacuna in the report: it did not face up to the growth of Zionist violence and terror in Palestine. Although the

Jewish Agency made no secret of its control of the Hagana, an ostensibly clandestine military force of some 60,000 soldiers, it alternately dissembled or disavowed two separate but kindred branches of a far-flung shadow army of about 6,000 irregulars sworn to Revisionism. Menachem Begin was in command of Irgun, which was significantly larger than Lehi (full name: Fighters for the Liberation of Israel), led by Yitzhak Shamir. The fighters in these two small guerrilla armies struck indiscriminately against British officials and installations and Arab civilians. In 1948, with independence, Begin and Shamir joined forces to transform Irgun and Lehi into Herut, or the Freedom Party—which in 1973 became Likud, or the Unity Bloc.

As early as January 1944, Irgun called on the Yishuv to rise up against the British occupation of the Holy Land, and in the course of the year the underground carried out several attacks on the Mandatory Power's administrative and security offices. This campaign took a dramatic turn on November 6, 1944, in Cairo, when two Lehi operatives assassinated Lord Walter Edward Moyne and his driver. Scion of the Guinness beer empire and former leader of the House of Lords, Moyne was the British minister of state in charge of the Allied war effort in the Middle East. All along, Ben-Gurion had kept a safe political distance from the allegedly irresponsible actions of Irgun and Lehi, which were said to threaten the further complication of relations with London; now and then the Hagana even collaborated with the Mandatory authority's drive against the clandestine underground. Moyne's murder reinforced the resolve of both Ben-Gurion and the Jewish Agency to keep the Revisionists at arm's length.

But following the end of the war Ben-Gurion ordered the Hagana and the Palmach—its volunteer elite unit, set up in 1942—to start guerrilla warfare against the British in cooperation with Irgun and Lehi. This became known as the Jewish Resistance Movement. Issued in early December, 1945, this command all but coincided with the establishment of the Anglo-American Commission of Inquiry and the Arab League's announcement, on December 12, that the creation of a Jewish state would mean war. Between the fall of 1945 and the summer of 1946 Palestine was swept by a wave of more or less coordinated attacks on military outposts, police stations, telephone exchanges, and railway installations. There was a tacit division of labor: the Hagana, including Palmach, sought to spare human life and focused, increasingly, on furthering clandestine immigration; Irgun and Lehi were left to imbrue their hands in blood, as in the attack on a British officers' club in Jerusalem that took some twenty lives. These assaults intensified following the publication of the Inquiry report on May 1, 1946.

The British High Commissioner, General Alan Cunningham, pressed London to authorize firm action against the Jewish Agency and the underground, and to break off Anglo-American discussions bearing on the Palestine problem. Refusing to have "their hand forced by terroristic methods," Attlee and Bevin approved taking stronger measures. But the foreign secretary, not about to risk endangering Britain's lifeline to America, refused to have talks with Washington "even partially suspended." On June 29—later known as Black Saturday—the local British authorities, having mustered 17,000 soldiers and considerable ordnance, summarily arrested about 2,700 Zionist officials and activists, including Sharett and three other members of the Jewish Agency Executive. Ben-Gurion, then in Paris, remained at large. Forewarned, the top military leadership of the Resistance Movement went into hiding.

Both Weizmann and Ben-Gurion began to have doubts. Although the Hagana was ordered to cease operations, it was not directed to make a clean break with Irgun and Lehi. Irgun then perpetrated what turned out to be the single most spectacular and bloody terrorist assault in the history of the Mandate. Apparently according to a plan cleared with the Hagana and the Jewish Agency, on July 22 Irgun activists blew up the southern wing of the grand King David Hotel in Jerusalem, which served as the headquarters of the British civil, military, and intelligence administration. Of the ninety-one killed, forty-one were Arabs, twenty-eight Britons, and seventeen Jews; forty-five others were wounded. On July 30, in retaliation for the execution of several of its militants, Irgun seized two British sergeants and hanged them.

This shift from inanimate to living targets, including the innocent, forced into the open the bitter rift within the Jewish Agency and in the Yishuv at large over the strategy and tactics of the struggle for statehood. Typically, Ben-Gurion performed another about-face, calling the Irgun an "enemy of the Jewish people." Simultaneously he held the policy of His Majesty's Government responsible for having provoked all the Jewish violence, including the King David atrocity. Ingenuously or not, Weizmann claimed to have been in the dark about the unholy alliance in the Jewish Resistance Movement. Insisting that the "political crimes" prefigured by Lord Moyne's assassination were an "abomination" by virtue of implicating the "whole community in the guilt of a few," he assured British officials that the Zionist leadership would go "to the utmost limit of its power to cut out, root and branch, this evil from its midst." The mounting terror, besides being utterly "un-Jewish," rather than change "the intentions . . . of our enemies [could only] provide them with a convenient excuse [and help them] justify their course before the bar of public opinion." Terrorism perverted "the purely defensive function of the Hagana" and poisoned the political process.

Four days after the explosion at the King David, Martin Buber addressed the Jewish Agency in the pages of the oldest and most prominent daily, *Haaretz*: it was "not sufficient" for officials to express "our . . . abhorrence [and] repugnance" for this crime, since "we were all accomplices . . . by virtue of [our] positions of influence." He blamed the leaders of the Yishuv for dispensing with the "rule of the sacred law" and for raising the young on the "false teaching that the rebirth of a people can be accomplished by violent means." No wonder the call condemning the spread of violence "was heard neither yesterday, nor the day before, nor any time in the past until today." Since the Yishuv was hardly unaware of what was happening, it had no right to say, in the words of Deuteronomy, "our hands have not shed this blood, neither have our eyes seen it." While it was "too late for mere words," it was not "too late for deeds." Buber prophesied that "unless the Yishuv repents and changes [its] ways . . . an even greater catastrophe [will] befall us."

In the two years prior to September 1947, when the UK announced its withdrawal from Palestine, there were some 350 deaths by civil violence. About half the victims were British; the other half was nearly equally divided between Jews and Arabs. The British reaction was relatively mild, in large part because London was careful not to enrage further the Yishuv's supporters in the U.S. at a time when a crucial loan was being debated in Congress, and when Anglo-American negotiations on the Palestine Question were at a critical stage. Arabs of most persuasions were incensed by this moderation, contrasting it to the ferocity of Britain's repression of the intifada of 1936–9. Whatever the diplomatic and political reasons for this double standard, in Arab eyes it reflected plain anti-Arab bias.

Magnes feared that, by defying the British and the Arabs simultaneously, the Zionist leadership was steering headlong into a spiral of civil violence and warfare. He warned against embracing the mantra that "the only way to get a Jewish State . . . is through the use of arms." Jabotinsky, "the prophet of the Jewish State," had advanced this argument "long years ago," and although he had been "ostracized and condemned and excommunicated" for his martial outlook, Magnes noted that "almost the whole Zionist movement adopted it," without publicly crediting Jabotinsky and the Revisionists "for their loyalty to this idea, which all these years was exceedingly unpopular, at least on the surface." Jabotinsky's reason was now being appropriated by those "who pilloried him," demonstrating that "ideas have a way of marching and of accomplishing themselves long after they have been subjected to derision and opposition." Uneasy about this mutation, Magnes stood aghast at the prospect of Jewish youth being taught, "mistakenly," that the "Jewish people is doomed everywhere . . . and that Judaism, the Jewish spirit, the Jewish religion, and Jewish culture are all in danger of deterioration, if not extinction, if there be no Jewish State." The killing and kidnapping of British soldiers and the sabotage of bridges were "the logical and the natural and the inevitable consequence of the theory our youth is being taught, that without a Jewish state we are lost—if not today, then tomorrow."

This concern with the militarization of Zionism gave Ihud the resolve to promote Jewish–Arab cooperation at the grass roots prior to negotiation of the binational state put forth in the Inquiry report. In the summer of 1946 Buber undertook to imagine a common polity built from the bottom up rather than the top down, rejecting the prevalent belief that "by its nature" the Jewish–Arab problem was insoluble. Palestine society was in the grip of a "political 'surplus' conflict," Buber maintained, brought about by the extreme politicization of "real conflicts" of religious belief, economic interest, and social custom. Insisting on their irreconciliability, politics provoked them "to the point of making them non-real," in the process subordinating the "demands of life" to the "demands of politics." Ihud's principal mission was to "fight the excessive growth of politics" by laying bare "the real interests and . . . the true bases of the conflicts between [Jews and Arabs]." He considered this "de-politicization" a precondition for conciliation and compromise. A year later Buber noted ruefully that the "continuing growth and domination of the political element" increasingly interfered "with the creation of . . . mutual trust while the Jewish and Arab peoples [by] living alongside [rather than among] each other" only became more desirous of a mutually exclusive autonomy. Neither people needed a separate state "to develop its potential freely . . . The demand for an Arab state or a Jewish state in the entire land of Israel falls into the category of political 'surplus.'" Both parties could realize their goals "within the framework of a joint binational socio-political entity," with each party "responsible for the particular matters pertaining to it, but the two working jointly to order their common concerns."

This censuring of official Zionist policy was vilified in the Yishuv. Back in July 1945 Irgun had distributed a broadside reviling Ihud as a coterie of Hebrew University professors issuing "quiet, refined, and reproachful" pronouncements from the "moral" heights of Mount Scopus. Scorning to participate in "what takes place down below," these intellectuals "adduce biological, sociological, economic, political, and historical" reasons why "the land of Israel," if it is to have a future, must "propose and seek a compromise at any price." Yet these "omniscient professors . . . make a fundamental error of historical fact and of principle." Ostensibly steeped in the Jewish tradition, the professors claimed that the Torah prescribed compromise as a ground rule of action. But whereas the books of Moses commanded the practice in "minor matters," they forbade it "with respect to the major issues . . . that shape the character of the [Jewish] nation and individual." The Hebrew nation had endured through the ages precisely because it "refused to compromise" with idolatrous peoples and had no desire "for them to compromise with us." Except for this thoroughgoing "refusal to compromise," the Jews would "long since have been assimilated among the gentiles." By the same token, in the "spirit of the past, present, and future martyrs of Israel," there could be no accommodation "on matters of supreme importance" with the British and the Arabs, as advocated by "the professors of Mount Scopus."

Buber answered for Ihud. They were not to be caricatured as cloistered and detached; nor did they embrace compromise "without reservation." In itself compromise was "neither good nor evil," but one had to be alert to "situations [where it] provides the only way out," short of violating principle. The present was precisely such a moment, when compromise was needed and could be sought without endangering the "foundations" or perverting the "maxims" of Zionism. Although "in all matters bearing upon the absolute, compromise must be ruled out . . . for the sake of the absolute it is permissible and defensible to act within the sphere of the relative as the situation demands." In the Middle East the issue was not survival regardless of cost, but survival with honor. There could be no imagining, let alone forging, a worthy future for the "remnant of Israel . . . in isolation, surrounded by hate and mistrust." The moment called for a "great peace . . . with the neighboring peoples . . . not a fictitious or dwarfed peace that is no more than a feeble intermission." All these years, rather than lay the foundations for a genuine peace with neighbors at home and abroad, the Zionists had developed the Yishuv's economic life "as a barrier rather than as a point of contact," preferring to make ever greater demands on the Great Powers than were "compatible with the realities of the situation."

*   *   *

Of all the Zionist factions, Ihud was the only one to consider the Anglo-American Commission's report a plausible basis for a bina-tionally-inclined middle course, steering clear of the violence inherent in a syncretism of Messianic and Revisionist Zionism. The Zionist leadership found itself on the horns of a dilemma: to spurn the Inquiry's proposal was to forfeit the instant immigration of 100,000 DPs—the movement's plan and prime moral imperative; to accept it was to forgo an all-Jewish state in the whole of Palestine that, with Biltmore, had become the sine qua non of the Zionist project. Although, of the two leaders, Ben-Gurion was more apt to be unbending than Weizmann, together they were nervous about the possibility Washington and London would pull together around an Inquiry report that had been strongly influenced by Ihud.

By now, however, even Weizmann knew the position of the U.S. would be decisive. While Truman supported the immigration of the DPs, he was unwilling to force them upon the British in Palestine. Skeptical of the reasons for Jewish statehood, and with violence in the Holy Land and opposition in the Arab world rising, the president was not "inclined to send half a dozen American divisions to Palestine to maintain a Jewish State." Yet in May, 1946, he notified Attlee that he approved the Inquiry's recommendation to admit 100,000 Jews to Palestine, while ignoring the report's other findings and proposals. On the far-reaching Palestine Question he hung back: close advisors as well as high officials of the State, Navy, and War Departments feared that a push for unrestricted immigration and a Jewish state would make tensions in Palestine worse, and jeopardize the West's interests throughout the greater Middle East at the dawn of the Second Cold War.

Meanwhile Attlee told the House of Commons that the report of the Anglo-American Commission needed to be considered as a whole, not piecemeal, and that before it proceeded His Majesty's Government would have to ascertain how much America was "prepared to share . . . the additional military and financial responsibilities." Presently Truman announced that the U.S. would take charge of the transport of 100,000 Jews to Palestine, though without assuming any of the other risks and burdens. In this whole matter Attlee and Bevin were worried about the DP imbroglio further aggravating Arab and Jewish rancor. In trying to square the circle, London had one major objective: to implicate Washington in solving the problem of Palestine without impairing America's preferential support for British interests in Europe and Asia. As Churchill, from the opposition bench, told the Commons on August 1, 1946, an agreement with America was all-important, and "any solution in which the U.S.A. would join us could be made to work." That "any," with its seeming openness to an Ihud-like plan, perturbed the Zionist inner circle.

To break the deadlock between Washington and London, at the suggestion of Loy Henderson, director of the State Department's Office of Near Eastern and African Affairs, Truman in June appointed a committee of delegates of the secretaries of state, war, and the Treasury. Chaired by Harry Grady, assistant secretary of state under Roosevelt, the group was instructed to advise the president on "such policy with regard to Palestine and related problems as may be adopted by this government." In July they headed for London to meet and negotiate with a British delegation headed by Herbert Morrison, the deputy prime minister. Their combined task was to propose ways of making the Commission of Inquiry's recommendations acceptable to both countries. The delegates submitted their report on July 24, 1946, three days after the attack on the King David Hotel, which redounded, locally and momentarily, to the benefit of the conciliators. Truman faced the rising pressure of the pro-Zionist lobby, while Attlee had to keep an eye on the turbulent situation in Palestine. The Morrison–Grady plan described Great Britain especially, but also the U.S., as caught between two equally hazardous alternatives: a binational state would entail establishing a long-term force of interposition; partition would touch off Arab–Jewish civil violence and regional war.

This report resembled the earlier one in its search for a compromise. It proposed the division of Palestine into an Arab and a Jewish province, with each enjoying a large measure of autonomy within a federal structure. During a period of transitional tutelage—again, as previously suggested—London would not only reign over Jerusalem, Bethlehem, and the Negev desert, but would continue to control military, diplomatic, and security affairs. Immediate admission of 100,000 DPs was again urged, but conditional on both Arab acceptance of cohabitation and on the agreement of the High Commission. The report recommended American economic assistance for Palestinian Arabs and nearby Arab states. Another assumption that had been implicit in the original Inquiry also survived: under the interim regime the two communities would either hammer out a confederation of their provinces or reach an impasse leading to partition, with all its likely perils. In other words, a binational solution remained a historical possibility, even if the odds against it were long. Rather guardedly, Magnes welcomed Morrison–Grady for providing "at least the outline for a binational Palestine," or one that could "at least be implemented in this spirit." But he did react to the size of the projected "Jewish

Province" of 1,500 square miles as "much too small"; how many more than 100,000 new refugees could it absorb, he wondered. He also criticized the plan for excluding Jews and Arabs "from really active participation in the central government." They should be appointed members of the high commissioner's executive council and heads of central government departments, and "some kind of central federated council" should be set up. Magnes regretted that, in political terms, the plan proposed "a kind of spoon-fed self-government . . . intended for infants" at a time when "the appetite of both peoples" for self-rule was "big and healthy." Needless to say, the official Zionists rejected the Morrison–Grady road map outright. And so did the Arabs.

At first, backed by Secretary of State James Byrnes, Undersecretary of State Dean Acheson, and Navy Secretary James Forrestal, Truman was inclined to endorse the new blueprint. But, sensitive to the pro-Zionist lobby during an election season, Truman informed Attlee in August that "the opposition in this country to the plan has become so intense that it . . . will be impossible to rally . . . sufficient public opinion to give it effective support." As if conscience-stricken, and mindful of Britain's quandary in Palestine, Truman chose this moment to announce that he would ask the Congress to open America to a greater number of displaced persons than the present quotas allowed. Eight months later an altogether improbable bill was introduced calling for the admission of 400,000 DPs, regardless of religion. It was not until July, 1948, after the creation and recognition of the state of Israel, that a pared-down bill was finally passed, admitting 200,000 immigrants over several years, of whom no more than 40,000 were expected to be Jewish.

The Zionist leadership fiercely attacked the autonomist–confederal model for Palestine as fatal to the idea of Jewish statehood. Even its vague timeframe ran counter to the sense of extreme urgency that galvanized the Zionist campaign. In America, though long-time adversaries, Stephen Wise and Abba Silver joined forces to do battle against Morrison–Grady. Influential congressmen and prominent public figures fell in, with direct representations to the White House.

Although confounded by the renewed American desistance, Attlee and Bevin, with little hope of success, sought to convince moderate Zionists and Arabs in the Holy Land and beyond to entertain the autonomy plan seriously. But London meant to stay on Washington's good side come what might. At about this time Bevin received the first intimations that the Zionist directorate, doubtful that either Britain or America would empower its reach for the whole of Palestine, was beginning to consider settling for part of it, perhaps with borders approximating those delineated in the Peel Report of 1937. Simultaneously Churchill, who as recently as November 1942 had said he had not "become the King's First Minister to preside over the liquidation of the British Empire," became increasingly critical of Labour's handling of imperial retrenchment. He proposed that London walk away from Palestine's ulcerating wound, forcing Washington to take over treatment: "If the United States will not come and share the burden of the Zionist cause [that it encourages] we should now give notice that we will return our Mandate . . . and will evacuate Palestine within a specified period." Churchill repeatedly dwelled on the forbidding annual cost of between £30 million and £40 million to maintain 100,000 soldiers in Palestine to police Jewish terrorism and Arab–Jewish enmity. He spoke for much of Britain's political class in downgrading the importance of Palestine at a time when England was preparing to get out of India and Egypt, in particular, but also Burma and Ceylon, and was ceding its sway over Greece and Turkey to the U.S.

At a meeting of the Jewish Agency Executive in Paris in August 1946, Nahum Goldmann, fearful of anti-British terrorism spinning out of control and alienating the Western Allies, proposed abandoning the Biltmore Program in favor of partition. Although Ben-Gurion, who was known to agree, abstained, a majority embraced this reorientation, which repudiated both the Inquiry and Morrison–Grady, and hence the prospect of binationalism. Goldmann hastened across the Atlantic, not the English Channel, to pitch the idea of "a viable Jewish state in an adequate area of Palestine" to the American Zionist directorate and to broader political and official circles in the U.S.

The establishment of a sovereign Jewish state in a partitioned Palestine, as in an undivided one, could be realized only by force of arms. On this score the Zionist leaders had few illusions, and were tempted in any case, as Magnes had noted, by Jabotinsky's wall of bayonets. They must also have known that the Great Powers were not likely to do their fighting for them. Truman would not send American soldiers to secure a Jewish state in the face of a hostile Arab world. His new secretary of state, General George Marshall, who quite agreed that a "certain degree of force may be required [for] any solution," likewise stood against U.S. military intervention. As Britain moved to jettison its Mandate, Bevin, mindful of Churchill and Truman's different priorities, let it be understood that "British troops who fought for freedom in the late war shall not now be used to enforce a policy by force in Palestine."

Goldmann arrived in Washington to discover that Marshall, Lovett, and Henderson at the State Department, and Forrestal at Defense, were opposed to partition, as were some members of the National

Security Council. Besides a distaste for deploying forces in distant and troubled lands, they were wary of alienating Arab countries whose oil was thought to be crucial for the economic recovery and political restabilization of western Europe. A mighty oil lobby also staked a claim on the matter: since 1939 the output of Middle Eastern oil had risen to one-quarter of total world production, and the interests of U.S. oil companies in the region had grown correspondingly. Spokesmen for the oil industry stood behind the nascent foreign-policy elite that was charged with defining America's longer-term geo-economic and geostrategic interests in the greater Middle East, which called for naval and air bases and control of vital sea lanes. One and all cautioned against an overly pro-Zionist policy that could drive the Arab world into Soviet Russia's arms. As yet relatively composed about the perils of communism, Truman, disregarding national security experts and oil lobbyists, paid more attention to domestic than to geopolitical calculations. On October 4, 1946, the eve of Yom Kippur, he issued a statement reiterating his efforts to relieve the plight of Jewish refugees by liberalizing immigration into the U.S. and admitting 100,000 DPs to Palestine. But the president said something new: the American government and people could support a partition of Palestine between Arabs and Jews that would create a "viable Jewish state in an adequate area of Palestine" in control of its own immigration and economy.

The Day of Atonement fell close to the mid-term elections of 1946, in which the Republican opposition had strong conservative winds in its sails. The Republicans swept the field. For the first time in twenty years the Democrats were defeated in New York City: Governor Thomas Dewey was reelected by a huge margin over Senator James M. Mead, and former Governor Herbert Lehman ingloriously lost his race for the Senate by 250,000 votes. The victory of Dewey, by far the most likely and credible G.O.P. candidate for the presidency in 1948, meant an uphill battle for Truman, who still stood in the shadow of F.D.R. Besides, the Republicans had been courting the Jewish vote that was concentrated in a few large cities within a handful of large states that carried great weight in the electoral college. From 1945 onwards, Rabbi Silver and his associates exhorted senators and representatives, regardless of party, to advocate American support for a bold Zionist course in Palestine—a political strategy in keeping with the growing role of the lobbies and pressure groups of minorities in electoral politics.

Within American Zionism the hardliners continued to be in the ascendant, and the abandonment of Biltmore for partition was seen as a retreat, if not a betrayal. In October of 1946 the convention of the

Zionist Organization of America reaffirmed the Jewish people's right
to "the whole of mandated Palestine, undivided and undiminished."
Although Silver, as president, criticized the Executive of the Jewish
Agency for yielding ground too readily, he nevertheless indicated that,
in extremis, partition might be acceptable should Washington get
behind it. The American chapter of Mizrachi, for its part, held fast to
"the historical claim to an independent state with historic boundaries
as ordained by the Torah." The American Jewish Committee alone,
presided over by Judge Joseph Proskauer, accepted partition, adducing
the labored reason that, besides providing a home for the DPs, the
projected state would occupy an area of Palestine in which Jews were
in the majority, and thus in keeping with Wilson's right of self-
determination. Proskauer typified the American Jewish community's
original non-Zionist and anti-Zionist elite: their preeminence challenged by the Eastern European Jews and themselves destabilized by
the Judeocide, they gradually came to develop greater empathy for the
Zionist project. This mutation eroded Magnes' support in America.

The Final Solution radically changed the composition of the Jewish
diaspora. The Jews of the United States, who by and large were the
descendants and rememberers of the murdered Jews of Eastern Europe,
took their place as the host of Zionism. During the immediate postwar
period, America counted over half a million Zionists in a Jewish
community of 5 million, whose donations in support of the Yishuv
far exceeded those of all other Jews combined. This sudden ascendancy
of American Jewry in world Zionism coincided with the prodigious
growth of the power and influence of the U.S. in the world system.

In 1942 the Biltmore convention had voted the maximalist platform:
a state embracing all of historic Palestine. In December 1946, meeting
in Basel, the first postwar World Zionist Congress was asked to ratify
the fallback position: an "adequate" part of a partitioned Holy Land.
Of the 385 delegates, 121 were American, and of these 56—the largest
single bloc—were sworn to Silver, who still stood against partition.
Ben-Gurion, leading the influential Mapai delegation from the Yishuv,
threw his lot in with Silver, less to oppose partition than to defeat the
compromisers who, like Weizmann, advocated backing Bevin's last-
ditch offer to mediate between moderate Zionists and Arabs in
London. Two motions in favor of staying with Biltmore won the
day by a small margin, thereby derailing Weizmann's reelection to the
presidency of the World Zionist Organization.

Having only recently stood with Silver to denounce the deficiencies of
the Morrison–Grady proposal, Stephen Wise now broke with him and
with the Zionist Organization of America. His allegiance remained with

the "Zionism of Weizmann, Brandeis, Nordau, and Herzl," and he feared the overreach of the newly elected executive agencies of both world and American Zionism. Richard Crossman, who had served on the Inquiry, had his own disenchanted reaction to the proceedings in Basel: Silver and most of his colleagues, though "experts in the arts of American politics," were "completely ignorant of the Middle East," with the result that they did not consider "the Palestinian Jews . . . a nation but colonists who must obey the instructions of World Jewry, which means, in effect, the American Zionists."

Starting in mid 1946, a group of Arab moderates in Haifa, Mandatory Palestine's model binational municipality, founded Falastin al-Jedida (New Palestine), an organization similar to the League for Arab–Jewish Rapprochement and Cooperation. It was headed by Fauzi Darwish al-Husseini, a cousin of the Mufti, who had taken part in the first intifada in 1929. During the turbulent years that followed he had a change of heart. Now he declared publicly that Arabs and Jews, taking the principle of mutual nondenomination as their starting point, should work for a binational state "based on political parity and full economic, social, and cultural cooperation." By fostering just that, together with the League, New Palestine meant to reduce Buber's "political 'surplus' conflict."

In August, at a gathering in the home of Kalvarisky, Fauzi declared that Arab moderates had not yet taken "serious actions" comparable to those taken by Ihud and the League. But, aware of the abuse the dissident Zionists had endured, he recognized that "we, too, will have great difficulties, the more so since political conditions have changed for the worse." Lately "the popularity of extremism has grown," benefiting his cousin Jamal al-Husseini and the Mufti, who were powers in the Arab Higher Committee. In rethinking his position following the earlier uprisings, Fauzi had come to realize that "there was no sense in this way," not least because "imperialistic policy was playing with . . . Arabs and Jews alike," which should incite them to work together to liberate and develop their common land. On November 11, 1946, leading members of Falastin al-Jedida signed a protocol of collaboration with the League for Jewish–Arab Rapprochement and Cooperation.

Feared and denounced for defying the Arab intransigents, Fauzi was gunned down on November 23, presumably by a nationalist loyal to the official leadership. At the funeral Jamal eulogized him in keeping with the hardliners' sentiment: he "got his just deserts for his misstep."

5

COLLISION COURSES

London had repeatedly insinuated that Britain was about to pull out of the Holy Land. Finally, on April 2, 1947, it asked that Palestine be placed on the agenda of the next session of the General Assembly of the United Nations—successor, in 1945, to the League of Nations and institutional heir presumptive of the Mandate. Unwilling to execute alone a decision abhorrent to Jews and Arabs alike, His Majesty's Government moved, at a special session on April 28, that a commission be established to examine the question. Five Arab states—Egypt, Iraq, Lebanon, Saudi Arabia, and Syria—unsuccessfully sought to amend London's draft resolution to include a call for "the termination of the Mandate over Palestine and the declaration of its independence." No major power or permanent member of the Security Council was expected to serve on the proposed committee of eleven members, who were given the task of finding a way out of the impasse. Of the eleven, the majority favored, or were prepared to consider, partition. Only multi-ethnic India and Yugoslavia, with large Muslim populations, refused, as did all-Muslim Iran. There was an unspoken meeting of minds on only one point: Britain's stewardship over Palestine should be ended forthwith.

On May 14, the day before the United Nations Special Committee on Palestine (UNSCOP) was formally chartered, the Soviet Union was the first Great Power to go on record in favor of partition. In a speech at the General Assembly, Andrei Gromyko, Russian ambassador to the U.N., declared that should a binational solution "prove impracticable . . . it would be necessary to consider . . . the division of Palestine into two independent states." This solution, however, could "only be justified in the event . . . relations between the Jewish and Arab populations were actually so bad that they could not be improved upon and their peaceful co-existence could not be ensured." His defense of the Kremlin's position was arresting, and his wording showed an understanding rooted in Russia's own loss of well over 20 million lives. During the Second World War "the Jewish people experienced exceptional calamities and sufferings which defy description." Gromyko spoke of the "almost complete extermination" of the Jewish people in the territories ruled by the "Hitlerites and their allies," and cited the figure of 6 million victims. The U.N. could not be indifferent to the plight of those who had survived this nightmare, especially the hundreds of thousands deprived of "homelands, shelter, and means of subsistence." He made a direct connection between the failure of the western European states to ensure the "elementary rights" and physical security of the Jewish people in the recent past and their "aspiration" today to "create [their] own state." Yet despite the emotive rhetoric, Soviet Russia's policy, like that of all the other members of the Security Council, was impelled less by honor than by geopolitical and geo-economic imperatives.

There is no grasping Zionism's critical turn toward partition without noting that the Anglo-American Inquiry and the multinational UN-SCOP were framed at the end of the Second World War and the start of the Cold War. By 1946 the U.S. was beginning to project its far-reaching naval and air power into the Indian Ocean and eastern Mediterranean, which together became the first proving ground for the Soviet–American confrontation. In March of that year, Churchill, sharing a platform with Truman, delivered his defining Iron Curtain speech in Fulton, Missouri. In February 1947, London asked Washington to assume its military and naval watch in Iran, Turkey, and Greece. Alarmed by the growing prospect of Soviet-backed international communism, Washington rushed to fill the vacuum being left by the failing *Pax Britannica*. The next display of America's unrivaled international reach came in June 1947: in an imperial speech at Harvard University, George Marshall proffered massive U.S. aid for the twinned economic recovery and political stabilization of Europe.

In the globalizing Cold War, the Middle Eastern and European theaters were thought to be intimately related. Washington assumed it needed to secure a steady and cheap supply of oil from Mesopotamia, Arabia, and Persia if it was to win the day in the First World, and Western Europe in particular. The Soviet Union was more eager to foil this connection than to secure such strategic raw materials for itself. The two nascent superpowers were about to compete for power and influence in the Middle East, though unequally; America was as yet unaware of the full extent of the Soviet Union's economic and military exhaustion. Because of the accident of its location, Palestine became caught up in this contest whose nature—though not its intensity, import, or force of arms—recalled the Anglo-French rivalry of the era of the First World War. The territory was still not desirable in itself, though the contingencies had changed. Most of Europe, including Russia, was guilt-stricken over the Judeocide, and inclined to be deferential to Zionism; and anti-colonial nationalism was sweeping the Middle East. But however preoccupied the White House and the Kremlin might be with the region, neither was concerned with the powerlessness of the Palestinian Arabs. The Palestinian Jews and the Zionist movement, confident of their morally charged strength, looked to cooperate with UNSCOP and affect its deliberations; the Palestinian Arabs and the Arab states decided on a boycott.

Presided over by Emil Sandstrom, a distinguished Swedish jurist, UNSCOP arrived in Jerusalem in June 1947. Palestine was in a state of cold civil war, and the British were preparing to leave India. On the eve of the committee's arrival, Weizmann dismissed a "binational state, or a sort of federal solution, or . . . the Morrison Plan" for having none of "the advantages of partition, which is final, definite, and crystallized." To legitimize this claim before the committee, the Zionist leaders invoked Biblical, religious, historical, and legal arguments, and steeled their case by invoking the unique infamy of the Judeocide. The long overdue establishment of a sovereign Jewish state in an adequate area of Palestine would provide a safe haven and self-respecting society not only for the survivors of the recent catastrophe, but for Jews who in time to come might again face persecution.

On July 8, 1947, Ben-Gurion told the eleven commissioners that, since no one "could guarantee that what happened to us in Europe" could not happen again, there was no "safeguard other than a homeland and a state." He asked that the part of Palestine not included in the Jewish state and remaining under a provisional trusteeship be kept open to unlimited immigration. "We are ready," he said, when asked to clarify his position, "to consider the question of a Jewish state in a significant part of Palestine all the while reaffirming our right to the whole of Palestine." Like the position of the hardliners at the time of the retreat from Biltmore, this response was not just tactical; it was premonitory.

Remembering the strong impression the internal critics had made on the Anglo-American Inquiry, Ben-Gurion made a point of criticizing their position. Tomorrow's Jewish state would have to be a national home for the 600,000 Jews in the Holy Land and for "the millions of Jews who are still left in the world." A Jewish minority in an Arab state, "even with the most ideal paper guarantees, would mean the final extinction of Jewish hope, not in Palestine alone, but for the entire Jewish people." Having made their case, the Zionist leaders again maneuvered—without success—to prevent the advocates of binationalism from addressing a world forum.

Magnes came before UNSCOP on July 14. In advance he submitted a memorandum and oral testimony from Ihud to the Anglo-American Inquiry; what he was about to say was "inseparable" from them. Magnes reiterated the call for "an undivided binational Palestine composed of two equal nationalities . . . irrespective of who is the majority or the minority"; for "the transfer of Palestine, for an agreed transitional period, to the trusteeship system of the United Nations" to prepare measures of self-government and draft a constitution with a Bill of Rights; for the establishment, following this transition, of a binational Palestine as an "independent constitutional state [working] in close cooperation . . . with the neighboring countries of the Middle East." Magnes pressed for the "speediest possible" admission of 100,000 DPs. "During the period of trusteeship" at least 600,000 more immigrants should be let in, mainly from North Africa, Hungary, and Romania, "to reach a numerical parity with the Arabs." Thereafter immigration would be "agreed upon between Jews and Arabs under the binational constitution," the principle of numerical parity being related to the principle of political parity.

Magnes did not broach the issue of partition in his oral deposition, nor had Ihud raised it. The chairman asked if he could oblige. Magnes responded that he and his associates had "wanted to present a positive case for a united binational Palestine on its own merits," without engaging in "polemics with the advocates of partition, whom we greatly respect." But he was "ready to formulate our arguments" against it, and devoted the remainder of his testimony to doing so. The position was further elaborated in a supplementary memorandum requested by UNSCOP. Ihud had "religious, historical, political, and economic" reasons for not embracing partition, which was "impracticable"; if it were "carried through [it] would be a great misfortune for both Jews and Arabs." Magnes held that since the "great majority of Arabs . . . and large numbers of Jews, both extremists and moderates . . . were against it," partition could only be "imposed" at the cost of a war bound to be unending given irredentist claims by both sides. To be sure, a binational state might also have to be "imposed," but whereas the two partitioned states would have to be created *ex nihilo*, a binational state already existed. Inasmuch as Jewish and Arab Palestinians lived in the same land, there was no need to draw "new boundaries" or to "persuade anybody that that part of the country is land for the Arabs and this part of the country is land for the Jews." Growth could occur organically.

Above all, Ihud had "no wish [for the Jews] to be segregated from the Arabs." There should be no yielding to the "defeatist cry" that Jews and Arabs "must be separated politically and territorially so as not to kill one another," though "the political leadership on either side may have worked itself up into this state of mind." But most of the "plain people" felt differently, and partition "would [only] stir up animosity that does not exist at the present time." Besides, segregation was not only "undesirable and unnecessary . . . but impossible." Any Jewish state, whatever its borders, would necessarily include "a very large Arab minority"—all the more so since "the important urban centers have a mixed population." Economic boundaries would be equally problematic: "The larger the Jewish state, the more impossible becomes the existence of the Arab state." It would be difficult equitably to divide the region's scarce water resources essential for economic development in both would-be states. Although "satisfactory 'national' boundaries" were said to be of paramount importance, they were perilous to draw *de novo*. Any delineation, Magnes argued, was bound to "create irredentas on either side of the border," with the "chauvinism taught in the schools" keeping the "war spirit" stirred up. Ominously, one of the chief advocates of partition had recently encouraged the acceptance of presumably inadequate borders by saying they need not be "eternal," implying that "the partitioned Jewish Palestine would be a bridgehead for the further conquest of the whole country." Magnes "found it strange" that anyone could commend partition for having the merit of "at least" providing "finality." To the contrary, it "seemed to be but the beginning of real warfare—warfare perhaps between Jew and Jew, and warfare between Jew and Arab."

Echoing Ahad Haam and Buber, Magnes placed the highest emphasis on Arab–Jewish relations, which he considered "the kernel of the problem." Cooperation was "not only necessary . . . but possible." In never having made it a "chief objective of policy," the Mandatory Government, the Jewish Agency, and the Arab leadership had committed a "great sin of omission." The two peoples had equally legitimate claims on Palestine. The Arabs had "great natural rights" by reason of their long presence and the "graves of their fathers" in the Holy Land, whose soil they had tilled "throughout all these centuries." There were "remains of Arab culture at every turn," exemplified by the Al-Aqsa mosque, Islam's third-holiest, and the Omar mosque, one of its "great architectural monuments."

The Jews had "great historical rights" they had never abandoned in the Exile; the very Book of Books was composed "in this city by [our] ancestors." Through "hymns, prayers, and voyages," memories of Jerusalem and the Holy Land had "been engraved in [our] hearts." Partition would keep them from "religious and historical associations with the whole country" and block access to "large parts" of it. A Jewish state without Jerusalem was "inconceivable."

Between the natural rights of the Arabs and the historical rights of the Jews, Magnes urged an "honorable and reasonable compromise." Palestine should become one of those states in which "the equality of basic national rights of different nationalities making up the state are protected against majority rule." Switzerland was a worthy model: "It gives full protection to [its] various religions . . . national languages, cultures, institutions, and yet, with all of that, there is full allegiance to the political state." Given the so far neglected opportunity to work and create together—by way of "life itself" and of "bridge-building " rather than "through discussion"—Jews and Arabs should take some such multinational road.

Here Sandstrom interrupted. Doubtless Magnes knew that the differences of "mentality . . . general outlook on life . . . ways of living, and standards of life" were not as great in the multinational states—Switzerland, Yugoslavia, Soviet Russia—or the binational ones—Belgium, Canada, Czechoslovakia—of which he had spoken. Magnes conceded the point only so far. To segregate Jew from Arab would be unwise. Such differences were not "insuperable" given the "will to face them together." In any case, "they cannot be faced by trying to put the Arabs into one compartment of an insane house, and the Jews into another." Sandstrom wondered about another singularity: since the Arabs "resent[ed]" as an "invasion" the immigration of the Jews with whom they would be asked to share self-government, they were not likely to embrace a binational scheme. The term "invasion" might be fair, Magnes admitted, and he expressed "great sympathy" for the Arabs' "fear of Jewish domination." Still, he felt neither side should seek ascendancy over the other. Although the Arabs might deny the "substantiality" of the "spiritual links" of the Jews, compared to their own, the Jewish ties were no less valid for being less "material."

Aware that Magnes did not represent multitudes, Sandstrom wanted to get some sense of the support his ideas enjoyed. Magnes answered that, should a binational solution be officially proposed, considerable segments of the Yishuv and the diaspora Jews would go along regardless of their "present views." Asked to elaborate, he characterized Ihud as a "small political group, a club" that published a monthly, in Hebrew, with a circulation of 1,300 copies that have "thousands and thousands of readers." In the February just past, Ihud had published *Towards Union in Palestine: Essays on Zionism and Jewish–Arab Cooperation* (edited by Buber, Simon, and himself, and subsequently submitted to UNSCOP), whose 2,500 copies had quickly sold out; 4,000 copies of Ihud's testimony before the Anglo-American Inquiry, recently published in New York, had done similarly well. Ihud was "partners" with Hashomer Hatzair in the League for Jewish–Arab Rapprochement and Cooperation, and in the last elections for the Vaad Leumi (National Council), the Hashomer Hatzair candidates, advocating binationalism, won "over 25,000" votes. The Communists too favored that outcome. Ultimately, however, Magnes had "no doubt and [was] ready to admit that the majority of the Jewish population was in favor of a [uninational] Jewish state."

In closing, he reflected that the Palestine problem, which had developed over "hundreds, perhaps one might say thousands of years," was so complex that it could not be settled "once and for all." Eschewing a solution claiming "finality," Magnes pleaded in the name of Ihud for a "practical approach," a

> framework for the development of common interests between the Jews and Arabs, who are both going to remain here unless the Arabs drive the Jews into the sea, as they say they once drove the Crusaders into the sea, or the Jews drive the Arabs into the desert, as some think perhaps they should be driven.

The Palestinian Arabs and the Arab states, though they had been approached by UNSCOP, remained aloof. They dismissed the U.N.'s authority to decide Palestine's future: self-determination could have only one meaning. The Arab Higher Committee specifically rejected the Zionist pretense to any kind of "historical" title to Palestine. To admit the principle of a timeless association would be to sanction the contesting and redrawing of borders—no matter how old—the world over. Even if one were to concede the Jews' claim, the Arabs' was, if anything, all the more compelling, since over the centuries it was they, not the Jews, who had reclaimed and worked a land that was never "without a people." As for the need for a haven for the Jewish people in general and the present-day refugees in particular, meeting it at the expense of the Palestinian Arabs, who had had no part in the ancient Christian persecution of the Jews, would be morally untenable.

This coldness was a default strategy dictated by the pervasive powerlessness of disarray. When the Palestine question came to a head at the end of the Second World War, the nationalist movement had not recovered from Britain's suppression of the second intifada of 1936—9. Its leadership was beset by rivalries among the old notable families of city and country, compounded by growing generational tensions in the cities and between the big landowners and the *fellahin*. The Arab Higher Committee, dispersed during the war but set up again in Bludan, Syria, in June 1946, was unable to agree on an effective executive. The Mufti had just returned to Cairo from his questionable travels in Europe and sought to retake control. But besides being spurned by the Allies, he was more than ever distrusted for his inordinate ambition by nearly the entire Arab Palestinian political class, as well as by the Hashemite sovereigns of Transjordan and Iraq and the rulers of Egypt, Saudi Arabia, and Syria.

Validating Buber's plaint that they were neglecting the "intra-national" for the "international" side of the Arab Question, the Zionist leaders paid little attention to the political infighting among Palestinian Arabs. Instead they were busy tracking the diplomatic moves of Emir (shortly King) Abdullah of Transjordan (soon to be Jordan). Throughout the life of the Mandate, in making overtures to that *soi-disant* sovereign, Weizmann, Sharett, Sasson, and Golda Meyerson (from 1956, Meir) practiced the old diplomacy of Herzl. Starting in 1922, when the British contrived the Emirate of Transjordan and enthroned Abdullah in Amman, there were sustained contacts between him and Zionist officials, beginning with Weizmann. All along, both parties explored the eventuality of the Emir's securing the lands on the western bank of the Jordan River in exchange for supporting the establishment of a Jewish state. In the mid 1930s Abdullah again met Weizmann, and then Sharett. Following the second intifada, which disconcerted him, Abdullah eyed the Peel Report, which had first bruited the possibility of partition, more favorably.

But, like his younger brother Feisal I, whom the British had elevated in Baghdad (succeeded by Feisal II in 1935), Abdullah was a proud son of the late Ibn Ali Hussein, Sherif of Mecca, who had died in 1931, and whose outsized ambition he made his own. For years Abdullah's extravagant, though tacit, aim was to unite or confederate Jordan and Iraq with Syria, Lebanon, and Palestine, under the Hashemite banner. Banking on British support, the Emir thought to ascend in the Middle East by reconstituting a chimerical Greater Syria. Egypt and Saudi Arabia were determined to block his reach. In October 1944 Cairo initiated the formation of an Arab League, including all of these states plus Yemen. Together they declared that to do violence to the Palestinian Arabs would be "to endanger the peace and stability of the entire Arab world."

Imperial America had so far refrained from direct intervention, keeping an eye on Saudi Arabia and its oil, while Britain, whose staying power the Arab elites vastly overestimated, barely held on. It was not until March 1946 that Transjordan became a fully sovereign state (eventually renamed the Hashemite Kingdom of Jordan) as part of a treaty of alliance between London and Amman: the British would keep a garrison in place and command and finance Jordan's Arab Legion, by far the best army in the Arab world.

With the war's end, the contacts between the Jewish Agency and Abdullah resumed. Sasson, chief of the Agency's Arab section, met with the king in August 1946 following the Morrison–Grady proposal, which both opposed. Abdullah again, in talks with his British over-lords, intimated his acceptance of the partition of Palestine, with one proviso: territory and population not included in a Jewish state and reserved for a would-be Arab Palestinian state were to be placed under his aegis and united or leagued with Jordan. On November 17, 1947, twelve days before the General Assembly voted to partition Palestine, and in utter disregard of the leaders of Egypt and Syria, Abdullah repeated his position in a secret meeting with Golda Meir, Sasson's successor. Although he would make a show of endorsing the Arab League's opposition, he was widely understood to be the only Arab leader to countenance partition, largely in the expectation of expand-ing his own realm.

The divisions within Palestinian civil and political society and among the Arab states coincided with the continuing clamor for nationalism throughout the wider Middle East. The contradiction between these conflicting self-interests and the shared interest in self-determination resulted in frustration that found an outlet in the struggle for a sovereign Arab state in Palestine and against Zionism. This debilitating mix of infighting and diversionary ideological in-vestment may well be one of the keys to the decision by the Arab Higher Committee and the Arab League to boycott UNSCOP: both lacked the coherence to parry and thrust credibly in an alien inter-national forum. As supplicants, furthermore, the Palestinian Arabs and their Arab advocates were without the Jews' aura of recent martyrdom, and were stigmatized as a people.

After spending a month taking testimony—concerning the holy places and the future of Jerusalem—and making on-site visits in Palestine, UNSCOP traveled from Jerusalem to Damascus, Beirut, and Amman. On July 22, in Beirut, Hamid Fragié, Lebanon's foreign minister, presented to the eleven commissioners, without discussion but in the name and presence of the representatives of the Arab states, their views on the Palestinian Question. With the right of self-determination as its foundation, Fragié's memorandum called for the end of the Mandate and the creation of a sovereign Arab Palestinian state in the whole of Palestine. It repudiated the Jews' "natural right of self-defense" in the event of their establishing, by force, a Jewish state.

Since King Abdullah had deliberately sent no representative to the Beirut meeting, Chairman Sandstrom and six other members of UNSCOP came to him. After feigning solidarity with the other Arab leaders, Abdullah restated his by-now-transparent position: he would go along with partition if Jordan came into control of the territories assigned or left to the Palestinian Arabs. To his patrons in London he gave the same assurance. Musa al-Alami, one of Magnes' early contacts, told his British confidants that to prevent the Arabs from going to war against a forcibly imposed Jewish state, the Great Powers would be well advised to offer control of these territories instead to the Mufti, Abdullah's sworn rival. Al-Alami, a scion of one of Jerusalem's great families who had read law at Cambridge, had impeccable credentials as a Palestinian nationalist. After collaborating with the British, supporting the second intifada, and repeatedly meeting Ben-Gurion in the late 1930s, late in the war he had set up a modest Palestinian-Arab propaganda organization, which operated in foreign countries to present the Arab side of the explosive Arab–Jewish confrontation to a wider world.

When it came to propaganda, as with other means of self-promotion in the West, the Arab Higher Committee and the Arab governments were no match for the Jewish Agency and the World Zionist Movement. The carefully staged odyssey of *Exodus 1947* revealed the full extent to which they were outclassed in concept, technique, and ingenuity.

The scheme was conceived with a view to discrediting the British "raj" in Palestine by defying the White Paper of 1939, with its strict limits on immigration. While the Irgun and Lehi partisans continued to harass the mandatory authority, the Hagana and Palmach concentrated on running the blockade. Already in a clear majority, the Arabs had an annual population growth of 30 per 1,000—one of the world's highest—compared with a Jewish increase of less than 18 per 1,000. With the disinclination of American Jews to emigrate to Palestine from their gilded exile, only an influx of survivors of the Judeocide and Jews from North Africa could help redress this imbalance.

The approximately 700,000 Jews of the Arab countries were an obvious reservoir of potential immigrants—and soldiers. But, quite apart from being practically untouched by Zionism, they were not esteemed by the Zionist leadership, which was solidly Eastern European (Ashkenazic). Even so, the Jewish Agency began to plan the *aliyah* of these mostly Sephardic Jews, representing them as living proof of the vain hope of the coexistence of Jews and Arabs on terms of equality. But what mattered immediately was the transmigration of the surviving East-Central European Jews, and not primarily for humanitarian and demographic reasons. They were wanted as a symbol. The Zionists proposed to use the DPs to dramatize the resolve of the Jews, following their recent near-extinction, to help build the *Judenstaat* in Eretz Israel. Rather than continue to run refugees into Palestine on the quiet, the Hagana and Palmach were ordered to undertake a large-scale, conspicuous rescue operation to coincide with the hearings of UNSCOP in Palestine and the debates in the U.N. General Assembly. The idea was to impress the eleven commissioners and world opinion with the determination of the Zionist leadership, and to exalt the raw courage of the refugees themselves, sufficiently traumatized to brave the Mandatory power's blockade. In the process the Zionists looked to embarrass the British, rally the Yishuv, and daunt the Arabs. There was no achieving these objectives without a focused propaganda campaign.

Thus was launched Operation Haganah Ship Exodus 47. With the connivance of the French government, some 4,500 refugees, primarily young men and women with pro forma Colombian visas on counterfeit identity papers, were brought to France from Eastern Europe for passage to Palestine. There they were packed onto the S. S. *President Warfield*, anchored at Sète, a discreet port south of Montpellier. A converted steamship ferry from Chesapeake Bay, this passenger transport stole away after midnight on July 11, 1947. British warships proceeded to track it doggedly. Six days later the *Exodus*, as it had been rechristened, was off the Palestinian coast at Gaza. After closing in on the ship, sailors of the Royal Navy moved to take it over and sail for Haifa for the quarantine of the passengers, pending their forced return to Europe. With a mixture of premeditation and spontaneity, the crew and passengers sought to fight off the British boarding party during the night of July 17–18. Although neither side used firearms, in the melee, with British soldiers resorting to force, two immigrants and one crew member were killed, and at least 150 were injured. Within a few days the immigrants were put on three ships that made for Port-de-Bouc, near Marseilles, where 130 of them agreed to disembark. The others, defiant, were taken to Hamburg, in Germany's British zone, and confined to two nearby camps until after the foundation of the state of Israel.

Not all the vicissitudes of the *Exodus* had been anticipated. Chairman Sandstrom and several other members of UNSCOP happened to be present as British men-at-arms bore down upon the refugees to get them to board the ships that would carry them back to the dark hold of the DP camps. The correspondent of the *Christian Science Monitor* reported from Haifa that the "Jews here believe that one 'illegal' ship may be worth 10 million words in helping to convince the Committee." An abundance of newspaper, radio, and newsreel reporters, some of them traveling with the *Exodus*, covered the event, and their stories stirred compassion and outrage in the West while sealing the diaspora's engagement with the Yishuv and the Zionist cause. The whole endeavor had been largely paid for and publicized by the American Zionists.

Much to the discomfort of the official Zionists, Irgun and Lehi stepped up their terrorist operations in mid July, at first independently of the ongoing *Exodus* saga. On July 12 Irgun took two British sergeants hostage, in the hope of dissuading the high commissioner from executing several of their colleagues who were facing death sentences. Irgun, Lehi, and Palmach attacked military posts near Haifa in an effort to force the release of the *Exodus* refugees. The British, unshaken, executed three Irgun militants. On July 30 the Irgun kidnappers hanged their two hostages and weighed down the bodies with explosives, causing one British soldier to be wounded when untying them. Incensed, British soldiers went on a rampage in Tel Aviv, killing five Jews and wounding several more.

Once again, the official Zionists tried to differentiate two illegal lines of action and to distance themselves from their sometime partners. Ben-Gurion was irate that the vileness of Irgun's latest deeds had eclipsed the nobility of the drama mounted by the Hagana. He considered *Exodus* a greater "epic" than the resistance in the wartime ghettos: whereas the Jews in Warsaw "had had no choice," the DPs had traded the safety of France for the hope of Zion. The exploit of the *Exodus* was "one of the most remarkable examples of Jewish combativeness, pride, and attachment to Eretz Israel"—whereas "the Irgun acted like the Nazis." "Who, after such a crime," asked Ben-Gurion, "can still be interested in the battle being waged by 5,000 Jews?" As they had after the explosion at the King David Hotel, the leaders of the Jewish Agency assured the high commissioner, General Sir Alan Cunningham, that in cooperation with the British they would restrain Irgun and Lehi. Meanwhile the vengeful cycle of Arab–Jewish clashes increased in and around Tel Aviv and Haifa, to which the Hagana contributed as much as the

Revisionist terrorists, whom the Zionist directorate kept at arm's length so as to be able to disavow them.

Against this background of escalating turmoil in Palestine, the members of UNSCOP traveled to Geneva to write up their findings, which were submitted to the secretary-general of the UN at the end of August 1947. Within less than a month, while a subcommittee of the General Assembly was deliberating, Britain's colonial secretary, Arthur Creech-Jones, stated in New York that His Majesty's Government, anticipating the possibility of an unsatisfactory settlement, was drawing up plans for an early withdrawal of military and civilian personnel from Palestine. By late November, the contingency had become a timetable: the Mandate would end on May 15, 1948, and the last soldier would leave by August 1. This unilateral rescript was as reckless as the edict of June 3 issued without concern for the subcontinent's explosive communal tensions, announcing Britain's imminent departure from India. The impatience of the government was triggered by the unbearable cost of imperial overstretch, and by Labour's resolve to blackmail Washington into becoming the backstop for a spent Greater Britain in the rapidly and radically changing world system.

The eleven UNSCOP delegates were aware, within limits, that the Middle East was at a crossroads in the refiguration of its subordinate and contested place between the fading *Pax Britannica* and the rising if indeterminate *Pax Americana*. Although they were divided on key issues, they agreed that the Mandate was no longer tenable given that the Arab and Jewish positions were so far apart and so combustible. The time had come to recognize Palestine's independence, but only if neither Jews nor Arabs would dominate. A majority of seven delegates proposed the establishment of two states linked by an economic union, and an internationalized Jerusalem administered by the U.N. During a two- to three-year transition, a U.N.-appointed authority would fit them each with a constitution safeguarding the rights of minorities as part of the passage to sovereignty.

The map for the projected partition of Palestine bore a strong resemblance to the one proposed by the Peel Report of 1937. The Arab state, covering about 43 per cent of the Mandatory territory, would comprise a population of 730,000, with a minority of about 10,000 Jews dispersed in about thirty-five settlements. It was configured to include western Galilee, the West Bank except for Jerusalem, and the coastal plain (the later Gaza Strip) from the Egyptian border to south of Tel Aviv. The Jewish state, covering about 55 per cent of the territory, would have 900,000 people, including over 400,000 Arabs and 90,000 Bedouins. With close to 85 per cent of the Jews centered in and around the three major cities and owning less than 10 per cent of privately held land, it was all but impossible to carve out a sizable, contiguous territory—"a viable Jewish state in an adequate area of Palestine"—with a clear Jewish majority but without a large Arab presence. The roughly 5,500-square-mile area would include the northern coastal plain, eastern Galilee, and the bulk of the Negev. Given the demographic dynamics of the two communities, this state would before long face the dilemma of being either swamped by Arabs or tempted to expel large numbers of them.

The recommendation for these vexed borders was signed by the delegates of Canada, Czechoslovakia, Guatemala, the Netherlands, Peru, Sweden, and Uruguay. Besides being Christian, all these countries were within the Anglo-American orbit except for Czechoslovakia. At the time Prague was still trying to act as a bridge between the West and the Soviets—a role made redundant once Moscow began to favor the two-state solution. Australia abstained.

Three UNSCOP delegates rejected partition in favor of a two-state federation. The elections to one of the chambers of a bicameral legislature would take account of the demographic factor. There would be a common citizenship and a federal authority to deal with foreign policy, defense, and economic affairs. Divided into separate Jewish and Arab municipalities, Jerusalem was designated the capital. The Ihud-like minority solution was endorsed by India, Iran, and Yugoslavia. With large Muslim minorities, India and Yugoslavia were concerned to guarantee minority rights and reduce intercommunal friction. Besides being the chief seat of Shiism, Iran had other reasons to vote against partition, fearing that it might help to reopen the door to the return of Anglo-American oil interests—a prospect it fought until the American-engineered overthrow of the elected Iranian prime minister, Mohammad Mossadegh, in 1953. All three countries were beginning to look for a third, nonaligned way between Washington and Moscow—as were the internal critics of Zionism.

The Jewish Agency and Zionists the world over by and large seconded the majority position with enthusiasm, and considered it a sound basis for discussion. Despite reservations about the forfeiture of Jerusalem and western Galilee, official Zionists were relieved that binationalism was at long last on the wane. No doubt settling for less than the whole was made more tolerable because of a belief, shared by Ben-Gurion, in the impermanence of borders. Irgun, by contrast, lambasted UNSCOP's plan as a violation of Zion, and charged its Jewish proponents with treason. It would fight on for an undivided Eretz Israel by any means necessary. No "normal and decent" man, Begin declared, could stand for his "homeland being cut up with scissors." A nation can be torn apart "by force," but it could hardly be expected to take such a dismemberment lying down. Irgun would not: on September 29 its operatives blew up the British police headquarters in Haifa, killing an estimated ten Britons and Arabs, and wounding a score of others.

The Arab–Muslim reaction to the UNSCOP vote was predictable. To a man—except for King Abdullah—the leaders were up in arms. Again they denied the authority of the U.N. to cede Arab lands to anyone, let alone the Zionists, and called on it to recognize the inalienable right of the indigenous population to their own state in the whole of mandatory Palestine. Eschewing proposals or counter-proposals, the Arabs pointed to the naked inequity of partition as further evidence of disproportionate Zionist influence in so many critical quarters. Voicing the conviction that the Zionists would never settle for anything less than mastery over all of Palestine, these spokesmen insisted their countries could not be bound by an illegal prescript, and if need be would resist it by force.

At this crucial juncture—and exactly as the internal critics had feared over the years—there remained no channels or even impulses for direct talks between Jewish and Arab Palestinians. Not only had nothing been done to temper the escalating friend–enemy dissociation, but the arbitrariness of the proposed partition could only intensify distrust, hostility, and cynicism. The future of both peoples was being negotiated in distant councils of state, and by special interests, in the spirit of Metternich's realpolitik at the Congress of Vienna in 1814–15, rather than of Woodrow Wilson's self-determination at the Paris Peace Conference of 1919.

Manifestly, the outcome of UNSCOP's findings would be decided by London, Washington, and Moscow acting through the U.N. General Assembly, in which the ascendancy of the U.S. became evident overnight. Pressed by Harold Laski—recently chairman of the Labour Party, a staunch advocate of Indian independence, and a leading socialist intellectual—and by Churchill, Bevin got behind the majority report, though he considered it grossly unfair to the Arabs. He and Attlee were as desperate to get out of Palestine as they were to get out of India, Burma, and Ceylon. They were determined not to waste any of the manna of the Marshall Plan, announced in June 1947, on keeping troops in Palestine to enforce one embattled alternative or another. American loans and credits eventually also swayed the governments of several other nations, including France, to support partition.

Determining the fate of partition would ultimately fall to Washington. Throughout September the Defense and State Departments, including Secretary of State General George Marshall, continued to press their opposition. But as Truman, facing an uphill presidential election, became more attentive to domestic politics, the pro-Zionist lobby exerted its pull. Marshall, who had quickly proved his diplomatic mettle, could be trusted to put aside his own judgment and work for a Jewish state without endangering relations with key Arab states and the flow of oil essential for the European Recovery Program. Besides, with the Soviets ever less equivocal about partition, Truman felt he had to match or best them. On October 11 Washington threw its weight behind UNSCOP's majority recommendation. With Stalin and Truman equally ignorant and unconcerned about the Palestinian Arabs, their cause was left to the Arab countries to champion—and to use for their own ends.

Starting in late September, a subcommittee of the General Assembly debated the UNSCOP report for two months. These deliberations resulted in minor changes to the majority plan: Jaffa and Beersheba were reallocated to the projected Arab–Palestinian state in order to reduce the Arab population of the Jewish state by about 100,000, to 325,000; and the life of the temporary authority to prepare the establishment of the two states was reduced from between two and three years to two months, making a peaceful transition unlikely if not impossible.

On November 25, in the General Assembly's ad hoc committee on Palestine, twenty-five member states voted for partition, thirteen against, and there were seventeen abstentions. A simple majority was necessary to forward the recommendation to the plenary session of the General Assembly, scheduled to vote two days later, when a two-thirds majority would be needed. Desperate for time to rally wavering governments, the pro-Zionist lobby, with the help of Washington, secured a postponement of the day of reckoning to Friday, November 29. Importuned by senators and representatives, as well as by influential Jews and Zionists, President Truman and his inner circle instructed American officials to lean on Liberia, the Philippines, and several Latin American countries to vote for partition. Dean Rusk, head of the State Department's U.N. desk, noted later that the "pressure and arm-twisting applied by American and Jewish representatives in capital after capital to get that affirmative vote are hard to describe."

Even so, it can scarcely be stressed enough: because of the complex of guilt and horror over the Judeocide, much of the Christian world was in favor of a Jewish state. Without that public sentiment, the campaign of backstairs diplomacy would have had less traction. The Palestinian Arabs had no such reservoirs of sympathy to plumb—let alone voting constituencies or lobbies to rally. Some of the Arab states were counting on support from oil interests in the West, but these were momentarily marginalized politically: Washington and London concluded that the oligarchies of Mesopotamia and Arabia, with their fortunes tied to the capitalist world economy, had nowhere else to go.

The vote on U.N. resolution 181, taken on November 29, included thirty-three for partition, thirteen against, and ten abstentions. Since Monday, though the nays had remained unchanged, the yeas had risen by eight and the abstentions were down by seven. Except for Cuba and Greece, the dissenting countries—no longer wards of the British or French empires—were Muslim or had a significant Muslim minority (they included Afghanistan, Saudi Arabia, Egypt, India, Iran, Iraq, Lebanon, Pakistan, Syria, Turkey, and Yemen). The abstentions included Britain, China, Ethiopia, and Yugoslavia, and six Latin American nations (Argentina, Chile, Colombia, El Salvador, Honduras, and Mexico). As for the affirmation, it was carried by two African countries, five Anglo-Saxon countries, thirteen Latin American countries, thirteen European ones, including the Soviet Union, Belorussia, and Ukraine. Although the last three had communist regimes at war with the old religion, the thirty-three countries voting for partition, including the Philippines, were of entirely Christian lineage.

Following the General Assembly vote, Walter Zander, permanent secretary of the Friends of the Hebrew University, argued in "Is This the Way?," a remarkably probing pamphlet, that "the task of rebuilding a state of the disintegrated parts of the Jewish people . . . would have been difficult enough even under conditions of peace and general approval." A non-Zionist of Ihud-like persuasion, he stressed that it would be "disastrous to underrate the strength and significance of the resistance" to partition as reflected in the "determined and powerful opposition" in the U.N. The states that had voted against had a population of about 480 million, he noted—or 28.9 per cent of the total population represented in the General Assembly; those that had abstained, 625 million, or 37.5 per cent; and those that had voted in favor, 560 million, or 33.6 per cent. The "proportion of those in favor" would probably have been "even smaller" were one to take into account that "more than 400 million people (including the peoples of North Africa, Burma, Manchuria, Indonesia, and Japan) were not represented at all." More important still, "the neighbors of the new Jewish state, without any exception . . . were united in their opposition, whilst most of those that declared themselves for the Jewish state were far removed from the scene of action." And whereas the latter had "only a small real interest in the matter . . . the Arabs and their supporters feel strongly in the matter, and most of them consider the issue as their own."

The UN's writ for the establishment of a "viable" sovereign Jewish state in an "adequate area of Palestine" was greeted with frenzied jubilation in the Yishuv and the diaspora. In their exaltation, rank-and-file Zionists everywhere put out of mind the enormous material and human costs of establishing and consolidating Herzl's *Judenstaat*, which was presupposed by Ben-Gurion, Weizmann, and Silver. Among the Arabs, the flagrantly inequitable partition whipped up anti-Zionist, anti-imperialist enmity to new heights. Both the Arab Higher Committee and the Arab League swore to follow up on their threat to resist.

When His Majesty's Government resolved that British troops would not enforce the U.N. resolution but would quit Palestine in the summer of 1948, Zionists and Arabs were left to face each other head-on. The risk, if not certainty, of violence—intercommunal and regional—did not intimidate the Zionist leaders. They had had ample warning from the British, Americans, Arabs, and internal critics that partition could not be implemented peacefully. Their immediate and subsequent expressions of offended shock over the Arabs' refusal to deliver up the keys to Palestine without a fight were feigned and politically calculated. During the night of November 29 Ben-Gurion confided to his diary: "This night the crowd is dancing in the streets, but I cannot dance. I know that war is in the offing and that in it we will lose the flower of our youth." From the first, when forced to draw the sword against the Arabs, he and his closest associates were prepared not just to defend the borders fixed by the U.N. resolution but to thrust beyond them. At the time of the Peel Report, Ben-Gurion had said that the words of the Bible, for Zionists, counted for more than the provisions of the Balfour Declaration, and that "after the formation of a substantial army within the context of an established state we will abolish the partition and will spread over the whole of Palestine." Now, ten years later, and following a world and Jewish catastrophe without compare, he held that "the establishment of a Jewish state will not depend on the UN resolution [but] given the time to mobilize all our resources, on our capacity [and] will to win through."

Right after the U.N. vote Menachem Begin, speaking for the lay Revisionists, publicly voiced a similar aspiration, if more belligerently: partition was "illegal" and "execrable." Vowing "never to recognize" the rump state, he declared that an undivided Palestine, with Jerusalem as "our capital," would be "restored, forever . . . to the people of Israel." He called for the preparation not of "local defense" initiatives but of "vast strategic plans aiming to repel attacks and to prepare the offensive of the new Hebrew army." Reportedly, Nathan Yalin-Mor, a leader of Lehi before becoming one of Begin's close confederates, also advised against "hesitating to cross the boundaries marked off arbitrarily by the . . . United Nations in order to establish ourselves firmly along the Jordan river."

Since the U.N. resolution did not provide for a peacekeeping force, hostilities between the two communities erupted almost immediately. Within a fortnight of November 29, around 160 people were killed, most of them Arabs. By the end of February 1948, the number of dead and wounded had risen to an estimated 870 Jews and 1,910 Arabs. Both sides prepared for all-out conflict. Toward the close of 1947 the American consul-general in Jerusalem warned Washington that "if the U.N. expects to be able to partition Palestine without forces to help maintain order and enforce partition, its thinking is most unrealistic and its efforts will be in vain." The growing bloodshed bore out the arguments of the opponents and skeptics of partition in the General Assembly and the State Department, encouraging them to renew their stand against it. What worried the Zionist leaders most were plans by the anti-partitionists in the State Department to reconsider an international trusteeship as preparation for some form of a binational Palestine. They took it as a bad omen that on December 5 Washington imposed an embargo on arms shipments to the Middle East. The Hagana had just signed its first contract for Czech arms, brokered by the Soviet Union, which began to arrive in late March, 1948.

As even Truman soon noted, the Zionists failed to understand that they were "not the only ones to be considered in the Palestine question." Marshall, Lovett, Henderson, and Warren Austin, the U.S. ambassador to the U.N., did not consider it on a level with the problems America had to confront in Eastern Europe (notably in Poland and Czechoslovakia) and in the eastern Mediterranean (Greece and Turkey). In their diplomatic, military, and economic calculus,

Europe was a higher priority, as was the flow of Arab oil to the Continent. By early March, Washington's foreign policy establishment, which still had relative political autonomy, began to back away from partition. On March 19, as instructed by Marshall but without the president's explicit approval, Austin proposed to the Security Council, in view of the mayhem in Palestine, that partition be suspended in favor of "a temporary [U.N.] trusteeship," so as to give Jews and Arabs another chance to come to an agreement on the future government there.

Truman had become increasingly irritated with the relentless pressure of the Jewish pro-Zionist lobby, and most probably condoned Marshall's search for some middle course. To stymie this effort, which they attributed to anti-Semitism in the State Department, top Zionists arranged a private meeting for Weizmann with the president the day before Austin's U.N. intervention. Truman reassured him of his own and America's continuing commitment to a two-state solution, claiming later that the "first [he] knew" about the State Department's having "reversed my Palestine policy" was what he read "in the papers."

Just after the meeting with Weizmann, however, Truman issued a remarkably forthright statement. Since Britain was leaving Palestine on May 15, without "emergency action . . . there will be no public authority . . . on that date capable of preserving law and order." With "violence and bloodshed . . . descending upon the Holy Land . . . large scale fighting" among its people would be "inevitable [and] would infect the entire Middle East." To prevent such a sequence of events the U.S. proposed a trusteeship not "as a substitute for the partition plan but as an effort to fill the [impending] vacuum." To propitiate Weizmann and the pro-Zionist lobby, Truman stressed that the trusteeship, intended to "establish the conditions of order . . . essential to a peaceful solution," would not "prejudice the character of the final political settlement." The White House itself had resuscitated the historical possibility of a solution other than a hard-and-fast partition.

In the meantime the Zionist movement and Jewish communities worldwide, but especially in America, lashed out at Washington for reverting to Bevin's binational scheme. Denouncing Austin's declaration of March 19 as a "new Munich," Rabbi Silver and his associates orchestrated a spate of mass rallies, telegrams to elected officials, and public petitions urging the president not to forsake partition. Truman was in a difficult contest to stay in office, and the Republicans too were attacking him for wavering on the Palestine issue.

But on the ground in Palestine the civil war was beginning to go the Yishuv's way. The Hagana, bearing Czech arms, on April 6, 1948 reopened the corridor from Tel Aviv to Jerusalem, and the Zionist leadership in Palestine and in the U.S. began to hurl defiance in all directions. In April the Zionist General Council announced that it would proclaim the establishment of a Jewish state on May 15—the end of the Mandate—in the territory assigned to it by the U.N. resolution. Twice Marshall cautioned Sharett: the Zionists were running a "grave risk." Should they get into trouble, they ought not to "come running to us for help." But Dean Rusk, chief of the U.N. desk at the State Department, strongly doubted that Truman would "ever put himself in a position of opposing [their] effort [should] the U.S. opposition . . . be the only thing that would prevent it from succeeding."

On May 12, Truman summoned Clark Clifford, Robert Lovett, and Marshall to the Oval Office to deliberate upon whether or not the U.S. ought to recognize the unstoppable Jewish state. Clifford, a staunch pro-Zionist and Truman's chief political advisor, argued that it should, to honor America's long-time commitment to Zionism, and to comfort the Jewish people after its recent ordeal. Lovett and Marshall advanced the standard geopolitical arguments against this course, voicing in particular their concern that in the event that Arab armies besieged the Jewish state, Washington might have to dispatch ground troops to an explosive Middle East. The president was undecided, and the meeting adjourned. Truman was again in difficulties. Thinking back, Marshall remembered telling him that "the counsel offered by Mr. Clifford was based on domestic political considerations, while the problem that confronted us was international." A political neophyte, the secretary of state feared that the "transparent" bid for the Jewish vote, even assuming it succeeded, would "seriously diminish . . . the great dignity of the office of the president."

The protean anti-communism and anti-Sovietism of the revived Cold War bore upon all such discussions. The critics of hardline Zionism in the State Department kept warning that communism pervaded the Zionist movement and the Yishuv. Just as in May, 1947, Moscow had got behind partition, so a year later it was said to be on the verge of recognizing the Jewish state, presumably to secure a foothold in the Middle East. For electoral, propaganda, and geopolitical reasons Truman, pressed by Clifford, decided he could not equivocate any longer. Late in the day of May 14, partly to steal a march on the Soviets, the president announced that since "a Jewish state has been proclaimed in Palestine, and recognition [having] been requested by [its] provisional government, the U.S. recognizes the provisional government as the de facto authority of the new state of Israel." He followed only by minutes Ben-Gurion's proclamation in Tel Aviv of "the creation of the Jewish State of Palestine that will take the name of Israel."

Since the special session of the U.N. was still debating the American-sponsored plan for an interim trusteeship, this recognition by the most pious champion of self-determination among the five Great Powers nonplussed many delegations, including its own, for being underhanded and peremptory. Repudiated a second time, Warren Austin resigned.

November 29 had marked a bitter defeat for Ihud, Hashomer Hatzair, and their confederates. The official Zionists had won out. In both the Yishuv and the diaspora their critics and opponents, except for the Revisionists, were in headlong retreat. Ihud lost most of its residual political and financial support in America: during the winter of 1947–8 many once sympathetic Jewish personalities switched from opposing to backing partition, if skeptically. The foreclosure of the historical possibility of a binational solution became all the more dispiriting as the worsening situation in Palestine confirmed Ihud's most somber analyses, apprehensions, and forewarnings.

A letter of February 4, 1948, from Magnes to Herbert Lehman, one of his once steadfast but now wavering companions, betrays the internal critics' blighted hopes: "The kind of pressure that was used at the U.N. Assembly . . . to put through . . . partition [was] as evil as partition itself." He felt "ashamed that [the] Holy Land should have been made into a bargaining counter." Troubling also was the influence this "mighty" American government had "exerted . . . on countries dependent on it." Although "delegate after delegate stood up" to express reservations about partition, together they voted for it "inasmuch as they were told that it was the only alternative to chaos." On the contrary, "partition was creating chaos," Magnes concluded ruefully. In fact, when Washington reverted to the trusteeship broached by Austin on March 19, Magnes and Buber yet believed a non-confrontational approach might have another opportunity. Still, with Palestine raked by civil strife and cross-border war with neighboring Arab countries, they knew moderation had at best a slim chance. Magnes himself finally realized that, in the end, whatever anyone might propose, America, the unbound empire with the largest and most powerful diaspora, would dispose.

The critics of partition in the State Department and the American Jewish community resolved, without Magnes' knowing, to recruit him in their rearguard effort to keep alive the trusteeship plan and use it to reconfigure the U.N. resolution of November 29. In early April 1948 Lovett apparently authorized Loy Henderson to issue an official invitation to Magnes, insisting that "at no time has there been a greater need for a courageously conciliatory attitude such as yours." In his own message, Henderson emphasized that for "such an attitude to prevail, cooperation on the part of moderate and conciliatory Arabs and Jews is essential." At first independently, then in collaboration with Henderson, a distinguished group of Magnes' allies also joined this entreaty. The animators of this effort were primarily of Central European lineage and belonged to the American Jewish Committee's dissenting faction that doubted the wisdom of creating an all-Jewish state.

Magnes arrived in America in late April, when Jewish and Arab Palestinians were locked in battle and the Arab armies were being deployed along the disputed borders of the would-be Jewish state. He came primed to work for a U.N.-mediated and enforced ceasefire in Jerusalem that he hoped could be extended to the four corners of the Holy Land, and to rally political and public support for the American-sponsored trusteeship plan—if necessary also imposed by the U.N. In New York Magnes conferred with Austin, Creech-Jones, and Mo-hamed Fawzi Bey, Egyptian Ambassador to the U.N., as well as with a broad range of Jewish leaders, including Nahum Goldmann. In Washington he met officials of the State Department, and on May 5 and 6, respectively, he waited on Secretary of State Marshall and President Truman to present his case.

Even if futile, Magnes' eleventh-hour appeal was neither a dream nor a delusion. He and his brother band fought staunchly for their alternative in the face of enormous odds. The hardline directorates of the Jewish Agency and the American Zionist Federation, backed by a maturing Jewish electorate, left too little space for disseminating the precepts of moderation and tolerance, essential to any Arab–Jewish rapprochement. Magnes proved his political probity by continuing to emend and debate Ihud's position until his death, in the U.S., on October 26, 1948. If the idea of binationalism has survived to become the moral touchstone for critical spirits in Israel and the diaspora, as well as among Palestinians, that is only because those who first mined and worked it were public intellectuals of uncommon historical vision and civic courage.

*   *   *

Palestine was a cauldron between 1944 and 1949. This stretch of polymorphic violence had three distinct phases: from mid 1944 to November 29, 1947, the Zionists fought an offensive guerrilla war against the British; from December 1947 to May 14, 1948, the civil war between Jewish and Arab Palestinians escalated; from mid 1948 to mid 1949 a cross-border war was fought between the army of the rudimentary state of Israel and the armies of the neighboring Arab states. In all three phases the Palestinian Arabs were the underdogs and the losers, and during the second and third phases first the Yishuv and then Israel significantly expanded the U.N.-drawn frontiers of the Jewish state. Not untypically, the civil strife of this Jewish–Arab struggle was more ferocious than its conventional warfare. The large-scale massacres in 1948 of Deir Yassin (April 3), the Mount Scopus Run (April 13), Kfar Etzion (May 2–13), and Tantura (May 22–23) are emblematic of the avenging fury unleashed on both sides.

To contend that the Palestinian Arabs were the assailants in December 1947, and the Arab states the aggressors in May 1948, is to beg a basic question: could any Palestinian or Arab leader have accepted that 60 per cent of the mandatory Holy Land would be turned over to a minority of about one third of the population to form a state in which close to half its inhabitants would be Arab Palestinian? And what of the prevalent suspicion that the Zionists would never abandon their reach for the whole of Palestine? If a Jewish majority in an expanding Jewish state were to be secured, that could only entail the expulsion of legions of Arab Palestinians.

It is not to undervalue the work of revisionist Israeli historians who of late have questioned the innocence of Zionist and Israeli leaders during the critical hinge of 1944–9 to recall Buber's article "Let Us Make an End to Falsities," published in October 1948. Tormented by the violence of foundation, Buber questioned the official version of who was responsible for it—and, implicitly, for the earlier civil strife. He noted that the Israeli press claimed the war was one "of defense, because, surely, we have been attacked." But Buber recalled that, starting in the late nineteenth century, "small groups of the people who had lived in this land two thousand years ago" infiltrated into Palestine in ever larger numbers "with the intention of . . . establishing a basis for [their] concentration." With the settlers making increasingly "political" demands, the people who had long ago come to live in this same land showed increasing "signs of dissatisfaction, opposition, and hostility." With time the Arab Palestinians developed the "conviction that the newcomers were undermining their entire existence," and the U.N. having granted them "political power in the important part of the country, the conflict has broken out." Hammering away at the mantra "We have been attacked," Buber asked "Who attacked us?" In an atmosphere of patriotic self-righteousness and of acutely felt endangerment, he gave the maverick answer: the assailants were "essentially those who felt that they had been attacked by us, namely by our peaceful conquest." And when the Palestinians accused the settlers of being "robbers," and the Zionists responded, "this was our country two thousand years ago," Buber closed with two questions: "Do we genuinely expect this reason to be accepted without argument? Would we accept it were we in their place?"

From the mid 1920s the internal critics had warned that, by condescending to the Palestinian Arabs and the Arab states and by giving priority to relations with London and Washington at the price of dependence, the Zionist leaders could not avoid being trapped into using violence as a first resort rather than an *ultima ratio*. This not only precluded compromise on the ground in both Palestine and the greater Middle East, but entailed a spiraling nationalization and militarization of political and civil society. Despite himself and his protestations to the contrary, Ben-Gurion followed in Jabotinsky's footsteps, leading to the "iron wall" and not the bargaining table. He too set his eyes upon the Jordan River and contemplated the transfer of Arab populations beyond the borders of the future state.

In January, 1949, three months after his article and after the cross-border war had turned in Israel's favor, Buber presaged "the danger that peace, when it comes, will not be . . . a real . . . constructive, creative peace." It would be "stunted," or a mere state of "non-belligerency, which at any moment [with some] new constellation of forces, is liable to turn into war at any moment." Living in the shadow of a "hollow peace," the question was how to "combat the 'spirit of militarism' " nurtured by "the leaders of extreme nationalism . . . who easily convince the young that . . . this spirit is essential for the survival of the country."

When Ben-Gurion and his de facto cabinet proclaimed the birth of the Jewish state on May 14, 1948, they intended to put an end to the continuing discussion of trusteeship. Back in April, when one of his closest associates had asked him about the possible state borders, Ben-Gurion replied that there was no need to specify them, particularly since "we do not know them ourselves." The post-Yishuv would "not go against the U.N., should [it] hold fast." But in the event of war with the Arab states, the Jewish state's armed forces would set their sights on western Galilee and the route to Jerusalem: "provided we have sufficient forces [these territories] will become part of the state."

Ben-Gurion became prime minister of a provisional government charged with consolidating the fledgling state by securing defensible borders, which remained studiously undefined. Although the Revisionists were not represented in the thirteen-member cabinet, they were represented in the legislative council—and this despite Irgun's and Lehi's intermittently reproved transgressions of the law that, following the raid on the King David Hotel, had culminated in the massacre of Deir Yassin.

Since the U.N. was neither empowered nor able to replace the Mandatory power as an effective governing authority, the Zionist leaders ordered the Hagana to prepare to take control, on the heels of Britain's withdrawal, not only of the area allocated to the Jewish state but also, where possible, of Jewish and Arab settlements beyond those ill-marked boundaries. Irgun too thought big, setting its territorial objectives to include Jaffa, Jerusalem, the Lydda–Ramle area, and the Nablus–Tul Karem–Jenin triangle. Ben-Gurion shortly after fixed almost the same strategic goals for the Hagana.

During the winter of 1947 and spring of 1948, the Palestinian Arabs seemed to have the upper hand, forcing the Hagana to stay on the defensive and suffer considerable casualties. The Arab forces aimed to expand their tenuous hold on major cities with mixed Arab–Jewish populations, and to cut off predominantly Jewish cities, notably Tel Aviv. By January 1948, the Palestinian leadership had given up on this guerrilla-based urban strategy and switched over to a decentralized drive against isolated Jewish villages and settlements, especially in the Jordan Valley, eastern Galilee, and the Negev. This naturally included laying siege to main roads with a view to severing the supply lines of major cities, primarily Jerusalem and Haifa. That same month, Arab irregulars, here and there assisted by villagers and volunteers of the Arab Liberation Army, attacked a score of villages and settlements in the Galilee and north of Hebron. In every instance the Jewish forces drove them back, inflicting heavy casualties. The Jews sustained their own losses, particularly in the critical battle of the supply routes, prompting fierce retaliation by the Hagana and Palmach, as in the assault on Saas in mid February 1948. All in all, the Arab forces were held at bay, although they continued to wreak havoc along several strategic routes. In particular the main highway linking Tel Aviv and Jerusalem remained under attack, leaving the Holy City's Jewish community of 100,000 dangerously exposed. In late December 1947 several of Irgun's operatives exploded a bomb at an Arab bus stop near

Haifa's oil refinery, taking six lives. Arab workers responded by killing some forty of their Jewish co-workers. In reprisal the Hagana struck a nearby village, home to Arab refinery workers, leaving about sixty dead.

To avoid being caught up in the escalating crossfire, members of the Palestinian Arab upper and middle classes began to leave Haifa, Jaffa, and Jerusalem to seek temporary refuge in the capitals of neighboring Arab countries—close to 30,000 by the end of March. The flight of this elite—the vanguard of the future exodus—most probably reduced the reservoir of political leadership for the emergent Palestinian resistance.

Clearly, both camps took it for granted that the violence would continue to spiral upward. The Yishuv's political and military leaders expected the insurgency not only to persevere but to be joined by the armies of the border states immediately upon the end of the Mandate. This they prepared to turn into an opportunity. Under the direction of General Yigael Yadin, they drafted a master war plan, both defensive and offensive. Its near-term objectives were to break the siege of isolated Jewish settlements and of Jerusalem, and to prepare to block the invasion of the Arab armies. These maneuvers were conceived as the necessary prologue to securing control of all the territories assigned to the Jewish state under the U.N. Partition Plan, and to reclaiming Jerusalem. To reach these goals the armed forces were ordered to launch actions "against enemy settlements [and villages] located within or near our own settlement areas" that were certain to be "used as bases for actively hostile armed forces." In order to "gain permanent control," such operations would entail "pacifying" villages and, "in the event of [continuing] resistance . . . eliminating the [dug-in] forces and expelling the villagers beyond the borders of the [future] state."

As ambitious as it was, this strategy, named Plan Dalet—or "D"—was also in keeping with the official Zionist intent to expand the state beyond the allocated territory. It was certainly not in a "fit of absence of mind"—an earlier British historian's rationale for how the empire had come to be acquired—that before long the armed forces of the inchoate Jewish state increased its designated 5,400 square miles by 2,300 square miles. This territorial extension was almost completely cleansed of its Arab Palestinian population. Plan D was activated in late March 1948, coincident with the arrival of urgently needed Czech arms. Within six weeks the Hagana and underground forces seized some 180 Arab villages and five Arab cities, most of them on the far side of the U.N. lines. Breaking the indigenous resistance, they occupied Tiberias, Haifa, and western Jerusalem during the second half of April and Safad, Jaffa, and Acre during the first half of May. Many of the Arab inhabitants escaped or fled to neighboring countries, and the victors appropriated their land and property.

The willed or forced departure of about 380,000 Arabs during these months considerably enhanced the ethnic homogeneity of the state-to-be. But what was in part an historically routine politico-military campaign was otherwise marked by the worst horrors of irregular and unconventional warfare: arbitrary executions, massacres, rape, arson, looting. These unexpected but neither adventitious nor minor savageries of war gave wings to the fleeing Arab Palestinians. In 1948 there were at least twenty massacres carried out by Jews, five of them claiming more than seventy victims each. More often than not the assailants were army officers and common soldiers who thought they were carrying out orders. There is no record that any were ever called to account, and in some instances higher military and civilian leaders had tacitly given their approval. Irgun and Lehi militants were implicated, but enjoyed their customary impunity.

Deir Yassin was one of the most heinous of these early outrages at the start of the five-year civil and foreign war of independence, occurring in the course of the drive to secure the passage between Tel Aviv and Jerusalem. Situated southwest of the Holy City, the village of around 700 inhabitants was relatively prosperous, the bulk of its labor force involved in mining and processing the high-grade limestone of a local quarry. Because of its location near the vital highway, Deir Yassin had a modicum of strategic value. By agreement with neighboring Jewish settlements, ratified by the Hagana command, it promised to keep clear of the fighting and scrupulously kept its word. Even so, before long Zionist ultras spread the rumor that the village was a redoubt of local and foreign agitators.

In the early hours of April 9 an Irgun–Lehi posse some seventy strong stormed Deir Yassin. Initially the villagers fended off the intruders, wounding several of them, until a unit of the Palmach arrived. A terrible fury followed. At least 100 villagers were slaughtered—mainly old men, women, and children. But the rage of the marauders was beyond measuring. They mutilated, raped, and looted, and blew up and scorched unevacuated houses. Finally, several traumatized residents were forced into an open truck and taken to Jerusalem. Accompanied by jubilant Jewish soldiers brandishing rifles, they were driven through jeering Jewish neighborhoods before returning to a summary execution in Deir Yassin.

Zionist leaders and the Hagana registered an official disgust over the massacre, and denied any responsibility for it. Ben-Gurion took special pains to assure King Abdullah, the most receptive of the Arab sovereigns, that the assault was perpetrated by refractory terrorists. But as after the King David incident, the furtive collaboration between the official and the covert forces continued. In the field there was not even the semblance of shame. When advancing upon Arab villages and towns, the soldiers of the Yishuv terrified the enemy by using bull-horns to warn of another Deir Yassin. Meanwhile the Palestinian fighters and their Arab supporters dwelled on the massacre as further proof of the iniquity of Zionism, magnifying and exploiting the event to make irresistible the cry for vengeance.

Years later Menachem Begin, past master of terror, would claim over-simply that the panic propagated by Deir Yassin had made the population only cut and run, as if Palestinian Arabs hadn't also given battle; flights from combat zones turned into "frantic and unruly" stampedes. Yet with some candor he conceded that Deir Yassin and the massacres that followed were not a sufficient cause of the mass exodus, whose "economic and political significance [for the future of Israel] was difficult to overestimate." Fleeing systematic terror head-long, "of the about 800,000 Arabs living in the [post-1949] territory of the state of Israel, only about 165,000 are still there."

In February and March 1948 the Palestinian Arabs had struck three times in the Jewish section of Jerusalem, killing at least fifty civilians and injuring about 100. On April 13, four days after Deir Yassin, they struck again, this time in explicit reprisal. The secular pinnacle of the new Jewish Jerusalem, Mount Scopus in East Jerusalem was home to Hebrew University and Hadassah Hospital. A garrison of the Hagana was also there. Doctors, nurses, and students, as well as soldiers, moved back and forth in weekly convoys that also transported vital supplies from the Jewish section of West Jerusalem. Much of the two-and-a-half-mile drive passed through the Arab section, whose autho-rities had agreed to the arrangement. The convoy en route to Mount Scopus that day was typical, comprising two armored cars, two armored ambulances—one of them transporting two Irgun partisans wounded at Deir Yassin—two buses, and four supply trucks. After a squad of guerrillas detonated a powerful bomb that wrecked the lead car and cratered the road, a host of armed Arabs waiting in ambush charged. Some of them fought off British and Hagana forces. Shouting "*Deir Yassin!*" others rushed the buses and set them on fire, taking some seventy-five lives, mostly of medical personnel.

A month later, on the cusp of the proclamation of the Jewish state, the Arabs struck again. Founded in 1943, Kfar Etzion was the largest of a cluster of four Jewish religious agricultural settlements, with 130 inhabitants. Chosen for its strategic location, it lay 12 miles south of Jerusalem on the main road to Bethlehem and Hebron, in an area assigned to the Arab state under the UN partition plan. Emboldened by Deir Yassin, and in concert with the Hagana, the settlers harassed traffic on the thoroughfare before ultimately blocking it. On May 4 the Arab Legion and local irregulars reopened the corridor. A week later some 300 Arab Palestinian partisans, determined to secure the road against renewed onsets, besieged Kfar Etzion with a view to dismantling it. Following a two-day struggle, on May 13 some fifty settlers and soldiers, including twenty women, surrendered after a hundred Jews had died in battle. The perpetrators, also said to have made "Deir Yassin!" their battle cry, brutally murdered all but four of the survivors. Kfar Etzion, hours before the British pull-out, stands out as the Yishuv's worst defeat and bloodletting. For the Palestinians, it was Tantura, 15 miles south of Haifa, where from May 22 to 23 some 200 mostly unarmed young Palestinians were shot after their village had surrendered.

The contested and bloody birth of Israel was like the foundation of almost any nation-state. For the Palestinian Jews the price was loss of life; and they argued that, as the aggressors, the Arabs had to pay the wages of their defeat in the coin of displacement and dispossession. That cost for the Arabs was compounded by a greater loss of life and a rush into an exodus beyond recall.

The five-year Arab–Zionist/Israeli conflict was not a war like any other in the middle of the twentieth century. The age of colonial wars, annexations, and border demarcations was virtually at an end: the timeless torment of the Jews—even in its latest realization—could not justify a historical throwback to a colonial war whose time had passed, especially since the Arabs were not among the tormentors. Yet the Zionists/Israelis took up the sword as if shouldering the "White Man's burden," treating their enemy with a swaggering scorn rounded off by Old Testament righteousness. The outlook came even more naturally to a political class now confident of superior military power and prowess. Ben-Gurion, Meir, and Sharett, and later Begin and Shamir, showed little moderation, tolerance, or *virtu* in their dealings with the Palestinian Arabs and the Arab states, except with Transjordan. The rare concession was nothing but a gift—never a give-and-take between equals—unless dictated by the imperial patron. Absent any sense of limits, geographic or otherwise, the Jews in Palestine embraced the time-tested precept that "possession is nine-tenths of the law."

With the shift from the second to the final phase of the five-year violence of foundation, what started as individual exile of, or panic-driven flight by, the Palestinian Arabs gradually turned into their premeditated expulsion. The war that drove this banishment was both expansionist and ideological: its purpose was to expand the U.N. borders and to improve the demographic balance in favor of the Jews in a state whose cultural identity was imperiled by a dangerously growing Arab–Muslim minority.

In mid-July 1948 Jewish forces took control, without resistance, of the twin cities of Lydda (Lod) and Ramle, southeast of Tel Aviv, with a total population of more than 50,000. When asked what to do with the local people, Ben-Gurion was said to have told Yigal Allon and Yitzhak Rabin, both seasoned Palmach officers, to "expel them." Colonel Rabin duly gave the order "to expel the inhabitants of Lydda quickly, irrespective of their age"; the order should "be executed instantly." Since they refused to leave of their own accord, "there was no alternative to using force and firing warning shots to run them out" in the direction of Ramallah. Over 200 Arab civilians and prisoners were killed before the start of this forced exodus of untold thou-sands—some estimates run to several tens of thousands—of towns-people. Before the start of the final drive for control of western Galilee, Ben-Gurion intimated that, should "the fighting in the north resume, the Galilee will be cleansed and empty of Arabs."

As for the emptying itself, there were not only the intentions and designs of war but also its contingencies. Some Arabs were driven to flee by raw fear and wild rumor; others ran off in the train of notables and leaders whose motives and interests did not necessarily coincide with their own; and still others were escaping atrocities committed by Jewish officers and soldiers acting on their own. Nonetheless, all were a product of the Jewish state's territorial expansion outward and Judaist ascendancy within. Bias underlay both developments, as well as the predisposition of Zionists to deny the same population the right to construct its own nationalism with a territorial base in Palestine. It was part of the Arab nation, said the Jews, as if pan-Arabism had won the day and the Arab world were not subdivided into so many sovereign states. First Herzl, then ever more explicitly the political leaders of the Yishuv and the infant Israel, spoke of maneuvering the Palestinian Arabs into the neighboring Arab states and Iraq. The larger the Jewish state became, the greater the number of estranged Arabs, and the more profound their tragedy.

Although the Revisionists became the most strident advocates of a large, Arab-free Jewish state, it was Herzl who had first entertained resettlement—an idea taken up by Weizmann and Ben-Gurion. Eventually, on October 11, 1961, during a debate over giving Palestinians a choice between returning home and being compensated for staying away, Ben-Gurion expressed his conviction that the first, an "insidious proposal," was "designed and calculated to destroy Israel." There was "only one practical and fair solution for the problem of the refugees: resettle them among their own people in countries with plenty of good land and water and that are in need of additional manpower."

As we shall see, neither the leaders of Israel or of the Arab countries, nor the Palestinian Arabs themselves, expected refugees to become the crux of the Israeli–Palestinian problem. But Ihud did expect it. Eventually Buber decried Ben-Gurion's position for

> contradicting not only repeated U.N. resolutions . . . but also all the principles that the civilized world has come to accept out of humanitarian considerations as well as the Declaration of the Rights of Man, and as a result of which a vast number of refugees, among them many Jews, have returned to their former homes.

Buber appealed to the leaders of all nations to "extend their help" to the governors of Israel and the Arab states to achieve "an agreed solution to the Arab refugee problem as a first step toward a real peace in the Middle East."

May 15, 1948, marked a new defeat for the Palestinian resistance. The Arab Higher Committee's campaign to defy the U.N. prescript of November 29 had failed. The Committee continued to be torn by feuds, and as Palestinian members rushed into exile, there was a leadership vacuum. A lack of a command structure and overall strategy meant their thrusts against the Zionists were essentially local, and therefore relatively easy to fend off. Thousands of Palestinian irregulars took to arms and blocked roads, but they fought as members of ill-trained, undisciplined, poorly armed, and uncoordinated militias; their raids could harass but not overwhelm isolated kibbutzim and moshavim, let alone towns. In a sense they were pre-political primitive rebels without a prophetic or utopian ideal. Barely touched by the rising anti-Zionist nationalist movement, theirs was, to borrow the words of Eric Hobsbawm, an "improvised, archaic, spontaneous" popular resistance still smarting from the repression of 1936–9. The few volunteers from the wider Arab world who joined them during the next intifada added little muscle. But the mass exodus of 350,000 Palestinian Arabs before May 15 was surely the most dramatic and stigmatizing measure of their powerlessness, made more acute by the knowledge that there was no Great Power to intercede on their behalf.

There remained one hope: the intervention of the five Arab neighbors whose forces were substantial and relatively well-trained and equipped, though in want of a military doctrine. Yet even their military heft was considerably compromised. Except for Egypt, they were rudimentary states. Their coalition was divided and incoherent. With competing interests, they could not agree on common war aims, harmonize their diplomatic policies, or coordinate military plans and operations. Jordan was the most problematic of them all: it combined a pivotal adjacency to Palestine with a disproportionately large and battle-worthy army—subsidized and commanded by the British. And the transparent territorial and dynastic designs of King Abdullah were not necessarily incompatible with the long-range plans of Israel. Its leaders continued the Zionist policy of courting him while turning to good account the diplomatic and military discordances in the Arab camp.

By contrast the Yishuv—as ancient Israel *redivivus* and supported by post-Judeocide Jewry—was a juggernaut. The battle for national existence and individual survival dissolved ideological and partisan divergences into a solid *union sacrée*. On the left, the Marxist–Zionist Mapam and Hashomer Hatzair parties went out with the tide, while on the right the Revisionists rallied to the Ben-Gurion-dominated government, though they were free to press their maximalist program. Morale was only one of the Zionists' advantages during the struggle of foundation. In terms of potential manpower, their fighting forces were way outnumbered, but they had long ago started to compensate for this fearsome handicap. By June 1948 the Hagana and Palmach were the mainstay of Tsahal (the Hebrew acronym for the Israeli Defense Forces), formed on May 31, 1948. Almost overnight their self-made officers had fashioned a precise military instrument with a single nerve-center and a clear chain of command. They also made tactics of speed and mobility serve an overextended army fated to fight simultaneously on several fronts.

Having started a major military buildup after November 1947, by the following May the Hagana counted between 50,000 and 60,000 men-at-arms, Palmach 3,500, Irgun 4,000, and Lehi 1,000. A draft in 1948–9 raised the total to 95,000 in a Jewish population of 600,000. Many had experience in the volunteer Jewish Brigade in the British Army, in partisan bands in Eastern Europe, and as guards in the kibbutzim.

Somewhere between late 1944 and the spring of 1947—the midpoint in the Jewish–Arab civil war—weapons and munitions were in short supply, though the Palestinian Arabs were no better off. The Czech arms deal turned out to be crucial. It was signed with Gromyko in January 1948, and the first shipment arrived in late March and early April 1947. By May 15, the Jewish forces had received over $10 million worth of rifles, machine guns, and cannons, complete with ammunition. American Jews financed the bulk of this ordnance. While the Czech contract was being sealed, Golda Meir, on a fundraising trip to the U.S. as a member of the Executive of the Jewish Agency, raised an additional $50 million.

The burgeoning army of Israel was like that of a First World colonial outpost in the Third World. Its political and military leaders had a Western concept of warfare suited for a literate soldiery primed to use modern weapons. In the greater Middle East not even Jordan's British-led Arab Legion approached Tsahal in numbers or fire power. Without this intellectual command of modern warfare and the financial energy of the American diaspora, Israel could not have fielded armed forces that, in all major respects save sheer manpower, were superior to those of the combined Arab armies lined up against it. Israel's decision-makers, civil and military, had a far more realistic and therefore sanguine estimate of the balance of forces than the population at large. Gripped by a siege mentality, the Israeli population saw itself as a small, weak, and peaceful people surrounded by a boundless Arab world bent on its destruction. As history's uniquely righteous, innocent, and imperiled victims, so the perception went, the Jews virtually required such an outlook. The Crusades, the Inquisition, the Russian pogroms, and the Nazi persecution were so many milestones to the present endangerment, which was prefigured in the unprovoked uprisings of 1929 and 1936–9. Such a founding myth could not accommodate the reality that the Crusades and the Inquisition had savaged Arabs too, and that the Zionists had to take their share of responsibility for the first and second intifadas.

The split between the public and official temper was patent in Ben-Gurion's charge to the supreme command to prepare a battle plan for an attack on Lebanon, Transjordan, and Egypt. Written on May 24, 1948, nine days after the start of the War of Independence, his directive bespoke vigor and confidence. Ben-Gurion considered Lebanon "the weakest link in the Arab coalition" on account of its fragile internal equilibrium, making it "easy to contest the domination of the Muslims, [which] was artificial." The objective should be to "establish a Christian state whose southern border would run along the Litani River," to be ratified by a treaty. (Since 1907, Zionist leaders had looked to extend Eretz Israel northward to include the hydrostrategic

Litani River basin, predominantly inhabited by Shia Muslims.) In turn, by "breaking the power of the [Arab] Legion and bombing Amman we would also be done with Transjordan, and Syria's fall would follow." Should Egypt "persist in fighting on, we will bomb Port Said, Alexandria, and Cairo." By virtue of Golda Meir's agreement with King Abdullah at Naharayim in the northern Jordan Valley on November 17, 1947—renewed in Amman on May 10–11, 1948— the Arab Legion was not likely to advance beyond the Cisjordanian territories assigned to the Arab Palestinian state (the West Bank), allowing Tsahal to shift scarce resources to other fronts. Even though Ben-Gurion now and then must have trembled, he knew he was speaking from a position of strength.

On the final day of Britain's withdrawal, May 15, the military forces of Egypt, Iraq, Lebanon, Syria, and Transjordan came at Israel from every direction, joined by two detachments of Saudi Arabians and Yemenis. The Arab League's army of about 25,000 men shared a language, traditions, religion, and a consuming anti-Zionism. Yet while there was fear, there was no panic among the Jews; the new state's political and military class was steady and defiant. They had expected war, and were prepared for it. Since they aspired to expand the borders of November 29, they may even have welcomed an engagement sooner rather than later, assuming time was on the Arab side. Certainly they had done nothing constructive to reduce the risk of hostilities. With Jabotinsky, they understood the enemy legions to be primitives that a 35,000-man modern army should find relatively easy to keep at bay. They knew also that they were unified and supported internationally; the Arabs were neither.

The attack by the five Arab states, despite their anti-Zionism, was not a jihad intended to drive the Jews into the sea. Only the Grand Mufti, chief of the Palestinian nationalist movement, thought in such eschatological terms, and he was scorned and ostracized by both Farouk and Abdullah. Although the Arab leaders exploited endemic anti-imperialist nationalism to justify the decision for war, their chief reason for the Egyptian-driven intervention was not to leave the field to Abdullah, who probably intended to extend his reign over Syria, Lebanon, and Palestine. At his own and Baghdad's insistence, Abdullah became supreme commander of the Arab armies, whose most proficient formation was Jordan's Legion: under British command and with London's blessing—and Ben-Gurion's awareness—it was not supposed to advance beyond the West Bank. The Arab League's principal field army crossed the Jordan River not to strangle the new-born Jewish state, but to grab the Arab part of Palestine for annexation to Transjordan, in the process aborting the birth of a Palestinian state, with Israel's connivance.

Notwithstanding Tsahal's multiple advantages—including, beyond those already cited, familiar terrain and internal lines of defense—the battles of the first weeks were hard-fought and indecisive. Several settlements were taken or surrounded, Jerusalem lay open, and some ground was abandoned in the Galilee and the Negev. But, in making those gains, several of the five enemy armies dangerously overextended their lines and exhausted supplies. With the Israelis and Arabs equally desperate for a break, they soon accepted a truce urged and negotiated by Count Folke Bernadotte, the U.N. mediator in Palestine. It went into effect on June 11, to last until July 7. Troubled by the war they had predicted, Truman and his advisors proposed using this breathing spell to press for a revision, more favorable to the Arabs, of the lopsided partition of November 29. London fell in with this stratagem.

Days after internal and cross-border violence had erupted following Britain's withdrawal, the U.N. General Assembly had sent Count Bernadotte to the region with instructions "to promote a peaceful adjustment of the future situation." Nephew of the king of Sweden and a distinguished international lawyer, the Count, acting for the Swedish Red Cross, had saved thousands of lives during the Second World War, including those of many Jews. His first move after arriving on May 31 was to broker the ceasefire. At the end of June he submitted a blueprint for a renegotiation of the partition, intended to "supersede . . . the existing indefinite truce . . . by a formal peace." Looking to make the U.N. boundaries "more equitable, workable, and consistent with existing realities in Palestine," Bernadotte recommended exchanging the Negev, allocated to the Jewish state but now partly occupied by Egypt, for western Galilee, originally assigned to the Arab state but presently in Israeli hands. Jerusalem and its environs should be included in the Arab state, with full autonomy for the Jewish community there. The ports of Jaffa and Haifa and the airport of Lod should have a free status. Transjordan should merge with a binational Palestine composed of the projected Jewish and Arab state. A joint council of the two states would regulate their common interests, including immigration. And the Arab refugees should have the right to return or to receive compensation.

Abdullah could not have been more receptive, but the other Arab leaders and Israel were utterly against the scheme, which Bernadotte forwarded to Trygve Lie, secretary-general of the U.N. The Arabs charged that the plan only served to advance Abdullah's Hashemite ambitions. The Israelis rejected the territorial modifications, and were ferocious over even the possibility of a cap on immigration. Nor would they hear of the shared sovereignty implied by the Arab–Israeli council that once again raised the specter of binationalism. Ben-Gurion and Sharett also explicitly opposed any return of the Palestinian refugees. After nearly two more months, they reaffirmed their intransigence through indirection: Sharett advised Bernadotte in the middle of August that "there were vast potentials for the absorption of refugees in Iraq and Syria."

Bernadotte's efforts to extend the ceasefire came to nothing. Both sides had used the four-week military lull to raise more troops and procure more weapons. The Arabs increased their numbers to about 40,000, the Israelis first to about 70,000, and by December to around 95,000. Partly because the Arab states needed soldiers for homeland security, they were hard put to match those levels. Meanwhile both managed to bring in additional weapons, with the Israelis unexpectedly coming into armor and aircraft from Europe by mid 1948.

When hostilities resumed on July 9, the Israelis had an even greater edge over the Arab forces in both soldiers and armaments than they had had in May, and they had also improved their battle formations and logistics. Ben-Gurion's directive of May 24 to the general staff also made for an expeditious deployment. Tsahal immediately went on the offensive, and stayed on it until the end of the war. On the central front, Lod, Ramle, and Ramallah—way-station to Jerusalem—fell in quick succession to Israeli troops, largely because the Arab Legion retreated for fear of suffering irreparable losses. The advance to the north was equally swift, with the enemy driven out of Nazareth and southern Galilee. After ten days of fighting, entirely to Israel's advantage and with the flood of refugees rising, the Security Council imposed a second ceasefire, effective on July 18.

All in all, except in the far north and far south, Israel had the ascendancy. On August 6, Israel offered to open direct negotiations with the Arab states by way of Bernadotte. Although there was no reply, he stayed the course. Taking account of the criticisms of his June proposal and of the evolving situation, he revised his recommendations. Israel had radically improved its position by dint of extraordinary resolve and prowess. Besides, the fledgling state was recognized by ever more states, including two more permanent members of the Security Council. If the Arab states and the Palestinian Arabs did not go along, there would be no headway. Yet now that the Israelis had the whip hand, they were even less receptive than before to mediation and compromise.

Perhaps too sure of approval from significant circles in Washington, London, and the U.N., on September 16 Bernadotte presented his revised blueprint. The whole of Galilee was still included in the Jewish state, and the Negev south of a line running from the sea near Majdad (Ashkelon) east-southeast to Faluja (Kiryat Gat) would still go to the Arabs. Although he retained the idea of the fusion of the Arab–Palestinian territories with Transjordan, he dropped any suggestion of an attendant union of the Arab and the Jewish state. Jerusalem was to have international status, as stipulated in the November resolution of 1947. Bernadotte forwarded his revised plan to Trygve Lie. The belligerents, save Jordan, were certain to refuse it point blank, but there would be enough other U.N. members determined to keep mediation alive. The provisional government of Israel and its supporters and sympathizers in the diaspora had become increasingly nervous about Bernadotte's effort to amend the plan of partition. Not a few pro-Israeli voices called for an end to his mission, and questioned his bona fides; he was charged with systematically contravening Israeli interests, especially in Gaza and Jerusalem. Regarding Bernadotte as an obstacle to their goal of a Greater Israel, Irgun and Lehi demanded his recall.

On the afternoon of September 17, the day after dispatching his report to the U.N., Bernadotte was assassinated in Israeli-controlled Jerusalem, together with his assistant, Colonel André Sarot of France. There are strong reasons to believe that a Lehi commando wearing Israeli uniforms carried out this political murder, with Yitzhak Shamir's blessing. There was worldwide indignation, and the provisional government condemned the act and impugned any suggestion of its own culpability. Holding the Israeli authorities responsible, the Security Council asked Tel Aviv for an investigation and a report—but in vain. No one was ever arrested or tried.

Ralph Bunch, Bernadotte's successor as U.N. mediator, tried to move the opposing sides toward the negotiating table. The Arab states balked, despite their defeats and disabilities; Israel did so because of its successes and prepotency, trusting the facts on the ground to give it the last word. The Security Council lacked the agency to break the deadlock. In the same month the Palestine Question was on the agenda of the General Assembly, meeting in Paris. There was considerable support for certain revisions of the partition along the lines suggested by Bernadotte. On September 27, Secretary of State Marshall issued a statement accepting the slain diplomat's recommendations as "a generally fair basis for settlement," while Bevin sought to convince the defiant Arab leadership that they offered "the least disadvantageous solution." Compared with the expanse of contested territory occupied so triumphantly by the Israelis, the Arabs had no bargaining power.

The Israelis were in fact prepared to violate the U.N. truce and fight the Egyptians for the Negev—the only unsecured land of consequence that Washington and London might be tempted to deny them. To foreclose that possibility, Tsahal launched a full-scale advance into the desert on October 15, with air cover flown by volunteer diaspora pilots, capturing the town of Beer Sheva in less than a week. Ben-Gurion's assumption that Jordan would remain neutral was confirmed when Abdullah chose to ignore King Farouk's plea for help. A third U.N.-brokered truce went into effect on October 31, before Tsahal had completed its southern sweep but not before it had driven out what remained of Lebanese and Syrian forces in the Galilee, along with countless Palestinians. With an impunity they took for granted, Israelis again broke the truce on December 22: they advanced south toward the northern shores of the Red Sea and crossed into the Sinai south of Gaza, then into the outskirts of El Arish. Urged by Britain and America, Tel Aviv and Cairo agreed to a ceasefire on January 13, 1949, to be followed by a U.N.-sponsored armistice on February 24, at which point Egypt conceded the entire Negev, except for the Gaza strip, to Israel.

Such an outcome was possible only because Israel, before forging ahead militarily, had applied pressure on Truman. At the height of the American presidential campaign the previous fall, Clark Clifford notified Robert Lovett that the president, probably swayed by the pro-Zionists, had "ordered [him] to send a telegram to the Secretary of State in Paris completely disavowing the statement made by the Secretary on September 21 in support of the Bernadotte Plan." In an exceedingly close race, first Dewey and then Truman re-endorsed the original partition assigning the Negev to the Jewish state—there should be no changes not acceptable to it, they added for good measure. Their blessing coincided with the first American loan to Israel, whose Mapai-dominated provisional government started to distance itself from Mapam and Hashomer Hatzair. Under the slogan "From a Class to a Nation," Ben-Gurion began to transform Mapai into a nationalistically-informed party of more moderate social reform. The logic of the Cold War demanded no less.

Reporting to the U.N. in September, 1948, Bernadotte had emphasized the problem of the refugees, in terms of both their number ("approximately 360,000") and character (many of them "vulnerable . . . infants, children, pregnant women, and nursing mothers.") Since they were "not citizens or subjects of Egypt, Iraq, Lebanon, Syria, and Transjordan," the countries they had fled to, these homeless people "understandably look to the United Nations for effective assistance." He held that "responsibility for their relief should be assumed by the United Nations in conjunction with the neighboring Arab States [and] the Provisional Government of Israel," thereby meeting "one of the minimum conditions" for advancing "efforts to bring peace to that land." There was another: the U.N. should "affirm . . . the right of the Arab refugees to return to their homes in Jewish-controlled territory at the earliest possible date [or to receive] payment of adequate compensation for the property of those choosing not to return." On December 11, by a vote of thirty-five to fifteen, the General Assembly blessed Bernadotte's last work by adopting Resolution 194 (III):

> . . . that [Arab Palestinian] refugees wishing to return to their homes and live at peace with their neighbors should be permitted to do so at the earliest practical date and that compensation should be paid for the property of those choosing not to return.

Israel's seizure of the Negev—along with the decisive defeat of the Egyptian army, which daunted the rest of the Arab coalition—ushered in the transition from volatile ceasefires to longer-term but still fragile armistice agreements: a regional peace in the sense of a momentary absence of war. Between February 24 and July 20, 1949, Israel signed such agreements with Egypt, Lebanon, Transjordan, and Syria (with no shared border, Iraq simply withdrew its forces). These suspensions of hostilities between armies were declared to be "indispensable step[s] toward the liquidation of armed conflict and the restoration of peace in Palestine." They also embodied "the principle that no military or political advantage should be gained" from success on the field of battle. Being "dictated exclusively by military, not political considerations," the agreements were understood not to prejudice the rights and interests of any of the parties in final settlement negotiations. Although Israel was in a military position to dictate armistice lines that included territories not allotted to it by U.N. Resolution 181, it did not secure a legal right to them. The accord with Transjordan was by far the most important. The partition voted by the U.N. transmuted into a transaction between Israel and Transjordan—at the expense of the Palestinian Arabs. With Churchill's imperial design and Jabotinsky's territorial imperative as their guide, Abdullah and Ben-Gurion played by the rules of the old diplomacy, treating people as chattels.

There existed, of course, an understanding about a division of the spoils; but no borders had ever been agreed on. Now that Tel Aviv and Amman proposed to delineate them, much depended on the battle-lines and the balance of forces. Israel had the means to seize the West Bank, and many of its leaders favored this course. But Ben-Gurion and his inner circle demurred, conscious of the risk of being "saddled with a hostile Arab majority," as well as courting serious diplomatic and financial complications. With a "larger than expected territory liber-ated," Israelis already had their work cut out for them for "two or three generations"; after which—in what became a formula—"we will see."

No doubt overestimating the exhaustion of Tsahal and Ben-Gur-ion's eagerness to come to terms, Abdullah, in an access of over-confidence, grasped for control of Lydda (Lod), Ramle (Ramla), and Jerusalem, and to make Jaffa (Yafo) into a free city. But once the Jewish forces, having routed the Egyptians, reached Eilat on March 11, Amman settled for a ceasefire. Negotiated by Yigael Yadin, Israel's Chief of Staff, an armistice was signed by the two states on April 3, on the island of Rhodes.

With minor adjustments, Transjordan came into the territory west of the Jordan River allocated to the Palestinian Arab state. In early December 1948 this land had gone by the name of the "western zone" of the Hashemite Kingdom of Transjordan, whose name was changed to plain Jordan in March 1950. Within a month the West Bank of the Jordan River was formally incorporated into Abdullah's realm. With Tel Aviv's consent, and taking advantage of the U.N.-dictated parti-tion plan, Jordan annexed a territory with over 500,000 native Palestinians and a large proportion of the more than 700,000 Pales-tinian Arabs who had either fled or been driven out of the Jewish state, in the process depriving them of a homeland of their own. By joining his fortunes with Ben-Gurion's, Abdullah secured a vast expansion of his kingdom, even if it fell short of his phantasmagoric Greater Syria, which only London and Washington could have procured for him. The envy of his fellow Arab sovereigns, he was denounced for this grand maneuver of self-interestedness. On July 20, 1951, an extremist Palestinian nationalist, Mustapha Shukri Usho, assassinated King Abdullah on the esplanade of the Al-Aqsa mosque.

The costs to the Arabs of the first war with Israel are recorded by no hard or even estimated data, except in the case of Egypt. Cairo claimed some 5,700 casualties, of which 1,500 or so were fatalities. It gauged war-related expenditures at £35 million, or about $140 million. The Palestinian Arabs counted many thousands of dead, and at least

700,000 voluntary and forced refugees. Regardless of the numbers, the ignominy of the defeat left a legacy of wounded pride and repressed vengeance throughout Islam that accumulated over time, particularly in the Arab world and Iran.

From November 29, 1947 through to the signing of the last ceasefire with Transjordan on March 11, 1949, Israel registered some 6,000 dead—about 2,000 civilians and 4,000 soldiers, 2,100 of the total after the second truce of July 18, 1948. The financial cost ran to at least $500 million, not counting collateral property damage. The violence of foundation claimed the lives of 1 per cent of the population, or of 10 per cent of all adult males between the ages of 18 and 21. This blood sacrifice, for a cause felt to be both venerable and existential, secured an additional 2,300 square miles, or a one-third expansion of Israel's U.N.-specified borders. That meant control of at least 75 per cent of Mandated Palestine, including West Jerusalem and the Galilee. Except for the Gaza Strip, the remainder was in the hands of Jordan.

Beyond mere acreage, the Palestinian Arabs lost hundreds of villages and towns to the Jewish state. Many of the villages, sometimes with their cemeteries, were completely destroyed during or after the fighting. Before long the names of villages, including razed ones, were changed beyond recognition or substituted entirely. In Arab districts of cities the occupiers also swept the past clean. Presently the new names were recorded on maps, without any trace of the preceding, age-old toponymy. This psychic rape went hand-in-hand with the expropriation of the land of Palestinian Arabs who had fled or been driven out. All in all, they were divested of 4.5 million of the 6.5 million acres of Mandate Palestine. In 1947 the Jews owned less than 10 per cent of the privately held land in Palestine; three years later they possessed 85 per cent. The ink was barely dry on the armistice agreements when the young Knesset voted a succession of laws ratifying and regulating this wholesale expropriation of land, some of it for military purposes.

The violence to map and cadastre betrayed Israel's commitment to a policy of no return. Those Arabs remaining were reduced from a majority of over 800,000 to a minority of between 160,000 and 170,000. With the help of the U.N., over 600,000 refugees—beyond the 30,000 to 40,000 early, high-status exiles—found shelter in some fifty camps, the bulk of them near big cities: twenty on the West Bank (Judea, Samaria, East Jerusalem) harbored 200,000; in Lebanon, thirteen held 100,000; in Jordan, ten held 100,000; in Syria, ten held 50,000; and in the Gaza Strip, eight held 200,000. Like all such emergency camps, these were crowded, squalid, and unhealthy. Yet the refugees, rather than succumb to anomie, reconstituted their communities in the camps. Though they had Islam in common, they conceived of themselves in terms of family and clan, as well as local tradition and dialect, rather than as Palestinians—let alone members of the greater Arab nation that so many Zionists and Israelis persisted in seeing as the refugees' natural homeland and destiny.

It would take some time and effort before the parochialism in the camps could evolve into anything like a national self-consciousness. Members of the professional class inside and outside the camps partly filled the political vacuum left by the notables of village and town who had taken residence in major cities, especially capitals, of the Arab host countries. Hardly veteran nationalists themselves, the members of this elite—occasionally in uneasy collaboration with mullahs—proceeded to raise the horizon of the refugees beyond the camp, village, or town, to Palestine itself. As the wait for the return, initially expected to be short, began to seem interminable, the cadre played crudely on the refugees' desolation, bitterness, and misery to aggravate their *mal du pays*, incubator of resistance.

6

THE COLD WAR:
ISRAEL IN THE WORLD

The armistice suspended but did not end Israel's War of Independence (1948–9). In Israeli eyes this first Arab–Israeli war was exclusively the doing of the Palestinian Arabs and the Arab countries, which continued to threaten the newborn state. The lines of the armistice agreements validated the war- and state-craft of the Zionist directorate embodied by Ben-Gurion and his core group, and dangerously engorged their pride. While the new state fulfilled the dream of Herzl, Nordau, and Weizmann, it delivered on the nightmare of Ahad Haam, Buber, and Magnes. For Israel, surrounded by hostile states and culturally and politically estranged, the end of war was an uneasy truce that entailed maintaining a level of preparedness likely to turn it into a garrison state run by generals and imbued with a fortress mentality.

The unstable armistice was as much political as military. Largely benefiting Tel Aviv, it served also to prevent the foreclosure of Eretz Israel's future by a premature drawing of borders. As Ben-Gurion said in committee when ceding the West Bank to Jordan, "we will see later." The Revisionists were impatient with such temporizing. The political heirs of Jabotinsky, who since the 1920s had trumpeted Zionism's title to lands on both banks of the Jordan, now noisily criticized the government for yielding part of the homeland, including half of Jerusalem, to London's last remaining vassal in the Middle East. The left opposition, which considered an armistice a necessary but provisional step to peace negotiations, suspected that the deal with Jordan meant Ben-Gurion was not about to push for the establishment of a Palestinian state, freestanding or in federation.

Although the creation of Israel lit the light of heaven for a Jewish people emerging from darkness, this making threw off its own murk. Half of Mandatory Palestine's population of 1947 had left their homeland—of those, half had taken flight and the other half had been expelled. Israel was left with a residue of only 160,000 to 170,000 Arabs. Among this putative non-people, most were now displaced persons whom the newly landed Jews, flouting international law and U.N. Resolution 194, would not allow to come home. Nor would they offer compensation. Return would endanger the nation's security and erode its ethnic homogeneity.

The position reiterated official Zionism's old readiness, from Herzl on, to resettle or if need be drive out the Palestinian Arabs. This animus toward the refugees and the supremacism implicit in it were exposed by the internal critics, starting with Ahad Haam. The Yishuv's failure to address the Arab Question empathically, which Magnes had called Zionism's "sin of omission," became the original sin of Israel's foundation. Certainly, the leaders of the Arab states exploited the issue for their own political purposes. But by not taking steps to allay the Arab League's rancor about the degrading armistice agreements and the Palestinians' rage over their plight, Israel's governors chose to play with fire, supremely confident of their ability to contain it.

In 1950, just when Ben-Gurion and his team decided to block the return of and compensation for the Palestinian refugees, the Knesset unanimously adopted the Law of Return, allowing any Jew of the diaspora to immigrate and acquire Israeli citizenship. According to Ben-Gurion this law embodied "the aim of the 'ingathering of the exiles' " rooted in Hebrew prophecy, canonical prayer, and Herzl's vision. It was one of the first of many rulings intended to shape a state unlike any other, and was charged, in its prime minister's words, with "the redemption of Israel." The new nation would be impregnated with Hebraic values by way of the public school and citizen army. The State Education Law of 1953 directed the school system to inculcate "love of the homeland," "the values of Jewish culture," and "loyalty to the state and to the Jewish people." The universal values of the Declaration of the Rights of Man or the American Bill of Rights were passed over in silence. Near the end of his long life, Ben-Gurion ranked the Education Law and the Law of Return as "the highest laws of the State of Israel . . . that point the direction in which [it] wishes to and must go if it is to exist and fulfill its historic mission."

The army too was conceived as a school of the nation. The Israel Defense Forces' orientation and educational programs were to forge a Jewish consciousness and sense of Jewish history in recruits from a multiplicity of backgrounds. In a special ceremony following induction, the men and women of war were issued a rifle and a Hebrew

Bible. In its preface, Shlomo Goren, Ashkenazi Grand Rabbi of Israel and first Chief Rabbi of the IDF, told the soldiers that "this Book of God's Law [Torah] is given unto you . . . to be unto you a fortress of strength, a source of courage and salvation, a fount of divine inspiration and a pillar of fire to lead you along the way." Whatever and wherever the battle stations "on land, at sea, or in the air, in times of peace and as you draw near to war [this book] will not depart from your mouth and you shall meditate upon it day and night." The Lord "the God of the hosts of Israel"—here, as in the Hebrew, the armed forces of Israel are punningly equated with the heavenly hosts—shall "light the way before you in which you shall walk and the deeds you shall perform"; he will "crown you with the crown of victory." The Torah should be "a perpetual memorial to you before the Lord, for [it is] the Lord your God who walks with you to do battle for you with your enemies [and] to save you." The IDF's insignias and the new state's flag, anthem and official seal, as well as its national holidays, were designed around symbolic, traditional, and historic materials of a heavily religious nature. Unbelievers themselves, Ben-Gurion and his associates projected the State of Israel not just as an instrument of power, but (Goren again) as "the light of salvation and redemption."

The establishment of an independent Jewish state in partitioned Palestine foreclosed the historical possibility of a binational solution. Henceforth the internal critics, with rare exceptions, were ostracized, becoming in effect internal exiles. Following the Judeocide, the unequivocal need for a sanctuary for the surviving Jews had facilitated rallying around a state that Ahad Haam's intellectual heirs considered to be congenitally flawed. Now the issue was no longer its form, but its very soul. They continued to argue that sovereignty was incompatible with Judaism's culturally and theologically enjoined refusal of violence. Others read this enshrined if mythical singularity differently: in exile, as a metahistorical people, the Jews could afford to live by a moral and religious code that abjured deadly violence, especially when the foreign Other was collective. But now that they had re-entered history as a people claiming the right and obligation to look after their own security and welfare, force and violence would be essential and legitimate tools in the service of a sovereign commonweal. The effect of using them was precisely what many of the internal critics dreaded.

After independence they remained focused on their traditional issues—fostering Jewish–Arab understanding within Israel, promoting reconciliation with the surrounding Arab world, and questioning the excessive dependence on an imperial power—and added two more:

warning against growth of the garrison nation and rejecting the sacralization of state and society. There was no addressing the Arab Question equitably without tempering the official charge that Arab–Jewish enmity was exclusively due to the Arab refusal to accept the Zionist project and Israel. Yet the new state claimed the innocence of the Judeocide's victims for itself. That purity provided a moral cornerstone for the in-migration of some 350,000 displaced Eastern European Jews in 1949—perceived as the sixth *aliyah*, or god-sanctioned ascent—and served partially to justify the expulsion of Palestinian Arabs. And from a position of insuperable strength, Ben-Gurion and his closest military and political collaborators saw no reason not to keep creating facts on the ground. The logic of the power of possession became a prologue that culminated, after 1967, in the reach for control of East Jerusalem, the West Bank, the Gaza Strip, and the Golan Heights. Such a policy confirmed the Arabs' worst suspicions about the Zionists' ultimate goal.

As predicted by Jabotinsky, the military and political spheres were destined to become indivisible in Israeli policy. The longer the expansionist reach, the more central the military factor in Israel's ideological stance and diplomatic strategy. Not just the religious fundamentalists but the secular ultra-nationalists clamored, at a minimum, for all the land between the Mediterranean Sea and the Jordan River, to be seized if necessary by force of arms. That aspiration produced a unique cadre of leaders. A successful career in the Hagana, Palmach, Irgun, Lehi, or, more recently, the Tsahal, has been the formative experience of countless Israeli politicians, and for many the royal road to the highest reaches of public office. Dayan, Allon, Rabin, and Barak are the linear descendants of Ben-Gurion, while Begin, Shamir, Netanyahu, Sharon, and Olmert are the offspring of Jabotinsky. But whether as leading members of Labor, Likud, or National Unity Governments, and notwithstanding differences in "dress of thought" and public comportment, one and all were driven by the idea of expanding first the 1948 and then the 1967 borders in the quest for a Greater Israel.

The victory over the Arab armies in 1947–9 was prototypical: it effected a considerable extension of the boundaries specified in U.N. Resolution 181, and the noncompliance with U.N. Resolution 194, calling for the return or compensation of the refugees, went unpunished. The Arab world's chronic incoherence and the unflagging support of three of the five Great Powers—the U.S. most importantly—meant there was little risk in practicing the politics and diplomacy of might rather than right. Israel's crushing military predominance made such a posture possible, as did the single-mind-edness of the emergent political–warrior class concerning the inade-quacy of U.N.-mandated borders. Bound by a deep consensus and braced by an expansive military establishment, these men became all but ascendant in government, providing an important source of continuity in a political system with restive and unsteady cabinets. Civilian leaders without their soldierly credentials were required to adopt the same mindset and modus operandi.

In April 2006, Prime Minister Ariel Sharon unwittingly divulged, in public, the previously unspoken premise that had informed the decisions of Israeli policy-makers through the decades, regardless of party. The War of Independence, he said, rather than having "ended [it] was just one chapter" in Israel's uphill struggle for life. The country was "certainly capable of defending itself," but that was not the same as "living in security." Given this persistent vulnerability, Sharon declared, it could not be said that "we have completed the work and can rest on our laurels."

If Martin Buber was the Cassandra of the violence of foundation, Yeshayahu Leibowitz became the Jeremiah of the post-Independence stratocratic and expansionist state. Besides sapping the nascent poli-tical and civil society's "humane and Jewish essence," it would sooner or later sunder it from both the diaspora and "the continuity of Jewish history and tradition." From the beginning of the occupation and settlement of the newly conquered land, Leibowitz warned that this course of action would expose Israeli society "to all sorts of violence and particularly to acts of terrorism," and risk becoming "a cancer certain to erode and destroy" whatever was sound and healthy in Eretz Israel. He even forewarned of the "danger of the state of Israel becoming a fascist state" should its leaders fail to "end the domination and repression" of the Palestinians in occupied territories through good-faith negotiations.

Post-Independence Israel bordered four hostile Arab states that could count on support from several others in the larger Arab–Muslim world. Together they imposed a comprehensive boycott, including a maritime blockade: the Suez Canal and the Strait of Tiran were closed to Israeli and foreign ships. This collectively articulated *no* to Zionism and to Israel was a further tie among the peoples of the greater Middle East, who were already bound by affinities of religion, language, and culture. Yet the Arab world was no more unified than Europe had been throughout most of its history. The Shiite–Sunni Muslim schism was analogous to that between Catholics and Protestants. There were rivalries among the leaders of the different countries, and between the oil-rich and poor, tensions between the traditional elites and the new middle classes, and struggles between conservatives and social radicals. European and American oil interests and the Cold War added torque to these intramural stresses.

The staying power of the Palestinian exiles and refugees was one of the great but unexpected singularities—how the Cold War affected them was another—of an otherwise unexceptional historical constellation. With most exiles and refugees living in makeshift camps in the countries adjacent to Israel, it wasn't long before resistance emerged, and partisans began to steal across the border. Incursions from Egypt and Jordan started almost immediately after the signing of the armistice agreements in 1949. The infiltrators were largely refugees on a vain quest to reclaim their property, though some robbed and murdered Israeli civilians. At first the Egyptian and Jordanian border patrols tended to look the other way, but by early 1953 the Egyptian authorities were suspected of sending their own operatives, and the Israeli military began to take preventive measures. While confrontations were still of low frequency and intensity, Ben-Gurion ordered the creation of Unit 101, a special self-directing commando unit. Ariel Sharon, who had served as an infantry captain and been gravely wounded in the War of Independence, was given command of the small battle group, with the rank of major.

This special force's initiation came in August 1953, with a stealth attack on the El-Bureij refugee camp in the center of the Gaza Strip, where Egyptian intelligence was said to be encouraging cross-border raids. But the unit did not come into view until October 1953, when it reacted to an incursion by *fedayeen* from Jordan who had killed a mother and her two young children in Yehud, an Israeli town east of Tel Aviv. Jordanian officials denounced the assault and offered to help find the culprits. But without delay Unit 101 was ordered or authorized to mount a retaliatory operation against Qibya, a border village of some 2,500 inhabitants in Jordanian-controlled Palestine, northwest of Ramallah. The special forces struck late on October 14, with instructions to show no mercy, the objective being to set an example and deter further border raids. With Major Sharon directing operations, Unit 101, after pacifying the village, razed about forty houses and destroyed the local school, police station, and mosque. At least fifty villagers died—mostly women and children, many of them trapped and killed when their houses were blown up.

Whereas Deir Yassin rang up the curtain on the civil and cross-border war of 1947–9, Qibya prefigured the routinely disproportionate counterattacks of Israel's war against the Palestinian resistance. At first Ben-Gurion sought to exonerate the army by laying blame on local citizens seeking revenge. But when the U.N. Security Council censured Israel and Washington temporarily suspended financial aid, the Israeli government switched to equivocating, as became its wont, and made only cosmetic changes in the policy of deterrence. In early 1954 Unit 101 was stripped of its relative autonomy and was integrated as a unit into an airborne brigade. Nevertheless it continued to carry out attacks for another two years, and Sharon kept his command. No charges were brought, and there were no reprimands.

After the War of Independence Israel fought four discontinuous cross-border wars with Arab countries—in 1956, 1967, 1973, and 1982—and an all but continuous internal war with the Palestinians, many operating from neighboring countries of refuge or exile. But there is no separating the latter from three of the former: the justification for what were considered preemptive or preventive foreign wars (excepting 1956) was to strike at Palestinian guerrillas or terrorists operating beyond Israel's unsettled frontiers. The invasion of Lebanon in June 1982 was meant, typically, to destroy their military bases once and for all, most of which were by then under the aegis of the Palestine Liberation Organization (PLO)—since 1964 the nerve center of the fast-expanding refugee resistance.

No matter how much he looked down upon his Arab neighbors and the Palestinians, Ben-Gurion knew that Israel could not face them alone while proceeding with nation-building. Although Moscow's help had been critical in 1947–8, and notwithstanding the lingering leftist proclivities of Zionism, the core of the political class turned full-force toward Washington, seeing in it a more expedient partner for its increasing militarism. Starting in 1951 with the Korean War, Israel chose sides in the Cold War. The fledging country offered the U.S. use of its airfields and ports, and otherwise stepped forth as the unreserved ally of the American-led West in a Middle East pulsating with anti-colonial nationalism. There was no playing such a role in this region ingenuously or with impunity. Sited in the midst of one large domain of the wretched and awakening Third World, Israel was also near to the world's most prized oilfields, and at the crossroads of strategic pipelines and seaways. For the modern world, oil had already assumed critical importance during the era of the First World War, but during and after the Second it became a matter of economic and military life or death.

In the 1930s oil was discovered in Kuwait and Saudi Arabia, with Standard Oil of California making major discoveries there in 1936. As early as June 1943, President Roosevelt promised the king of Saudi Arabia that "no decision would be reached altering the basic situation in Palestine without full consultation with both Arabs and Jews." It remains uncertain whether the Big Three discussed the Palestine problem at the Yalta Conference of February 4–11, 1945, but on February 14, during his voyage home, FDR met Ibn Saud on the U.S.S. *Quincy* in the Suez Canal. His purpose was to repeat the previous pledge and to assure the king that, in exchange for preferential access to Saudi oil, the U.S. would provide his dynasty with military protection. In the midst of the war, Secretary of State Cordell Hull had advised the president that "no great power [should be allowed to] be established in the Persian Gulf opposite the American petroleum development in Saudi Arabia." Now the U.S. was about to supplant Britain as the leading economic and political force in the greater Middle East (eclipsing France in the process) chiefly by gaining control of the Arabian peninsula and the Persian Gulf—specifically Iran—and securing the oil production there.

Until the mid 1950s Europe's two major colonial powers went to great lengths to save face and wrest their remaining interests from the voracious American empire. Suddenly negligible in the Middle East, France briefly became Israel's principal arms supplier. After the forced abdication of King Farouk in July 1952, and during Nasser's rise to power, in 1955 Britain finally quit the Suez Canal Zone. Even so, it still hoped to make Egypt the naval linchpin of a regional security pact to include Turkey, Iraq, Iran, and Pakistan, with the eventual reunion of Iraq and Jordan. Such a grandiose plan exceeded London's palsied grasp. But America's grip was entirely adequate to its reach, now truly vast. At first giving Nasser's anti-colonialism the benefit of the doubt, Washington used its matchless financial, naval, and air power to refigure Western hegemony in the region, extended to include Afghanistan and Pakistan, completing the *cordon sanitaire* around the Soviet Union.

Whereas the U.S. was obsessed with the danger of Soviet Russia and communism, Nasser considered Israel's threat to the Arab world by far the greater and most immediate peril. To counter Tel Aviv's unrelenting military buildup, he gave high priority to the modernization and expansion of Egypt's armed forces. The Cold War left its first major mark on the Middle East when, in the fall of 1955, Washington's refusal of military assistance compelled Nasser to turn to Moscow for up-to-date land, air, and sea weapons, along with instructors. By this time, with French help, Israel had developed a formidable armory and was starting a nuclear program. Naturally

both Tel Aviv and Cairo insisted their forced-draft military preparedness was purely defensive.

An anti-colonial nationalist committed to self-sufficiency and social
reform, Nasser proposed to develop Egypt by means of rapid state-
directed industrialization. The country had little oil; its chief export
was cotton, depressed by unfavorable terms of trade. Following
feasibility studies inspired by the harnessing of the Tennessee River
under the American New Deal, and the Dnieper as part of the Soviet
Five-Year Plan, Nasser decided to construct a dam across the Nile at
Aswan. The electricity generated would provide Egypt with some
energy independence. Such a monumental public work would carry a
charge that Nasser expected to kindle his political prestige and ignite
Egyptian nationalism.

To finance this pharaonic project Nasser turned to the Western
powers and the World Bank for loans. In July, 1956 Washington again
turned Cairo down, insisting that, given the "instability of [its]
regime" and the "deplorable condition of [its] economy," Egypt
was in no condition to undertake a project of that scale. Rather than
accept Soviet funding in exchange for cotton, Nasser resolved to
nationalize the Anglo-French Suez Canal Company, with the aim
of using future toll revenues to help finance his grand design. To turn a
lucrative icon of Western imperialism into a spectacular symbol of
anti-imperial rebellion and economic self-reliance was to tempt fate, as
had been demonstrated by Mohammad Mossadegh's nationalization
of the Anglo-Iranian Oil Company in 1951 and its sequel.

Mossadegh was another anti-imperialist nationalist bent on reclaiming his country's political and economic sovereignty. A wealthy
notable and experienced bureaucrat, he was a popular prime minister,
and his National Front established a reformist secular democracy,
fiercely opposed by the Tudeh Communist Party. To consolidate and
enhance his regime, Mossadegh sought the withdrawal of Soviet
troops from Iranian Azerbaijan and the domestication of the Anglo-Iranian Oil Company. Although he relied on the Tudeh members
of parliament to further his twofold project, he remained a moderate
reformist and proposed to follow a neutralist course in foreign policy.
By taking over the oilfields, Mossadegh invited the all-out hostility of
both the crumbling British and the unbound American empires, local
rivals. Inside Iran, however, the nationalization, perceived as an anti-
imperial stand, won near universal support, especially among the
subaltern classes of town and country.

With the atrophy of London's military muscle, Washington was
forced to act. John Foster Dulles at the State Department and Allen

Dulles at CIA persuaded President Dwight Eisenhower that Mossadegh, alleged to be a Soviet puppet, was about to take Iran into the communist orbit, with dire consequences for the West in the vital Persian Gulf. Acting on orders from Washington, Kermit Roosevelt, the CIA's head man in the Middle East, set about destabilizing Mossadegh's regime in cooperation with General Fazollah Zahedi. On August 19, 1953, Mohammad Reza, Shah of the Pahlavi dynasty, certain of full U.S. backing, cashiered Mossadegh and designated Zahedi to take his place. In the face of an explosion of popular protest, the Shah fled the country. He returned four days later, accompanied by Allen Dulles. By then General Zahedi, at the head of the army, had gained the upper hand in Tehran.

Mossadegh was the first victim of Western, primarily American-engineered "destabilizations" of postcolonial secular regimes headed by strong nationalist leaders with social reformist agendas that endangered the economic and strategic interests of one or more of the great Western powers. When arraigned before a court of the triumphant Pahlavi–Zahedi successor regime, Mossadegh made a seemingly grandiose but disarmingly true confession: "My only crime is that I nationalized the Iranian oil industry and removed from this land the network of colonialism and political and economic influence of the greatest empire on earth."

Nasser knew of Mossadegh's fate when he announced the nationalization of the Anglo-French Suez Canal Company on July 26, 1956—the fourth anniversary of King Farouk's fall—at a mass rally in Alexandria, Egypt's largest port city. British ships made up one-third of the canal's traffic, and two-thirds of Europe's oil supplies passed through this waterway. Nasser was perceived as threatening not only the economic interests of England and France, but also one of the West's most strategic lifelines. In the wake of France's defeat at Dien Bien Phu in Vietnam, Paris for good measure charged Nasser with aiding and abetting the new nationalist revolt in Algeria. Even before his latest defiance, large segments of the Free World's media portrayed Nasser as a multifaceted demon: part Mussolini and Hitler, a crypto-communist, and an anti-Semite. To go along with the Egyptian president would be to encourage him and his followers throughout the Third World, Israel's other neighbors especially. In fact, as a self-assertive left-populist nationalist and secular reformer, Nasser alarmed the old elites of the Arab countries as he did the establishments of the West and Israel.

For both the American and Soviet cold warriors, the mid-1950s was the peak Manichean moment. Although he was very much his own man, Nasser was increasingly vilified in Washington as a dangerous pawn of Moscow. Not yet a pan-Arabist nor an Islamist, he still carried the banner of anti-imperialist nationalism, which remained a sufficient cause to rally the Arab street within and beyond Egypt. It also moved him to join other nationalist leaders who were desperately looking, as Mossadegh was, for a way to avoid the baneful embrace of either Washington or Moscow. In April 1954, at the Bandung Conference in Indonesia, the would-be non-aligned nations sought to form a neutral third bloc. Apart from Marshal Tito of Yugoslavia, one of Bandung's founding fathers, this was an assembly of the leaders of 29 Asian and African countries that had recently won their independence. They had gathered to decry a decolonization that was essentially political, without concern for the continuing economic indigence and dependency of the new nations, the lamentable legacy of colonial imperialism. Nasser was among the prime movers of the Non-Aligned Movement, along with Nehru, Indonesia's Sukarno, and Burma's U Nu. Zhou En-lai attended from China and Ho Chi Minh from Vietnam.

Although zealous about finding a third way, Nasser realized that, given the military and economic impotence, as well as the lack of unity, of the ex-colonized nations, the idea of Bandung would go nowhere. The U.N. General Assembly, where the Third World countries led the way, was after all no match for the Security Council. In the short run, with Israel aligned with the West and arming furiously, and with the U.S. replacing Britain as the hegemon in the Middle East and refusing arms to Cairo, Nasser saw no alternative but to turn to Moscow for modern weapons. In the fall of 1955, Czechoslovakia again became the conduit.

Britain and France seized on the moment of Nasser's nationalization of the Suez Canal to make their last major imperial stand. At France's suggestion Israel was asked to play a pivotal role in the Anglo-French invasion, reoccupation, and seizure of the Canal Zone, which it readily agreed to do. For Ben-Gurion, it was an unhoped-for opportunity to help deal a lethal blow to Nasser. The incentives were loss of access to the Canal and the Gulf of Aqaba, as well as the increasing *fedayeen* cross-border raids and anti-Israeli propaganda. Convinced that, militarily, time was on Nasser's side, Ben-Gurion—pressed by Moshe Dayan, chief of staff, and Shimon Peres, director general of the Defense Ministry—was eager to participate in what he considered a preventive war that Israel could not afford to wage on its own.

In secrecy, top British, French, and Israeli politicians and generals contrived a ruse. Claiming they were hunting down terrorists, the

Israelis would invade the Sinai and move on Suez. With the IDF's tanks rolling ahead, Paris and London would issue an ultimatum condemning the assault, calling for a ceasefire, and enjoining both sides to withdraw ten miles from their shores of the Canal. Certain that, unlike the Israelis, the Egyptians would spurn this intervention, Anglo-French forces would then move in to "protect" the Canal and cripple Egypt's air force. Although each of the three governments had its own reasons for the assault on Suez, all expected that a quick and decisive military defeat of the Egyptian army would precipitate the end of Nasser's regime and discourage militant anti-Western nationalists throughout the Third World.

Everything went precisely as planned until the two superpowers interceded. On October 29 Israeli forces crashed into the Sinai and raced for Suez; the next day Britain and France issued their twelve-hour ultimatum. Following Nasser's predicted response, on October 31 Britain and France launched their attack by land, air, and sea. Within a week troops landed at Port Said, at the Mediterranean end of the Canal. But before they could occupy the zone their stratagem was frozen by the Cold War. None of the actors had notified Washington of their adventure, which happened to coincide with the anti-Soviet rebellion in Hungary. Even while Moscow was cracking down on Budapest, on November 5 Soviet Prime Minister Nikolai Bulganin threatened to intervene on behalf of Nasser. Eisenhower, caught completely by surprise, pressured America's three allies to accept a ceasefire and withdraw from Egypt. With the Cold War in East-Central Europe his first priority, he would not risk opening a second front. Britain, France, and Israel drew back.

London and Paris at last had to recognize Washington's unchallengeable dominance in the greater Middle East, and their reliance on the U.S. to secure their oil supply; Israel, its utter and manifest dependence on the U.S. for survival itself. Now Egypt and other Arab nations would move closer to Moscow in pursuit of an alternative source of arms. Meanwhile Nasser's prestige soared not only in the region but throughout the Third World. He had succeeded, according to the consensus, where Mossadegh had failed. In London the Suez fiasco contributed to Prime Minister Anthony Eden's resignation, and in Paris, not long thereafter, to the fall of Guy Mollet, followed by the collapse of France's Fourth Republic. Experienced by the Arabs as a victory, the second Arab–Israeli war raised an already heated anti-imperialist nationalism to incandescence, demonstrated by bursts of political radicalization in Egypt, Iraq, and Syria, and explosions of civil strife in Lebanon and Jordan.

Unlike its senior allies in the Suez venture, Israel achieved its minimum objectives. In return for the withdrawal of IDF troops from the Sinai and Gaza, the U.N. deployed an Emergency Force to patrol the Egyptian–Israeli border with a view to ending the *fedayeen* raids, and the U.S. guaranteed freedom of navigation in the Gulf of Aqaba, securing trade in and out of the Israeli port of Eilat. Cairo took instant umbrage at the presence of U.N. peacekeepers, stationed as they were on the Egyptian side, not the aggressor's, of the 1949 armistice line. More seriously, Israel signaled its status as a de facto protectorate of the Americans. But whether in the West or the Middle East, the Palestinian refugees were still not even a blip on the radar.

Israel's modest, contingent gains that November came at the expense of heavily burdening its near future. By lending itself to such a flagrant variation on the old gunboat diplomacy, Israel blazoned its readiness to continue defying and alienating the Arab world. But, to say it once again, Israel's collaboration with the imperial powers was not inevitable. Ben-Gurion and Dayan need not have gone along. Did they fear jeopardizing Israel's relations with France, as yet its chief supplier of the arms essential for a hardline policy? No matter, the longer-term costs of that policy rendered its achievements pyrrhic: a dramatic widening of the friend–enemy dissociation; radicalization of the regimes of several Arab countries; further inflammation of Arab nationalism; and a necessary dependence on the U.S. The stockpiler of bayonets became a loyal spear-carrier for the Eisenhower Doctrine, which promised help to governments battling international communism at home and abroad—a rank also attained by Afghanistan, Iran, Iraq, Lebanon, Libya, Pakistan, Saudi Arabia, and Turkey.

The causes of the Second Arab–Israeli, or Suez War of 1956 also brought about the third—the 1967 War—although several geopolitical factors were new: the resistance of the Palestinians and their supporters was coming of age; the Soviet Union had taken root in the Middle East, chiefly in Syria and Egypt; the U.S. had definitively supplanted Europe's colonial powers and turned into a global imperial hegemon; and Israel had become implicated in America's worldwide battle against communism and drive for predominance in the Third World.

Though the enmity between Israel and the Arab nations had necessarily become more virulent, its dynamics were unchanged. Arab leaders, having no other strength to project, continued to brandish the moral issue of the refugees, and to hint at an imminent surge of the Arab–Muslim masses. Israel's governors trusted and flaunted their military omnipotence in defense of a land set upon by all its neighbors—refusing, as victims of the Judeocide, any new martyrdom. Diplomacy and compromise with the Palestinians and the Arab world were clean off the agenda. The only forms of dialogue left were military gesticulation and bellicose rhetoric; both now escalated. In addition to the conflict over control of the Jordan River, a crucial source of water, there was an increase in Palestinian cross-border raids. These were more than matched by Israeli retaliatory strikes. In Tel Aviv the hawks kept pressing for preemptive war to forestall an allegedly impending Arab assault.

In the early 1960s Syria, whose regime was being radicalized along Egyptian lines, especially encouraged guerrilla infiltration, though Palestinian partisans also entered from Jordan in the south. The number of total yearly raids rose from between thirty-five and forty in 1965 and 1966 to as many in the first quarter of 1967 alone. These incursions and counter-incursions blew up into a fatal spiral of vengeance. As it had brutally retaliated against Qibya in 1953 and the headquarters of the Egyptian army in Gaza in 1955, killing about forty Egyptian soldiers, Israel again willfully overreacted to a succession of border incidents. On November 13, 1966, commandos struck at Al Samu, south of Hebron, killing some twenty soldiers and civilians and wounding about fifty; on April 7, 1967, planes attacked Syrian artillery positions and shot down six Syrian fighter jets—Soviet MiGs—over the outskirts of Damascus.

Israel was certainly not unopposed. From 1955 to 1975 Egypt's armed forces depended heavily on the Soviet Union, which provided grants and loans, advisors and equipment—particularly fighter planes and defense systems, tanks, and anti-tank missiles. But on the whole Moscow was not nearly as forthcoming as Cairo hoped. It held back on providing the latest military hardware, leaving Egypt at a disadvantage to Israel, which received the most advanced weapons from the U.S. and had highly skilled indigenous military cadres. Because of this stark imbalance of power, the boundaries between Israel and its neighbors would have remained calm apart from the stepped-up border raids. Until the mid 1960s these were relatively few in number. But gradually some of the Arab governments, chagrined by a second-class geopolitical status, began supporting the Palestinian resistance to demonstrate their own anti-Zionist and anti-colonialist bona fides. It bears emphasizing that the exiles and refugees who had conceived and raised the resistance were only half-welcomed and half-tolerated in their host countries.

Until nearly the eve of the 1967 War, and although they had been an important background factor in the first two Arab–Israeli wars, the displaced Palestinian Arabs were all but consigned to oblivion. The elites among them—the old landed class, the mercantile bourgeoisie, the established professionals—became privileged exiles in the capitals of the Middle East. The rest, largely tillers of the soil, wound up as refugees in the crowded and noxious camps, most of them near cities in the West Bank, Gaza Strip, and Arab states. These preserves of traditional and religious peasant communities became forcing houses of anger over deracination and dispossession; as such they provided the political activists and militants who would energize, or themselves become, *fedayeen*. The interaction between camp-based refugees and city-based exiles would bear significantly on the course of the resistance's engagement with Israel and relations with the host Arab states.

The leaders of the Palestinian movement emerged from cities that were centers of ideological disputation and higher education, Cairo then chief among them. Nationalism, pan-Arabism, Islamism, and socialism were all in the air. These sons of mostly well-to-do Palestinian families included Yasser Arafat. Typically for his class, he studied architectural engineering at Cairo's King Fuad University, a hotbed of student activism centered around social-reformist anti-Western nationalism. In 1952 Arafat became president of the local Union of Palestinian Students. The Ecole Normale Supérieure and American University there, as well as Beirut's American University, also produced their share of activists. Driven by the idea of an early return to Palestine, one and all militated against Zionism and Israel, while recognizing themselves in Colonel Nasser and his defiance of the West.

After their studies in Cairo and Beirut a number of these young men found employment in the oil industry of the Gulf States, which was how al-Fatah came to be charted in October 1959, in Kuwait. Arafat was among the less than a dozen founding members, along with Abu Jihad, Faruk Kaddumi, and Abu Ijad—all of them from the new middle class. Given the powerlessness, division, and irresolution of the Arab states, Fatah saw no alternative to liberating Arab Palestine on its own and by force of arms, starting with commando raids from Gaza, Jordan, and Lebanon. This was the beginning of the organized Palestinian resistance. Similar groups were soon formed, such as the Marxist-oriented Popular Front for the Liberation of Palestine (PFLP), headed by Dr. George Habash, with headquarters in Lebanon. The Palestine Liberation Organization was established in May–June 1964. Where the first meeting of Fatah had been an intimate and clandestine affair, 422 mostly upper-class Palestinians from some ten Arab countries convened in a major hotel in Jordanian-controlled East

Jerusalem to charter the PLO. It assumed the mandate of coordinating the policies and actions of the fractious Palestinians in the struggle to reclaim their land. The effort to translate the organizational zeal at the top into the systematic and disciplined mobilization of refugee activists and militants at the base would take considerable time. By 1967 the armed resistance of those partisan bands was still embryonic. The rate of organized cross-border raids rose slowly, and took a relatively small human toll.

Lacking an autonomous territorial and financial footing, the early resistance depended desperately on the collaboration and support of its host countries, whose Palestinian policies were driven mainly by their own national and dynastic interests. Nasser furthered the establishment of the PLO, hoping to control and use it to advance his own agenda. Its first leader, approved by the Arab League, was a Nasser faithful, Ahmad Shuquairi. Eventually, however, the militant Palestinians became a force to contend with, which was dramatically revealed by the bloody showdown in 1970–1 between the Jordanian government and the resistance forces it had permitted to operate on and from its soil. Though for different reasons, the Arab states and Israel took decades to recognize that the Palestinians were resolved and able to act independently.

Resistance and terror coexist uneasily. Terror can serve as an instrument of resistance or oppression, hence the adage, "One man's terrorist is another man's freedom fighter." With few exceptions, terror through the ages has been a collective affair. Once a thoroughly religious phenomenon, it has assumed political forms only in modern times. More recently it has become a mix of politics and religion (whether revealed or secular), with nationalism a factor in both. Eventually this form of terror on both sides of the divide fanned the flames of the Zionist/Israeli–Palestinian and Israeli–Arab conflict. This instrumentalization of religion, while not unprecedented, has gained momentum. The bomb-throwing Revisionist Zionists and Palestinian *fedayeen* of the first hour acted largely spontaneously and on their own; so did individual religious zealots in both camps, Baruch Goldstein and Yigal Amir becoming the most notorious religiously-driven terrorists on the Israeli side. As terror became more organized, it became more intentional in pursuit of larger, if inconstant and contested, political objectives. Attacks produced more innocent victims. Those who survived were often radicalized.

Each side has sought to portray the other as a terrorist monolith. Yet the Palestinian national movement, like most national liberation movements, has a political and a terrorist wing, which both complement and rival each other, making for chronic ideological tension and tactical dissonance. The political arm defines the goals of the struggle; the masterminds and operatives of terror strike to advance and sometimes enlarge them. Unlike field and guerrilla armies, the terrorists can fade into the street or countryside without worrying about their lines of communication and supply. With its overwhelming might, the Israeli army can inflict severe punishment on such fighters and their infrastructures throughout the Middle East; it cannot root them out. And, just as violence against civilians by Palestinian terrorists alienates their sympathizers and supporters in many quarters, the "collateral human damage" of Israel's disproportionate strikes has similar political effects.

Ultimately the rise of reciprocal cross-border raids was less damaging than the intensified rhetorical violence they set off. Syria's Baathist regime, close to Nasser, broke new ground not only by backing the *fedayeen*, but by emboldening them with increasingly aggressive anti-Israeli declamations. The hardliners in Tel Aviv seized on this stridency to hold Syria responsible for all cross-border terrorism, and in general used its support, along with Egypt's, to deny the autonomy and justice of the Palestinian resistance. The post-independence leaders of Israel could not conceive of the refugees becoming the embodiment and representation of the Arab–Israeli conflict. Nor could they fathom that al-Nakba ("the disaster"), the Palestinian defeat and exodus of 1948, had served to precipitate a Palestinian identity and consciousness distinct from, if related to, the far-spread and inchoate Arab nation.

After a Syrian attack on a kibbutz in northern Galilee, on April 7, 1967, Israeli planes, as has been noted, shot down six MiGs deep inside Syria's air space, not far from Damascus. On May 11 Prime Minister Levi Eshkol, Ben-Gurion's successor, stated that "in view of the fourteen incidents of the past month alone [Israel might] have to adopt measures no less drastic than those of April 7." Undoubtedly mindful of the Syrian–Egyptian pact of mutual defense, within forty-eight hours Eshkol raised the ante by declaring that, although the "focal point of the terrorists is in Syria," the Israeli government had "laid down the principle that we shall choose the time, the place, and the means to counter the aggressor." On May 12 the correspondent of the *New York Times* reported from Tel Aviv that "some Israeli leaders have decided that the use of force against Syria may be the only way to curtail increasing terrorism."

On May 19, U.N. Secretary-General U Thant noted that although "intemperate and bellicose utterances . . . are unfortunately more or less routine on both sides of the line in the Near East," they were becoming more ominous. Judging by recent reports, "high [Israeli] officials" were making "statements so threatening as to be particularly inflammatory" and likely to "heighten emotions and thereby increase tensions." On May 22, in a speech announcing the closing of the Gulf of Aqaba, Nasser referred to a recent statement by Israeli commanders that they "would carry out military operations against Syria in order to occupy Damascus and overthrow the Syrian government." Even though Cairo and Damascus were highly apprehensive of an attack by Israel's armed forces, they stood their ground, encouraged by the Soviets who, in pursuit of their own regional interests, kept supplying them with critical military and economic aid. On May 26, Nasser, with nervous bravura, announced that, should Israel "embark on an aggression against Syria and Egypt, the battle against it would . . . not be confined to one spot on the Syrian or Egyptian borders." As they had not in 1956, other Arab states would "send troops," and the "battle will be a general war and our objective will be to destroy Israel." Dr. Nureddin al-Atassi, the Syrian president, wanted Israel to know that "the Palestinian *fedayeen* will continue their activities until they liberate their homeland."

Nasser protested that, whereas the whole Western world was in an "uproar because of the closure of the Gulf of Aqaba . . . nobody speaks about peace or threats to peace . . . when Eshkol and Rabin threaten Syria." Quite apart from not liking the "progressive" Arab regimes, the Western powers "ridicule and despise" the Arabs, whose rights they "disavow." The time had come to tend not only to the "material . . . but also the spiritual aspects . . . of the renaissance of the Arab nations." By closing the Gulf of Aqaba and securing the withdrawal of the U.N. Emergency Force, Egypt was "restoring Arab honor and renewing Arab hopes." Of pivotal importance for the Arab awakening was "the revival of the Palestine Question." Egypt was "demanding" that the Palestinians recover "the full rights" of which they had been deprived in 1948, and was doing so with the support of "India, Pakistan, Yugoslavia, Malaysia, the Chinese People's Republic and the Asian and African states." To Saudi Arabia, Jordan, and Iran—older regimes tied to the West that had formed an Islamic Alliance—Nasser said the best way for them to "serve the Palestine Question" would be for Iran to stop supplying Israel with oil via Eilat.

On November 4, 1966, Syria and Egypt had signed a mutual defense pact. On November 13, Israel raided the Jordanian village of al-Sammu. Eighteen civilians were killed and over 100 wounded, and 130 houses were demolished, as well as a school and a clinic. By the end of the following May, even Jordan's normally Israel-friendly and cautious King Hussein went to Cairo to sign a mutual defense pact and agree to a joint command with Egypt. Concerned about unrest among the 700,000 Palestinian refugees who now constituted over 50 per cent of Jordan's population, Hussein was prepared to secure domestic peace through diplomatic brinkmanship and, if need be, foreign war. On June 4 Iraq joined up as well. But where Hussein had eschewed polemics, the Iraqi premier, Abd ar-Rahman Arif, declared roundly that war would provide an "opportunity to wipe out the ignominy that has been with us since 1948" and "wipe Israel off the map." On paper, at least, the four signatories could deploy some 460,000 troops, 3,000 tanks, and 800 aircraft along Israel's borders. But the Arabs' bark was worse than their bite, and Israel's power elite most certainly knew it.

The leaders of the frontline Arab states came under mounting domestic criticism for not responding, except rhetorically, to the uncommonly heavy raids on Damascus and al-Sammu. Israel's warnings further stirred up the Arab street. To stem the erosion of his popular authority and his standing abroad, Nasser took the risk of defying Israel with more than just language. Between May 15 (Israel's Independence Day) and May 22, 1967, he took three bold steps: in addition to demanding that the U.N. Emergency Force leave Egyptian territory in the Sinai, he ordered two divisions across the Suez Canal into the Sinai to the 1957 ceasefire line; and he reaffirmed Egypt's right to close the Strait of Tiran—and soon did so—severing Israel's vital southern supply and trade route. This last maneuver was meant to test the resolve of the U.S., which in 1956–7 had assured Israel of its right of access to the Gulf of Aqaba, and hence to the Red Sea. Attuned to the constraints of the Cold War, Nasser made his moves without consulting Moscow but confident of its support, just as Israeli hardliners were sure of Washington's.

Premier Eshkol promptly declared in the Knesset that "any interference with the freedom of navigation in the Gulf and Strait is a flagrant violation of international law [and] constitutes an act of aggression." That same day, May 23, President Lyndon Johnson stated that America "considers the Gulf an international waterway and feels that a blockade of Israeli shipping is illegal and potentially disastrous to the cause of peace." But Eshkol and Johnson privately took Nasser to be merely rattling his saber, and were disposed to resolve the confrontation by diplomacy.

Eshkol, however—even more than Nasser—shortly came under intense pressure to go on the offensive. The core of Israel's political–military caste, backstopped by latter-day Revisionists, kept urging

Eshkol to form a national unity government with Menachem Begin, leader of Herut and of the parliamentary opposition. He should yield his defense portfolio, they felt, to Moshe Dayan, who was affiliated with Rafi, the hawkish breakaway faction of Mapai headed by Ben-Gurion and Shimon Peres. The leaders of the IDF called for instant war, spreading rumors that a military *coup d'état* was in the works. Dayan was at one with Yitzhak Rabin, the chief of staff, who kept stressing that the "military and diplomatic stranglehold [that was] tightening around [Israel]" was fraught with extreme danger and that to "deliver a decisive blow to Nasser [would be to] change the entire order in the Middle East." Major General Ariel Sharon, now head of the training division and about to assume an important field command, was equally bellicose: "The problem is not the Straits. The problem is the survival of the people of Israel." In early June, while Washington, embroiled in Vietnam, was still urging caution on Tel Aviv, Sharon contended that the time had come to stop "kowtowing" to the Great Powers, for if "we want to survive here, we [will] have to stand up [by ourselves] for our rights." Dayan was all for taking the offensive, insisting that it would be "lunacy to wait" for the Egyptians to attack first.

In 1967 Nasser was still the firebrand, but hoped the blazes he was setting to dramatize the Arab cause would not burn out of control. While his stature kept rising throughout the Third World, he feared that Israel would take his posturing as an existential challenge it could not fail to answer. Nasser, as it happened, was not deploying his or his allies' troops either for a full-fledged invasion or a first strike. He was too conscious of Israel's military superiority, and the best he could hope for was a standoff that would leave the door open for a nonmilitary resolution of the crisis. On the morning after Israel's overwhelming victory, Rabin said he "[did not] think Nasser wanted war" and noted that the "two divisions he sent to Sinai would not have been sufficient to launch an offensive war." To put it plainly, "he knew it and we knew it." Eshkol held too that "the Egyptian [battle array] and general build-up . . . in the Sinai testified to a militarily defensive Egyptian setup, south of Israel." The experts in the State Department in Washington had made a similar assessment. They advised President Johnson that, though Nasser "may well fulminate against Israel," they thought that "practically there was no possibility that he will strike or provoke the Israelis within the foreseeable future."

Against his better judgment, on May 31 Eshkol bowed to political and popular pressure: he formed a national unity government with

Begin as minister without portfolio, and the next day appointed Dayan as minister of defense. On June 4 the new cabinet unanimously ordered "military operations to liberate Israel from the current siege and to preempt the impending attack from the forces of the United Arab Command." The Israeli decision-makers, confident of the IDF's incontestable military superiority, were disposed to seize the occasion. A timely preventive war would set back the Arab states' military buildup, further increasing Israel's advantage. The caste-like nature of its leadership ensured there were no oppositional voices to argue for using the nation's dominant position to press for negotiations.

The war of 1967 started with a massive preemptive strike: as June 5 dawned, Israeli planes, without warning, destroyed practically all the aircraft and airfields of Egypt, Syria, and Jordan. This surprise attack was calculated to provide almost complete aerial immunity for the ground forces that advanced full-speed upon the Suez Canal, the Jordan River, and the Syrian Heights. Within less than a week the IDF reached its objectives: it utterly routed the allegedly formidable Arab armies, destroying nearly 70 per cent of their heavy armaments and killing almost 20,000 of their soldiers, half of them Egyptians. Israel lost some thirty airplanes, and between 500 and 1,000 men; about 2,500 were wounded.

Israel found itself suddenly in possession of the whole of Mandatory Palestine, all but nullifying the 1947 partition of U.N. Resolution 181. Tripling its 8,000 square miles, it wrested the West Bank and the eastern part of Jerusalem from Jordan. It also captured the Sinai Desert as far as Suez and the Gaza Strip from Egypt, as well as the Syrian Heights (the future Golan Heights). This Greater Israel was neither God's latest six-day creation nor the payoff of an ingenious ground plan. It was the predictable outcome of greater brute strength.

In Israel and in the diaspora, however, the undisputed lightning victory was greeted as a sign of divine intervention, Jewish exceptionalism, and Israeli invincibility. The reunification of Jerusalem, in particular, caused a resurgence of religious and messianic sentimentality even among non-practicing and non-Jewish Jews. Immediately following the occupation of the Holy City, General Dayan proclaimed at the Western Wall: "We have returned to the most sacred of our holy places, never to part from it again"; Rabbi Goren, the chief rabbi of the IDF, blew the shofar on the Western Wall. Starting the same day, Ben-Gurion repeatedly celebrated in his diary the reunification of Jerusalem. A large Jewish presence should be established in the Old City and Jews settled "in abandoned Arab houses" in Jerusalem and Hebron. He urged also the demolition of an alien "building attached to the Wailing Wall," the removal of a sign in Arabic and English, and the "razing of the wall that Suleiman the Magnificent had built [around the Old City] 400 years ago, in 1542." To tear it down in a fit of iconoclastic exultation would be "to unify Jerusalem and facilitate [its] expansion to the east, south, north, and west." On June 8 Golda Meir, secretary-general of Mapai, opened a meeting of its executive committee with the traditional prayer of thanksgiving, the *Sheheyanu*: "Blessed are You O Lord Our God, Ruler of the Universe, who has enabled us to see this joyous day." Even a prominent member of Mapam, previously sworn to binationalism, concluded that "the world has revolved, we have liberated the land of Israel, and now it is ours."

This spiritual rapture obscured the profane political consequences of victory, beginning with the acclamation of the governing caste and its statecraft. The exodus of some additional 250,000 to 300,000 Palestinian refugees, mostly from the West Bank and Gaza Strip—about 100,000 of them fleeing for the second time—went unnoticed. Once again, many villages were leveled, and six new DP camps sprang up in Jordan. Although the Eshkol government vouched that it would only administer the new territories pending negotiations with the defeated Arab nations, by June 27 the Knesset had voted to annex East Jerusalem. The first settlement was founded on the Syrian Heights on July 15 (in 1981 the Knesset voted to rename them the Golan Heights, and annexed them), a second near Hebron in September. Within a year a total of some fifteen settlements had been founded on the Golan, in the Jordan Valley, and near the northern reaches of the Dead Sea. By 1977 there were about 35,000 colonists in the West Bank. Some were driven by secular ultra-nationalism or religious messianism, others by the prospects of cheap housing and a better quality of life. While not all, then, were prompted by the revival of the Zionist pioneering spirit, all served to invigorate it further. In no time at all, generous government and faith-based subsidies became available for anyone inclined to pick up the pilgrim's staff.

While the settler movement had a certain spontaneity, there was nothing unruly about it. As early as July 26, 1967, the Allon Plan—named for its author, famed general and Eshkol's deputy premier Yigal Allon—proposed the implantation of settlements in a thinly populated zone 10 miles wide running up and down the Jordan Valley, deemed by the military to be of vital strategic importance for Israel's security. Supported all along by Labor, the Allon Plan sought to come into as much land as possible, inhabited by a minimum of Arabs. It was the birth certificate and warrant of the settlement movement.

Other settlements were projected in the Yehuda Desert along the Dead Sea. A separate plan, favored by Dayan, called for colonies in the heavily populated mountainous regions of Samaria, north and west of Jerusalem on the West Bank. All were determined to add to Israel's prewar territory of 8,000 square miles. The issue was not whether, but how to fortify its position in the newly occupied territories, bearing in mind the strategic importance of the Jordan River, Golan Heights, and Tiran Strait.

As the victors sorted out their gains, the vanquished were left to inventory in horror their latest and most thorough humiliation. Israel's resounding, single-handed triumph discredited the Arab regimes in the eyes of both their own people and the Palestinian refugees. Nasser's prestige plummeted, along with the appeal of the Egyptian–Syrian model of nationalist revival and development. Only King Hussein, master temporizer, survived unbroken. He did so despite the loss of the West Bank and East Jerusalem, and the influx of more refugees, who now accounted for 60 per cent of Jordan's population. The Arabs repaired to Khartoum on September 1 to consider their paucity of options. Though losers and powerless, the front-line states could still be as stubborn and unrealistic as Israel: mindful of their influence and stiff-necked with pride, they refused to recognize the Zionist state, and they would not negotiate without its complete and unconditional withdrawal from the newly occupied territories. The Gulf States, unhinged by the shaming of the Arab and Muslim world, promised to provide financial aid, particularly to Egypt and Jordan. This went against the Israeli assumption that, with their backs to the wall, the Arabs would come to terms, conceding the legitimacy of an expanded state in exchange for return of some of the captured Syrian and Egyptian territory. Repatriation or compensation of some of the Palestinian refugees as a gesture of reconciliation was never contemplated.

Israel remained unbending largely because the U.S. now stood squarely behind it. Washington welcomed the discomfiture of Egypt and Syria. The Soviets, in no position to rescue their client states and with Nasser's days numbered, were losing additional ground in the Middle East. Having proved its mettle, Israel became America's foremost strategic outpost and ally in the greater Middle East—especially now that its right-leaning National Unity Government, now including Begin as minister without portfolio, passed ideological muster.

The war also confirmed Israel's heavy reliance on America, which had replaced France as its major and most indispensable supplier of the latest weapons. No longer concerned about Nasser inspiring North African rebels, and having extricated France from its Algerian impasse, President Charles de Gaulle set out to improve relations with the Arab world, in keeping with his resolve to sail a course apart from both Washington and Moscow.

On June 2, 1967 he had cautioned the Israelis—whom he later referred to as an "elite people, self-confident and domineering"— about the treachery of hubris. By December he wrote to Ben-Gurion that the "worrisome" blockade of the Gulf of Aqaba, combined with the "flood of anti-Israeli invective," had rightly outraged and frightened the Israelis. But he doubted the wisdom of Israel's "having gone to war and taken possession, by force of arms, of Jerusalem as well as of several Jordanian, Egyptian, and Syrian territories." In resorting to

> repression and expulsions, the inevitable consequence of an occupation tending to annexation, and by declaring that the conflict can only be resolved on the basis of keeping rather than evacuating the conquered territories, Israel is violating the precept of elementary moderation.

In return for the "withdrawal of its forces" a solution might be found. Along with the "recognition of Israel by its neighbors," he suggested, there ought to be three stipulations: security guarantees on both sides of the borders, backed by "international arbitration"; "dignified and equitable" arrangements for "refugees as well as minorities"; and "free navigation for all nations in the Gulf of Aqaba and the Suez Canal" within the framework of the United Nations. Under certain conditions France would be disposed to "contribute" to such a plan of action "not only on the political level but on the ground as well." The life of any nation, new or old, "depends on the policies it adopts," and these stand the test "only provided they take account of realities."

In the fall of 1967 the U.N. Security Council took up the Middle East crisis with a view to moving the deadlocked belligerents to the negotiating table. The idea was to arrange for an exchange of land for peace, based on the premise that "the acquisition of territory by war" was contrary to international law. Whereas the Soviet Union, supported by the Arab states, pressed for Israel's withdrawal from all the occupied territories, the U.S., in concert with Israel, chose to translate the phrase in the Soviet draft as simply "territories"— suggesting only certain territories. Except for Israel, the members presumed that the less rigorous formulation was intended to allow for relatively minor reciprocal rectifications of the pre-June 5 armistice lines. The Soviets yielded on the wording, and on November 22, 1967 the Security Council unanimously adopted U.N. Resolution 242, calling for the "withdrawal of Israeli armed forces from territories occupied in the recent conflict." It also affirmed the "right . . . of every State in the area . . . to live in peace within secure and recognized boundaries, free from threats or acts of force." Steering a middle course, the resolution further laid down the "necessity . . . to guarantee freedom of navigation through international waterways in the area [and] to achieve a just settlement of the refugee problem." The text fixed no timeframe, but it was generally understood, save by Israel, to be about six months.

Though with great reluctance, Tel Aviv, Cairo, and Amman signaled that they would comply with the U.N. resolution, which in itself was a milestone. Practically, however, both camps all but ignored it. It soon became clear that, rather than think about exchanging land for peace, Israel was preparing the ground for "secure" borders: the pre-June 5 boundaries having been perilously vulnerable, they called for more than minor adjustments. In a moment of supreme mastery, Israel's leaders might have considered carrying not only a gun but an olive branch. But they stayed as unyielding on boundaries as they were on refugees, the two being inseparable. A "just settlement" of the problem, after all, would require the seeing of injustice by eyes that were blinded.

Resolution 242 made no explicit mention of Palestine or Palestinians. It was assumed that, with the return of the West Bank to Jordan, the Hashemite Kingdom would morph providentially into a Palestinian state. The mortification of the Palestinians, sharpened by the inglorious Arab defeat and now sealed by diplomatic perfidy, raised their national self-consciousness and radicalized their politics. Forced to fend for themselves and powerless in the face of Israel's armipotence, they turned to partisan and terrorist warfare from staging grounds in neighboring countries and inside the occupied territories. The victorious conventional war, then, followed by hard-bitten conventional diplomacy in pursuit of imaginary borders and elusive security, had determined the pursuit of unconventional warfare by a momentarily humbled but irrepressible people.

Among the defeated, the Palestinians paid the heaviest price for the war of 1967—inauspiciously the twentieth anniversary of the Nakba. Israel not only took possession of the rest of historical Palestine, but ravaged more homes and villages and made more exiles. The Waterloo of the Arab governments and armies meant that they could not be counted on for support in the near future. At such a moment even the most politically savvy Palestinians could not imagine that this latest debacle would turn out to be a blessing in disguise: it caused a gradual mutation in the ideology, organization, and strategy of the resistance that had stood by helplessly while the second Nakba unfolded. A powerful drive emerged to reduce the Palestinians' political dependence on the Arab states, and to translate rhetoric into more frequent and forceful militant action. The two impulses came as much from anonymous refugees and *fedayeen* in the camps as from middle-class political leaders prominent in Fatah and the PLO. Henceforth the main cleavage in the Palestinian movement would be between factions determined to combine armed struggle with politics and diplomacy and those favoring guerrilla warfare and terror. Many of the latter were also committed to struggling for a radical economic, social, and cultural transformation of liberated Palestine.

Still largely without central direction, cross-border attacks from Jordan and Lebanon resumed and increased in 1968–9. Israel reacted with its usual disproportion, overland and by air. The incident at Karameh, a village east of the Jordan River where Fatah was thought to have set up a base, was a harbinger of things to come. On March 21, 1968, Tel Aviv launched a raid intended to punish recent attacks and to deter any further buildup of partisan bases near the Jordanian border. The armored unit that charged the village met with stiff resistance from *fedayeen* backed, unexpectedly and decisively, by a unit from the Jordanian army. The Israeli commando suffered about thirty killed and nearly ninety wounded. The several wrecked armored vehicles it left behind, including tanks, became the backdrop for a carefully staged nationalist celebration hailing what Arafat extravagantly extolled as the first victory of Palestinians over the Israeli army in regular battle.

Israel in fact had come away the winner. It wrought heavier losses on the Arabs than it took itself, and its vastly superior weaponry and firepower left no doubt that, even once the *fedayeen* were better organized and equipped, they could not hope to measure themselves against the Israeli forces in urban or open-field combat. Almost overnight a hard core of militant Palestinians resorted to new forms of unconventional warfare at the same time that they joined in calling for the radicalization and streamlining of the PLO. An umbrella organization, the PLO set up a panoply of divisions probably modeled after those of the Zionist movement during the life of the Yishuv: a military department, a department of political and information affairs, and a Palestine national fund department.

Pressed by Fatah and the PFLP, the PLO took three steps in quick succession: the number of delegates to its National Council, the Palestinian parliament in exile, was reduced from 422 to 300; a revised version of the PLO's Covenant was adopted; and Arafat, chairman of Fatah, the premier guerrilla organization, was elected chairman of the new executive committee. The PFLP and its offshoot, the Democratic Front of the Liberation of Palestine (DFLP), along with several other mini-groups, joined the PLO to become an obstreperous left-radical opposition. By 1974 both the PFLP and the DFLP impatiently had broken away.

Whereas the PLO's original Covenant of 1964 had stressed the all-Arab nature of the cause, the revised Charter of July 1968 emphasized its intrinsic Palestinian character. Palestine was the "homeland of the Arab Palestinian people" and constituted an "indivisible territorial unit," which only the Palestinian people could "legitimately claim as its homeland." The Charter "rejects any solution short of the total liberation of Palestine . . . with the boundaries it had during the British Mandate." As for the Palestinian identity, it was "genuine, essential, and inherent," and "transmitted from parents to children." From this point onward, "anyone born of a Palestinian father . . . inside Palestine or outside, is also a Palestinian." Accordingly, "Jews who had normally resided in Palestine until the beginning of the Zionist invasion will be considered Palestinians." The Charter stated that it was a "national duty to bring up individual Palestinians in an Arab revolutionary manner . . . to [prepare them] for the armed struggle . . . to win back [their] homeland." According to Article 9, since "armed struggle [is] the only way to liberate Palestine . . . it [is] an overall strategy, not merely a tactical phase." The "commando action constitutes the nucleus of the Palestinian popular liberation war [and] the fighters and carriers of arms . . . are the nucleus of the popular army."

The Charter declared that the "partition of Palestine in 1947 and the establishment of the state of Israel are entirely illegal," since they were "contrary to the will of the Palestinian people and to their natural right in their homeland, and inconsistent with the principles embedded in the Charter of the United Nations, particularly the right to self-determination," which made the "Balfour Declaration . . . null and void." Judaism was "a religion," but not an "independent nationality [nor] a single nation with an identity of its own." Zionism was a "political movement organically associated with international imperialism and antagonistic to all actions for liberation and to progressive movements in the world." Israel was "the instrument of the Zionist movement," which was "racist and fanatic in nature, aggressive, expansionist, and colonial in its aims, and fascist in its methods." The state was a "geographic base for world imperialism placed strategically in the midst of the Arab homeland to combat the hopes of the Arab nation for liberation, unity, and progress." Israel was "a constant source of threat vis-à-vis peace in the Middle East and the whole world." The liberation of Palestine was "a national duty and it attempts to repel the Zionist and imperial aggression against the Arab homeland, and aims at the elimination of Zionism in Palestine."

The basis, then, for the shift from an Arab-centered position in the 1964 Covenant to a Palestine-centered position in the amended Charter of 1968 lay in this sense of mission: the "destiny of the Arab nation, and indeed Arab existence itself, depend upon the destiny of the Palestinian cause." The "interdependence" of these two fates explained the "Arab nation's pursuit of, and striving for, the liberation of Palestine," with the Palestinian people playing "the vanguard in the realization of this sacred [national] goal."

The leaders of the PLO had no ideology other than anti-imperialist nationalism of the sort rampant throughout much of the Third World after the Second World War. While Arafat and his associates embraced the principle of progress, which subsumed social regeneration, they left George Habash and Nayif Hawatmeh, co-founder of the PFLP and one of its left-wing leaders, whom they failed to bring round, to espouse variants of Marxism, which they grafted onto nationalism. Islam was not part of the picture. Insofar as the organization had a project for post-exodus or liberated Palestine, it envisaged a political and civil society that would be democratic, secular, and progressive, within a binational frame. The PLO also sought to "achieve unity among the different groupings," to include Saiqa—a radical group of Marxist Muslim Palestinians with ties to Syria—and the Arab Liberation Front (ALF), connected to Iraq. The two inclusions pointed to the continuing if reduced weight of the Arab states and street.

Notwithstanding the PLO's resolve to break free of the Arab countries, the Palestinian resistance remained hopelessly dependent, in what would be an enduring love–hate relationship. To begin with, Egypt, Jordan, Lebanon, and Syria would necessarily host the bases, hideaways, and other logistic support systems for the commandos, while the oil states—Kuwait, Libya, Saudi Arabia—would be the paymasters. These host and donor nations would naturally attach strings to their assistance as they continued to pursue their not always compatible national and dynastic interests. Vulnerable to retaliatory strikes by Israel, the front-line states sought off and on to restrain *fedayeen* operating from within their borders. The oil states, although fiercely hostile to Israel, carefully avoided a falling-out with the Western powers—especially the U.S., which shored up their economies and regimes. Still, shaken by the great defeat, the Arab leaders encouraged the resistance to replace the failed armies in combat, and hailed the *fedayeen* for serving the cause and assuaging the wounded pride of their people.

The swift development of Fatah and the PLO transformed any residual nostalgia for the lost homeland into a broad-based popular movement and underground for the liberation of Palestine, to culminate in the establishment of a fully sovereign state. By 1970 the countries bordering Israel, Jordan above all, quartered a profusion of partisan organizations, including guerrilla groups, which the PLO labored to streamline and coordinate. Although the consolidation of the PLO, the amendment of the Charter, and the Karameh affair riveted the attention of Palestinians and Arabs, most of the rest of the world took little interest in the refugees, let alone their national cause. That Israel ignored them, when not stigmatizing their resistance as spurious and barbaric, contributed to this dismissal. In 1968 the headlines were dominated by the assassination of Martin Luther King, the student rebellion throughout much of the First World, and the Soviet repression of the Czech uprising. Such cursory mention as there was of cross-border raids by *fedayeen* focused on the defenseless and innocent Israelis, pictured and identified. The Palestinian and Arab victims of Israel's retaliatory raids remained nameless and faceless.

The disagreements and rivalries among the several guerrilla groups and factions were an expression of vitality even amid weakness. In many respects the conflicts ideologically mirrored those between the General Zionists, Laborites, and Revisionists of previous years; in tactical terms, they resembled those among the Hagana, Irgun, and Lehi. According to Abu Iyad—close to Arafat and, like him, a leading founder of Fatah and the PLO—"alone the armed struggle bids fair to overcome ideological differences and serve as a unifying catalyst." Whatever their disaccords, all involved were fast becoming impatient with the inefficacy of the commando raids. Presently they looked to mount, as Abu Iyad put it, "spectacular operations . . . to strike the imagination" of four distinct constituencies:

the Israelis, whom we want to impress with our existence; the Palestinians, whose resolve to pursue an autonomous struggle we mean to bolster; the Arab regimes, at whom we hurl defiance; and world public opinion, which ignores or pretends to ignore the fate allotted to our people.

The two stratagems they settled on soon overshadowed ordinary guerrilla operations and caused a growing rift in the PLO: the taking of hostages, and the unprecedented hijacking of commercial airliners.

This radical turn was principally the work of the PFLP, not Fatah. Between mid 1968 and mid 1972, out of some thirty hijackings, half were successful. Some fifteen Israelis and many more others were killed. This brief spell of international aerial terrorism also saw the dramatic seizure and murder, by the tiny Black September terrorist group, of ten Israeli wrestlers and their coach at the 1972 Olympic games in Munich. The political significance of the new violence far exceeded its number of victims. Its novelty and degree of moral contravention shocked the world into recognizing the existence of the Palestinian refugees, and led to their cause assuming its rightful place on the world's diplomatic agenda.

It all started with the skyjacking, on July 28, 1968, of an Israeli airliner on a flight from Rome to Tel Aviv, which was forced to land in Algiers. This curtain-raiser, which took no lives, was followed on December 26 by an attack on an El Al plane at Athens airport, killing one Israeli passenger. A dozen equally brazen and terrifying, but relatively non-lethal assaults and hijackings followed, some of them on non-Israeli carriers. Then, on September 8, 1970, PFLP operatives hijacked three civilian airliners: TWA and Swiss Air flights were forced to land at Zarqa, in Jordan, and a Pan Am flight was forced to land in Cairo. In exchange for the release of several Arab terrorists imprisoned in Western Europe, all the hostage-passengers were freed unharmed; the PFLP blew up the planes.

The triple skyjacking had the most serious political effects in Jordan, where tensions between the Palestinian resistance and King Hussein's regime had been rising. With 60 per cent of the population being Palestinian, and by virtue of its long border with post-1967 Israel, Jordan had become the Middle East's primary commando base and center of political agitation. The refugee camps were home to most of the thousands of militants and partisans, most of whom affiliated with Fatah. In addition to stirring up the youth, Fatah began to build community support by establishing hospitals and social centers. For a few years relations between its leaders and Hussein had been cordial. After the Karameh incident the king praised the guerrilla fighters, declared that the PLO was rightfully opposing the unlawful Israeli occupation, and reaffirmed Jordan's advocacy of the implementation of U.N. Resolution 242.

But as the camps developed into a state within a state and the resistance became more radical, Hussein was increasingly hedged in.

When the guerrillas stepped up their cross-border forays, the Israelis ratcheted up their retaliation. Within five months of Karameh there were hard-hitting raids on Irbid and As Sadt, northwest of Amman. The attacks claimed civilian victims whose deaths stirred the resistance among the Palestinians and a faction of PLO sympathizers in Hussein's inner circle. With their help, the PFLP and DFLP meant to destabilize, if not overthrow, the Hashemite regime with a view to making Jordan the main staging area for a popular or revolutionary assault on Israel, with the Palestinian *fedayeen* on the frontline.

On May 9, 1970 there was an attempt on King Hussein's life. Soon thereafter he sought an accommodation with the PLO and Fatah, whose factions Arafat tried with difficulty to prevent from splintering. Several Arab heads of state unsuccessfully tried to act as facilitators of this effort. By this time the *fedayeen* were encroaching on several towns in the north and precincts in Amman, while Habash was rumored to have framed the rebel slogan "All power to the resistance!" that the king took to be a call to topple his regime.

The triple skyjacking, with the Swiss Air and TWA airliners forced to land 20 miles northwest of Amman, violated Jordan's sovereignty, defied its government, and risked provoking fierce Israeli reprisals. On September 17, Hussein ordered the royal army to take over the refugee camps and reassert firm control over the country generally. The leaders of Syria and Iraq threatened to intervene on the side of the *fedayeen*, but did nothing. During a ten-day civil war the insurgents were left to fight on their own, while Washington tacitly backed the king by deploying units of the Sixth Fleet in the eastern Mediterranean. Israel stationed troops along the border with Jordan and other frontline states. Arafat, while trying to outflank Habash, probably discovered that many of Fatah's *fedayeen* were beyond his reach and operated on their own. Fighting separately, the partisans of Fatah and the PFLP were no match for the Jordanian forces, and paid dearly for their valor.

As leader of Fatah and the PLO, Arafat was emerging as a credible and valued interlocutor. With his fighters at bay, he was desperate to avoid a total disaster. On September 27, at the urging of Arab leaders, including Nasser, Arafat met with King Hussein to agree to a ceasefire, to the immediate withdrawal of Fatah's armed militias from Jordan to positions "appropriate" for the continuing battle with Israel, and on a mutual release of prisoners. Scrimmages continued intermittently, especially in Amman, but also to the north, in Irbid and Jarash. On October 13, in a codicil, Arafat agreed that all *fedayeen* would pull back from towns and villages to the camps and be prohibited from carrying arms outside them. At a cost of at least 3,000 lives on all sides, the showdown of "Black September" reinforced Jordan's sovereignty, the authority of its army, and Hussein's rule. Within less than a year those *fedayeen* who had not yet fled to either Lebanon or Syria were run out of the kingdom, along with their military and political cadres.

Having routed the core of the Palestinian resistance, King Hussein felt strong enough to resume posing as the chosen herald of the Palestinian diaspora everywhere. In March 1972 he proposed the establishment of a "united Arab kingdom" to consist of a confederation of "a Jordanian [and] a Palestinian region," with himself as supreme sovereign and commander-in-chief of the armed forces. The king, along with some Zionists and Israelis, subscribed to the equation "Jordan is Palestine and Palestine is Jordan," as propounded by one of his foreign ministers. However covetous Hussein remained of the West Bank, for all intents and purposes he recognized Israel and welcomed the majority of refugees, continuing to extend citizenship to them.

Meanwhile, from Israel's perspective, Jordan was still potentially by far the most tractable Arab state, all the more so now that it was truncated and no longer the main springboard of the Palestinian resistance. Because Israel's leaders would not credit the resistance, they also could not fathom the import of the Jordanian *fedayeen* relocating massively to Lebanon and Syria as well as going underground in the occupied territories—with the refugees in the camps providing an inexhaustible source of recruits. Lebanon became the new hub of the resistance along Israel's borders. It was there that some of the *fedayeen* regrouped under the Black September ensign to mark their fierce repression by Hussein, which, for those who survived it, meant a second expulsion.

The attacks against Israel were undiminished by this forced relaunching of the resistance. Two of the most spectacular new-style strikes took place in 1972, both directed from beyond Jordan's borders. On May 30 a commando of three Japanese landed at Tel Aviv's Lod Airport on board Air France flight 132. In an operation apparently engineered by the PFLP in Lebanon, the gunmen, taking their weapons from violin cases, randomly mowed down twenty-six passengers and injured eighty in the terminal. Of the twenty-six dead, ten were Jews, and sixteen were Puerto Ricans on a pilgrimage to the Holy Land.

More infamously still, on September 5 a Black September commando of eight armed Palestinian Arabs burst into the quarters housing the Israeli athletes in the Olympic Village outside Munich.

One coach and one athlete were killed, and nine others were taken hostage. The terrorists, all refugees from Palestine, demanded the release of 234 Palestinian Arab prisoners, including members of their families, from Israeli jails. The plan is thought to have been conceived by Abu Daoud, chief of Black September, allegedly with the complicity of Arafat and Mahmoud Abbas (*nom de guerre*, Abu Mazen—another founding member of Fatah). With Israel refusing all negotiations, a rescue attempt by the German police degenerated into a murderous firefight in which all the hostages and five terrorists were killed, with three terrorists being taken prisoner. On September 9 Israel retaliated with heavy air raids on supposed Fatah–PLO bases in Lebanon and Syria, and a unit of the Mossad—one of Israel's three major intelligence agencies, which was focused on counter-terrorism—undertook operation "Wrath of God," charged by Premier Golda Meir with "strik[ing] at the terrorist organizations wherever we can reach them." A few weeks later, on October 29, a Palestinian commando hijacked a Lufthansa jetliner, which it traded for the release of the three Black September militants being held for trial in Germany.

From the Palestinian point of view the impact of the new violence was equivocal: on the one hand, it fulfilled the aim of putting the refugees on the map; on the other, it vindicated the enemy, alienated sympathizers, and heightened intramural rivalries. But at the time its bearing on the Israeli–Egyptian confrontation was what mattered most, enabling Israel to say, in effect, "You see what these people are all about."

Although neither Nasser nor Nasserism recovered from the defeat of 1967, for Israel the border with Egypt—280 kilometers (174 miles)—remained by far the most dangerous because of the size and quality of Cairo's army and the entanglement of the two superpowers. Nasser strengthened his positions along the Suez Canal and lobbed small-caliber artillery shells over Israel's frontlines. The Israelis built the fortified Bar-Lev Line of some thirty outposts along their side of the Canal, and answered these pinprick volleys with air strikes against Egyptian positions. The number of mutual incursions continued to rise. On May 1, 1969, a blustering Nasser declared a "war of attrition" as he sought to implicate Moscow in his last-ditch but cautious effort at reviving his political fortunes and improving his negotiating position in the diplomatic opening he meant to create.

Israel's military–political caste had little patience for this "war of attrition." Although both Allon and Dayan had their eyes set on the premiership, following Eshkol's death the Labor Party put forward Golda Meir, who had been confirmed as prime minister on March 17,

1969. While she publicly cultivated an image of a winsome and reassuring grandmother, the political establishment knew her to be an unbending hardliner. Begin resigned as minister without portfolio, insisting that Israel not renew the ceasefire with Egypt without a dictated peace. Meir stated publicly that Israel would counter enemy attacks, from whatever quarter, with an "asymmetrical response," and sought to convince Washington to bear with Israel's intransigence. Yet the Soviets and the Americans were equally weary of another escalation of potentially explosive tensions along the Middle East's main line of demarcation. Each was undoubtedly more apprehensive about Tel Aviv making trouble than about Cairo doing so. There was widespread agreement among those nations directly concerned about the urgency of taking steps to implement Resolution 242, whose tacit rationale was that, in the words of King Hussein, "Israel may have either peace or territory, but she can never have both."

The U.N. pressed for a renewable ceasefire of at least three months, during which Egypt and Israel would move from the theater of their phony but hazardous war to the conference room. On December 9, 1969 William P. Rogers, President Nixon's first secretary of state, advanced a plan suggesting that Israel withdraw to the pre-June 1967 boundaries in exchange for security and peace. Rogers postulated that "any changes in the preexisting [border] lines should not reflect the weight of conquest and should be confined to insubstantial alterations required for mutual security." America, he added, does "not support expansionism." This first U.S. proposal to exchange "land for peace," to be mediated by special U.N. envoy Gunnar Jarring, also addressed, even if only vaguely, the issue of Jerusalem. And perhaps heeding the convulsion in Jordan, Rogers insisted that "there can be no lasting peace without a just settlement of the problems of those Palestinians whom the wars of 1948 and 1967 have made homeless." Washington was "prepared to contribute generously, along with others," to resolve this vexed question. Stressing the importance of "taking into account the desires and aspirations of the refugees and the legitimate concerns of the governments of the area," Rogers cautioned that "the problem posed by the refugees will become increasingly serious if their future is not resolved."

Egypt and Jordan, the two major frontline states, were favorably disposed, as was Russia. But Israel rejected the Rogers Plan outright; so did Syria and the PLO's hardliners—the latter because it still addressed the refugee problem without envisaging a Palestinian state. Even President Nixon and Henry Kissinger, his national security advisor, turned their backs on the Rogers Plan. Kissinger in particular was loath to ask anything of Israel's leaders that might weaken their unconditional support for the U.S. in the Cold War with Soviet Russia, which in the Middle East meant keeping the pressure on Nasser.

The miscarriage of the Rogers Plan strengthened the hardliners not only in Israel but also in Egypt, Syria, and Iraq, as well as within the PLO. Following Israel's rebuff, Nasser asked Moscow for additional arms, with limited success. Washington's backsliding encouraged first Eshkol and then Meir not to yield. Israeli Mirages flew ever more daring missions across the Canal until, on July 30, 1970, they downed six Egyptian MiGs with Soviet pilots at the controls. The Americans and Russians imposed a ceasefire on August 7. The Egyptians were strengthening their anti-aircraft defenses west of the Canal when Nasser, weakened by diabetes, died of a heart attack, aged 52, on September 28. His funeral, attended by millions, had the appearance of an apotheosis.

Anwar Sadat, his generally unknown and disprized vice-president and successor, was even more determined to move from confrontation to negotiation. By February 4, 1971, after an unsuccessful approach to Kissinger, in a speech to the Egyptian parliament he announced his readiness to "sign a peace agreement with Israel through the efforts of Dr. Jarring," premised on a Rogers-like exchange of peace for land, notably for the occupied Sinai and Gaza Strip. Simultaneously, convinced that the U.S. was master of the game in the Middle East, he signaled his eagerness to restore diplomatic relations with Washington and his willingness to reopen the Suez Canal. After several hints of his disposition to reduce Cairo's ties to Moscow, in July 1972—apparently without incurring the Kremlin's wrath—he asked the Soviets to withdraw their 20,000 military advisors and cadres from Egypt.

Golda Meir fended off all diplomatic advances and proposals for a reduction of tensions and an opening for negotiations. Israel continued its military buildup, with emphasis on the acquisition of the latest jet fighters, tanks, and naval missile launchers, largely paid for with American credits and low-interest loans. It also persevered in the development of its nuclear capability. The military budget rose threefold within less than a decade, partly because of the cost of lengthening universal military service and reserve duty. As Martin Buber had predicted, Jewish Palestine was turning into a garrison state—one dominated by a caste of generals still stamped with the old Western supremacism. This expressed itself in a frank and sweeping contempt for the Arab nation. General Ezer Weizman, chief of operations of the General Staff during the Six Day War, held that war "was not for the Arabs." General Yehoshafat Harkabi, of Army

Intelligence, found that at "crucial moments of combat the Arab soldier," rather than benefit from the support of "a tightly-knit unit [is] abandoned to his own devices [while] his combat unit disintegrates [and leaves] each soldier to look out only for himself." Shortly before the next Arab–Israeli conflict, Defense Minister Dayan, speaking to the members of the General Staff, attributed the Arabs' weakness to "factors so deeply rooted that they cannot, in my view, be easily overcome: the moral, technical, and educational backwardness of the soldiers." The Israelis' presumed moral superiority was conveniently confirmed by one further advantage (first identified by Jabotinsky): "The balance of forces is so much in our favor," Dayan continued, that it would deter the Arabs from an "immediate renewal of hostilities"—an assessment shared by General Rabin, the Chief of Staff during the 1967 War. All took it for granted that the latest American weapons—tanks, planes, missiles—gave the IDF the ultimate edge.

Given these judgments, as well as strategic buffer zones and divisions in the Arab world, Israel's leaders unsurprisingly saw no reason to trade land for peace, let alone give thought to the Palestinian refugees. Nor were they about to heed Sadat's repeated warnings in 1972–3 that, should Washington and Tel Aviv continue to spurn his outstretched hand, he would have to reach for the sword. He began to lay plans for a joint military move with Hafez Assad, the new Baathist president of Syria, and ordered the deployment of additional forces along the Suez Canal, which the Israelis took to be a military exercise. Meir dismissed Hussein's secret and personal warning, on September 25, that an invasion by Syria was imminent.

Having exhausted his diplomatic options, and confident of the advantage of a first strike, in concert with Assad, Sadat launched the bruited attack on October 6, 1973. The Third Egyptian Army rushed to cross the Suez Canal, and Syrian tanks broke into the Golan. Coinciding with the highest holidays of both Judaism and Islam, the Yom Kippur or Ramadan War—the Fourth Arab–Israeli War—lasted three weeks. The two Arab armies thrust into Israeli-occupied Egyptian and Syrian territories with the limited objective of reclaiming lost lands and precipitating negotiations. The Egyptian and Syrian leaders knew they were in no position to defeat Israel completely. Even the financial help of Saudi Arabia and the ever hoped-for but problematic oil embargo—the Arabs' ultimate weapon—would not have enabled them to win through.

Even so, many thousands of Egyptian foot soldiers and hundreds of tanks succeeded in overrunning the Bar-Lev Line, and dug in some 10 miles east of the Canal. In the north, Syrian troops and armor penetrated into the Golan Heights, advancing close to and ultimately breaching the 1967 ceasefire lines. On both fronts Israeli troops, caught off guard, were forced to fall back before beginning a counter-attack, with difficulty, on October 8. With the arrival of reservists the tide began to turn on October 10–11. In the north the IDF reconquered the Golan Heights and moved into Syria. In the Suez theater, however, the counteroffensive stalled, with the Egyptians exacting a heavy toll of Israeli lives, planes, and tanks. The loss of advanced weaponry was such that it in fact raised Israeli fears about the depletion of its arsenal.

Both the force and speed of the two-front attack caught Israel's leaders unawares, especially since it gave the lie to their credo of innate Arab military dysfunction. Their momentary bewilderment was tinged with panic. At dawn on October 9 several senior officers broached the idea of resorting to nuclear arms, and Dayan himself appears to have advocated the option. Marginally less alarmed, Premier Meir—backed by General Allon, among others—demurred. Instead, with the support of the cabinet, she flew to Washington to supplicate Nixon and Kissinger for instant help. Apparently Meir invoked the possibility that, *in extremis*, Israel might resort to the ultimate weapon, which Kissinger seemed to consider a sign of "either hysteria or blackmail." But something worked. A massive airlift of military supplies began on October 12, helping Israeli forces to seize the offensive: they reoccupied the western shore of the Suez Canal on October 16 and surrounded Egypt's Third Army on October 21. By then the IDF had advanced to within 20 miles of Damascus. On October 17 the Arab oil states, meeting in Kuwait, placed a monitory embargo on oil, which quadrupled the price of black gold within a year. Moscow started its military airlifts to Damascus and Cairo, and threatened to send in troops.

For the fourth time the intervention of the superpowers simultaneously aggravated and limited an escalation of the 25-year-old Arab–Israeli conflict. Presently the U.S. and the Soviet Union again conspired, respectively, to check further Israeli gains and stem further Arab losses while they applied pressure and held the ring for negotiations—as always to the advantage of Washington and Tel Aviv. On October 22 the Security Council unanimously adopted Resolution 338 calling for an immediate ceasefire, for the "implementation" of U.N. Resolution 242 "in all of its parts", and for negotiations "aimed at establishing a just and durable peace in the Middle East." An Israeli–Syrian ceasefire was signed that day, with Israel returning the Syrian territory it had occupied during the hostilities but holding on to the

Golan Heights. Since the IDF continued to encircle the Egyptian forces west of the Canal, the Israeli–Egyptian ceasefire was delayed until October 26. The U.S. brokered an agreement that gave Egypt control over both shores of the Suez Canal, including a strip several miles inland from the eastern bank. It also provided for a U.N. force to monitor compliance with the ruling along the waterway. Had it not been for the threatened damage of the oil embargo to the capitalist world economy, Kissinger would probably not have pressured Israel to make even these marginal concessions. The blow was softened when Washington quadrupled its annual financial aid for Tel Aviv to over $2 billion—most of it to purchase American weapons—and promised to have no truck with the PLO. Cairo received a pledge of limited American aid and of support for the implementation of Resolution 242, soon followed by the restoration of diplomatic relations.

It had taken Sadat's head-on military assault, the attendant consternation in Israel's political and civil society, and the shock to the international system to secure even small repossessions, and to open the road to negotiation that Israel had been determined to keep closed. But that road would be uphill. The balance of military and economic forces in the region was unchanged, with Israel the confirmed colossus. Just as forbidding, the Arab territories captured by Israel in 1967 remained under occupation: the West Bank and Gaza, most of the Sinai, and the Golan Heights. Inside Israel ever more latter-day Revisionists—both secular and religious—pressed for the settlement of the territories with an eye to incorporating them into a Greater Israel. In the Arab world the increasingly radical hardliners in the Palestinian resistance and their champions gained influence and strength. So although the latest war had had nothing to do with the Palestinian refugee problem, it managed to give the issue greater salience in the domestic and international politics of the Middle East.

The most avoidable of the cross-border Arab–Israeli wars, the war of 1973, took a greater human and material toll on Israel than the three previous wars combined: approximately 2,600 killed and over 7,000 wounded; about 100 aircraft and 400 tanks destroyed. Egypt and Syria together suffered at least three times as many fatalities. In the aftermath, Israeli politicians, public intellectuals, and editorialists held the governing class responsible for the military unreadiness and intelligence failure that had brought on the costly fiasco of the first week. But there was no suspicion that the cause of the setback might have been a fundamental arrogance. By daring to go up against Israel, Sadat had unwittingly struck and exposed its Achilles heel. Nevertheless, despite the comfortable victory, the country was in a profound state of shock. For the first time since 1947, the overweening self-confidence of veteran Zionists and first-generation Israelis was shaken. The taste of failure, however fleeting, of the IDF—formerly presumed invincible—was a reminder of their personal vulnerability. The pretense of self-reliance was also shattered: there simply was no way to avoid owning up to Israel's utter military, diplomatic, and economic dependence on the U.S. As Ben-Gurion and Abba Silver had realized even before the Biltmore conference in 1942, there was no alternative to enlisting American power, as well as the political and financial muscle of the American Jewish diaspora, for the establishment and consolidation—for the very survival—of the Jewish state.

The political consequence of the victory, though inglorious, was not only to revalidate the policy that had provoked the war and to harden the incumbent governing and ruling class, but to embolden the composite right-wing opposition. Certainly the initial Egyptian and Syrian breakthroughs also forced reappraisals on the nongovernmental left, particularly among those who questioned the wisdom of holding on to the occupied territories at the cost of intensifying Arab resistance, especially among the refugees. But, compared with the hawks, these emergent doves were for the most part without political pedigree, organization, or public echo. The hawks, temporal and religious, advocated the settlement of all of historical Palestine plus the Golan Heights for a wild mix of nationalist, Biblical, and security reasons. Certainly the political suasion of Uri Avnery and Yeshayahu Leibowitz counted for nothing against the trumpet-calls of the ultra-nationalists.

In the parliamentary election of December 31, 1973, Likud increased its representation from twenty-nine to thirty-nine in a Knesset of 120, and the religious nationalists of Mafdal won ten seats. Begin refused to join the cabinet, preferring to keep a free hand in order to head this growing right-wing opposition. Except for the portentous rightward tilt among the deputies and in the electorate, there was no change in Israel's political leadership or orientation. This continuity was confirmed on April 11, 1974, when Golda Meir stepped down and General Rabin, her successor, made Shimon Peres, ordnance expert and father of Israel's nuclear program, his defense minister, and General Allon his foreign minister.

In Cairo, Sadat's prestige soared. He basked in the glory of Egypt's army having broken through the fortified Bar-Lev Line. This success was said to be due not to the Israeli forces' having been caught off guard, but to the Egyptian forces' mastery of modern warfare.

Infantry, tanks, and air force had engaged the enemy together, in perfect coordination. Although Sadat had distanced himself from Moscow, his army made good use of its surface-to-air and anti-tank missiles. Even defeat had its dignity. During the retreat, the Sinai divisions fell back without panic or disorder. The army had acquitted itself well, leaving Egypt still the Arab world's major military power. In the streets and ruling circles there was, this time, quiet pride—even a whispered sentiment that Israel might be vincible after all. Yet, in the refugee camps and among the leadership of the PLO, Sadat's policy met with great skepticism. He was criticized for pursuing Egypt's national agenda without regard for the common regional interests— diplomatic, economic, political—of the other Arab states, and for neglecting the plight of the Palestinians. Nothing about the 1973 War and its aftermath held out any promise of improved prospects for the refugees.

Under the circumstances the Palestinian resistance continued to be torn between Arafat and Habash. The latter stayed on the offensive, as if to remind the Israelis and Egyptians, as well as the world at large, that the Palestinians could not be passed over in silence. Of the ten terrorist incidents in 1974, the bloodiest were the work of the PFLP and DFLP. Arafat professed to be outraged, in a reaction not unlike that of the Yishuv's leaders to Zionist terrorism in the 1940s. The Israelis indiscriminately and unwisely condemned the entire Palestinian resistance as a group of murderers, thereby hardening the friend–enemy divide. There were three major terrorist incidents inside Israel, two near the Lebanese border: on April 11, 1974, eighteen Israelis were killed (including eight children) and sixteen injured in Kiryat Shmona; on May 15, twenty-seven were killed (most of them children) and 134 injured in Ma'alot. The terrorists killed and injured many of their victims during battles with Israeli forces seeking to rescue hostages. Premier Meir lost no time warning that Israel "regarded the government of Lebanon and its people who collaborated with the terrorists [as] responsible for these murders." Shortly thereafter, an Israeli air strike killed some sixty civilians in southern Lebanon. On November 18, four Israelis were killed and twenty-three injured in Beit Shean, 2 miles from the Jordanian border. Defense Minister Peres served notice that Israel would increasingly strike terrorist bases "in their centers in Lebanon and in their roots on both sides of the border."

All this while Arafat, probably inspired by Sadat, was looking for a diplomatic venue. Several Arab heads of state endorsed the call for the establishment of a sovereign Palestine in the occupied territories. In October 1974, a summit of twenty Arab countries in Rabat, Morocco's capital, proclaimed the PLO the sole legitimate representative of the Palestinian people. Partly to help Arafat keep his own ultras in check, several governments urged that the Palestine Question be placed on the docket of the U.N. General Assembly. On October 14, at the request of fifty-five member-states, this more sympathetic body invited the PLO, "the organization of the Palestinian people . . . the principal party" in this matter, to participate in plenary sessions concerning the Palestine Question. Arafat, as chairman of the executive committee of the PLO, addressed the General Assembly on November 13—the first delegate of a national liberation movement, not a member-state, to do so. In a forum in which the countries of the Third World, many of them postcolonial nations, were in the ascendant, Arafat declared the struggle of the "people of Palestine" to be part of the larger struggle against "colonialism, imperialism, neocolonialism, and racism." He well understood "the close connection between Cecil Rhodes, who promoted settler colonialism in south-east Africa, and Theodor Herzl, who had settler designs upon Palestine." In exchange for support from the British in this enterprise, the early Zionists had promised them "an imperialist base in Palestine," which became "an arsenal of weapons." It followed naturally in Arafat's construction that, having seized the Palestinians' land, Israel, this "racist entity," should "support the Secret Army Organization in Algeria [the French military and settlers opposed to independence], bolster the settler colonialists in Africa, and back the South Vietnamese against the Vietnamese revolution."

Arafat charged that, although they had appropriated countless Palestinian homes, pastures, and orchards, the Israelis embraced the "myth" that our "homeland was a desert until it was made to bloom by . . . foreign settlers [and] that it was a land without a people." He was there to say the Palestinian people defied this negation of its existence. It was only after it had "lost faith in the international community which persisted in ignoring its rights [that it had] no choice but to resort to armed struggle." To denounce the Palestinians as "terrorists" was to tar past and present freedom fighters with the same brush: the American colonists who fought the British; the Europeans who resisted the Nazis; and the peoples of the Third World who struggled against colonialism and neocolonialism. There was a time when "many of you who are in this Assembly hall today were considered terrorists."

Speaking to the delegates of the First and Second Worlds, Arafat emphasized that the Palestinian movement was never "motivated by racial or religious factors, [that] its target was never the Jew as a person, but racist Zionism and undisguised aggression [and that] while it maintained its opposition to the colonialist Zionist movement, it respected the Jewish faith." By the same token, Palestinians "deplore all those crimes committed against the Jews [and] all the real discrimination suffered by them because of their faith." Yet Arafat asked why the Palestinian people should "have to pay the price" for this persecution and why it should be held "responsible for the problems of Jewish immigration." In appealing to the delegates "to help our people's return to its homeland," Arafat wanted them to know that "when we speak of our common hopes for the Palestine of tomorrow we include in our perspective all Jews now living in Palestine who choose to live with us there in peace and without discrimination."

Yet there was no denying that Israel was making "feverish" preparations for a "fifth war of aggression . . . against us." Though he would not submit and deliver up his arms, Arafat reiterated his "faith in political and diplomatic struggle as a complement [and] enhancement of our armed struggle." His conclusion was at once a warning and an appeal. After declaring that he had come before them "bearing an olive branch and a freedom fighter's gun," he exhorted the members of the General Assembly: "Do not let the olive branch fall from my hand. I repeat: *Do not let the olive branch fall from my hand.*"

Yosef Tekoah spoke for Israel in the afternoon, following Arafat's speech in the morning. A seasoned diplomat, he had served as ambassador to Brazil and the Soviet Union before becoming Israel's permanent representative to the U.N. in 1968. He spoke not only "on behalf of a nation that has struggled through twenty centuries for its liberty and equality and for the restoration of its independence," but also in the name of the "entire Jewish people . . . of whom one third was annihilated in the Second World War that gave birth to the United Nations." Whereas a "million Jewish soldiers [fought] in the Allied armies and in partisan ranks" to help "make the United Nations a reality," most of the Arab states did not "know the struggle that made the world safe for the United Nations," and some of their "leaders collaborated with the forces of darkness against the United Nations." These were the states that were "in the vanguard of a fanatical assault on the Jewish people, an assault that tramples to dust the ideals of the United Nations."

On October 14, Tekoah continued, when it voted to invite the PLO to participate in its debates, the General Assembly "turned its back on the U.N. Charter, on law and humanity [by] virtually capitulating to a murder organization." It as good as "hung out a sign reading

'Murderers of children are welcome here,' " and that very morning the "chieftain" of these murderers had "defiled . . . the rostrum" of the assembly. Tekoah characterized the PLO as sworn to "willful, cold-blooded, carefully prepared, bestial assaults on innocent and defenseless children, women, and men in towns and villages, in schools and market places, at airports, in the air, and on the ground." This violence explained why "associations of anti-Nazi freedom fighters have repeatedly condemned the PLO atrocities as crimes reminiscent of Nazi savagery." There was no concealing that Arafat, "as commander of El Fatah–Black September," was both the "gangster who received $5 million from President Muammar el-Qaddafi of Libya as prize for the slaughter of Israeli sportsmen at the Olympic Games at Munich [and] the criminal who personally directed the murder of diplomats at Khartoum." Charging Arafat with preferring "Nazi methods," Tekoah maintained that the "murderers" of Israel's athletes and "the butchers" of Ma'alot's children "do not belong in the international community." Israel would "see to it that they have no place" in the peace process.

The U.N. had not discussed the plight of "the Kurdish people, [which was] subjected to a continuing war of annihilation by the Iraqi Government." Nor, Tekoah argued, had it "tried to avert the massacre of half a million non-Muslim Africans in South Sudan" or addressed "the fundamental human and political rights of hundreds of millions who live under totalitarian regimes." So why should it take up the problem of the "Arabs of Palestine" who were not starving like "almost 500 million people in Asia, Africa, and Latin America"? Clearly, the United Nations was not leaving them "without assistance as it has [left] tens of millions of refugees all over the world, including Jewish refugees in Israel from Arab lands." Tekoah contended that there was "one and only one . . . reason for the special consideration accorded to questions concerning the Arabs of Palestine: the continuous exploitation of these questions as a weapon of Arab belligerency against Israel." Besides, the PLO neither "emerged from within the Palestinian community" nor was "representative" of it. Rather, it was "a creation of the Arab governments themselves" that conceived the PLO as an "instrument for waging terror warfare against Israel."

No nation, Tekoah went on, "enjoyed greater fulfillment of its political rights" and was "more abundantly . . . endowed with territory, sovereignty, and independence" than the "Arab nation," which has a "common language, culture, religion, and origin." This was the nation that "stormed out of its birthland in the seventh century and conquered one people after another until its rule encompassed the entire Arab peninsula, the Fertile Crescent, and North Africa." Of all the cultures and peoples that it replaced and vanquished, the Jews alone "refused to disappear and shed [their] national identity."

Now the Arab nation, having acquired "territory by war [for] centuries," was "represented in the United Nations by twenty sovereign states," among them "the Palestinian Arab State of Jordan." And in point of fact, Tekoah asserted, "geographically and ethnically Jordan is Palestine." The two banks of the Jordan river were "parts of the land of Israel or Palestine . . . until Jordan and then Israel became independent." The nomad Bedouins were only a small minority in Jordan's population. As for the majority sedentary population, even on the East Bank, it was "of Palestinian West Bank origins, [and] without the Palestinians, Jordan would be a state without a people." Moreover, he continued, "the vast majority of Palestinian refugees never left Palestine." Rather, "as a result of the wars of 1948 and 1967, they [merely] moved from one part of the country to another." Tekoah was categorical: since

> most Palestinians continue to live in a Palestinian State. The vast majority of Palestinian Arabs are citizens of that Palestinian State . . . It is, therefore, false to allege that the Palestinian people has been deprived of a state of its own or that it has been uprooted from its national homeland.

No matter how "civilized" the terminology of Arafat,

> behind it looms . . . the design to deprive the Jewish people of its independence, to liquidate the Jewish state, and to establish on its ruins another Arab state in which Jews would again live as a [persecuted and tortured] minority as they do today . . . and did in the past

in so many Arab countries. By recognizing the PLO on October 24, the General Assembly had opted "for terrorism and savagery." The assembly must know that none of its resolutions could

> wash the hands of Yasser Arafat and his henchmen clean of the blood of their innocent victims; . . . could confer respect on a band of cutthroats; . . . could establish the authority of an organization . . . that does not represent anyone except the few thousand agents of death it employs.

Israel too had "made its choice": instead of "paying homage to bloodshed and bestiality," it would "pursue the PLO murderers" and act against "their organization and their bases until a definite end is put to their atrocities." The Jewish state would "not permit the establishment of PLO authority in any part of Palestine." The world should know that, since the

> Jewish people . . . had defended its rights, fought and bled for centuries, outlived empires, and survived holocausts [it was not about] to be swayed from its course by a gang of murderers who thrive on Jewish blood or by the whims of regimes that claim to seek justice for Palestinian Arabs, but openly deny it to Jews.

While dealing with the PLO was out, Tekoah insisted that Israel was nevertheless ready and willing "to reach a peaceful settlement with the Palestinian Arab State of Jordan in which the Palestinian national identity would find full expression." He reconfirmed his government's declaration of July 21, 1974, promising to "work towards negotiating a peace agreement" with the "Jordanian–Palestinian Arab state east of Israel" in which the "specific identity of the Jordanians and Palestinians would find expression in peace and good-neighborliness with Israel."

Tekoah's jeremiad overwhelmed Sherif Abdul Hamid Sharaf, Jordan's permanent representative to the U.N., who followed him on the rostrum and was expected to be by far the least hostile of the Arab spokesmen. Sharaf called attention to the stark contrast between Arafat's speech, in which, "despite tragedy and agony . . . he pleaded for peace . . . and asked . . . for justice," and Tekoah's reply, which exemplified the core obstacle, which was "a state of mind . . . that closes itself to the realities [and is a] captive of its own mythology and dogmatism." The Palestinians were merely the "first Arab victims" of an "aggressive state" bent on expansion with "illegitimate and manipulated support from many quarters of the world." Like so many Zionist and Israeli spokesmen, past and present, the "representative today [made] an attempt to solve the problem semantically." In place of a known history, a succession of myths had been propagated: that "Israel descended upon an area that was empty"; that the people of Palestine "hardly existed"; that the Arabs "were the aggressors and were besieging Israel"; and that the "Arabs were trying to throw Israel into the sea while Israel was pleading for peace." Sharaf insisted that Tekoah's "injection of Jordan into the debate" was in keeping with this tried way "of fabricating facts" and using rhetorical ruses. However one designated Jordan—"Palestine," "Syria," "X," or "the name of any Arab country"—from 1947–8 Israel had "expelled a million people"; and in 1967 it had attacked three Arab countries, "one of which—and call it by whatever name you wish—now has a million people under Israel's occupation." For the Israeli representative to describe Jordan as Palestine in no way made it so. "Can anybody justify taking over Jordan and Syria" and telling the people living there to "go live with their brothers" in other countries of the Arab nation?

Sharaf argued that, after twenty-five years, debate over the Palestine Question ought to move from "acrimony" and "closed, rigid, and dogmatic positions" to "dialogue . . . and the opening of new avenues, minds, and spirits." Though Tekoah had spoken of "negotiating" with Jordan, that was "precisely what Israel had not been doing for the last seven years." Perhaps, once pressed by its own people, the Israeli leadership might want "to make an agonizing reappraisal." To "come to terms with the realities" meant recognizing that Israel "must end the occupation" of the West Bank which, together with "1.5 million Palestinians in refugee camps," was "the root of the problem." Short of such a change of course, the situation would continue to deteriorate, with Israel in "continuous confrontation with its neighbors," which, according to Sharaf, precluded furthering the "coexistence of Jews and Arabs" in the Middle East.

Digressive in nature, the Jordanian's address could not counter Tekoah's ferocious repulsion of Arafat and the Palestinians. Since the creation of Israel in 1947, its leaders had categorically refused the return of the refugees, and were no less determined to eliminate Fatah. Tekoah toed the mark, treating the complex world of the Palestinians as monolithic. In not recognizing them at all, the Israelis necessarily missed any differences of class, status, education, religion, or generation among both exiles and refugees. Similarly, they gave little thought to differentiating between Arafat, Habash, and Abu Nidal—the terrorist mastermind who broke with the PLO in the mid 1970s. Their sweeping dismissal precluded any dialogue or negotiation whatsoever.

But Tekoah's oratory was no more outrageous or intractable than the Revisionist program of the ascendant Likud party, now focused on annexation and settlements rather than on boundaries and cross-border wars. Hereafter Israel's running fight would be ever more with the Arab Palestinians in the occupied territories and host countries. Roughly half of the displaced Palestinians were under direct Israeli rule within the post-1967 frontiers, the other half being dispersed in Jordan, Lebanon, Syria, and the oil states.

The PLO, meanwhile, was making headway in its campaign to be recognized as the chief representative of the highly diverse, syncretic, and fractious universe of Palestinian exiles and refugees. Among them were several formations of *fedayeen* with ties to hard-line Arab states—notably Syria, Libya, and Iraq. But these extremist forces, sworn to recover occupied Palestine for the refugees by any means necessary, were a small minority in the PLO. Still, they affirmed themselves through increasingly dramatic terrorist acts that were, however execrable, no worse in kind than Israel's retributive and preemptive raids.

By now there was a growing disposition within the PLO to combine the "armed struggle" for the return to Palestine with a campaign to establish, by way of negotiation, a separate and sovereign state for Palestinians on the West Bank and in the Gaza Strip. The drive for non-member observer status—with the right to speak, but not to vote on resolutions—and Arafat's address in the General Assembly were steps in this direction, as was an insistent demand by Sadat for Israel's withdrawal from all occupied territories.

The General Assembly provided a platform for the articulation of Third World grievances after decolonization. All the Palestinian leaders understood the plight of their people to be inseparable from this great historical mutation, and certainly Arafat's address of November 13, 1974 was cast in this perspective. He knew, as did his audience inside and beyond the U.N. headquarters, that resolutions of the General Assembly were nonbinding and essentially symbolic—a naked demonstration of the enduring powerlessness and dependency of yesterday's colonial and semi-colonial world. An outpost of the First World in the Middle East, as well as shielded and financed by it, Israel kept ignoring the General Assembly's resolutions concerning the Palestine Question, including the refugees.

A year later, on November 10, 1975, the General Assembly voted Resolution 3379, designating Zionism "as a form of racism and racial discrimination." It was sponsored and supported by the Arab, African, and other nonaligned nations, in concert with the countries of the Soviet bloc. To legitimize this infamous counter-charge to Israel's stance, as expressed by Tekoah, the Resolution recalled that, on December 14, 1953, the General Assembly had condemned "the unholy alliance between South African racism and Zionism"; that in mid 1975, in Mexico City, the World Conference of the International Women's Year had proclaimed that "international cooperation and peace require the achievement of national liberation and independence, the elimination of colonialism and neo-colonialism, foreign occupation, Zionism, apartheid and racial discrimination in all its forms"; that in late July 1975, in Kampala, the Assembly of Heads of State and Government of the Organization of African Unity had declared that "the racist regime in occupied Palestine and the racist regimes in Zimbabwe and South Africa have a common imperialist origin, forming a whole and having the same racist structure and being organically linked in their policy aimed at repression of the dignity and integrity of the human being"; and that, in August 1975, the Conference of Foreign Ministers of the Non-Aligned Countries had "condemned Zionism as a threat to world peace and security and called upon all countries to oppose this racist and imperialist ideology." Resolution 3379 was adopted by seventy-two votes to thirty-five, with thirty-two abstentions.

In Israel and the Jewish diaspora the accusations of racism and imperialism, and the conflation of Israeli and South African discrimination, were greeted with moral outrage and a shudder: the November 10 vote took place on the anniversary of Kristallnacht. The resolution registered unavoidably as anti-Semitic. But, like the Arafat–Tekoah standoff, it also exposed the clash of two distant world views—one embedded in a narrative of colonial domination, the other in Jewish suffering. Superadded to the extreme imbalance of power between Israelis and Arab Palestinians was the non-simultaneity of their historical condition. The Jews had ended their wandering in the desert; the Palestinians had just started theirs.

The PLO did not generally play a significant role in the corridors of power until after the October 1973 War. Arafat's invitation and address to the General Assembly heralded this breakthrough, and bespoke a burgeoning awareness in many quarters that there was no moving toward a negotiated settlement of the Middle Eastern imbroglio without engaging the PLO, whose leadership was headed, haltingly, in that direction. In June 1974 the twelfth Palestinian National Council, meeting in Cairo and encouraged by Sadat, adopted a ten-point program that reaffirmed its rejection of U.N. Resolution 242 "for ignoring the national right of our people and treating our cause as a refugee problem." Point 2 of this program, in addition to reiterating the primacy of "armed struggle," called for the establishment of a "people's national, independent, and fighting authority on every part of Palestinian land that will be liberated." Four months later came the Arab summit's recognition of the PLO as "the sole legitimate representative of the Palestinian People." Even King Hussein signed on, his negotiations with Israel for his partial control over the West Bank having come to nothing. For now he not only renounced the West Bank, but acceded to the PLO's speaking for the Palestinian refugees in Jordan, most of whom had been granted Jordanian citizenship.

Very gradually Cairo, the PLO, and Amman began to entertain the idea of accepting Israel within its pre-1967 borders. The Marxist PFLP predictably rushed to form a "Rejectionist Front" to stem the new course. Starting in the spring of 1974, a loose minority coalition, including the DFLP, launched a series of cross-border raids, of which those already cited—on Kiryat Shemona, Ma'alot, and Beit Shean— were the most deadly. But they could not stop the PLO, in league with Fatah, from developing its political influence as it worked out a formula in which diplomacy and armed struggle were complementary. The thirteenth session of the Palestinian National Council, meeting in Cairo in March 1977, agreed "to escalate the armed struggle . . . on the occupied soil" with a view to promoting the Palestinian nation's "right to return, to self-determination, and to the establishment of its national independent State on its independent soil." Such language implied a readiness to envisage a two-state solution.

Israel's leaders remained immovable. They were furious, frustrated, and bitter about the growing recognition of Arafat, and continued to portray him in the darkest of colors. Typical was Defense Minister Peres' outcry against the "stormy ovation at the United Nations" received by "the chief representative of the murder gangs" that had assaulted Ma'alot and Beit Shean. This stance made the Israeli and Palestinian rejectionists objective allies in the battle against Arafat. Israel's political class construed any intimation that the PLO might settle for a rump state alongside Israel as nothing but a sly maneuver to secure a staging area for the reconquest of the entire Holy Land. The rise of the secular and religious right, culminating in the formation of the first Likud government in June 1977, served to reinforce Israel's willful negation of the Palestinian resistance and its resolve to under- mine the PLO—if necessary by abetting its sworn internecine rivals.

Aided by Henry Kissinger's shuttle and step-by-step diplomacy, the 1973 War was ended by disengagement agreements between Israel, Egypt, and Syria. Israel was, to all intents and purposes, once again in control of the Golan Heights. On January 18, 1974, an initial accord with Egypt called for the evacuation of Israeli forces from the areas west of the Suez Canal; for the restoration of a buffer zone east of the Canal; and for the return of a U.N. force of interposition. So-called Sinai I marked the first withdrawal by Israel from conquered Arab land, although it held on to most of the Sinai Desert. Under Sinai II, in

September 4, 1975, Israel ceded additional land: its forces fell back to the eastern end of the supposedly strategic Mitla and Gidi passes through the Sinai mountains, and vacated the Abu Rudeis and Ras Sudar oilfields on the Gulf of Suez. The pact further provided for a demilitarized zone controlled by the U.N. and a string of early warning stations; and it held out, once again, a promise of American economic aid to Egypt.

Much of the Sinai remained in Israeli hands. Just as important—and more premonitory—was the fact that, in a secret annex to Sinai II, the U.S. renewed its pledge not to "recognize or negotiate with the PLO so long as [it] does not recognize Israel's right to exist and does not accept Security Council Resolutions 242 and 338." Israel was concluding the fourth cross-border war at the same time that it faced a growing and more defiant "internal" enemy on both sides of its borders.

Sadat wanted to complete the Israeli–Egyptian disengagement by multilateral negotiations for a comprehensive settlement of the Arab–Israeli conflict. But first Prime Minister Rabin, and then, starting June 21, 1977, his successor Menachem Begin, hung back. A strong Likud and its associates were confident of the backing of the American Jewish community for their hawkish course, even though Jimmy Carter, the new president, showed signs of favoring a Sadat-like initiative. In March 1977 Carter expressed support for the idea of a homeland for the Palestinians. By October 1, Cyrus Vance, his secretary of state, and Andrei Gromyko, the Soviet foreign minister, in effect jointly floated the suggestion of a Geneva conference with the participation of the "representatives of all the parties involved in the [Middle East] conflict, including those of the Palestinian people." The PLO took heart—and the Begin government demurred. Moshe Dayan, the hawkish foreign minister, pressed Washington to reconsider. On October 5 the State Department issued a statement attenuating the discreet Vance–Gromyko initiative.

In the face of Israeli obduracy and Arab skepticism, Sadat decided to go the distance. On November 9 he stunned the whole world: in a speech to Egypt's People's Assembly, with an unsuspecting Arafat in the audience, he announced his intention to journey to Jerusalem. Sadat's foreign minister resigned in protest, the Syrian president spurned his invitation to join him on his journey, and the leaders of Fatah and the PLO urged him to desist so as not to squander the political and psychological dividends of the Ramadan War.

On November 20, the heir of Jabotinsky and erstwhile commander of the terrorist Irgun chose high-handedly to finesse the irony of welcoming the olive-branch-bearing Sadat to the Knesset by declaring that Israel itself had "always wanted peace" and had forever extended "a hand of peace . . . to all neighboring countries and people." But Begin went on to say that he felt duty-bound to affirm the "truth" that "our hand outstretched for peace was [never] grasped." To the contrary, immediately following the Jewish people's "renewed" independence, "we were attacked on three fronts, and we stood almost without arms, the few against the many, the weak against the strong" who meant to "strangle [us] at birth, to put an end to the last hope of the Jewish people, the yearning renewed after years of destruction and holocaust." Unabashed, Begin averred that "we do not believe in might . . . and never based our attitude toward the Arab people on might." And yet, in all these years, "we never stopped being attacked by might" bent on "exterminating our people, destroying our independence, denying our rights." The premier of Israel wanted the president of Egypt to know that "the commanders of all the underground Hebrew fighting organizations," as well as "the veteran commanders and captains" of the IDF were "sitting in this democratic house." Though they "belong to different parties," they were at one in wanting peace "for our nation . . . and for our neighbors."

To this end, Begin invited the leaders of the other border states to follow in Sadat's footsteps and "come to discuss with us" in Jerusalem, or, should they "invite us to go to their capitals, we will accept their invitations." Israel was even "ready to sit" with them at a peace conference in Geneva, "once it is ready, to discuss . . . on the basis" of resolutions 242 and 338. Though "everything can be negotiated," Begin wanted it understood that "this country," which was "eternal," belonged to "our people." It would not be "taken from us," because when that had happened in the past, it ultimately led to the murder of "millions of our people, among them 1.5 million of the little children of Israel," and "nobody came to save them, not from the East, nor from the West." In consequence, Israel's "generation of extermination and revival" has taken a "solemn oath . . . never again to put our people in danger." Like Ben-Gurion, Begin claimed all of Jerusalem, and breathed not a word about the refugees or possible points of negotiation.

Sadat addressed the Knesset as "president of the biggest Arab state, which bears the heaviest burden and the main responsibility pertaining to the cause of war and peace in the Middle East." He conceded that, after he had announced his decision to go to Jerusalem, "most of those who contacted [me] expressed their objection because of the feeling of utter suspicion and absolute lack of confidence between the Arab states and the Palestine people on the one hand, and Israel on the other." Sadat blamed this enormous deficit of trust for the "fruitless discussions on the procedure for convening the Geneva conference." There was "neither victor nor vanquished . . . amidst the ruins of what man has built," he insisted; "all of us must rise above all forms of obsolete theories of superiority . . . and never forget that infallibility is the prerogative of God alone." He had not come to Jerusalem to seek "a separate agreement between Egypt and Israel . . . a partial peace [or] a third disengagement agreement in Sinai, Golan, or the West Bank." Any such limited step would merely postpone "the ignition of the fuse." The time was past due to confront head-on the obstacles to "a durable peace based on justice," and this required overcoming the "psychological barrier of suspicion . . . rejection . . . fear [and] deception—70 per cent of the whole problem." It also called for mutual frankness and "direct confrontation" with the core issues.

Sadat reminded the assembly of his willingness "to sign a peace agreement with Israel" in February 1971, and that he had "called for an international conference to establish a permanent peace based on justice" in October 1973. Now, again, Sadat proclaimed in "all sincerity" that "we welcome you among us with full security and safety . . . with all the international guarantees you envisage and accept." But, like Begin, he had a "truth" of his own to impart: a peace "worth its name" cannot be based "on the occupation of the land of others." Israel will "have to give up once and for all its dream of conquest . . . and its belief that force is the best method for dealing with the Arabs," especially since by now it should be clear that "missiles, warships, and nuclear weapons cannot establish security." Israel continued to occupy Arab territories "by force" and to seek a "special status" for Jerusalem within a framework of "annexation or expansion." There could be neither a permanent peace nor a move toward "coexistence" without the "complete withdrawal from all territories, including Arab Jerusalem," that had been "occupied . . . by force of arms after 1967."

Yet, even should there be peace between the Arab states and Israel, Sadat continued, it could not be "durable" without addressing the "Palestine cause," which was "the crux of the entire problem." Certainly, "nobody in the world could accept today slogans propagated here in Israel, ignoring the existence of the Palestinian people" to the point of "questioning even their whereabouts." The U.S., no less— Israel's "first ally"—now recognized this as "the cause and essence of the conflict," and that the "Palestinian people [were] entitled to legitimate rights." Without them, he said in conclusion, "there can be no peace," and to "overlook" this problem or leave it "unresolved" would be to "aggravate" it and invite "unpredictable consequences."

Sadat spoke truth to power, knowing full well that his primary audience was neither the members of the Knesset nor the Israeli public, but the Arab political class and street, as well as the geostrategists in Washington. Sadat and Begin were not unduly worried about speaking past each other inasmuch as both understood, ahead of this wondrous strange occasion, that Israel would swap the rest of the Sinai Peninsula for peace with Egypt. Even the most zealous Zionists never imagined the Sinai as part of Eretz Israel. Sadat had therefore used the opportunity to raise the very issues that Begin—and Israel along with him—had avoided for ideological, political, and diplomatic reasons.

Begin had his own agenda and addressed his own public. He and his cabinet were sworn to reach for a Greater Israel, with the radical messianic settler movement Gush Emunim, which was formed after the 1967 War, conferring on it eschatological legitimacy. One could hardly expect less from a government with Begin at its helm, Dayan at the Foreign Ministry, Weizman at Defense, and Sharon at Agriculture, where he was charged with the establishment of settlements in the West Bank and Gaza. Though not devout himself, Begin held that Greater Israel necessarily included the lands once controlled by King David and King Solomon. Dayan, having long since forsaken Labor, argued that since "we possess the Holy Book and consider ourselves to be the people of the Holy Book, we need to possess the land of the Holy Book as well." With irredentism assuming an increasingly religious edge, it risked awakening what Ben-Gurion had once called the Islamic "demon." And the unstable mix of nationalism, Zionism, and the Bible would prove just as demonic and volatile in the region as that of nationalism, Arabism, and the Koran.

As early as February 1971, well before the Yom Kippur/Ramadan War, Sadat had proposed normalizing relations with Israel in exchange for the Sinai. Eventually Abba Eban, worldly U.N. delegate and Labor foreign minister, admitted that once Begin and Sadat had agreed on the principle of trading the Sinai for peace, the signing of the treaty was "only a matter of a short time" away. Washington played a crucial role, holding out the carrot of economic aid for both parties, in pursuit of its own interest: the delineation of Israel's border with the major Arab power so as to stabilize the Middle East and secure America's regional hegemony in a critical theater, and moment, of the Cold War.

The accords reconfiguring Egyptian–Israeli relations were negotiated at Camp David from September 5–17, 1978. They consisted of two parts not contingent on each other. The first spelled out the exchange of land for peace between Egypt and Israel. The second, in the form of an annex, set forth a framework for three-step negotiations to create a "fully autonomous [Palestinian] authority" to be elected, under Israeli military occupation, in the West Bank and Gaza. Relations with neighbors would be hammered out by Egypt, Israel, and Jordan in a final status agreement. To begin in no more than three years' time, these negotiations were expected to be completed within five years. The delegations of Egypt and Jordan could "include" Palestinians from the occupied territories and elsewhere, but only on condition that they were "mutually acceptable" to the three negotiating states. There was no mention of either self-determination or a sovereign state for the Palestinians. In the meantime, Israel's occupation of the West Bank, Gaza Strip, and East Jerusalem continued, as did the settlement drive. The Camp David annex remained a dead letter—mostly because Begin would have nothing to do with Palestinians, let alone the PLO. In August 1980 the Knesset declared Jerusalem the "eternal and undivided capital" of Israel, and in December 1981 it voted the annexation of the Golan Heights. Begin joined the chorus of true believers who urged that, henceforth, the West Bank should go by the Biblical name of Judea and Samaria.

Back in Cairo, Sadat had become a marked man for having turned his back upon the Soviets, the Nasserite reformist left in Egypt, and the PLO. By reclaiming the Sinai and securing American economic aid to the tune of $1 billion each year—rising to $2.3 billion by 1988 and $3 billion by 1998—he advanced Egypt's national interest without regard for the other confrontation states or the Palestinians. Implicitly, and counter to his soaring address to the Knesset, Sadat accepted Israel's occupation of conquered Arab lands along with its sovereign disregard for the refugees. While the West extolled the Camp David accords, the Arab world was incensed and alarmed. By going it alone, the most populous and militarily powerful Arab state had greatly weakened the anti-Israel front and the Palestinian cause. The ineffectual Arab League, with Syria, Iraq, and Libya voicing particular disgust, expelled Egypt for breaking ranks. The Palestinian front of rejectionist parties echoed their sense of Cairo's betrayal, and Arafat denounced Egypt for having "sold the national rights of the Palestinian people for a handful of desert sand."

In Cairo too there was rancorous opposition; but Sadat used his breakthrough on the world stage to consolidate his personal rule and steel Egypt's political system. He curbed Nasserite, pan-Arabist, and Islamist critics of his go-it-alone diplomacy, his compact with Israel, and his turn to America. On October 6, 1981, as he and Vice-President Hosni Mubarak observed a military parade in Cairo marking the eighth anniversary of the start of the 1973 War, Sadat was assassinated. As he fired the fatal shot, Khalid al-Islambuli, an army lieutenant with alleged links to the Cairo-based Islamic Jihad, was said to have cried out "Glory to Egypt!"

All in all, Sadat's two excursions proved to be of enormous benefit to Israel. With the neutralization of Egypt, what little Arab solidarity there had been was as good as shattered. The recognition of Israel by Cairo broke an Arab taboo. Sadat's visit to Jerusalem (including Yad Vashem) lent legitimacy to Israel's claim to the Holy City, undivided, as the new Zion's capital. By agreeing to come to terms separately, the Egyptian president confirmed the country's resolve to fight shy of multilateral negotiations. Israel remained free to tighten its control of the occupied territories and expand the settlements. With the Arab camp in disarray, Washington reassured, and the PLO isolated, Israel's leaders had little incentive to rethink the Palestinian problem.

Yitzhak Rabin might as well have spoken for the entire political–military caste when he asserted that Egypt was "the key" and that "militarily Syria alone was no problem whatsoever." As for terrorism, it posed "no threat to Israel's existence." Indeed, Rabin "wished that the so-called PLO were the only problem facing" the country, for this would mean that "Israel would have no problem."

The war against Lebanon in 1982 was Israel's fifth with the Arabs. But unlike the four previous conflicts, which had been conventional wars with sovereign Arab states, this was a massive raid on a powerless and fragile state, intended to destroy the PLO root-and-branch. It was less an Israeli–Arab than an Israeli–Palestinian war. Lebanon's army—more of an overgrown constabulary—did not trouble its southern neighbor; Syria's presence was fit for policing Lebanon's chronic internal factional strife, but not for battling Israel's armed forces. The militias of the Christian Phalange were the most credible military force, and they were certain to be Israel's accessory. With Egypt disengaged, Israel was free to move at will into Lebanon without risk.

A primary objective of the invasion of Lebanon on June 6, 1982, was to go after the bases of the *fedayeen* in southern Lebanon, and to decapitate the PLO's main command and administrative center, then located in Beirut. In some Israeli political–military quarters, there was also an unavowed hope and plan to exploit the indeterminacies of a lightning military campaign to expel the Syrians, to create a Christian-dominated and pro-Israeli new order in Lebanon, and to revive Chaim Weizmann's and Ben-Gurion's notion of expanding Israel's border northward to the Litani river in southern Lebanon—a valued source, like the Jordan, of scarce soft water. The attack was planned and executed by Begin's first and second Likud governments. "Operation Peace for Galilee" proceeded in tandem with a drive to tighten Israel's administrative control across the territories, particularly in the West Bank. The unspoken dream was to incorporate Judea and Samaria into Israel, and eventually to drive the greater number of refugees across the river into "Palestinian" Jordan. While Likud took the initiative, there was a broad national consensus concerning the ways and means of dealing with the Palestinians in both the occupied territories and over the borders—Lebanon's in particular. Not all of Labor subscribed to the Likud-like blueprint for a Greater Israel, or to its strategy for achieving it; but the reservations of the moderates tended to be tactical and partisan, rather than substantive.

Between 1970 and 1980 the total number of Palestinian refugees rose from roughly 1.4 million to over 2 million. Within Lebanon their number jumped from about 175,000 to over 250,000, out of a population of around 2.7 million. Soon after its modern borders had been drawn in 1920, Lebanon became an all but independent republic of many faiths and cultures. Though a rough equilibrium obtained among some fifteen confessional communities, it was inherently unstable. The rapid influx of Palestinians, who were predominantly Arab Muslims, inevitably strained this delicate balance: traditionally a Maronite Christian was president of the Republic, a Sunni Muslim president of the Council, and a Shiite Muslim president of the Chamber of Deputies. To avoid rocking the boat—and unlike in Jordan—the refugees were denied citizenship. As stateless foreigners they did not qualify for work permits either, with grave economic and social consequences for a community over 60 per cent of whose population was under the age of eighteen.

In Lebanon the Palestinians made their homes in twelve camps. Seven of these were located between the Phoenician ports of Tyre and Sidon along the Mediterranean, and two of them, Sabra and Chatila, were situated in the south of West Beirut. At the outset the camp elders belonged to the traditional elite. But soon after the PLO had set about organizing and recruiting in the camps, the old guard was overtaken by militant novices with a vigorous political, ideological, and military agenda. This change became particularly pronounced after Black September in 1970, when the political leaders and *fedayeen* of the Palestinian resistance were forced out of Jordan and made their way to Lebanon—the only remaining neighboring state with a long frontier permitting cross-border raids into Israel/Palestine. Presently the PLO, including the rejectionist factions, brought all the camps, along with much of southern Lebanon, under its influence. With headquarters in West Beirut, it set about developing not only a military network but also a would-be political authority and a far-flung social service organization. The Lebanese state, weak and forbearing, gave as much running room to the PLO as it did to the Christian Phalange. But sufferance of the PLO burdened its sovereignty with the vicissitudes of Israel's cross-border counter-terror. From the early 1970s, then, the Israeli–Lebanese frontier became increasingly strife-ridden. After one of the terrorist incidents of mid 1975, Shimon Peres, Rabin's minister of defense, issued a particularly stark warning: "We mean to put an end to all civil life in Lebanon if it continues its policy of supporting the Palestinian organizations."

By this time Lebanon was itself drawing near civil war. The Palestinian refugees, the PLO, and Fatah had polarized the country's forces of order and forces of movement. The former rallied around the predominantly Maronite-Christian Phalange, headed by Pierre Gemayel, who was determined to preserve Lebanon's political and social status quo, including its ethno-religious compact, as well as its pro-Western orientation in the Cold War. He and his son Bashir, commander of the Phalangist militias, denounced the other Arab states for saddling Lebanon with a mass of indigent Palestinians. The forces of movement coalesced around the Druze-based National Movement of Lebanon, headed by Kamal Jumblatt. Of Nasserite persuasion, he called for a secular and progressive Arab Lebanon, unbound from the West. To achieve this goal Jumblatt collaborated with the Palestinians, whom he considered exponents of the radically progressive nationalism that he saw stirring elsewhere in the Arab world.

While Peres uttered threats, Pierre Gemayel pressed the Lebanese government to restrain the Palestinians and put an end to the *fedayeen*'s military operations near and along the southern border. But with no army to speak of, and lacking cohesion, the Lebanese authorities could do little, leaving civil war to smolder and spread. The Gemayels approached Israel for arms and ammunition to help bring the Palestinian refugees, exiles, and partisans to heel. To complicate matters further, Syria, concerned about Lebanon's descent into chaos and the PLO's social radicalism, boosted its military presence in Lebanon to over 10,000 men.

During the first quarter of 1978 four terrorist attacks in Jerusalem and one in Tel Aviv, claiming the lives of close to forty Israeli civilians, infuriated the government and the population at large. In mid March Begin sent more than 20,000 troops into southern Lebanon to establish a 6-mile-deep security zone along the border and to ward off future

incursions. From there to the Litani river, Israeli forces policed the
territory jointly with the Christian militia of Major Saad Haddad, the
self-styled South Lebanon Army. For reasons of both military security
and economic advantage, Israel proposed henceforth to trust only
itself—not a U.N. or Great Power peacekeeping force—to stand guard
in southern Lebanon.

Meanwhile, with all manner of rejectionist factions and partisan
bands beyond their control, the Palestinian leadership became increasingly worried that the PLO and Fatah would suffer the same fate in
Lebanon as they had in Jordan a decade before. In this infighting,
Arafat was the supreme realist, at odds with Abu Nidal, Habash, and
even his early comrade-in-arms Abu Iyad. Since 1977, following Camp
David, he had actively sought openings with western European leaders
and politicians, as well as Israeli personalities, intermittently using Dr.
Issam Sartawi as his personal emissary. These overtures coincided
with the Palestinian National Council's backing away from its claim
for a return to an undivided Palestine in favor of the establishment of a
state in the territories occupied in 1967: the West Bank and Gaza were
to be evacuated by or liberated from Israel. In June 1980 the nine
members of the European Economic Community issued a statement
reaffirming Resolution 242 and suggesting that the PLO be asked to
participate as an "associate" in future negotiations. Because the EEC
did not acknowledge the PLO as the sole representative of the
Palestinians, the PLO repudiated the gesture. Yitzhak Shamir, Begin's
foreign minister, rejected it too, telling the Europeans, who "want us
to pull back to the ghetto-borders of 1967" to "leave us alone." A year
later, in August 1981, King Fahd of Saudi Arabia put forward a plan
for a Palestinian state on the West Bank and in Gaza. After Arafat
viewed it with favor, the Israeli government dismissed it as a "maneuver of propagandistic deception" and a call "for the destruction of
Israel."

Begin had set his face against any negotiation whatsoever, in
violation of both the spirit and letter of the Camp David accords.
So inflexible was he that even Foreign Minister Dayan and Defense
Minister Weizman, both inveterate hardliners, resigned their posts in
October 1979 and May 1980 respectively. Not that the ship of state
was about to change course: in the second Begin government, inaugurated in summer 1981, Shamir, having earlier replaced Dayan,
continued as foreign minister, and Sharon replaced Weizman. Their
collective rigidity played into the hands of the rejectionists in the PLO
as well as in Syria, Libya, and Iraq. The Abu Nidal faction was as
determined to assassinate Palestinian moderates—among them Issam

Sartawi—as it was to murder Israelis. The Jewish state, however, took no steps to strengthen Arafat's position against his own extremists.

This was the context for the 1982 invasion of Lebanon, which took place against a backdrop of the religious revolution in Iran, the Iran–Iraq War, and the Soviet intervention in Afghanistan. Operation Snowball, renamed Operation Peace for Galilee, was the external side of Israel's policy of consolidating and expanding its hold on the occupied territories. One tactic of the internal policy was to put in place a civil administration, under the exigent eye of the military, charged with reconciling and uplifting the local population for eventual integration into a Greater Israel. Rather than promote a transitional regime of autonomous self-government as laid out at Camp David, this civil authority also proposed to cultivate collaborators who would help check the emergence of a nationalist Palestinian leadership and the implantation of the PLO.

By virtue of his long experience as commanding officer of large military and commando units, as well as promoter of aggressive settlement in the occupied territories, Ariel Sharon, embodied Israel's two-pronged forward course. But though he would later be demonized as its chief architect, he was no more for it than any other member of the politico-military caste he belonged to. Few if any of them advocated capitalizing on Israel's unmatched position of strength to propose points of discussion and compromise, or to launch a peace offensive.

The spring and summer of 1981 brought not only an escalation of regional tensions, but also portents of Israel's rising bellicosity. In late March, determined to continue exacting two eyes for one, Tel Aviv's planes and ships continued to strike Palestinian targets deep in Lebanon. During one of these sorties Israeli fighters shot down four Syrian planes, followed by a stern warning to Damascus not to deploy missiles in east Lebanon's Bekaa Valley. On June 7, in a preemptive strike licensed by the U.S., and at a time when Israel was developing its own nuclear capability, Israeli aircraft destroyed Iraq's Osirak nuclear reactor 18 miles south of Baghdad, 700 miles away. On July 17, in retaliation for a rocket attack on Nahariya that killed four and wounded eight, Israel bombed the general headquarters of the Palestinian resistance in West Beirut, leaving over 100 dead and about 600 injured—mostly civilians. Egypt objected, but since its hands were tied by the treaty with Israel and its financial links to Washington, there was no Arab power fit to back up the protest. Left to his own devices, Arafat declared the PLO to be "in a state of war."

It was an open secret that Israel was preparing to move into Lebanon, with the primary aim of putting down the organized resistance once and for all. Although aggressively importuned by the ultras, Arafat sought to cool the atmosphere, convinced that Tel Aviv was looking for a pretext to march on Beirut. Haunted by Black September, Arafat apparently appealed to Begin, through a U.N. envoy, to reconsider. Conceding that he had "learned more from you than [from] any other resistance leader about how to combine politics with military tactics," Arafat is said to have told Begin that he, "of all people, should understand that it is not necessary to face me only on the battlefield." He implored the Israeli premier "not to send a military force against me [and] not to try to break me in Lebanon [because] you will not succeed"—and he all but defied him to try.

The attempted assassination in London on June 3, 1982, of Shlomo Argov, Israel's ambassador to the Court of St. James, provided a welcome if feeble pretext for war. Argov was shot and wounded by a commando, presumably directed by Abu Nidal from Syria and supported by Iraq. Although Abu Nidal had allegedly tried repeatedly to have Arafat—his sworn political enemy—killed, Begin fixed the responsibility for the attack on the PLO. The next day Israel again raided PLO headquarters and bombed several refugee camps. In retaliation, *fedayeen* fired rockets across Israel's northern border.

After sundown on the June 5 Sabbath, the cabinet met at Begin's private residence in Jerusalem to decide on a course of action. The prime minister was reportedly grave, and suggested that the "alternative" to not acting decisively would be to invite another "Treblinka." Begin, Sharon, and Chief of Staff Rafael Eitan laid out a plan to end terrorist attacks on settlements in the north, by establishing a 25-mile-wide security zone north of the Israeli–Lebanese border. In pursuit of this minimal goal, the cabinet approved a lightning thrust into Lebanon; the invading troops were to make every effort to avoid engaging Syrian forces. It is not generally known whether there was any discussion of aims beyond the immediate aim of clearing the *fedayeen* out of the projected buffer zone. But, given subsequent events, the cabinet members are likely to have seen eye to eye on the hoped-for and probable end result of Operation Peace for Galilee: destruction of the nerve center of the PLO, establishment of a pro-Israeli order in Beirut, and termination of the Syrian presence.

The dawn of June 6 saw an armed force of 100,000 pouring into Lebanon, overwhelming U.N. observers and setting upon, at most, 20,000 Lebanese and Palestinian men-at-arms. The Israeli air force had full control of the skies; Syrian ground and air forces were hopelessly outnumbered. Within three days the IDF surrounded southern Lebanon and beyond. But between the difficult terrain and the Palestinian irregulars, who slowed down the invading forces, any assumption that the march toward Beirut would be a promenade proved wide of the mark. Resistance was particularly heavy and costly in and around the refugee camps in the Mediterranean littoral. The Israelis had failed to reach their larger objective by June 11, when the Soviets, pressed by Syrian President Assad, and the Americans, who had other priorities, tried to impose a ceasefire, which Begin ignored. The Israeli forces continued to advance, and on June 13 linked up with the Maronite Christian militias in East Beirut, in accordance with the recent agreement between Sharon and Bashir Gemayel.

Although the Phalangists did not hesitate to enlist the Israelis to help them maintain or improve their position in Lebanon's destabilized political and civil society, the most exacting and politically explosive work they would leave for the Israelis to take care of alone. Concerned about their future in an increasingly turbulent environment, as Arab-speaking Christian Maronites they left it to the Israelis to take over West Beirut, which, besides being heavily Muslim, was a Palestinian stronghold, the site of the PLO headquarters, and a Syrian redoubt. Sharon and Eitan gave the order to lay siege to this Gomorrah. They summoned the PLO and the *fedayeen* to surrender, leave the city, or take the consequences. On June 25 the Israeli forces were in the heart of West Beirut, and seized the main airport. The siege began on July 3 and lasted for ten weeks, taking a terrible toll. The districts controlled by the PLO were bombarded and struck from the air. Electricity, water, and provisions were severely curtailed. Easily 15,000 Arabs were killed in the first Lebanon war, between 5,000 and 6,000 of them in Beirut—probably 80 per cent of them civilians. There are no reliable estimates of the number of wounded. Slightly over 650 Israeli soldiers lost their lives.

Operation Peace for Galilee glaringly exceeded whatever scope it may have had at the outset. Washington roiled: Secretary of State Alexander Haig, deemed to have been overindulgent with the Israeli military for its yeoman service in the Cold War, was replaced by George Shultz. Even in Israel questions were being raised about a war that, compared with the previous four self-professed wars for survival, seemed aggressive and intemperate. Once the offensive bogged down, Labor spoke up. But the criticism was too hesitant to convince anyone. The party was as eager as Likud to put an end to the PLO. Besides, there was something unconvincing about its whispered reproach that Begin and Sharon had furtively enlarged the scale of the campaign: as consummate insiders, the Labor leaders would have understood its ambitious design from the start. Eventually Rabin recalled how Begin and Sharon had informed him, Peres, and Haim Bar-Lev, former chief of staff, of the "Big Plan" in April, two months before the start of hostilities. And on the night of June 5 Peres allegedly reported to his inner circle that "the war in Lebanon would commence the next morning, with the operational intention of reaching Beirut to join up with the Christian forces."

On August 12, Begin accepted an agreement with Arafat, brokered by the U.S., to evacuate the PLO and the *fedayeen* from Lebanon. Whether by coincidence or not, that same day Israeli forces pounded West Beirut from the air, leaving between 200 and 300 dead, most of them civilians. Finally, international pressure and mediation did their work. Between August 23 and September 3 some 15,000 *fedayeen*, under Franco-Italian protection and defiantly brandishing their guns, put out to sea. Most of them sailed to Algeria and Tunisia. Several thousand were relocated under Syrian influence to the Bekaa Valley. The night before this embarkation, a strong majority of the Lebanese parliament, under the watchful eye of Israeli soldiers, elected Bashir Gemayel president of a country that was in total disarray. On September 1 he met Begin to sign a peace treaty, which never materialized. Two weeks later, on September 14, a Syrian agent killed Gemayel and twenty-five of his followers in an explosion at the Phalange's military headquarters. Just as the attempted assassination of Ambassador Argov had been the pretext for the invasion of Lebanon, so the assassination of President Gemayel triggered the massacres at Sabra and Chatila.

Before sailing for Athens on August 30, Arafat had urged that an international force of intercession assume guardianship of the two nearby refugee camps. These were home to many of the families of the departed *fedayeen*, now defenseless and vulnerable to any avenging animus of the Phalange. But apparently Sharon and his staff did nothing, and by September 15, in violation of the evacuation agreement, Lebanese Christian militiamen and Israeli soldiers moved into West Beirut, presumably to restore and maintain order. While Sharon and his staff claimed to suspect that the remaining Palestinians were concealing weapons in their camps, and that some 2,000 terrorists were hiding in Sabra and Chatila, they limited Israeli forces, under Chief of Staff General Eitan, to surrounding the periphery, and left it to the Phalange to secure the camps themselves, saying that "the business of going after terrorists could be handled much more effectively by Arab-speaking Lebanese familiar with the local accents and with the PLO's urban *modus operandi*."

Between September 16 and 18, crack Phalangist units, with the complicity of Israeli soldiers, bent on cleansing greater Beirut of what remained of the Muslim Palestinians, went on a rampage in both camps. There was little resistance. Besides slaughtering an estimated 700–2,000 men, women, and children, the Maronite soldiers took to beating, mutilating, and raping many of their victims. This outrage became the climax of Operation Peace for Galilee.

The gratuitous violence in Sabra and Chatila, not the devastating invasion itself, which had enjoyed broad political and popular support within Israel, provoked critical questions. The siege of Beirut and the massacres played in the international media as episodes analogous to the *Exodus*, this time—fortuitously—with the Palestinian refugees and partisans as the beneficiaries. Within a week, the hastily formed Israeli Committee Against the War in Lebanon, joined by Peace Now (the land-for-peace movement begun after Sadat's 1978 visit) and its Labor affiliates, rallied over 300,000 people in the heart of Tel Aviv to call for an independent investigation of the carnage at the camps, and for the resignation or dismissal of those responsible. Under mounting pressure, Begin charted a commission of inquiry chaired by Chief Justice Yitzhak Kahan. Although its report of February 8, 1983 held Begin and Shamir in some sense accountable, it found Sharon, as minister of defense, "personally" responsible for "having disregarded the prospect of acts of revenge and bloodshed by the Phalangists against the population of the refugee camps and for having failed to take their danger into consideration." The Commission recommended he be removed from office. Both Sharon and Eitan resigned.

Sharon was out of one post but not out of the cabinet. He was promptly named minister without portfolio, while Moshe Arens, another certified hawk, replaced him at Defense. In October, when Shamir succeeded Begin, he appointed Sharon minister of industry and trade. This purely cosmetic reshuffle signaled that the "business" of the camps was nothing to be disavowed. On the contrary, so far from being incidental to Operation Peace for Galilee, it was intrinsic to Israeli policy generally concerning the Arab Question, now firmly embodied in the PLO and Fatah, the terrorists, and the refugees. Carried by a broad and deep-rooted social and political base, Likud pursued the eradication of the PLO along with the consolidation of Greater Israel. Following Begin, who had been premier for six years, Shamir served cumulatively for seven—from 1983 to 1984, and from 1986 to 1992. During the National Unity Government of 1984–6, he was vice-premier and foreign minister under Labor's Shimon Peres—the very model of Israel's bipartisanship—before again becoming prime minister. This enduring *consensus omnium* continued to swing rightward, with Likud embracing the rapidly emergent religious right and Labor preparing to court it, however uncomfortably at first.

But religious passions on both sides of the Great Divide were increasingly permeating politics. While public protest in Israel over Sabra and Chatila moved Jewish fundamentalists to rally around the secular Zionist ultranationalists, the massacre, combined with the second major defeat of the Palestinian resistance, stirred their Islamic counterpart, wary of the PLO's secular directorate. Among Palestinians, and with the Arab street now hearkening to theocratic Iran, Operation Peace for Galilee aroused sympathy for the Shiite Hezbollah, the Sunni Hamas, and Islamic Jihad. Following 1985, when Israel withdrew from Lebanon, it kept control of the buffer zone north of its border by means of a Lebanese-Christian phalanx. The Islamist *fedayeen* took root in this contested and permeable region facing their sworn enemy.

If the extinction of the PLO and the cowing of the Palestinian resistance as a whole were the primary objectives of Operation Peace for Galilee, it was an unequivocal failure. The PLO simply relocated its command center, and the *fedayeen* redoubled their implantation in the occupied territories. At the same time, this latest defeat quickened the radicalization of the nationalist movement, especially among the younger generation in the refugee camps and their sympathizers, and began to change its dynamic from secular and Marxist to Islamist and fundamentalist. But Israel's political class was unconcerned about this mutation. There was no sense that the government's victory had cost more than it was worth.

7

THE IRON DIPLOMATIC WALL

Following the establishment of an Islamic theocracy in Iran in 1978–9 and the Soviet intervention in Afghanistan, the geostrategists in Washington counted more than ever on Israel to help contain Moscow's reach into the greater Middle East, beginning with Soviet support of Syria. But this military calculus had to be reconciled with the Western powers' need for safe access to the oilfields and supply lines of the Arabian peninsula, whose ruling elites continued to abet the Palestinian resistance. The new Reagan administration, nervous about the destabilizing effect of Tel Aviv's forward policy, resolved to intercede. The president accepted Haig's resignation, and special U.S. envoys to the Middle East Philip Habib and Morris Draper mediated the safe evacuation of the PLO, Arafat, and the *fedayeen*.

Washington soon launched a major initiative. On September 1, 1982, in a television address, President Reagan dramatically outlined a comprehensive peace plan, prepared in consultation with King Hussein and other Arab heads of state, but not with Israeli leaders. The latest Arab–Israeli war had demonstrated, he said, that the PLO's military losses had "not diminished the Palestinian people's yearning for a just solution of their claims." Nor could the gains of Israel's regionally unsurpassed armed forces, without political give-and-take, "bring a just and lasting peace to Israel and her neighbors." The "next step" on the road charted at Camp David in 1978 should be a return to negotiations to deal with the "legitimate rights of the Palestinian people" as part of a general settlement of the Arab–Israeli conflict.

Reagan recommended giving the Palestinians of the West Bank and Gaza "full autonomy over their own affairs." Rather than call for a sovereign and independent Palestinian state in the occupied territories, Reagan suggested "self-government by the Palestinians of the West Bank and Gaza in association with Jordan." Free elections for a "Palestinian authority" would be followed by a five-year transition to blunt this authority's "threat to Israel's security." America would support "neither the annexation nor permanent control" of the territories by Israel, nor the establishment, during the five years, of additional settlements, which were "in no way necessary for Israel's security." In fact the "immediate adoption of a settlement freeze . . . more than any other action, could create the confidence needed" for negotiations. Jerusalem would remain united under Israeli control pending final status talks. And the Arab states would recognize Israel in exchange for its withdrawal "on all fronts," in accordance with U.N. Resolution 242.

Begin dismissed Reagan's plan outright: he was against exchanging land for peace, and was deeply offended, along with the pro-Israel lobby, for having been kept in the dark. In his view, this latest road map foreshadowed a major change in American policy, and was altogether one-sided. Privately, he felt only a "traitor" could accept it, since it would spell "national suicide" for Israel. Begin justified this categorical rejection in a personal letter to the President, dated September 5. Two months before, the IDF had entered Lebanon, Reagan should understand, "not to conquer territory but to fight and smash the armed bands operating from that country against our land and its citizens." Nor had Israel previously conquered "what some call the 'West Bank,'" but in fact is "Judea and Samaria." No doubt "cynics" would continue to "deride history," but Begin would

> stand by . . . this simple historical truth: millennia ago there was a Jewish Kingdom of Judea and Samaria where our kings knelt to God; our prophets brought forth the vision of eternal peace; and we developed a rather rich civilization [which] we took with us in our hearts and minds, on our long global trek for over eighteen centuries; and with it we came back home.

In 1948 not Israel but King Abdullah had "conquered parts of Judea and Samaria . . . by aggressive war and invasion," while in 1967, "after being attacked by King Hussein, we liberated, with God's help, that portion of our homeland." Besides, this territory being "mountainous," potentially it could be used to "hit every city, every town, each township and village, and last but not least, our principal airport in the plain below." Equally worrisome, should Judea and Samaria ever be "given to Jordanian jurisdiction . . . in no time we and you will have a Soviet base in the heart of the Middle East." In closing, Begin said he was certain that, since America and Israel were "friends and allies," Reagan would "not put his ally in jeopardy [which] would be the inevitable consequence" should Washington's "positions become reality." To hallow his flat refusal he invoked Isaiah: "For Zion's sake I will not hold my peace, and for Jerusalem's sake I will not rest."

Just weeks prior to the letter Washington had deployed 1,500 Marines to help evacuate the PLO and *fedayeen*, and to assist the Lebanese government in securing Beirut as a first step to restoring sovereignty over its unhappy land. Then came news of the atrocities at Sabra and Chatila. On September 18 Reagan issued a statement expressing his horror: "All people of decency must share our outrage and revulsion at the murders that included women and children." During the negotiations concerning the PLO's withdrawal from Lebanon, he said, "we were assured that Israeli forces would not enter West Beirut [and] that following withdrawal, Lebanese Army units would establish control over that city."

After Gemayel's assassination the U.S. "opposed Israel's move into West Beirut . . . both because we believed it wrong in principle, and for fear that it would provoke further fighting." The presidential declaration in vain asked Israel to turn to "serious negotiations for . . . the earliest possible disengagement of its forces from Beirut" and to work out "an agreed framework for the early withdrawal of all foreign forces from Lebanon." Although Sabra and Chatila moved Reagan to press ahead with his peace plan, it soon died on the vine, killed off by Israel's categorical refusal to enter multilateral negotiations or engage with the PLO. The Jewish community in America, more particularly the pro-Israel lobby, was all for the posture.

The immediate reactions of the PLO to the Washington initiative were cautiously positive. Faruk Kaddumi, head of the political section of the Executive Committee, judged that Reagan's proposal offered room for discussion. But the PLO Central Committee balked, as did the Sixteenth National Council, meeting in February 1983 in Algeria. At this session George Habash spoke for the rejectionists: "Since the Reagan Plan says no to the PLO and to the Palestinian State, we respond no to the United States." The head of the PFLP reiterated his standard argument that the Palestinian resistance had to continue the "armed struggle . . . and improve the military balance in its own favor before turning to political action."

But this refusal, encouraged by Israel's rigidity, was not absolute. The miseries of the Lebanese war had accelerated the PLO's shift from a focus on military struggle for the liberation of an undivided Palestine to a militant political and diplomatic campaign for a Palestinian state in the occupied territories. Its expulsion from Lebanon entailed the final abandonment of regular and guerrilla warfare for terrorism. To adapt Clausewitz's axiom, terrorism became "the continuation and implementation of political and diplomatic transactions" by the "admixture of other means." The pragmatists of the PLO were determined to hold out for autonomous and active agency, rather than helpless subjectivity, in the inevitable search for a negotiated settlement. With time, as even Israel realized it would not go away, the PLO secured a seat at the bargaining table. Preliminary political and diplomatic probes had actually started before the Lebanese war. In 1980 Leonid Brezhnev presented a plan calling for the return of all occupied territories; the creation of a sovereign Palestinian State in the West Bank and Gaza, with East Jerusalem as its capital; the mutual recognition by Israel and the PLO of one another's sovereignty, independence, and territorial integrity; and an international security guarantee.

Almost coincident with the Reagan plan, on September 9, 1982 the Arab states, minus Egypt, meeting in Fez, Morocco, adopted a revised version of King Fahd's initiative of the previous year. It coincided with Brezhnev's plan except on two points: it explicitly affirmed the right to self-determination of the "Palestinian people" along with compensation "for those not wishing to return," to be negotiated by the PLO, "its unique and legitimate representative"; it stipulated that "the Security Council should guarantee the peace among all the states of the region, including the independent Palestinian state." Even though the latter clause did not explicitly recognize Israel, it was a tacit move in that direction. The Algiers meeting of the National Council that rejected the Reagan plan accepted the Fez plan as a "minimum for . . . political action." King Hussein and Egyptian President Hosni Mubarak backed it as well, in the hope of getting Washington to align the Reagan plan closer with the Arab position, which was all but endorsed by the PLO. But there were two sworn intransigents. One was Libya's Qaddafi: he charged the Arab states with "high treason." The other was Shamir, Israel's then foreign minister, who dismissed the Fez plan as "yet another declaration of war . . . with an eye to the destruction of the Jewish state."

During the first quarter of 1983 Arafat carried on discussions with Hussein about the modalities for confederating a Palestinian state composed of the West Bank and Gaza with the Kingdom of Jordan, as proposed by Reagan. The main stumbling block was the question of whether the PLO or Hussein would represent the Palestinians of the occupied territories. Negotiations faltered momentarily at about the same time that the Middle East was jolted by yet another of its characteristically eloquent political assassinations. On April 10 Issam Sartawi was gunned down while attending a congress of the Fourth

Socialist International in Albufeira, 185 miles south of Lisbon, Portugal. Point man in Arafat's search for reconciliation and negotiation, Sartawi had intensified his efforts to build bridges to the democratic left in Europe and to the embryonic peace camp in Israel—the latter centered around Uri Avnery, Peace Now, and the Israeli Council for Israeli–Palestinian Peace. His murder by an Abu Nidal agent was widely read as an admonition by the radical fringe to the pragmatists of the PLO. Shamir contended that the killer of Sartawi was just another phantom of the Palestinian resistance, no more than the latest in a band of homicides. Besides insisting that only the errant policies of the Western powers kept the PLO alive, he maintained that "the PLO had to disappear from the political scene" before any steps toward peace could be taken. Shamir's dictum found a considerable echo in the U.S., where Reagan's roadmap thus came to a dead end.

Syria became the chief sponsor and sanctuary for the terrorist arch-nationalists of the Palestinian resistance. Hafez Assad was consumed by an atavistic ambition to restore a Greater Syria that would consist of a confederated Syria, Lebanon, Jordan, and a Palestinian state composed of the West Bank and Gaza. He pared his inordinate ambition to fit Syria's limited military and economic means, temporarily augmented by Soviet aid. The loss of the Golan Heights to Israel served as a stark reminder of weakness. To safeguard its security and consolidate its position as a credible actor in the greater Middle East, Damascus meant to perpetuate the fragility of Lebanon's ethnic and political society, forestall a Palestinian–Jordanian union, and gain a hold on the PLO. Assad began to fund Hezbollah in Lebanon and to open lines to Iran and Libya. Eager to use the Palestinian ultras for his own ends, he encouraged the PFLP and DFLP to fix their main seats in Damascus. This persuaded Arafat to establish the PLO's headquarters elsewhere.

From mid 1983 onwards, Syria also provided military support to the anti-Arafat factions in the Bekaa Valley, which it controlled. By late December, Arafat returned from Athens to be with 4,000 of his beleaguered *fedayeen* in the port city of Tripoli, who were being forced to decamp a second time. Thanks to the intercession of Saudi Arabia, the U.N., and the U.S., and protected by French naval units, Greek ships took them to safety in various places.

On his way to Tunis—which, unlike Damascus, favored negotiations—Arafat stopped off in Cairo to confer with Mubarak. At this juncture the two leaders needed each other: Mubarak looked to Arafat to help Egypt rejoin the concert of Arab nations, partly to appease the Cairo street; Arafat needed Mubarak to strengthen the PLO in its dealings with Damascus and Amman, as well as to serve as a go-between with Washington. While Arafat's rapprochement with Cairo met with approval in the Arab capitals—not counting Damascus, Tripoli, and Baghdad—and in the occupied territories, Tel Aviv reproved Mubarak for contravening the Camp David accords and dining with the devil. As usual, overly heedful of Israel, Washington failed to back him, probably against its own better judgment.

Although condemned separately by Syria, his own ultras, and Israel, Arafat persevered, now resuming a dialogue with King Hussein. Arafat wanted statehood in the occupied territories first, to be followed by talks on a confederation in which the PLO would be the main representative of the Palestinian people. As a condition for an international conference Hussein wanted the U.N. to sponsor, he demanded the PLO accept Security Council Resolution 242. Apparently Arafat retorted that, while the PLO was "prepared to recognize all U.N. resolutions" concerning the Palestine question, it was not disposed to accept "a single one, all by itself."

Without breaking with the PLO, the ultras, centered in Damascus, as well as Fatah's left, coalesced to denounce and fight the "new Hussein–Mubarak–Arafat axis" for favoring "an American solution seeking the liquidation of the Palestinian cause." In Israel, even if some Laborites—at least verbally—countenanced the Arafat–Hussein talks, the political class rejected the "Jordanian option"; neither Likud nor the successor National Unity Government did anything to further it. Even Hussein responded to Arafat's overtures and sought out Mubarak largely because he feared that Israel would not only hold on to the occupied territories but shunt the West Bank Palestinians into Jordan, in keeping with the axiom, last articulated by Begin and Tekoah, that the Hashemite kingdom was the chosen land of the Palestinians.

Conscious of all the intra-Palestinian and intra-Arab dissension, and with Washington looking the other way, Israel was less motivated than ever to accommodate. Territorial concessions and any contact with the PLO were out of the question. Iraq, Syria, and Libya seized on this implacability to malign the compromise-mongers and close ranks with the militants. In Damascus, splinters of the PLO—the PFLP, the DFLP, the Saiqa, and the Palestinian Liberation Front—clustered around a National Alliance that broke away from the PLO.

There were fewer than twenty terrorist incidents in Israel during the second half of 1985—six were killed and about fifty injured—but this period also saw a recrudescence of terrorism beyond its borders. All of it was perpetrated by the irreconcilables, primarily the Fatah Revolutionary Council of Abu Nidal, who struck out against whosoever,

Palestinian or otherwise, would make possible the least gesture toward a two-state solution, which he considered a betrayal of the cause. In August a bomb exploded in a tourist resort near Athens, injuring thirteen, and an attack on the Israeli embassy in Cairo killed one staff member and wounded two. The next month forty people were injured in a grenade attack on a café in Rome. In November a commando hijacked an Egyptian airliner and forced it to land in Malta, where six passengers were killed. At year's end there were simultaneous attacks on passengers at El Al's ticket counters at airports in Rome, Madrid, and Vienna, taking twenty lives and wounding over 100.

Over three decades, Nidal masterminded terrorist acts in some twenty countries. He never had more than a few hundred followers and militiamen, and was neither populist nor popular. He became notorious for both using and serving the secret services of the rejectionist states. There were even rumors of contacts (though never substantiated) with the Mossad. From the Israeli point of view, if Abu Nidal had not existed, he would have had to be invented: he was too perfect for demonizing the entire PLO—indeed the Palestinian Other and resistance as a whole.

While the Abu Nidal scourge was widely reported and debated, bringing the Palestine question into sharper relief, it was soon overshadowed by even more dramatic and incendiary operations. On September 25, 1985 three Israelis, probably secret service agents, were murdered by a breakaway PLO group on board an Israeli yacht anchored in Larnaca, Cyprus. Begin's government seized on this incident, coming after a string of attacks at home and abroad, to launch a major retaliatory raid. The cabinet selected the target of the PLO headquarters in the village of Hamman el-Shat, on a Tunisian beachfront, to which the PLO had repaired from Lebanon. Arafat was not directly implicated in any of the attacks, and expressed indignation out of one side of his mouth; out of the other he insinuated approval of terrorism in advancement of the Palestinian cause. The tactic was not original: Ben-Gurion had used it himself during the late Mandate.

On October 1, 1985 eight Israeli F-15s, refueled in flight by Boeing 707s, flew 1,300 miles to drop their load. They destroyed nearly the whole PLO complex, including the office of the chairman, who happened to be away. Over sixty Palestinians and Tunisians were killed, and another seventy wounded. Save for the U.S., who abstained, the U.N. Security Council denounced the attack unanimously as an "act of armed aggression" in violation of international law and Tunisian sovereignty. This incursion was answered on October 7 when four terrorists of the Abu Abbas-led paramilitary Palestine

Liberation Front hijacked the Italian cruise liner *Achille Lauro*, sailing from Alexandria to Israel. In an act of grotesque vengeance the hijackers shot and killed Leon Klinghoffer, a 69-year-old disabled American Jew, dumping his body and wheelchair into the sea. When the ship returned to Egypt, Mubarak's government allowed the terrorists to fly to Tunisia on an Egyptian airliner. The plane was intercepted by U.S. jets and forced to land at a NATO airbase in Sicily, where the terrorists were arrested. Abu Abbas having fled abroad, an Italian court sentenced him *in absentia* to five life terms. Unlike Abu Nidal, Abu Abbas never broke with the PLO. The headquarters of the PLF were also in Tunisia, where he collaborated with both the PLO and Fatah. In 1984 he had been elected to the Executive Committee of the PLO and, ultimately, favored negotiations with Israel and the Oslo accords. Even though the PLF turned increasingly militant and mounted ever more attacks in the north of Israel, Abu Abbas, with Arafat, kept hold of the olive branch.

The PLO and Fatah realized that this train of events served only to hasten the abandonment of guerrilla warfare in favor of terrorism. Militarily outclassed, the leaders of all resistance organizations and the militants in the refugee camps yielded to the temptation.

Terrorism was no more of a political, social, psychological, or moral disorder than warfare with conventional weapons, especially in an era in which the difference between military and civilian victims had become fatally blurred. It was a political act intended to achieve political ends. Its tactical objectives were psychological, not military; the strategy was to foment fear, to shatter morale, to mobilize sympathizers, and inspire recruits. Yet the hardliners in Israel seized on this surge in terrorism, which their policies had fed, to discredit the PLO's apparent turn toward a two-state position, holding Arafat responsible for each and every incident. This indiscriminate response became a conditioned national reflex. Of course, the remnant of the internal critics had their reflexes too: the small and beleaguered peace coalition kept the faith, searching for a way to strengthen the hand of the PLO moderates. One wing had ties to several members of the Labor Party who discreetly sympathized with its cause. But there was no loyal opposition to challenge the perpetual policy concerning the PLO, the occupied territories, and the Arab states.

From mid 1977 to mid 1992 Israel was ruled by the far-right Likud, apart from during the National Unity Government of 1984–6, led by Peres. In the thick of blinding nationalism, secular and religious, and an all-consuming Cold War during most of those years, the militant left dissidents had no impact on official policy concerning the Arabs.

Certainly, an Israeli peace initiative, which alone might have made a difference, was not in the realm of historical possibility; and it was U.S. backing that had long given its client state the privilege of such obduracy.

The PLO could not break the deadlock except at the price of surrender. Although, in Abu Iyad's words, "after Jordan [Black September] we had a sense of defeat, after Beirut we had a sensation of victory," it was only a victory of morale. By evacuating Lebanon, albeit with honor, the PLO lost its major base in a frontline country; Tunisia was remote from the theater of operations. On top of that, the PLO was internally torn, the Arab nations remained disconcerted, Syria was antagonistic to it, and Israel was mightier than ever. Given the radical imbalance of power (which obtained also between Russia and America), there was no alternative to seeking an opening for negotiation. The situation was unpromising, if not desperate, except for the commonwealth of refugees, who continued to be more responsive to Arafat than to the irrreconcilables. But while the PLO was weakened by dispersion, the refugees remained territorially and politically gathered in by the occupation—and made singularly susceptible, by Israel's own doing, to the ever more radical appeals of Palestinian nationalism. The enemy was no longer at the gates, but within them.

The fall of the Soviet Union in 1989 confirmed America's unqualified victory in the Cold War, its position as the sole superpower, and its ascendancy in a resurgent and expanding global capitalism. These radical changes were disastrous for the Arab world generally, and for those countries and movements in particular that rejected any compromise with Israel. The Arabs could no longer threaten to turn to the Kremlin for military and economic aid. Having lost its Soviet patron, Syria ceased to be much of a threat, and Israel continued to improve relations with Egypt and Jordan. With America unequivocally at its side, in strictly military terms Tel Aviv no longer had anything to fear.

The intifada of 1987–93 was a popular uprising against Israel's twenty years of occupation of the West Bank and Gaza. Compared to the first intifada of 1928–9 and the second of 1936–9, this third "shaking off" was deep-rooted and widespread. The first spontaneous outburst, in early December, took the leaders of both Israel and the PLO by complete surprise. Scattered and uncoordinated demonstrations exploded into a full-scale revolt that became more organized and politicized as a function of the severity of Israel's response.

Since 1967 Israel, irrespective of which party held power, had spared no effort to consolidate and expand its control of the occupied territories, and to exploit their human and economic resources. Military, legal, and administrative measures were used to coerce the local population into forfeiting much of the land desired for permanent colonization. Between 1967 and 1987, in a predominantly agrarian society, Israel had expropriated some 50 per cent of the West Bank, including the Jordan Valley, and 15 per cent of the Gaza Strip. Some was commandeered for military bases and security zones, some for the construction of about 130 settlements for roughly 200,000 settlers. Valuable water sources were seized in the process. This land-and-water grab undercut local agriculture, pressed Palestinian peasants into the reserve army of cheap labor for Israel, and undermined the social and political sway of the traditional landed Palestinian elite—which served to empower younger and more radical elements. That many of these would turn to activism, even to underground combat, was a given: in a heavily dependent and largely stagnant economy, there were few jobs for high school and university graduates. Not everyone had a bad time of it: there were breadwinners who made a virtue of necessity by collaborating with the occupying authorities. But there were more losers than winners. Israelis kept expenditures for health and social services to a strict minimum, and the safety net was no more than gossamer.

Besides laying themselves open to social and political unrest, the occupiers and settlers came up against the demographic time-bomb. In the occupied territories there was no ignoring the imbalance between Jews and Arabs. The annual birth rate there dashed the prospects for a Jewish Greater Israel. The implantation of settlements and *nahalim* (military bases eventually turned into civilian colonies) was intended to promote both military and civil security. With time, however, in the West Bank the stress was increasingly on thwarting the emergence of a territorially contiguous and cohesive geographic entity headed for Palestinian statehood. The new colonizing drive was intended to further fragment such a space by establishing settler communities near major Arab cities, by placing *nahalim* in militarily strategic locations, and by expanding entire Israeli cities beyond the Green Line of 1967. These Israeli–Jewish settlements, linked by a restricted network of secure roads, many of them built on confiscated farmland, became an archipelago in a vast Arab–Muslim sea.

By the second decade of the occupation, Palestine's forced and rapid socioeconomic deterioration was matched by an acceleration of dissent. Israel's military and civil administration responded by instituting a comprehensive system of control and repression: checkpoints, roadblocks, curfews, travel restrictions, school closings, mass arrests, deportations, house demolitions. This grinding occupation regime—particularly its practice of arbitrary and collective punishment—nourished the lifeblood of resistance, now coursing in the veins of a new generation: the old emotions of frustration, resentment, and humiliation.

In 1987, up until November, there were fifteen partisan or terrorist attacks against Israeli targets. Eighteen of the twenty killed were soldiers, as were fifty-three of the sixty injured. Five of the assaults took place in Jerusalem, three in Tel Aviv, and one in Haifa. The prime targets were military buses, border crossings, and police stations. During these same months there was also an upswing of disorders and riots in the occupied territories, particularly in the Gaza Strip, which was home to over 700,000 Palestinian refugees out of a total population of 1 million. Most lived in eight severely overcrowded and woefully deprived refugee camps, breeding grounds for young *fedayeen* who, unlike their counterparts outside the 1967 territories and the first generation of exiles and PLO leaders, experienced the indignities and miseries of Israeli occupation firsthand.

The third intifada seems to have risen up on December 6, 1987, when an Israeli businessman was stabbed to death in Gaza. Two days later four Arab workers were killed and seventeen wounded when an Israeli truck collided accidentally with two vans in which they were returning to Gaza from their day jobs in Israel. The victims were residents of the Jabalia camp, north of Gaza City, and a rumor soon spread through its 60,000 refugees that the putative accident had in fact been an act of vengeance for the previous day's murder. On the morning of December 9 a riot broke out in the camp, which Israeli forces tried to contain. A Molotov cocktail was thrown at an IDF patrol, which shot dead a Palestinian youth. That night the funeral procession for all the victims morphed into large-scale and raucous political demonstrations. The unrest blazed throughout the Gaza Strip and jumped to the West Bank. On December 10–11 Nablus and the nearby Balata refugee camp witnessed anti-occupation demonstrations. Here confrontations with Israeli forces left five Palestinians dead and fifty injured. On December 13 protesters took to the streets of East Jerusalem, and two days later, following Friday prayers, Israeli policemen and soldiers used tear gas to disperse a demonstration on the Temple Mount. Jenin, in the far north, was the next big city to see unrest. There was considerable street violence in all areas: activists and militants threw stones and hurled firebombs at occupation forces and offices.

The uprising, initially spontaneous, acquired a political voice and direction. While young refugee stone-hurlers stood for the grammar of the third intifada, an end to the Israeli occupation and a fully sovereign Palestinian state became its logic. This demand almost instantly issued from ad hoc political committees, which articulated it in public meetings and handbills. Within three weeks Fatah, the PFLP, and the DFLP were working together to set up the United National Command (UNC) to guide the protest. Since these and other resistance organizations were affiliated, some of them uneasily, with the PLO, its Executive Committee, headed by Arafat, took charge. Presently the UNC became the PLO's operational branch. Largely on its own, it coordinated a campaign of civil disobedience that called for the boycott of Israeli products, the closing of shops, the refusal to pay taxes, and the resignation of Palestinians working for the occupation authorities.

This nonviolent resistance went relatively unnoticed compared with the mayhem recorded and magnified by the media. Yet much of the violence of the third intifada, which continued irregularly for six years, was modest and homegrown. Almost from the start, Arafat warned that firearms should not be used, so as not to give the Israelis a pretext to "commit massacres." The strength of the Palestinian resistance, he insisted, was "rooted not in the nature of its weapons but the right-eousness of its cause." With time, however, Palestinian militants resorted to more lethal weapons and methods, largely in response to the ferocity of Israeli retaliation and deterrence. During the first four years the IDF reported that Palestinians had mounted some 3,600 attacks with incendiary grenades, 100 with hand grenades, and 600 with guns. These had resulted in the deaths of 16 Israeli civilians and 12 soldiers in the occupied territories, and left some 1,400 Israeli civilians and 1,700 soldiers wounded. During the entire intifada Israel lost about 150 lives, 50 of them civilians; on the other side, about 1,200 mostly young Palestinians died in the uprising, around 200 of them under the age of 16. Between 20,000 and 30,000 were injured by live ammunition, rubber bullets, or beatings. In addition, by the end of 1988 the Israelis had made some 50,000 arrests.

As in 1973, the government was at first not especially alarmed. Committed only to anathematizing Fatah and the PLO, Israel was not about to examine with fresh eyes the reality that had incited them. Shamir and his cabinet saw "no reason for concern"; having "over-come this kind of thing in the past," the country would be able to "do so now and in the future." On an official visit to Washington, when the unrest broke out, Defense Minister Rabin reassured his hosts that it would "all be over by Christmas," confident the IDF could take the uprising in its stride. By the end of January 1988 he announced that, with the use of "force, power, and blows," Israel would "make it clear who was running the territories." Still convinced that his soldiers could easily prevail without resorting to firearms, Rabin is said to have instructed them "to go in and break the bones" of the stone-throwers, which they did with clubs and rifle-butts. They were also ordered to arrest and detain demonstrators and to impose strict curfews in unruly areas. But as the uprising escalated, repression became increasingly violent.

The intifada at once revived and redefined the PLO. Its leadership was uneasily ensconced in its headquarters south of Tunis, which two years before had been all but wrecked by the Israeli air strike. This extravagant attack had boosted the political stock of the PLO at a time when the external and internal resistance were tangling over strategy and tactics in a manner reminiscent of the discord between the resistance inside France and General de Gaulle in London during the Second World War. Overnight the third intifada shifted its focus from advancing its cause through politics and diplomacy in the corridors of power, to autonomous direct action by the refugees in the occupied territories. Arafat and his inner circle had to come to terms with this new nerve-center and its accompanying dynamic: young, unpracticed militants mobilizing a downcast society of villages, towns, and, above all, refugee camps—a society waiting to be empowered.

From the outset, the PLO and Fatah had been cast in the mold of Third World national liberation movements. The PFLP and DFLP were, in addition, Marxist-inspired. Typically of such groups, their leaders were all fiercely secular: Arafat, Abu Jihad, Abu Iyad, Habash, and Nayif Hawatmeh would have no truck with Islam, which, like all religions, they considered retrograde. The internal resistance, however, anchored in the tradition-bound refugee culture and society, had to take account of religion and mosque. The burgeoning Islamic movement among the Palestinians was indigenous, but supplemented by the influence of Egypt's Muslim Brotherhood and Iran's theocratic regime. Step by step, both Arab and Israeli politicians and clerics instrumentalized religion, feeding their own and each other's fundamentalism.

The clash over the Wailing Wall in 1929, during the first intifada, had been an early portent. Twenty years later, Ben-Gurion's decision, at the foundation, to Judaize the nation guaranteed the future use and abuse of religion. The annexation of Jerusalem in June 1967, followed by its sanctification as Israel's "indivisible and eternal capital" in July 1980, incensed the true-believers across the Arab–Muslim world, not just in its Palestinian precincts. These were so many milestones on the road to the premeditated visit of Ariel Sharon, leader of Likud, to the Temple Mount in September 2000, accompanied by party deputies and bodyguards.

In 1971, the far-right Kach party ("Only Thus," also known as the Jewish Defense League) called for the establishment of a theocratic state in Biblical Eretz Israel, to be grounded in Jewish scripture. The Arab Palestinians, the latter-day Canaanites, should be removed and their mosques and monuments demolished, as mandated in Exodus and Deuteronomy. As for answering terror with terror, the adepts of Kach were fiery descendants of Irgun and Lehi, of early Begin and Shamir, except that, as a further refinement, like a sect of illuminati, they urged that Jewish infidels—in their eyes trimmers and appeasers—be tormented.

Religion advanced in a similarly erratic manner on the Palestinian side. None of the great leaders of the anti-Israel states were Islamists, let alone fundamentalists. Nor were they non-Muslim Muslims, since they publicly practiced mainstream Islam for the sake of appearances. The real faith of Nasser and Sadat, Assad and Saddam Hussein, was anti-colonial secular nationalism. They all feared and resisted but hesitated to confront the revivalist Islamism that had begun to catch on among the underclasses. The relatively soft confrontation in Egypt between Nasser, Sadat, Mubarak, and the Muslim Brotherhood was exemplary. It was only following the triumph of the Shia in Iran in 1979, and the combative intractability of Israel—best attested by its invasion of Lebanon—that Islamism broke to the surface, taking the form of the Shiite Hezbollah there, and of the Sunni Hamas and Islamic Jihad in the occupied territories just before the third intifada. Although the later Al-Aqsa Martyrs' Brigades consisted of secular nationalists, their origins were inseparable from the religiously conditioned fourth intifada of 2000.

Hamas ("zeal" or "bravery") emerged in the late 1970s, founded by its spiritual guide, Sheikh Ahmed Yassin. The Islamic Resistance Movement, as it was also known, was native to the occupied territories, being based in the Gaza Strip. Following Egypt's Muslim Brotherhood, Hamas considered undivided Palestine a Muslim land and a province of the Islamic world, which it saw being swept by a religious and cultural revival. A religiously animated state was the goal. A secular and democratic state was sacrilege enough, but a Marxist or Socialist state was Hamas' nightmare. The PLO, Fatah, the

PFLP, and the DFLP were all equally odious; and yet Hamas shared in the opposition of the latter two to a two-state solution, especially since it feared the loss of full title to Jerusalem. The leaders of Hamas used the rostrum of the mosque to disseminate their articles of faith and developed welfare, educational, and cultural centers. Bent on transforming social into political influence, Hamas catered especially to the wretched of the camps and simultaneously built an underground of activists, *fedayeen*, and, finally, suicide bombers. Saudi Arabia and the Gulf States provided much of the financing.

While Hamas too looked to the Iranian revolution for guidance, it was the intifada of 1987 that provided the momentum for the once embryonic sect to grow. As a mass movement, it was sustained by the distress and ferment among the Palestinian refugees first in Gaza, and then the West Bank—notably Hebron and Nablus. The mushrooming growth of Hamas astonished the Israelis and the PLO as much as had the intifada itself. For a few years in the late 1970s, the Israeli occupation administration had actually been encouraging and funding the party–movement, but its stratagem had been to use Hamas as a stalking horse to weaken the popular support of the PLO and to disconcert its inner circle. During the third intifada Hamas defied both the Israelis and the PLO. With mounting local support it helped energize the anti-Israeli resistance, at the same time avoiding the uprising's United National Command. Above all, it challenged the PLO's claim to be the sole legitimate representative of the Palestinian people, its decision to seek a compromise solution through negotiations with Israel, and its refusal to embrace the idea of an Islamic Palestinian state. Hamas' covenant proclaimed that there was "no solution for the Palestinian Question except through Jihad." It charged that "after Palestine, the Zionists aspire to expand from the Nile to the Euphrates" and beyond, their plan being "embodied in the 'Protocols of Zion,'" the infamous nineteenth-century Russian forgery regarded as gospel by the religiously-animated nationalists, and according to which the Jews sought world domination. Hamas vowed to fight to the death to destroy Israel and raise "the banner of Allah over every inch of Palestine." And there was no winning through without also doing battle against the unregenerate PLO and its craven leaders.

Hezbollah, or "Party of God," was forged in 1982 in the heat of the Lebanon war. Inspired and funded by Iran in particular, its members championed the establishment of a Shiite theocracy in Lebanon, the end of Western influence in the Middle East, and the destruction of Israel. Besides exerting influence in Beirut's political society, Hezbollah operated a network of social service missions that won over thousands of sympathizers and supporters among Palestinian refugees. The military branch of a small but hardcore group of militants provided security forces in the Shiite-dominated areas: in sections of Beirut, in southern Lebanon, and in the Bekaa Valley. It also trained and deployed operatives for terrorist attacks—kidnappings, bombings, and hijackings—on American, Israeli, and European targets in Lebanon, before focusing exclusively on Israel. Early notoriety came with the suicide truck bombings of the U.S. embassy in Beirut in April, 1983, leaving 63 dead, 17 of them Americans, and of a U.S. Marine barracks in October of the same year, when 260 American servicemen died and 160 were wounded. By virtue of Syria's unremitting military and political sway in Lebanon, Damascus soon supplanted Tehran as Hezbollah's main backer.

The Palestinian Islamic Jihad bore a strong family resemblance to Hamas and Hezbollah. In keeping with the credo of their reawakened faith, all three were implacable enemies of Israel, and sought to establish an Islamic Palestinian state in its place. They vilified the secular PLO, the moderate Arab states, and the corrupting Western world. Islamic Jihad, like Hamas, was another offspring of the Muslim Brotherhood. Two Palestinian students, Fathi al-Shaqaqi and Abd al-Aziz Odah, had gone to Cairo in the late 1970s, where they were inspired by the Iranian Revolution, and associated with members of the Muslim Brotherhood at Cairo University. When these young Egyptian rebels were suspected of involvement in Sadat's assassination in 1981, their two alleged coadjutors, along with other Palestinian Islamic radicals, were expelled to the Gaza Strip, where they founded the Islamic Jihad. Shaqaqi was deeply impressed by the Islamization of Iranian society, and by Imam Khomeini's advocacy of collaboration between Sunnis and Shiites. He and his associates took issue, however, with the idea held by the Brotherhood and common in the Arab–Muslim world that pan-Arabism and pan-Islamism were the keys to the liberation of Palestine. Instead, the Islamic Jihad looked to the Holy War against Israel and the liberation of Palestine to further Islam's redemption and renewal.

This relatively small and opaque organization recruited militants among the impatient radicals of the Muslim Brotherhood, and from leftist critics within the PLO, a number of whom were natives of the refugee camps. By the late 1980s, Arafat's inner circle had become worried about the lure of Islamic Jihad, which was penetrating different quarters, including the forward wing of Fatah. Still, compared with Hamas, Islamic Jihad was and would remain a small phalanx of *fedayeen,* concentrated on training for irregular warfare, including terrorist operations, rather than on developing a social service network.

It was Hamas that became the intifada's most audible, effective, and unsettling champion of Palestinian Islamic nationalism. By proclaiming the fight against colonialist occupation, material dispossession, and cultural alienation as the key to the rebirth of Islam, Hamas was fundamentally at odds with the PLO, which conceived of the struggle with Zionist Israel in profane and political terms. Yet they became inseparable if uneasy brothers-in-arms. Once Arafat and Abu Jihad had got the upper hand in the Committee of National Unity, they had to contend with two factions more militant than Fatah. While Hamas stood apart, the PFLP became the main radicalizing force within the joint command. The one preached a strident theocratic nationalism, the other a fierce secular ultra-nationalism. George Habash of the PFLP pressed for the intensification of civil disobedience and boycotts, and called on Israel to put an end to the settlements and pull out its garrisons. But, while making these tactical and short-term demands clear, he pronounced within the CNU and wherever he could be heard that the ultimate aim of the uprising was the establishment of an undivided Palestine with Jerusalem as its capital.

During the third intifada the terrorist strikes inside Israel continued as before. From 1988 to 1992 there were 48 incidents, killing some 60 Israelis and injuring 130. At least ten of the operations were carried out by *fedayeen* who had crossed into Israel from Lebanon and Jordan. The proportion of military victims declined substantially. Fifteen of the assaults—nearly a third—took place in Jerusalem. Between 1988 and 1990 the Israeli security forces undertook three major actions in the Holy City, all of them centered around the two hallowed mosques on the Temple Mount. These alleged retaliations claimed 18 Palestinian lives and nearly 300 wounded. East Jerusalem—sometimes even the entire city—was put under curfew. The struggle for Jerusalem proceeded apace. Israel, supported by the U.S., stayed on the offensive: in March 1990, first the U.S. Senate and then the Knesset adopted resolutions declaring undivided Jerusalem the capital of Israel, in the second case specifying that its status was non-negotiable. The following October, and again in November, Ariel Sharon, then minister of housing, announced a faster pace for residential construction in East Jerusalem beyond the Green Line. Since 1967 the number of its settlers had reached nearly 120,000; 100,000 were in the other occupied territories. The Palestinians continued to respond to every inflection—symbolic, physical, political—of Israeli violence against them.

The PFLP and Hamas were together fastened on the immutability of this forward policy. They not only opposed negotiating with Israel from a position of weakness, but also intensified their criticism of Arafat and his closest associates for proposing to exploit the glory and blood of the uprising to promote a two-state solution. In this Habash and Yassin spoke to a new generation of activists, most of them children of the camps and the occupation, who balked at Arafat's caveat against excessive reliance on the gun. Both the PFLP and Hamas rallied the internal resistance to turn against appeasers as collaborators.

With this schism, the third intifada became fratricidal. Palestinians are estimated to have killed between 700 and 1,000 of their own during its course—more than ten times the number of their Israeli victims. This obviously played into Israel's hands. There were even suggestions that its own agents may have had a hand in some of the high-profile assassinations, as in the case of Abu Iyad (Salah Khalad), responsible for the PLO's internal security, who was murdered in January 1991 in Carthage, outside Tunis. Without offering proof, the PLO charged that "the hand that killed [Abu Iyad] was beholden to the Zionist enemy."

There was no uncertainty, however, about who took out Abu Jihad (Khalil al-Wazir). Prime Minister Shamir asked his coalition cabinet to approve the assassination of the head of the PLO's military branch, also responsible for the occupied territories, claiming that he was actively radicalizing the intifada. His chief ministers, including Rabin at Defense, were in favor, except for Weizman and Peres, who worried about the risk of diplomatic fallout. Major General Ehud Barak, deputy chief-of-staff, planned the raid, which was carried out by an elite paratroop brigade in mid-April 1988, north of Tunis, under the command of Moshe Ya'alon. Such political murders merely enhanced Arafat's standing in the world, and made it more difficult for the Palestinian intransigents to charge him with exploiting the intifada in the search for a political solution. Abu Mazen replaced Abu Jihad.

Chief of the external resistance, Arafat had at best a limited hand in the violent grammar of the internal resistance in the camps. But almost from the start of the third intifada he and his associates defined its political logic. Paradoxically, the radicalization of the uprising— including the spiraling Palestinian fratricide and Israeli repression— put wind in Arafat's sails.

The intifada's first major unintended diplomatic consequence, beneficial to Arafat, was the implosion of King Hussein's design to recover the West Bank, annexed in 1948 by his grandfather. From 1967 until the eve of the uprising in 1987, he had refused to recognize the

PLO as the representative of the Palestinians, for whom he himself presumed to speak. In some administrative matters, such as the appointment of mayors in the occupied territory, Amman cooperated awkwardly with Tel Aviv. But Hussein never ceased to be apprehensive about Israel's long-term intentions and about Palestinian loyalty. The intifada foregrounded a second factor: the Palestinians of the West Bank, remembering Black September of 1970, scrapped the idea of a contingent autonomy under a Jordanian Palestinian federation, in favor of the promise of and struggle for independence. Hussein feared that the fever of events would spread to the kindred Palestinians, who comprised 60 per cent of his kingdom. And Israel's hardline cabinet might make it an occasion to drive the West Bank Arabs across the Jordan River—the ultimate goal of a long line of Zionists.

Hussein recalculated, choosing to forswear the Hashemite claim to the West Bank. By doing so he knew he would smooth the way for the PLO not only on the ground but in the diplomatic arena. In early June 1988 the Arab League held an emergency summit in Algiers to discuss the intifada. The delegates agreed to back the uprising, to support the Palestinian people's right to self-determination and an independent state, to endorse the call for a U.N.-sponsored conference on the issue, and to recognize the PLO as the sole representative of the Palestinian people. King Hussein now conceded that right, renounced any claim to "even the smallest parcel of Palestine," and "sever[ed all] legal and administrative ties" with the West Bank.

The path was now clear for Arafat to envision the establishment of a sovereign Palestinian state to consist of the West Bank and Gaza, and to accept U.N. Resolution 242, which he had so far resisted for mentioning neither Palestine nor a Palestinian people with a voice of its own. He was encouraged to take this course by Faisal Husseini, a grand notable of East Jerusalem recently arrested for supporting the uprising. An early champion of Israeli–Palestinian dialogue, Husseini came to believe that both sides needed "to abandon [their] dreams because dreams are not negotiable." On July 31, 1988 he published a "Project for a Declaration of Independence," proposing negotiations linking the independence of Palestine with the recognition of Israel.

The following September, Arafat addressed the Socialist members of the European Parliament in Strasbourg. Speaking in the name of the "people of the Intifada," he proposed that the U.N. convene a peace conference whose participants would accept one of two options as a basis for discussion: "all U.N. resolutions relevant to the Palestine question, including Security Council Resolutions 242 [1967] and 338 [1973]"; or U.N. Resolutions 242 and 338 "along with the legitimate rights of the Palestinian people, foremost among them their right to self-determination." For how could the Palestinians be "asked to accept Resolution 242 and forget the other [relevant] resolutions?" How could the U.S. and Israel embrace General Assembly Resolution 181 (1947) providing "for the creation of two states . . . and simultaneously reject . . . Resolution 194 [calling] for the repatriation of the Palestinian refugees or the payment of compensation for those choosing not to return?" Arafat further stressed that, following Jordan's recent move, the PLO's representation of the Palestinian people at any future international parley could no longer be open to question. At a press conference following his speech he declared that "what Israel and all of us need is an Israeli De Gaulle." Assuring all Israelis that "we are proposing peace to you," Arafat called on them to "vote, in the next elections, for the peace camp, for those who do not sound the trumpet of war."

In November 1988, a year after the start of the intifada, Arafat asked the Nineteenth Palestine National Council meeting in Algiers to approve the new course. After lengthy and heated debate by some 310 delegates, a large majority called for an international conference to discuss the establishment of an independent Palestinian state in accordance with Security Council Resolutions 242 and 338. They also "reject[ed] terrorism in all its forms, including state terrorism," but without renouncing the right to resist foreign occupation and to fight for independence by other means. With considerable encouragement from other nations, the PLO launched a diplomatic offensive in search of a two-state solution.

On November 15, at the close of the four-day conclave, Arafat read out the Declaration of Independence drafted by Mahmoud Darwish, bard of Palestinian nationalism and member of the PLO's Executive Committee. Invoking "the national, historical, and legal rights . . . of the Palestinian Arab people" to their land, the charter enshrined their "aspiration for liberation, progress, democracy, and unity." Resolution 181, from 1947, which had originally "partitioned Palestine into two states . . . still provided the conditions of international legitimacy that ensure the [Palestinians'] right . . . to sovereignty." The U.N. charter and resolutions "recognized the Palestinian Arab people's national rights, including the right to return" of the "majority of Palestine's civilian inhabitants," who had been displaced and expelled with the help of "organized terror." Moved by a "revolutionary irreversible impulse," the intifada was "elevating awareness of the Palestinian truth and right into still higher realms of comprehension and actuality" and bringing the "history of Palestine [to] a decisive juncture." The Declaration proclaimed "the establishment of the State of Palestine on our Palestinian territory with its capital Jerusalem (Al-Quds Ash-Sharif)." Committed to "the settlement of regional and international conflicts by peaceful means," the state rejected the threat or use of force, violence, and terrorism "not only against its [own] historical integrity or political independence" but also against the "territorial integrity of other states." The Palestinians, however, would "continue the struggle until the occupation ends."

In 1948, when Ben-Gurion had proclaimed the independence of Israel, his provisional government had exercised effective control over its embattled territory; the Palestine National Council had none over any of the land it aspired to. The Declaration of Independence was at bottom a symbolic act intended to invite recognition of the would-be state and its would-be government in the community of nations. While the document did not explicitly recognize Israel's right to exist, implicitly it did—a giant step for Arafat, whose eyes were trained on ongoing and upcoming diplomatic negotiations in which he would be guided by Faisal Husseini's blueprint for reciprocity. Rather than commend the new course, Israeli leaders dismissed it as "just another step in the terrorist organization's war against Israel's independence and existence" (Prime Minister Shamir), and a "smokescreen . . . of moderation [for] a more extreme position" (Foreign Minister Peres).

The PLO leaders realized that America was the ultimate master of the diplomatic and military game in the greater Middle East. "Nothing can get done . . . without the United States," Arafat understood, and "alone Washington, putting imperial interest ahead of domestic political calculation," might conceivably pressure Israel to come to the negotiating table. He needed to go further still in meeting U.S. preconditions for dealing with the PLO. Toward the end of Reagan's presidency, Secretary of State George Shultz countenanced the secret efforts of Sten Anderson, the Swedish foreign minister, and five dovish American Jewish personalities led by Rita Hauser, a prominent lawyer, to meet a Palestinian delegation, which included Darwish and Yasser Rabbo, a politician close to Arafat. The delegation proposed to craft a wording of the PLO's new position, mindful of U.S. concerns regarding the recognition of Israel and the renunciation of terror. Their joint statement, published in Stockholm on December 7, 1988, was signed by Arafat and other senior PLO figures. In it the Palestine National Council called for an international conference to be held "on the basis of U.N. Resolutions 242 and 338 and the right of Palestinians to self-determination"; accepted the "existence of every state in the region"; confirmed again their rejection of "terrorism in all its forms, including state terrorism"; and "called for a solution to the Palestinian refugee problem" in accordance with "international law and practices and relevant U.N. resolutions (including right to compensation)."

Shultz granted that the Stockholm text marked a step forward, but still deemed it insufficient. Arafat, meanwhile, had prepared to travel to New York to address the annual session of the General Assembly and seek international support for his initiative. To practically universal consternation, on November 26, on orders from the State Department, the American consul in Tunis denied Arafat's application for a visa, alleging that his connections with terrorism endangered the security of American citizens. Unexpectedly, by 121 votes against 2— the United States and Israel—the General Assembly adopted a resolution, introduced by Egypt and Jordan, to transfer its plenum to Geneva.

On December 13, Arafat told 159 delegates at the site of the late-lamented League of Nations that he took their vote to give him a hearing in Geneva, "after an unjust U.S. decision . . . as evidence that our people's just cause has taken root in the human conscience." Fourteen years after he had first spoken to them, he could speak "with a louder voice, stronger determination, and greater confidence." Invigorated by the "masses of our blessed uprising," he brought greetings from "the stone-throwing children who are challenging the occupation and its aircraft, tanks, and weaponry." Even so, noting "the distance between this situation and the dream," the PLO was searching for "realistic alternative formulas" to bring about a solution of the Arab–Israeli conflict "based on possible and not absolute justice." But Israel had rejected all peace initiatives, including those of the U.N. and the great powers. It had responded instead by "building more settlements, escalating its expansionist policies, and exacerbating conflict," most recently and egregiously in Lebanon, the scene of the Sabra and Chatila massacre. Arafat found it particularly "painful and regrettable that the U.S. government alone should continue to support [Israel's] expansionist and aggressive plans [and] to refuse to recognize the right of six million Palestinians to self-determination."

After reiterating the main points of the Palestinian Declaration of Independence and the Stockholm statement, Arafat emphasized, once more, that he "condemned terrorism in all its forms." At the same time, he again "saluted" all those U.N. delegates who had been "accused by their executioners and the colonialists as terrorists during the battles for the liberation of their land from the yoke of occupation." Welcoming the new "climate of international detente," Arafat called on Israelis to have done with "weapons of destruction . . . occupation, coercion, humiliation, killing, and torture," so as to help clear the way for "the peace of the brave." This time around, he concluded with his vision of "the flag of our independent Palestinian state flying over the hills of the homeland."

On December 15 the General Assembly took note of the Algiers Declaration by 104 votes to 2, with 36 abstentions, and a good majority of states recognized the virtual state of Palestine. But the U.S. continued to find Arafat's protestations unsatisfactory. Shultz still balked at the PLO's refusal to swear off violence in its struggle for liberation. He also took exception to the PLO's unilateral claim to East Jerusalem as the capital of an independent Palestinian state, rather than leaving it to be negotiated. Nevertheless, he instructed the American ambassador in Tunisia to begin a dialogue with representatives of the PLO.

However reluctantly, in the political precincts of the resistance, most of the secular radicals endorsed Arafat's new diplomatic turn. Loath to give the Israelis the "pleasure" of seeing them break ranks, George Habash announced that, whereas his motto had been "revolution until victory," he now supplemented it with "unity until victory." Yet he also maintained that the Palestinian cause could not advance without armed struggle, as the intifada had shown. Whatever Arafat's concerns about the hardliners, secular and religious, in both the internal and external resistance, they did not significantly temper his drive for an opening for negotiations. Much of the world had considerable sympathy for the intifada, and the PLO saw no reason not to play on it.

Meanwhile, Israel's leaders were not simply immovable; they did their best to thwart Arafat's efforts, primarily by applying pressure through the pro-Israel lobby in Washington. Shamir kept denouncing the chairman's moves as "monumental acts of deception." He and Moshe Arens, Peres' successor at the Foreign Ministry, were opposed to Shultz's cautious overture to the PLO, and would not brook the idea of exchanging land for peace. Whereas, until recently, they had abused Arafat for playing fast and loose with language and documents, Israeli officials now became less discreet in their disregard for Resolutions 242 and 338 (Resolution 194, on the right of return and compensation, having long been ignored). Almost the entire politico-military caste continued to see Arafat only as a terrorist, both directing and obeying fundamentalists and Islamists who were in fact among his detractors. Shamir, for one, was impatient for him "to leave the political scene . . . and all I wanted to know was how he would disappear."

The third intifada finally awakened Israel to the magnitude of the oppositional force. For twenty years the country had looked to the occupied territories to provide military security, economic benefits, and psychic income. Overnight the West Bank and Gaza had turned into a source of insecurity more threatening than the neighboring states. Rabin was among the first to see reason. His prediction the year before that the suppression of the PLO would be child's play turned out to have been facile. Now he was troubled about the IDF becoming bogged down in a quagmire and, of necessity, transmuted into a police force to crush rebels, protect settlers, and restrain Jewish ultras. He worried about their prestige and morale, and even about their proficiency at a task they weren't trained for—counterinsurgency.

Not that the garrison state was ineffectual. Fierce repression had largely subdued the intifada by 1992. West of the Green Line, however, this quashing of the revolt of the stones had broad psychological and political consequences. The same critical spirits in Israel that had taken to the streets and editorial pages at the time of the Sabra and Chatila massacre were again feeling the pangs of conscience. Voices at the far left of the political spectrum cried out that the systemic transgressions of the occupation ran counter to Jewish and Zionist principles. But at the other end, secular and religious zealots still insisted that these same commandments called for Judea and Samaria to be incorporated into Eretz Israel, at whatever cost. The intifada forced the issue of the future status of the West Bank, which the PLO had designated the epicenter of the imagined Palestinian state, onto the political agenda in Israel, and onto the diplomatic agenda of the community of nations.

Whatever one felt about the Palestinians, it became more and more difficult to continue denying their existence as a self-determining people, the possibility of their having a state, and the legitimacy of the PLO. A speech like Tekoah's in 1974, neatly negating all three, had now become inconceivable. But, as much as they had been traduced since Israel Zangwill had deemed their home "a land without a people for a people without a land," the Palestinians—most of them exiles and refugees—had grown in self-awareness, self-affirmation, and sheer number: close to 1 million in Israel and Gaza each, about 2 million in Jordan, and an equal number in the West Bank. Yet, despite this consolidation of national identity and evolution of political consciousness, Israel's political caste was not to be moved. Suspicious and intolerant of dissidents pursuing dialogue with their Palestinian counterparts, in 1986 the government had amended the "Anti-Terrorist Ordinance" to forbid direct contacts between Israeli citizens—

including members of the Knesset—and members of the PLO. This proscription echoed Ben-Gurion's efforts to keep Magnes and Buber from having such contacts and testifying before British and U.N. inquiry commissions before Israel's foundation in 1948. It was not until January 1993, after Rabin succeeded Shamir and Washington pressed Israel to take the road to Madrid and Oslo, that this interdict was repealed.

The diplomatic deadlock of the late 1980s and early 1990s was finally broken by three interrelated factors: the international environment, and the changing internal politics of both the PLO and Israel. Internationally it was the time of the Soviet Union's collapse, the Iran–Iraq War, and the war to evict Saddam Hussein from Kuwait. The after-effects of all three benefited Israel, although the stamina of the Islamic regime in Tehran encouraged Hamas and the Islamic Jihad. Among the Palestinians, there was, as we have seen, a momentous change in the PLO's readiness to negotiate and accept a two-state solution. And in Israel there was also a political mutation, though less marked.

The Israeli elections of June 1992 were held in an atmosphere charged with disenchantment. Apart from a two-year interval, Likud had been in power since June 1977. But even during the Peres-led National Unity coalition of September 1984–October 1986, Labor was hardly free to change course: Shamir remained minister of foreign affairs until he regained the premiership. Likud, then, wrapped in promises of a secure, extravagant Eretz Israel, had a long and nearly unbroken record on which to be judged. Both at home and abroad it stood for incessant fighting for a goal that allowed at best a token degree of autonomy for the occupied territories. Shamir's refrain had been Begin's: Israel would never give up Judea and Samaria, even for peace. Likud's slate was all but closed to negotiations, whether bilateral or multilateral.

The secular ultra-right was estranged from the outside world, which it considered hostile, partial to the Arabs, and latently anti-Semitic. Even the U.S. could not be trusted. Likud's inordinate self-reliance and unilateralism were the natural instincts of a combined ghetto–fortress mentality that was perhaps the most salient feature of Israeli society. The requirements of such an outlook had saddled the party with a domestic record worn ragged by exorbitant expenditures for the armed forces, the occupation, and the settlements. The economy was tailing off, unemployment was high, housing was in short supply, and social services were being starved. Significantly, and in a development related to that discouraging picture, immigration declined, while emigration increased.

General Yitzhak Rabin headed the Labor ticket. His pedigree as a member of Israel's politico-military caste was even better than Peres': field general, chief of staff, minister of defense, prime minister, and ambassador to Washington. A right-centrist in his party, he was not about to mount a radical challenge to the established Likud–Labor consensus in foreign or domestic policy. He left it to the party platform and to individual candidates for the Knesset to engage Likud on the domestic issues, while he focused on the Palestine Question: occupation, settlements, negotiation. Here his positions mirrored Likud's: he favored settlements in what even Labor called Judea and Samaria, rejected the idea of a Palestinian state, claimed East Jerusalem, and opposed the Palestinian right of return. As a military man, Rabin invoked first the imperative of security when justifying the continued colonization and military control of the territories—part of the geostrategic plans put in place immediately after the victory of 1967. Accordingly, he distinguished between "security" and "political" colonies. While he favored the maintenance and expansion of the former, he had reservations about the latter for not bringing any economic or military benefits. Yet he did not question the growing dormitory communities that spilled across the Green Line.

The election campaign, then, turned on matters of style rather than of substance. Rabin and Labor favored a process of continuing bilateral negotiations with the Palestinians as well as close cooperation with the U.S., the mediator of choice. But, opposed to a Palestinian state as he was and determined to hold on to most of the occupied territories, Rabin was not about to engage with the PLO and Arafat. Instead, he proposed to further the election of local Palestinian officials prepared to collaborate with Israel in exchange for limited autonomy and self-government. For that he was prepared to make minor territorial concessions; the sidelining of the PLO was an unspoken aim.

Only the leaders of Meretz—a left-of-consensus party combining Mapam, Shinui, and Retz—spoke of the need for mutual concessions in negotiations that would include the PLO. They also called for a halt to settlement construction and were open to the idea of a sovereign Palestinian state. But the rest of the field was rife with right-wing parties, mostly religious, catering to hawkish voters opposed to talks and clamoring for the annexation of the occupied territories. The two major parties, Labor and Likud, competed for the vote of the center, which put security first and countenanced some degree of autonomy for the territories apart from the security zones and settlements. Rabin even took credit personally for Labor's having been in the vanguard of the settlement project, for which he had provided the military reasoning since 1967. Labor scored points against Likud not by criticizing its settlement policy as such, but by charging Shamir with having furthered it at the expense of domestic economic and social programs.

The election result reduced Likud's Knesset delegation from forty to thirty-two seats. But by capturing seventeen seats, several arch-conservative parties—Shas, Moledet, Tehiya, Zomet, and the National Religious Party—more than compensated for this minor loss. The Labor representation, at forty-four seats, was practically unchanged. The emergence of Meretz, which won twelve seats, was the great surprise of the election, measuring the extent of the restiveness with the Likud–Labor course, whose latest failing had been the third intifada. Needing 61 out of 120 votes to form a government, Rabin asked both Meretz and Shas to join his cabinet. Shulamit Aloni, the head of Meretz, became minister of education, a sign that the desecularization of society might be slowed. Consensual Laborites assumed the crucial portfolios: Rabin took on Defense and Interior besides the premiership; Peres became foreign minister; and Barak remained chief of staff. There was certain to be a strong continuity in policy.

In his inaugural address of July 13, 1992 before the Knesset, Rabin made the search for peace one of his chief priorities. He was anxious about the deleterious effect of long-time service on the IDF's combat-readiness in the rebellious occupied territories. He also had growing doubts about Israel's ability to curb the Palestinian resistance by arms alone. Still confident of the country's overall military might and strongholds across the territories, including the Golan, Rabin was open to Washington's insistent proposal to open a dialogue with the PLO and convene an international conference.

Relations with the U.S. had emerged as an important issue in the election. Under Likud they had gone from bad to worse because of Shamir's refusal to address concerns about the settlement drive, which the U.S. considered a prime obstacle to the lowering of tensions. As a former ambassador to the U.S., Rabin had a sophisticated understanding of the nature and importance of the American connection, as well as that of national-security and party politics in Washington. He seemed much better suited than Shamir to mending fences, and then seizing the opportunities and mastering the risks of multilateralism. And as a renowned general he could speak the language of the Pentagon, which held the key to the continuing incontestability of Israel's military might.

If Labor agreed to a change in method, however, it was also with an eye to the American Jewish community, whose political support was a matter of life and death—something else Rabin had come to appreciate during his various visits. The pro-Israel lobby—via the American Israel Public Affairs Committee and the Conference of Presidents of Major American Jewish Organizations—had grown into one of America's most powerful and effective foreign-policy pressure groups, raising money to support congressional races, mobilize the Jewish vote, run think tanks, and publish journals of opinion. There was also a critical mass of independent pro-Israel Jewish government officials, experts, journalists, and public intellectuals. This collective and individual attachment of American Jewry was unimpeachable because of the fundamental convergence of the geo-political interest of the two countries.

The U.S., as the self-proclaimed indispensable power, enabled Israel to pursue a forward policy at the same time as intermittently seeking to restrain it. This inconsistency stemmed from American policy being driven by the calculus of imperial interest—Israel's strategic location, proximity to oil, and military capability—and the reason of domestic politics: the pro-Israel lobby and electorate. The former counted for more than the latter, which, like the oil lobby itself, significantly influenced but did not dictate policy. But by virtue of there being no answering Arab-American—let alone Palestinian-American—lobby, the pro-Israel lobby, in step with Tel Aviv, helped tilt U.S. policy disproportionately away from the Palestinians. But more than tilting was involved. For years successive Israeli governments had stonewalled Washington's efforts to delineate a roadmap and arrange a diplomatic venue for negotiations with the neighboring Arab states, or with the Palestinians. Israel turned down the Rogers Plan (1970), the Reagan Plan (1982), and the Shultz Plan (1987–8). In each instance Tel Aviv enlisted the American pro-Israel lobby to help scuttle the initiative, rather than make constructive counterproposals.

Even before the start of the third intifada, Shultz had sought to include the PLO in negotiations, if need be through the good offices of Jordan. In October 1987 he maintained that "the Palestinians must be involved in the peace process if it is to mean anything." There could be no role, however, "for a people [that] refuses to renounce violence [and] to recognize that Israel is there as a state." After the start of the intifada, in January 1988, Shultz proposed an international conference, to take U.N. Resolutions 242 and 338 as its starting points, with a joint Jordanian–Palestinian delegation representing the Palestinians. The objective was to work out some form of autonomy for the West Bank to be administered, jointly, by Israel and Jordan during a three-year transitional period. Both the PLO and the Israelis refused.

Shultz kept at it, insisting that while "Israelis were free to argue for annexation [and] the Palestinians . . . for independence," the U.S. would "support neither of these positions during negotiations." Presently the intifada changed the parameters for his determined diplomatic effort: King Hussein renounced the West Bank, while Arafat disavowed terror and accepted Resolutions 242 and 338. Just before George Bush Senior succeeded Reagan, and James Baker took over at the State Department, Shultz authorized the start of the dialogue with the PLO. This time, rather than straight-arm Washington outright, Israel proposed instead the election of representatives in the West Bank and Gaza with whom to negotiate an interim autonomy agreement. Impatient with the diplomatic stalemate produced by the intifada, and with a mind to court Washington, in August 1989 Egyptian President Hosni Mubarak put forward a ten-point program that linked the Israeli proposal for elections with "an Israeli commitment to the principle of exchanging land for peace"—anathema to Shamir.

Unmoved by the concessions of Arafat and the intercessions of friendly governments, Israel failed to budge, partly because the intifada had begun to falter. In the first half of 1989 the occupation forces stepped up the repression. Soldiers and policemen more readily used live ammunition, rubber bullets, and tear gas to ward off stone-throwing rebels. The Civil Administration also stepped up punitive house demolitions and arrests, with long prison terms for proven or suspected leaders, many of whom were deported. The rising costs of defying the IDF intensified not only the rivalry between Palestinian pragmatists and zealots but also the persecution of informers and collaborators.

Between George Bush's accession to power and the start of the Iraq crisis, Secretary of State Baker, building on the proposals of Shultz and Mubarak, intensified the search for a framework and agenda for negotiations. His five-point plan of October 1989 assigned an active, but unofficial and limited, role to the PLO in a delegation of non-PLO Palestinians mandated to engage in Israeli–Palestinian discussions. Despite reservations, the PLO accepted—whereas Israel insisted that the PLO be excluded altogether and that no topic be broached other than municipal elections in the territories. As Shamir had declared on the floor of the Knesset on May 17, 1989, "we shall not give the Arabs one inch of our land, even if we have to negotiate for ten years." A few weeks later, he insisted that "settlement in Judea, Samaria, and Gaza will continue," and that no part of "Greater Israel" would be off limits to latter-day Jewish pioneers. "All terror and violence" would have to be stamped out "before any negotiations [could] get under way," Shamir declared, and should these come about, there "will be neither negotiations with the PLO [nor a] Palestinian state in the land of Israel."

Soon the Iraq crisis of 1990 and then the Gulf War of 1991 snapped the thread of diplomatic exploration. In the eyes of many Palestinians, Iraq was the last bastion of militant Arab nationalism: with an army aiming to measure itself against the IDF, Saddam Hussein continued to champion their cause. Vulnerable to pressure from his own intransigents, but also in keeping with a tried if treacherous historical logic, Arafat sided with Iraq. In the era of the First World War the British empire had drawn the borders of Iraq and installed King Feisal; during the Cold War the American empire had supported Saddam Hussein's rise to power in the 1960s and helped him in his war with Iran in the 1980s. Following the end of the Cold War, Washington became the policeman of Iraq's borders even against Hussein himself, before eventually forcing a regime change in Baghdad in 2003. The unspoken objective of both Gulf Wars was the maintenance of an American-controlled status quo in Mesopotamia and the Arabian peninsula, thought to be essential for the stability of the world's largest and richest reserve of oil. In words that Churchill and Balfour, even Clemenceau, would have appreciated, President Bush and other high officials, faced with Hussein's move on Kuwait, asserted that America would resort to war not only to uphold the U.N. charter but to protect its "longstanding vital interests" in the Persian Gulf, among which safe access to oil was primary.

Ingenuously, Arafat set out, together with King Hussein, to mediate an all-Arab solution of the Gulf crisis. The chairman and the king sympathized with the Iraqi leader's crafty if unreal effort to tie the withdrawal of his troops from Kuwait to Israel's withdrawal from the occupied territories and Syria's withdrawal from Lebanon. Needless to say, with the Arab world sharply divided and off balance, they were out of their depth. Some of Arafat's closest associates warned him of the political risk of drawing a moral equivalence between Saddam Hussein's invasion of Kuwait and Israel's occupation of the territories. But the damage was done. Unlike King Hussein, Arafat paid a steep price for his diplomatic misstep. Kuwait expelled some 400,000 Palestinian refugees into Jordan, and along with Saudi Arabia cut off all financial support for the PLO. Mubarak felt affronted by Arafat's going it alone. Even for Western sympathizers, Arafat's steadiness and prestige were tarnished, and the moral capital of the PLO pragmatists fell sharply. The expiring Soviet Union was no longer in a position to support the Arab states, which further weakened the PLO's diplomatic hand. Above all, the effortless defeat of Saddam Hussein by the U.S.-led coalition confirmed America's unchallenge-able hegemony in the greater Middle East.

Immediately after the Gulf War, Secretary Baker resumed his drive to defuse the Arab–Israeli conflict. Saudi Arabia and Syria, which had joined the anti-Iraq coalition, were more disposed to seek a peaceful settlement than before. Tel Aviv remained the obstacle, as hardliners used the forty Iraqi Scud missiles that had struck Israel during the Gulf War as a scare tactic. In 1991, Baker traveled eight times to the Middle East to corral the Arab states, Israel, and the Palestinians into attending a conference in Madrid late in the year. The most proble-matic issue was that of the makeup of the Palestinian delegation: Shamir and his cabinet kept insisting on the exclusion from this delegation of representatives from the PLO, from east Jerusalem, and from exile communities. They successfully pressed Baker to circumscribe the agenda as well, and urged on him the idea of having the negotiations proceed along two parallel tracks and in several phases.

By now the PLO had no weight left to throw around. Even though the search for a PLO-friendly international conference had been driven by the intifada, its subsequent reflux favored Israel, making America's role all the more decisive. Yet a sizable faction of the Palestinian political class advocated agreeing to nothing less than a self-chosen and fully independent PLO delegation. Given the balance of forces, with Arab backing no longer guaranteed, Arafat settled: a joint Jordanian–Palestinian group would include no representatives from the PLO, which nevertheless stood firm in its demand for a sovereign Palestinian state, if necessary preceded by a brief transitional regime of self-governing autonomy.

At long last the U.S. and Russia invited Egypt, Israel, Jordan, Lebanon, Syria, and the Palestinians to meet for three days in Madrid, starting on October 30, 1991. This opening conference, meant to be essentially ceremonial, would be followed by "direct bilateral [as well as] multilateral negotiations." Those "between Israel and Palestinians who are part of the joint Jordanian–Palestinian delegation [would begin] with talks on interim self-government arrangements," to be concluded "within one year." Whatever was agreed upon would "last for a period of five years," with negotiations "on permanent status" to start "beginning the third year" of the interim period. As if to relax what was bound to be a strained atmosphere in the palace of King Juan Carlos I, the invitation mentioned that the conference had "no power to impose solutions on the parties or [to] veto agreements reached by them"; had "no authority to make decisions for the parties"; and could not be reconvened without "the consent of all the parties."

The speeches at the opening sessions were forthright. After affirming "the inadmissibility of the acquisition of territories by force and the right of all states to live in peace and security," Amr Moussa, the Egyptian foreign minister, staked out the basic Arab position: the "legal status of the Palestinian people should not be challenged"; the "West Bank, Gaza, and Golan are occupied Arab territories subject to the full implementation of Security Council Resolution 242"; and the "settlements established in territories occupied since 1967, including Jerusalem, are illegal." Declaring the "Arab–Israeli dispute [to be] in essence an Israeli–Palestinian conflict," he said the "time has come to free the Middle East from sources of tension, weapons of mass destruction, primarily nuclear," so as to free up resources for "development needs, common welfare, and prosperity." Kamil Abu Jabir, the Jordanian foreign minister, recalled that although the "Israelis themselves knew and were aware of our innocence for the crimes against the Jewish people," it was Jordan's fate to "live with, suffer, and contain the powerful forces of extremism" driven by "Israel's indignant outrage." The Palestinians and Jordan "have paid the price . . . of the passions of injured Zionism . . . unleashed by the Nazis and others," and they continue "to pay for the sins of others" in the form of the "brutally created . . . new realities and manufactured facts on the ground." Abu Jabir thought that any future solution should be guided by "the formula of land for peace," which he judged "to ring more meaningfully true than any other principle or slogan." Predictably more strident than his Arab colleagues, Syria's foreign minister, Fariq al-Shara, refused to consider the occasion "a ceremonial event," as the sponsors had framed it. He held Israel's "continuing intransigent position" responsible for the "incalculable dangers" facing the Middle East. The Arabs wanted peace, and "the Jews, and Oriental Jews in particular, know better than anyone that they have lived among Muslim Arabs throughout history wherever they coexisted without suffering any form of persecution or discrimination, either racial or religious." Israel refused to recognize that "peace and the usurpation of the land of others cannot coexist." Al-Shara emphasized that "especially following the Gulf crisis . . . double standards are no longer acceptable . . . and United Nations resolutions, not brute force, have to be applied." Obviously Israel was "not interested in implementing resolutions 242 and 338 on the basis of the principle of land for peace," yet expected to join in "negotiations on economic cooperation" with neighboring states "while perpetuating its occupation of Arab territories"—entirely against the "objective" for which the conference had been convened.

Haydar Abd al-Shafi spoke as leader of the Palestinian delegation. Son of a notable Gaza family and a surgeon, al-Shafi had been a member of the first PLO executive committee. He was twice imprisoned by Israel and deported to Lebanon before founding and presiding over the Palestinian Red Crescent. Respected in all quarters, al-Shafi was a reasoned critic of Arafat's moderate course. His address was both plaint and recrimination. The Palestinian people had for "too long . . . gone unheeded, silenced, and denied," their existence and identity negated for reasons of "political expedience." The intifada was "testimony to their . . . perseverance and resilience" in the face of this "willful blindness." The Palestinian delegation was not a "supplicant" nor was it "seeking. . . an admission of guilt after the fact [or] vengeance for past iniquities." Starting in November 1988 the PLO had launched a "peace initiative," and since then it had "responded positively" to all subsequent "serious" peace moves. Israel had only obstructed them. Al-Shafi pointed to Israel's "illegal and frenzied settlement activity [as] the most glaring evidence of its rejectionism, the latest settlement [having been] erected just two days ago."

Shamir spoke next. He recalled the universal persecution of "homeless" and "defenseless" Jews through the ages: "Some countries tolerated us; others oppressed, tortured, slaughtered, and exiled us." Finally, in "this century . . . the Nazi regime set out to exterminate us." But the prime minister made a special point of stressing that, although the Holocaust had contributed to the "world community [having] recognized our rightful claim to the Land of Israel . . . the rebirth [of Israel] made the world forget that our claim is immemorial." The Jews were "the only people to have lived in the Land of Israel without interruption for nearly 4,000 years . . . and to have had an independent sovereignty" there, with Jerusalem as capital. Having for thousands of years "encouraged each other with the greeting 'Next Year in Jerusalem,' " for Jews "any other country, no matter how hospitable, is still a diaspora, a temporary station on the way home." The unprovoked "Arab hostility" during the refoundation of Israel had not only cost Jewish lives, but also "brought tragic human suffering to the Arab people." In addition to "tens of thousands . . . killed and wounded . . . hundreds of thousands of

[Palestinian] Arabs . . . were encouraged by their own leaders to flee from their homes." Many of these were living "in slums known as refugee camps." Shamir charged the Arab states with using the "plight" of the refugees "as a political weapon against Israel," in the process blocking Israel's "attempts . . . to rehabilitate and house them." In Israel there was "an almost total consensus on the need for peace," though there were differences "on the best way to achieve it." To the contrary, "in most Arab countries the opposite seems to be true," save for differences "over the ways to push Israel into a defenseless position and, ultimately, to destruction." Shamir called on the Arab delegations "to denounce the PLO covenant [of 1968] which called for Israel's destruction" and on the Palestinian Arabs "to renounce violence and terrorism . . . and stop exposing their children to danger by sending them to throw bombs and stones at soldiers and civilians." Claiming that Israel's "pursuit of accommodation and peace was relentless," Shamir took credit for having helped to bring about "today's gathering," which was in keeping with Israel's fixed belief "that only direct, bilateral talks . . . between Israel and its neighbors . . . can bring peace . . . and reach an agreement on interim self-government arrangements with the Palestinian Arabs." He knew that Israel's negotiating partners would "make territorial demands on Israel." They would do so despite the fact that the conflict was not about land, inasmuch as "it raged well before Israel acquired Judea, Samaria, Gaza, and the Golan in a defensive war." Whereas Israel was "a nation of 4 million [and] controlled only 28,000 square kilometers," "the Arab nations, from the Atlantic to the Gulf, number 170 million [and] possess a land mass of 14 million square kilometers." Manifestly "the issue was not territory," but whether Israel should exist at all, and to "focus the talks primarily and exclusively on territory" would be "the quickest way to an impasse."

In exchange for allowing Baker to drag him to Madrid, Shamir had in effect dictated the direction of the conference. The three-day plenary session approved a proposal to proceed along two tracks: multilateral negotiations, to include the twelve European U.N. members, bearing on regional issues like economic development and cooperation, water, the environment, arms control, refugees; and bilateral negotiations to resolve past conflicts and agree on peace terms. The multilateral negotiations were a nonevent. The bilateral talks continued for nearly two years, and ended in a peace treaty between Jordan and Israel. More generally, they meant that Israel had finally gone beyond its talks with Egypt in the 1970s to direct political negotiations with other neighbor states.

Predictably, several Madrid meetings between Israel and the Palestinians—starting on November 3, immediately after the conference—came to nothing, although the October 1991 conference was the first time since 1947–9 that Israelis and Palestinians had met officially face-to-face. Although the Israelis had insisted that the Palestinians from the occupied territories embedded in the Jordanian–Palestinian delegation have no ties to the PLO, half of the twenty-eight-man delegation (which sat separately and acted on their own) were Palestinians whom Arafat had been closely involved in selecting, beginning with al-Shafi. It also included fellow-travelers of the PLO and Fatah, but no one connected with the secular and Islamist radicals, who had denounced the conference. When the Israelis vetoed the inclusion of Faisal Husseini and Hanan Ashwari, a prominent academic and champion of human rights, Arafat appointed them, respectively, coordinator and spokeswoman of the Palestinian delegation. In concert with other members of the PLO present in Madrid, they consulted with its headquarters in Tunis during the conference.

Both Arafat and Shamir were poised to seize the occasion: Arafat to advance the peace process, thereby hastening independence and strengthening the PLO; Shamir to delay or derail negotiations in order to gain time for the expansion of settlements, as well as to pacify or further subjugate the occupied territories. After assuming power in mid 1992, Rabin by and large carried on this policy. That, and frustration with the diplomatic paralysis, continued to stir the embers of the intifada. In late 1992 there was greater violence than at any time since the start of the uprising, with declining economic conditions in the occupied territories adding further fuel. In December, 415 Palestinian militants were expelled into the demilitarized zone in southern Lebanon. By March 1993 the Israeli government decided to seal off the occupied territories, denying Palestinians who didn't live there access to East Jerusalem, and all but closing Israel to Palestinian workers.

Indirectly, Madrid turned out to be a milestone on the circuitous way to Oslo and the White House South Lawn. Strange to say, the impasse of over a dozen rounds of low-level bilateral Israeli–Palestinian negotiations in Washington, along with the renewed flare-up of the intifada, gave a push in that same direction. A confirmed hardliner, Elyakim Rubinstein, chairman of the Israeli delegation, was intractable across the board. During the Madrid discussions al-Shafi, taking issue with the increase in settlement expansion, threatened to resign, only to be dissuaded by his colleagues. But his dissension, along with others, encouraged the opposition to Arafat's moderate course among the Islamist militants in the Palestine National Council, and in Fatah. The members of the Palestinian delegation traveled to Amman in mid 1992 to meet Arafat publicly. Both the State Department and Rabin roundly blamed them for violating the ground-rules regarding contact with the PLO. The Washington negotiations continued to go nowhere.

In Israel, voters weary of their government's unchanging policy of conspicuous occupation and settlement were vindicated by the protracted intifada, while their own worsening economic conditions were now aggravated by the lockout of Palestinian workers. Among officials and the public at large there was growing awareness that ever-rising military expenditures were starving the domestic budget. Elected partly because of this issue, Rabin sought a way out. The disquiet about the military–economic nexus especially heightened his sense of the overwhelming importance of continuing American support, which promised both to dictate and smooth the way for a tactical engagement with the PLO.

Where the stalled negotiations and persistent intifada vexed Rabin, they shook Arafat. The two factors together eroded his political support in the PLO and the territories just when, abandoned by most Arab leaders following the Gulf War, his diplomatic leverage was at its lowest point. In his predicament Arafat too looked to America, though from a pitiful position compared with that of the Israeli prime minister. Rabin would know how to exploit the chairman's vulnerability at the same time as his government was prepared to risk paying the domestic political cost of engaging in direct but circumscribed talks with the PLO.

The talks were arranged through Johan Jorgan Holst, the Norwegian foreign minister, and Terje Roed-Larsen, a Norwegian sociologist. Director of Oslo's Institute of Applied Social Science, and a keen student of the Palestinians' living conditions in the West Bank, Roed-Larsen prepared the terrain with two Israeli academics and Ahmed Qurei (a midlevel PLO official also known as Abu Ala, who would later become prime minister of the Palestinian Authority). Before long, highly secret negotiations got under way in and around Oslo, to run parallel to the all-but-public talks in Washington. With the sanction of his mentor, Foreign Minister Shimon Peres' deputy, Yossi Beilin, headed a small Israeli team in the early stage of what became known as the Oslo negotiations. In May 1993 he was joined by Uri Savir, director-general of the Foreign Ministry, while his Palestinian interlocutors were joined by Mahmoud Abbas of the PLO's Executive Committee. As mutual distrust receded and indications surfaced that the Palestinians might go for a provisional arrangement, the Israelis proposed that the Gaza Strip be ruled as an autonomous region by a Palestinian authority, pending the signing of a final peace treaty, within a period to be specified. Arafat agreed, provided the jurisdiction of the interim government include a symbolic fragment of the West Bank—the town and immediate environs of Jericho, north of the Dead Sea. Israel was willing. There was no settlement colony near this legendary city of 15,000 inhabitants.

The Israelis most probably considered it a sign of weakness that Arafat would accept so little, even though he held fast to his demand for a fully sovereign state in accordance with U.N. resolutions. The Gaza Strip measures 139 square miles (360 square kilometers), with a width ranging between 3.72 and 8.68 miles (6 and 14 kilometers) and a Mediterranean coastline of 24.3 miles (40 kilometers). With a population of over 750,000, nearly half of them refugees, and with arable land making up only 13 per cent of its land area, Gaza was overcrowded, economically barren, politically unruly, and militarily of scant importance to Israel. Lacking Biblical and cultural markers, it had no place in the storehouse of Jewish memory. For some time Israel's leadership had actually been contemplating a withdrawal from Gaza, which was difficult and expensive to police. The problem was less a partisan matter than one of fundamental political calculus: to evacuate Gaza might encourage the cry for a withdrawal from Judea and Samaria—an inflammatory issue where the stakes were perceived to be infinitely higher.

By the summer of 1993 the negotiators had agreed on the broad outlines of an accord, built on the Gaza–Jericho understanding, which would not be made public until August. Presently the members of the Palestinian delegation in Washington, who had been constantly frustrated, were indignant to learn that Arafat had surreptitiously been entertaining far more narrow and forbearing terms. Husseini, Ashwari, and again al-Shafi, came close to resigning. Beyond feeling personally ill-used, they criticized Arafat, intimating that he was "subverting" the intifada by settling for so little, and postponing all fundamental questions regarding Palestinian sovereignty to an indeterminate future.

The preliminary Declaration of Principles, or the Oslo accord, concerning "Interim Self-Government Agreements," was formalized on August 19, 1993, in the Norwegian capital. Validated by Peres and Abbas, it spelled a peace process that, in the form of the "road map" of 2003 sponsored by the so-called Quartet—the U.S., the European Union, Russia, and Great Britain—stumbles along fitfully to this day because it is honored mainly in the breach, especially by the U.S. The

Oslo accord stipulated the withdrawal, in stages, of Israeli forces from the Gaza Strip and the whole of the West Bank, along with the right of Palestinians to self-government in these territories by means of a Palestinian National Authority. This rule would last for an interim period of no more than five years, in the course of which, starting no later than May 1996, a final status agreement would be negotiated. There was no explicit mention of such salient and divisive issues as Jerusalem, boundaries, settlements, and refugees. Israel would grant this authority to govern in phases. Simultaneously the West Bank and Gaza would each be divided into three zones: the first (A—by far the smallest, covering 4 per cent of the land) fully controlled by the Palestinian Authority; the second (B), with Palestinians exercising civil control, and the Israelis military control; the third (C), fully controlled by Israel.

Three weeks later, on September 9, to strengthen the Declaration of Principles, the two parties exchanged letters of joint recognition that entailed mutual acceptance of the principle of partition. "The PLO recognizes the right of the State of Israel to exist in peace and security," Arafat wrote Rabin, with Holst as courier, "and accepts United Nations Security Council Resolutions 242 and 338." Committing the PLO "to the Middle East peace process," Arafat declared that, since the agreement of August 19 inaugurated "a new epoch of peaceful coexistence . . . the PLO renounces the use of terrorism and other acts of violence [and] assumes responsibility over all PLO elements and personnel," in order to secure "their compliance, prevent violations, and discipline violators." In the spirit of the latest false dawn, the Chairman assured Rabin that "those articles of the Palestinian Covenant which deny Israel's right to exist, and the provisions of the Covenant which are inconsistent with the commitments of this letter, are now inoperative and no longer valid." He promised to recommend that the Palestinian National Council "approve these changes." In his covering letter to Holst, Arafat confirmed that the PLO would "encourage and call upon the Palestinian people in the West Bank and Gaza Strip to take part in the steps leading" to the new deal. Rabin answered Arafat, via Holst, within forty-eight hours. His reply consisted of a single sentence:

> I wish to confirm to you that, in light of the PLO commitments included in your letter, the Government of Israel has decided to recognize the PLO as the representative of the Palestinian people and commence negotiations with the PLO within the Middle East peace process.

Given the nature and extent of Arafat's concessions, and the conciliatory tone of his letter, Rabin's letter was wooden and condescending, the correlative of Israel's—and Zionism's—inveterate refusal to bend when it came to the Arab Question. Nevertheless, this exchange of letters concerning the Declaration of Principles marked the first official engagement between the state of Israel and the PLO. But there was still need for a formal start to the peace process—an appearance of good faith expressed publicly by both sides. The U.S. now stepped forward, consistent with its weight with both parties and with its unquestioned hegemony in the region. On September 13, Arafat and Rabin were summoned to seal their understanding on the White House South Lawn in the glare of publicity, with President Clinton officiating. Using a shorthand for what was agreed to in the Declaration of Principles and the epistolary exchange, the president explained that the PLO and Israel had agreed to recognize each other's "natural, legitimate, and political rights."

Arafat had been in the U.S. only once, in 1974, to address the General Assembly in New York. As recently as November 1988 he had been barred as a terrorist from making a second appearance. Alluding to his first visit, when he had figuratively carried both a pistol and an olive branch, this time he had come "with two olive branches." Arafat, now 64 years old, must have been amazed and exhilarated to find himself at the center of such an occasion. In his remarks at the White House, after thanking President Clinton "for sponsoring this historic event," Arafat told the American people that "we share your values of freedom, justice, and human rights, values for which my people have been striving." Once again, there was no reference to Islam or the Koran. He expressed the hope that the Declaration of Principles about to be signed would mark "the beginning of the end of pain and suffering . . . and will usher in an age of peace, coexistence, and equal rights" in the Middle East. The move "toward the final settlement," involving the resolution of "all the issues of Jerusalem, the settlements, the refugees, and the boundaries" would be the "responsibility" not only of Palestinians and Israelis but of "the international community." Arafat welcomed the chance to "address the people of Israel and their leaders, with whom we are meeting today for the first time [to] assure them that the difficult decision we reached together was one that required great and exceptional courage." He wanted them to know that "our people do not consider that exercising the right to self-determination could violate the rights of their neighbors or infringe on their security." To the contrary, to "put an end to their feelings of being wronged and of having suffered an historical injustice is the strongest guarantee for the achievement of coexistence and openness between our two peoples."

Rabin had decided to go to Washington in person only after serious hesitation. His demeanor was of a piece with the letter to Arafat— stilted, wary, and cold. The signing of the Declaration, he began, was "not so easy—neither for myself, as a soldier in Israel's wars, nor for the people of Israel, nor to the Jewish people in the diaspora, who are watching us with great hope, mixed with apprehension." It was "certainly not easy for the families of the victims of violence, terror, and war, whose pain will never heal [nor] for the many thousands who defended our lives . . . and even sacrificed their lives for our own," and for whom "this ceremony has come too late." He stressed that he had "come from Jerusalem, the ancient and eternal capital of the Jewish people," and represented "an anguished and grieving land" that had "not known a single year . . . or month in which mothers have not wept for their sons." Turning more directly to the Palestinians, Rabin said he spoke in the name of "soldiers who have returned from battle stained with blood [and] have seen our relatives and friends killed before our eyes." He said to all listening, "in a loud and clear voice: enough of blood and tears," especially since "we are destined to live together, on the same soil in the same land." With "no desire for vengeance . . . harbor[ing] no hatred toward you . . . let us pray that a day will come when we will say, enough, farewell to arms."

Rabin's peroration was frankly religious. Claiming that "our strength, our higher moral values, have been derived for thousands of years from the Book of Books," he quoted Ecclesiastes: "To every thing there is a season . . . A time to kill, and a time to heal . . . A time of war, and a time of peace." At the time of Rosh Hashanah, with "the Jewish people celebrating the beginning of a new year," Rabin proposed to "pray that the New Year will bring a message of redemption for all peoples [and] a good year for Israelis and Palestinians [as well as] for all the peoples of the Middle East." In conclusion, Rabin invited the close to 3,000 officials and guests assembled in the Rose Garden to join him in the "Jewish tradition" of saying "Amen" upon completing his recitation of the closing words of the daily prayer recited by Jews: "May He who makes peace in His high heavens grant peace to us and to all Israel. Amen." With that "us," he had effectively compelled all present— including Arafat and the Palestinians, ten foreign ministers, two former presidents (Carter and Bush), eight former secretaries of state, and several national security advisers—to bless only the Jews.

There was no prearranged ending to the ceremony—certainly not the handshake between Arafat and Rabin seen round the world, with

Clinton hovering over them. Throughout the proceedings the Chairman had appeared genial and at ease, while the prime minister had pointedly shunned him. Finally, Arafat advanced toward Rabin and artlessly extended his hand. Rabin held back, then took it grudgingly, after what appeared to be a prompt from Clinton. The Israelis present followed their leader's decorum and avoided the Palestinians. This reserve also pervaded the vote in the Knesset on September 23: after a heated debate it ratified the Declaration of Principles, including the coming withdrawal from Gaza and Jericho, with sixty-one in favor, fifty opposed, and eight abstentions. Although the PLO's Executive Committee was split down the middle, the vote in the Central Council, on October 12, was considerably more decisive: sixty yeas, eight nays, and three abstentions. According to a contemporary opinion survey, the Palestinians of the occupied territories were in rough accord: 67 per cent were for, 30 per cent against. Less reassuringly for Arafat—and for Rabin—the same poll showed that some 17 per cent of Palestinians favored Islamist groups over the PLO, a significant increase from 10 years previously.

In light of Zionist and Israeli policy since 1987, it took an enormous leap of faith for Arafat to assume that within five years, counting from Israel's instant withdrawal from Gaza and Jericho, a "permanent settlement" based on Resolutions 242 and 338 could be brought to a happy end. While during the White House ceremony Arafat (and Abbas) had specifically referred to the core issues that Oslo had left for final status talks, Rabin and Peres kept clear of them. In exchange for a mere promise, without any guarantee, of self-determination and a sovereign state, the PLO extended unconditional recognition of Israel—its only bargaining chip of any real value, except for the threat of another intifada.

The historic compromise-in-the-making symbolized by the famous handshake was fiercely skewed. The PLO had conceded to Israel 78 per cent of the expanse of historical Palestine, including more than two-thirds of Jerusalem. But while the Palestinians were waiting to come into 22 per cent of the land, Israel remained in full control of practically all of it. The expansion of settlements, the confiscation of property, and the construction of bypass roads and military installations proceeded apace. The number of settlers in the occupied territories rose from 106,000 in 1992 to 150,000 in 1996. True, Rabin and Peres, unlike Begin and Shamir, agreed that the empowerment of the Palestinians should also be territorial. But they thought in terms not of an independent, sovereign, and contiguous Palestinian state, as Arafat did, but of some sort of autonomous polity subordinated militarily and economically to Israel.

The persistence, after Oslo, of the settlement drive was part of this design, continuous with that conceived immediately after 1967. In other words, starting with Rabin, Israel's chronic equivocations and delays in the establishment of the interim self-governing authority and the advance to permanent status negotiations were not circumstantial, but systematic. And they provided Palestinian extremists with all the incentive in the world to sabotage Oslo and Arafat together. Their continued commando actions in turn motivated Likud to attack Labor, and encouraged extremist settlers to launch their own vigilante raids, hoping both to foil negotiations and bring down Rabin. His calculated irresolution, then, sowed the wind that became the whirlwind that blew the peace camp to kingdom come.

Unmindful, however, of the political consequences in the Palestinian camp and the Arab–Muslim world generally, and as usual cocksure of Israel's military, economic, and technical superiority, its leaders counted on Arafat's weak hand. Their plan was to lull and outwit the PLO's middle-of-the-road leadership while extending indirect rule in the occupied territories with the help of Palestinian collaborators, whose numbers they expected would increase. But this was grossly to underestimate the vigilance and impatience of the PFLP and the DFLP, of Hamas and Islamic Jihad—not to mention that of the population itself. By conceding so little so reluctantly and ungraciously, the Israelis forced this hardening and expansion of opposition, which continued to trade on deteriorating social and economic conditions in the occupied territories.

8

THE WAGES OF HUBRIS

Oslo and the Declaration of Principles, which were heralded with the flourish of trumpets on the White House lawn, gave rise to the illusion of imminent peace. The Palestinians naïvely expected the occupation regime to soften and the prisoners in Israeli jails to be released. They also took it for granted that neither side would spare any effort to work out and implement the two-phase road map: first Gaza–Jericho, then final status. The Oslo agreement was more process and timetable than substance, but as Israel's leaders were in no hurry to quit Gaza and Jericho, they were mostly to blame for the six-year delay, from mid 1996 to mid 2002, in the start of the final status negotiations.

Israel stalled because of a de facto consensus on the Palestinian Question between the political caste and the far right, which agitated rabidly against Oslo. Shlomo Goren spoke for the religious Zionists. Chief rabbi of the IDF for over twenty years, in 1967 he had conspicuously heralded the Jewish people's return to the Wailing Wall in Jerusalem and the Cave of the Patriarchs in Hebron. He was also a prominent advocate of the destruction of the mosques on the Temple Mount. Having left the army in 1972, he became Israel's chief Ashkenazi rabbi for ten years. Fiercely hostile to Oslo and the PLO, in 1993, as a retired but respected Orthodox religious oracle, Goren held that soldiers had the right to disobey orders to dismantle settlements in the occupied territories, and suggested that Arafat should be "eliminated" for "belonging to the world of death." The plan for Palestinian autonomy was "satanic" for portending "the destruction of Israel and the creation of a Palestinian state governed by the chief of the PLO terrorists." Such virulent negations articulated what was implicit in Likud's seemingly more reasonable position.

In the Palestinian camp, except in Arafat's inner circle, there was a strong belief that, notwithstanding all the fanfare, Oslo was a grossly inequitable blueprint for peace, and a case of the all-powerful victor laying down humiliating terms to the vanquished. In short, the secular and Islamist radicals accused Arafat of a treacherous surrender. Al-Shafi's disavowal of Oslo and spurning of the White House ceremony showed that this view was not confined to the world of the extremists. The criticism multiplied once it became clear that Israel would now go all out to extirpate the resistance, which it continued to stigmatize as terrorist. Since, under the Declaration of Principles, the PLO was answerable for all Palestinian violence, the Israelis demanded that Arafat repress "his" terrorists.

Negotiations for an interim regime of self-rule in Gaza and Jericho began shortly after the White House ceremony—and soon nearly foundered over three issues: control over border crossings, the size of the Jericho enclave, and protection of the settlements in the Gaza Strip. The Israelis dragged their feet on all three questions. On November 25, 1993, Rabin warned that, unless Israel's security concerns were met, its troops would not respect the agreed schedule for withdrawal, which was set to begin on December 13 and to be completed four months later. Barring an agreement on the "delimitation of the Jericho zone to be evacuated, the protection of the Jewish colonies, and the control of the borders with Egypt and Jordan . . . all dates would cease to be sacred, whether December 13, 1993, or April 13, 1994." Disregarding the anemic protests of Arafat, Rabin had his way. Unless and until challenged by either the U.S. or the Palestinian resistance, Israel could set the tone and pace. Arafat, convinced that Rabin had played him false, was reduced to licking his wounds, as the withering critique of Arafat and Oslo by the secular and religious militants resonated increasingly among ordinary Palestinians.

In Israel, meanwhile, Rabin did nothing to generate popular support for the process, and peace activists took advantage of the listlessness of the Oslo process to step up their attack on the Labor government. But on February 25, 1994, halfway between the two framing withdrawal deadlines, Israel and the Arab world were shaken by the Hebron massacre. In the Muslim calendar, that Friday was the second fasting day of Ramadan. For Jews it was Purim, celebrating their deliverance from Haman's massacre in the sixth century BC. Hebron was sacrosanct to Muslims and Jews for being home to the Tomb of the Patriarchs, the presumed burial site of Abraham, Isaac, Jacob, and their wives. Jews had lived in Hebron through the centuries until 1928–9, when many of them were killed and wounded during the first intifada (1929), which had triggered the dispersion of their community. They had returned to Hebron after 1967. Most of the 400 new settlers were ultra-orthodox and far to the right. They established their principal colony at Qiryat Arba, south of Hebron, on a hilltop overlooking the city. A number of extreme militants were among its members, most of them followers of Rabbi Meier Kahane, the American-born founder of Kach. He was a member of the Knesset from 1984 to 1988, when the courts barred him from standing for reelection. The settlers of Qiryat Arba were religiously-inspired enemies of the Rabin government.

A Brooklyn native, Kahane disciple, and resident of Qiryat Arba, Dr. Baruch Goldstein claimed he felt a religious calling to stop the Oslo negotiations. The fated Friday morning he burst into the Ibrahim Mosque, where some 500 worshippers were at prayer. With his army-issue assault rifle he began firing at point-blank range, killing twenty-three Arab Muslims and wounding over 120 before he was over-powered and bludgeoned to death by the congregants.

Once again the classic combustibles of politics and religion threatened a crisis. Rabin hastened to express his condolences to Arafat, then balked when several cabinet members urged the removal of the settlers from the city of the Patriarchs. Rabin reminded them that, under the Oslo accords, the question was one for the final status talks. The PLO broke off all negotiations and called for the evacuation of all Israelis from Hebron. The radicals felt vindicated in their refusal of Oslo and their mistrust of Rabin. Throughout the territories the IDF put down demonstrations by Palestinians who poured into the streets to protest against the massacre—and con-tinued to turn a blind eye to outrages committed by settlers. These were exempt from the curfew imposed in Hebron, while the Pales-tinians paid the price of the emergency closure of the West Bank and Gaza Strip.

Hamas, breathing vengeance, chose this moment to launch a series of terrorist strikes against Israeli civilians. The opening salvo was the blowing-up, in April 1994, of two buses in northern Israel, killing fifteen and wounding seventy. By the end of the year that toll had doubled. This new violence served Rabin as an excuse to continue temporizing, and provided ammunition for his right-wing critics. Henceforth Hamas was in the line of fire of the security forces of both Israel and the embryonic Palestinian National Authority, head-quartered in Gaza. But since Oslo had brought few, if any, peace dividends, and with Israeli forces still killing countless civilians during their search and destroy operations, Hamas gained popular support. It also benefited from the martyr status of Sheikh Ahmed Yassin, held in an Israeli jail since 1984. Even assuming Arafat had wanted to go against Hamas and Yassin, such a task was way beyond his power. Besides, had he tried to do so he would have undercut the social base of the PLO and Fatah by appearing once again to truckle to Israel, with nothing to show for it.

On May 4, 1994, after eight months of acrimony, the Gaza–Jericho Autonomy Agreement, or Oslo I, was finally signed in Cairo. It stipulated that Israel would withdraw its military forces from the Gaza Strip and the Jericho Area within three weeks, and would transfer the authority of its Civil Administration to a Palestinian National Authority. Composed of twenty-four PLO-appointed members, this ambiguous polity would exercise all legislative and executive powers, and assume broad judicial functions. It would also create a constabulary of 9,000 men to enforce law and order. Beyond that, the PNA's powers were essentially limited to the civil sphere of education and culture, social welfare, tourism, health, and taxation.

Israel ceded far less power than it kept for itself, retaining exclusive control of all settlements, military installations, bypass roads, and border crossings. Given the undiminished and growing importance of the settlers' domain, these security arrangements were the most problematic part of the Gaza–Jericho Agreement: forces would not really be withdrawn after all. The Jews in Gaza were less than 1 per cent of the population, entrenched among over 800,000 Palestinians, yet their fifteen colonies occupied 30 per cent of the territory and coastline, and consumed 40 per cent of its soft water. The settlements in both enclaves, linked to Israel by corridors, would require constant military protection.

Arafat knew the agreement was pitifully skewed against the Palestinians, but strained to put the best face on it. At last his people had the embryo of a state, complete with the customary badges of sovereignty: flag, postage stamps, passport, and currency pointed beyond mere autonomy. Long suspicious of Arafat's stratagem, Likud and Israel's far right lambasted these concessions as so many steps to perdition. From a broad front of Islamist and international critics came the opposite charge: Arafat and the PLO had capitulated in Cairo as they had in Oslo and Washington. The moral prestige of their cause had been thrown away on the Declaration of Principles—which amounted to what, in the end? The Palestinian hardliners concluded that, in the boast of one Israeli official, whereas the Israelis "got control," the Palestinians "got the symbols." Worse, the Palestinian Authority was sworn to enforce order and security, understood by Rabin to mean the repression of all anti-Israeli violence. Any movement to extend the autonomous territory and advance toward final status negotiations was made contingent on the rigorous fulfillment of this impossible charge—meaning that the Authority was put on de facto probation for the five-year interim period.

The autonomy agreement gave Arafat and his associates leave to move to the "liberated" territory to set up the Palestinian National Authority. On July 1, 1994, in a long line of cars, they crossed the border into the would-be homeland from Egypt at Rafah, the southern tip of the Gaza Strip. Despite the secular and religious opposition— Hamas denounced the return as a "humiliating submission before the enemy government"; the Palestine Popular Struggle Front said it took place "under the canopy of the Zionist occupation"; and the PFLP General Command called it a "Sadatist visit"—along the road and in the streets of Gaza City, Arafat was greeted with wild jubilation. Some 80,000 people gathered in the central Square of the Unknown Soldiers to mark the occasion. Though critics of Oslo, Ashwari and al-Shafi figured prominently among the notables gathered on the platform from which the Chairman addressed the crowd. Even in this moment of exultation he put unity in the foreground. "We are here today," he began, "to tell Ahmed Yassin that we will not rest or be silent until you are with us, by our side, here." He honored, too, the other political prisoners, the Palestinian casualties of the intifada, and the stone-throwing youth. Recalling the martyrs of Hebron, Arafat pledged to pray for all Palestinian martyrs in Jerusalem. He appealed to the Israeli public to recognize the reality of Jerusalem as a holy site for Muslims, Jews, and Christians, and to "support Rabin" in making progress on the road to peace. Whatever the difficulties ahead, he was "sure that with the cooperation and in coordination with our neigh- bors the Israelis, we will have the ability to protect the peace of the brave and to implement accurately and honestly what has been approved."

On July 2 Arafat traveled northeast, to Jabalya, the Gaza Strip's largest refugee camp. Oslo I had marked the subsidence rather than the extinction of the third intifada, without which Oslo itself would not have been possible. The uprising had begun in Jabalya, and he went to assure a crowd that he was "proud to be in the birthplace of the intifada." He had come there to "speak frankly," as if to admit the shortfall of Oslo: "The accord may not please some of you, but it is the best deal we could get under existing circumstances in the interna- tional community and the Arab world." The following day Arafat went by helicopter to Jericho, flying over Israel and the West Bank rather than traveling by land. The idea of his passing through Israel and possibly stopping for prayer at the al-Aqsa Mosque was no doubt unthinkable to most Israelis.

Though Oslo I was in reality a triumph for Israel, the secular hardliners denounced the idea of land for peace along with its perpetrators: reviled for dealing with an "assassin" and a "terrorist organization," Rabin was charged with "treason." A committee of settlers looked ahead to the day when "Jews would cease to dance the macabre dance, known as the peace process, and bring the peace criminals to justice."

Once it set about the business of governing, the PNA faced a redoubtable task, which was complicated rather than facilitated by the Israeli government—and with full intent. Ever more settlements were planted along the West Bank border and around Jerusalem, keeping Judea and Samaria fragmented into isolated cantons. This push was consistent with the strategy of continued territorial control, which included the effort to foil Palestinian economic autonomy. Gaza had scarcely any to begin with, and now it was further wasted by the cost of the intifada and the burden of the refugees, half of them under 18. Unemployment was rife, and the GNP and wages, even for Gazans working in Israel, were in free-fall. All the occupied territories remained utterly dependent on the Israeli economy and on foreign aid. This culture of poverty was all the more galling for its stark contrast with the transparently easier circumstances in Israel and the settlements.

Another grievance was the almost daily vexation of Israeli domination, connected with the war against the resistance but visited on the entire population: indiscriminate detentions, house demolitions, and assaults by settlers. Border closures aggravated economic conditions by shriveling wages earned in Israel, which accounted for more than 30 per cent of Gaza's GNP. Delays and harassment at the checkpoints rubbed salt into wounds of morale. Despite the lift following Arafat's triumphal return to Gaza, within two weeks a "bread intifada" broke out at Eretz, the main northern checkpoint between Gaza and Israel. When workers grew agitated over debasing searches and a lengthy queue that had been forming since before dawn, the Israeli guards simply cut off that day's crossing. In the ensuing melee an Israeli soldier killed three Gazans, and Palestinian policemen killed an Israeli guard. To this kind of methodical, daily indignity, the Palestinian workforce responded with a predictable increase in resentment and unrest.

Between 1992 and 1995, under Rabin's government, the number of settlers in Gaza and the West Bank rose by 50 per cent, from 100,000 to 150,000, not counting the increasing number of settlers in East Jerusalem. These years also saw a considerable expansion of the network of exclusive expressways, bypass roads, and military checkpoints, all three of which furthered the Israeli control and fragmentation of the territories. Arafat was expected to work for peace from within a small and divided fiefdom that was now quaking with anger. He was caught between the unbending Israelis and the Islamists, particularly Hamas militants, backstopped by the secular radicals, who could feed continuously on the disillusionment and hardships of Palestinians throughout the territories. By the fall of 1994 there was a surge in terrorist attacks. On October 9 two Palestinian militants opened fire indiscriminately in a bustling pedestrian mall in Jerusalem, killing two and injuring fifteen. Two days later Hamas operatives abducted an Israeli soldier near Tel Aviv airport and threatened to kill him unless Israel released Sheikh Yassin, along with 200 other political prisoners. A week after that, a suicide bomber blew apart a bus in the center of Tel Aviv, killing twenty-two passengers and wounding twice as many. In November an Islamic Jihad suicide bomber blew himself up at the army post outside the Netzarim settlement south of Gaza City, killing three Israeli officers and injuring eleven, including several Palestinian bystanders. On December 25 a member of the Palestinian Authority's police force did the same at a Jerusalem bus station, wounding twelve. A month later, two Islamic Jihad militants killed twenty-one Israelis, mostly soldiers, at the Beit Lid crossing southeast of the West Bank town of Tulkarm.

Tensions rose between the Palestinian Authority and the intransigents; Arafat repeatedly imposed curfews in Gaza. In a fiery speech in Gaza City's packed Yarmuk Stadium, interrupted by catcalls, he denounced those seeking to "wreck the peace" at the same time as he called for the liberation of Yassin and all Palestinian prisoners. But Arafat did not limit himself to verbal scolding and disciplinary gestures. On November 17, 1994, in an assault on a Gaza mosque, his security forces killed fourteen and wounded about 100 suspected supporters of Hamas.

In the meantime Israel pursued the bilateral track of the peace process, most earnestly with Jordan. Tel Aviv and Amman had a Palestinian problem in common, and their leaders found it easier to negotiate with each other than to deal with Arafat. With a huge Palestinian population and a long border with the West Bank, Jordan could not stay on the sidelines. King Hussein felt threatened by the likely emergence of some form of sovereign Palestinian entity, with the West Bank as its center of gravity. The prospect of a Jordanian–Palestinian confederation, championed widely for so many years, became an ever less plausible historical possibility. On both sides of the Jordan River, few if any Palestinians favored giving the Hashemite dynasty yet another chance at reaching for Cisjordania.

Without oil or other natural resources, Jordan was nearly as much of an economic wasteland as the Gaza Strip: of its total population of 2.8 million, half were Palestinian refugees and one-third hovered between bare survival and destitution. Following the Soviet collapse and the Gulf War, Jordan, like Egypt, looked to the U.S. for aid, and sought an accommodation with Israel. Both regimes stood against the spread of Islamism, and aspired to mediate between the Western world, including Israel, and the Arab–Muslim world, in which Cairo remained the regional heavyweight.

In keeping with a long tradition dating back to the Yishuv, in mid 1994 Rabin and Hussein held several secret meetings. On July 24 they met in Washington to sign, under President Clinton's aegis, a declaration ending a nearly forty-six-year state of war, and promising promptly and fully to normalize relations between their two countries. By October 26, the premier and the king shook hands publicly on a peace treaty at the Araya border crossing in the Wadi Araba desert. Israel wanted an agreement with Jordan comparable to the one it enjoyed with Egypt. For Jordan, however, the central issue was not territorial. After Oslo, Hussein looked to refigure Jordan's place in America's new co-prosperity sphere in the Middle East. But any adjustment would have to be accompanied by a firm understanding that Jordan was neither Palestine nor the ultimate dumping ground for Palestinians. In addition, acutely conscious of his country's economic fragility, Hussein wanted assurances that the PLO and the U.S. would recognize Jordan's privileged economic ties with the West Bank. As well as the issue of the Jordan and Yarmuk rivers, this meant banking and trade, of which Hussein sought an enlarged share. Above all, remembering Sadat's calculus on his way to Camp David, Hussein sought U.S. debt relief and economic assistance.

Israel had its own stratagem: to make Jerusalem a bone of contention between Amman and the PLO. Rabin of course intended to keep the capital undivided: there would be no yielding the eastern part of the Holy City as the capital of a future Palestinian state. Instead, Israel now recognized Jordan's "special role" as administrator, custodian, and sponsor of Jerusalem's Muslim holy sites. Since 1967—while clinging to the hope that Cisjordania, with East Jerusalem, would eventually revert to Jordan—King Hussein had paid the salaries of the clerics and staff of the Jerusalem mosques and underwritten the renovation of the Mosque of Omar.

Accusing Jordan of complicity in denying the Palestinians control of the eastern part of the city, contrary to Oslo, Arafat launched an impossible diplomatic and political attack on this clause of the July

Washington declaration. The Palestinian Authority declared all employees of the holy sites in the occupied territories, including Jerusalem, to be "under its jurisdiction." On October 26, 1994, some 1 million Palestinians in the West Bank and East Jerusalem joined in a strike and observed a "day of mourning" to protest against the treaty between Israel and Jordan. King Hussein stood his ground, although at the Islamic summit in Casablanca in mid December he held out the airy promise that he would yield protection of the holy places to the PLO as soon as it exercised "territorial rule in East Jerusalem." Jordan's political class more than suspected that there was no pacifying the Middle East without an equitable resolution of the Israeli–Palestinian conflict; only a minority of the 1.4 million refugees cursed Hussein outright for bending the knee to Israel. The general unease, however, was reflected in Jordan's parliamentary vote on the peace treaty that November: against fifty-five yeas there were twenty-three nays and two abstentions.

By contrast, the Knesset approved it overwhelmingly, by a vote of 105 to 3, with 6 abstentions. The entire political establishment and electorate welcomed an agreement compatible with Israel's policy of consolidating "facts on the ground." Relations with Jordan had been "Egyptianized" without cost or risk. That Rabin's cabinet meant to press on was confirmed in late April 1995, when it approved the largest confiscation of Arab land in fifteen years for the construction of 2,500 housing units on a hill in southeastern Jerusalem known in Arabic as Jabal Abu Ghueim, about to be renamed Har Homa. The objective was to tighten the ring around the city's southern edge, to eliminate any geographic link between the Old City's Arab Palestinian population and the P.A.-controlled West Bank, in the process dashing Arafat's hope for a capital in East Jerusalem. This decision foreshadowed the next decade of accelerated construction of housing units, and the increase of settlers in and around an expanding, united Jerusalem. Rabin and all his successors ignored the protests of Arafat and the Arab world, the censures of the U.N., and the caveats of Washington. Domestically, except for the emphatic but inconsequential dissent of Peace Now, there was near-universal public support for staking the eternal claim.

On September 28, again under Clinton's auspices, Rabin and Arafat signed the Oslo II interim agreement in Washington. Marking the end of the first stage of Palestinian autonomy, this accord extended self-rule to additional sectors of the West Bank for a period not to exceed five years. Oslo II again marked the subdivision of the West Bank into three zones with different ratios of Israeli and Palestinian jurisdiction.

In Zone A, which comprised seven major Palestinian cities and their environs—Jenin, Qalqilia, Tulkarm, Nablus, Ramallah, Bethlehem, and Hebron—the Palestinian Authority was slated to assume full responsibility for civil affairs, internal security, and public order. Zone B embraced the other 450 towns and villages (except several refugee camps) of the West Bank, in which Israel would exercise "overriding security responsibility" in a diarchic administration. Zone C covered the sparsely populated areas, inclusive of all settlements, military bases, public lands, and strategic roads, over which Israel retained full security and nearly all civil control.

Oslo II thus replicated the inequities of Oslo I and earlier agreements. Rabin yielded full and partial control, respectively, over only about 3 per cent and 25 per cent of the territory, with a combined population of over 1 million Arabs, while retaining over 70 per cent of the territory. That portion counted about 140,000 Jewish settlers, or almost half of the 300,000 Israelis living in the territories occupied in 1967, the other half clustering in the Arab–Palestinian neighborhoods annexed to Jerusalem since then. In Zone A, Hebron, City of the Patriarchs, was never in fact given over to the Palestinian Authority: with some 450 settlers ensconced among 100,000-plus Palestinians, Israel retained all but complete control. Although Oslo II allowed for "safe passage" for Palestinians traveling between the West Bank and Gaza, it also specified that the provision "shall not prejudice Israel's right, for reasons of security and safety, to close the crossing points to Israel and to prohibit or limit the entry into Israel of persons and vehicles from the West Bank and Gaza." By empowering the Palestinian Authority to maintain order and combat terrorism in Zone A, Oslo II made the PLO a handmaiden in the enforcement of a status quo favorable to Israel.

The Interim Agreement of September 1995, like that of July 1994, made only minimal concessions to the PLO, and mostly met Israel's concerns. Essentially dictated by Tel Aviv, it fortified Jerusalem with further satellite blocs, and formalized settlements within the post-1967 borders. In other words, Oslo II cemented the foundations of Greater Israel. Yet throughout the West the media, and simple-minded purveyors of hope, celebrated Oslo II as a just historic compromise: Israel was said to have ceded control of most of the Biblical West Bank to the Palestinians as an additional step toward a sovereign state. Even in public, however, Rabin and his associates played down this latest, far from final, installment in an indeterminate peace process: they were concerned with how extravagant readings of it would affect the rightist opposition.

Far from being a mentally deranged loner, Yigal Amir was a Jewish fundamentalist embedded in a broad syncretic movement of extreme Zionism—both secular and religious—that enjoyed long established ties with kindred political parties. His act grew out of a campaign of anti-Oslo demonstrations increasingly trained on Rabin. Incitement to manhandle the "peace criminals," of whom Rabin and Peres were deemed the worst, was orchestrated by such leading figures of the Likud as Benjamin Netanyahu and Ariel Sharon. It was they and their confederates who encouraged this *fronde* by embracing its cause in the media and at mass meetings. They were seconded by cabals of West Bank settlers and Orthodox rabbis. *Hashavna* (The Week), a leading ultra-Orthodox paper, carried an interview with Sharon denouncing the government's policy as more abject than Marshal Pétain's during the Second World War. In the summer of 1995, when the assault on Oslo began to reach a crescendo, *Hashavna* charged Rabin and Peres with "leading the state of Israel and its citizens to annihilation," and cried for them to be hauled "before a firing squad," for which certain Orthodox rabbis provided a religious sanction. On the eve of Rabin's murder, the weekly predicted that "the day will come when the Israeli public will bring Rabin and Peres before a court" that would decide between sending them to "the gallows or an insane asylum." Sharon was no more delicate. Writing in June, he accused members and followers of Peace Now of being "spiritually closer to PLO murderers than to [the settlers] of Judea–Samaria and Gaza." By September, he was deriding the idea that the threats against Rabin were serious:

> Perhaps [the perceived danger] is the paranoia of leaders in decline. One mustn't compare, but does anyone remember the blood libels of Stalin, through which he carried out the 'great purges'? He wiped out the old leadership and the top brass of the Red Army, he liquidated Jewish men of letters. It all began then with 'news reports' or 'assessments' about supposed intentions to assassinate the tyrant . . . Where are they leading us with the new libel they are spreading?

Those in the U.S. from similar far-right and Orthodox circles, who plied their Israeli counterparts with ideas and money, mounted a similar campaign, treating the Labor leaders as traitors and calling for their removal. Rabbi Mordechai Friedman of Brooklyn, president of the American Board of Orthodox Rabbis, imprecated Rabin and Peres for "persecuting" the settlers and turning the IDF into an "ultra-radical, left-wing . . . militia." In Israel, this same tone spilled into the streets of Tel Aviv and Jerusalem; at public protests the ultra-right and ultra-Orthodox crowds reviled Rabin, the designated demon of Oslo. The prime minister was a "traitor," "assassin," and "Arafat's henchman," who followed in "Hitler's footsteps." By participating in these rhetorical autos-da-fé, prominent political leaders condoned even the worst excesses. This was only too evident on October 5, at a mass rally in central Jerusalem: two future prime ministers (Netanyahu and Sharon) and one future president (Moshe Katsav) spoke as fellow true believers, not in the idiom of a loyal opposition. By now they felt at home in a crowd that held aloft posters and distributed leaflets picturing Rabin in the uniform of an SS officer, or wearing Arafat's trademark kaffiyeh.

Rabin had to have been aware of this opposition to the supposed peace process, of which the crowds were but a token. Polling data suggest that a large majority was reluctant, if not hostile, with less than 20 per cent explicitly favorable. Rabin was taunted in public. Yet, curiously, he and his ministers did little to sell their overall plan. Perhaps they were inhibited by their own lack of candor. Rabin knew perfectly well that Oslo II did not match its buildup in the minds of the doves and their sympathizers who, despite their lack of clout, kept hoping against hope. Politically unsteady, the government also failed to counter the hard right-wingers (who went on taking advantage of its equivocation), a task complicated by their being wrapped in both flag and prayer shawl. Labor, like Likud, had long played along with the religious element in Israel's founding myth and civil religion, and for the same instrumental reasons. In 1967 Rabin himself had hailed the capture of the Holy City in Biblical terms, intoning the vow of an eternal and unified Jerusalem that became policy.

As the political climate deteriorated, Rabin was rumored to be considering changes in the Oslo timetable and in the phases leading to complete withdrawal. He was also seeking ways to shore up his popular support on the left of the political spectrum. On November 1, in a television interview, he sought to rebut his fiercest critics by asserting that, "as a partner in the process of reconciliation Arafat . . . is putting an end to terrorist attacks." Untypically, Rabin cited the cleavages in the Palestinian camp, insisting that "Hamas and the Islamic Jihad" were the chief perpetrators of anti-Israeli terror. Three days later, over 100,000 doves gathered for a rally in Tel Aviv's Melchai-Israel Square. The scurrilous assault of the far right, supported by Likud, had galvanized leftists and centrists to make a stand. Apparently on the initiative of Shlomo Lahat, ex-mayor of Tel Aviv, the crowd had been drawn from Peace Now, Meretz, and Labor.

Unexpectedly, Rabin and Peres turned up at the rally to mix with a crowd that was not theirs. Rabin stepped to the podium to make some improvised remarks. As a long-time "military man . . . who fought so long as there was no chance for peace," he felt that now there was a "great chance" to achieve it. He commended those who had come "to demonstrate, together with many others who [had] not come [for] desiring peace and opposing violence," also because "violence erodes the basis of Israeli democracy." To those "trying to hurt us" by "torpedo[ing] the peace process," Rabin wanted to say, "bluntly, that we have found a partner for peace among the Palestinians as well"— the PLO—which had "ceased to engage in terrorism." His government would "demand that they do their part for peace, just as we will do our part . . . in order to solve this most complicated, prolonged, and emotionally charged aspect of the Israeli–Arab conflict: the Palestinian–Israeli conflict."

Shortly after concluding his seemingly forthright, if expedient statement, at about 9.45pm, Rabin walked through a passageway to his car, where Yigal Amir fired his two deadly bullets. A 27-year-old law student of Yemeni origin, Amir had come out of the same milieu of settlers as Baruch Goldstein, whose funeral he had attended. Arrested on the spot, Amir told police he had planned his deed for some time, and had "acted alone, on God's order." Subsequently he told prosecutors that he had meant to put a stop to any further surrender of "our land to the Arabs," and to all Arab–Israeli negotiations.

As acting premier, Peres proposed to hold Rabin's course, which the two had jointly charted. Although the assassination was cheered in several West Bank settlements, overall the Israeli citizenry was shaken and shamed, provoking a small upswing of support for Labor. But the appearance of an even divide between Labor and Likud was momentary, and the center-right consensus held: yield no more than an absolute minimum to the Palestinians, and do so at the slowest pace and with maximum chicanery. Israeli officials, regardless of party colors, acted with scant wisdom but consummate cunning, always with the tacit aim of gaining time to maximize "facts on the ground." The left-of-center flank—Meretz and Peace Now—was no match for Shas, the National Religious Party, and the newly formed Yisrael Ba'aliya, the party headed by former Soviet dissident Natan Sharansky, representing immigrants from the former USSR. In Israel's multi-party system the assorted religious parties and the ultra-nationalists were in a position to make or break governments of any stripe— Likud, Labor, or National Unity.

Of the two major parties, Labor was now the least coherent. Given the rightist and religious groundswell since 1967, and fearful of losing its centrist constituencies, it sought not to be perceived as leftist or radical. While claiming Ben-Gurion as its tutelary guide, it disguised its lineage to Mapai and Histadrut, let alone Mapam. Rabin had stolen a march on Peres largely by virtue of his military prestige in a country obsessed with security. Soon Barak, casting himself in Rabin's likeness, even changed his party's name from Labor to "One Israel"— though it never caught on. Laborites were hardliners, though on certain issues some displayed an intermittent flexibility; the party spoke more softly than Likud, but it carried as big a stick. Even after Rabin's murder, its leaders went out of their way to make a show of toughness. They had difficulties, however, matching Likud's strident ultra-nationalist and right-populist sloganeering, which appealed, in particular, to the separate and unequal communities of North African and Russian Jews. Labor was also handicapped by its reticence in discussing its "final stage" objectives, about which it remained outwardly uncertain, though in truth artfully vague.

In accordance with Oslo II, by the end of December 1995 the Israeli army had carried out the phased withdrawal from the West Bank towns of Zone A, except Hebron. Under Oslo II there were to be additional redeployments from Zones B and C in three stages, at six-month intervals, thus within 18 months. Permanent status talks— bearing on Jerusalem, settlements, borders, and refugees—were to begin no later than May 4, 1996, to be completed within three years. But all these steps and negotiations were put on hold pending an election scheduled for the end of May. For the first time, Israelis were going to the polls to elect a prime minister directly—Peres or Netanyahu—and a new Knesset. The peace process became the election's all-consuming issue. Rather than stand on Rabin's Oslo legacy, Peres prevaricated—as Rabin himself had done—and sought to counter the charge that Labor was soft on the Palestinians and an advocate of appeasement.

For five months before Rabin's death and several weeks after, there were no terrorist attacks. This lull was broken following the assassination by Israel, on January 6, 1996, of Yahya Ayash in the Gaza town of Beit Lahia. A Hamas militant reputed to be an expert bomb-maker, Ayash was held responsible by army intelligence for several earlier bus attacks. Apparently for electoral reasons, to prove his military mettle and daring, Peres approved in advance his liquidation by a booby-trapped cellphone—a feat unabashedly celebrated by the Israeli media.

Thousands of Palestinians of all political persuasions attended Ayash's funeral. A moderate member of the Palestinian Authority "came to register [his] protest and anger at Israel's . . . alarming act of terror that came precisely when we had reached an agreement with Hamas." He suggested the act "was deliberately intended to bring the break-down of the agreements" and "show[ed] a lack of respect for the Palestinian Authority." A senior security official lamented that "the peace and quiet we achieved over the past five months" had made no impression on the Israelis despite the Authority's efforts "to safeguard Israeli security by persuading Hamas to become a political movement and reach an agreement with us."

This remote-controlled assassination triggered several revenge attacks inside Israel that—as Peres might have anticipated—redounded to the benefit of Likud. On February 25, bombs exploded in two buses in Jerusalem, killing twenty-six and wounding seventy-seven, followed by suicide bomb attacks in Tel Aviv and Ashkelon that took an additional thirty lives. Practiced at turning popular outrage and fear to good account, the right blamed Peres and Oslo, as well as Arafat. Overnight the left lost in the polls whatever small lead it may have had going into the elections. Arafat considered the Hamas operations a "disaster," convinced that the PLO was in "the same boat as Shimon Peres": should Rabin's heir "capsize . . . we and the peace accords will drown with him." No doubt he agreed with the *Jordan Times* of March 4 that the bombs of the Palestinian militants were "aimed at peace." He denounced the intransigents and vowed to bring them to heel, in cooperation with Israeli security forces, in the Palestinian Authority's realm. During the following two months Arafat cracked down on Hamas and the other radical formations, making hundreds of arrests.

Just after Rabin's martyrdom, there had been an upswing of sympathy and support for Arafat among Palestinians and Israeli Arabs, as well as in the moderate Arab countries. But Israel's wonted overreaction to the terrorist strikes reversed this trend overnight. Peres sealed off the West Bank and Gaza for months on end, causing acute hardship to countless Palestinians whose livelihoods depended on day-work in Israel. This latest collective punishment for the acts of a few extremists produced, predictably, an equal collective indignation throughout the Arab world. Peres' struggle in Israel's electoral cam-paign was not lost on Clinton or Arafat. Both knew the latest cycle of violence would strengthen Netanyahu and the right, and each set out to help Peres, *faute de mieux*.

By 1995, terrorism against American interests and within its borders had motivated the Clinton administration to make fighting it a top priority. The first bombing of New York's World Trade Center in 1993 was followed by the explosion at the Murrah Federal Building in Oklahoma City in April 1995. Shortly thereafter the President declared that it was America's "duty to purge ourselves of the dark forces which gave rise to this evil." But it was the insurgent and repressive state terror in the troubled Holy Land that prompted Clinton to call a "Summit of Peacemakers" the next year. Twenty-nine kings, presidents, prime ministers, and sheiks met on March 12, 1996, at Sharm el-Sheikh, an Egyptian resort town on the Red Sea, for a one-day meeting. President Mubarak was host and co-chair. King Hussein flew in with Clinton, joining Peres and Arafat, and nine other Arab leaders, along with heads of state and representatives from Britain, Canada, France, Germany, Ireland, Italy, Japan, Norway, Russia, Spain, and Turkey. Syria and Lebanon stayed away, charging that the event was designed to favor Israel at the expense of the Palestinians and Arabs generally. The formal part of the hastily improvised gathering consisted of less than a half-day exchange of platitudes intended to lubricate the peace process and open what Clinton called a "working group" of world leaders to propose strategies for staunching terrorism. In part for lack of follow-through, this effort came to naught. The prestige of the assembled "peacemakers" managed nevertheless to rub off on Peres and Arafat, leaving Netanyahu aura-less. In this dramatic setting Peres enjoined Arafat to crush the Palestinian terrorists; yet it was Israel, Arafat answered, that was aggravating the "poverty and misery . . . that foment violence and extremism" and preventing "getting out of this impasse" by locking Palestinian laborers into the Gaza Strip and West Bank, a misbegotten "collective punishment."

Peres' reward for his part in the high-profile parley was not long in coming. After stopping off in Israel, where he addressed the Knesset, Clinton asked Congress for $100 million to provide Israel with the latest counter-terrorism equipment, and to organize a joint American–Israeli counter-terrorism task force. Presently the FBI opened offices in Tel Aviv, Cairo, and Riyadh, while Washington tightened sanctions against Iran, Sudan, Libya, and Iraq.

Beset on all sides, with barely a crumb from the high table, Arafat had no alternative but to continue his efforts to bolster Peres. Oslo I had stipulated that the Palestinian National Council repeal the clauses of the Palestinian National Charter that denied Israel's right to exist and sought its destruction. As was customary in the peace process, Arafat tarried, looking for a quid pro quo: confirmation that Israel would abide by the agreement to start final status talks no later than May 1996. But he also waited for a newly elected National Council to convene in Gaza to give formal approval to the necessary changes. In the Palestinian elections of January 1996, Arafat and his supporters had swept the field, marking a political and moral victory for the Oslo line. All but 10 per cent of the voters endorsed Arafat as chairman. In April, six weeks after the summit, the twenty-first session of the Council voted 504 to 54, with 14 abstentions, to nullify the notorious articles—albeit in a resolution that was contorted and vague. Nevertheless, they remain in the document still.

On May 4, less than a month before the Israeli elections, Arafat informed Peres by letter that, in keeping with the Madrid Conference and the Washington negotiations, the Council had voted to amend the Charter "by canceling the articles that are contrary to the letters exchanged between the PLO and the Government of Israel on September 9–10, 1993." And in a separate letter to Secretary of State Madeleine Albright he confirmed he had "specified the articles which had been fully abrogated." With the Charter as good as revised, the Palestinians "had every right to expect" that Israel would fulfill its "contractual obligations under the Oslo accords." In a less distracting moment, Peres and Labor might well have benefited from Arafat's honoring of the earlier promise, a gesture magnified when Clinton immediately invited the president of the Palestinian National Authority to the White House and extended financial aid.

But Israel's nervous northern borders took precedence as a campaign issue. In 1982, with Operation Peace in Galilee, Israel had sought to root out the infrastructures of Hezbollah and all other guerrilla organizations in southern Lebanon. The objective of ensuring tranquility had entailed driving out much of the local population, establishing a security zone in southern Lebanon and a friendly government in Beirut. Judging by Sabra and Chatila alone, the human and moral costs had been exorbitant, and civil political relations with Lebanon were out of the question. The self-proclaimed security zone in southern Lebanon turned out to be anything but: Hezbollah's primitive rockets could easily fly over it, and the zone itself became a target. Eleven years later, in July 1993, Hezbollah operatives, backed by Syria, killed seven Israeli soldiers in the security zone and fired several Soviet-era Katyusha rockets into upper Galilee, causing material damage. In retaliation Rabin, with Barak as chief of staff, launched Operation Accountability. Israeli planes and guns heavily bombarded and shelled an area north of the buffer zone, without regard for civilians. Within a few days more than 100 were killed, nearly 500 were injured, and some 1,000 houses were destroyed. Thousands fled in terror.

In April 1996, after the Israelis killed an adolescent in the security zone, Hezbollah again killed seven soldiers and fired several rocket salvos into Kiryat Shmona, in northwestern Galilee, injuring some thirty Israelis and causing considerable property damage. Nearly three years after Oslo, still guided by the same operating code as his predecessors in 1982, Peres—acting prime minister and defense minister, now with Barak at the Foreign Ministry—launched Operation Grapes of Wrath. Heavy bombing and shelling of southern Lebanon again killed scores of civilians and forced fearful thousands northward. The Israeli navy blockaded the ports of Beirut, Sidon, and Tyre, and, after warning the inhabitants to evacuate, bombarded Tyre on April 13. Over the next two days the air force struck power stations southeast and east of Beirut. Four days into the operation Hezbollah militants had launched some 140 rockets that took few if any lives, while the IDF had fired several thousand artillery shells and made hundreds of bombing runs. On April 16 Israeli helicopters hit Ein el-Hilweh, Lebanon's largest refugee camp, near the coastal city of Sidon. Two days later artillery shells rained down on a U.N. compound sheltering some 800 civilian refugees in Qana, a village in southern Lebanon, leaving 102 dead. Such was the collateral damage of this latest military operation, intended to pressure the Lebanese and Syrian governments to disarm Hezbollah and turn Beirut against Damascus. Operation Grapes of Wrath produced a harvest of denunciation. The *Jordan Times* observed that the *soi-disant* retaliatory operation "lack[ed] even the semblance of credibility in its disproportion." Some of its own friends and patrons censured Israel for pursuing a policy of punishing thousands for the acts of a handful. To Israel's contempt for international law was added—particularly in the eyes of the Global South—the charge of scorn for Arab life.

The timing of the Israeli incursion was transparently tied to the forthcoming election: it began on April 11 and continued until four weeks before the vote on May 29. No doubt Peres launched the operation out of a genuine perception of national interest. Before inheriting Rabin's mantle, he had been a pillar of the defense establishment, serving six years as director-general of the Defense Ministry (responsible for weapons and nuclear programs), six years as deputy-minister of defense, and three years as minister of defense. Although never in the field, he was experienced in what Napoleon called "the business of barbarians." But in addition to being tried in military affairs, he had also been chairman of the Labor Party for fifteen years, minister of foreign affairs for five, and prime minister for three. Accused by Netanyahu of knuckling under to Arafat and the Palestinians, Peres seized the moment to combine the search for security with the pursuit of political advantage: by acting energetically in Lebanon, he could appear authentically hardline during the final weeks of the uphill campaign.

To make war or peace, that was the question: whether it was wiser to stay with Oslo or end it. The country was deeply divided over what it took to be an existential issue. Given the almost even polarization, in a multi-party system the limited-issue parties of the ultra-Orthodox Jews, the recent Russian *aliyah*, and the disadvantaged North African Jews would weigh unequally in the balance, mostly against accommodation. Only the Israeli Arabs would bend the other way. Labor's election platform opened with a section on "peace and security." It promised "to reach [for] a new Middle East in which there will be no more wars and terrorist acts," the proximate aim being a "cessation of the Arab–Israeli conflict by the year 2000." Where the opposition whipped up fear, Labor declared that, although "the terror of Hezbollah, Hamas, and the Islamic Jihad is the enemy of individual freedom in Israel [and] harms normal life," it was not "a strategic danger to Israel since it is not powerful enough to jeopardize the existence of the nation." The urgent assignment was to continue "negotiating for peace while simultaneously fighting against the remnants of the old Middle East, the fundamentalist and terrorist forces that seek to destroy the peace process."

To harden its "defensible borders and essential security arrangements," Israel needed to "continue to develop its qualitative advantage over the Arab armies and give high preference to independent [home-grown] military research and development and to the expansion" of local "production of innovative, highly sophisticated military equipment." So as to leave no doubt about its resolve to maintain Israel's regional military hegemony, the party would "oppose the arming with weapons of mass destruction of any regime with an ideology of hatred and destruction . . . primarily including Iran." Its government would "act in both regional and international frameworks to prevent the catastrophic link between a fundamentalist ideology and nonconventional weapons" and would forge ahead with "the Strategic Alliance and the Alliance for War Against Terror between Israel and the United States." Israel appreciated American assistance "and [its] guarantee that Israel's qualitative [military] superiority will be preserved." Security and peace through overwhelming military strength were keys to achieving a "final settlement with the Palestinians." In future negotiations Labor would stand fast on a "Jerusalem . . . united and undivided under Israeli sovereignty and jurisdiction." The old–new capital would encompass "the area surrounding" it, to include "Ma'ale Adumim, Giv'at Ze'ev, the Etzion Bloc and the area northwest of the Dead Sea." Labor would bar the PLO from discussions on Jerusalem during the interim period, and in the permanent status talks would stress Jordan's historic role in administering the Moslem holy shrines there. Although Meretz scolded Peres for courting the religious parties and settlers, it supported him in opposing the division of the Holy City.

The other objectives were equally vaulting and imperious: "the Jordan River will be the eastern security border of Israel [with] no other army west of it"; Israel will exercise "sovereignty over the Jordan Valley, Northwest Dead Sea area, the Etzion Bloc, and areas essential to the security of Israel"; the "Palestinian refugee problem" will be settled "outside the borders of Israel," which meant "rejecting the right to return"; and the state will "maintain jurisdiction over most of the settlers, ([though] no new settlements will be established)." With Likud and kindred parties calling for the unceasing expansion of settlements, the Labor leaders went out of their way to reassure the settlers and the electorate at large that the colonies in the territories would continue their "natural development" and would remain under Israeli military control. Under the final status agreement Labor would not "remove" or "evacuate" any settlements, but neither would it "add new ones"—"the difference between us and the Likud." The platform thereby concealed what the electorate well knew: since the Oslo accords, and in violation of them, the Labor government had continued to expand settlements, confiscate land, and construct bypass roads in the West Bank. Although on April 25 the party abandoned its opposition to the creation of a Palestinian state, Peres advocated enlarging the settlement blocs, particularly in the region of Greater Jerusalem, for annexation to Israel, and also favored fostering "separation which will answer the needs of security and national identity."

Where Labor was in accord with Oslo, however reluctantly and cagily, Likud was unambiguously not. Although Netanyahu grudgingly accepted the agreements as a grim reality, he and his party embraced no more than the creation of some form of Palestinian autonomy, without sovereign statehood. Likud would "restore to the peace process . . . the principle that we are taking full and exclusive responsibility" for security throughout the territories, "including those areas under total Palestinian authority." In short, Israel would keep control of Judea and Samaria. Likud called for the continued and virtually unlimited construction of settlements. Together with the religious movements and parties Netanyahu asserted that undivided Jerusalem would be the "political and spiritual capital of Israel and the Jewish people." He also stood squarely for a more authentically Jewish civil society. Although the party did not endorse all the religious and cultural demands of the fundamentalist United Torah Party and of Shas, like Labor it was ready to exchange political favors with them. As he played up the latest resurgence of violence, Netanyahu ignored the boldness of Operation Grapes of Wrath. He blamed the compromises of Oslo for encouraging the terrorists, whose actions proved that Arafat was either unwilling or unable to subdue Hamas; he probably even supported the group. Netanyahu attributed the whole sorry scene to Peres, insisting that his ways would "bring us neither peace nor security," and vowed that Likud would not leave the "security of our children in Arafat's hands." It was an open secret that the Clinton administration preferred Peres, which the acting premier sought to turn to his advantage. Labor all but took credit for ties between Israel and the U.S. "having reached a peak in terms of the quality of the relations and the deep friendship between us and the administration, Congress, and the American people."

Netanyahu looked to harness to Likud's foreign and domestic policy another America that he knew well. After graduate studies at MIT and Harvard, Netanyahu had served for two years in the U.S. as deputy chief of mission in Israel's embassy in Washington, followed by four years as ambassador to the United Nations (1984–8). He had become attentive then to the rising conservative Republican majority in Congress, many of whose values and strategies he shared, while also getting close to the conservative and Orthodox elements in the corridors of the leading pro-Israel lobbying group, the American Israel Public Affairs Committee. Since then, following the Republicans' triumph in the midterm elections of 1994, he and his associates in America had developed ties to the anti-Clinton elements in Congress, which for partisan reasons opposed a peace process that would redound to the political benefit of the left in both the U.S. and Israel. In 1996—an election year in the U.S. as well as Israel, both for president and Congress—Clinton and the Democrats risked being considerably weakened. By then Netanyahu and Likud were also commending themselves to the ascendant free-market, libertarian, and evangelical right, with their call to speed up the privatization and deregulation of Israel's residually "socialist" economy. They bruited about that, in America, they would be sailing with the wind.

With a voter turnout on May 29, 1996, of nearly 80 per cent, Netanyahu edged out Peres by just under 1 per cent. Results in the Knesset were nearly as close: Labor won thirty-four seats, with 26.8 per cent of the vote; Likud, in coalition with Tzomet and Gesher, won thirty-two seats, with 25.1 per cent. But the statistical picture misleads. The composite left was distinctly in decline against the composite right, where the religious and secular ultra-nationalists were on the rise. An "ethnic" breakdown of the vote for prime minister shows that, without the heavy Israeli Arab vote for Peres, Netanyahu would have won by 11 per cent, rather than less than 0.9 per cent. Except for the revulsion over Lebanon, this Arab vote would have been considerably higher. Yet it still would not have compensated for the abandonment of Peres by Jewish voters. This defection was consonant with Labor–Meretz's loss in the Knesset of nearly a quarter of its seats, and a decline from 44 per cent to 34 per cent of the popular vote, leaving the composite left with forty-three deputies.

Meretz appears to have contributed significantly to this setback. Its candidates had campaigned for an attenuation of the Judaization of civil and political society with a view to safeguarding democracy, which it saw as contingent on the separation of state and synagogue. Labor had made Jewish values and symbols its own since before the creation of the state, and the right easily charged it with being hypocritical and heretical for condoning Meretz's call for the all-out secularization of army, school, and culture. This vision—redolent of Herzl's dream of an enlightened Voltairian state for Jews—was profoundly disturbing, especially for Oriental or Sephardic Jews, most of whom tended to live by the Book. Such strident secularism, together with the endorsement of Oslo, helped to mobilize the alienated and underprivileged silent majority. The exceptionally high voter turnout of 80 per cent among Jewish Israelis chiefly benefited the national–religious formations.

Among those, Likud stood closest to Tsomet and Gesher, respectively headed by Raphael Eitan and David Levy, sworn hardliners for a Greater Israel. With Levy rallying the vote of the Oriental Jews in particular, the three parties together secured the thirty-two Knesset seats. Tsomet was in fact secularist, but by throwing in its lot with Likud, it strengthened the messianic–clerical rightists who distrusted or opposed Oslo. That camp was joined by Yisrael Be'aliyah, the Russian immigrants' party led by Natan Sharansky, which won seven seats. But perhaps the most striking and weighty outcome of this election was the growth of the popular vote and parliamentary representation of three ultra-Orthodox parties: Shas, the National

Religious Party, and the United Torah Judaism Front between them won nearly 600,000 votes, or 20 per cent of all votes cast, for a total of twenty-three seats in the Knesset. The number of religious members rose to thirty—a quarter of parliament—if one counts the true believers in the nonreligious parties. In addition, Gush Emunim, the movement of radical settlers, blended Jewish messianism and nationalism.

Netanyahu's narrow victory mattered less than his likely coalition with partners even more hawkish than Likud. With a nervous eye on Washington, in the weeks before forming a government, Netanyahu continued to pay lip-service to the peace process as the left continued to bad-mouth the prime minister elect and his supporters. Yet with the election past, each side fell habitually to the shared task of securing a Greater Israel, locking arms in a de facto National Unity Government. Netanyahu soon patched together a cabinet of nine parties—as good as monolithic on the matter of Palestine and far more religious than the last. Nearly all twenty-one members of Rabin's government had come from or lived in greater Tel Aviv, the mainly Ashkenazi bastion of secularism, guided culturally and politically by the comfortable middle and professional classes. By contrast, well over one-third of Netanyahu's ministers were of Sephardic origin, and had their residence in Jerusalem; only three of the seventeen lived in Tel Aviv, and seven were religious. Many more were anchored in inland regions of cultural and political traditionalism, carried by Shas. The key portfolios were held by a notably uncompromising group: Likud ran Defense and Finance; Shas oversaw Interior, Labor and Social Affairs. Gesher was at Foreign Affairs; Yisrael Be'aliyah (Sharansky) at Trade and Commerce; and the National Religious Party at Education, Culture, and Religious Affairs. There was to be no letup in the drive to strengthen legislation extending religious control over education, marriage, divorce, burial, conversion, and nationality—nor in providing subsidies for Orthodox religious institutions and exemptions from military service for students in rabbinical seminaries.

The final composition and approval of the cabinet was delayed for several weeks because of Sharon, Netanyahu's fierce rival yet indispensable party coadjutor. Claiming credit for having engineered the rightist victory by convincing the leaders of Gesher and Tsomet to stand with Likud, Sharon held out for either the Defense or Finance positions. When David Levy refused to serve as foreign minister unless Sharon were given a major portfolio, Netanyahu offered him the newly charted but expansive Ministry of National Infrastructures, which would bear on the occupied territories. As Sharon was one of the earliest and most outspoken of the original advocates of rampant settlement, his appointment announced a program, and was a signal to Clinton. Whereas the Labor government had at least paid lip-service to the notion of "land for peace," Likud explicitly spurned it in favor of the motto "peace through strength." On June 18 the Knesset confirmed the new cabinet by a vote of sixty-two to fifty.

Arafat and the wider Arab–Muslim world were profoundly troubled by the outcome of the Israeli elections. Mubarak and Assad called for a meeting of the Arab League to take stock and adopt a common position toward the new government. In the first week of June 1996, Mubarak, King Hussein, and Arafat conferred in Aqaba, and Mubarak, Crown Prince Abdullah of Saudi Arabia, and Assad met in Riyadh. On June 9 Assad, Abdullah, and Mubarak announced from Damascus that the first Arab summit since 1993 would convene in Cairo during June 21–23. Hussein and Mubarak urged that, rather than defy Netanyahu directly, they should give him some limited time to show his colors. The deadline for the twice-postponed second stage of redeployment of Israeli troops from Hebron had been June 12. Though there was as yet no sign of compliance, in their closing communiqué the Arab leaders, after blandly reaffirming their commitment to the peace process, did no more than caution Israel not to scuttle it. They could do little else. Relative to Israel's abiding and overwhelming military superiority, they remained defenseless—a condition compounded by their persistent and crippling internecine divisions. To measure the Israeli–Palestinian imbalance in simply economic terms: the West Bank and Gaza's gross per capita production and per capita income were between a quarter and a third those of Israel, whose purchase on America's political society and Jewish community further guaranteed it a wide spectrum of economic and social aid.

In July 1996, Netanyahu went for a five-day visit to the U.S. Rather than bank exclusively on the Clinton White House and State Department, the new premier looked to the Republican majority in Congress to support his drive to gut the peace process and privatize critical sectors of an economy foundering under the weight of chronically overburdensome military expenditures. He also courted the conservative and Orthodox elements that continued to gain ground in America's Jewish community. Although strong-armed by Clinton and Warren Christopher, Netanyahu, confident of the support of his own intransigents, including Sharon, refused to yield an inch on Hebron. When he grudgingly met with Arafat on September 4 at the

Erez checkpoint, the talks were idle.

It took seven months and intense American pressure for Israel finally—on January 15, 1997—to sign the Hebron Protocol, in fulfillment of the 1993 Oslo accords. Though determined to be fiercer than his predecessors, Netanyahu did more or less what would have been expected of Rabin or Peres. Hebron was divided in two unequal parts. Israel withdrew its troops from 80 per cent of the city, but kept enough in place to protect not only some 400 settlers living in an enclave—a self-chosen ghetto—within the city, but also the more than 5,000 ultra-religious settlers in nearby Kiryat Arba. The agreement transferred civil and police authority from the rest of Hebron to the Palestinians, though Israel reserved the right to keep greater Hebron and its population of 130,000 under surveillance. This redeployment in no way presaged further withdrawals from the West Bank and Gaza Strip, as pledged. Instead, the new government quickened the consolidation and expansion of Israel's settlements across the territories. Jerusalem remained non-negotiable. Since 1967, well before the rise of the religious parties, every government—Labor or Likud—had supported moving into the surrounding Palestinian towns and villages, as well as the Muslim and Christian quarters of Jerusalem's Old City.

Before daybreak on September 24, 1997, Ehud Olmert, the ultra-Likud mayor of Jerusalem, who had opposed the Camp David accords and the withdrawal from the Sinai, did the government's bidding and opened the Hasmonean Tunnel that links the Wailing Wall with the Via Dolorosa. Dating from the first century BC, this passage runs under the Temple Mount. Manifestly the intent was to express Israel's sovereignty over an indivisible Holy City; the announced motive was to give tourists easy access to the Muslim Quarter. The Arab–Muslim world was irate over what it viewed as a threat to the time-honored autonomous status of Haram al-Sharif, site of the Dome of the Rock and the Al-Aqsa Mosque. The expanse of some 40 acres was Islam's third-holiest ground. All Palestinians considered the tunnel opening to be in keeping with a long series of provocations and desecrations there that had started in the time of the Yishuv, and had reached its first climax in 1928–9. After 1967, Israeli zeal to challenge the Islamic presence on the Temple Mount had matched the exponential growth of the ultra-religious themselves. The most extreme among them even looked to raze the Al-Aqsa Mosque to make room for the construction of tomorrow's Third Temple, in celebration of the Jewish people's return to Zion.

The Palestinians' over-suspicious if understandable attribution of a religious rather than territorial meaning to the tunnel operation was made more fervent by their rising rage over Hebron, the continuing settlement drive, the refusal to free political prisoners, and the willed economic decline of the occupied territories. Violence predictably erupted in several places in the West Bank and Gaza on September 25. In Jerusalem there were clashes between Palestinian and Israeli security forces. In no time the unrest boiled over, leaving four Palestinian civilians and three policemen dead. In and around Ramallah and Bethlehem, surrounded by Israeli troops, several hundred Palestinians were wounded—mostly young stone-throwers. The next day Israeli soldiers, using automatic weapons and supported by Cobra helicopters, killed some 40 Palestinians, half of them in Gaza, and injured around 700; they lost 7 of their own. On September 27 Israeli soldiers burst into the Al-Aqsa Mosque, taking the lives of three worshippers and wounding over 100. The Israelis suffered 14 dead and about 50 wounded. It was the worst violence since the intifada of 1987. Netanyahu cannot have expected that the opening of the underground passage would go unnoticed, or that Arafat, let alone his radical critics, would absorb the offense. Whatever the mixture of spontaneity and predetermination in the breach of the peace, Arafat exploited it to redirect international attention to the perils of the Arab–Israeli conflict, the hard fate of the Palestinians, and the frailty of the peace process. This suited Netanyahu, who had his own reasons for fishing in these same troubled waters.

While many European and Third World governments and public intellectuals reproached Israel, Clinton sought to ward off another intifada. He invited Arafat, Netanyahu, Mubarak, and King Hussein to an emergency meeting in Washington on October 3–4, about a month before the American elections. Despite himself, and notwithstanding opposition within his coalition, Netanyahu could not beg off, but Mubarak declined to attend. In the event, Netanyahu refused to shut the tunnel temporarily pending negotiations, and the meeting came to naught—as did his second meeting with Arafat at the Erez checkpoint on October 8, when the disentanglement of Hebron still hung in the balance. The Israeli premier looked not to the White House but to Newt Gingrich—Speaker of the House, grandmaster of the fast-rising new conservative majority and a confederate of the waxing religious right, which had long since signaled its unqualified support of Likud's hard line.

Back in January, when his cabinet had approved the Hebron protocol by eleven votes to seven, Netanyahu had proclaimed that he would "work to protect the conditions and necessary requirements for the existence, security, and livelihood of the Jewish community in

Hebron." Only the government of Israel, he said, "would determine the details of the next stage of redeployment in Judea and Samaria." The subsequent announcement of the construction of sixty new housing units in Ma'ale Efrayim, in the Jordan Valley, was the first of a series of similar notices in the following months, during which the government accelerated the settlement drive in the occupied territories. In flagrant defiance of Oslo, it expanded existing settlements, created new ones, and legitimized the illegal emplacement of mobile homes on hilltops as makeshift outposts. Economic and tax benefits for settlers still obtained, protective fences were built, privately owned Palestinian lands confiscated, bypass roads laid out, and military facilities reinforced and enlarged. Resistance to this encroachment was met with military repression, arrests and imprisonments, demolition of houses, and destruction of olive groves. Much of this punishment was collective.

At the end of February 1998, Netanyahu approved the construction of 6,500 housing units in Har Homa—the Arab neighborhood of Jabel Abu Ghmeim, along the southeastern rim of Jerusalem, long ago annexed and prospected by his predecessors. Sharon's ministry as usual played a central role. Within a week the PLO called a one-day general strike to protest against the decision and the settlement policy in general. On March 18, the day construction began, the Palestine National Authority broke off peace negotiations. Although no one was killed in the crackdown on the Har Homa protests that month, hundreds of Palestinians were injured and arrested, and thousands more politicized. The U.S. campaigned against a Security Council resolution censuring the Har Homa move, and against a General Assembly resolution calling on Tel Aviv to halt construction and end all other settlement activity. America vetoed the first and voted against the second, joined by Micronesia.

King Hussein, who with Mubarak had urged giving the new Israeli premier the benefit of the doubt, was by now moved to anger. When Israel refused to let him fly Arafat to Gaza in his personal jet, he wrote Netanyahu a scathing letter. Reviewing Tel Aviv's recent transgressions, the king cautioned the premier not to allow conditions to "slide towards an abyss of bloodshed and disaster, brought about by fear and despair." They slid. In Hebron the settlers hectored Netanyahu to stand firm, and the Palestinians continued to endure delays in the peace process. Throughout 1997 the City of the Patriarchs witnessed numerous incidents, usually set off by local Jewish zealots. In April a settler shot and killed a Palestinian, setting off a riot. The Israeli security forces struck back, killing 2 and wounding around 100. Three days of clashes in mid June left over thirty-five Palestinian casualties. In July settlers taunted Palestinians with anti-Muslim profanities. In August the government authorized several thousand true believers to travel to Hebron to participate in a rally marking the thirtieth anniversary of the return of the Jews to Hebron, and the fiftieth anniversary of the foundation of Israel. In Hebron alone, the year's tally of suffering came to at least 10 Palestinians dead, 250 injured, and 220 imprisoned.

Especially after Oslo, the vicious cycle of avenging violence increasingly took the form of civil rather than cross-border wars, with the bulk of casualties on both sides being civilians. The furies of this bitter struggle were intensified by religion and the animus peculiar to the encounter between colonialist master and native subaltern. The rash of terrorist strikes in the occupied territories and in Israel in the years following Oslo, most of them probably perpetrated by Hamas operatives, must be seen in this context—one in which the unrelenting settlement drive weakened Arafat against his opposition. Following protests over Har Homa and Hebron, on March 22, 1997, a Palestinian detonated a bomb in a restaurant in Tel Aviv, taking three Israeli lives. On April 2, another bomb struck a bus on the West Bank, wounding eleven Israeli soldiers. Two suicide bombers detonated their explosive charges in Jerusalem's Maham Yehuda market on June 30, killing thirteen and wounding nearly 170. On September 4, three suicide bombers blew themselves up in the Ben Yehuda pedestrian mall, leaving four Israelis dead and some 150 injured. On each occasion Netanyahu reiterated Israel's refusal to return to the conference table until the Palestinian authorities had eliminated terrorism completely. The Israeli government also ordered the customary deterrent and punitive measures, including military incursions and indiscriminate arrests in territories now under Palestinian control.

In his fixation on settlements, Netanyahu eagerly used this violence to justify not turning over large parts of the West Bank to Arafat, as stipulated in the Oslo accords. As we have seen, it took nearly a year, until October 8, 1997, and steady American muscle, for the two leaders to meet again at the Erez checkpoint—to no end. Ten days later in Ramallah Dennis Ross, Clinton's special envoy, brought them together once more. Netanyahu repeated that Israel would not implement any of the scheduled redeployments until the PNA had demonstrated its good faith in eradicating terrorism. In the meantime Israel would persevere with its expansion program. Ross left empty-handed, as he knew he would. In January 1998 the Israeli government authorized the construction of a substantial number of additional housing units in the Efrat and Elkana settlements, as well as several towns along the Green Line, not far from Hebron. By now the supply of housing in the territories actually outran demand.

Netanyahu's government began to develop serious fissures, for reasons of domestic and foreign policy. In October Foreign Minister Levy resigned. First spokesman for the disadvantaged Sephardic communities, he protested at the budget's neglect of social programs, which was largely a result of exorbitant military outlays—a function, in turn, of the hardline policies he nevertheless favored. Sharon replaced him. Defense Minister Mordechai then gave notice of his intention to resign over the handling of the peace process, though he and other party stalwarts were less critical of the policies themselves than of the truculence in implementing them. The tactics were also politically divisive in the U.S. The greater this opposition, the more the premier turned to those furthest to the right, where he sought the support of the small Moledet party, which called for the transfer—the old euphemism for expulsion—of all Palestinians to Arab countries.

As Netanyahu strained to shore up his support in the cabinet and Knesset, Clinton kept at him, requesting his and Arafat's presence in Washington for talks during January 20–23, 1998. To restart the stalled peace process Clinton asked Netanyahu to agree to a three-stage redeployment, spread over four months, of 12 per cent of Area C of the West Bank; he would not. In a gesture to Clinton, Arafat assured him that the Executive Committee of the PLO would ratify the changes of the Palestinian Charter within a month—which it did not. A week later the American secretary of state flew to Tel Aviv to press for 10 per cent of Area C, still in vain. Although Albright blamed both sides for the continuing stalemate, she implied that Washington might cease trying to mediate should Israel "continue to display a stubborn and uncompromising attitude toward the Palestinians." Netanyahu began to negotiate, in a niggardly fashion: Israel would consider 9 per cent. Not until July 20 did his cabinet accept an American proposal to withdraw from 13 per cent of the West Bank on condition that 3 per cent of it be turned into a nature reserve to be policed jointly.

That still left a considerable reneging on Oslo. Arafat and the Palestinians resorted to a bold stratagem. When he had asked Clinton, in Washington, to recognize a Palestinian state, the president had been evasive. After launching several trial balloons, Arafat announced in April 1998 that unless Israel agreed to fix a timetable for further withdrawals and to freeze new settlement construction, the Palestinians would declare their state unilaterally on May 4 the following year, when Oslo I's five-year deadline expired. Netanyahu warned—

and did so again five months later—that, should the Palestinian National Authority issue such a proclamation, Israel would annex part of the West Bank and repudiate all previous accords.

Arafat's theatrical dare could not have displeased Clinton, who for political reasons would not push Netanyahu, and may have prompted the prime minister (in turn careful not to rile Clinton) to agree to meet Arafat in Washington in late September, when both would be in New York to address the annual session of the General Assembly. While there the two leaders shook hands on the 13 per cent proposal. Quite apart from settling for 20 per cent less territory than he had asked for, Arafat was also apparently persuaded to make no mention of his planned declaration of independence in his U.N. speech on September 30. A week later, they met again at the Erez checkpoint and agreed to a summit for comprehensive negotiations, to start on October 15 at the Wye River Plantation in eastern Maryland. Within forty-eight hours of his talk with Arafat, Netanyahu attended a ceremony consecrating the 16,000-strong Ariel settlement, halfway between the Green Line and the Jordan Valley, as a full-fledged city; he authorized the construction of 150 additional housing units in the Ma'ale Mikmas settlement east of Ramallah; and he announced Sharon's appointment as foreign minister.

The peace process having gone nowhere for nearly a year and a half, it took Clinton's most charismatic coaxing to bring the Israelis and Palestinians back to the table. Whatever his authentic solicitude for both peoples, his primary investment in the conflict concerned America's imperial interests in the greater Middle East, focused on oil. The negotiations at Wye were difficult. It took eight days to reach an agreement, with Clinton using increasingly bigger carrots—over $1 billion in financial aid for Israel, $350 million for the Palestinian National Authority—and a terminally ill King Hussein bringing to bear his uncommon political wits. The final Wye River Memorandum, signed on October 23 at the White House by Arafat and Netanyahu, stipulated that Israel was to withdraw from 13 per cent (including the nature reserve) of the occupied West Bank, in three stages, within four months. In addition Israel agreed to release 750 of its 3,000 Palestinian prisoners, to open the airport and an industrial park in Gaza, and to provide two corridors for the safe passage of Palestinians between the West Bank and Gaza. The PNA agreed to reinforce its fight against anti-Israeli violence, applying zero tolerance in arresting terrorists, confiscating weapons, and extraditing individuals suspected by Israel of having committed terrorist acts. These and other security measures were to be furthered by "bilateral Israeli–Palestinian" cooperation,

and monitored by U.S. security agents. Arafat also promised to curb
rhetorical incitements to violence, and to eliminate the articles of the
Palestinian Charter calling for Israel's destruction.

Only a partial implementation of the Oslo accords, the Wye
protocol guaranteed a vexed future in which all the major issues
remained to be resolved. It provided for an Israeli–Palestinian committee to discuss further troop deployments, and called for "the two
sides . . . to immediately resume permanent status negotiations on an
accelerated basis [in] a determined effort to achieve the mutual goal of
reaching an agreement by May 4, 1999." The last paragraph, titled
"Unilateral Actions," was invocatory: "Recognizing the necessity to
create a positive environment for [these] negotiations, neither side
shall initiate or take any step that will change the status of the West
Bank and the Gaza Strip in accordance with the interim Agreement."
In brief, the Palestinians were not to unilaterally proclaim their
independence as a state; the Israelis were not to continue their
settlement drive. Powerful critics in both camps fulminated against
their leaders for having made heretical concessions. The Wye Memorandum made Netanyahu's cabinet and parliamentary position more
precarious. The task of appeasing his own diehards and Washington
simultaneously was impossible. In November, the Knesset approved
Wye by a vote of seventy-five to nineteen, with nine abstentions. Only
twenty-nine members of Netanyahu's coalition of around sixty approved the accord. The composite left, particularly Labor, provided
the mainstay of the support, without voicing any qualms about the
fundamentals of Netanyahu's policies—the reaching for space and the
playing for time.

Despite the Wye agreement, the settlement drive stayed on course.
After signing the Memorandum, the government almost daily announced the enlargement of established settlements and the foundation of new ones in and around Jerusalem, Bethlehem, Hebron, and
Nablus—with the Knesset readily allocating the necessary funds.
More bypass roads were built, with Sharon encouraging the settlers
"to move, run, and grab as many hilltops" as possible, "because
everything we now take will remain ours." Sanctioned, safeguarded,
and subsidized, they burned and uprooted olive trees, and confiscated
Palestinian lands with impunity. Netanyahu reassured his supporters
that, should the Palestinians proclaim their independence or not live
up to their word, Israel reserved the right to consult its own interests
and protect its own security. Like all his predecessors, he gave no
thought to the importance of building confidence among Palestinians—whether through military, political, or economic measures.

During the third week of November 1998, he began quietly—in a gesture that was probably for American consumption—to redeploy Israeli troops from a small section of the West Bank. He did release some 250 prisoners, but more than half turned out to be common-law criminals rather than political detainees. And while Tel Aviv authorized the opening of the Gaza airport, Israel retained full control of the airspace over all the territory ceded to the Authority.

Immediately after taking these minimal steps, the government seized on several terrorist incidents first to delay and then suspend its implementation of the Wye River accord. Besides overdramatizing them, it imputed each and every one to Arafat and the Palestinian Authority, and stiffened the conditions for any further compliance. On December 2 a Palestinian crowd killed an Israeli soldier near Bet El, a settlement northeast of Ramallah, and an Israeli militant fatally stabbed a Palestinian in East Jerusalem. Parity in terror was followed by disparity: the next day the cabinet voted to freeze all troop withdrawals and relocations. Political concerns fed Netanyahu's resolve to give the quietus to Wye. Four more of his cabinet members had resigned—Benny Begin, Dan Meridor, Yitzhak Mordechai, and Yaakev Neeman. Like David Levy before them, they stepped down not because they disagreed with the policy in the territories, but because of the heavy-handedness of its execution. They may have feared, too, that Netanyahu was needlessly antagonizing the White House. With his cabinet and coalition coming apart, rather than risk being brought down by a vote of no confidence, he opted for early elections in which he meant to rally hardliners and hawks, including the silent majority, around himself as well as around a Likud revivified by the far right. On December 21 the Knesset, by a large margin, voted for elections to be held May 17, chilling negotiations for five months and ensuring that the Oslo deadline of May 4 would go unhonored.

The Wye Memorandum, and the ways in which the Israelis sought to vitiate it, widened the schism between moderates and extremists among Palestinians and their supporters across the Muslim Middle East. Once again Arafat had secured few tangible advances for the national pride, daily life, and personal dignity of the average Palestinian. Yet he had agreed to take on the militants, whose taunting stones and deadly bombs spoke the only language the Israelis had shown any evidence of understanding. The extremists were now increasingly obliged to fight on two fronts: against the Palestinian National Authority and against the Israeli government. Representatives of the main Palestinian resistance organizations condemned the Wye accord, and pledged themselves anew to the armed struggle.

Toward the end of October 1998 there was a large protest rally in Gaza. Soon after, secular and Islamist radicals demonstrated in Damascus and burned Israeli and American flags in Ain al-Hilweh, Lebanon's largest refugee camp, near Sidon. On December 11 delegates of the various movements held a "national conference" in Gaza to keep the pressure on Arafat. Terror continued its bloody business. On October 26 a Jewish settler was killed near Kiryat Arba. Three days later, tele-guided by Hamas, a Palestinian driver crashed his car into a convoy of army jeeps and a school bus, killing one Israeli and wounding three. A week later, Islamic Jihad sent an operative to blow himself up in a car near Jerusalem's Mahane Yehuda market, injuring twenty-one.

Just as during the elections following Rabin's assassination, Arafat knew perfectly well that developments in his own camp—especially the staying power of the extremists—were bound to have an impact on the upcoming electoral campaign. His hope was to give the Israeli right as little help as possible. Netanyahu himself had to navigate between the far right and Clinton, Arafat between his militant gainsayers and the U.S. president, without whose intervention he would have scarcely any leverage. Arafat and his people opted to make a substantial if halting good-faith effort to comply with the Wye River accord. The PNA's intelligence and security forces extradited, arrested, tried, and imprisoned a substantial number of militants. It also issued and enforced an anti-incitement decree and, in the name of a recent weapons control act, confiscated illegal arms and munitions.

As early as October 24, 1998, the Authority took into custody several militant Fatah members in Ramallah who were on Israel's wanted list, precipitating popular demonstrations in which a 16-year-old Palestinian was killed by local police. A fiery sheik in Nablus was arrested, along with the leader of Islamic Jihad in Gaza. Following the Hamas suicide attack of October 29, Arafat's security forces rounded up Hamas members and supporters, and consigned Sheik Yassin to house arrest for two months—only a year after his release from eight years in an Israeli prison. In November and December, Palestinian security forces dispersed several demonstrations clamoring for the release of political prisoners held by Israel and by the National Authority. In a nod to Washington they also broke up protests against American air attacks on Iraq.

Yet close to 50 per cent of the Palestinian population critical of Wye harbored serious support for Arafat's rivals—especially when confronted with the overbearing pride of the settlers, whose behavior was in every way countenanced by their government. Arafat was increas-

ingly on the defensive in his own camp. On November 14 he renewed
his threat to "declare our independent state with Jerusalem as its
capital on May 4, 1999." Pressed by activists of all persuasions, the
PNC convened in special session to explore ways to stem Israel's
continuing confiscation of lands and construction of bypass roads.
Their latest distress was well-founded. Netanyahu and Sharon, convinced that delay was of the essence, stuck to a strategy of stalling. By
late November they had cleared only 2 of the 13 per cent of territory to
be transferred to the Palestinians; the release of prisoners was equally
fitful. After the December ambush of an Israeli soldier, cited above,
the Israeli government stopped even playing along with the accord; the
vote for early general elections was now pending.

Arafat and Clinton each had a stake in seeing to it that, counter to
Netanyahu's plan to rally the right, the hawks should not be strengthened. They all but conspired to have the PLO fulfill yet another Wye
requirement: the de-fanging of the Palestinian Charter with regard to
Israel. Arafat convened some 450 members of the PNC at the Shawwa
Center in Gaza City on December 13, 1998, to expurgate the PLO's
founding covenant formally before hundreds of other Palestinian
notables, including several former guerrilla fighters and suspected
terrorists. To confer the ultimate legitimacy on the occasion, he made
so bold as to invite the American president to attend. Clinton agreed,
momentarily escaping the embarrassment of the impeachment proceedings against him. He arrived by helicopter and seized the hour to
inaugurate the Gaza airport officially.

On the opening day, the delegates stood and solemnly raised their
hands in near-unison to vote for revising the Charter. The next day
Clinton spoke and commended them for "rejecting—fully, finally, and
forever—the passages . . . calling for the destruction of Israel." Twice
he insisted that by doing so they had sent "a powerful message not to
the government but to the people of Israel," and Clinton wanted the
Israelis to know that the Palestinian people themselves were behind the
peace process. Although Palestinians' "lives are hard, jobs are scarce,
prospects are uncertain, and personal grief is great," and for "too
many" of them the "[peace] process [had] remained remote"—in spite
of all that, they lent their support. Turning then to the Palestinian
people, Clinton assured them he was sensitive to their "history of
dispossession and dispersal," and "understood [their] concerns about
settlement activity, land confiscation, and home demolitions." He
repeated too the qualms of both Palestinians and Israelis "about
unilateral statements that could prejudge the outcome of final status
negotiations." It was "profoundly wrong," he cautioned, "to equate

Palestinians in particular and Islam in general with terrorism, or to see a fundamental conflict between Islam and the West." Conceding that, when in their own minds they and their representatives "had a hundred good reasons to walk away, you didn't," he concluded: "Palestinians must recognize the right of Israel and its people to live safe and secure lives today, tomorrow, and forever; Israel must recognize the right of Palestinians to aspire to live free today, tomorrow, and forever."

By his grave and empathic address to the Palestinian nation as a whole, Clinton hugely enhanced the legitimacy of its cause. And in promising the PNA additional funds "to support the development of the Palestinian people," he had implicitly recognized the Authority's sovereignty. Netanyahu, already blamed for having abused Israel's relationship with Washington, was put on the defensive. Clinton's primary concern, however, was again simply to breathe new life into the peace process. The day after his speech, he compelled Arafat and Netanyahu to meet on the Israeli side of the Erez crossing. Netanyahu stood fast, refusing to give any timetable for the resumption of withdrawals or the release of prisoners. The effect of Clinton's efforts would have to await the outcome of the elections.

In 1999 peace seems to have been less of a campaign issue than in the 1996 elections. This time there was too little violence for Netanyahu to play on. Eager not to gratify the right, Arafat fell quiet on his declaration of statehood, compelled Hamas to stay its hand during the campaign, and urged Israeli Arabs to vote against Netanyahu and Likud. Yet there were no major policy differences on the Palestinian question between Netanyahu and Ehud Barak. A war-tested hardliner, Barak teamed up with David Levy of Geshen, a mini-party that had seceded from Likud over its failure to include Sephardim in its leaderships, and with Meimad, the minuscule moderate Orthodox party. In addition, on key issues he was at one with Yitzhak Mordechai, who at the last minute pulled out of the race for premier. A non-ideological member of the Likud, Mordechai defected to form the Center Party, together with Dan Meridor, another apostate from Netanyahu's cabinet. In the race for the premiership, Barak could also score well with the "left of the left"—Meretz and Shinui—which were ready to make a virtue of necessity.

Labor and Likud were agreed that the Oslo peace process should be resumed and that the American connection, as vital as ever, needed to be kept front and center. There was also a broad if unspoken consensus on what was precluded: withdrawal to the borders of

1967, a re-division of Jerusalem, renouncement of the West Bank settlement blocs, and a right of return for the refugees. While both Netanyahu and Barak were reconciled to the establishment of some form of Palestinian autonomy, neither entertained the prospect of a fully sovereign and independent state. The Palestinian leaders could never be co-equal negotiating partners, and remained only supplicants to be propitiated with trivial concessions. Netanyahu and Barak did differ on how much to concede to the Palestinians in terms of territory and political rights, and on some aspects of settlement policy; but they were equally extreme in their refusal to envisage any curtailment of the de facto outposts of Greater Israel. Netanyahu's coalition, which included a powerful "right of the right," was driven by a religiously tinged, politically expedient, and totalizing ideology proclaiming Judea and Samaria to be part of an indivisible "holy land." Labor, renamed One Israel, was organized around a secular pragmatism, implicitly expansive but without an explicit end-goal. Likud hastened the foundation of scores of colonies near Nablus, Ramallah, and Hebron; Labor, beginning with the Etzion Bloc, favored the development of the Maale Adumim, Gi'vat Ze'ev, and Har Homa complexes around Jerusalem. Yet settlements per se, ostensibly rooted in Zionism, had for both parties become constitutive of the very state of Israel.

But settlements were hardly the only concern. Much more than in 1996, the election of 1999 was informed by socio-economic issues which, in turn, were widely assumed to have a profound effect on the future course of the peace process. Israel's unrelenting Palestinian and regional foreign policy greatly aggravated domestic tensions: the allegedly necessary military and security expenditures continued to bleed the exchequer of funds for economic, social, and cultural programs for the rapidly growing disadvantaged sectors of Israeli society, both Jewish and Muslim. These mounting inequalities were made more pernicious by rising ethnic cleavages. Fifty years after the foundation of the state, the Ashkenazim were a fast-shrinking but still dominant minority. The Jewish population of 5 million was now over half Oriental or Sephardic. Relatively newly-fledged Zionists and recent immigrants, they were radically different in mental outlook, cultural capital, and religious practice from the preceding European aliyahs, which recognized themselves in the worldviews, languages, and mores of the Founding Fathers. Barely touched by either the promise or the treachery of the Enlightenment, the members of this population became the chief social bearers and agents of a certain re-Judaization of civil and political society. Israel's Ashkenazim scorned the Jews from the Arab and Muslim Middle East in much the way that

Western and Central European Jews had historically disdained their brethren in and from Eastern Europe. In turn, the Sephardic communities blamed the old establishment for relegating them to second-class economic, cultural, and social status.

Shas especially, but other religious parties too, turned this broadly grounded alienation to good political account—as did Likud, though its religiosity was superficial. In fact, the relation between these parties and their would-be constituencies was synergistic: ultra-nationalism and Orthodoxy stoked each other. The disadvantaged half of Israel's Jewish population ever more actively opposed renouncing any of the occupied territories. And under the spiritual guidance of Ovadiah Yosef, former Sephardic chief rabbi, it supported strengthening the role of religion: the synagogue, conservative and Orthodox, increasingly held the prerogative in matters of nationality, conversion, marriage, divorce, and burial. From 1989 to 1999 Shas had raised its representation in the Knesset from four to seventeen seats. It succeeded in large part because it did not limit itself to preaching from the pulpit and electioneering, but developed a vast network of nurseries, pre-schools, summer camps, and welfare services in ways the leaders of Hamas and Hezbollah could appreciate. With time the party came to rely increasingly on government subsidies to finance this social outreach. In exchange for state aid, it sold its political support to the highest bidder—be it a Likud- or Labor-headed coalition. Shas sought cabinet seats. It was not likely to become a force for accommodation with the Palestinians.

Russian immigrants were another significant bloc. The first wave had fled the Soviet regime from 1980 onwards for political and cultural reasons; the second came after 1989, in search of economic opportunity. At the turn of the millennium, the total of 500,000 Russians accounted for 10 per cent of Israel's Jewish population. In contrast to the Oriental or Sephardic Jews, they were on the whole non-Jewish Jews. They were also, on average, much better educated—many of them with advanced degrees; and they had smaller families. Yet their social isolation as newcomers, coupled with a visceral anti-collectivism, caused the Russian community to affiliate with the secular and muscular right. Yisrael B'Aliyah, headed by Sharansky, and then Yisrael Beiteinu (Israel Our Home), led by Avigdor Lieberman, established close ties with Likud. In the last analysis, the Russian community was anything but a font of support for social reform and the peace process.

In May 1999 only Netanyahu and Barak survived to square off for the premiership, while 31 parties contested the parliamentary race.

Under the proportional voting system, fifteen of them won representation in the unicameral Knesset.

In the campaign for the head office, style counted beyond measure. Netanyahu's candidacy was laden with all the misjudgments and effronteries, including his clumsy defiance of Clinton, that had brought down his government in the first place. Barak's political track record did not stand out, but as a former field general, head of Army Intelligence, and chief of the general staff he had the swagger and aura so valued in Israel. During his 35-year military career he had served under Begin and Shamir, Peres and Rabin. In 1982 he had been deputy commander of the IDF during Operation Peace in Galilee. From mid-1995 through mid-1996 he was first minister of interior and then minister of foreign affairs under Peres. His credentials qualified him for membership in Israel's select caste of warrior-politicians.

Although during the election campaign Barak dodged the Palestinian Question, his thick cluster of military decorations made him immune to Netanyahu's charge that he would jeopardize Israel's security by surrendering crucial strategic positions and being soft on Arafat and the "terrorists." That left him free to criticize the outgoing Likud government for its Thatcherite ultra-liberal economic and social policies, which had fallen disproportionately and onerously on the swelling underclass. Not that Barak proposed to cut back military expenditures or revive anything of the social contract devised between 1930 and 1977. Rather he fell in with Labor's march to the center, much as Clinton and Tony Blair had taken their parties in a similar direction. The American president's electoral strategists were even called in to help manage his campaign.

Whereas Barak was distant and cautious, Netanyahu was brash and categorical. The latter preached to the converted and appealed to the silent majority of the forgotten. Barak, taking the left for granted, reached into the center and center right, not least because he meant to reassure and cajole foreign capitals, especially Washington. On May 17, 1999, Barak decisively defeated Netanyahu by a majority of almost 400,000, gathering 56 per cent of the popular vote. But in the election for the Knesset, One Israel, with only 20 per cent of the vote, barely captured 26 out of 120 seats. Even with the addition of the 10 Meretz and 6 Shinui representatives, with a combined popular vote of 12.6 per cent, the left-of-center held only 42 seats, 19 short of a majority.

All in all, the elections marked a substantial rightward shift in the domestic balance of power with consequences for the new administration's Palestinian and foreign policy. The rise of the ethnically based and Orthodox religious parties was a convulsion: Shas, United

Torah Judaism, and the National Religious Party together secured 27 seats, nearly one quarter of the house and 21 per cent of the vote. With 17 representatives and 13 per cent of the vote Shas emerged as the third-largest party after One Israel and Likud. Far short of a parliamentary mandate, Barak chose to forge a coalition that left him beholden to the center right, in which there were few, if any, supporters of land for peace.

A breakdown of the vote maps the socio-geography of the new political forces. In Haifa and Tel Aviv Barak got, respectively, 68 per cent and 62 per cent of the vote; the militantly secular parties 14 per cent and 19 per cent; Shas, 6 per cent and 11 per cent. In Ariel, Maale Adumim, and Jerusalem, Barak scored 16 per cent, 27 per cent, and 35 per cent, with the secular parties 7 per cent, 9 per cent, and 12 per cent, and Shas at 8 per cent, 14 per cent, and 17 per cent. In the southern cities of Ashkelon, Bersheva, and Kiryat Gat, Barak took between 40 per cent and 45 per cent of the vote, Shas between 21 per cent and 26 per cent. In the rapidly growing interior and southern cities in general, in which the upper and professional middle classes were less ascendant than in the northern, cosmopolitan Mediterranean littoral, Shas and the religious parties made the greatest inroads while the secularist parties failed to enlarge their narrow social and political base.

Just as Barak's victory was not a victory for the center-left, so the defeat of Netanyahu and the reflux of Likud from forty-two Knesset seats in 1992 to nineteen in 1999 was not a defeat for the center-right. This loss redounded largely to the benefit of the religious parties—and also the two Russian parties, which won ten seats. On the far right, with four, stood the expulsionist Moledet.

A staid centrist, Barak, the left's anti-hero, would have to enlist several parties to form a working majority, one of which would have to be Likud or Shas. Although he initiated discussions with Sharon, Netanyahu's successor at the head of Likud, he soon came to terms with Eli Yishai, the chairman of Shas—presumably because he would keep a relatively freer hand in the peace process, his urgent priority. The cost would come in domestic policy, particularly state–synagogue relations. And opting for Shas meant contending with the National Religious Party and Torah Judaism as well. All three religious parties were opposed to repealing the draft exemption for *yeshiva* students and, with minor variants, espoused the idea of Greater Israel.

After nearly two months of hard factional bargaining, Barak presented his cabinet to the Knesset. Like Rabin, he kept the Defense portfolio for himself. In a sign that he proposed to work for a minimalist Oslo—which he had originally opposed—Barak made

David Levy, his hard-line One Israel partner, foreign minister; Peres was perceived to be too soft. Shas was compensated with four ministries that were most likely to guarantee the wonted subsidies and reassure its votaries: Labor and Social Affairs, National Infrastructures, Health, and Religion. The crucial Education portfolio went to Yossi Sarid, the leader of Meretz, who threatened to go into opposition should it go to Shas. Yet Shaul Yahalom of the National Religious Party became Sarid's deputy minister. With Sharansky at Interior, the conservative tilt was unmistakable. Limited by law to eighteen cabinet ministers, there remained not all that many posts for Labor, and few of them were pivotal. Shlomo Ben Ami was assigned to Internal Security and Yossi Beilin to Justice, but Peres was relegated to the new and untested Ministry for Regional Cooperation. As for the Palestinian Israelis, even though they gave nearly all their 520,000 votes to Barak, they continued to be politically excluded. On July 6, 1999—the very day that Barak delivered his policy speech and introduced his cabinet—he asked that it be legally enlarged to twenty-four (it was) in order to assign additional portfolios to the faltering Labor Party, so long ago disenchanted of its hope, coherence, and engagement.

Barak's coalition mirrored the unprecedented factionalism in parliament and political society at large, which itself reflected the rifts in civil society. As heterodox and precarious as the coalition was, Barak, himself an Oslo skeptic, thought it necessary and adequate for reviving the peace process, taking up once again the Wye River accord.

In Israel and the diaspora the doves celebrated the ascension of a candidate they genuinely considered one of their own, not merely the lesser of two evils. They tended to ignore the fact that, under Rabin, Barak had opposed Oslo, and that on the essentials of the peace issue he and Netanyahu had more in common than not. But the doves also balked at the decisively rightist orientation of the new government coalition, which was bound to redouble Barak's diplomatic rigidity, already grounded in his firm belief in a Greater Israel and in the nation's insuperable might.

While the White House cannot have been so sanguine about the reconfiguration of the Knesset, it was no doubt relieved. The new premier lost no time reassuring Clinton that Israel's recent defiance of Washington was a thing of the past. What Barak was most concerned about was that, by scuttling the Wye Accord and needlessly disparaging the peace process, Netanyahu had prompted the President to move closer to Arafat, at Israel's expense. Barak adopted a different demeanor, acting more prudently as he prepared to resume negotiations with the Palestinians—as well as with Syria, which held the key to Lebanon, headquarters of Hezbollah.

After weeks of Israeli–Palestinian negotiations, on September 4, 1999 Barak and Arafat signed a revised Wye Accord in Sharm el-Sheikh. The agreement fixed a timetable for three further reductions in Israeli forces from areas of the West Bank (chiefly in the Nablus–Jenin region and south of Hebron) before their transfer to either full or partial Palestinian control: on September 5, 7 per cent of the area would be transferred; on November 15, a further 2 per cent; and on January 20, 2000, a further 6.1 per cent. Israel would still have direct military and civil control of roughly 60 per cent of the West Bank. The memorandum also committed Israel to the release of 350 prisoners, and enjoined the two parties to work out a protocol for establishing two safe-passage routes between Gaza and the West Bank. Within five months from September 13, they would formulate a set of principles to guide final status negotiations, looking to the completion of a permanent peace settlement by September 13, 2000—seven years after the signing of the Oslo accords. The Israeli cabinet approved the Sharm el-Sheikh understanding by twenty-one votes to two. Barak adhered to its terms for about two months. Rather than treat the redeployments as occasions to build trust, he turned a succession of trivial land disputes into so many tests of will, thereby ensuring intensified suspicion among the Palestinians. This was the old tactic of stalling for time to establish facts on the ground. On March 21, two full months after the deadline, Israel finally authorized the last transfer. Just as the prevarication on redeployment maintained the bad blood, so did the delay in the release of prisoners.

Final status talks proceeded at a similar deliberate crawl. David Levy and Mahmoud Abbas met, as agreed, on September 13 at the Erez checkpoint, and their delegates followed suit in Ramallah on November 8. The Israeli and Palestinian delegations, headed by Oded Eran and Yasser Abed Rabbo respectively, began talks on January 30, 2000. Immediately it became clear that Eran was under instruction to dictate Israel's unsparing terms, rather than to negotiate. On February 2 Arafat implied that Barak's *démarche* was fundamentally no different from Netanyahu's, and his encounter with the Prime Minister—their first since September 4—at the Beit Hanun crossing led him to allege that Barak was an even worse partner. With the peace process again stalling, the Chairman started to let it be known that, if there were no deal by September 2000, he would have every right to declare Palestinian statehood.

To end the shadow-boxing, in April Rabbo presented Eran with a restatement of the Palestinian delegation's starting position: the denial of the legitimacy of Israeli settlements; non-acceptance of an Israeli military presence inside Palestine's pre-1967 borders; and refusal of the settlement of Palestinian refugees outside their homeland. As for procedure, core issues like Jerusalem and the refugees should not continue to be dismissed. On May 19 the Israeli delegation submitted a final status map outlining a scattering of autonomous cantons totaling 66 per cent of the West Bank and the annexation of 20 per cent of it by Israel, leaving the remaining 14 per cent under Israeli control pending future negotiations. The deadlock was complete. All but powerless, Arafat could only continue to make noises about a declaration of independence. Barak cautioned, like Netanyahu, that were Arafat to go any further, Israel would proceed to annex certain areas of the West Bank. With hostilities threatening once again, Clinton issued an invitation, in early July, to a three-way summit at Camp David.

The Barak government, meanwhile, religiously honoring Oslo in the breach, approved the expansion of existing settlements and the creation of new ones, along with more bypass roads, checkpoints, and road-blocks, and further demolitions and confiscations of land. Settlers commandeered more hilltops and uprooted the fruit trees and vines of Palestinian villagers, not infrequently with the tacit support of the occupying military and civil authorities. In all this Barak merely followed in the steps of his post-1967 predecessors. Whereas he promised, disin-genuously, not to build any new settlements, he also pledged not to dismantle any of the existing ones. And on September 14, the day following the beginning of the final status talks, Barak offered unflagging support for the still burgeoning Maale Adumim complex. Up to the time of Camp David II, while it was supposed to curb settlement activity, the Israeli government pushed ahead with expansion and development in the districts of Bethlehem, Hebron, Ramallah, and Nablus on the West Bank, as well as in Neve Dekalim in southern Gaza. In January and March 2000, Barak approved the expropriation of hundreds of dunams of Palestinian land for the construction of several bypass roads in these districts. In May and June the government released additional funds for the further spread of Maale Adumim, the Etzion Bloc, Har Homa, and Efrat. During the first half of 2000 alone, there was an increase of some 96 per cent in construction over the preceding year.

Although during the fall of 1999 the Yesha Council—the lobby of the religious settlers, and tied to the coalition religious parties—kept quiet, that winter it resumed agitating against any return of Judea and Samaria. The militant true believers in Jerusalem never let up. In July they twice staged incursions into the Al-Aqsa Mosque. That same month Yitzhak Levy, the housing minister, invited tenders for the construction of forty-five units for ultra-Orthodox Jews in Shuafat, in East Jerusalem. From the U.S. came renewed calls for the American embassy to be moved from Tel Aviv to Jerusalem. Burger King announced that it planned to open a branch in Maale Adumim, and Disney World in Florida was preparing an exhibit entitled "Jerusalem, Capital of Israel." Under pressure from key Arab states, both corporations desisted.

In the fall of 2000 the Housing Ministry issued invitations for bids to build new housing units in Givat Zeev, Maale Adumim, and the Etzion Bloc, while the construction of Har Homa raced ahead. Mayor Olmert reaffirmed, with Barak's blessing, the right of Israel to exercise sovereignty over an undivided Jerusalem. At no time since Oslo had there been any relaxation in the drive for a Greater Jerusalem. The undisguised settlement activity during the time that the supposedly Oslo-minded Barak was believed to be engaged in the peace process was not lost on the Palestinian insurgency. Throughout the occupied territories there were demonstrations, especially near settlements, which invited retribution by Israeli security forces. Settlers and Palestinian militants perpetuated their cycle of violence and vengeance.

As always, there were many more Palestinian than Israeli casualties. Most of the former were killed or wounded by the IDF, not by extremist settlers, who nevertheless inflicted considerable material damage and severe psychological harm; between 1,500 and 1,600 political prisoners remained in Israeli jails. Israelis had their own grievances. During the first six months of Barak's premiership there were five terrorist attacks—in Tiberias, Haifa, Netanya, Jerusalem, and Hadera, where twenty-six were wounded in an explosion at the market. The PLO seized upon the fifty-second anniversary of the Nakba, on May 15, 2000, to call a one-day general strike, which offered an outlet for cumulative resentment over the settlement drive, the glacial final status negotiations, and the calculated delay in the release of prisoners. In some precincts the strike triggered unrest that continued for several days, often resulting in confrontations with both the Israeli and Palestinian security forces. Several Palestinians were killed, and many hundreds wounded and arrested, particularly near the settlements of Bet El, northeast of Ramallah, and Netzarim, in Gaza. On May 21 Barak invoked this unrest to justify a suspension of exploratory negotiations in Stockholm. One month later General Shaul Mofaz, chief of the general staff and member of Likud, served notice that Israel's armed forces were primed to use heavy weapons, including helicopters and rocket bombs, to counter any future intifada. The threat had the predictable effect of rousing rather than deterring the PLO, let alone Hamas and Islamic Jihad. And it undermined the PNA's effort to coordinate security measures with Israeli authorities and bring to terms the religious and secular militants. With the situation worsening, the latter increasingly contested Fatah's leadership of the popular resistance.

On July 5 the White House announced that Barak and Arafat had accepted Clinton's invitation to the trilateral summit starting on July 11. The "negotiators having reached an impasse,", the objective was to see if they could not break out of it and reach "an agreement on the core issues that have fueled a half-century of conflict between Israelis and Palestinians." Besides these official reasons, Clinton wanted to make one last effort concerning the problem in which he had invested himself so earnestly. Having ostensibly stood by Arafat at Wye and Gaza, the President now intended to help Barak, who had asked for the summit as a way to shore up his fragile coalition. Washington was anxious too about threats to its own strategic interests. Barak had good reason to fret about the unsteadiness of his cabinet and parliamentary majority. Faced with a simultaneous nationalist defiance by the Palestinians beyond the Green Line and troubling socio-economic conditions at home, the far right folded its domestic discontent into the clamor for a Greater Israel that precluded even the semblance of negotiations with the Palestinians. Shas, the National Religious Party, and Yisrael Beliyah became aggressively refractory immediately before Camp David. By July 9, all three parties had pulled their ministers from the cabinet, forcing Barak to lean further to the right. They also abandoned the coalition in the Knesset, leaving it with only 43 out of 120 deputies. Barak's was a minority government when he arrived in Washington, and on the very eve of the summit it narrowly weathered a Likud-sponsored no-confidence motion. It barely survived two additional right-wing censure motions immediately following Barak's return. On August 3, Foreign Minister Levy resigned, wary that the premier would make unwarranted territorial concessions and flinch on Jerusalem. In short, even though Barak was anything but a dove, his wager on the far right was a losing one. The right's hold on the government reinforced his predisposition not to compromise on the core issues pitting Israelis against Palestinians.

Besides toting this heavy political baggage to Camp David, Barak brought along the same trunk of tactics and attitudes as his predecessors. The give-and-take of negotiation was replaced by bob-and-weave, always in order to permit further consolidation of the territories. To this was added a visceral condescension to Arafat: during the fortnight of talks the prime minister managed to avoid having a single face-to-face meeting with the Chairman. Barak's position consisted of four "red lines" in the sand: no return to the pre-1967 borders; no discussion of Israel's sovereignty over the whole of Jerusalem; no acceptance of legal, civil, or moral responsibility for the refugees, who would continue to be denied the right to return; and annexation of the settlement blocs on the West Bank, accounting for 80 per cent of the settlers. There was no thought of a fully sovereign Palestinian state, since Israel meant to keep strategic and economic control over the West Bank and Gaza. Barak would only offer concessions compatible with his constraining political exigencies and the intent to keep reaching for a Greater Israel. Ultimately he trusted in Israel's American-supported military power to enable him to impose a unilateral peace and avoid making tangible proposals or compromises.

Arafat had not asked for the summit; Clinton's invitation took him and his associates by surprise. He had to accept, but did so with reservations. Previous negotiations had not sufficiently narrowed the outstanding differences to make meaningful discussion possible. In keeping with Rabbo's position paper of April, Arafat drew his own red lines. Still embracing U.N. Resolutions 242 and 194, including the principle of land-for-peace, Arafat called for Israel to withdraw from the West Bank, East Jerusalem, and the Gaza Strip, as well as to recognize a fully sovereign Palestinian state in the evacuated territories. He was under immense pressure from the hardliners in the Palestinian Central Council and the militants to defy the Israelis. Like Barak, he too was instantly hounded for preparing to betray the cause of a free Palestine by making shameful concessions. Unlike Barak, however, Arafat approached Camp David in a flexible frame of mind. As always, he had no military and little diplomatic leverage to speak of, and he understood that, during the election season in America, the president, solicitous of the Jewish vote, was likely to be less attentive to the Palestinian people's plight. The specter of another intifada, more lethal than that of 1987, was Arafat's chief bargaining chip. Apparently before the summit convened, he apprised Clinton of his willingness to consider a swap of Palestinian lands with large settlements for equivalent Israeli land, an arrangement for Israeli sovereignty over certain settlements in East Jerusalem, and an agreement on the refugees that would strike a balance "between the Israelis' demographic worries and our own concerns." Barak eventually interpreted this last, not unreasonable, offer as a heinous act of blackmail—a threat to subvert the Jewish state by swamping it with Muslim Arabs.

Not that Arafat was any less manipulative than Barak, who both used and bridled Israel's intemperate militants. Arafat and his associates, quite apart from maintaining an equivocal relationship with Hamas, fell far short in their efforts to keep in check anti-Israeli propaganda in the Palestinian media, and to confiscate illegal firearms. By denying the blight of corruption and the deficit of democracy in the Palestinian Authority, they enabled Israel to vilify their governance, and by association their cause. No matter how many Hamas activists Arafat arrested and extradited, his security measures were belittled and mistrusted—just as Barak was unable to reassure the Palestinians by occasionally apprehending a direct-action settler.

The talks at Camp David focused on three core issues: refugees, the configuration of the Palestinian state, and Jerusalem. All remained explosive, as mediation was preemptively defeated by the old atmosphere of mutual suspicion and the disparities of power. Having inherited historical Zionism's unmindfulness of Palestine's indigenous Arab population, for fifty years Israel's political class and public intelligentsia had never seriously reexamined the problem, and nor had their supporters in the diaspora. To the extent that the matter was raised at all, it was to deny any responsibility—political, moral, economic, legal—for the plight of the refugees. With time it became only more difficult to come to terms with the nation's original sin, now stained darker by confiscation of countless dunams of Palestinian land and the destruction of scores of Palestinian villages.

Admittedly, by the turn of the millennium, partly thanks to revisions of the official rendering of the refugee story by a new generation of investigative journalists and historians, almost half of Jewish Israelis conceded that their country bore some measure of culpability for the mass exodus in 1948. Even so, most believed the refugees should either remain in their countries of exile or in a Palestinian state, whatever its eventual configuration and borders. In the year 2000 there were some 3.7 million Palestinian refugees in the diaspora, including 720,000 in Gaza, 600,000 on the West Bank, 1.2 million in Jordan, 400,000 in Lebanon, and 460,000 in Syria. Of these, nearly 1.4 million were spread among fifty-nine camps. The refugees' existence was the crux of the Israeli–Palestinian imbroglio: the Palestinian political class considered and represented them as fundamental to their cause; the Israeli political class privately negated them, while publicly charging that their Palestinian counterparts were using the refugees as a stratagem.

Yet Barak, and certainly Clinton, knew that in the final status negotiations at Camp David there could be no side-stepping the issue. After all these years, Arafat simply could not be expected to postpone it to the end of time. U.N. Resolution 194 of December 1948 had laid down that "the refugees wishing to return to their homes and live in peace with their neighbors should be permitted to do so at the earliest practicable date [and] compensation should be paid for the property of those choosing not to return." Although Arafat swore by the right of return, he was realistic about the need for a compromise, as long as Israel admitted its share of blame for the exodus. But Israel would not. Barak categorically gainsaid any obligation to contend with the refugees. Arafat indicated that he understood the need not to "destabilize the demographic balance in Israel." Apparently there was vague talk not only of allowing some 100,000 refugees to return on humanitarian grounds of family reunion, but also of a multinational compensation fund. Ultimately, however, Israel did not submit any credible proposals toward a compromise on the right to return. For Barak it was ideologically and politically unthinkable.

He was scarcely more forthcoming on the geography and constitution of a future Palestine. He offered to transfer to the Palestinians the whole of Gaza (145 square miles) and 81 per cent of the land area of the West Bank (2,200 square miles). The territories to the east of Israel and west of the Jordan would be divided into two disconnected cantons on either side of the highway running from Jerusalem to the Dead Sea. An enclave around Jericho would form a third canton; Gaza would be the fourth. Presented only orally, this was even less of an offer than met the ear: quite apart from being broken into four shards, the state would have no meaningful sovereignty. Ultimate control of its armed forces, airspace, border crossings, diplomacy, highways, water resources, and economy—these Israel reserved to itself. There were to be three additional curtailments: Israel would "lease" the Jordan Valley; the settlements would not count as Palestinian territory; and Jerusalem remained all but untouchable. Ostensibly for reasons of security, Barak demanded that Israel have jurisdiction over large areas of the Jordan Valley for up to twenty-five years. The time "limit" on this fertile 10 per cent of the West Bank would allow for expanding the forty settler colonies there, complicating any future withdrawal. Besides that, in the event of a military threat from across the Jordan river, Israel reserved the permanent right to deploy troops in the region.

By mid 2002 the number of settlers in the occupied territories stood at about 200,000, not counting those in East Jerusalem. The archipelago they constituted covered about 5 per cent of the West Bank and over 10 per cent of Gaza. The attendant bypass roads, checkpoints, roadblocks, and military bases set up to protect and service their settlements were themselves naturally a further constraint on Palestinian sovereignty. Whereas Israel would guarantee these settlements an extraterritorial status in the future Palestine, three blocs adjacent to Jerusalem would be annexed outright: Maale Adumim, Efrat, and the Etzion Bloc. Counted together with three small communities to the north, Maale Adumim was the largest. Spread over about 17,000 acres and stretching eastwards to the outskirts of the Jericho enclave, it all but bisected the West Bank. Israel also proposed to exercise direct control over Ariel and several nearby rural settlements extending deep into Palestinian territory to the north. The idea was to allow their residents direct and safe access to Israel by way of the so-called Trans-Samaria highway, which was off-limits to Palestinians. Kiryat Arba, near Hebron, would be similarly connected. To compensate for these expropriations, where 60 per cent of the settlers lived, Israel offered to transfer back to the Palestinians one unit of Israeli land for every nine taken. Although Arafat was amenable to an exchange of territory, he was not about to accept terms so transparently inequitable.

What Barak proposed for Jerusalem—not an original plan, but prefigured as far back as Ben-Gurion—was equally shameless. A few weeks before Camp David, Barak had declared that

> only those who do not understand the depth of the total emotional bond of the Jewish people to Jerusalem, only those who are completely estranged from the vision of the nation, from the poetry of that nation's life, from its faith and from the hope it has cherished for generations—only persons in that category could possibly entertain the thought that the State of Israel would actually concede even a part of Jerusalem.

Although Arafat gingerly laid claim to East Jerusalem as the capital of the future Palestinian state, Barak was persuaded that, with Clinton's support, he could prevail on him to renounce it, probably confident that Arafat, unlike himself, would hesitate to press such a religiously sensitive political demand.

As an inducement, Barak suggested that certain of the city's outlying Palestinian villages, including Abu Dis and Sawahre, be incorporated into the West Bank. Within Arab East Jerusalem he would grant the Palestinians a large degree of self-rule in several outer Arab neighborhoods, including Beit Hanina and Shuafat, which would remain noncontiguous. But then, while trying to bargain Arafat out of East Jerusalem, Barak went too far: he demanded authority over the Temple Mount, or Haram al-Sharif, holy to Palestinian Muslims and to Islam worldwide. Until that point only zealots had called for Jewish control of the site. First in 1929, and most recently in September 1996, the incitement of the Temple Mount activists had precipitated deadly riots. The leaders of the Yishuv and of Israel knew only too well that to defy the sanctified complex governed by Jerusalem's Supreme Islamic Council and Trust was to risk inflaming religious passions across the whole Middle East.

Yet, through Clinton's would-be mediators, Barak not only insisted on taking over the Temple Mount, which he now called the "holy of holies," but also explicitly vindicated the right of Jews to worship on the sacred hill. The architects of this pretense fantasized about building a synagogue next to Islamic holy sites. In Palestinian eyes Israel, with U.S. backing, seemed to be speaking—and preparing to act—like the ultra-Orthodox sect that, with government support, had turned Hebron into one of the chief flashpoints of Israeli–Palestinian violence. The Palestinian Authority responded by insisting on full control of all four quarters of the Old City, though Israel was to have free access to the Jewish Quarter and the Wailing Wall. Eventually the Israelis envisaged conceding dominion over the mosques to the Palestinians, while retaining control of the land they occupied. But Arafat, though he overlooked the emergence of the religious factor in the negotiations, could not dissociate the issue of the Temple Mount from Barak's claim to more than the whole of Jerusalem.

Judging by the nature of Israel's proposals, Barak went to Camp David not to try to adjust conflicting claims but only to lay down terms. In keeping with Israel's political class as a whole, Barak lacked all sense of limits. Since Camp David II was intended to advance final status talks in line with the Oslo accords, he might have marked out judicious parameters for pursuing a global settlement. Such a *démarche* would have involved not simply striking piecemeal bargains, but conceiving them as part of an overall design that would allow for the vital interests of the Palestinians, in pursuit of a historical reconciliation. But like those earlier leaders, Barak never seriously entertained the idea of a sovereign Palestinian state. All he had envisioned and was prepared to endorse was a collection of fragmented enclaves literally marginalized by settlements—a pseudo-state under Israel's sway.

*　　*　　*

Camp David II marked the failure of the Oslo peace process. Barak and Arafat, dug in along their respective "red lines," made no measurable headway on the four core issues. Clinton's anything-but-even-handed ministrations did not help. The token concession by Barak to allow the villages of Al Eizarya, Abu Dis, and Sawahre, which until 1967 had been outside East Jerusalem's city limits, to serve as an extraterritorial and encircled capital of a virtually non-sovereign Palestinian state exposed again the immutable haughtiness of Israel's political caste.

Prior to Camp David, Barak had sought an accommodation with Syria and Lebanon. Eighteen years after Operation Peace for Galilee had forced the PLO out of southern Lebanon only to see the Syrian-backed Hezbollah take its place, and despite a considerable security zone, Israel's northern borders remained porous and unsafe. To reduce the loss of life and free up troops to pacify the West Bank and Gaza, Tel Aviv pressured Damascus and Beirut to accept terms favorable to Israel. After this diplomatic initiative miscarried, as he had intimated it would during his election campaign, Barak ordered a pullout from southern Lebanon, to take place in May 2000. Intransigents and hawks denounced the move for emboldening the terrorists, while their Palestinian and Arab counterparts celebrated what they took to be a glaring victory for Hezbollah and a vindication of their blind trust in armed resistance. Hezbollah promptly took advantage of Israel's redeployment. Except in military terms, however, the conflict with Syria was less urgent than the struggle with the Palestinians—less charged emotionally, symbolically, and politically, and therefore ultimately easier to contain and compromise over.

Barak's temporizing before, during, and following Camp David shattered the rising expectations generated by Oslo and the establishment of the autonomous Palestinian National Authority. With the new order delivering few material, psychological, or political dividends, frustration gave way to rage in the refugee camps of the West Bank and Gaza Strip. The secular and Islamic militants encouraged the rising disenchantment, with a view to strengthening the hand of Arafat and contesting what they considered to be his false-hearted policies and methods. The Chairman was caught between the militants of his own Fatah and of the rival Islamist formations, who urged him to stand his ground, and the Israelis, who made the neutralization of both the first condition both for implementing existing agreements and for further negotiations. Too weak to join battle with his radical opposition, but unwilling entirely dispense with it entirely, Arafat could not close his eyes to the risk of a fratricidal war among Palestinians that could only benefit Israel.

Barak and his cabinet were alert to the rising social ferment in the territories and the political infighting in the Palestinian resistance. But, rather than help Arafat by meeting him part of the way, they made minimal concessions in what they considered a zero-sum game to be won by force and ruse. The government continued on its invasive course, and General Mofaz declared the year 2000 "the year of preparedness" for the impending explosion of violence in the West Bank and Gaza Strip. There was nothing conciliatory or considerate in Barak's ways of dealing with the Palestinian leadership and the population of the territories. He kept testing limits that he took to be nonexistent, impervious to the Palestinians' broken hopes and hardships.

Though Barak professed to be a man of peace and to have offered the Palestinians the "best deal" imaginable for all time, he was a hawk who, no less than any of his predecessors, had internalized Jabotinsky's expansionist and military logic. Presently, however, he was trapped by his own charade: the Israeli right pounced on what they regarded as generous giveaways to accuse him of being soft on Arafat and terrorism; the Palestinians decried the same gestures as deceitful, and portrayed Barak as just the latest in a long line of Zionist and Israeli irreconcilables. Ariel Sharon, the ultra-militant wing of Likud, and the true believers were lying in wait. Among the Palestinians, Marwan Barghouti emerged as a popular tribune critical of Arafat's failings and in favor of unity between Fatah and Hamas, in anticipation of a fourth intifada.

A deceptive two-month calm after Camp David was broken by Ariel Sharon's ascent to the Temple Mount, which Barak condoned. This event revealed the dynamics, both internal and international, of the Israeli–Palestinian contest. On September 25, 2000, Sharon, the presumptive leader of the Likud after Netanyahu's defeat, announced his intention to "visit our holy sites" on the Temple Mount on September 28. He meant to affirm a jurisdiction over the sacred ground that only extremist individuals and voluntary associations like the Temple Mount Faithful had ever presumed to assert. This time it would be done with great fanfare and in the glare of the media. Concerned that Sharon's "visit" might provoke the Palestinians—who were bound to suspect its political motives—Israeli and Palestinian security officials conferred, and agreed to take certain precautionary measures. The chief of the West Bank's Palestinian Preventive Security Organization is said to have told his Israeli counterpart that, provided Sharon did not set foot in the mosques on the Temple Mount, there should be "no reason for concern"; yet it is unlikely that Jibril Rajub was told of the impending intrusion. But Arafat assumed the worst. After unsuccess-fully urging Barak to head it off, the Chairman told his associates that "having started at Camp David, the battle of Jerusalem will continue with Sharon's visit to the Haram"; both the city and the Al-Aqsa Mosque were "in danger." Saeb Erekat, Arafat's chief diplomat, and the Arab–Palestinian members of the Knesset shared this apprehen-sion.

Even President Clinton, who had unduly blamed Arafat, and only Arafat, for the failure of Camp David, cautioned Tel Aviv to recon-sider. But at the height of America's presidential race, and with Clinton about to leave the White House, Sharon and Israel's compo-site right favored George W. Bush and the right-wing Republicans, including their born-again confederates, over Al Gore and the centrist Democrats. During his recent trip to the U.S., Sharon had met with key leaders of the pro-Israel lobby which, hostile to Oslo, was mobilizing support for the Republicans as well as for the hardliners, including the settlers, in Israel.

At 7.30 a.m. on Thursday, September 28, Sharon passed through the Maghrabi, or Western Gate, on his impious pilgrimage to the hal-lowed plaza. He advanced shoulder to shoulder with six Likud members of the Knesset: Moshe Arens, Reuven Rivlin, Naomi Blu-menthal, Yehoshua Matza, Gideon Ezra, and Ayub Kara. For security reasons, the delegation had a military escort of over 1,000. On reaching the site Sharon was said to have exclaimed "the Temple Mount is in our hands," as if to echo the cry that had burst forth at the capture of East Jerusalem in 1967. As minister of defense, if not prime minister, Barak must have approved the deployment of the praetorian guard. No doubt he went along because he and Sharon basically agreed on Jerusalem: apart from their relatively close personal ties, they were sworn to the same military and political operational code, as was Mayor Olmert. In the event neither Sharon nor any of his companions entered a mosque, and the "visit" ended by 8.30. An hour was enough, however, to reignite the fire that had last crackled in 1996, when Netanyahu had ordered the piercing of the Hasmonean Tunnel. Though bitter rivals, Sharon and Netanyahu—both secular extremists and political pyromaniacs—were alike unscrupulous in their instru-mentalization of religion.

Several Palestinian lawmakers and Arab-Palestinian Knesset mem-bers were among the approximately 150 men at prayer in the Al-Aqsa Mosque at the time of Sharon's visit. Some of them joined a crowd that, having assembled, hurled stones at the security escort as the political pilgrims turned back to the Western Gate. This clash was an almost ritualistic prelude to the genuine and widespread violence triggered by Sharon's calculated provocation. The next day, at 1.30 p.m., following the solemn Friday prayer, a host of young Muslims gathered to protest, again pelting the police with stones. This time over 500 Israeli policemen, under the command of the chief of the Jerusalem District, charged onto the Temple Mount. Against demonstrators they knew were unarmed, they began firing grenades and shooting rubber bullets, perhaps overreacting for fear the unrest would spill over into the plaza of the Wailing Wall below during Rosh Hashanah. Four Palestinians were killed and over 200 wounded.

The turbulence soon swept all over Israel–Palestine, turning into the fourth, or Al-Aqsa, intifada. Acknowledging no evil of its own making in the general plight of the Palestinians, the Israeli government blamed the latest upheaval entirely on their leadership: it was Arafat, the PLO, and the extremists who were guilty, not Barak's scuttling of Camp David. Of course, Israel was not alone in using religion, but both Sharon and Barak would have understood the logic of the situation: once the Temple Mount had been symbolically taken, the Noble Sanctuary would be perceived as violated and in imminent danger of further assault—and the tocsin would be rung.

Demonstrations duly erupted throughout the occupied territories, as well as in Arab communities within the borders of Israel. On September 30 nine Palestinians were killed and well over 100 injured, principally in and around Al-Bira, Hebron, and Nezarim. Over the next three days twenty more died and 500 more were wounded; Israel lost two soldiers. When the IDF pulled back after a confrontation in Nablus, Palestinian militants beset Joseph's Tomb. The first week of the Al-Aqsa intifada counted, on the Palestinian side, seventy-five dead and 3,000 injured; on the Israeli side, three soldiers and one settler were killed, and thirty-five armed men wounded. There were also clashes in Hadera, Jaffa, Nazareth, and Tiberias, where a mosque was desecrated. Israel sealed off the territories, shut down Gaza Airport, and closed the Rafah–Egypt crossing.

On October 7 Hezbollah took three Israeli soldiers hostage along the Lebanon border. Barak issued an ultimatum for their release. Five days later a Palestinian mob lynched two Israeli reservists in Ramallah. In reprisal Israeli bombs and missiles struck Gaza, Hebron, Jericho, Nablus, and Ramallah, destroying military installations and police stations, as well as radio and television towers, along with the usual collateral damage. Arafat answered by releasing Hamas prisoners from Palestinian jails—a tonic to the morale of the resistance. By the end of October, over 150 Palesinians were dead, many of them minors, and over 5,000 wounded.

Like most broad-based revolts, the intifada swelled up from below, and undoubtedly its scope and intensity took Arafat and the Palestinian political class as a whole by surprise. In mid October Shimon Peres judged that, although Arafat "had not started the intifada, once it was under way he directed it," in uneasy but inextricable collaboration with the militant left and Islamists. Israel's military had used its habitual excessive military force during the uprising, honed this time in keeping with General Mofaz's recent proclamation of "the year of preparedness." As latter-day Revisionists, he and his staff were primed to deal the resistance a death blow, and force the Palestinians, once and for all, to accept the inevitable: unconditional submission.

The Al-Aqsa intifada was far deadlier than the uprising of 1987–92, with a broad-based popular rebellion of stone-throwers joined by guerrilla fighters and suicide bombers. Since Oslo, although Israel retained full military control on the ground and command of the airspace, it had removed its occupation forces from the Arab towns, villages, and camps of the West Bank and Gaza (except for the guards of the religious sites in Bethlehem and Nablus, and the constabulary in Hebron). Accordingly the fury and violence were increasingly directed against settlers in the territories and civilians inside Israel. Religion now also played a greater role, judging by the creeping Islamization of Fatah alone. Hamas and the Islamic Jihad sent commandos into Israel and harnessed the popular rancor to pressure Arafat and the PNA to abandon the path of compromise and conciliation. They were confident they could reap the benefits of the Israeli aggression that had produced an abasement of everyday life.

The Temple Mount/Noble Sanctuary had long ago emerged as one of the world's most sensitive holy sites; and it was Barak who had made it only more so, perhaps unintentionally. By raising the issue of sovereignty at Camp David, he had emboldened Israel's ultra-religious to force a showdown between the holiest site of Judaism and the third-holiest site of Islam. Even if the history behind both claims was partly apocryphal, and their ancestral carriers imagined, such myths could still potentiate a nationalism that was hardly less idolatrous.

The tensions in the territories refused to subside. On November 20 a roadside bomb exploded alongside a school bus carrying settler children from Kfar Darom to Katif, in the Gaza Strip. Two adults accompanying them were killed, and nine others, including five children, were injured—the work of Tanzim, the radicalized military arm of Fatah. Sharon called on Prime Minister Barak to order the

assassination of Mohammed Dahlan—a prominent Fatah leader close
to Arafat, and head of an internal security organization—whom he
blamed for the attack. To put an end to the terror, Barak announced
that Israel would act "with all force necessary, without restraint." The
armed forces proceeded to strike offices, buildings, training camps,
port installations, and a television relay station. Soldiers also ravaged
nearby orchards and homes. Well over 100 Palestinians were injured,
half of them minors. Two days later, inside Israel, a car bomb
exploded on Hadera's main street, killing two civilians and injuring
over fifty. Shortly thereafter, the Israeli Land Administration issued a
tender for seventy-six new housing units in Elkana, a settlement south
of Qalqilya in the northwest West Bank. On December 8, near Jenin,
the guns of an Israeli tank killed four members of the PNA security
forces and a civilian. Many more Palestinians were wounded around
the same time, during several other clashes in the West Bank and Gaza.
At year's end some fifty Israelis were wounded by another car bomb in
Netanya, and a hand grenade ripped apart a bus in Tel Aviv, injuring
fourteen passengers.

Earlier that fall, the outside world had sought to intervene. Arafat
and Barak met in Paris on October 4 under the auspices of Jacques
Chirac and Madeleine Albright. The mediation foundered when the
Israeli prime minister, backed by the American secretary of state,
stood against an international investigation of the causes of the new
intifada. Three days later, by a vote of fourteen to zero, with the US
abstaining, the Security Council "deplore[d] the provocation carried
out at Al-Haram Al-Sharif . . . and the subsequent violence . . .
resulting in over eighty Palestinian deaths and many other casualties."
The resolution also "condemn[ed] acts of violence, especially the
excessive use of force against Palestinians." There followed a summit
at Sharm El-Sheikh on October 16. Arafat and Barak in vain met in the
presence of Kofi Annan, Clinton, King Abdullah of Jordan, Mubarak,
and Javier Solana, the European Union's external envoy.

Within a week the U.N. Commission on Human Rights, meeting in
Geneva, censured Israel's "grave and massive violations of the human
rights of the Palestinian people" and established a committee of
inquiry. Before adjourning, it condemned, by a vote of nineteen to
sixteen, with seventeen abstentions, Israel's "disproportionate and
indiscriminate use of force," and dispatched Mary Robinson, former
president of Ireland and then U.N. high commissioner for human
rights, to evaluate the situation in the territories, where she and her
entourage were then harassed by settlers, in Hebron especially. The
U.N. General Assembly approved a similar text. Israeli officials and

their supporters accused Arafat and his associates of playing the innocents to advance their cause.

On October 25, 2000, a week before the American elections, the House of Representatives, by a vote of 365 to 30, denounced the U.N. resolutions for being unfair to Israel, blamed the Palestinians for the recent violence, and enjoined Arafat to put an end to it. It also voted to extend a $3 billion aid package to Israel for the next fiscal year—close to 20 per cent of all American foreign aid. Just after November 8, however, the State Department announced the formation of an international commission to inquire into the uprising. Chaired by ex-Senator George Mitchell, who was coming out of a successful mediation of the troubles in Northern Ireland, it was composed of ex-Senator Walter Rudman, Turkey's ex-President Suleiman Demirel, the E.U.'s Solana, and the Norwegian foreign minister, Thorbjorn Jagland.

Between September 28 and mid December, the Israelis had killed close to 240 Palestinians and wounded close to 10,000, nearly half of them minors; many thousands had been arrested and imprisoned. By comparison, Israeli casualties were slight. The economic and social wounds were similarly disproportionate. Barak was not faring well. Since the elections of May 1999, he had not only failed to deliver on his promise to make meaningful progress on the Palestinian Question, but seemed unable to stop the spiral of violence. Sharon, spurred on by the secular and religious far right, was burning to challenge Barak and force early elections. His turn on the Temple Mount had been at least as much a move to boost Likud's political stock as to mark Israel's absolute claim to Jerusalem.

Consenting to Sharon's maneuver had weakened Barak. Caught in a double-bind and fearing a further erosion of his coalition in the Knesset, by October 12, in keeping with past practice, he invited Sharon to join a national emergency or unity government. Talks broke down when Sharon, confident that Barak's right-wing coalition partners would bend his way, insisted on a veto over the resumption and direction of the stalled peace process. Barak resigned as prime minister on December 9. Since the Knesset refused, by a vote of sixty-nine to forty-nine, to dissolve itself, Barak and Sharon were left to face off for the premiership, without an attendant vote for a new parliament. The election was set for February 6, 2001. In a garrison democracy in which critical thought and oppositional politics had atrophied, the electorate would be asked to choose between rival factions of the Greater Israel consensus, with no left to offset the secular and religious far right.

On the Palestinian side there was a similar radicalization of the resistance, now more clandestine, combative, and defiant. A pseudo-government, the inchoate Palestinian Authority lacked the "monopoly of the legitimate use of physical force" to enforce the order that was essential to guarantee its own ascendancy, and to fulfill its commitments to Israel. The growth of extremism in the secular if increasingly religionized left, in competition with mainline Fatah and the implacable Hamas and Islamic Jihad, testified to the fragility of Arafat's rule. The militants of the fourth intifada named themselves the Al-Aqsa Martyrs Brigades. An offshoot and now rival of Fatah, the name proclaims the circumstances that provoked the religionization of the uprising: Sharon's incendiary visit to the Temple Mount, the Al-Aqsa Mosque's iconic power. Although they resorted to the rhetoric of Islamic fundamentalism, the Al-Aqsa combatants were Palestinian nationalists worried about Hamas and the Islamic Jihad stealing their political thunder. Many of them were of a younger generation, graduates from the battles and jails of the intifada of 1987, and inspired by Hezbollah. They meant to rally popular support to harry the Israelis out of the West Bank, East Jerusalem, and Gaza—not drive them into the sea. Like the Tanzim, the Al-Aqsa Martyrs' Brigades, besides countervailing the Islamists ideologically and militarily, exerted pressure on Arafat and the Palestinian Authority to be less compromising in negotiations with Israel. They also railed against the corrupting sway of older landowners, businessmen, and political appointees in the executive and administrative leadership of the Palestinian Authority and Fatah.

At first the Tanzim and the Al-Aqsa Martyrs' Brigades struck mainly Israeli soldiers and settlers in the West Bank and Gaza. In early 2002, however, they turned increasingly to attacking civilians inside Israel. By then 1,000 Palestinians had died in the intifada, and the militants of Hamas and Islamic Jihad were embarrassing and defying Arafat and Fatah. None of this is to minimize the extent to which Arafat and Fatah, even if uneasily, at once bore down upon and supported the Tanzim and the Martyrs' Brigades. All things considered, however, at this stage Arafat and his inner circle, concerned about the moral, political, and diplomatic fallout of attacks on civilians inside Israel, strongly preferred stepping up the armed resistance to the occupation forces and settlers within the territories of the Palestinian para-state.

The political infighting of both the Israelis and Palestinians moved to an international stage. For partisan reasons, Barak pressed for a meeting to resume the peace process and end the intifada. Trailing

Sharon in the polls by at least sixteen points, less than three weeks before the election, scheduled for February 6, 2001, Barak concluded that nothing but a dramatic breakthrough in negotiations might give him an even chance. It was a sign of his desperation that he sought such an encounter even though he was neither disposed nor in a position to make compromises that he had resisted making at Camp David and after. Nor could Arafat afford to be any more forthcoming than he had been. And just as Likud, Sharon, and the religious right were poised to assail Barak for the slightest accommodation, so the secular and religious radicals on the Palestinian side were set to go after Arafat. Though he suspected that no serious agreement was possible, Arafat nevertheless agreed to the talks, motivated, like Barak, to keep Sharon from the premiership and to reassure the international community of the Palestinian people's commitment to détente.

They met on January 21, 2001, at Taba, an Egyptian Red Sea resort in the Sinai. The talks were bilateral, without a mediator. America observed from afar: George W. Bush was not focused on either the greater Middle East or the Israeli–Palestinian conflict. Putting little stock in the hastily improvised parley, Egypt sent a second-ranking official of the Foreign Ministry as an observer. Israel's delegation included the prominent doves Yossi Beilin, the minister of justice, and Yossi Sarid, leader of Meretz—both lately sidelined. But they took a back seat to Shlomo Ben-Ami, the foreign minister, Ammon Lipkin-Shahak, former chief of staff, and Gilad Sher, one of Barak's closest advisors. The Palestinians were headed by Ahmed Qurei, speaker of the Palestinian National Council, and also included Rabbo, Erakat, and Dahlan, by now chief of security. Representative of the impatient younger generation in Fatah, he had only recently been on Sharon's hit list for his alleged role in the bombing of the Gaza school bus.

The delegates broke up into four committees, each to deal with one of the four perennial issues: territory, including settlements; security; Jerusalem; and refugees. Both sides made crumb-sized offerings, and they were unable to narrow the overall divide. Barak came to realize that his eleventh-hour attempt to wrest some kind of consequential concession from Arafat—without a corresponding quid pro quo, and without Clinton's intercession—was wishful thinking. Ten days before the election he broke off negotiations and fixed to hang the whole stalemate on Arafat, apparently canceling a—potentially politically ruinous—scheduled meeting with Arafat in either Davos or Stockholm.

Not blameless himself, but unwilling once again to be made the scapegoat, Arafat lashed out preemptively the next day. The venue had changed from the desert to the Alps—at the World Economic Forum, in Davos. On January 28, with Peres on the dais, Arafat charged "the current government of Israel [with] waging, for the last four months, a savage and barbaric war as well as a blatant and fascist military aggression against the Palestinian people" in which it was "using . . . weapons and ammunitions [containing] depleted uranium." Its policy was one of "collective punishment . . . occupation, and settlement, as well as of aggressive and armed expansion." Barak and his cabinet "as well as the preceding government of Netanyahu" had "practiced the policy of economic strangulation, closure, and siege," with the result that in the occupied territories "the percentage of those living under the line of poverty has risen to 75 per cent."

Disinhibited by the occasion, Arafat had momentarily lost sight of his desire to see Sharon defeated. Collecting himself, he promptly gave an interview to Israeli television in which he spoke respectfully of the prime minister as "Rabin's successor." Barak disdained the gesture. In a long interview in an Israeli daily, and straining to make himself out to be as tough as Sharon, he expressed pride for having exposed, at Camp David and Taba, the innate rigidity of Arafat and the Palestinians: "In their culture," he said—in a textbook display of unreconstructed orientalism—"there is no compromise, which is a Western notion." The Palestinians considered the Israelis to be reduced to choosing in the forthcoming elections between what Barghouti called "the bad and the worse," but Rabbo and Hawatmeh, among others, urged Israel's Arab community of 1.2 million to vote at least to prevent Sharon from gaining power.

Barak ran against the principal representative of the forces favoring a muscular, merciless drive for the realization of Greater Israel. Since 1953, when he had formed the first anti-terrorist commando unit (dubbed "the Avengers"), Sharon had been a stalwart champion of territorial expansion with little regard for the local Arab population. After serving as field commander in the wars of 1967 and 1973, he joined Herut, the forerunner to Likud, and became defense minister in Menachem Begin's first government, in 1982. In that capacity he had masterminded and directed the invasion of Lebanon; in the massacres at Sabra and Chatila he had much to answer for. By this time he had also emerged, in the Likud and nationally, as a leading architect of Israeli settlement on Arab land. His recent ascent to the Temple Mount had provoked the latest wave of violence. A confirmed rightwinger, Sharon was a typical member of Israel's military–political caste, which gave primacy to military, foreign, and Palestinian affairs, devoting little if any concern to socio-economic and cultural questions, except for the issues vital to the Orthodox and ultra-Orthodox communities, whose votes he needed.

Like Barak, Sharon made peace a theme in his campaign. Opposed to Oslo, he advocated the negotiation of successive interim agreements rather than of a near-term final settlement. He refused the division of Jerusalem, the dismantling of settlements, and withdrawal from the Jordan Valley. But like Netanyahu before him, he declared security his overriding concern, insisting there would be no negotiations until all violence was brought to an end. He presented himself as uniquely qualified to "bring peace," but on Israel's unyielding terms.

Having been elected mainly on a peace platform in May 1999, in his race for reelection Barak would stand or fall on that issue, which he had made into the be-all and end-all of his administration. Whereas at the time of his first run, close to 70 per cent of Jewish Israelis had supported the Oslo accords, by February 2001 this proportion was inverted. The escalating violence of the Al-Aqsa intifada, for which Barak was held accountable, was central to the rejection. Though he had pledged to bring peace with the Palestinians and the neighboring Arab states, Camp David had also collapsed on his watch. He could not explain away the contradiction between posing as the herald of the left and center-left with a roadmap for peace, and his continuation of settlement and brutal repression in the territories.

Much of Barak's natural electorate was disoriented by the violence that greeted an occupation policy that it had been told—first by Rabin—was forbearing and welcomed by the Palestinians. What remained of the peace camp had fallen apart when enough of its members allowed themselves to be taken in by Barak's claim that he had offered Arafat and the Palestinians "nearly everything," only for them to spurn his generosity with deadly force. Sharon's people used the same claim to accuse Barak of making alarming concessions to an enemy which, according to the Prime Minister himself, was incapable of change and bent on destroying Israel, as attested by Arafat's allegedly brand-new and identity-threatening demand for the right of Palestinian return. Compared with the equivocations of Barak's electoral message, Sharon's was consistent and direct. At bottom, in fact, they were similar. But whereas Barak spoke with two voices, Sharon addressed the Arab Question boldly.

The vainglorious precepts of the right were apposite for the inchoate, ethnically divergent electorate of an embattled and disoriented society. This target population had five components: non-

Orthodox Ashkenazi Jews, non-Orthodox Sephardic Jews, Arab Israelis, Orthodox and ultra-Orthodox Jews, and recent immigrants from Russia. The right appealed especially to the Russian, Sephardic, Orthodox, and ultra-Orthodox communities, which were heavily anti-establishment, super-patriotic, hawkish, and anti-Arab; together with the ultra-right, it excelled at transmuting the fears and resentments of these forgotten men and women, especially in the development towns, into a nationalism marked by Arabo- and Islamo-phobia. Rather than address the urgent needs and concerns of Israel's expanding multi-ethnic Jewish underclass, the left trusted in its time-honored but nearly obsolete meliorist message and historical aura to resonate with the Ashkenazim and Israeli Arabs.

Sharon's victory on February 6, in which he scored 62 per cent of the popular vote, was tarnished by a singularly low turnout: only 60 per cent, as compared with about 80 per cent in past elections. Since 3 per cent cast a blank ballot, Sharon may be said to have been chosen by only 35 per cent of the electorate. The trouncing of Barak and Labor was the result of the high rate of abstention among two groups who shunned them without, however, switching to Sharon. In 1992 and 1999 Rabin and Barak had prevailed by dint of the Arab vote, with Barak securing some 95 per cent of it. But the failure of Camp David and the deaths of thirteen Israeli Palestinians in the early repression of the fourth intifada had taken their toll. Under pressure from the rank-and-file, the Arab parties called for a boycott of the election, which was widely followed, except in the Druze villages in northern Israel. Barely one fifth of the 13 per cent possible voted for Barak. In keeping with the ethic of a colonialist democracy, the settlers had the right to vote, unlike the Palestinians of the West Bank and Jordan, and cast over 80 per cent of their ballots for Sharon.

Disenchanted too were the ranks of the mostly Ashkenazi left and center. Barak paid a heavy electoral price for betraying so many hopes concerning his signature issues, but it was the renewal of violence that proved his undoing. His support from this cohort had plummeted by nearly a half since May 1999. He also lost some 20 per cent of the Russian vote, Sharansky having abandoned him. But the desertion of a signifi-cant percentage of Labor and Meretz voters confirmed the accelerating erosion of the peace camp and the far left. Sharon's overwhelming defeat of Barak—by 25 percentage points—was as much a measure of the enfeeblement of the left as of the vitality of the right.

Into the fifth month of the Al-Aqsa intifada, and despite his sweeping victory at the polls, Sharon faced the same acute crises, foreign and domestic, as had Barak, including a sharply divided Knesset. Like all Israeli politicians, he spoke much of peace and the need to find a solution for the Palestinian problem, though his thoughts remained those of his caste, hewing to Moshe Dayan's reasoning of 1977, inspired by Ben-Gurion—"The question is not 'What is the solution?' but 'How do we live without a solution?' "—while continuing to create new "facts on the ground." Since Dayan's time, however, the center-right had been considerably radicalized, and the Revisionist idea of imposing a unilateral, expansionist peace by force had prevailed. Sharon's "interim agreements" were to metamorphose into a permanent solution disproportionately favorable to Israel on all major counts.

In the evening of February 6, after the votes were counted, Sharon went to Likud headquarters to give his victory speech. He started by thanking the leaders of Likud, Shas, Yisrael b'Aliyah, Yisrael Beiteinu, and the National Religious Party for standing with him. Next he expressed his appreciation to David Levy, former foreign minister; Rabbi Menachem Porush, chairman of Agudat Israel and grand champion of the Jewish recovery of the Temple Mount, and his son, Rabbi Meier Porush, leader of United Torah Judaism; Michael Kleinert, leader of Herut and of the campaign to establish Jewish sovereignty over the Temple Mount; and Mayor Olmert.

Before speaking of the task ahead, Sharon told the gathering that "a few moments [ago] when I was already in the building . . . President Bush called me, and asked me to present his best wishes to you [and] told me that [the United States] wants to cooperate very closely with the government under my direction." He "reminded me of the trip I took with him through Samaria and the Jordan Valley, and that at that time he said to me, 'No one believed then . . . that I would be president and that you would be prime minister.' " Yet, " 'despite the fact that no one believed us . . . I have been elected president, and you have been elected prime minister.' "

The significance of the moment, said Sharon, was that Israel would "embark on a new path of domestic unity and harmony" in pursuit of "security and a true peace." In his quest for that cohesion, he proposed a coalition with Labor that would "fly the social flag side-by-side with the flag of security and peace." But above both these flags would be hoisted the "flag of Zionism, the flag of national honor, immigration and settlement"—in allegiance to which his government "would strive to strengthen and consolidate united Jerusalem, the capital of Israel and the eternal capital of the Jewish people." Sharon closed with a citation from Psalm 137: "If I forget thee, oh Jerusalem, may my right hand forget its cunning. May my tongue cleave to the roof of my mouth if I do not remember you, if I do not make Jerusalem the chief of my joys."

Even during the election campaign Sharon had intimated that he might seek to collaborate with Labor, possibly with Barak himself. Should Labor set too high a price on its cooperation, he warned, he would form an out-and-out right-wing government. He need not have worried. Peres, impatient to get back at Barak, was craving to be Sharon's foreign minister; Benjamin Ben-Eliezer, a hawkish and politically ambitious retired career general and Barak's deputy prime minister, eyed the defense appointment. Between them, one would act the part of Oslo, while the other would be a lightning rod for left-wing criticism of the militarist policy.

Sharon took a full month to put together his "unity" cabinet, drawing representatives from eight political parties, though it was predictably right-wing. Of the twenty-six positions—the most ever—Likud and Labor each got eight; five went to Shas, two to National Union, and one each went to Yisrael b'Aliyah, Yisrael Beiteinu, and One Nation. Demographically the cabinet mirrored profound changes in Israeli civil and political society: twenty of the ministers were born after 1940, while nine were born in North Africa and the Middle East, and six in Jerusalem. This coalition would control 73 of 120 Knesset seats. All cabinet members subscribed to guidelines calling for the negotiation of "interim accords" envisaging "a new deployment . . . in the territories of Judea, Samaria, and the Gaza Strip . . . insofar as it does not constitute a threat to Israel's security." While "no new settlements [would] be constructed," the government would "provide solutions and tend to the ongoing natural development needs in the current settlements"; Lebanon and Syria would be pressed to "prevent acts of terror that threaten the peace and security of residents of the North and IDF soldiers." Domestically, steps would be taken "to reduce the social gaps . . . in Israeli society"; "new incentives" for the "liberalization of trade policies" and for the "creation of a favorable atmosphere for investment" would receive "top priority."

Sharon—the fifth prime minister in less than six years—presented his national unity government for confirmation to the Knesset on March 7, 2001. Before the vote he stressed that, in the search for security, his government was prepared to resume negotiations for a "political settlement" and to "ease the suffering of the Palestinians," but only on condition that they "abandon the way of violence, terrorism, and incitement." The vote of confidence was passed by seventy-two to twenty-one, and was followed by thunderous applause.

At no time between February 6 and March 7 were Labor's leaders moved to reevaluate their own actions. Instead, they tended to attribute Barak's defeat to the poor judgment or treason of the defectors and abstainers. Arafat and the Palestinians also came in for their share of the blame.

The tone and substance of this left-wing self-justification was neatly captured in an opinion piece by Amos Oz following Sharon's victory. He declared Sharon to be "Arafat's gift to the Israeli and the Palestinian people." After celebrating Rabin, Peres, and Barak, along with Sadat and King Hussein, for being "men of their time," he charged Arafat with lacking their "courage to compromise and make peace even while their [own] people call them traitors." In Oz's reading, at Camp David Barak had "proposed the establishment of a Palestinian state in the West Bank and the Gaza Strip, with slight reciprocal border modifications, including East Jerusalem as its capital." He even "agreed, with great anxiety, to put the controversial Temple Mount under the auspices of the Muslim authorities." "Had the Palestinians agreed to this offer," Oz wrote, Barak would have won the election. But rather than demand "to further narrow the border modifications" or "reply with yea [or] nay," the Palestinians "replied with fire: with the Al-Aqsa Intifada, a religious war with the declared goal of cleansing the disputed holy sites of Jewish presence." Their added "demand for 'the right to return' . . . was nothing but a codename for the destruction of Israel."

There was more. "Part of the Palestinian leadership" had decided, "immediately following Camp David . . . to initiate a wave of violence aiming to take down Barak and push Israel into the hands of the extremists." By so spurning Barak's "dramatic concessions," Arafat and his men calculated that they could drive the Israelis to "despair"— and to choose Sharon, who would isolate Israel and court disaster, as Slobodan Milosevic had done in Serbia. Barak had no alternative but "to react with force" to the Palestinian assault, making it probable that Israelis would "fall into the Palestinian trap and vote for Sharon . . . out of discontent with the peace process, out of anxiety, rage, and fear of unyielding violent Palestinian extortion that will not stop until Israel's destruction." Oz thought it was

> too early to say whether Sharon will fall into the same trap and play the role that the Arab rejection front has written for him: the role of an Israeli Milosevic who will be dragged into unruly militant reactions that will tear apart Israeli society and turn it into an international pariah.

To take this course would be to risk Israel "either collapsing from within or giving in to the dictates of the Arab world."

This manifesto of impenitence—and insolence—showed by how much Labor had forfeited any role of genuine opposition. Like his political kind, Oz did not breathe a word about his party's fundamental agreement with Likud—not only on the objectives of reaching for a Greater Israel, but on the ways and means of doing so. Since 1967 Labor had been sometimes the leader and never less than a partner in the thrust for an undivided Jerusalem and the creation—and subsequent expansion—of the settlement blocs. The establishment of 200,000 settlers in the five developments girdling Jerusalem—two of them extending deep inside the West Bank—along with a network of strategic bypass roads, had been its handiwork; and whether spearheading or collaborating, Labor kept voting for military expenditures that it knew would cut seriously into funds for any social agenda. The party lost its moorings by virtue of radical changes in the Israeli economy, society, and culture that rendered its political precepts and formulas out-of-date and ineffective. Its leaders and office-seekers became increasingly estranged from the swelling religious, oriental, and Russian communities.

While Labor shifted to the center, Likud moved from the moderate to the far right, exercising a growing if never perfect cooperation with the religious parties. Both major parties now subscribed to ultra-liberal economics, and with the military throttling the social budget, the bulging ethno-economic underclass was likely to continue seething with discontent and *ressentiment*. With Labor floundering, should the anti-Arab, super-nationalist, expansionist invocations of Likud cease to divert or soothe the pains of everyday life, the underclass might become increasingly receptive to the predications of religious parties that combined the promise of religious and national salvation with a social, economic, educational, and cultural plan.

When Sharon asked Labor to become a junior partner in his unity government, he was counting on its political weakness and cowardice. While he figured to use what remained of Labor's moral capital to legitimize his hardline course, Peres and his ilk convinced themselves that by joining the coalition they could act as a moderating force, even in a cabinet that tilted far to the right. Their conceit may even have deluded them into believing that they might be able to prevail on Sharon to steer a more moderate course than they had ever managed themselves.

The Palestinians—even those who saw little to choose between Barak and Sharon—had watched the Israeli elections nervously. All had scoffed at Sharon's presentation of himself as a de Gaulle-like figure uniquely qualified to wrest peace from the jaws of war. In the midst of the campaign, Hanan Ashrawi had expressed the general skepticism, based on the contradiction at the heart of the Israeli position:

> On the one hand Sharon claims to be able to deliver peace . . . while promising, on the other, to annex Palestinian territory, maintain all Israeli settlements, impose Israeli sovereignty over Jerusalem, totally negate the Palestinian refugees' right of return, and wreak havoc among the Palestinians, should they dare to protest.

Arab and Palestinian reactions to Sharon's victory ran the gamut. Mubarak said he would "wait and see what Sharon will do"; the premier of Jordan said Amman would not prejudge the new government. Syria's official newspaper declared that "the Zionist entity had reached its highest level of extremism." Arafat struck a cautious note. He combined his "respect for the decision of the Israeli people" with his "hope [that] the peace process will continue." But Marwan Barghouti spoke for those who were "not concerned with Sharon, Barak, or Peres." Sharon was "the last shot in the arsenal of the Israelis," and he predicted confidently that, with time, "the intifada will persuade them of the futility of the occupation."

Weeks after the election, Saeb Erakat, the senior Palestinian negotiator, commenting on Sharon's speech in the Knesset, dismissed it as "too general . . . to analyze or discuss." It would take more than "lip service" to peace to reduce the violence and tension of the last few months. Should Sharon press to return to a pre-Oslo/Camp David starting line, there "will no longer be a peace process." Again left alone to face a hawkish government and formidable army backed by Washington, the Palestinian leadership resolved neither to start again from scratch, nor to take the path of endless interim agreements.

Sharon's big win stirred up the intifada anew. Here and there militants staged protests on what they trumpeted as "days of rage," provoking clashes with Israeli security forces. With Barak still in charge, on February 13, 2001 the IDF carried out two political assassinations. A rocket fired from an IDF helicopter killed Massoud Ayyad, a major in Arafat's Force 17 Presidential Guard, in a car outside the Jabalia refugee camp in northern Gaza; several passers-by were apparently wounded. Ayyad had been named as the brains behind a recent mortar attack on the Netzarim settlement and an abduction of Israeli soldiers nearby, though the Palestinian Authority denied the charges. In the evening of that same day, planes dropped bombs on Khan Yunis, a Gaza town near the Katif Settlement Bloc, wounding over 100. Another Fatah member and security official, Ayeh Abu-Houb, was killed in an ambush in the West Bank town of Ramin, east of Tulkarm. There was a growing suspicion that Israeli forces were fine-tuning new ways of decapitating the military and political leadership of the PLO and the Palestinian Authority.

The next day, February 14, a Palestinian driver from Gaza rammed his bus transporting Palestinian workers into a crowded bus stop near Holon (Azor Junction), south of Tel Aviv. Eight Israelis were killed—seven of them soldiers—and over twenty wounded, several of them seriously. It was the single deadliest onslaught within or beyond the Green Line since the start of the Al-Aqsa intifada. Hamas claimed credit for the attack, and Israel closed the occupied territories. Barak vowed that the perpetrators and their superiors would not go unpunished; Sharon spoke of renewed proof that, for the Palestinians, "there is no difference between Netzarim, the West Bank, the Lebanese border, and the country's very heart." On February 26, a spokesman for the Yesha Council of settlers declared Arafat an "enemy" who needed to be "assassinated . . . after seven years of war," in which he had sent "his own people to kill."

Before Sharon's investiture on March 7 there were two more attacks. On March 1 a car bomb exploded near the Mei Ami junction southwest of Afula, killing one Israeli and wounding nine. Three days later, a suicide bombing in central Netanya killed two Israelis and injured around sixty. Besides using excessive force, the Israeli military units surrounded Jericho and several villages west of Al Bira, blocking the road between Bir Zeit and Ramallah. Barghouti reiterated that "if Israel wants occupation and settlement it cannot have security."

On March 11, the settlers of Hebron celebrated the seventh anniversary of the massacre by Baruch Goldstein of twenty-three worshippers in the Ibrahim Mosque by pelting Palestinians with stones and bottles, and vandalizing several properties. Later weeks saw five attacks by Palestinians: three in Jerusalem, killing one Israeli and injuring thirty-five; one in Qalqilya, killing two and injuring four; and one in Hebron, killing an infant. On March 26 the IDF placed Hebron under curfew and fired shells and bullets fitfully, injuring sixteen Palestinians, while Israeli settlers smashed several Palestinian cars and ravaged the office of the local Islamic Waqf, or charitable endowment providing support for mosques, schools, and welfare organizations. After the funeral of the murdered baby, Sharon declared that the settlement in Hebron would stay "forever." The demonstrations in

Israel and the West Bank on Land Day—commemorating the fatal shooting on March 30, 1976 of 6 Arabs during peaceful protests in the Galilee against Israeli land confiscation—resulted in Israeli forces killing 5 Palestinians in Nablus and 1 in Ramallah, and injuring about 170 others.

Inside Israel, a steadfast but torpid Peace Now called a rally on March 12 in Tel Aviv to protest at the intensified siege of Palestinian towns and villages, and collective punishment generally. In a public notice its director, Moria Shlomot, lamented that "the day will come when we will have to explain to our children why the state of Israel starved a whole civilian population and how the army of a people who experienced the ghettoes cut off entire villages with ditches and barbed wire," the task made more awkward since "any rational person understands that this measure will not improve security." Not only would "determined terrorists cross any obstacle, but the despair caused by poverty and starvation will . . . push more and more people into the arms of Islamic fundamentalists." Unlike Amos Oz, Shlomot, recoiling from Labor, warned that "Sharon's assistants, Benjamin Ben-Eliezer and Shimon Peres, will never shake off the permanent stain of a policy whose only purpose is to appease the settlers."

There was no way to conclude this book, the story it tells being indeterminate except for the Jewish–Zionist logos. The external boundaries and internal landscapes of both Israel and Palestine—or of their binational/single-state accommodation—remain as contested and uncertain as ever. What point in bringing the story forward any further when ideas, issues, and agencies have themselves not budged? Instead I turned to writing the thematically framed Prolegomenon, whose perspective is at once long-term, short-term, and of the moment . . .

BIBLIOGRAPHY

Abu-Amr, Ziad, *Islamic Fundamentalism in the West Bank and Gaza: Muslim Brotherhood and Islamic Jihad*, Bloomington: Indiana University Press, 1994.

Aburish, Said K., *The Rise, Corruption, and Coming Fall of the House of Saud*, New York: St. Martin's Press, 1994.

————*Nasser: The Last Arab*, London: Duckworth, 2004.

Abu-Sitta, Salman H., *Atlas of Palestine, 1948*, London: Palestine Land Society, 2004.

Agha, Hussein and Robert Malley, "Camp David: The Tragedy of Error," *The New York Review of Books* 48, no. 13 (August 9, 2001): 59–65.

————"The Last Negotiation," *Foreign Affairs* 81, no. 3 (May/June 2002): 10–19.

AIPAC, Near East Report

Ajami, Fouad, *The Vanished Imam: Musa al Sadr and the Shia of Lebanon*, Ithaca, NY: Cornell University Press, 1986.

————*The Arab Predicament: Arab Political Thought and Practice Since 1967*, New York: Cambridge University Press, 1992.

al-Hout, Bayan Nuwayhed, *Sabra and Shatila: September 1982*, London: Pluto Press, 2004.

American Petroleum Institute, *Basic Petroleum Data Book: Petroleum Industry Statistics*, vol. 25, Washington, DC: American Petroleum Institute, 2005.

Anderson, Benedict, *Imagined Communities: Reflections on the Origin and Spread of Nationalism*, rev. edn, London: Verso, 1991.

Andrew, Christopher M. and A. S. Kanya-Forstner, *France Overseas: The Great War and the Climax of French Imperial Expansion, 1914–1924*, Stanford: Stanford University Press, 1981.

Ansprenger, Franz, *Juden und Araber in einem Land: Die politischen Beziehungen der beiden Völker im Mandatsgebiet Palästina und im Staat Israel*, Munich/Mainz: Grünewald, 1978.

Antonius, George, *The Arab Awakening: The Story of the Arab National Movement*, Philadelphia: J. B. Lippincott, 1939.

Armstrong, Karen, *The Battle for God*, New York: Alfred A. Knopf, 2000.

————*Islam: A Short History*, London: Weidenfeld & Nicolson, 2000.

Avnery, Uri, *Israel Without Zionists*, New York: Macmillan, 1968.

Bar-Zohar, Michael, *Ben Gourion: Le prophète armé*, Paris: Fayard, 1966.

Bauer, Yehuda, *Flight and Rescue: Bricha*, New York: Random House, 1970.

————*Out of the Ashes: The Impact of American Jewry on Post-Holocaust Jewish Europe*, Oxford: Pergamon Press, 1989.

Bayle, Pierre, *Les Relations secrètes israélo-palestiniennes*, Paris: Balland, 1983.

Beck, Robert J., ed., *Oil Industry Outlook, 1997–2001: Projection to 2005*, 13th edn, Tulsa: Pennwell Corp., 1996.

Begin, Menahem, *La Révolte d'Israël*, Paris: Editions Albatros, 1978.

Bein, Alex, *Theodor Herzl: A Biography*, Philadelphia: The Jewish Publication Society of America, 1962.

Ben-Eliezer, Uri, *The Making of Israeli Militarism*, Bloomington: Indiana University Press, 1998.

Ben-Gurion, David, *Memoirs: David Ben-Gurion*, New York: World Publishing Co., 1970.

Bensoussan, Georges, *Une histoire intellectuelle et politique du sionisme, 1860–1940*, Paris: Fayard, 2002.

Bentwich, Norman, *For Zion's Sake: A Biography of Judah L. Magnes, First Chancellor and First President of the Hebrew University of Jerusalem*, Philadelphia: Jewish Publication Society of America, 1954.

Benvenisti, Meron, *1986 Report: Demographic, Economic, Legal, Social, and Political Developments in the West Bank*, Jerusalem: West Bank Data Base Project, 1986.

———*City of Stone: The Hidden History of Jerusalem*, Berkeley: University of California Press, 1996.

———*Sacred Landscape: The Buried History of the Holy Land Since 1948*, Berkeley: University of California Press, 2000.

Bishara, Marwan, *Palestine/Israël: La paix ou l'apartheid*, rev. edn, Paris: La Découverte, 2001.

Brenner, Lenni, *The Iron Wall: Zionist Revisionism from Jabotinsky to Shamir*, London: Zed Books, 1984.

Brinner, William M. and Moses Rischin, eds, *Like All the Nations: The Life and Legacy of Judah L. Magnes*, Albany: State University of New York Press, 1987.

Brownfield, Peter Egill, "Judah Magnes: A Disappointed American Zionist," *Issues* (Spring 2005).

Buber, Martin, *I and Thou*, New York: Scribner, 1970.

——— *Paths in Utopia*, London: Routledge, 1949.

——— *Israel and the World: Essays in a Time of Crisis*, 2nd edn, New York: Schocken, 1963.

Buber, Martin, Judah L. Magnes, and Ernst Simon, eds, *Towards Union in Palestine: Essays on Zionism and Jewish–Arab Cooperation*, Jerusalem: IHUD (Union) Association, 1947.

Calaprice, Alice, ed., *The New Quotable Einstein*, Princeton: Princeton University Press, 2005.

Caplan, Neil, *Palestine Jewry and the Arab Question, 1917–1925*, London: Frank Cass, 1978.

———*Futile Diplomacy*, 4 vols, London: Frank Cass, 1983–97.

Carré, Olivier, *Septembre noir: Refus arabe de la résistance palestinienne*, Bruxelles: Editions Complexe, 1980.

Chaliand, Gérard, ed., *Les stratégies du terrorisme*, Paris: Desclée de Brouwer, 2002.

Charbit, Denis, ed., *Sionismes: Textes fondamentaux*, Paris: Albin Michel, 1998.

Chomsky, Noam, *The Fateful Triangle: The United States, Israel, and the Palestinians*, Boston: South End Press, 1983.

———*Middle East Illusions*, Lanham, MD: Rowman & Littlefield, 2003.

Cohen, Aharon, *Israel and the Arab World*, New York: Funk & Wagnalls, 1970.

Cohen, Amnon, *Political Parties in the West Bank Under the Jordanian Regime, 1949–1967*, Ithaca, NY: Cornell University Press, 1982.

Cohen, Arthur Allen, *Arguments and Doctrines: A Reader of Jewish Thinking in the Aftermath of the Holocaust*, New York: Harper & Row, 1970.

Cohen, Israel, ed., *Speeches on Zionism*, London: Arrowsmith, 1928.

Cohen, Michael J., *Palestine, Retreat from the Mandate: A Study of British Policy, 1936–1945*, New York: Holmes & Meier, 1978.

———*Palestine and the Great Powers, 1945–1948*, Princeton: Princeton University Press, 1982.

———*Truman and Israel*, Berkeley: University of California Press, 1990.

Cohen, Morris R., *The Faith of a Liberal: Selected Essays*, New York: Henry Holt, 1946.

Cole, Juan, *Sacred Space and Holy War: The Politics, Culture, and History of Shi'ite Islam*, London: I. B. Tauris, 2002.

Conklin, Alice L., *A Mission to Civilize: The Republican Idea of Empire in France and West Africa, 1895–1930*, Stanford: Stanford University Press, 1997.

Corbin, Jane, *Gaza First: The Secret Norway Channel to Peace Between Israel and the PLO*, London: Bloomsbury, 1994.

Cypel, Sylvain, *Les emmurés: La société israélienne dans l'impasse*, rev. edn, Paris: La Découverte, 2006.

Debray, Régis, *Le feu sacré: Fonction du religieux*, Paris: Gallimard, 2003.

Dershowitz, Alan, *The Case for Israel*, Hoboken, NJ: John Wiley, 2003.

Dieckhoff, Alain, *L'Invention d'une nation: Israel et la modernité politique*, Paris: Gallimard, 1993.

Djahili, Mohammed-Reza, *Géopolitique de l'Iran*, Bruxelles: Editions Complexe, 2005.

Doyle, Michael W., *Empires*, Ithaca, NY: Cornell University Press, 1986.

Eban, Abba, *The Arab Refugees: Road to a Solution*, New York: Israel Office of Information, 1955.

———*An Autobiography*, New York: Random House, 1977.

Elazar, Daniel J. and M. Ben Mollov, *Israel at the Polls, 1999*, London: Frank Cass, 2001.

Elazar, Daniel J. and Shmuel Sandler, eds, *Israel's Odd Couple: The 1984 Knesset Elections and the National Unity Government*, Detroit: Wayne State University Press, 1990.

———*Who's the Boss in Israel: Israel at the Polls, 1988–89*, Detroit: Wayne State University Press, 1992.

———*Israel at the Polls, 1992*, Lanham, MD: Rowman & Littlefield, 1995.

———*Israel at the Polls, 1996*, London: Frank Cass, 1998.

Elon, Amos, *Herzl*, New York: Holt, Rinehart, and Winston, 1975.

Enderlin, Charles, *Le Rêve brisé: Histoire de l'échec du processus de paix au Proche-Orient, 1995–2002*, Paris: Fayard, 2002.

———*Paix ou guerres: Les secrets des négociations israélo-arabes, 1917–1997*. rev. edn, Paris: Fayard, 2004.

Epstein, Simon, *Histoire du peuple juif au xx siècle*, Paris: Hachette, 1998.

Esposito, John L., ed., *The Iranian Revolution: Its Global Impact*, Miami: Florida International University Press, 1990.

———*The Islamic Threat: Myth or Reality?*, 3rd edn, New York: Oxford University Press, 1999.

————*Unholy War: Terror in the Name of Islam*, New York: Oxford University Press, 2002.

Evans, John, *OPEC and the World Energy Market: A Comprehensive Reference Guide*, 2nd edn, Burnt Mill, Essex: Longman Current Affairs, 1995.

Finkelstein, Norman G., *Image and Reality of the Israel–Palestine Conflict*, 2nd edn, London: Verso, 2003.

————*The Holocaust Industry: Reflections on the Exploitation of Jewish Suffering*, New York: Verso, 2000.

————*Beyond Chutzpah: On the Misuse of Anti-Semitism and the Abuse of History*, Berkeley: University of California Press, 2005.

Flapan, Simcha, *The Birth of Israel: Myths and Realities*, New York: Pantheon, 1987.

Friedman, Thomas, *The Lexus and the Olive Tree*, New York: Farrar, Straus, and Giroux, 1999.

Friling, Tuvia, ed., *Critique du post-sionisme: Réponse aux "nouveaux historiens" israéliens*, Paris: In Press, 2004.

Fromkin, David, *A Peace to End All Peace: The Fall of the Ottoman Empire and the Creation of the Modern Middle East*, New York: Henry Holt, 1989.

Gallagher, John, and Ronald Robinson, "The Imperialism of Free Trade," *Economic History Review*, second series, 6:1 (1953): 1–15.

Ganlin, Zvi, *Truman: American Jewry and Israel, 1945–1948*, New York: Holmes and Meier, 1949.

————*An Uneasy Relationship: American Jewish Leadership and Israel, 1948–1957*, Syracuse: Syracuse University Press, 2005.

Gerson, Jospeh and Bruce Birchard, eds, *The Sun Never Sets . . .: Confronting the Network of Foreign U.S. Military Bases*, Boston: South End Press, 1991.

Gilbert, Martin, *The Routledge Atlas of the Arab–Israeli Conflict*, 7th edn, New York: Routledge, 2002.

Goldhill, Simon, *The Temple of Jerusalem: The Extraordinary History of a Site Sacred to Jews, Christians, and Muslims*, Cambridge, MA: Harvard University Press, 2005.

Goldmann, Nahum, *Autobiographie: Une vie au service d'une cause*, Paris: Fayard, 1971.

————*Mein Leben als deutscher Jude*, Frankfurt: Ullstein, 1983.

Goodman, Moshe, ed., *The Magnes–Philby Negotiations, 1929: The Historical Record*, Jerusalem: The Magnes Press, The Hebrew University, 1998.

Goren, Arthur, ed., *Dissenter in Zion: From the Writings of Judah L. Magnes*, Cambridge, MA: Harvard University Press, 1982.

Gorny, Yosef, *Zionism and the Arabs, 1882–1948: A Study of Ideology*, Oxford: Clarendon Press, 1987.

Gregorian, Vartan, *Islam: A Mosaic, Not a Monolith*, Washington, DC: Brookings Institution Press, 2003.

Greilsammer, Ilan, *La nouvelle histoire d'Israël: Essai sur une identité nationale*, Paris: Gallimard, 1998.

Gresh, Alain and Dominique Vidal, *Palestine 47: Un partage avorté*, 2nd edn, Bruxelles: Editions Complexe, 1994.

Grose, Peter, *Israel in the Mind of America*, New York: Schocken, 1984.

Grossman, Richard H. S., *Palestine Mission: A Personal Record*, New York: Harper, 1947.

Gurr, Ted Robert, *Why Men Rebel*, Princeton: Princeton University Press, 1970.

Hass, Amira, *Drinking the Sea at Gaza: Days and Nights in a Land Under Siege*, New York: Henry Holt, 1999.

Hazony, Yoram, *The Jewish State: The Struggle for Israel's Soul*, New York: Basic Books, 2001.

Hersh, Seymour M., *The Samson Option: Israel's Nuclear Arsenal and American Foreign Policy*, New York: Random House, 1991.

Herzl, Theodor, *Der Judenstaat: Versuch einer modernen Lösung der Judenfrage*, Vienna: M. Breitenstein, 1896.

——*Altneuland*, Leipzig: H. Seeman, Nachf, 1902.

——*Tagebücher, 1895–1904*. 3 vols, Berlin: Jüdischer Verlag, 1922–3.

——*Gesammelte zionistische Werke*, 5 vols, Berlin: Jüdischer Verlag, 1934–5.

Himelstein, Shmuel, ed., *The Grand Mufti: Haj Amin al-Hussaini, Founder of the Palestinian National Movement*, London: Frank Cass, 1993.

Hirst, David, *The Gun and the Olive Branch: The Roots of Violence in the Middle East*, New York: Harcourt Brace, 1977.

Hourani, Albert, *Europe and the Middle East*, Berkeley: University of California Press, 1980.

——*A History of the Arab Peoples*, Cambridge, MA: Harvard University Press, 1991.

Huntington, Samuel P., *The Clash of Civilizations and the Remaking of World Order*, New York: Simon & Schuster, 1996.

Hurewitz, J. C., ed., *The Struggle for Palestine*, New York: Schocken, 1976.

——*The Middle East and North Africa: A Documentary Record, British–French Supremacy, 1914–1945*, 2nd edn, New Haven: Yale University Press, 1979.

International Energy Agency, *Oil Information/Données sur le Pétrole: 2005 with 2004 data*, Paris: OECD/IEA, 2005.

International Energy Analysis Group, *The World Petroleum Market: Perspectives to the Year 2010*, New York: International Energy Analysis Group, 1995.

Jansen, Johannes J. G., *The Neglected Duty: The Creed of Sadat's Assassins and Islamic Resurgence in the Middle East*, New York: Macmillan, 1986.

——*The Dual Nature of Islamic Fundamentalism*, Ithaca, NY: Cornell University Press, 1997.

Jenkins, Gilbert, ed., *Oil Economists' Handbook*, 5th edn, 2 vols, London: Elsevier Applied Science, 1989.

Johnson, Chalmers, *Blowback: The Costs and Consequences of American Empire*, New York: Metropolitan/Owl Books, 2004.

——*The Sorrows of Empire: Militarism, Secrecy, and the End of the Republic*, New York: Metropolitan Books, 2004.

——*Nemesis: The Last Days of the American Republic*, New York: Metropolitan Books, 2006.

Johnson, James Turner, *The Holy War Idea in Western and Islamic Traditions*, University Park, PA: Pennsylvania State University Press, 1997.

Journal of Palestine Studies

Kaminsky, Catherine and Simon Kruk, *Le monde arabe et Israël aujourd'hui*, Paris: Presses Universitaires de France, 1999.

Kapeliouk, Amnon, *Enquête sur un massacre: Sabra et Chatila*, Paris: Seuil, 1982.

——*Arafat l'irréductible*, Paris: Fayard, 2004.

Kaplan, Eran, *The Jewish Radical Right: Revisionist Zionism and Its Ideological Legacy*, Madison: University of Wisconsin Press, 2005.

Karpin, Michael, *The Bomb in the Basement: How Israel Went Nuclear and What That Means for the World*, New York: Simon & Schuster, 2006.

Kayyali, A. W., *Palestine: A Modern History*, London: Croom Helm, 1978.

Keay, John, *Sowing the Wind: The Seeds of Conflict in the Middle East*, New York: Norton, 2003.

Kent, Marian, *Oil and Empire: British Policy and Mesopotamian Oil, 1900–1920*, London: Macmillan, 1976.

Khalidi, Rashid, *British Policy Towards Syria and Palestine, 1906–1914: A Study of the Antecedents of the Hussein—McMahon Correspondence, the Sykes–Picot Agreements, and the Balfour Declaration*, London: Ithaca Press, 1980.

———*Under Siege: PLO Decision Making During the 1982 War*, New York: Columbia University Press, 1985.

———*Palestinian Identity: The Construction of Modern National Consciousness*, New York: Columbia University Press, 1997.

Khalidi, Rashid, Lisa Anderson, Muhammad Muslih, and Reeva S. Simon, eds, *The Origins of Arab Nationalism*, New York: Columbia University Press, 1991.

Khalidi, Walid, ed., *From Haven to Conquest: Readings in Zionism and the Palestine Problem until 1948*, 2nd edn, Washington, DC: Institute of Palestine Studies, 1987.

———ed., *All that Remains: The Palestinian Villages Occupied and Depopulated by Israel in 1948*, Washington, DC: Institute for Palestine Studies, 1992.

Khoury, Gérard, Ilan Halevi, and Maha Baaklini Laurens, "Hommages à Maxime Rodinson," *Revue d'études Palestiniennes* 93 (Fall 2004): 10–53.

Kimche, Jon and David Kimche, *A Clash of Destinies: The Arab–Jewish War and the Founding of the State of Israel*, New York: Praeger, 1960.

———*La Première guerre d'Israël—1948*, Paris: Arthaud, 1969.

Kimmerling, Baruch, *Zionism and Territory: The Socio-Territorial Dimension of Zionist Politics*, Berkeley: University of California Press, 1983.

———*The Invention and Decline of Israeliness: State, Culture and Military in Israel*, Berkeley: University of California Press, 2001.

———*Politicide: Ariel Sharon's War Against the Palestinians*, London: Verso, 2003.

Kohn, Hans, *Martin Buber: Sein Werk und seine Zeit: Ein Beitrag zur Geistesgeschichte Mitteleuropas, 1880–1930*, Cologne: Joseph Melzer, 1961.

———ed., *Nationalism and the Jewish Ethic: Basic Writings of Ahad Ha'am*, New York: Schocken, 1962.

Laqueur, Walter, *A History of Zionism*, 3rd edn, London: Tauris Parke, 2003.

Laqueur, Walter and Barry Rubin, eds, *The Israel–Arab Reader: A Documentary History of the Middle East Conflict*, rev. edn, New York: Penguin Books, 1984.

Laurens, Henry, *Le Retour des exilés: La lutte pour la Palestine de 1869 à 1997*, Paris: Robert Laffont, 1998.

——— *La Question de Palestine*, 2 vols, Paris: Fayard, 1999/2002.

"Le Conflit Israélo-Arabe," *Les Temps Modernes*, special issue, no. 253 bis (July 1967).

Lenczowski, George, *The Middle East in World Affairs*, 4th edn, Ithaca, NY: Cornell University Press, 1980.

Levitt, Matthew, *Targeting Terror: U.S. Policy toward Middle Eastern State Sponsors and Terrorist Organizations, Post-September 11*, Washington, DC: Washington Institute for Near East Policy, 2002.

Lewis, Bernard, *The Crisis of Islam: Holy War and Unholy Terror*, New York: Random House, 2004.

Lowenberg, Peter, *Fantasy and Reality in History*, New York: Oxford University Press, 1995.

Luz, Ehud, *Like All the Nations?*, Jerusalem: Herod's Gate, 1930.

——*In The Perplexity of the Times*, Jerusalem: Hebrew University, 1946.

——*Parallels Meet: Religion and Nationalism in the Early Zionist Movement (1882–1904)*, Philadelphia: Jewish Publication Society, 1988.

Magnes, Judah Leon, and Martin Buber, *Arab–Jewish Unity: Testimony Before the Anglo-American Inquiry Commission for the IHUD (Union) Association*, London: Victor Gollancz, 1947.

Magnes, Judah Leon, M. Leon Reiner, Lord Samuel, E. Simon, and M. Smilansky, *Palestine—Divided or United? The Case for a Bi-national Palestine Before the United Nations*, Jerusalem: IHUD (Union) Association, 1947.

Manceron, Gilles, *Marianne et les Colonies: Une introduction à l'histoire coloniale de la France*, Paris: La Découverte, 2003.

Mandel, Neville J., *The Arabs and Zionism Before World War I*, Berkeley: University of California Press, 1976.

Ma'oz, Moshe, *Syria and Israel: From War to Peacemaking*, Oxford: Clarendon Press, 1993.

Masalha, Nur, *Expulsion of the Palestinians: The Concept of "Transfer" in Zionist Political Thought, 1882–1948*, Washington, DC: Institute for Palestine Studies, 1992.

——*The Politics of Denial: Israel and the Palestinian Refugee Problem*, London: Pluto, 2003.

Massoulié, François, *Les Conflits du Proche–Orient*, rev. edn, Paris: Casterman, 1994.

Mattar, Philip, *The Mufti of Jerusalem: Al-Hajj Amin al-Husayni and the Palestine National Movement*, New York: Columbia University Press, 1988.

McDowall, David, *Palestine and Israel: The Uprising and Beyond*, London: I. B. Tauris, 1989.

——*The Palestinians: The Road to Nationhood*, London: Minority Rights Publications, 1994.

McTague, John J., *British Policy in Palestine, 1917–1922*, Lanham, MD: University Press of America, 1983.

Mearsheimer, John, and Stephen M. Walt, *The Israel Lobby and U.S. Foreign Policy*, New York: Farrar, Straus, and Giroux, 2007.

Meir, Golda, *My Life*, New York: Putnam, 1975.

Mendes-Flohr, Paul R., ed., *A Land of Two Peoples: Martin Buber on Jews and Arabs*, New York: Oxford University Press, 1983.

——ed., *Martin Buber: A Contemporary Perspective. Proceedings of an International Conference Held at the Israel Academy of Sciences and Humanities*, Syracuse, NY: Syracuse University Press, 2002.

Middle East Quarterly

Migdal, Joël, *Palestinians: The Making of a People*, New York: Free Press, 1993.

Miller, Aaron David, *Search for Security: Saudi Arabian Oil and American Foreign Policy, 1939–1949*, Chapel Hill: University of North Carolina Press, 1980.

Millis, Walter, ed., *The Forestall Diaries*, New York: Viking, 1951.

Moore, Donald J., *Martin Buber: Prophet of Religious Secularism*, Philadelphia: Jewish Publication Society, 1974.

Morris, Benny, *The Birth of the Palestinian Refugee Problem, 1947–1949*, Cambridge: Cambridge University Press, 1987.

————*1948 and After: Israel and the Palestinians*, New York: Oxford University Press, 1990.

————*Israel's Border Wars, 1949–1956: Arab Infiltration, Israeli Retaliation, and the Countdown to the Suez War*, Oxford: Clarendon Press, 1993.

————*Righteous Victims: A History of the Zionist–Arab Conflict, 1881–1999*, London: John Murray, 2000.

————*The Road to Jerusalem: Glubb Pasha, Palestine and the Jews*, London: I. B. Tauris, 2002.

Morris, Benny, Hussein Agha, and Robert Malley, "Camp David and After: An Exchange," *New York Review of Books* 49, no. 10 (June 13, 2002): 42–9.

————"Camp David and After—Continued," *New York Review of Books* 49, no. 11 (June 27, 2002): 47–9.

Muslih, Muhammad, *Toward Coexistence: An Analysis of the Resolutions of the Palestine National Council*, Washington, DC: Institute for Palestine Studies, 1990.

Nevo, Joseph and Ilan Pappé, eds., *Jordan in the Middle East: The Making of a Pivotal State, 1948–1988*, London: Frank Cass, 1994.

Nordau, Max, *Zionistische Schriften*, Cologne/Leipzig: Jüdischer Verlag, 1909.

Norris, Pippa, and Ronald Inglehart, *Sacred and Secular: Religion and Politics Worldwide*, Cambridge: Cambridge University Press, 2004.

Onfray, Michel, *Traité d'athéologie: Physique de la métaphysique*, Paris: Grasset, 2005.

Oren, Michael B., *Six Days of War: June 1967 and the Making of the Modern Middle East*, New York: Oxford University Press, 2002.

Pape, Robert A., *Bombing to Win: Air Power and Coercion in War*, Ithaca, NY: Cornell University Press, 1996.

————*Dying to Win: The Strategic Logic of Suicide Terrorism*, New York: Random House, 2005.

Pappé, Ilan, *Britain and the Arab–Israeli Conflict, 1948–51*, Basingstoke, Hampshire: Macmillan, 1988.

————*The Making of the Arab–Israeli Conflict, 1947–51*, New York: St. Martin's Press, 1992.

————"Critique and Agenda: Post-Zionist Scholars in Israel," *History and Memory* 7:1 (1995): 66–90.

————*A History of Modern Palestine: One Land, Two Peoples*, Cambridge: Cambridge University Press, 2004.

————*Les Démons de la Nakbah: Les Libertés fondamentales dans l'université israélienne*, Paris: La Fabrique Editions, 2004.

Pavlowsky, Agnès, *Hamas, ou le miroir des frustrations palestiniennes*, Paris: L'Harmattan, 2000.

Perlmutter, Amos, *The Life and Times of Menachem Begin*, Garden City, NY: Doubleday, 1987.

Picaudou, Nadine, *Le Mouvement national palestinien: Genèse et structures*, Paris: L'Harmattan, 1989.

————*La Décennie qui ébranla le Moyen-Orient, 1914–1923*, Bruxelles: Editions Complexe, 1992.

————*Les Palestiniens: Un siècle d'histoire*, rev. edn, Bruxelles: Editions Complexe, 2003.

Porath, Yehoshua, *The Emergence of the Palestinian–Arab National Movement, 1918–1929*, London: Frank Cass, 1974.

———*The Palestinian Arab National Movement: From Riots to Rebellion*, vol. 2: *1929–1939*, London: Frank Cass, 1977.

Quandt, William B., ed., *The Middle East: Ten Years after Camp David*, Washington, DC: The Brookings Institution, 1988.

———*Peace Process: American Diplomacy and the Arab–Israeli Conflict since 1967*, Washington, DC: The Brookings Institution; Berkeley: University of California Press, 1993.

Quandt, William B., Fuad Jabber, and Ann Mosely Lesch, *The Politics of Palestinian Nationalism*, Berkeley: University of California Press, 1973.

Rabinovich, Abraham, *The Yom Kippur War: The Epic Encounter that Transformed the Middle East*, New York: Schocken, 2004.

Rabinovich, Itamar, *The Road Not Taken: Early Arab–Israeli Negotiations*, New York: Oxford University Press, 1991.

Raider, Mark A., Jonathan D. Sarna, and Ronald W. Zweig, *Abba Hillel Silver and American Zionism*, London: Frank Cass, 1997.

Rashid, Ahmed, *Taliban: Militant Islam, Oil, and Fundamentalism in Central Asia*, New Haven: Yale Nota Bene, 2001.

———*Jihad: The Rise of Militant Islam in Central Asia*, New Haven: Yale University Press, 2002.

Reinharz, Jehuda, *Chaim Weizmann: The Making of a Zionist Leader*, New York: Oxford University Press, 1985.

Report on Israeli Settlement in the Occupied Territories

Ricca, Simone, "Heritage, Nationalism and the Shifting Symbolism of the Wailing Wall," *Jerusalem Quarterly* 24 (Summer 2005): 39–56.

Rodinson, Maxime, *Israël et le refus arabe: 75 ans d'histoire*, Paris: Seuil, 1968.

———*L'Islam: Politique et croyance*, Paris: Fayard, 1993.

Rogan, Eugene L. and Avi Shlaim, eds, *The War for Palestine: Rewriting the History of 1948*, Cambridge: Cambridge University Press, 2001.

Ro'i, Yaacov, *Soviet Decision Making in Practice: The USSR and Israel, 1947–1954*, New Brunswick: Transaction Books, 1980.

Roosevelt, Kermit, *Countercoup: The Struggle for Control of Iran*, New York: McGraw–Hill, 1979.

Roy, Olivier, *L'Islam mondialisé*, new edn, Paris: Éditions du Seuil, 2004.

Rubenberg, Cheryl, *The Palestine Liberation Organization: Its Institutional Infrastructure*, Belmont, MA: Institute of Arab Studies, 1983.

Rubin, Barry, *The Arab States and the Palestine Conflict*, Syracuse, NY: Syracuse University Press, 1981.

———*Revolution Until Victory? The Politics and History of the PLO*, Cambridge, MA: Harvard University Press, 1994.

Rubin, Barry, and Judith Colp Rubin, *Yasir Arafat: A Political Biography*, New York: Oxford University Press, 2003.

———eds, *Anti-American Terrorism and the Middle East: A Documentary Reader*, New York: Oxford University Press, 2002.

Rubin, Barry, and Thomas A. Keaney, eds, *Armed Forces in the Middle East: Politics and Strategy*, London: Frank Cass, 2002.

Said, Edward W., *Arabs and Jews: Possibility of Concord*, North Dartmouth, MA: Association of Arab-American University Graduates, 1974.

———*Orientalism*, New York: Pantheon, 1978.

———*The Palestine Question and the American Context*, Beirut: Institute for Palestine Studies, 1979.

————*The Question of Palestine*, London: Routledge, 1980.

————*Covering Islam: How the Media and the Experts Determine How We See the Rest of the World*, rev. edn, New York: Vintage, 1997.

————*The End of the Peace Process: Oslo and After*, 2nd edn, London: Granta Books, 2002.

————*Freud et le monde extra-européen*, Paris: Le Serpent à Plumes, 2004.

Said, Edward W. and Christopher Hitchens, eds, *Blaming the Victims: Spurious Scholarship and the Palestinian Question*, London: Verso, 1988.

Salmon, Yosef, *Religion and Zionism: First Encounters*, Jerusalem: The Hebrew University Magnes Press, 2002.

Sanbar, Elias, *Palestine 1948: L'expulsion*, Washington, DC: Les livres de la Revue d'études Palestiniennes, 1984.

————*Figures du Palestinien: Identité des origines, identité de devenir*, Paris: Gallimard, 2004.

Sand, Shlomo, *Les mots et la terre: Les intellectuels en Israël*, Paris: Fayard, 2006.

Sarig, Mordechai, ed., *The Political and Social Philosophy of Ze'ev Jabotinsky: Selected Writings*, London: Vallentine Mitchell, 1999.

Sayigh, Yazid, *Armed Struggle and the Search for State: The Palestinian National Movement, 1949–1993*. Oxford: Oxford Press, 1997.

Schaeder, Grete, *Martin Buber: Hebräischer Humanismus*, Göttingen: Vandenhoeck & Ruprecht, 1966.

Schechtman, Joseph B., *Postwar Population Transfers in Europe, 1945–1955*, Philadelphia: University of Pennsylvania Press, 1963.

Schulz, Helena Lindholm, *The Reconstruction of Palestinian Nationalism: Between Revolution and Statehood*, Manchester: Manchester University Press, 1999.

Seale, Patrick. *Abu Nidal: A Gun for Hire*, New York: Random House, 1992.

Sears, David, *Compassion for Humanity in the Jewish Tradition*, Lanham, MD: Rowman & Littlefield, 1998.

Segal, Rafi and Eyal Weizman, eds, *A Civilian Occupation: The Politics of Israeli Architecture*, London: Verso, 2003.

Segev, Tom, *1949: The First Israelis*, New York: Free Press, 1986.

————*The Seventh Million: The Israelis and the Holocaust*, New York: Hill & Wang, 1993.

————*One Palestine, Complete: Jews and Arabs Under the British Mandate*, New York: Metropolitan, 2000.

————*Elvis in Jerusalem: Post-Zionism and the Americanization of Israel*. New York: Metropolitan Books, 2002.

Shafir, Gershom, *Land, Labor and the Origins of the Israeli-Palestinian Conflict, 1882–1914*, Berkeley: University of California Press, 1996.

Shapira, Anita, *Land and Power: The Zionist Resort to Force*, New York: Oxford University Press, 1992.

Shavit, Yaacov, *Jabotinsky and the Revisionist Movement, 1925–1948*, London: Frank Cass, 1988.

Shlaim, Avi, *Collusion Across the Jordan: King Abdullah, the Zionist Movement, and the Partition of Palestine*, Oxford: Clarendon Press, 1988.

————*The Politics of Partition*, Oxford: Oxford University Press, 1990.

————*War and Peace in the Middle East: A Critique of American Policy*, New York: Viking, 1994.

————*The Iron Wall: Israel and the Arab World*, New York: W. W. Norton, 2000.

Silberstein, Laurence J., *The Post-Zionism Debates: Knowledge and Power in Israeli Culture*, New York: Routledge, 1998.

Simon, Akibah Ernst, "Jewish Adult Education in Nazi Germany as Spiritual Resistance," *Yearbook of the Leo Baeck Institute*, ed. Robert Weltsch: 68–104, Oxford: Berghahn Books, 1956.

————*Brücken: Gesammelte Aufsätze*, Heidelberg: L. Schneider, 1965.

————*Sechzig Jahre Gegen den Strom: Briefe von 1917–1984*, Tübingen: Mohr Siebeck, 1998.

Simon, Leon, ed., *Essays, Letters, Memoirs—Ahad Ha'am*, Oxford: East and West Library, 1946.

Sivan, Emmanuel, *Radical Islam: Medieval Theology and Modern Politics*, New Haven: Yale University Press, 1990.

Stein, Leonard, *The Balfour Declaration*, New York: Simon & Schuster, 1961.

Sternhell, Zeev, *Aux Origines d'Israël: Entre nationalisme et socialisme*, Paris: Fayard, 1996.

Stevens, Richard P., *American Zionism and U.S. Foreign Policy, 1942–1947*, New York: Pageant Press, 1962.

Stone, I. F., *Underground to Palestine*, New York: Pantheon, 1978.

Strachey, James, ed., *The Standard Edition of the Complete Psychological Works of Sigmund Freud*, vol. XIII (1913–14), London: Hogarth Press, 1955.

Sykes, Christopher, *Crossroads to Israel, 1917–1948*, 2nd edn, Bloomington: Indiana University Press, 1973.

Talmon, Jacob L., *The Unique and the Universal: Some Historical Reflections*, New York: Braziller, 1966.

Teveth, Shabtai, *Ben-Gurion and the Palestinian Arabs: From Peace to War*, New York: Oxford University Press, 1985.

————*The Evolution of "Transfer" in Zionist Thinking*, Tel Aviv: Shiloah Institute, 1989.

————*Ben-Gurion and the Holocaust*, New York: Harcourt Brace, 1996.

Thobie, Jacques, *Ali et les 40 voleurs: Impérialismes et Moyen-Orient de 1914 à nos jours*, Paris: Messidor, 1985.

Thual, François, *Géopolitique du Chiisme*, Paris: Arléa, 2002.

Tivnan, Edward, *The Lobby: Jewish Political Power and American Foreign Policy*, New York: Simon & Schuster, 1987.

Tomeh, George J., *United Nations Resolutions on Palestine and the Arab–Israeli Conflict, vol. 1, 1947–1974*, Washington, DC: Institute for Palestine Studies, 1987.

Van Creveld, Martin L., *The Sword and the Olive: A Critical History of the Israeli Defense Force*, New York: Public Affairs Press, 1998.

————*The Changing Face of War: Lessons of Combat, from the Marne to Iraq*, New York: Presidio Press, 2006.

Veblen, Thorstein, "The Intellectual Pre-Eminence of Jews in Modern Europe," *Political Science Quarterly* 31, no. 1 (March 1919): 33–42.

Vidal, Dominique, *Le Péché originel d'Israël: L'expulsion des Palestiniens revisitée par les "nouveaux historiens" israéliens*, Paris: Editions de l'Atelier, 2002.

Vital, David, *The Origins of Zionism*, Oxford: Clarendon Press, 1975.

————*Zionism: The Formative Years*, Oxford: The Clarendon Press, 1982.

————*Zionism: The Crucial Phase*, Oxford: Clarendon Press, 1987.

Wagner, Yigal, *Martin Buber: Kampf um Israel—Sein zionistisches und politisches Denken*, Potsdam: Verlag für Berlin-Brandenburg, 1999.

Warschawski, Michel., *Israël–Palestine: Le Défi Binational*, Paris: Editions Textuel, 2001.

Warschawski, Michel and Michèle Sibony, *A Contre-coeur: Les voix dissidents en Israël*, Paris: Editions Textuel, 2003.

Washington Report on Middle East Affairs

Wasserstein, Bernard, *The British in Palestine: The Mandatory Government and the Arab–Jewish Conflict, 1917–1929*, London: Royal Historical Society, 1978.

Webb, Beatrice, *The Diary of Beatrice Webb, vol. IV (1924-1943)*, Norman and Jeanne MacKenzie, eds, Cambridge: Harvard University Press (Belknap), 1985.

Weizmann, Chaim, *Trial and Error: The Autobiography of Chaim Weizmann*, New York: Harper, 1949.

Wiener, Daniel, *Shalom: Israels Friedensbewegung*, Reinbeck bei Hamburg: Rowohlt, 1984.

Wilson, Mary C., *King Abdullah, Britain and the Making of Jordan*, Cambridge: Cambridge University Press, 1987.

Wright, Robin, *Sacred Rage: The Crusade of Modern Islam*, New York: Linden Press/Simon & Schuster, 1985.

———"Islam and Liberal Democracy: Two Visions of Reformation," *Journal of Democracy* 7.2 (1996): 64–75.

———*The Last Great Revolution: Turmoil and Transformation in Iran*, New York: Knopf, 2000.

Wyman, Mark, *DPs: Europe's Displaced Persons, 1945–1951*, Ithaca, NY: Cornell University Press, 1998.

Yalin-Mor, Nathan, *Israël, Israël: Histoire du groupe Stern*, Paris: Presses de la Renaissance, 1978.

Yergin, Daniel, *The Prize: The Epic Quest for Oil, Money and Power*, New York: Simon & Schuster, 1991.

Zander, Walter, *Is This the Way? A Call to Jews*, London: Victor Gollancz, 1948.

Zertal, Idith, *From Catastrophe to Power: Holocaust Survivors and the Emergence of Israel*, Berkeley: University of California Press, 1998.

———*La Nation et la mort: La Shoah dans le discours et la politique d'Israël*. Paris: La Découverte, 2004.

Zipperstein, Steven J., *Elusive Prophet: Ahad Ha'am and the Origins of Zionism*, Berkeley: University of California Press, 1993.

INDEX

Abbas, Abu 307–8
Abbas, Mahmoud 66, 67, 68–9, 269, 336, 337, 383
Abdullah I, King of Jordan 114, 115, 201–2, 203, 208, 225, 228, 229–30, 232, 234, 302
Abdullah II, King of Jordan 67, 397
Abdullah, Crown Prince of Saudi Arabia 366
Abdullah, King of Saudi Arabia 68, 87
Abu Ghraib prison 13
Abu-Houb, Ayeh 409
Acheson, Dean 189
Achille Lauro hijacking 307–8
Acre 221
Adenauer, Konrad 62–3
Afghanistan 15–16, 46, 83, 295
Africa, North 2
Ahmadinejad, Mahmoud 18, 46, 47, 53–4, 55–7, 59, 87
Ain al-Hilweh 375
Al Samu 250
al-Alami, Musa 158, 203
al-Aqsa Martyrs Brigades 399
Al-Aqsa Mosque 12, 367–8, 385, 394–5
Al-Bira 395
Albright, Madeleine 397
Alfei Menashe 21
Allenby, Sir Edmund 115, 121
Allon, Yigal 20–1, 224, 240, 258, 269, 273, 275
Allon Plan 20–2, 258–9
Aloni, Shulamit 327
al-Qaeda 31, 48, 71, 83
al-Sammu 254
Ambassador Award 29
American Arabian Oil Company (Aramco) 5
American Emergency Council 164
American Israel Education Foundation 30
American Israel Public Affairs Committee (AIPAC) 29–32, 53–4, 58–9, 328, 363
American Zionist Federation 216
Amir, Yigal 252, 353, 355
Anderson, Sten 321
Anglo-American Commission of Inquiry 173–81, 187–8
Anglo-Iranian Oil Company 245
Anglo-Persian Oil Company 96
Annan, Kofi 397
Anti-Defamation League xi
Anti-Imperialist League 94
anti-Judaism x–xi, 2, 3, 89, 143, 172
anti-missile defense system 57, 74–5
anti-Oslo demonstrations 353–5
anti-Semitism 2, 30

anti-Zionism 171
Antonius, George 158, 165
appeasement 156
Aqaba 366
Arab Higher Committee 145, 146, 150, 158, 200–1, 202, 225
Arab League 61, 170, 176, 201, 228, 252, 290, 319, 366
Arab Legion 223, 226, 228, 230
Arab Peace Initiative 68
Arab Question xii–xiii, 91–3, 103, 105, 240; and the Anglo-American Commission 174, 175–7, 180–1; Brit Shalom and 120; Epstein on 108–9; expelled from discourse 165; and the first intifada 135–6; Haam on 105–8; Jabotinsky and 124–7; Jewish Agency advisory committee 167–8; Lawrence and 110–11; Magnes on 198–200; population transfer 149–50, 157; situation during 1920s 111–13; Zangwill on 109–10; Zionism and 6–7, 91–3; Zionist neglect of 105–10
Arab Revolt 98
Arab–Israeli War, first 93, 228–35, 237, 240–1
Arab–Israeli War, second 248–9
Arab–Israeli War, third 16, 19, 40, 249–61
Arab–Israeli War, fourth 272–6
Arab–Jewish understanding, call for 118–21
Arab-Palestinian question 72–3
Arabs: approach to the Axis 152; Ben Gurion on 126–7; British support for 97–9; collision with Zionism 3–4; discrimination against 64; fratricide 200–2; Israeli 73–5; lack of unity 241–2; leverage 157; moderates 120–1; national awakening 13; and the Peel Report 149–50; and the PLO 264–5, 284–5; population growth 203; portrayal as aggressors 217–18, 223; reaction to UNSCOP findings 208; and the third Arab–Israeli War 259; uprising of 1920 114–15, 116–17; voting patterns 73–4, 364; Western view of 89
Arafat, Yasser 10, 12, 55–6, 60, 62; and the 1996 elections 366; accused of surrender 344; addresses the World Economic Forum 401; agrees to ceasefire 267–8; and the Al Aqsa intifada 396; background 251; and Barak 383–4; and Black September 269; calls for international protection of refugee camps 298; Camp David II talks 386–92; elected chairman of PLO executive committee 263; Erez checkpoint meetings 368, 370, 372, 377; and extremists 295; and the first Gulf War 330–1; ideology 264;